EXPANDED SECON[D]

D1118128

DEFRAUDING AMERICA

A Pattern of Related Scandals

Makes the Godfather Saga Pale By Comparison

Dirty Secrets Of the CIA and Other
Government Operations

Written by an insider
Rodney Stich
Author of *Unfriendly Skies*
With Extensive Input From Deep-Cover CIA Personnel

Copyright © 1994 by Rodney Stich

Library of Congress Catalog Card Number 93-074654

Stich, Rodney

Defrauding America

EXPANDED SECOND EDITION

1. Corruption–Government; 2. Government–corruption; 3. Judges–California and federal–corruption; 4. Courts–bankruptcy–corruption; 5. Congress–corruption; 6. Government–U.S. Department of Justice–corruption; 7. Drug trafficking–United States–CIA and DEA; 8. Intelligence services–United States; 9. Intelligence service–Israel; 10. Savings and loan association–United States–corrupt practices; 11. October Surprise; 12. Cocaine habit–United States; 12. Airlines–accidents; 13. Aeronautics, commercial–accidents;
14. Inslaw; 15. Bank of Credit and Commerce International–corrupt practices; 16. HUD–corruption; 17. Bishop, Baldwin, Rewald, Dillingham, & Wong; 18. Nugan Hand Bank; 19. Whistleblowers.

Soft Cover ISBN: 0-932438-08-3

Published and printed in the United States of America.

Supporting title: *Unfriendly Skies—Saga Of Corruption*.
ISBN 0-932438-05-9

Order from:
Diablo Western Press, Inc.
P.O. Box 5, Alamo, California 94507
or
Diablo Western Press, Inc.
P.O. Box 10587, Reno, Nevada 89510
or
Telephone orders: 1-800-247-7389

10 9 8 7 6 5 4 3 2

CONTENTS

Introduction; About the Author; Dedication; Applicable Quotations

INTRODUCTION

This book is a thirty-year chronology of corruption inflicted upon the American people, as seen and related through the eyes of government insiders. The author was formerly a federal investigator holding federal authority to make the determinations and charges that he makes in these pages. His discovery of shocking corruption associated with a series of fatal airline crashes, and the felonious coverup by every known government and non-government check and balance, motivated him to become an activist against corrupt government.

These activities brought him into contact with whistleblowers from the Central Intelligence Agency, the Drug Enforcement Administration, law enforcement personnel, and other insiders. They all contributed to the exposure of hard-core corruption which continues to inflict great harm upon the American people and the United States.

The author knows of no other book in which a group of concerned former government people, in key positions, possessing sensitive information on criminality in government, has spoken like this. Never before in the history of the United States have the inner details of organized corruption within the federal government been described by insiders in this manner. This book provides strong support for the charge that there is a parallel and corrupt government in control of the United States, that has executed, without the public's recognition, a coup d' etat against the American people.

Most of the facts described in these pages are supported by what the author and others personally discovered or witnessed; dozens of secret and confidential government documents; statements given to the author by a group of deep-cover whistleblowers formerly or currently with U.S. intelligence agencies; cross-check of these statements with other whistleblowers; various forms of legally recognized evidence. Many of the events were personally discovered while a federal investigator, a private investigator researching for his activist and book activities, and when he became a victim of efforts to silence him. Over a thousand hours of deposition-like questioning of many former deep-cover CIA and DEA personnel, hundreds of secret and confidential documents, intensive cross-checking, constitute *prima facie* evidence of a frightening secret and corrupt government.

Many people will have difficulty accepting the events described in these pages. This is partly due to having been shielded from reality by the disinformation and withholding of data by the establishment media.

As in any book encompassing this great amount of data, there may be occasional errors of relatively minor facts. These would not negate the major facts.

If the contents shock your sensibilities, then consider this a novel.

Because of the continuing nature of the corruption described within these pages, and the continuing receipt of additional information from my deep-cover contacts, this book will be repeatedly updated.

ABOUT THE AUTHOR

The author spent most of his adult life in aviation, and during federal and private investigations. He was a pilot and flight instructor in the U.S. Navy during World War II and an airline pilot for many years, flying throughout most of the world for numerous airlines. He was one of the first pilots licensed by Japan, holding pilot license number 170. He has flown aircraft licensed in the United States, Japan, Iran, Jordan, and Djibouti. His early flying in the Middle East took him into numerous interesting experiences, including being caught in an Iranian revolution when the Shah overthrew Mossadegh in 1953.

In the early 1960s he became a federal air safety investigator, responsible for airline programs that were experiencing a continuing series of fatal airline crashes. It was here that he first discovered the pattern of corruption within the federal government, which motivated him to become an activist against corrupt government. During the past thirty years he witnessed the explosion of government corruption to a degree that is almost beyond comprehension to most Americans.

Seeking to silence him, many of the same people implicated in various segments of the related corruption have misused the powers of the United States government to inflict great harm upon the author, showing the price that patriots or whistleblowers must pay.

The author, and those former government people who confided in him, had nothing to gain and everything to lose by fighting the overwhelming corruption that is now epidemic in the government of the United States.

DEDICATION

This book is dedicated to the memory of those who have directly suffered so grievously at the hands of corrupt federal personnel. It is dedicated to those very few patriots who have been willing to take on and fight the corrupting elements in government.

Thanks are given to those former or current CIA and DEA people, FBI and private investigators, who contributed much information to these pages. They had nothing to gain and much to lose by coming forward, including criminal prosecution by renegade Justice Department prosecutors, and risk joining the long list of whistleblowers, informants, and concerned citizens, who were killed or mysteriously died. Special thanks are given to Gunther Russbacher; his wife, Rayelan; Robert Hunt, Stewart Webb; Russell Bowen; Basil Abbott; Jim Rothstein; John Cole; and others. Some of my informants were themselves a part of the corruption described within these pages, having done so under orders. I make no judgment on these prior acts, and focus on their willingness to come forward, helping expose great crimes against the American people. For this, they must receive credit.

Appreciation also goes to the talk show hosts who allowed me to appear and inform their audiences of the great harm inflicted upon the American people by corrupt federal officials in control of key government entities. Appreciation also goes to the few newspapers who have reported in detail certain of the criminal enterprises described within these pages, including the *Spotlight*,[1] *Napa Sentinel*, *Arkansas Gazette*, and others. The *Arkansas Gazette* published a series of articles exposing CIA drug trafficking in Arkansas, and Governor Bill Clinton's coverup of it. The *Spotlight*, a national weekly, exposed several of the major scandals described within these pages. The *Napa Sentinel*, even though it is a small local newspaper near San Francisco, exposed many of the criminal activities described here, and which were covered up by the mass media.

This edition of *Defrauding America* will be updated and enlarged periodically, bringing to the readers' attention additional information and supporting documentation and evidence, in the hope that the American public will eventually recognize and respond to the harm inflicted upon them.

---

[1] *Spotlight* is a weekly newspaper, 316 Independence Ave., S.E., Washington, Washington, D.C.

APPLICABLE EUROPEAN QUOTATION

In Germany they came first for the Communists, and I didn't speak up, because I wasn't a Communist. They then came for the Jews, and I didn't speak up, because I wasn't a Jew. Then they came for the trade unionists, and I didn't speak up, because I wasn't a trade unionist. Then they came for the Catholics, and I didn't speak up, because I was a Protestant. Then they came for me, and by that time no one was left to speak out.

Attributed to Martin Niemoeller

COMPARABLE U.S. QUOTATION

I didn't speak up when the secret government brought about wars in Laos, Burma, Vietnam, and Central America. I didn't speak out about the deaths of 58,000 Americans in Vietnam, or the tens of thousands of CIA-directed assassinations in Central and South America. I didn't speak out when the savings and loans were looted. I didn't speak out when courageous individuals spoke out about the October Surprise operation. I didn't speak up when other people reported the CIA drug trafficking into the United States. I didn't speak up when I learned of the looting of peoples' assets in Chapter 11 by corrupt federal judges and others.

I chose to remain ignorant about the depth of corruption by government officials and judges. I ignored the pattern of coverup and criminal activities by members of Congress. I ignored the patterns of corruption. They didn't affect me directly. I ignored my responsibilities as a citizen, and was indifferent to the tragic plight of those people who were directly affected by the massive corruption in government. I shirked my responsibilities by eagerly believing the disinformation and denials given by the media and federal officials.

I am now paying the consequences, and I share the blame for what is happening to the United States, to the American people, including those specifically targeted, and to myself.

CHAPTER ONE

FRAUD–RELATED AIR DISASTERS

In the 1950s and 1960s United Airlines experienced a series of brutal airline disasters, one after the other, far greater than any other airline in the United States, and far more than its size justified. The government accident reports blamed almost every crash on "pilot error," which indicated something was seriously wrong with United's training program. federal officials covered up serious violations of important federal air safety requirements by United Airlines management, and the record-falsification associated with the practice. The reason for these crashes was known to federal air safety investigators, but this knowledge was withheld from official accident reports. Withholding this information allowed serious safety violations to continue, along with related crashes.

It was during these series of air disasters that the FAA asked me to accept assignment to the United Airlines' training center at Denver. This new assignment required that I transfer from the Los Angeles office where I was working with airlines such as American and Western, who had good safety standards and attitudes, and very few crashes. Almost none of those crashes were due to the training-program-induced ignorance accompanying those at United Airlines. The decision to accept the United Airlines assignment altered the course of my entire life.

I had been a Navy and airline pilot for many years prior to joining the Federal Aviation Administration in 1962, and had worked for airlines throughout the world. (Frequent pilot layoffs in those days required changing employers frequently.)

In addition to the many senseless airline crashes United Airlines experienced in the 1950s, 1960s, and 1970s, it experienced on December 16, 1960, the world's worst air disaster (at that time). On that fateful day a United Airlines DC-8 jet plunged into the heart of New York City, killing 134 people, while narrowly missing thousands more. Several months later it experienced another crash at Denver that became another industry classic for its senselessness. Most of the crashes at United Airlines fit the same pattern.

If the truth had been told in the accident reports, the criminality associated with the deaths would have rocked the government and United Airlines, showing that United Airlines' management virtually controlled the government agencies. The coverup continued the pattern of senseless and fraud-related crashes for the next twenty years. To this day the corruption that caused or made these many fatal crashes possible has been kept from the public.

FAA management reacted to the New York City and Denver crashes. They transferred the FAA inspector, Frank Harrell, who had been most vocal about the corruption the inspectors discovered at United Airlines. Following demands by United Airlines' management, the FAA transferred the inspector from United's Denver training base to Puerto Rico, and then asked me to volunteer for the position. FAA people warned me that the position was difficult, that United had a poor record of compliance with federal regulations, and that they had high FAA management on their side. However, I was told that the FAA was right behind me. As it eventually turned out, the FAA was far behind me when I sought to correct the serious problems that I found at the airline and within the FAA Denver District Office and the Western Region offices.

No one had to tell FAA management what the reasons were for the many crashes. The FAA files were full of reports filed by FAA inspectors reporting serious safety problems and unprecedented violations of federal air safety laws.

The air disaster that occurred in the New York City area was the result of extremely poor and dangerous piloting technique, a problem that would have been prevented by adequate training and checking of crewmembers' competency. United's DC-8 had entered a low-altitude holding pattern in the New York City area at a speed of approximately 500 miles per hour, twice as fast as it should have been going. The faster an aircraft flies, the greater the amount of airspace necessary to remain in a circular or racetrack holding pattern. There was no low-altitude holding pattern in the United States designed for such an excessive speed.

As the fast-moving United DC-8 turned into the holding pattern it quickly departed its protected airspace, ramming into a TWA Constellation aircraft making an approach to nearby LaGuardia Airport. The impact ripped open the TWA fuselage, sucking one of TWA's passengers into a jet engine of the DC-8. The TWA Constellation broke into millions of pieces, spewing passengers from the spinning fuselage as it fell onto Staten Island. United's DC-8, now partly disabled, continued in a descending flight path directly toward the heart of New York City.

Skimming past many crowded buildings containing thousands of people, the United jet finally rammed into the street between apartment buildings in Brooklyn. When it was over, the death toll was 134 people.

There was only one survivor in the two airplanes: Stephen Baltz, a young boy, who survived for a few days.

FALSIFIED TRAINING RECORDS

Several months before this New York City crash, FAA inspectors traveled from United's Denver training center to its maintenance base at San Francisco. The purpose of the trip was unprecedented for a scheduled airline. Inspectors had long suspected that the United Airlines FAA-approved company check airmen were not performing the legally required training and competency checks of the crewmembers. Certain of the United Airlines check airmen were then falsifying records to show that the lawful safety requirements had been accomplished. The unannounced inspection trip was to cross-check aircraft maintenance records at San Francisco against flight training records at the Denver training center.

The unexpected cross-check revealed that the aircraft used for flight training and competency checks were only in the air for thirty to forty-five minutes. It required over three hours to complete the required training and check maneuvers, and that is the time that it took when there was an FAA inspector present. Obviously, United flight instructors and check airmen were violating federal law and then falsifying the records showing that the specific maneuvers had been completed, when they had not been. This would explain the pattern of air disasters that plagued United Airlines for a thirty-year span.

These were serious offenses, especially in the presence of continuing fatal crashes. Under federal criminal statutes, these air safety and criminal violations became, arguably, capital offenses[2] when death resulted. Some people call it murder.

Following the cross-check of records, FAA Inspector Frank Harrell prepared a report, signed by other inspectors (October 16, 1960), that described what was found. Instead of taking corrective actions as internal FAA directives required, the FAA sequestered the report and commenced harassing Inspector Frank Harrell. After the New York City crash occurred, the NTSB[3] joined the coverup by omitting any reference to the pattern of misconduct at United Airlines or the FAA. In its final report, instead of blaming the airline and FAA management for the unlawful and fraudulent training program, the NTSB blamed the crew for the crash and deaths. Of course, the crew was directly at fault, but the underlying cause was elsewhere.

Under federal law it is a crime to submit or prepare a statement to any department or agency of the United States that is knowingly false, or conceals or covers up. United Airlines management repeatedly falsified important records to feloniously suggest that it had provided the lawfully required training and competency checks of its crewmembers.

CORRECTIVE ACTION—REMOVE THE REPORT!

After that report was filed as a government document, and before the New York City crash occurred, FAA Western Region officials engaged in a coverup causing the continuation of the safety violations. These acts

---

[2] Title 18 U.S.C. §§ 34 and 35.

[3] At that time the government equivalent of the National Transportation Safety Board (NTSB) was the Civil Aeronautic Board Bureau of Air Safety.

implicated them in the subsequent New York City crash, and others that followed. FAA inspector reports of serious misconduct at United Airlines continued, as did the resulting crashes.

Instead of forcing United Airlines to comply with the law, and provide the legally required training and check safeguards, FAA officials sequestered the report and harassed the inspectors, and particularly Frank Harrell. United Airlines management warned me that they pressured FAA officials in the Western Regional Office to remove Harrell from the inspection program and to transfer him to an undesirable position in Puerto Rico. Duplicating what they had done to other federal inspectors, United's management repeatedly threatened me when I reported the same safety violations that Harrel had done. My exercise of tact and persuasion with United's management, trying to halt the serious safety violations, was ineffective.

THE NTSB SEQUESTERED THE BLOCKBUSTER REPORTS

Federal law required the NTSB to include these sequestered FAA reports in the accident report. But the NTSB aided and abetted the serious problems, making them accomplices in the causes of many subsequent airline crashes. As the NTSB investigative staff finished their investigation and prepared their technical report, they presented their findings and recommendations to the politically appointed NTSB Board members, who issue the official cause of the crash. The Board's report withheld the FAA reports and the criminal falsification of government-required safety records. I witnessed these coverups by FAA and NTSB officials for years after that. A few of the many subsequent crashes will be briefly described in the following pages.

UNION RESPONSE

Many of the pilots and their union, Air Line Pilots Association (ALPA), knew of the serious irregularities in United's training program, and said nothing about them. Despite knowing that coverup would continue the practices that caused their own pilots to perish, ALPA took no action to expose these serious problems. Instead of revealing the serious problems that resulted in the crashes, ALPA fabricated excuses that only people poorly knowledgeable in aviation could accept. In the New York City crash, ALPA laid the blame on the controllers who cleared United to remain inside the holding pattern, which it failed to do.

WARNINGS TWO DAYS BEFORE THE CRASH

Ironically, two days before this crash, the head of the Federal Aviation Agency, Air Force General E.R. Quesada, testified before the House Commerce Subcommittee on airline safety. Quesada identified the obstacles confronting aviation safety. He identified pressure groups and tactics which blocked efforts to improve safety, including the Air Line Pilots Association (ALPA) and the Aircraft Owners and Pilots Association (AOPA). *Aviation Week & Space Technology* reported his testimony:

> *Quesada Blasts AOPA and ALPA during FAA report to Congress—Washington—The Federal Aviation Agency Administrator E.R. Quesada accused Aircraft Owners and Pilots Assn. and Air Line Pilots Assn. last week of attempting to undermine Federal Aviation Agency's safety rules and enforcement during a farewell appearance during a*

House Commerce Subcommittee report on the FAA's two-year existence. In his two-hour, forty-seven page testimony, Quesada told the sub-committee that when he became Administrator of the newly created agency on Nov. 1, 1958: "I was by no means naive as to the history of the AOPA as a self-serving group. But I must admit I was not fully prepared for the intensity of their invective or for the imaginative and sometimes devious methods they employ."

Declaring that he refused to allow the pressure groups to intimidate him or the FAA inspectors, Quesada presented a case-by-case list of AOPA and ALPA attacks on government safety activities. He urged the subcommittee to insist on effective administration of the new government air safety agency. FAA Administrators come and go, and Quesada probably did not know the bureaucratic corruption that existed deep within the FAA which was especially rampant in the FAA Western Region.

United's executive offices were in Chicago, and the FAA office at Chicago should have held safety responsibilities for United's operations. But United had control of FAA officials in the Los Angeles FAA Regional Office and pressured the FAA not to transfer the certificate.

Outspoken FAA Administrator Quesada issued a statement based upon the evidence shown by the DC-8 flight recorder and other data, warning that unless the FAA and the airlines paid greater attention to basic safety requirements the tragedies would continue.

United management and the Air Line Pilots Association each had an ax to grind against Quesada. Neither took kindly to Quesada's requirement that the crews meet the stiffer training and competency standards that Quesada initiated. Even though this air tragedy showed the importance of training, and the danger arising from lack of such training, the airline and ALPA blamed Quesada for the crash and resisted the training requirements. Despite Quesada's warnings, the Chairman of the Senate Aviation Subcommittee, Senator Mike Monroney of Oklahoma, condemned Quesada's control of the FAA, and eulogized the very groups that shared blame in the crash. The respected trade magazine, *Aviation Week*, wrote:

Monroney Increasingly Critical of the FAA. Sen. A.S. Mike Monroney (D-Okla.) made it clear last week that he intends to keep a closer, more critical eye on the Federal Aviation Agency as his Aviation Subcommittee continued its investigations of air safety. He made it clear that he has some misgivings about the uncritical support he gave the agency during its first two years and that he intends to keep FAA operations under close surveillance. Commending ALPA on its testimony ... Sen. Monroney again raised the issue of whether the FAA has exerted its full powers to promote air safety, and commented, "This is not a very good record. I don't think we're doing a good job."

POLITICAL FRIENDS

Monroney received large financial contributions from ALPA and United Airlines, as did many other members of Congress. Under the direction and insistence of Attorney General Robert Kennedy, the United States Department of Justice acted to relieve United Airlines of considerable financial responsibility for the crash. This caused the American taxpayer to assume a greater portion of the financial liability arising out of the air disaster. A *World News Digest* article stated:

> **U.S. to Pay in Air Crash.** *It was disclosed Oct. 22 that the federal government [i.e., the taxpayers] had agreed to pay 24% of the damages of verdicts agreed on in law suits growing out of the Dec. 16, 1960 collision over N.Y. between a United Air Lines DC-8 jet and a Trans World Airline Lockheed Super-Constellation. (The death toll was 134 people.) United Air Lines was to pay 61% of lawsuit damage costs, Trans World 15%. The government was a co-defendant in the suits because the planes' instrument landing approaches were being guided by Federal Aviation Agency controllers when the collision occurred. A tentative government agreement to bear such a share of the damages had been canceled by FAA administrator Najeeb E. Halaby, but his decision was over-turned by the Justice Department. [See Vol. XXII, P. 256B-C3]*

In the *Journal of Air Law and Commerce* a description appeared of the government's settlement of the lawsuits arising out of the United DC-8 crash into New York City.

> *On October 23, 1963, the United States government, specifically the Department of Justice, agreed to pay 24 percent of whatever damages are fixed as a result of claims and lawsuits arising from the collision of a United Air Lines DC-8 jet with a Trans World Airlines Super Constellation over Staten Island on December 16, 1960. United Air Lines and Trans World Airlines agreed to pay sixty-one and 15 percent respectively.... It is interesting to note that if the case had been tried and lost, the Justice Department would have been responsible for paying the judgment out of its budget. However, since the case was settled, the FAA is liable out of its budget.*

The article raised the question of whether political considerations caused Kennedy to have the American public assume much of the liability belonging to United Airlines: "Would ... political considerations cause these standards to be stretched beyond those of even the most liberal court?"

Voicing strong disapproval of this settlement, FAA Administrator, Najeeb Halaby (who followed Pete Quesada when his outspoken position caused his removal as head of the FAA), lambasted the settlement in an internal FAA communication:

> *I opposed this settlement formula at every level in the Department of Justice up to and including the Attorney General. My opposition was based on the fact that the system (referring to the air traffic control system) cannot either then or now reach out and prevent an accident involving an airplane which flies 12 miles past a holding fix at a great rate of speed .... The Air Traffic Control system is very much like the system furnished to the highway users. The government authorities furnish the stop signs, the red and green traffic lights and the rules for their use.*

The air traffic control system cannot physically prevent a pilot from disregarding a stop signal any more than the highway traffic control system can physically stop a vehicle whose operator disregards a red light and plunges through it. Both systems are dependent on and require responsible compliance on the part of the operator of the vehicle with the traffic rules. When a pilot is told to hold at a particular holding pattern and says he will, it is up to him.

The controller on the ground cannot pilot or navigate the airplane for him ... the system in December 1960 was not capable of stopping those who did not comply with directions from the controllers. Neither does it today, despite the many advances made in the past three years. Nor will it in the future, because it is generally agreed that ultimate responsibility must reside with the pilot ... the system was not violator proof nor will it be.

NO CHANGES

Nothing changed within the FAA Denver district office and Los Angeles regional offices, or at United Airlines. FAA inspectors continued to complain among themselves about the poor training and standards at United Airlines, and the blocking of any corrective actions by FAA management. Harrell was gone, and the inspectors were demoralized. They rarely filed written reports of the continuing safety violations and safety problems, and limited their complaints to grumbling among themselves.

One of the key obstacles faced by FAA inspectors trying to make United Airlines conform to the air safety requirements was harassment by the chief of the FAA Air Carrier Branch in Los Angeles, Lynn Ashwell. He sought industry support to become the first career Administrator of the FAA, at a time when most Administrators were political appointees. To obtain industry assistance in reaching his goal, Ashwell applied pressure to inspectors, and threatened them not to report unsafe or illegal practices. I encountered this problem when I joined the FAA, which multiplied many times after I accepted the United Airlines DC-8 assignment.

UAL WAS CATALYST FOR FAA FORMATION

Ironically, Congress legislated the Federal Aviation Administration through the Federal Aviation Act of 1958 because of an earlier United Airlines crash over the Grand Canyon, after a United DC-7 crashed into a TWA Constellation (June 30, 1956). Both planes plunged into the Grand Canyon with the loss of all 128 people on board the aircraft. Even today the remains of the two aircraft can be seen in the Grand Canyon.

The former government air safety agency, the Civil Aeronautics Administration, was managed by indifferent bureaucrats, very responsive to political and vested-interest groups. The Act granted the FAA the authority and responsibility to make and enforce air safety rules, but brought into the new agency the same government bureaucratic mentality existing in the CAA.

The public soon forgot the horror of the New York City disaster. The people at United Airlines and within the FAA responsible for the disaster continued in highly sensitive air safety positions, and were promoted to other sensitive positions. Tactics that had proven so profitable in the past,

continued. The American public would pay a terrible price in years to come.
DENVER TRAGEDY
For the next twenty years the air safety and criminal misconduct that I and other federal inspectors discovered at United Airlines and within the FAA continued, as did a long series of resulting air disasters. The first of these occurred seven months later. A United Airlines DC-8 crashed during landing at Denver's Stapleton Airport, in full view of the United Training Department, where the underlying cause of the crash had its origin. The DC-8 had experienced a hydraulic failure enroute to Denver, a common occurrence following the introduction of the jets into airline service. This was no big problem on the DC-8, but certain steps had to be taken which should have been common knowledge to the crew, and which were stated in the emergency procedures the crew should have followed. One of the corrective actions that the crew had to take required actuating a lever releasing high pressure nitrogen into the hydraulic lines that hold the engine reverse mechanism in position after landing. The crew did not do this, and didn't recognize what would probably happen upon applying reverse thrust after touch-down.

As friends and relatives watched from the terminal building, the DC-8 touched down on the runway, and as the crew applied reverse thrust, they experienced loss of directional control. As the crew applied power, expecting all engines to be in reverse thrust, the two engines on the left side of the aircraft went into forward thrust mode, causing the left wing to move forward, while the two right engines remained in reverse thrust, slowing the forward movement of the right wing. Veering from the runway, the aircraft crossed over rough ground, causing the landing gear to rip off. Careening crazily from the runway, the jet rammed into a truck, crushing to death a maintenance worker eating his lunch.

At this stage everyone on board the aircraft was unharmed and should have safely left the aircraft. But there were other problems. United's emergency evacuation training was as bad as their pilot and flight engineer training, and this resulted in many of the people being cremated alive in the ensuing fire.

NTSB[4] Board members falsified the accident report, covering up for the serious air safety and criminal violations at United Airlines and within the FAA. The report identified the errors made by the crew, but covered up the airline's safety violations and the FAA aiding and abetting of these violations.

I arrived at the United Airlines training base in Denver shortly after this latest air tragedy, and it didn't take long for me to discover the cause of the string of crashes. Other inspectors already knew the relationship between the corruption and the crashes and deaths.
DISREGARD FOR THE LIVES
OF THE PASSENGERS AND CREW
Despite the continuing tragedies, United Airlines management continued and even escalated their violations of federal safety laws. They refused to

---

[4] At that time the NTSB was called the Civil Aeronautic Administration and the responsibility for aviation safety matters rested with its Bureau of Aviation Safety.

meet safety standards and requirements found at most other airlines. I accepted the United Airlines assignment to clean up the problems, and was determined to do just that. Other inspectors had simply given up and transferred to other assignments, or looked the other way. Some joined the corrupt practices, receiving the many benefits that came with that approach.

FAA management was paid and entrusted to support me (and other inspectors) when I reported the major safety violations and safety problems, and tried to take corrective actions. This was what we were being paid to do and entrusted to do. I was naive. FAA management already knew about the violations, and wanted me to do something about the continuing series of crashes without addressing their causes.

My reports of safety violations and safety problems in the United training operations were similar to those of my predecessors. I reported into the official FAA records that United Airline officials corruptly violated the spirit and intent of federal air safety laws and violated federal safety requirements. This included denying legally required and industry accepted training, and corrective training, to crewmembers. United's management covered up for the serious safety violations by falsifying training records. These were criminal acts associated with death on a wholesale level. I reported that United management refused to allow inspections of their safety records, which constituted a major violation of federal air safety laws. Other inspectors and I reported that the training was grossly inadequate and the resulting level of flight crew competency was at a dangerous level. I reported that United check airmen lowered the acceptable level of competency to dangerous and illegal levels to compensate for the inadequate training.

RETALIATING AGAINST FEDERAL INSPECTORS

United Airlines management, including senior check airmen approved by the FAA, threatened to get me removed from the program, as they admitted they did with prior inspectors. FAA officials assisted United's efforts, applying pressure, threats, and intimidation of the inspectors to stop their reports.

Despite the threats from FAA and United management, I continued reporting the unsafe and unlawful conditions, including the criminal falsification of safety records. The airline saved tens of millions of dollars a year by violating the specifics and the intent of federal air safety requirements. My exposure actions threatened to raise the training costs to the level accepted by most other airlines, and threatened to expose prior corruption within the FAA and at United Airlines. I was obviously a threat to them, and something had to give.

FAA HATCHET MAN

Washington reacted to the developing crisis by sending a replacement supervising inspector to the Denver District Office, replacing Dave Haley. Chuck Stacy arrived in the Denver Air Carrier District office, where he was assigned during the New York City and Denver crashes. He fully knew the serious problems at United Airlines and within the FAA, as reported by other inspectors.

The first clue that Stacy was a "hatchet man" came within a few days. Almost before he knew where his office was, let alone learn of the complex problems, Stacy wrote a two-page memorandum accusing me of being unable to get along with others in a work situation. He sought to support this charge on the basis of my critical reports of United's training program irregularities. These reports were similar to those reported by other inspectors for years, and they constituted one of our primary job functions. Stacy's memorandum stated in part:

> I have reviewed considerable correspondence prepared by you relating to technical subjects and training requirements ... for United Air Lines. Today, during our discussion concerning the adequacy of UAL's flight engineer training and checking, the subject was again recognizable.

Stacy was referring to a morning staff meeting when one of the inspectors stated: "If we push this," referring to the correction of United's training program deficiencies, "United will buck us, and not do anything."

I replied, "The Agency has the authority and responsibility to take immediate corrective actions when safety irregularities are suspected. What United thinks doesn't alter these responsibilities." Stacy's memorandum continued:

> With respect to our discussion of UAL flight engineer training ... the intent of the majority of your correspondence, although in numerous places it is inferred, or implied, is that UAL flight engineers are not meeting the CAR requirements. In view of the above, it is requested that you give careful consideration to the above subject.

The only consideration remaining for me was to violate the safety functions expected of me as a federal safety inspector, thereby pleasing the group whose conduct left a trail of horror and death in its path. My nature didn't permit me to accept that alternative. During several conversations, Stacy said to me, "Your reports are a thorn in the side of the Agency. They'll get the office in trouble if an accident investigation is made." It became clear that Stacy's function was to block my reporting of the corruption.

LONG–TERM KNOWLEDGE

As Stacy's harassment continued, I called Al Butler, Chief of the Air Carrier Branch, in Los Angeles, to arrange for a meeting to discuss the serious matters. During the meeting I described the multitude of safety irregularities and violations at United Airlines, the FAA blocking of corrective actions, and Stacy's obsession with blocking the duties of the federal air safety agency.

"I've had these problems myself..."

Butler sympathized, "I know, Rod, I've had these problems myself when I was on the United assignment." (Butler had held the primary DC-8 safety responsibilities at United *during* the New York City and Denver crashes, and knew the consequences of these same irregularities.) I later learned that he was present during the cross-check of United's training and maintenance records when the inspectors discovered that United had falsified the flight training records.

I complained about the high accident rate for Western Region air carriers, for which Butler held safety responsibilities, and the incestuous relationship between FAA and United management. "I'm concerned about it also," Butler replied. But his actions did not reflect concern. In Butler's possession, unknown to me at the time, was a recently received Washington evaluation report equating the high number of airline crashes with internal FAA problems in the Western Region.

I told Butler that Stacy's incessant attacks were forcing the continuation of the same problems that caused earlier crashes. Again, Butler sympathized. Butler was a weak-minded individual and was simply doing what he was told. He had no initiative to buck the hierarchy. My efforts to obtain help failed.

I felt higher FAA management was calling the shots: Lynn Ashwell (Chief of the Western Region Air Carrier Branch); or William Krieger (Chief of Flight Standards in the Western Region).

The harassment to block reporting of serious safety problems escalated after Stacy arrived from Washington. The probability was that the pressure was directed from Washington.

Interference with the FAA's safety functions increased. Stacy was on a literal rampage, blocking every report unfavorable to United Airlines. I requested another meeting in the Western Regional office, which occurred on February 2 and 3, 1965. During this meeting I again described the serious problems and their relationship with a series of United Airlines crashes. Among those present was the chief of the air carrier division, Al Butler; head of the Denver Air Carrier District Office, Chuck Stacy; and chief of the Flight Standards Division, William Krieger.

These were serious charges and shouldn't be ignored. But they were ignored, and Krieger said, "Get on the team or get out." To which I replied: "I won't be a party to these activities!" I added: "If I have to request a Congressional investigation, I'll do it." I also stated I would file an employee grievance protesting the safety irregularities and coverup.

"An investigation of the entire
FAA Flight Standards is necessary."

After the conference ended, and before I left the building, the Chief of the Air Carrier Division, who was not part of the corrupt mentality, guardedly wished me luck. He sympathized, knowing the gravity of what I was trying to expose, but smart enough to realize nothing would be done to correct the problems. Before leaving the FAA building on Manchester Avenue, I visited the legal counsel's office to discuss the problems with an attorney friend, Rick Street. He knew the FAA problems and its inability to investigate itself. He candidly stated, "An investigation of the entire FAA Flight Standards is necessary."

My intention to file an employee grievance protesting the coverup and misconduct was similar to an FBI agent using the FBI employee grievance procedure to expose, for example, FBI ties to the Mafia. (Recent revelations about J. Edgar Hoover make the Mafia connection no longer absurd.) The FAA management group commenced actions to discredit me, seeking to block an exposure of the corruption. In that way FAA officials could respond to

Congressional or other inquiries by claiming the grievance hearing related to employee problems. These actions constituted obstruction of justice.

Before my assumption of the United assignment, and while working with American and Western Airlines in the Los Angeles area, the FAA had several times written letters praising my technical ability and expressing appreciation for my attitude and hard work. They now had to reverse themselves by criticizing everything I did.

THE PSYCHIATRIC APPROACH TO
FAA SAFETY RESPONSIBILITIES

Among the stunts these FAA officials pulled was charging me with psychiatric problems for reporting the safety irregularities. Stacy gave me a written memorandum and order:

It is requested that a medical examination be made of Inspector Stich to determine his fitness for duty. It is believed the above request is warranted [because] I have found his performance to be marginal in the following areas: ... use of snap judgment ... I have found in his conversation and correspondence, contradiction in some cases of facts; his method of communication [referring to the government reports required by my position] frequently involved distortion, insinuations and innuendos ... has frequently expressed quivering of lips, flushed face and inability to speak normally. This usually occurs during conversation wherein he has become argumentative, or is in the process of expressing his dislike of certain procedures, policy, etc., pertaining to the Agency.

Stacy would later testify at the safety grievance hearing that my reports of violations and safety problems at United Airlines supported his allegations. Apparently, inspectors reporting safety violations at a powerful airline such as United were guilty of psychiatric problems. My reports were similar to reports other inspectors had reported for years. In the eyes of FAA management, did they too have psychiatric problems?

IMAGINATIVE USE OF EMPLOYEE
GRIEVANCE PROCEDURE

The entire FAA office, as well as United Airlines management, knew of the retaliation for having reported the safety problems, discouraging other FAA inspectors from reporting the problems. At the request of FAA officials, Dr. Robert Fleming, flew to Denver from Los Angeles to conduct a psychiatric examination of me. Its intent was to discredit me and be a warning to other safety inspectors. We met for breakfast at the motel where he was staying. For a couple of hours I described the problems that other inspectors and I had uncovered, and the actions being taken to silence me. He recognized that he was being used, and immediately returned to Los Angeles. I then filed the employee grievance reporting the pattern of corruption that other inspectors and I had discovered.

The resources of the FAA Western Region were misused to discredit me and cover up for the rampant corruption at United Airlines and within the FAA. The particulars of the many harassing and threatening actions are described in *Unfriendly Skies*.

A month before the start of the hearing, I filed a report (March 5, 1965) with the Director of the FAA Western Region, Joe Tippets, detailing air safety and criminal acts other inspectors and I had discovered, and preceded the factual section of the report with a general statement:

An actual investigation of these alleged conditions discloses startling findings that affect aviation safety with past catastrophic effects. An impartial hearing officer will discover conditions of grave concern to the Federal Aviation Agency during the investigation of this grievance ... unsafe operating practices, standards and procedures ... low standards of [certain United check airmen] ... marginal and in some cases deplorable piloting ability on the part of certain senior pilots including check pilots themselves ... refusal of FAA personnel, primarily management, to correct or allow inspectors to correct obvious safety shortcomings and non compliance with Washington directives... The record of fatal and catastrophic accidents of the air carrier, along with obvious serious conditions, required immediate corrective actions. These were not accomplished.

An investigation of FAA management [and the part they played in certain] accidents may reveal startling implications affecting the structure of the Federal Aviation Agency, and the relationship of the crashes to their attitudes and actions involving safety activities.

[referring partly to destruction of official government reports] refusal to take corrective actions when inspectors disclose safety shortcomings or non compliance with Agency directives, when such action is not only authorized but demanded by job directives.

Numerous safety deficiencies exist today due to failure of FAA management to function as their job requires. The authority and responsibility ... to take corrective actions were ignored.

Many safety shortcomings exist. There is probably no other office in the United States with the massive and serious shortcomings that has resulted in a continuing series of fatal airline crashes, and many more will follow if corrective actions are not promptly taken.

Unknowingly, I stated problems similar to an earlier internal FAA investigation in 1964 by a Washington inspection team, but my statements were more blunt. The warnings were prophetic.

CHAPTER TWO

FAA KANGAROO COURT

Federal directives require the head of any federal agency to report any criminal allegations made by an employee to the U.S. Department of Justice. Since I had made serious allegations it is safe to assume that Justice Department officials knew of my charges, knew of the tactics used to silence me, and had approved the actions. Also, prior to the start of the hearing, I made formal complaints of criminal misconduct to the Federal Bureau of Investigation and the U.S. Department of Justice, putting them on notice of the charges. Instead of conducting an investigation, they engaged in a coverup. Not once, to this day, did the FBI or any other division in the U.S. Department of Justice examine my evidence or receive my testimony. The coverup had, of course, tragic consequences.

The FAA Administrator appointed an attorney from his staff, William Jennings, to act as the hearing officer. This hearing to receive testimony and evidence continued for approximately six weeks, followed by two months for submitting opening and reply briefs.

FORTUITOUS FINDING SHOWING THE PRIMARY
CAUSE OF THE WORLD'S WORST AIR DISASTER

I paid Denver attorney J.E. Kuttler to represent me at this hearing, but his performance was so grossly unsatisfactory that I dismissed him before the end of our first hour of the FAA hearing. It appeared he was deliberately sabotaging me, or was incompetent. As Kuttler gathered his folders from the conference table to turn over to me, he accidentally picked up one of many folders belonging to FAA attorney Donald Boberick, and gave it to me, thinking it was one of mine. That one act resulted in discovery of a document detailing criminal activities by United Airlines that played a role in some of the nation's worst air disasters.

After the first day's hearing, I carried home three suitcases containing copies of FAA reports to be introduced during subsequent hearings. As I worked late into the night preparing for the next day's presentation, I discovered the folder Kuttler accidentally picked up. Inside was a sequestered government document that was dynamite. The October 16, 1960, document, prepared and signed by several FAA inspectors, described the pattern of falsified training and competency-check flights and the falsification of records by United management. Arguably, the revealed criminal activities made the air safety and criminal violations into capital offenses.

If this report were known to the public and its importance recognized, the financial liabilities of United Airlines to the next-of-kin would skyrocket. Huge punitive damages, not covered by insurance, would be justified. United Airlines stock could plummet, and cause huge losses to individuals and corporations holding the stock. An exposure would show the nation's primary air safety agency engaging in rampant corruption.

The report didn't expose anything that the inspectors didn't already know, but it was hard evidence to enable others to recognize the gravity of the corruption associated with several recent air disasters involving United Airlines.

FAA attorney Boberick knew about the criminal activities that played a causative role in recent air disasters. He had the hidden report, knew of highly critical Washington reports, and had received complaints from other FAA inspectors. Despite this knowledge, and despite the brutal price that would be paid if the corruption was not exposed, this FAA attorney, and the FAA legal division, spent the few months of hearing and brief-writing, lying about the problems.

THE HIDDEN REPORT WAS A BLOCKBUSTER

The sequestered government report did more than anything else to explain why the New York City, Denver, and earlier crashes occurred. It was a blockbuster. The report stated in part:

Mr. Butler stated, "following an inspection and cross-check of United's training and maintenance records," what had disappointed him was that when he or Harrell were on board, the check takes three to three-and-a-half hours, but on inspection of the [aircraft] log book to see how long they were taking when we were NOT on board, it had been taking one hour fifteen minutes to one hour thirty minutes, and we just could not understand how they could do all the required [training-check] maneuvers in that time when the second in command was also being checked.

A memorandum of that type was undoubtedly preceded by many other inspector reports, but I did not have subpoena power to get them. On the other hand, Boberick probably had many of them in his possession.

INTRODUCING THE EXPLOSIVE REPORT

At the start of the hearing the following day, the FAA legal counsel asked if I had found one of his folders. I admitted that I had, and that I was about to introduce a copy of the contents of the folder into the hearing record. Boberick strongly protested the introduction of that highly sensitive document, which was hardly indicative of the FAA's primary duty to expose safety problems. Hearing Officer Jennings, also an attorney, tried to prevent the introduction of the report. Over Boberick's strong objections the report was introduced.

I produced dozens of official reports prepared by myself and other inspectors, proving that United Airlines' management had a practice of falsifying records to fraudulently indicate that federal safety requirements had been accomplished. I produced reports showing serious safety problems that I sought to correct, and gave testimony concerning the threats that other inspectors and I had received from United Airlines and FAA management.

The safety problems that I reported, and the corrective actions I exercised, which FAA management sought to block included: dangerous piloting practices; high-sink-rate descents on final approach for a landing; lack of altitude awareness; lack of knowledge of aircraft systems and procedures; non-compliance with the emergency evacuation training program; and much more. These were the same problems that were resulting in fatal airline crashes.

Not a single person gave testimony contradicting my charges or the hundreds of government documents that I submitted. The only opposition was the fabrication by the FAA legal counsel, who had no aviation expertise and it was not his role in a safety hearing. As the hearing officer stated at the beginning of the hearings, any testimony that I gave, that was not contradicted by any other testimony, would be accepted as true.

PROPHETIC WARNING

Time and again I warned verbally and in writing of the consequences resulting from the reported misconduct and the coverup of the misconduct. One of the warnings that I placed in my closing brief at the Denver air safety grievance was prophetic:

Many safety shortcomings exist. There is probably no other office in the United States with the massive and serious conditions existing, affecting safety, as in Denver. Any one of these safety shortcomings can bring newspaper headlines into being. Safety is endangered by existing safety shortcomings at this time, any one of which can cause a fatal or catastrophic accident tomorrow. The repercussions from the perjury may be paid for in blood and guts. The Agency tolerates a worsening of the existing conditions to depths never before reached, of misconduct and dereliction of duties. A sinister attempt to undermine the United States' aviation security could not be anymore effective than the conditions shown here.

This warning was stated in 1965, and the history of gory air disasters caused by the same unsafe and unlawful conditions continued uninterrupted at United Airlines for many years.

HEARING COVERUP BY THE FAA ADMINISTRATOR

Hearing officer Jennings, an attorney and Executive Director of the FAA, reflected the mindset of the FAA. Jennings knew of the pattern of hard-core criminal activities associated with the series of United Airline crashes. He knew the significance of the hidden report, and the significance of the criminal coverup of the report. He saw the continuation of the crashes occurring during the hearing. On August 24, 1965, the Executive Director of the FAA issued his report, which was approved by the FAA Administrator.

The hearing decision falsely stated there were no safety problems, even though the uncontradicted evidence proved otherwise. Hearing officer William Jennings, an attorney on the Administrator's staff, falsely stated the safety picture had improved. The facts showed otherwise. Crashes were more frequent. No testimony or evidence was introduced into the hearing to support that statement. The hearing decision falsely stated that the safety problems and violations did not exist because I had never reported them.

I introduced dozens of copies of previously submitted reports into the hearing record, showing he lied. Further, not a single report was introduced into the hearing record indicating any change in the safety violations and safety problems. The decision stated that the problems, which the report earlier stated did not exist, had been corrected, even though there was not a shred of evidence implying such corrective actions had occurred.

The report chastised me for reporting safety problems "when the need was long gone." Referring to my reports of the non compliance with the emergency evacuation training program, the report stated:

It was also clearly evident in this hearing that when this condition was reported by the grievant, nearly two years ago, the necessary steps to correct this condition were taken by the personnel then responsible. Further, it was also evident that at all times subsequent to the time that the corrective action was taken, United Air Lines had been found to be meeting all the requirements of the regulations.

But there were no reports or testimony that any corrective action had been taken. On the contrary, I conducted an investigation while the hearing was in progress, and submitted a report showing that no corrective actions had been taken. I named in that report the UAL ground instructor in charge of the training who admitted that fact to me.

The Executive Director's decision refused to address the shocking report prepared by other inspectors prior to the New York City crash. Every safety problem and safety violation, and the criminal falsification of safety records, received the same coverup. This misstating of facts, omitting evidence, violated numerous federal criminal statutes cited in later pages. When criminal acts result in fatalities, they become capital offenses, like outright murder.

Following this hearing coverup I continued to report the criminality to many members of Congress, to the FBI, to the Justice Department, to the media, and every government and non government check and balance that I could find. Despite the enormity of the charges, despite the gory consequences if my charges were true, despite the fact I held federal authority to make these determinations, and that I had evidence supporting my charges, not a single one of these checks and balances responded.

My reports of criminal misconduct related to an ongoing series of very brutal airline crashes, and the refusal to receive my evidence, were in some ways similar to reporting the placement of bombs on large aircraft that subsequently blew up. Despite the ongoing crashes arising from the alleged wrongdoings, none of the checks and balances would listen.

Removing bodies from a United Airlines Boeing 727 at Salt Lake City, another in a long line of fraud-related air disasters.

United Airlines crash into New York City, resulting from a pattern of corruption at United Airlines and within the government safety agencies.

CHAPTER THREE

SUBSEQUENT CRASHES

The FAA hearing and coverup were over, and it was déjâ vu all over again. The corruption continued, as did the crashes and the deaths. But what else could be expected? Let's look at a few of the consequences brought about by the conduct of the FAA, the NTSB, Justice Department, and members of Congress. The consequences didn't wait for the FAA safety hearing to end; they occurred during the hearing and to this day.

LAKE MICHIGAN

A United Airlines Boeing 720 crashed into Lake Michigan[5] due to the pilots' lack of altitude awareness, a problem I reported and for which I had undertaken corrective actions. FAA management had ordered me to stop the corrective actions. During the grievance hearing, FAA attorneys charged me with fabricating this safety problem in my detailed reports. Every one on board was killed in this Lake Michigan mishap, including a former president of the Air Line Pilots Association, whose silence helped bring about his death.

SALT LAKE CITY

A Boeing 727 crashed at Salt Lake City[6] with the loss of forty-three lives, due to three key, specific areas that I had reported:

* The initial crash was due to the pilot's high sink rate approach. Ironically, I had reported in my official reports that same dangerous approach technique of that same pilot. I made that report following an enroute inspection flight from Chicago to Denver via Omaha. As required by FAA directives, I recommended that the captain be removed from line flying until satisfactorily completing recurrent training in approach and landing techniques. That was not done. Ironically, I had made similar reports of two United Airlines FAA-approved check airmen, and was

---

[5] August 16, 1965.
[6] November 11, 1965.

suspended from the program for two weeks in retaliation for making the report.

* The resulting fire that engulfed the aircraft and killed forty-three passengers was caused by the flight engineer's failure to turn off the fuel shutoff valves and the fuel booster pumps. After the crash landing, fuel lines broke open, and fuel poured out of the broken lines, under pressure from the operating fuel pumps, igniting as the aircraft slid down the runway for 2,000 feet. I had repeatedly reported the flight engineer training program to be dangerously inadequate, resulting in unqualified flight engineers who could not perform basic flight engineer duties. FAA management used these reports as the basis to charge me with psychiatric problems.

* Compounding the flight engineer's failure to perform, the crew poorly evacuated the passengers, even though time permitted everyone to be evacuated. I had repeatedly reported that United Airlines was falsifying its records to fraudulently indicate emergency evacuation training was given, when the training had not occurred. During the FAA grievance hearing, I conducted another examination of this training and filed a report stating the legal requirements were still being violated, as admitted to me by a UAL ground instructor responsible for performing the training. The FAA legal counsel and hearing officer falsely stated I never made any such reports. The reports entered into the FAA safety hearing proved these statements to be lies.

LOS ANGELES

A United 727 crashed shortly after departing Los Angeles International Airport[7] due to:

* Unlawfully dispatching the aircraft with an inoperative generator, the illegality having continued for over a dozen flights.

* Compounding the inoperative generator problem by dispatching an aircraft in which a second generator circuit panel was malfunctioning. Mechanics at Los Angeles tried unsuccessfully to fix the defective circuit panel.

* Flying aircraft without a backup flight attitude indicator powered by a battery source, making almost certain the loss of the aircraft if an entire electrical system failure occurred during instrument flight conditions. Every known airline in the world had a backup, battery-powered, attitude-indicator in case this failure occurred. Except United Airlines.

* Poor knowledge of the aircraft systems by the engineer and the pilots, who shut down one of the two engines with the operating generators, causing the entire electrical load, including the ship's galley, to be powered by a single generator. This action caused the remaining generator to fail and all electrical power to be lost to the aircraft and flight instruments. Without instruments, at night, in the clouds over the Pacific Ocean, the plane crashed, with the loss of everyone on board.

---

[7] January 19, 1969.

PHILADELPHIA

A United Boeing 737 crashed during takeoff from Philadelphia International Airport (July 19, 1971) when the captain rejected the takeoff long after the aircraft had passed the reject point. The aircraft had lifted off the runway when the crew heard an explosion caused by the left engine disintegrating. Because of United's poor training and sham check procedures, the captain reduced the power to idle on the remaining good engine, trying to land on the remaining runway. This was contrary to standard operating procedures. The plane touched down with only one thousand feet of runway remaining, when many thousands of feet were necessary to bring the aircraft to a halt. Everyone died.

PORTLAND

A United DC-8 crashed at Portland, Oregon (December 28, 1978), after all four engines ran out of fuel. An hour earlier, as the aircraft prepared to land, the landing-gear-down lights did not properly illuminate, indicating one of the three landing gears may not have been down and locked. This was a minor abnormality as the flight engineer could visually check within five minutes that the three landing gears were down and locked. But the crew didn't understand the system. Even worse, the crew didn't recognize the precarious position they put themselves in as the aircraft circled for an hour while the crew puzzled as to what action to take. The aircraft arrived in the Portland area with only one hour of reserve fuel, and this fuel had now been exhausted. When the captain finally decided to proceed to the airport and land, all four engines ran out of fuel, causing the aircraft to plunge to the ground several miles before reaching the airport. In darkness, the heavy aircraft crashed into the outskirts of Portland, causing many passengers to die.

SALT LAKE CITY

During a night approach to Salt Lake City Airport (December 18, 1977) a United DC-8 crashed into the side of a mountain, killing everyone on board. Pilot error was the cause of the crash, since the pilot held on the wrong side of a holding pattern, crashing into the mountains northeast of Salt Lake City.

DETROIT

A United DC-8 crashed during takeoff from Detroit on January 11, 1983, killing everyone on board. The captain allowed the flight engineer to make the takeoff, even though the engineer was unqualified to fly the aircraft and had flunked earlier pilot training. During the takeoff the flight engineer incorrectly set the horizontal stabilizer trim to an extremely nose-up position and the Captain didn't check the setting. Immediately after becoming airborne, the plane pitched up sharply, stalled, and crashed to the ground.

CHICAGO

A United Boeing 737 crashed into a Chicago residential area (December 8, 1972) during an approach, killing everyone on board, including the wife of Watergate figure E. Howard Hunt. She was reportedly carrying money to silence Watergate witnesses, and carried papers implicating President Richard Nixon in the coverup. A Chicago public-interest group, known as the Citizens

Committee,[8] believed that Justice Department personnel played a role in the crash of United Flight 553, and that they wanted key individuals on Flight 553 exterminated. Twelve of the people who boarded United Flight 553 had something in common relating to questionable Justice Department and Watergate activities.

There had been a gas pipeline lobbyist meeting as part of the American Bar Association meeting in Washington, D.C., conducted by Roger Morea. Among the lobbyists attending were attorneys for the Northern Natural Gas Company of Omaha; attorneys for Kansas-Nebraska Natural Gas Company; and president of the Federal Land Bank in Omaha. The Citizens Committee portrayed these people as a group determined to blow the lid off the Watergate case.

For many years Chicago resident Lawrence O'Connor boarded flight 553 like clockwork. He had no Watergate connections, but he had friends in the White House. On this particular Friday, O'Connor supposedly received a call from someone he knew in the White House, strongly advising him not to take Flight 553. The caller advised him to go to a special meeting instead of taking that flight.[9] Whether this was coincidental or to save his life is unknown to me, although the Citizens Committee considers it significant.

U.S. Attorney General John Mitchell, later indicted and sent to federal prison, and the Justice Department were putting pressure on Northern Natural Gas. The firm had subsidiaries that the federal government indicted on federal criminal charges in Omaha, Chicago, and Hammond, Indiana. (September 7, 1972.) Justice Department charges included bribery of local officials in Northwest Indiana and Illinois, to get clearance for installing the pipeline through their state.[10]

Allegedly to blackmail the Justice Department and cause them to drop the charges, the Omaha firm uncovered documents showing that Mitchell, while Attorney General in 1969, dropped antitrust charges against a competitor of Northern Natural Gas—El Paso Natural Gas Co. Just before the crash, Carl Kruger, an official with Northern Natural Gas Company, had been browbeating federal officials to drop the criminal charges.[11]

The Citizen Committee alleged that dropping these charges saved the utility 300 million dollars. Simultaneously, Mitchell purchased through a law partner a stock interest in El Paso Natural Gas Company. Gas and oil interests, including El Paso, Gulf Resources, and others, contributed heavily to Nixon's spy fund supervised by Mitchell. The Citizens Committee reported that Kruger had previously been warned he would never live to reach Chicago. Kruger carried these revealing documents on United Flight 553, telling his wife that he had irreplaceable papers of a sensitive nature in his possession. For months after the crash Kruger's widow demanded that United Airlines turn his briefcase over to her.

---

[8] Citizens Committee to Clean Up the Courts, 9800 So. Oglesby, Chicago, Illinois 60617.
[9] Report by Citizens Committee.
[10] *Chicago Daily News* September 8, 1972.
[11] *Chicago Tribune*, May 18, 1973.

CBS news reporter Michelle Clark traveled with Mrs. Hunt, doing an exclusive story on Watergate. Ms. Clark had already gained considerable insight into the bugging and coverup through her boyfriend, a CIA operative. Others knew of this exclusive interview, including the Justice Department.

According to some media articles, Dorothy Hunt conveyed offers of executive clemency with the financial payoffs to some of the Watergate defendants. Mrs. Hunt also reportedly sought to leave the United States with over two million dollars in cash and negotiables that she obtained from CREEP (Committee to Re-Elect the President).

Early in December 1972, Dorothy Hunt and her husband threatened to blow the lid off the White House if Hunt wasn't freed of the criminal charges and if they both didn't get several million dollars.[12] Hunt claimed, according to McCord, to have evidence necessary to impeach Nixon. McCord said matters were coming to a head early in December 1972. Dorothy Hunt was unhappy about bribing defendants and witnesses, and wanted out of the mess.

The Citizens Committee to Clean Up the Courts reported that over a hundred FBI agents were inexplicably in the area when the plane crashed, and that the FBI kept a medical team out of the crash zone. One member of the medical team said he heard someone in the crashed plane screaming for help.[13] Witnesses near the airport reported that the FBI agents were there before the fire department arrived. Something highly irregular appeared to be going on, involving the Department of Justice.

In *Secret Agenda*, author Jim Hougan makes reference to this intrigue and the request to the FBI by Michael Stevens (who supplied bugging devices to James McCord, allegedly under authority of the CIA) for protection. Stevens claimed he was to receive part of the money Mrs. Hunt was carrying, that his life had been threatened, and that he believed Mrs. Hunt's death had been a homicide.

MORE POLITICAL INTRIGUE?

The day after Flight 553 crashed, the White House appointed White House aide Egil (Bud) Krogh, Jr. to the post of Under-Secretary of Transportation, which controlled the FAA role in the investigation. His qualifications? Krogh was involved in the Ellsberg burglary caper and was part of the White House Plumbers group. In his new position Krogh had an important safety role supervising, or muzzling, the NTSB and the FAA. He could exert political influence over the NTSB investigation through the politically appointed NTSB Board members who establish the official probable cause of the crash.

Further control over the air safety process was demonstrated ten days later. On December 19, 1972 the White House appointed Nixon's deputy assistant and secretary to the Cabinet, Alexander Butterfield, former CIA aviation liaison officer, to head the FAA.[14] The officials controlling the FAA, the NTSB, and the Department of Transportation, had political loyalties

[12] See Memo of Watergate spy, James McCord, before the Ervin Committee. (*New York Times* 5/9/73).
[13] Testimony offered at the NTSB hearing on June 13 and 14, 1973.
[14] Jack Anderson's column, Chicago Daily News, 5/8/73.

to the White House. At the initial NTSB crash investigation hearings (February 1973), White House Appointment Secretary Dwight Chapin reportedly threatened media people with reprisals if they mentioned sabotage. These political appointees could influence matters affecting the nation's air safety.

UNITED'S CONNECTIONS IN GOVERNMENT

Five weeks after the crash, Nixon's appointment secretary, Dwight Chapin, became a top executive with United Air Lines in the Chicago home office, even though he had no previous business experience. Before the crash, Herbert Kalmbach, Nixon's personal attorney had been an attorney for United Air Lines.

Those federal officials were capable of carrying out reprisals against the news media through Clay Whitehead, Nixon's communication czar. The breakup of the networks on antitrust charges was always lurking in the wings. Threats of IRS harassment, Justice Department prosecution for vague federal offenses, fabricated charges, and news handouts, all played a part in government control of the news media.

NEVER IN LIVING MEMORY

Supporting the fact that these irregular actions occurred, NTSB chairman John Reed testified before the House government Activities Subcommittee on January 13, 1973, concerning Justice Department interference with the NTSB's investigative duties. Reed testified that he sent a letter to the FBI, claiming that never had the FBI acted as they had in this crash. Reed said fifty FBI agents came into the crash zone shortly after the crash, assuming the duties assigned by law to the NTSB.

The FBI confiscated the Midway Control Tower tape relating to Flight 553, interfering with the NTSB investigation. The FBI conducted twenty-six interviews, including the surviving flight attendants, obstructing the NTSB's safety responsibilities.

At the original NTSB accident hearings, Board members refused to consider the documentation and testimony provided by the Citizens Committee relating to suspicious FBI activities. The NTSB reopened the hearings after the committee sued the NTSB (June 13, 14, 1973). Over thirteen hundred pages of documentation were produced by the group and many witnesses were brought forward, establishing the obstruction of the accident investigation by the FBI. The final NTSB report ignored the committee's testimony and evidence.

The Citizens Committee alleged that a gang known as the Sarelli group came into possession of the highly sensitive documents carried by Mrs. Hunt. This discovery was made after the arrest of gang members on January 12, 1973, for an unrelated robbery.[15] The Nixon Strike Force in Chicago prosecuted the case against the Sarelli mob. What they didn't know was that their star witness against the gang was a staff investigator on the Citizens' Committee, Alex Bottos, Jr.

---

[15] U.S. Magistrate Balog's records, 72-41, U.S. Courthouse, Chicago.

There were many near-crashes that avoided becoming crashes by luck. Some of the United Airlines aircraft landed with only a few minutes of fuel remaining, avoiding a major disaster by a matter of minutes.

There were other crashes at United Airlines, and there were crashes at other airlines due to the corruption I uncovered.

A more thorough description of these events is found in *Unfriendly Skies—Saga of Corruption*, written by the author.

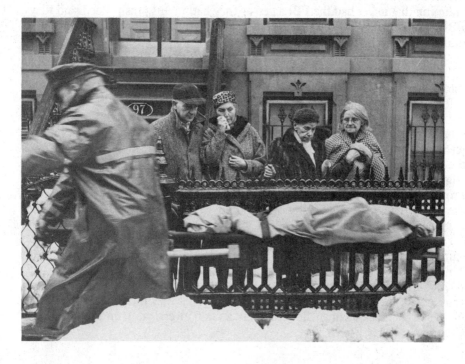

Removing Bodies From United DC-8 Crash In New York City

Removing Bodies From United DC-8 Crash In New York City

CHAPTER FOUR

CORRUPT AIR SAFETY
CHECKS AND BALANCES

Starting in 1964 and continuing for years, whenever an airline crash was associated with FAA misconduct, I petitioned members of Congress to receive my evidence and testimony showing the connections between the crash and the documented FAA, NTSB, and UAL misconduct. In the mid-1960s several members of Congress admitted the gravity of my charges and offered to investigate. But they quickly backed off, giving sham excuses, such as this matter was not in their area of responsibilities, even though they admitted that it was, prior to contacting Justice Department officials.

Hundreds of members of Congress were petitioned to receive my evidence. The few who expressed concern included Senators Robert Kennedy, William Proxmire, Mike Monroney; Representative Henry Gonzalez, and others. Senator Proxmire wrote that he hoped my charges would be given the "attention they seem to deserve." But he did nothing to get the attention other than wish me luck. His letter continued:

> It was good of you to go into such great detail regarding your accusation of criminal malfeasance in the Federal Aviation Administration. Frankly, I think you would be well advised to submit whatever evidence you have regarding this matter to the Aviation Subcommittee of the Senate Commerce Committee. This Subcommittee is chaired by Senator Monroney and has a great deal more experience in the field of aviation law than I have. I simply don't have the staff or the expertise to give this matter the attention it seems to deserve.

Over the next three decades I discovered that regardless of the gravity of the criminal acts I brought to their attention, regardless of their lawful requirement to receive evidence of criminal activities, not a single member of Congress would receive my evidence. Hundreds were contacted by petitions and letters, as I uncovered criminal activities as serious or far more so than what I had discovered in the aviation field. This refusal to perform a duty became even worse as my activist activities discovered corruption far beyond my realm of understanding at this stage.

PATTERN OF NTSB OBSTRUCTION OF JUSTICE

Officials in control of the NTSB were heavily involved in the aviation-related corruption. I first presented evidence of the criminality associated with a series of airline crashes in 1963. Before those reports, my predecessor on the United DC-8 program had done the same. Many crashes followed my warnings to the NTSB. Under federal statutory and case law, their coverup and refusal to perform their duty made them as guilty as the principals at United Airlines and the FAA. This deep involvement as co-conspirators prevents the NTSB from ever conducting an in-depth investigation into the underlying air safety problems.

Donald Madole, a former FAA attorney during the investigation of the New York City and Denver crashes [and subsequently chief of the air safety section of the Civil Aeronautic Board][16] knew the relationship between safety problems and the resulting crashes. He was the FAA attorney in charge of the NTSB hearing into the United Airlines DC-8 crash at Denver in the fall of 1961. Frank Harrell had contacted him in Washington prior to that crash, as well as prior to the United DC-8 crash into New York City, describing the rampant corruption within the FAA and at United Airlines. By now, Madole knew as well as anyone the price the public and the crews paid for the deeply entrenched pattern of corruption and coverups.

Several times I put the NTSB on notice in such a way that they could not sidestep the issues. I sent to the head of the NTSB a several-hundred-page document specifically identifying the pattern of air safety and criminal acts associated with a series of airline crashes in which the NTSB played a role through their coverups. I demanded a meaningful reply from the NTSB, and they refused to provide one.

I sought assistance by writing to Colorado Representative McVicker, who represented my home district in Colorado at that time. The letter explained the NTSB involvement in the scandal, the report that I had sent to the NTSB, and my inability to obtain a response. McVicker wrote to the NTSB and received a reply stating: "Our Bureau of Investigation [has] been unable to substantiate his allegations relating to safety hazards." The NTSB advised that the Congressman "will be ... advised ... if subsequent review produces any information relevant to a hazard in aviation safety."

The NTSB had access to thousands of pages of evidence that I introduced into the Denver grievance hearing, and had the proof supporting my charges. These were not difference-of-opinion or poor-judgment charges that I brought to their attention. They were hard-core air safety and criminal violations.

Certainty of recurring crashes from the uncorrected corruption didn't appear sufficient cause for either McVicker or the NTSB to address my charges. Seeking to force them into action, I wrote to McVicker nine months

---

[16] Later renamed National Transportation Safety Board.

later, asking that he inquire of the NTSB the status of their findings, which he did. The NTSB replied, "The investigator who has been reviewing this case is out of town and will not be available until the week of June 6. Upon his return a more detailed reply to your request will be prepared."

The NTSB investigator returned to Washington on June 6, and on June 12 the NTSB wrote to Congressman McVicker stating: "There is no evidence ... that Mr. Stich's allegations as to safety hazards ... [exist]."

The NTSB is a small organization, and the investigators are in close touch with FAA inspectors, enabling me to determine who was examining my material. I met an old friend, Ed Jensen, on May 26, at the FAA center in Oklahoma City, who invited me to join him and a friend, Bill Ayton. Ayton was none other than the investigator from the NTSB who was examining my material, and who would return to Washington on *June 6*.

During this fortuitous encounter the NTSB investigator referred to my 3500-page closing brief in the Denver safety hearing, stating *he* had the responsibility for reading my material. He said: "The report reflects poorly upon the Agency," adding, "I've worked on the material with Don Madole." This conversation indicated that Ayton considered the material serious, and that he was the one to whom the NTSB referred as having reviewed the material, and that the head of the aviation section knew about the charges.

I asked, "Why didn't the NTSB act on that report before the accidents that followed, as I warned they would?" Ayton replied: "You sent it to the wrong section, it should have been sent to the safety division. Why don't you send it now to the Board's Bureau of Safety?" Ayton was naive; it was the Board's Bureau of Safety that had referred the report to him. Further, anyone within the NTSB had a responsibility to insure that the proper people inside the NTSB are made aware of such serious charges coming from a federal inspector holding federal authority to make such determinations.

"The NTSB has their tit in the wringer..."

"The NTSB has their tit in the wringer now," I said, "especially since the Salt Lake City accident. It certainly doesn't want to admit *now* that it did nothing when advised, before the accident, of the problems that were later identified as the causes of the crash. It is going to take an outside investigation to bring this matter out." Ayton stated he had possession of my material and that it was the only copy the NTSB had. He admitted that the charges were very serious, and that he had looked it over, adding that he would look at it again when he returned to Washington. Ayton was obviously *the* person whom the NTSB told Representative McVicker was examining my material.

"Members of Congress have no authority..."

I explained to McVicker the coverup tactics by the NTSB and their earlier involvement in the criminal activities associated with several of the air disasters. McVicker responded, "I am sorry that the report is not more favorable, but as you know, members of Congress have no authority over agencies of the Executive Branch, and our only prerogative is to make suggestions or recommendations."

No authority? Members of Congress have oversight authority and responsibility over the agencies they create. They are constantly conducting investigations and asking other government agencies, especially the General Accounting Office (GAO), to conduct investigations for them. All government departments and their officers are accountable to Congress, acting and funded by virtue of the statutes creating them, and the GAO is one means of determining that the legislated agencies and programs are being properly operated.

The Supreme Court recognized the authority and responsibility of Congress to investigate wrongdoings in government departments and agencies, especially violations of Congressional laws. In *Watkins v. United States*[17], the Supreme Court stated:

Congress has the power to investigate "departments of the federal government to expose corruption, inefficiency or waste ... [and to make] inquiries concerning the administration of existing laws as well as proposed or possibly needed statutes."

Representatives Pete Stark, Jerome Waldie, Pete McClosky, and Senator Alan Cranston, plus many others, from my resident state of California, all refused to act when I reported the corruption to them. I sent detailed letters of the FAA misconduct to many other Congressmen.[18] Some acknowledged the seriousness of the problem. Some ignored my letters. None helped. Their excuses were all basically the same; the corruption wasn't within the scope of their responsibilities. None questioned the validity of my charges or the facts.

RESPONSIBILITIES OF THE NTSB

The authority over aviation safety is provided by the Federal Aviation Act, which provides that the Civil Aeronautics Board's Bureau of Air Safety, investigates aviation accidents, publish accident reports, and make safety recommendations to the FAA. (The Bureau of Air Safety has been changed to the National Transportation Safety Board.) This responsibility is stated in Section 102, which reads in part:

The Board shall consider the following, among other things, as being in the public interest ... assure the highest degree of safety [by] air carriers ... The promotion of safety in air commerce ... The Board is empowered to perform such acts, to conduct such investigations, to issue and amend such orders, and to make and amend such general or special rules, Regulations and Procedures, as it shall deem necessary to carry out the provisions of, and to exercise and perform its powers and duties under the Act.

Essentially, the Board is required to do anything necessary to investigate and correct air safety deficiencies or irregularities. Section 701 of the Act further states:

It shall be the duty of the Board to ascertain what will best tend to reduce or eliminate the possibility of, or recurrence of, accidents by conducting special studies and investigations on matters pertaining to safety in air navigation and the prevention of accidents.

[17] 354 U.S. 178.
[18] Senators Eugene McCarthy, Daniel Brewster, John Stennis, Russell Long, Gaylord Nelson, Strom Thurmond, Barry Goldwater, and many, many others.

Responsibility for the NTSB to conduct an investigation is spelled out in section 1002 of Public Law 85-726, otherwise known as the Federal Aviation Act, which states in part:

Any person may file with the Administrator [of the FAA] or the Board ... a complaint in writing with respect to anything done or omitted to be done by any person in contravention of any provisions of this Act, or of any requirement established pursuant thereto ... it shall be the duty of the Administrator or the Board to investigate the matters complained of.

POLITICAL PRESSURES UPON THE NTSB

Political pressure to alter accident reports is well known within the FAA and NTSB. Charles O. Miller, training seminar director of the Flight Safety Foundation (former director of the Bureau of Aviation Safety for the National Transportation Safety Board from 1968 to 1974), stated he left the Board because of a degradation of safety and technical competence brought about by political pressures on NTSB members.

SUICIDE BY NTSB BOARD MEMBER

The effects of political contributions and political interests affecting the NTSB was evident in the suicide of William Gingery of the NTSB. Gingery left a suicide note implicating Richard J. O'Melia, acting chairman of the Board at that time. Gingery's suicide note made reference to the obstruction of aircraft accident investigations through illegal political contributions by airlines. The Congressional subcommittee looking into these payoffs asked O'Melia about these charges. As could be expected, O'Melia denied the allegations.

O'Melia then accused Board member Timm of ordering him to discontinue these investigations, which Timm denied. I don't know who is lying, but bribing government officials, especially members of Congress, is certainly no secret. The subcommittee submitted evidence to the Justice Department revealing "a strong likelihood of highly improper and possibly criminal behavior on the part of the Board members themselves." That subcommittee reported that the material was being submitted "to see whether criminal prosecution is warranted." These were serious matters that would open a can of worms if exposed. Nothing came of it, of course.

The report continued: "When the interests of the industry and those of the consumer have diverged, the board has chosen to protect the industry at the expense of the consumer." This relationship dovetailed with my findings that the Board had repeatedly covered up safety and criminal violations associated with airline crashes. The United Salt Lake City crash was only one example of many of how safety and lives are sacrificed to protect vested interests, especially of politically powerful United Airlines. The relationship is often so subtle that neither passengers nor crewmembers recognize it. NTSB accident investigators frequently complained to me that they were pressured by political members of the Board to omit or change the official cause of a crash.

OBSTRUCTION OF JUSTICE BY
JUSTICE DEPARTMENT OFFICIALS

A contradiction exists. The Department of Justice is required to enforce federal laws, but also required to defend the government and its employees in federal lawsuits. Obviously, priority must be given to upholding the laws and Constitution of the United States, over protecting criminal acts by government employees and government officials. If Justice Department officials prosecuted, instead of covered up, the misconduct of federal officials, there would be no contradiction.

Controlling the conduct of the Department of Justice is the politically appointed U.S. Attorney General, whose responsibilities are stated in Public Law 89-554:

The Attorney General and the Federal Bureau of Investigation may investigate any violation of title 18 [federal criminal codes] involving government officers and employees ... any information, allegation, or complaint received in a department or agency of the executive branch of the government, relating to violations of title 18, involving government officers and employees, shall be expeditiously reported to the Attorney General by the head of the department or agency ...

Internal FAA directives require that allegations of criminal misconduct committed by federal employees be promptly relayed to the U.S. Attorney General. My letters to the FBI and other divisions of the Justice Department also insured that the Attorney General knew of the allegations, and surely examined the evidence I submitted into the FAA grievance hearing supporting the charges.

AMONG THOSE HOLDING RESPONSIBILITIES TO ACT

The coverup tactics during the FAA Denver grievance hearing constituted federal crimes, including perjury, subornation of perjury, withholding of information, obstructing justice, tampering with air safety, falsification of hearing records, and conspiracy to defraud. Justice Department officials had responsibilities to prosecute these crimes. This responsibility also fell upon the U.S. Attorney in Denver, where the criminal acts during the FAA air safety hearing occurred.

After the FAA transferred me to Oklahoma, I filed a complaint with the U.S. Attorney in Oklahoma City, reporting the corruption associated with several of the crashes. I identified myself as a government employee, briefly detailed the specific criminal acts associated with the Salt Lake City and other crashes, and requested that they contact me for further information and evidence.

Justice Department personnel never contacted me. The U.S. Attorney responded: "The matter you complained of occurred in Denver, it seems unlikely that any action by this office would be appropriate. However, we are double checking our own judgment on this with our superiors."

A private citizen does not have to run to the far corners of the country to report federal crimes. The local U.S. Attorney is responsible for making the *initial* investigation and then coordinating it with the U.S. Attorney at Denver. The Justice Department stonewalled me, preventing me from reporting these serious federal crimes. Officials in control of the Justice Department gave me phony excuses for not investigating what was the free world's worst air-disaster-related scandal. This stonewalling, or felony coverup, continues to this day. I would later discover that coverup and obstruction of justice are synonymous with those in control of the Justice Department when federal officials are implicated. When I received no reply, I wrote again:

> It is now almost five weeks since I submitted to your office charges of criminal acts gravely involved in air carrier safety. Is it possible that your office has no interest in this serious matter involving the public's welfare? I think we both realize the government scandal that would be uncovered if the material that you have is actually true.

Again, no answer. A month later I wrote again, stressing the urgency of the matter and stating that irregularities "would have a very important effect upon aviation safety, and delay can have a very adverse effect." No answer.

My letter to Alfred Hantman, Chief of the Criminal Division in the Justice Department, produced the following response:

> Please be advised that your letter of September 14, 1966, directed to the United States Attorney in this jurisdiction, and relative to certain allegations of perjury committed by unidentified persons in connection with a government safety hearing, has been referred to the Department of Justice for its consideration.

At that time I had not provided the Justice Department with any evidence. Their responsibility to investigate criminal activity required that they receive my evidence, unless they already knew of the crimes and were engaging in a coverup. I submitted another letter on October 9, followed by a third on October 30, emphasizing the gravity of the matter. I was a government safety investigator, holding federal authority to make these determinations. It was preposterous that I, a federal investigator, making such serious charges, was unable to get the nation's top law enforcement people to receive my evidence. I sought to circumvent this block by reporting the matter to FBI Director J. Edgar Hoover, stating in part:

> Possibly I should have made this request sooner [for an FBI investigation of my allegations] but I had expected other government agencies to act, who are now involved in the crime themselves. I also was not completely aware of the responsibilities specifically delegated to your bureau until analyzing the government Organization Manual, Executive Order 10450 and other material.
>
> I am requesting an investigation into the crimes of perjury, criminal misconduct, by government personnel, especially as it preceded the tragic and expected cremation of forty-three passengers at Salt Lake City from ... forcibly-continued unsafe and unlawful conditions. Unfortunately, we are beyond the point of euphemistic platitudes, and immediate corrective action, not whitewash, is required. The affront upon the public's welfare cannot continue ... I really think that at least one government agency should finally respond to this serious condition and its responsibilities before the public is made aware of the crime. Naturally, I am the one person with the information of the crime. May I have an acknowledgment from your Bureau of this letter and of its intentions, Mr. Hoover?

U.S. Attorney Hantman then wrote: "I feel certain that the Department of Justice will take whatever action may be necessary in connection with the information you have heretofore furnished." The Justice Department never contacted me.

Major airline crashes were continuing to occur as I sought to present evidence relating to their causes, and no one wanted to hear the evidence.

WHY WERE THE CRIMES COMMITTED?

FBI agent Don Sloatt came to my Oklahoma City home after I sent a letter to FBI Director Hoover. Sloatt explained that he wanted to make an initial contact to determine the general nature of my allegations. He made it clear that it wasn't an investigative or fact-finding visit, and he didn't look at my evidence or go into any specifics.

It turned out the real purpose of Sloatt's visit was to discourage me from pursuing the exposure activities. He advised that the FBI could not take action on government corruption unless they knew the reason for the crimes. "This is asinine," I retorted. "Giving the reason for the crime, much less proving it, would be virtually impossible. This requires looking into a person's inner thought processes." I added, "Your position is synonymous to a policeman standing indifferent as a crime is committed because he doesn't know the *reason* for the attack!" Not one of the federal criminal laws permits criminal acts to go unpunished because the *reason* for the crime is unknown. On the contrary, federal statutes and case law make it clear that the reason for the crimes being committed is immaterial. Sloatt then tried to justify FBI inactivity on the basis that the accident rate wasn't very high. Sloatt was not an expert or authority on air safety. Nor were criminal acts justified on the basis that the resulting accident rates were not high. Further, the accident rate **was** high.

REQUEST FOR A JUSTICE
DEPARTMENT INVESTIGATION

Recognizing that I wasn't buying his argument, Sloatt said: "This appears to be a matter for our fraud division to investigate. I'll recommend that the Justice Department conduct further investigations." Before leaving, Sloatt asked me to submit a letter outlining the general allegations in more detail, which I did. The silent treatment continued. I wrote directly to FBI Director J. Edgar Hoover, stating in part:

[My previous letter of October 31] made reference to what I considered to be a serious crime within government that is ... creating aviation chaos with one example being the intimate association with the Salt Lake City crash of November 11, 1965. To this date I have not been contacted for the details and evidence that I possess except for a brief discussion with a local FBI agent who of course wasn't equipped for conducting the intensive investigation ... the public is getting the short end of this failure to investigate.

Hoover never responded. In a later speech he said, "The best way to solve the crime problem is by swift detection, prompt prosecution and sure punishment." While still employed by the Federal Aviation Agency, I again tried to obtain a response from Hoover. I stated in my certified letter, "To this date the Federal Bureau of Investigation has never once contacted me for the specifics of the alleged crime that I brought to its attention, or looked over any of my myriad evidence, facts, and other material pertaining to my allegations."

FBI OBSTRUCTION OF JUSTICE

Accusing Hoover of coverup, I wrote: "If the crime actually exists, and it certainly does, then we have the added problem of the felony of harboring the crime which would be attached to anyone knowing of it and refusing to bring it to immediate justice."

I had been naive, thinking that all I really had to do was present evidence of the FAA corruption, the related crashes, and that Justice Department officials would swing into action. What especially bothered me was that they knew the FAA corruption and deadly consequences would continue if full-blown exposure and prosecution did not occur.

I seemingly ran out of federal agencies to whom I could appeal. I also hadn't done well with the legislative branch, but I kept trying. I contacted Representative Jerome Waldie (D-CA) on the basis that I had resided in California before I moved to Colorado. I described the FBI coverup and requested that Waldie obtain an explanation from Hoover, which he did.

HOOVER'S CONFIDENTIAL REPLY

Hoover's reply to Waldie's letter:

I have received your letter of February 10, and copies of official communications written by Mr. Rodney F. Stich. However, I did not receive the letter sent to you by this individual. In response to your inquiry and for your confidential information, Mr. Stich has been interviewed by a representative of this Bureau. Mr. Stich has also corresponded with this Bureau, and based upon the data he has set forth there has been no violation of federal law coming within the investigative jurisdiction of the FBI.

The FBI never asked for my evidence and never received any. The FBI was stonewalling, and lied about the FBI contacting me. They were covering up for crash and death-related criminal activities. It is understandable that Hoover requested Waldie to keep confidential the contents of the letter. Accidentally or on purpose, Waldie sent me a copy.

WHO'S LYING—HOOVER OR ME?

In my reply to Waldie's letter I described the discrepancies in Hoover's letter and requested that Waldie pursue the contradiction. Waldie answered:

Although I have read and re-read your letters of March 12 and March 14, I still cannot overcome the hurdle of J. Edgar Hoover's letter to me of February 27. The only way that I will feel free to proceed on this matter is to assume that Mr. Hoover is misinforming me as to the fact that his agency has examined your material and has concluded that no violation of federal law occurred. I am not willing to make that assumption. I am returning for your file, the information you have heretofore forwarded me and regret that I am not able to be of further service.

FBI Director Hoover was lying. Rather than let the matter drop, I asked Waldie to obtain the following information from Hoover:

1. The date that the FBI alleges to have contacted me and examined my material, from which determination was made that no violations of federal laws were involved. The mere coverage of the multitude of federal criminal, safety and Civil Service laws, for which the FBI has responsibility, would take at least several hours if not longer. There are at least eight criminal laws, a multitude of federal safety laws, and Civil Service Commission regulations included in this area of responsibility.

2. What material was examined? There are thirty-five hundred pages of hearing records, hundreds of pages of correspondence, some of which would imply fraud in statements to Congressmen. These specific areas would require considerable explanation to provide any investigator with an understanding of the allegations. To examine these, it would take at the very minimum, one day, and probably longer. I hardly feel that my memory is so bad that I recall none of these actions taking place.

Waldie surely recognized the significance of the implications. In an apologetic manner he asked Hoover for this information. Hoover refused to provide the requested data, writing:

As indicated in my letter to you of February 27, information which Mr. Stich has supplied the Bureau, both through correspondence and personal interview, has been considered and indicates no violation of federal law within the investigative jurisdiction of the FBI.

Waldie wrote back, "I would now suggest that you proceed through a civil court action." That was hogwash. It is totally impractical for a private citizen to use a civil action to address criminal misconduct by government officials in control of a large segment of the federal government. First, the cost would be out of sight. No attorney would tackle such powerful adversaries. A civil action did not have the subpoena power to force federal officials to testify.

Typical of members of Congress, Waldie said the right things for public consumption, totally alien to realities. In a newsletter to his constituency, Waldie later wrote:

It is readily apparent that there is an overwhelming lack of confidence in the integrity of the Legislative Branch. My concern with this ... stems from a conviction that each of the three Branches of government are experiencing a similar decline in the confidence of the general public, and if this is so, the Nation is deeply threatened because self-government simply cannot function unless respect for and confidence in its basic institutions exists among the governed.

"The part played by the FBI"

To set the record straight concerning Hoover's false statements, I sent the following letter to Hoover, while I was a federal investigator:

The purpose of this letter is to place into a single communication certain important facts known to both of us. The purpose being to clarify the conflicting facts between what you reported to Con-

gressman Waldie, and what we both know to be the truth ... [govern-
ment fraud] intimately associated with the deaths of airline passengers
by willful misconduct. If these allegations and facts are true, the part
played by the FBI is tragically manifest.

Hoover never replied. He had repeatedly appealed to the public to show
concern about crime, and to report any crimes to the proper security
departments. I did both, but encountered obstruction of justice by the FBI and
other divisions of the Department of Justice.

Upon learning that Representative Waldie was to be one of the seven
Congressmen named to a newly created House Committee to conduct an
investigation of crime in the United States, I wrote:

I understand you are one of the seven named to the newly created
House committee to conduct an investigation of crime in the United
States. The resolution as I understand it authorizes this committee,
including you of course, to conduct a complete investigation and study
of all aspects of crime in the nation ... I suppose you and FBI Director
Hoover would be working together, as you did when I requested your
help in exposing the serious aviation and government fraud associated
with the Salt Lake City and other air disasters. It pains me that so
many aid and abet the conspirators in this crime that has left such
horrendous human suffering in its wake. It further pains me that those
who give comfort and aid to the guilty, those in public positions of
trust, continue their pious-appearing roles.

Waldie never answered.

It was the legal responsibility of the U.S. Attorney in Denver to investigate and prosecute the crimes that I reported. My residence was in Oklahoma
City, so I filed a complaint with the U.S. Attorney in Oklahoma in 1965. The
complaint, filed under the responsibilities of federal criminal statutes,
including Title 18 U.S.C. § 4 requiring a citizen to report federal crimes to
a federal tribunal, identified myself as a federal investigator holding federal
authority to make such determinations. I briefly described the criminal acts
discovered as part of my official duties and requested that I be contacted so I
could submit my evidence and provide more detailed information.

The U.S. Attorney responded, "The matter you complained of occurred
in Denver. It seems unlikely that any action by this office would be appropriate. However, we are double checking our own judgment on this with our
superiors." That was the end of that. I then made a written complaint to the
U.S. Attorney at Denver, again identifying myself as a government investigator. U.S. Attorney Lawrence Henry replied: "We cannot see that this office
has any jurisdiction whatsoever in the matter, and accordingly, are taking no
action." I wrote back: "I suggest you correlate your letters with Oklahoma
City as the United States Attorney [at Oklahoma City] stated it was in your
area [of responsibility]."

DUTY TO INVESTIGATE AND PROSECUTE

Responsibility to act is shown in part by Public Law 89-554 which states:
"Each United States attorney, within his district, **shall** [investigate and]
prosecute all offenses against the United States." The U.S. Attorney, like the

U.S. Attorney General, is a political appointee, and although responsible for enforcing federal law, he is part of a vast political machine that routinely misuses the powers of the federal government to persecute and cover up.

GRAND JURY INVESTIGATION

Unable to proceed through the law enforcement agencies holding responsibility to do so, I tried circumventing the Justice Department's stonewalling, filing a complaint directly with the foreman of the federal grand jury at Denver. The jury foreman notified U.S. Attorney Henry to have me appear, which he reluctantly did. When the FAA refused to give me time off for the grand jury appearance, I requested of the grand jury that they subpoena me to appear, which they did.

Before leaving for the grand jury appearance I contacted attorney Clyde Watts in Oklahoma City for legal guidance. He and attorney Percy Foreman had defended General Walker, whom the federal government had incarcerated in a mental institution at the time of the early civil rights movement, to silence his anti-Justice Department position. Watts listened attentively, offering no encouragement. Recognizing the odds and the stacked deck I faced, he said I had very little chance of obtaining a grand jury investigation.

Watts felt it was virtually impossible for me to win with the awesome power of government against me. He seemed surprised that government attorneys hadn't made trumped-up psychiatric charges against me and had me locked up, or in some manner gotten rid of me. Watts told of the false arrest of General Walker by Justice Department attorneys, the General's placement in the federal prison at Springfield, and the difficulty in getting him released.

It is a standard practice for government officials to charge a whistleblower exposing corruption by federal officials with a crime, and then arrest the person. During incarceration the person may be forced to take drugs on the pretense of conducting a mental examination, which then affects the person's memory and conduct. The federal prison hospital at Springfield, Missouri, is a favorite location for these tactics. By claiming the person is mentally deficient the person can be incarcerated in the prison hospital indefinitely, forcibly injected with mind-altering drugs. I have talked to people who experienced this treatment after they sought to expose government corruption that is yet to be described within these pages.

According to Watts, the office of Attorney General was a vast and powerful political machine, making it an easy matter for United Airlines to influence government officials to take action against me, through political contributions or outright bribes. That reminded me of Attorney General Robert Kennedy's benevolent actions on behalf of United Airlines as he made a decision assuming for the U.S. taxpayers much of the financial responsibility for United Airlines' New York City crash. It was a simple matter to secretly donate a large sum of money to Kennedy's campaign chest and in return receive a Justice Department decision relieving them of hundreds of millions of dollars in compensatory and punitive damages.

Watts gave me some tips for my grand jury presentation, assuming the U.S. Attorney would thwart my presentation by tampering with the jury. Watts apologized for not being able to help me, advising that he had to appear before the United States Supreme Court on Walker's behalf the following week.

TAMPERING WITH A FEDERAL GRAND JURY

I was given a cold reception by a small but vocal number of jurors in the grand jury. They either resented my appearance, or they were carrying out the wishes of the Justice Department officials who had been covering up for the crimes. Most of the jury members were unsophisticated lay persons, unaware of the politics and corruption within the Justice Department. As a grand jury they are supposed to act independently. In practice, they serve as a rubber stamp for Justice Department prosecutors. A *Wall Street Journal* article (August 11, 1989) described this control by the U.S. attorney over the average unsophisticated jury member: "Prosecutors can get grand juries to indict a ham sandwich, the old adage runs."

I was ready to present evidence and testimony supporting my charges of massive corruption related to a series of airline crashes, but the U.S. Attorney blocked my presentation. He demanded that I cite the specific federal statutes pertaining to the various criminal acts that were violated, including fraud, perjury, conspiracy, subornation of perjury, and those under the Federal Aviation Act. A corollary to that would be a refusal of the police to respond to a call about a woman being raped unless the caller could cite the particular statute that the rapist was violating.

The U.S. Attorney already knew these statutes as part of his job, and it shouldn't be necessary for a government air safety expert to explain the criminal statutes to the nation's highest law enforcement agency. This was an obvious diversion tactic to block my testimony before the grand jury and tamper with the jury in an obstruction of justice maneuver. I just happened to have the numbers of the statutes, and read them off, but the U.S. Attorney expressed no interest, and didn't even write them down. If a member of the public tried to tamper with a grand jury they would end in prison, as Jimmy Hoffa did.

Certain grand jury members didn't want to hear my allegations or to look at my evidence. It was as if they were shills placed on the grand jury to control its actions. The proceedings took on the air of a circus. Aggravated and disgusted with this spectacle, irritated that the U.S. Attorney would tamper with a grand jury hearing, I rose, closed my briefcase, and said:

I have evidence here of a major aviation and government crime that is being openly harbored and protected, a crime undertaken by government personnel in positions of trust, realizing that death would occur. Death did occur, at Salt Lake City, in a United Airlines crash. Today, a former airline captain living here in Denver, is the scapegoat to protect the guilty in government.

As I started to return documents to my two briefcases, the jury disbanded. But a few came over to me and one elderly woman stated: "There must be something behind all this." I answered, "I wouldn't be here if there wasn't." Another juror stated, "I admire you for trying; we need more like you." They were average compliant and non aggressive middle-class citizens, no match for the aggressive behavior of the U.S. Attorney and the shills he appeared to have on the grand jury.

In *The FBI Nobody Knows*, author Fred J. Cook said of the FBI: "An autocracy that was superior to and above the law it was supposed to serve; an autocracy so powerful, so unchallengeable, that it intimidated, if at times it did not actually terrify, even senators and congressmen."

Possibly this fear was one reason many Congressmen shied away from this scandal. The FBI could destroy a political career by simply announcing that an investigation of a particular member of Congress was in progress. Worse, they could fabricate charges, labeling an otherwise legal and normal activity a crime. Further, the conduct of most politicians is such that filing charges against them takes no great amount of exaggeration.

SEEKING LEGAL HELP

I needed legal help in this fight and an attorney with a good knowledge of aviation and criminal law. It would take months to handle a matter of this complexity in the federal courts. But this was an almost impossible task. First, the cost would be prohibitive. Second, finding an attorney with these qualifications would be difficult. Third, any attorney can be manipulated by the powerful legal and judicial fraternities to sabotage any such effort. As I would later discover, there is a close bond between Justice Department attorneys and state and federal judges. When necessary, they join forces to block any exposure of government corruption. Much more will be stated about this relationship in later pages.

Some attorneys warned me that I would face serious dangers if I continued with these exposure activities, and that if an exposure did occur, I would have powerful interests viciously attacking me. I encountered attorneys who alluded to the seriousness of the matter, indicating they would look into it and possibly assist, but who became unavailable shortly thereafter. I felt the legal fraternity was under the influence of the Justice Department, a suspicion supported by later developments yet to be described.

Aviation attorney Lee Kriendler, highly experienced in the aviation accident field. He had written several technical books on aviation accident litigation, was a recognized authority in the field. I contacted him, giving him details of the crash-related corruption that I and other federal inspectors discovered. He replied:

Thank you for giving me the opportunity of reviewing these materials and, since I realize their importance to you, I am returning them herewith ... Since we do share ... a common interest in aviation safety and in view of your qualifications in this area, I would like to extend an invitation to you to visit our offices and talk further with us in this area should you ever have occasion to be in New York.

By refusing to offer assistance in exposing the corruption in the aviation environment, he helped keep the lid on the activities that led to subsequent air disasters in which his law firm profited handsomely. Kriendler appeared on a TV production call *The Aviation Revolution* (1969), discussing safety problems, and stating that airlines occasionally "sacrifice safety for economic considerations." Making reference to the show, I wrote: "I sometimes wonder [what crashes and what deaths would not have occurred] if you had given attention to the serious matters that I presented to you last winter."

One of the attorneys I contacted, who had previously worked for the Department of Justice, remarked: "I've never heard of anything like this!" Since he had been working on the Bobby Baker case and was going to Washington in a few days, he said he would check with his friends at the Department of Justice and get back to me when he returned. But Justice Department officials were heavily implicated in the corruption by their coverup and obstruction of justice. They would be the last to act on the criminal misconduct.

He never called, and my attempts to reach him were unsuccessful. However, when I called his secretary and told her I would pick up the data I had left, he was immediately available to authorize its release. When I picked up the material his associate was waiting for me, and wished me "lots of luck." Many wished me luck, but none would help.

"I wish to warn you once again..."

A Denver attorney with whom I had previous business dealings in the mid-1960s initially expressed a willingness to help. This too changed, and he wrote: "I wish to warn you once again that you are biting off an awful big piece when you take on United Air Lines and the people entrenched in the FAA. As you point out, this thing is getting bigger and bigger all the time ... There are many ramifications that might arise..."

Another of the nation's leading aviation attorneys, Stuart M. Speiser, expressed concern and appeared ready to help. He wrote: "I certainly appreciate the gravity of the situation described in your letter." In a subsequent letter he did not offer any help but stated he would "advise ... if there is anything further" he could do to assist me. On this letterhead I noted a change in the partnership; a name was added—Donald W. Madole, former Chief of the NTSB Hearing Section, to whom I had appealed for help while the FAA engaged in the criminal obstruction of justice during the Denver safety grievance hearing. I concluded that was the end of that relationship, and I was right.

"The matter is so serious..."

I pressed Speiser for a reason why he could not represent me. Speiser replied:

We found from looking over the material that you sent to us that the matter is so serious and complicated it would be physically impossible for us to do justice to your positions.

These words from one of the most knowledgeable aviation attorneys in our nation added further weight to the gravity of my charges.

Using another approach, I sent a letter to Ray Christensen, President of the Utah State Bar Association, offering help to the plaintiffs in the Salt Lake City crash, and requesting the names of the plaintiffs' attorneys. That confidential letter was directed to the Utah State Bar Association and belonged in the files of that association. Since there was no response, I sent a strong follow-up letter, but still no reply. Shortly thereafter, FAA legal counsel John Graziano, at Oklahoma City, whom I knew from earlier days when I worked out of the Los Angeles FAA offices, contacted me and asked if I had written to the Utah State Bar Association. Something was amiss.

Since I never kept my exposure activities from the FAA, I did not hesitate to answer yes. But his request raised questions. I wrote to the President of the Utah Bar Association, demanding to know what the bar association did with my letters. At first they ignored the matter. I finally forced an answer from the ethics committee. They wrote, "Mr. Christenson was at the time and is now retained as legal counsel by United Air Lines," and advised that he had received my letters, which he then sent to United Airlines and to the FAA.

My confidential letter offering to provide information of criminal misconduct to the attorneys representing the victims of the Salt Lake City crash was diverted from its destination, and given to the people most responsible for the deaths. Despite this gross misconduct by an attorney in a major Salt Lake City law firm and by the president of the bar association, the ethics committee refused to take any action. I then wrote to the American Bar Association and received a reply from its presidential assistant, James Spiro:

Let me clarify the situation so that the urgency of the matter is clear to you. I had then, and I have now, factual and evidentiary material pertaining to criminal misconduct and fraud preceding the Salt Lake City disaster, obtained through my official position as government safety inspector assigned to United Air Lines prior to that expected and forewarned air disaster.

In subsequent correspondence he circumvented his responsibility, stating:

It is assumed that you have been in touch with the attorneys for the plaintiffs in each of the cases which have been filed as a result of the ... United Airlines crash in Salt Lake City. May I suggest you also consider contacting our Standing Committee on Aeronautical Law so it may have the benefit of the special information you have about improper airline operations. The chairman of the committee is Mr. Sidney Goldstein ... Our wish is to be of as much help as our authority permits and we do hope you are convinced of our intentions in this regard.

Spiro also reminded me to again write to Goldstein, which I did. Goldstein never answered. I advised Spiro of this and he replied:

As a believer in persistent pursuit of solutions to problems, I am confident that you will be successful if you persevere.

Lack of perseverance is something of which I could not be accused. Several attorneys for the Salt Lake City crash victims eventually learned of my efforts and ability to help their clients. But their loyalty lay elsewhere. They refused to receive my testimony and evidence. For the next thirty years the legal fraternity blocked every attempt I made to expose the corruption that played a major role in several major air disasters, and later, other national scandals.

During a subsequent conversation with Graziano I told him the nature of the FAA corruption I encountered and the consequences in several specific airline crashes. Graziano became quite concerned, apparently unaware of the serious criminal acts and coverup by the FAA hierarchy. He was astute in security-type activities, but naive about the misconduct taking place within the FAA.

Mistakenly assuming that the FAA Administrator was unaware of the misconduct, Graziano requested that I prepare a report for the Administrator describing what I had stated to him. I felt the last thing the FAA Administrator wanted was to be confronted with more evidence of the scandal. "That's a great idea, John!" I immediately went to work preparing a sixty-page document for transmittal to FAA Administrator Bozo McKee.

"This is serious!"

After Graziano read the document he exclaimed, "This is serious!" adding, "You surely must keep your evidence under double lock and key and behind locked doors."

Internal FAA directives required that the FAA Administrator report the criminal charges to the Justice Department for further investigation.

Graziano was a competent attorney who clearly recognized the significance of my report. Several days later, as we were having lunch in the FAA cafeteria he said: "It's a lonely fight taking on the role of a crusader." I replied: "Yes, John, I know, lonely and rough." Graziano later headed the nation's Sky Marshall program dealing with skyjackers.

I waited for the FAA Administrator's reply, but it never materialized. Several months later I submitted a request to the FAA Administrator that I am advised "of the actions, or inactions, taken on my August 1 report." The FAA replied: "We ... know of no entitlement you might have to a reply..."

"You're going to get shot!"

Typical of the concern felt by some of my FAA friends was the statement by one FAA employee, "You're going to get shot! They're going to dynamite your house or your car!" Another inspector felt that the gravity of the problem was such that a hired killer would not be beyond the acts of present-day government. (Government involvement in the planned assassination of foreign leaders, CIA dirty tricks, didn't leave much doubt that this was a definite possibility.) My involvement expanded over the years into other areas of corruption implicating federal personnel.

Over a period of the next thirty years I became a confidant to a long list of deep-cover personnel in the Central Intelligence Agency, the Drug Enforcement Administration. These people, and others, had knowledge of very serious criminal activities perpetrated by federal officials against the United States and the American people. Their knowledge threatened to expose officials in control of the Justice Department, the CIA, the White House, members of Congress, and other government entities. Some of these people that I would be associated with mysteriously died, or would be killed. More about this in later pages.

I received phone calls and letters from friends who were concerned over my safety, asking for instructions about whom to contact if something suddenly happened to me. But to whom could I refer them? Certainly not the FBI or the Department of Justice.

I wasn't oblivious to the possibility of physical danger, and took precautions to protect myself, including keeping my not-too-docile Doberman Pinscher, "Savage," close at hand. I remembered the unsolved murder of a federal investigator, Henry Marshall. He uncovered the key to the Billy Sol

Estes scandal in Texas, and the ties to President Lyndon Johnson. He was murdered on a remote section of farm land near Franklin, Texas. The Billie Sol Estes scandal had not yet broken, and Marshall had the incriminating evidence and determination to expose it, threatening many federal officials, including President Johnson. It wasn't until 1989 that the part played by President Johnson in this murder was revealed. This is detailed in later pages.

CONSTANT THREAT OF HARM

Every time I started the engine of my car, I thought of how easy it would be to eliminate the threat I represented, by attaching explosives to the starter cables. Even today I wonder who may be lurking in the shadows.

Government employees, especially safety inspectors, cannot function when they are faced with threats that FAA inspectors on the United Airlines program received. The warnings given to me by other FAA inspectors reflect their *belief* that such things can happen. Little did they know how frequently it does happen.

ATTITUDE OF FEAR BY FAA INSPECTORS

An example of how government inspectors are prevented from correcting air safety violations and safety problems were revealed during a telephone conversation I had with senior FAA inspector Carl Whitman. He complained about the same safety problems that I and other inspectors found at United Airlines and within the FAA:

We had the problems in the Boeing program, though not what it was in the DC-8." The senior United pilots were on the DC-8 program and they possessed more clout than the junior pilots on other aircraft programs, such as the Boeing 720. We don't have any backing. They'd crucify us!

Referring to the threats and harassment experienced by, Frank Harrell, my predecessor on the United Airlines DC-8 program, Whitman said:

Harrell got into the same deal you did ... he went to Washington [to report the air safety and criminal acts] and when the chips were down, he was by himself.

Whitman added that he and another FAA inspector, George Sheridan, attempted to dissuade Harrell from going to Washington, realizing the futility of attempting to buck well-entrenched pressure groups within the FAA. Whitman related a conversation that occurred in a Denver restaurant and bar, the Blue Onion, preceding Harrell's departure for Washington.

"Don't do it!"

"Let it die! We told him. Whatever you do, *don't do it*," Whitman said to me. "It will take an out-of-Agency investigation ... you don't have any backing."

I was well aware of this, having been through the mill myself, having attempted to correct the same problems. I had battled longer and lost much more. Whitman continued, "They [United Airlines and the FAA] made it very uncomfortable for Harrell and he had to leave." (Harrell was transferred to Puerto Rico. United Airlines officials admitted to me they forced the FAA to remove the inspector, as they simultaneously warned me of my fate.)

"Like a pack of wolves..."

Referring to Hiram Broiles, the former Principal Inspector responsible for the United Airlines certificate, Whitman said: "Hi is sick of all these things." He continued: "We can't be professionals right now. You know, any time any of us questions industry, automatically, they all come upon us like a pack of wolves, you know, when a wolf gets a wound. It's like a big game. It is a weird damn life. Just like the FAA Western Region, what backing do we get? None!" Referring again to the reaction when inspectors attempt to function: "That's right, coercion, they'd crucify us!"

Whitman's primary responsibilities were the training and check programs at American Airlines, an airline with a good safety attitude and very few crashes, none due to extreme stupidity from lack of training that existed at United Airlines. Whitman was a good pilot with an interest in promoting safety. Referring to the inability of FAA inspectors to obtain compliance with the FAA safety requirements and the difficulty of obtaining enforcement with mandatory federal air safety requirements, Whitman said, "As soon as you enforce them, it hits them in the pocket. They go to the top in Washington and put pressure upon us."

"It would implicate a lot of people if this gets out."

"Fellows admire you, they really do; we thank you for your fortitude. There are a lot of us that have bowed back, have avoided collisions with industry." He said, "it would implicate a lot of people if this gets out."

Carl Whitman and George Sheridan were two men I admired from the time I joined the FAA in the Los Angeles area. They were sincere, dedicated to air safety, and had a good analysis of the problems. The FAA doesn't have many like them. Whitman showed more courage than most inspectors.

George Sheridan had also been on the jets since they first entered commercial service. In a telephone conversation following the NTSB hearing on the Salt Lake City crash, a year after the Denver grievance hearing, he gave his reactions to testimony given by United Airlines officials responsible for air safety: "If these are the people we have to work with at United, assign me to Edde Airlines!" This was reference to a small charter operator with far less air safety sophistication than would be expected from a large airline such as United Airlines. Sheridan had taken the FAA assignment with United after I left the FAA, and discovered the same safety problems and FAA obstruction tactics other inspectors and I had discovered earlier. Nothing had changed. It was too much for him, and he transferred back to Los Angeles.

Possibly in reaction to my charges, Congress passed legislation placing the FAA under the newly formed U.S. Department of Transportation.[19] But this did not change the mentality of the bureaucracy, and served more as an excuse to imply corrective actions were taken should the scandal ever erupt into the media.

---

[19] All functions, powers, and duties of the FAA were transferred to the Secretary of Transportation in the Department of Transportation by Public Law 89-670, October 15, 1966, 80 Statute 931 (also known as Title 49). The Bureau of Aviation Safety of the Civil Aeronautic Board was also transferred to the newly formed National Transportation Safety Board.

DEFINITION OF CRIMINAL ACTS

It is important for the reader to know what type of conduct constitutes federal crimes, since many of the actions or inactions by the people in the three branches of the federal government, the media, and others, described within these pages, were criminal acts. The following brief description of selected criminal statutes will help to make the association between the acts of people described within these pages and the crimes that they committed, and help to understand the gravity of these acts.

ACCESSORY BEFORE AND AFTER THE FACT

An accessory is a person who in some manner is connected with a crime, either before or after its perpetration, but who is not present when the crime is committed. (21 Am J2d Crim L § 115.) Title 18 U.S.C. § 3. An accessory *before* the fact is a person who contributes to a felony committed by another, and is too far away to aid in the felonious act. In some jurisdictions the accessory before the fact is also charged with the crime of those committing the actual act. An accessory *after* the fact is a person who knows a felony has been committed and who *comforts or assists the felon in any manner to avoid prosecution.* (21 Am J2d Crim L § 126.) An attorney in the Justice Department, a judge, a member of Congress, who knows of a crime and has the duty to expose it, and who doesn't, would be guilty of this criminal offense.

ACCOMPLICE

An accomplice is a person who knowingly, voluntarily, and with a common interest with others, participates in the commission of a crime as a principal, as an accessory, or aider and abettor.

AIDING AND ABETTING

Aiding and abetting is advising, counseling, procuring, or encouraging another to commit a crime. Any person who "commits an offense against the United States or aids, abets, counsels, commands, induces or procures its commission, is punishable as a principal." Any person who joins any conspiracy, even if they are unaware of the actual act committed by others, or why, become equally liable with the others. Title 18 U.S.C. § 3.

CORRUPTION

Corruption applies to many within these pages. It applies particularly to a government employee who acts under authority of his or her office, and **who impedes or obstructs the administration of justice.** (*United States v Polakoff*, 121 F2d 333.)

CONSPIRACY

Conspiracy is an agreement between two or more persons to accomplish an unlawful act. Conspiracy is a separate offense over and above whatever other acts the parties conspired to accomplish. The existence of a conspiracy is usually determined from *circumstantial evidence*, looked at collectively. This is usually the only means of determining a conspiracy,[20] and is generally established by a *number of indefinite acts, each of which, standing alone, might have little weight. But taken collectively, they point unerringly to the*

---

[20] *United States v. Calaway* (9th Cir. 524 F.2d 609.

existence of a conspiracy.[21] The existence of a conspiracy may be proved by *inference from conduct, statements, documents, and facts and circumstances* which disclose a common design on the part of the accused persons and others to act together in pursuance of a common criminal purpose. This offense is rampant throughout these pages. It is a common disinformation tactic to ridicule anyone claiming a conspiracy exists, when conspiracies are possibly the most common offense committed, being simply an agreement between two or more people to commit some act.

Title 18 U.S.C. § 371 Conspiracy to commit offense or to defraud United States. "If two or more persons conspire either to commit any offense against the United States, or to defraud the United States, or any agency thereof in any manner or for any purpose, and one or more of such persons do any act to effect the object of the conspiracy, each shall be fined not more than $10,000 or imprisoned not more than five years, or both."

The word "defraud" is used broadly to include obstructing the lawful operation of any government agency by any "deceit, craft or trickery, or at least by means that are dishonest."[22] To convict someone, including a federal official, under Title 18 U.S.C. § 371 it is only necessary to show that the person (1) entered into an agreement (2) to obstruct a lawful function of the government (3) by deceitful or dishonest means and (4) had committed at least one overt act in furtherance of the conspiracy.[23]

FALSE STATEMENTS WITHIN GOVERNMENT AGENCY

Making false statements to or within a government agency is a felony under several government statutes. (Title 18 U.S.C. §§ 35, 1001, 2071.) It is a crime under section 1001 to make a false statement in a "matter within the jurisdiction of a department or agency of the United States." Under the Federal Aviation Act it is also a crime to make a false statement, verbally or in writing, to a federal air safety inspector. This offense was repeatedly committed in the FAA and NTSB to cover up the facts by misstating the evidence or withholding evidence. This offense is common in Congressional "investigations."

Title 18 U.S.C. § 35. Imparting or conveying false information.

"(a) Whoever imparts or conveys or causes to be imparted or conveyed false information, knowing the information to be false, ... (b) or with reckless disregard for the safety of human life, imparts or conveys or causes to be imparted or conveyed, false information, knowing the information to be false, ... shall be subject to a civil penalty ... or imprisonment ...." This offense was and is rampant in the air safety proceedings, in Congressional investigations, and is shown throughout these pages.

Title 18 U.S.C. § 34 Penalty when death results.

If death results from violation of any criminal statute title 18 U.S.C. § 34 states: "Whoever is convicted of any crime prohibited by this chapter, which has resulted in the death of any person, shall be subject to the death penalty

---

[21] *State v. Horton*, 275 NC 651, 170 SE2d 466.

[22] *Hammerschmidt v. United States*, 265 U.S. 182, 188 (1924).

[23] *United States v. Boone*, 951 F.2d 1526, 1543 (9th Cir. 1991).

or to imprisonment for life, ..." Management at United Airlines, the FAA, and those involved in the complicity of coverup and obstruction of justice, would arguably qualify for this punishment.

Title 18 U.S.C. § 2071. Concealment, removal, or mutilation generally. Relates to the concealment, removal, or destruction of official records. federal case law, referring to section 1001 and the others related to it, makes it a crime to alter the contents of the records, leaving out pertinent facts, with the purpose to avoid learning the truth. U.S. v. Lange, 528 F.2d 1280. This criminal offense was especially common in the FAA proceedings.

Title 18 U.S.C. § 1101[24] makes it a federal crime for **anyone** within the jurisdiction of any department or agency of the United States to knowingly and willfully falsify, conceal or cover up by any trick or scheme a material fact, or to make any false, fictitious or fraudulent statement or representation. If the offense is committed by a federal employee, especially a federal judge or Justice Department attorney, the offense is made more serious. Included in these federal offenses, for instance, would be an airline covering up its violations of federal air safety requirements by falsifying the records they present to FAA inspectors; NTSB or Justice Department officials or federal judges making false statements as they seek to cover up crimes being reported; or a federal judge doing any of these acts.

FRAUD

Fraud is deceit, deception, or trickery operating prejudicially to the rights of another, and so intended, by inducing him to surrender some legal right. It is anything calculated to deceive another to that person's prejudice. It is an act, a word, silence, the suppression of the truth, or any other device contrary to the plain rules of common honesty. (23 Am J2d Fraud § 2.)

MISPRISION OF A FELONY

Misprision of a felony is a criminal offense, and arises from failure to inform a federal court or other authorities as to a felony that has been witnessed or that has come to the person's knowledge. It is also the failure to prevent a felony from being committed. (21 Am J2d Crim L § 7.) The federal offense of misprision of felony is the failure to disclose a felony coupled with some positive act of concealment, such as suppression of evidence, harboring of criminal, intimidation of witnesses, or other positive act designed to conceal from the authorities the fact that a crime has been committed. It is a felony not to promptly disclose and make known to a Judge of the United States, or to the Governor or some judge of a particular state, knowledge of the commission of any felony against the United States or the particular state. (Title 18 U.S.C. § 4) It is having knowledge of the commission of a felony and concealing it, or failure to report it to a proper civil authority. The statute

---

[24] **Title 18 U.S.C. § 1001 Statements or entries generally**
"Whoever in any matter within the jurisdiction of any department or agency of the United States knowingly and willfully falsifies, conceals or covers up by any trick, scheme, or device a material fact, or makes any false, fictitious or fraudulent statements or representations, or makes or uses any false writing or document knowing the same to contain any false, fictitious or fraudulent statement or entry, shall be fined ... or imprisoned ..."

addressing withholding of evidence on federal crimes is **Title 18 U.S.C. § 4. Misprision of felony**, which states: "Whoever, having knowledge of the actual commission of a felony cognizable by a court of the United States, conceals and does not as soon as possible make known the same to some judge or other person in civil or military authority under the Under States, shall be fined ... or ... imprisoned." This criminal offense would attach to a Justice Department attorney, a federal official, a judge, media personnel, and many others shown throughout these pages.

OBSTRUCTION OF JUSTICE

Obstruction of justice is the criminal offense of knowing of a crime and interfering with the administration and due course of justice. This applies to any government person having knowledge of wrongdoing or anyone who engages in deceit, fraud, or any other act that prevents exposure of a crime.

Title 18 U.S.C. § 1505. Obstruction of proceedings before departments, agencies, and committees

Whoever, with intent to avoid, evade, prevent, or obstruct compliance, in whole or in part [with any civil investigation] willfully withholds, misrepresents, removes from any place, conceals, covers up, destroys, mutilates, alters, or by other means falsifies any documentary material, ... or attempts to do so or solicits another to do so, ... or obstructs, or impedes the due and proper administration of the law under which any pending proceeding is being had before any department or agency of the United States, or the due and proper exercise of the power of inquiry ... shall be ... fined ... or imprisoned...

Title 18 U.S.C. § 1512. Tampering with a witness, victim, or an informant.

(a) Whoever ... prevents the attendance or testimony of any person in an official proceeding; (b) prevents the production of a record ... in an official proceeding; (c) prevent the communication by any person to a law enforcement officer or judge of the United States, of information relating to the commission or possible commission of a federal offense ... (2)(b) Whoever knowingly uses intimidation ... or threatens another person, or attempts to do so, or engages in misleading conduct toward another person, with intent to (1) influence, delay or prevent the testimony of any person in an official proceeding; (2) cause or induce any person to (A) Withhold testimony, or withhold a record, document, or other object, from an official proceeding; (3) hinder, delay, or prevent the communication to a law enforcement officer or judge of the United States of information relating to the commission or possible commission of a federal offense ... (c) Whoever intentionally harasses another person and thereby hinders, delays, prevents, or dissuades any person from (1) attending or testifying in an official proceeding; (2) reporting to a law enforcement officer or judge of the United States the commission or possible commission of a federal offense ... (3) arresting or seeking the arrest of another person in connection with a federal offense; or (4) causing a criminal prosecution ... to be sought or instituted, or assisting in such prosecution or proceeding, ... shall be fined ... or imprisoned ...

An understanding of that criminal statute will be invaluable in understanding the criminal acts by Justice Department attorneys, federal judges, and others, in later pages. It will help to understand how agencies of the United States have been made into literal criminal enterprises, helping to explain the constant exposure of scandals involving employees of the three branches of government.

Title 18 U.S.C. § 1513. Retaliating against a witness, victim, or an informant.

(a) Whoever knowingly engages in any conduct and thereby causes ... injury to another person, ... or threatens to do so, with intent to retaliate against any person for (1) the attendance of a witness or party at an official proceeding, or any testimony given or any record, document, or other object produced by a witness in an official proceeding; or (2) any information relating to the commission or possible commission of a federal offense ... shall be ... fined or ... imprisoned ...

This criminal statute applies to FAA officials who retaliated against me prior to the Denver FAA safety hearing. It applies to acts yet to be described, in which Justice Department attorneys/officials and federal judges, among others, sought to destroy my ability to continue with the exposure activities.

In later pages it will be shown that it is a routine practice for Justice Department prosecutors and federal judges to commit the criminal offense of retaliating against anyone who tries to expose federal corruption.

MISFEASANCE

Misfeasance is the improper doing of an act which a person can lawfully do, but done in an unlawful and injurious exercise of lawful authority. It is the doing of a lawful act in an unlawful manner.

MALFEASANCE

Malfeasance is the doing of an act which is positively unlawful or wrong, and which causes injury to another's person or property. It is the performance by a public official of an act in an official capacity that is wholly illegal and wrongful.

NONFEASANCE

Nonfeasance is the failure to act where duty requires, such as when a public officer neglects or refuses, without sufficient excuse, to do that which it is the officer's legal duty to do, whether wilfully or through malice or ignorance.

MAIL AND WIRE FRAUD

Under Title 18 U.S.C. § 1341 and 1343, mail and wire fraud is any scheme to harm another by false or fraudulent pretenses, dishonest methods, tricks, deceit, chicane, overreaching, or other wrongful acts. Among those who committed crimes, funded by the government of the United States, were FAA officials, and especially those at the FAA Denver grievance hearing; the Executive Director of the FAA, speaking for the FAA Administrator; the NTSB; attorneys with the Justice Department; members of the U.S. Senate and House; the news media, who covered up; and others. This group was joined by others, as the saga of corruption continues.

Except for FAA officials, who were directly implicated in the aviation crimes, the others had two basic decisions to make when I brought evidence of the government-funded corruption to them. One, they could expose and take corrective actions that would greatly reduce the number of airline crashes and deaths, but cause powerful people and powerful government and non-government institutions to be rocked with scandal. Or two, they could cover up, protect the guilty, and sacrifice lives that would be lost because of the coverup. Up to the date of this book's publication, every known check and balance took the second option. By doing so, they are implicated to a lesser or greater degree, in causing or permitting many air tragedies to occur, and the criminal activities that have yet to be described. None of the victims were any match for this group, acting in unison, funded and protected by the cloak of federal office.

PERJURY

Perjury is making false statements under oath. Anyone who subscribes or signs any material matter which he does not believe to be true, is guilty of perjury.

Title 18 U.S.C. § 2[25] provides that everyone becomes a principal to a criminal act who in any way aids or covers up for offense. This would include federal judges, Justice Department attorneys, members of Congress, the media.

FEDERAL SENTENCING GUIDELINES

Justice Department attorneys, federal judges, and federal officials, are not immune from prosecution if they commit any of these offenses. On the contrary, the crimes are made worse when committed by them, as they are in positions of trust, and know the acts that constitute a crime better than the average citizen. A longer prison sentence is required under the federal sentencing guidelines if the parties committing the offenses are in positions of trust. Obviously, most of the characters shown within these pages were people in positions of high trust, requiring them to prevent the crimes, punish the perpetrators, and provide relief to those harmed by the offenses.

Federal officials, federal judges and Justice Department personnel have escaped punishment primarily because they control the prosecution of criminal acts at the highest levels of the federal government.

---

[25] **Title 18 U.S.C. § 2. Principals**. "(a) Whoever commits an offense against the United States or aids, abets, counsels, commands, induces or procures its commission, is punishable as a principal. (b) Whoever wilfully causes an act to be done which if directly performed by him or another would be an offense against the United States, is punishable as a principal."   The legislative intent was to punish as a principal not only a person who directly commits an offense, but a person who "aids, abets, counsels, commands, induces or procures" another to commit an offense, and anyone who causes the doing of an act which if done by him directly would render him guilty of an offense against the United States. Case law decisions include *Rothenburg v. United States*, 1918, 38 S.Ct. 18, 245 U.S. 480, 62 L.Ed. 414, and *United States v. Giles*, 1937, 57 S.Ct. 340, 300 U.S. 41, 81 L.Ed. 493.

CHAPTER FIVE

The Imposters—
Who were they?

Many forces were at work blocking my exposure of the criminal activities that were getting worse. A friend in San Francisco, Edith Armstrong, tried to obtain publicity for my activities, resulting in a series of strange encounters with three mysterious men. Edith was a sales person in San Francisco from whom I bought supplies for my rental units. (I had over one hundred rental properties.)

Several days before the Salt Lake City crash I first told Edith about the mess I was trying to expose. The Denver safety grievance hearing had ended, and I was in California purchasing supplies for my apartment projects, while waiting for the FAA Administrator's assistant, William Jennings, to issue his final report. Edith was a public spirited person who had the backbone to try and do something about government corruption.

After I returned to Denver to await the outcome of the safety hearing, Edith started calling newspapers, radio stations, and members of Congress, generating considerable interest, making her a threat to those implicated in the scandal. She came to the attention of people who wanted her stopped.

THE MAGAZINE IMPERSONATORS

A person identifying himself as Ed Keating, editor of *Ramparts* magazine, telephoned Edith at her home, requesting a meeting to discuss what I had uncovered and about my exposure activities. He supposedly wanted to write a magazine article about these activities. *Ramparts* had been exposing CIA activities at that time, including the CIA's spying on college students. Both of us sought publicity for the scandal from any source, and welcomed their attention.

The next day a woman representing herself as Mr. Keating's secretary phoned Edith advising her that Keating was entering the hospital for an ulcer checkup, asking if Edith would meet with Keating's assistant, Dave Russo. That evening Edith received a call from the person identifying himself as

Russo, stating that he was Keating's assistant at *Ramparts*, and that he would like to meet with her as soon as possible to discuss the possibility of a story. They set a meeting for the following Saturday at Appy Knight's restaurant in San Mateo.

Edith's daughter, Minda, drove Edith to the restaurant. Sensing possible danger, Edith said, "If I'm not back in two hours call the police and then call Rodney."

THE WRONG QUESTIONS

Two men, Dave Russo, and Ted Crawford, both well dressed and in their forties, met Edith at the restaurant, representing themselves as *Ramparts* employees. They spent the first fifteen minutes of conversation on inconsequential matters and then for the next two hours the conversation centered on my activities. But the questions were not slanted to obtain the type of data needed for an article. Instead, they sought to determine Edith's reasons for assisting me and whom we thought were involved.

The men didn't want to know the specifics of the government corruption; it appeared they already knew and their questions reflected this. Edith asked them to provide identification. Russo said they did not carry identification because of their association with the magazine and because they were trying to avoid receiving frequent phone calls at home. The answer sounded suspicious but Edith decided to play along.

I was still with the FAA at that time, assigned to the FAA training center at Oklahoma City, and Edith and I were in almost daily telephone contact discussing the events taking place. We both suspected the men were not from *Ramparts*, I asked her to call the magazine and verify my suspicions, which she did. Ramparts confirmed our suspicions. No one by those names worked for the magazine.

We decided to continue the contacts in the hope of determining who the men actually were and their motives for the meetings. In hindsight we realized our approach should have been more sophisticated in order to be productive. We should have had another person in the background obtaining license plate numbers and other identification. But at that time I had my hands full with the FAA at Oklahoma City, making numerous appeals to members of Congress and others who had a responsibility to act.

Russo called Edith at home, explaining that he had assimilated the information, checked into it, and found the material too hot to handle. He warned Edith: "I don't have a clear understanding of how close the ties are between you and Mr. Stich, but if you are wise, you will take up sewing or golf."

"I never could sew," Edith answered, "and I've given up golf long ago."

"Do you think the CIA is involved?"

Next morning Russo called again, arranging an immediate meeting, which was held in the Southern Pacific passenger depot near downtown San Francisco. Edith met Russo and Rob Randall, who questioned her along the same lines as in the previous meeting. They still weren't concerned with details that would be the subject of the story they were allegedly writing. Instead, the questions centered around Edith's relationship with me; why she was being so loyal to me; was the CIA involved; were any government agencies involved; will Mr. Stich carry on; are you aware of the risk Mr. Stich is taking?

Three phone calls in as many weeks followed this meeting. During the last call Russo said that Randall was also on the line and they had a few more questions. Edith told them I was now in town and they could ask me directly. Russo said they would contact me later. They never did. Russo said, "We can determine the public's reaction to the events by learning how you react." Again, this sounded fishy, but Edith played the game.

AGAIN ASKING ABOUT CIA AND FBI INVOLVEMENT

"Do you have any knowledge of, or any material in your possession that would implicate the CIA in this matter?" Russo asked. "Do you think the FBI is involved?"

"How do these questions concern public reaction?" Edith asked.

"As long as you have access to information that Mr. Stich had given to you," Russo replied, "we can gain an insight into how the public will react." The excuses weren't getting any better.

"Mr. Stich is facing a stacked deck."

Randall telephoned Edith at home two weeks later and asked for my phone number, explaining that he had been out of town, and that Russo was back East. She asked Randall for the correct spelling of Russo's name, and Randall managed to avoid answering the question. He then asked basically the same questions as in previous conversations, including whether we thought the FBI or CIA were involved. Apparently he was concerned with what we may have discovered about their involvement. At this time the CIA was very active in undermining dissidents in college. At a later date I became a confidant to several CIA contract agents and operatives, and learned the CIA was heavily involved within the United States in covert activities against U.S. citizens. This is discussed in later pages.

About a week later, Russo called, and asked Edith if she had heard from Randall. He added, in an almost sympathetic voice, "Mr. Stich is facing a stacked deck; it's a rough go." Russo said that this was his last call and that he was leaving town, again suggesting that Edith and I discontinue our efforts.

That telephone call was the last contact Edith had with the three mysterious strangers. To this date we don't know their identity or from where they came. I felt they were with one of the government's security departments although it is possible that United might hire private investigators for a case like this. The nature of their questions concerning the CIA and FBI strongly suggests one or both of these two agencies *were* involved. Bizarre and very serious activities by the CIA would surface in my investigative activities at a later date, and these are described in later pages.

If we had been more sophisticated in the ways of private investigators we probably would have learned much about the three men's identities. We would probably have added still another dimension to this bizarre scandal. To whom could we turn? Certainly not the FBI or Department of Justice. The imposters could have come from either of these two agencies, or the CIA.

As the years went by, I came in contact with former government employees, including people who owned or headed companies that were fronts for the CIA and Justice Department covert activities. From them I learned that the type of activities of these three mysterious men were routine CIA tactics. The one key exception was that Edith didn't get killed, an event that I discovered was very common when high federal officials are threatened by informants or whistleblowers.

The intrigue continued over the years as various methods were used to silence me. I later wondered what a fool I was, to continue this hopeless task in an environment of endemic government corruption, media coverup, and public apathy.

My attempts to expose and correct the corruption within the FAA and NTSB weren't proving effective. All I managed to do was uncover more participants who willingly committed criminal acts of coverup, knowing that the only parties who would prosecute them were themselves implicated.

I exhausted my remedies within the executive and legislative branches of government. Even my attempts to circumvent the obstruction of justice by the Justice Department, by going directly to a federal grand jury at Denver, failed. The media could have blown this scandal sky high, but they kept a tight secrecy lid on this government corruption, making them co-conspirators.

I thought of another way to circumvent the block. Government officials can't force a government employee to work under corrupt conditions, especially when the corrupt conditions result in a continuing series of airline crashes. Internal FAA corruption forced me and other inspectors to cover up for air safety and criminal violations. This certainly was a basis for refusing to work. I stopped going to work, giving written notification to the FAA for my reasons, and waited for the FAA to take action to separate me from government employment. After the FAA took action to terminate my employment, I planned to exercise my administrative remedies by appealing to the Civil Service Commission and then, if necessary, seek judicial relief.

This plan was unorthodox, but with the breakdown in all checks and balances I had to take unorthodox actions, just as I did when I exercised the employee grievance hearing to bring out the pattern of criminality associated with a series of United Airlines crashes.

Circumstances caused me to change my plans. First, the FAA simply ignored my absence, although the problem had to be addressed eventually. Second, an early-morning phone call from California notified me that the manager of my apartment complex in the San Francisco Bay Area had died, requiring me to return immediately to California. This unexpected death and the realization that I could carry on just as well in California caused me to sell my home in Oklahoma City and move to California.

CALIFORNIA HERE WE COME

I loaded my three-manual Allen theater organ and other furniture into a rented truck, hitched the car to the back, and with my companion, Savage, the Doberman, headed for the home that I left five years earlier.

Just before pulling away, a neighbor, who worked for the NTSB accident investigative school at the FAA academy in Oklahoma City, came to me, saying the NTSB investigators admired me for my activities. She told of the pressures NTSB investigators encounter as the political Board members acted to conceal accident-causing misconduct reflecting adversely upon the FAA, itself, or a favored corporation.

Years earlier I had left California with my family, having accepted the United assignment with the FAA. I was now returning without them. Eighteen months earlier (May 1964), when the FAA pressures at Denver became too great, my wife moved out of the Denver residence and returned to her former home in Texas. We obtained an amicable divorce in 1966.

After arriving in California I tried to learn the true identity of the three men who had contacted Edith. In a telephone conversation with *Ramparts'* associate editor, Adam Hochschild, I again confirmed that the mysterious men who had met with Edith were unknown at the magazine. My inquiry raised Hochschild's interest. We met for dinner in Berkeley, and he reviewed some of my writings. He was especially intrigued by Edith's experience with the three men representing themselves as *Ramparts* writers. Hochschild and Edith met several times after that to discuss various aspects of the scandal and the part the three men played in it.

A couple of weeks later, Edith received a call from Hochschild, asking her to come immediately to *Ramparts'* San Francisco office. Waiting for her was internationally known detective Harold Lipset, who had a special interest in determining where FBI Director Hoover might fit into the picture. It wasn't until many years later that books and articles were written about Hoover's association with criminal elements, a fact that Lipset appeared to know at that time.

Referring to the almost incredible nature of the matter, Edith said, "No one would make up a story like this." Lipset replied, "Many would, but we've bought it." Edith described the meeting with the unknown men; the sympathetic and gentle attitude of one, and the needling by the second man. Lipset explained, "This was classic investigative procedure. Both were against you; neither was on your side." Lipset added, "This is the game they play. One tries to get the information in a sympathetic manner; the other uses an approach to get you angry, trying to get you to snap back with answers."

Lipset decided to stake out the FAA offices at the San Francisco Airport on the possibility that Edith might recognize one of the FAA people. William Buchanan, who was associated with Lipset for many years, checked the FAA offices the night before, learning the departure and arrival habits of the employees. The next morning Buchanan and Edith arrived early in a radio-equipped station wagon, and parked where they could observe FAA employees coming and going. It was like looking for the proverbial needle in a haystack. As I expected, it was non productive.

Lipset decided to do the same stakeout at the FAA Los Angeles Regional Office. The next afternoon Edith and Lipset boarded a Pacific Southwest Airlines plane at San Francisco Airport for Los Angeles. There were light moments in this intrigue. When they got on the plane Edith saw a close friend, Norris Seastrom, who was also on the flight. Edith, with her overnight bag in hand, and in the presence of Lipset, said to Norris: "This isn't what you think.

I'll tell you later!"

During the week I lived in Los Angeles, working at Flying Tigers Airline to prepare a pilot operating manual for the stretched DC-8s that they had ordered. I met Edith and Lipset that evening and we speculated as to whom the three men represented. I felt it was probably the FBI, another segment of the Justice Department, or the CIA, rather than the FAA, and that surveillance of the FAA regional offices would be fruitless.

Lipset thought covert CIA activities might be involved. At that time I was as ignorant as most Americans of CIA activities and had no thoughts on the matter. Today, based on my discoveries during the last few years, I recognize the many covert domestic operations the CIA had, and has, against the interests of the United States.

Lipset's Los Angeles assistant, Harry Grimm, was to drive Lipset and Edith to the FAA regional office the next morning. But because of heavy traffic, Grimm was late, requiring Lipset and Edith to go by cab to the FAA offices on Manchester Avenue. No Admittance signs caused the cab driver to stop short of entering the FAA area. Bags in hand, Edith and Lipset walked into the restricted area and watched the arriving personnel. Lipset said jokingly: "If anyone asks what we are doing here we are looking for a hit and run car." Surely this was Lipset's form of a joke.

They weren't stopped. When Grimm arrived, they all sat in his car parked in the restricted area and waited. Again, no one questioned them. After deciding they had seen enough from the outside and that all the employees had probably arrived, Lipset said, "Come on, we're going through the building."

After they were inside the FAA regional office building, they went from office to office, on the chance that Edith might recognize one of the men. Again, they received quizzical stares but no one questioned them as they wandered deep within the FAA inner sanctum.

Edith didn't recognize any of them. Lipset and Edith went back to the airport and caught a flight to San Francisco, but not with United. Lipset said he hadn't flown on United since reading of United's problems and that he wasn't about to do so. (United Airlines has many excellent pilots; the problem arose because the government-mandated checks and balances were not working and the routine requirement of additional or corrective training did not meet industry standards or federal requirements.)

"Could be a major public scandal."

Ramparts continued their interest in the case, and in a subsequent letter to me, Hochschild stated, "It looks good, I read the material with considerable interest. There obviously is quite a bit of inside information here on a subject that could be a major public scandal." In another letter he wrote that he hoped the magazine would "treat your story with the attention it deserves."

After the unproductive FAA stakeout, Hochschild flew to Washington to interview FAA officials for their reaction to my charges. He spoke with FAA Flight Standard officials who were part of the FAA misconduct. After talking with Joe Ferrarese, assistant to James Rudolph, Director of Flight Standards, and others, Hochschild returned to San Francisco.

Hochschild said, "They said *terrible* things about you." Obviously those people with a key role in the corrupt acts associated with the deaths of over a thousand people would not talk kindly of the person exposing their activities. And possibly, dirty politics of air safety was so ingrained that they couldn't accept being accused of wrong-doings.

My attention was diverted to the work I was doing at Flying Tigers, and my considerable real estate investments, causing me to grow tired of the lonely fight. If the scandal was exposed, I would be fighting all alone. Every check and balance had a vested interest in coverup and in the event the scandal blew, they would band together to discredit me. I had enough. Hochschild agreed to stop any further action on the story.

I never forgot the tragedies or those who had yet to become victims. I flew my Navion Rangemaster airplane to Idaho Falls and visited the grave site where Mrs. Bennett and her two daughters, victims of the United Airlines Salt Lake City crash, were buried. Standing at their graves, I thought of their final moments and it stirred me to fight again. Ironically, a short distance before reaching the cemetery entrance was a large billboard with the words, "The Friendly Skies of United." My rekindled outrage culminated in using judicial remedies to expose the corruption.

Some strange and powerful force stopped every investigation in its track. I wondered how they did it. Were they being threatened, paid off, or was the corruption in the United States, especially in the federal government, so extensive that an exposure was almost impossible? Did the Justice Department threaten members of the House and Senate to keep them quiet? Were so many people involved that no one could blow the whistle without implicating other members of their group? Were they trying to protect United Airlines, and prevent possible financial losses if the public reacted against the company?

STILL WITHOUT FRIENDS

My search for an attorney to help was just as futile in the 1970s as in the 1960s. A San Mateo attorney advised me to forget the exposure attempts. He warned that I would be virtually without friends and that I could be viciously smeared by powerful forces with unlimited funds, power, and resources, to discredit me and my exposures. He also said the Justice Department could come up with trumped-up charges against me, discrediting me to the point where the media misrepresented the facts, making me look bad in the public's eye. The attorney said the public isn't going to believe these outrages could happen. In the end, I would be seriously harmed if I continued. The truth of his warnings came to pass several years later.

It was frightening. Some of the attorneys I contacted reminded me of the high cost of legal actions, which could easily exceed several hundred thousand dollars. As I would also find out, the high government bloc controlled the legal profession, and could cause my own attorney to sabotage my defenses.

THE INFAMOUS DC-10 AND THE FAA

During the time frame that I was exposing FAA corruption in the Western Region the same management authorized the elimination of numerous previously required safeguards. These changes increased profits but brought with them a great number of deaths that would not have otherwise occurred.

One of the changes has already killed over 1,000 people, through elimination of a previously required mechanical backup for controlling the aircraft in the event all hydraulic systems fail, as periodically occurs.

In certifying the DC-10, FAA Western Region management covered up for outrageously dangerous design problems. In one accident resulting from the design problems, 346 people were killed. FAA management had ignored the unsafe outward-opening cargo doors; cargo door locking mechanism that permitted the doors to open in flight; cabin floors that lacked sufficient strength to avoid collapsing in the event of a cargo door opening; inadequate pressure equalizing vents between the upper and lower sections of the aircraft; and the elimination of the flight control backup for the occasional total hydraulic system failures. Company inspection reports and engineering changes were falsified to indicate changes were made on the DC-10 that had never been made. This was discovered by French authorities after 346 people perished in one of the most brutal air disasters of all time.[26]

Hard evidence of these previously reported dangers occurred during a ground pressure check of the fuselage at the Douglas plant in Long Beach, California, on May 29, 1970. During the pressure check of the aircraft fuselage, a cargo door suddenly exploded open when the defective locking mechanism failed on the outward-opening cargo door, causing the weak cabin floor to collapse and jam the flight controls. If the aircraft had been airborne, it probably would have crashed and the passengers killed.

Among the people who complained of the dangerous design was the head engineer, F. Applegate, Consolidated Aircraft in San Diego, one of Douglas's subcontractors. He warned his superior in a memorandum:

It seems to me inevitable, that in the twenty years ahead of us, DC-10 cargo doors will come open and cargo compartments will experience decompression for other reasons, and I would expect this to usually result in the loss of the airplane ... It is recommended that overtures be made at the highest management level to persuade Douglas to immediately make a decision to incorporate changes in the DC-10 that will correct the fundamental cabin floor catastrophic failure mode.

Correction will take a good bit of time. Hopefully there is time before the National Transportation Safety Board (NTSB) or the FAA grounds the airplane which would have disastrous effects upon sales and production both near and long-term. This corrective action becomes more expensive every day as production continues. However, it may well be less expensive than the cost of one plane load of people. **BUT WHO'S GOING TO PAY FOR IT!**

In response to Applegate's warning, Consolidated's DC-10 Support Program Manager, J. Hurt, in a reply memorandum wrote:

We have an interesting legal and moral problem, and I feel that any direct conversation on the subject with Douglas should be based on the assumption that as a result, Convair may subsequently find itself

---

[26] Paris DC-10 crash.

in a position where it must assume all or a significant portion of the costs that are involved.

NTSB officials were aware of the DC-10 problems since their inception, and did very little to prevent the inevitable. Numerous cargo door problems were reported. American Airlines experienced an inflight explosive opening of the door which jammed the flight controls, almost resulting in the loss of the aircraft and the occupants. The FAA, NTSB, Douglas, and the airlines still resisted corrective actions to forestall the inevitable slaughter that would surely happen.

IT FINALLY HAPPENED

Luck ran out, and instead of American citizens paying the price for America-bred corruption it was foreign citizens who paid with their lives. A Turkish Airlines DC-10 departed Paris for the short flight to London (March 3, 1974). Within ten minutes the same scenario that took place on the ground at Long Beach, and occurred on the American Airlines flight, again occurred. But this time the consequences were gory.

While climbing through 12,000 feet, the cargo door locking mechanism failed; the outward opening cargo door exploded open; the under strength cabin floor collapsed; the flight controls jammed; and the pilots lost control of the aircraft. The explosive cargo door opening ripped a large hole in the cabin floor, causing passengers to be ejected out the bottom of the aircraft.

"We've lost it."

As the aircraft dove toward the ground at almost the speed of sound, the captain said, *"We've lost it."* Shortly thereafter the CVR recorded the sound of the aircraft hitting the ground at nearly supersonic speed, and 346 people were dismembered as never before.

Investigative reporters discovered shocking evidence of corruption by the FAA, falsification of inspections and work performed, and massive indifference!

The corruption that made this great air disaster possible was so profound that several heavily documented books were written describing the criminal acts at the FAA and at Douglas Aircraft Company. Investigation by private investigators discovered that aircraft records were falsified and known serious safety problems covered up, knowing that crashes would occur. More details of this and many other crashes are found in my companion book, *Unfriendly Skies*.

The world's most experienced coverup body, Congress, duplicated their prior coverup tactics after I brought the air safety and criminal acts to their attention. This practice of coverup escalated in the 1980s and 1990s, with the help of a controlled media. This corrupt practice made possible many of the scandals described in following pages.

CONTINUING THE EXPOSURE ACTIVITIES
IN THE FEDERAL COURTS

The continuing crashes and deaths rekindled my attempts to expose corruption within the Federal Aviation Administration and those who made it possible. I had exhausted the checks and balances in the executive and legislative branches of government and that which the media should provide.

I decided to use judicial remedies, which took me into an entirely new area of corruption.

Title 18 U.S.C. Section 4, for instance, makes it a crime if a person knows of a federal crime and does not promptly report it to a federal judge or other federal tribunal. I exercised that right and that responsibility, and discovered the key role played by federal judges in some of the worst criminal activities ever perpetrated upon the American people.

Federal statutes and constitutional provisions guarantee to any citizen the right to file a federal action to halt wrongful conduct by a federal official. Title 28 U.S.C. § 1361,[27] for instance, gives a citizen the right to obtain a judicial order addressing misconduct by federal officials. Title 18 U.S.C. § 4,[28] makes it a crime if a person who knows of a federal crime does not report it promptly to a federal court or other federal tribunal and requires federal judges to receive evidence of the charges. The Federal Aviation Act[29] required federal courts to exercise jurisdiction when a lawsuit is filed charging violation of air safety matters.

Months were spent by me studying the law. When I felt competent to proceed, I filed two federal actions in 1974,[30] both of which invoked mandatory federal court jurisdiction. My first action was filed in the U.S. District Court at San Francisco. This lawsuit addressed the pattern of air safety and criminal violations I had uncovered while a federal investigator and those I subsequently discovered as a private investigator and author.

Under federal law[31] the allegations made in a complaint must be accepted as true until reaching the trial stage. Federal judges have a mandatory duty to

---

[27] Title 28 U.S.C. § 1361. Action to compel an officer of the United States to perform his duty. The district courts shall have original jurisdiction of any action in the nature of mandamus to compel an officer or employee of the United States or any agency thereof to perform a duty owed to the plaintiff.

[28] Title 18 U.S.C. § 4 (misprision of felony). "Whoever, having knowledge of the actual commission of a felony cognizable by a court of the United States, conceals and does not as soon as possible make known the same to some judge or other person in civil or military authority under the United States, shall be fined not more than $500 or imprisoned not more than three years, or both."

[29] Title 49 United States Code Section 1487 states:
Any party in interest may apply to the district court of the United States ... for the enforcement of ... this Act, or such rule, regulation, requirement, ... such court shall have jurisdiction to enforce obedience thereto by a writ of injunction or other process, mandatory or otherwise, restraining such person, his officers, ... from further violations of such provision of this Act or of such rule, regulation, requirement ... and requiring their obedience thereto.

[30] *Stich v. United States, et al.*, 554 F.2d 1070 (9th Cir.) (table), *cert. denied*, 434 U.S. 920 (1977)(addressed hard-core air safety misconduct, violations of federal air safety laws, threats against government inspectors not to report safety violations and misconduct); *Stich v. National Transportation Safety Board*, 685 F.2d 446 (9th Cir.)(table), *cert. denied*, 459 U.S. 861 (1982))(addressed repeated criminal falsification of official airline accident reports, omitting highly sensitive air safety misconduct, making possible repeated crashes from the same sequestered problems); Amicus curiae brief filed on July 17, 1975, in the Paris DC-10 multi-district litigation, *Flanagan v. McDonnell Douglas Corporation and United States of America*, Civil Action 74-808-PH, MDL 172, Central District California.)(addressing the long standing FAA misconduct, of which the coverup of the DC-10 cargo door problem was one of repeated instances of tragedy related misconduct).

[31] Federal courts must accept as true the allegations in the complaint and supporting affidavits as true. *Gardener v. Toilet Goods Assn.*, 387 U.S. 167, 172 (1967).

provide a court forum if the allegations in the complaint state a federal cause of action. Justice Department attorneys, who had blocked every attempt to report these criminal acts for the past ten years, and who had seen the gory consequences of their coverup, filed a motion to dismiss my action.

Justice Department attorneys sought to block my exposures by claiming I lacked standing to report and seek correction of the matters raised in the complaint, being the FAA and NTSB corruption. I had been a federal investigator holding federal authority to determine the existence of the corruption. No one else had the opportunity to make these discoveries. Attorneys representing the Justice Department argued that only those people who have been directly harmed by the wrongful acts could file an action seeking to report and halt the corruption charged in my complaint. But many of these people were dead, and others lacked the opportunity to discover the criminal activities, and lacked knowledge of them.

For argument, anyone who has occasion to be in the aviation environment has standing to obtain relief from corrupt acts by federal officials that affect the aviation environment. If a government investigator, who discovered the criminal acts during his official duties, who held federal authority to make these determinations of criminal acts, lacked standing, who could possibly have the knowledge and the standing to do so? Possibly the deceased victims?

Further, federal criminal statutes required that I report the criminal acts to a federal court or other federal tribunal. And if I failed to do so, I would be guilty of a crime.[32] I had a responsibility to report the crimes, and federal judges had the responsibility to receive testimony and evidence.

Federal statutes make it clear that federal judges must receive the testimony and evidence offered, especially when it is by a present or former federal investigator who had federal authority to make such determinations.

U.S. District Judge Richard Schnacke admitted the gravity of the allegations stated in my federal filing during the first status conference in 1974, and surely knew his responsibilities under federal crime reporting statutes. In clear violation of law, Schnacke dismissed the action, starting the first in a series of criminal acts involving the federal judiciary that escalated in the 1980s and 1990s. Today, the conduct of renegade federal judges constitutes one of the greatest dangers facing the American people. Schnacke's dismissal of the action was the first in a long line of judicial coverups and judicial involvement that continues to this day, linked to some of the major crimes against the American people.

Immediately after Judge Schnacke dismissed my federal filing, I filed an appeal with the U.S. Court of Appeals in San Francisco. I presented briefs and verbal arguments in 1975, heard by Court of Appeal Judges Herbert Choy, Warren Ferguson, and Anthony Kennedy (later appointed to the U.S. Supreme Court). During the verbal briefing the judges asked me why I didn't bring these matters to the attention of Congress. I stated that I did, but that Congress refused to receive my testimony and evidence. I also argued that

---

[32] Including Title 18 U.S.C. Section 4.

even though Congress had a duty to receive my evidence, federal statutes required federal judges to receive my evidence. In their decision upholding Schnacke's dismissal the Judges stated in part:

> *Stich appeals the dismissal of his petition for a writ of mandamus by the district court. He argues that the district court had jurisdiction and that he had standing to sue. Although appellant's concern for the safety of future airline passengers is commendable, in view of the recent decision of the United States Supreme Court in Valley Forge Christian College v. Americans United for Separation of Church and State, Inc., 102 S.Ct. 752 (1982), the judgment must be affirmed.*
>
> *Article III of the United States Constitution limits federal court jurisdiction to "cases or controversies." Consistent with this limitation, litigants may not make claims for relief in federal court without showing an actual or threatened personal injury. "[A]t an irreducible minimum, Art. III requires the party who invokes the court's authority to show that he personally has suffered some actual or threatened injury as a result of the putatively illegal conduct of the defendant ...." Valley Forge, supra, 102 S.Ct. at 758, quoting Gladstone, Realtors v. Village of Bellwood, 441 U.S. 91, 99, 99 S.Ct. 1601, 1608 (1979). Even absent an article III bar, this court should refrain from adjudicating disputes based on generalized grievances shared by all citizens. Warth v. Seldin, 422 U.S. 490, 499-500, 95 S.Ct. 2197, 2205-06 (1975).*
>
> *Stich's concern, the risk of future airline crashes, is real enough. That concern does not, however, rise to the level of an actual or threatened injury. The risk is shared by Americans generally. Absent an injury which threatens Stich in a way which distinguishes him from the populace as a whole, federal action is barred. [district court's dismissal is] Affirmed.*

The judicial dismissal and coverup were repeated many times in the next eighteen years, in what was to become an ever-increasing judicial Ponzi scheme blocking my access to federal court, opening up an entirely new area of corruption.

I filed a petition for writ of certiorari with the U.S. Supreme Court, invoking their responsibility to receive my evidence of federal crimes. Their duty to act on my petition was increased on the basis that judges and Justice Department attorneys, over whom they had supervisory responsibility, were implicated. The Supreme Court Justices turned down my petition in 1976, thereby becoming implicated in a series of continuing judicial coverup and obstruction of justice.

FRIEND-OF-THE-COURT BRIEF

In the Los Angeles action I filed a friend of the court brief[33] in the multi-district litigation arising out of the Paris DC-10 crash and which had the FAA

---

[33] *Stich v. National Transportation Safety Board*, 685 F.2d 446 (9th Cir.)(table), *cert. denied*, 459 U.S. 861 (1982))(addressed repeated criminal falsification of official airline accident reports, omitting highly sensitive air safety misconduct, making possible repeated crashes from the same sequestered problems).

as one of the defendants. Since I had insider information about FAA misconduct which no one else possessed, I had important information relating to the litigation that no one else possessed, and my brief should have been welcomed. A friend-of-the-court brief in this type of litigation required obtaining the written approval of the lead attorney, which I obtained. Judge Hall, who lost a member of his family in an aviation crash, refused to allow me to present evidence, thereby protecting the FAA, NTSB, Justice Department, and all the others who were involved in the duplicity.

With the involvement of all three branches of the federal government in this coverup there I thought of another way to circumvent this massive obstruction of justice, and that was to go public via a book. This was done in 1978 when I published the first printing of *Unfriendly Skies*. The book came out several weeks before a major air disaster occurred in San Diego, which took the record away from United's New York City crash as the most deadly to have ever occurred. This crash arose when a PSA Boeing 727 rammed into the back of a small plane while the 727 was maneuvering to land. The 727 then plunged into a residential area.

I investigated that crash for the purpose of updating my book (Unfriendly Skies). During this investigation I discovered evidence of all-night partying and drinking by members of the PSA crew, which greatly impaired their ability to safely fly the plane. I also discovered that FAA, NTSB, and Justice Department officials were following the prior pattern of covering up and sequestering this information.

The brutality of the crash caused daily media attention for weeks and the publication of my book occurred just prior to its occurrence. If the crew partying had been made public, the resulting outrage could have focused attention on the corruption I had identified. For either that reason, or simply the mindset that withholds from the public evidence of corruption by federal officials, every government agency that had a responsibility to address the drinking and partying withheld the information. By refusing to address the evidence, the entire accident investigation and final report was made invalid. The NTSB altered its accident report and shifted the blame for the tragedy elsewhere. Under federal crime statutes[34] it is a felony to conceal records to conceal the truth.

ACTION IMPLICATING NTSB CRIMINALITY

Under authority of the Federal Aviation Act, I petitioned the NTSB to reopen the accident investigation to admit evidence of the crew partying throughout the night until shortly before the flight took off from Sacramento. Even though the Act required the NTSB to receive my evidence, they refused to do so. This refusal was made worse by the fact that I was a former FAA inspector with qualifications far exceeding that of the average NTSB investigator.

---

[34] Including Title 18 U.S.C. Section 2071, Concealment, removal, or mutilation generally. Associated federal case law, referring to 18 U.S.C. § 1001 and other statutes, makes it a crime to alter the contents of the records, or to leave out pertinent facts for the purpose of avoiding the truth. *U.S. v. Lange*, 528 F.2d 1280.

I then exercised the next remedy in law by filing a federal action in the U.S. District Court at San Francisco, requesting the court to order the NTSB to reopen the accident investigation to receive my evidence. After I filed the 1980 action, assistant U.S. Attorney George Stoll in the San Francisco office contacted me by phone and agreed that the NTSB should be required to reopen the investigation. He said:

It's ridiculous that the NTSB did not investigate further into the reported partying. ... The investigation should be reopened. ... I am going to bring pressure on them [NTSB] through the Department of Justice to see if they won't reopen the investigation. ... the government has responsibility to see to it that its agencies do their jobs. ... I can go ahead and file a motion to dismiss in the next few days, but I'm not satisfied with that because I don't think in this case the government's skirts are totally clean, and I don't think it's my job to cover up. ... I agree with you that what she said [PSA passenger Helen Rhea] was far more than an investigator in many cases is reasonably likely to hear. It certainly is pregnant with some very serious implications. ... it is ridiculous [referring to the NTSB coverup].

Stoll stated that he was recommending to his superiors in Washington that the government support my action, and that the NTSB should be ordered to reopen the investigation and admit evidence of the crew partying. He also advised that he was recommending that the NTSB be investigated, as was obviously necessary.

The assistant U.S. Attorney was unaware of what Justice Department officials had done in the past to cover up for FAA and NTSB misconduct. I knew that Stoll's recommendations would be denied, and that is what Washington did. Typical attorney conduct, Stoll then reversed his earlier position and filed a motion for the judge to dismiss the action against the NTSB, stating in the motion: "There is no question in this case that the Board has performed its duty and conducted a substantial investigation." That was a 180 degree reversal from his prior position.

Judge Wiegel disregarded his duty to provide me with a federal court forum and to receive evidence of criminal activities. Misstating the law, he wrote in his opinion that I was appealing an order of the NTSB, and that it came under Title 49 U.S.C. Section 1903(d), requiring it to be filed in the Court of Appeals:

This is a matter that is properly before the Court of Appeals, and in a way I am sorry, because it is a fascinating subject and I would like very much to have it before me. But under the law, I don't think I properly can.

If, for argument, the complaint was filed in the wrong federal court, federal law[35] provides for the action to be transferred to the proper court rather than

---

[35] Title 28 U.S.C. § 1406 (c). "If a case within the exclusive jurisdiction of the Court of Claims is filed in a district court, the district court shall ... transfer such case to the Court of Claims, where the case shall proceed as if it had been filed in the district court."

dismiss the action. But I was not making money claims; I was seeking to force federal officials to comply with the law, and the Court of Claims had no jurisdiction for that issue. Another argument was that federal crime-reporting statutes, including Title 18 U.S.C. Section 4, provides for reporting federal crimes to any federal court (or other federal tribunal), and my federal filing did that.

Concurrent with this latest action, I released the second printing of *Unfriendly Skies*, which exposed the felony coverups by federal judges in the Ninth Circuit and by the Supreme Court justices. These two groups possessed enormous powers that could be criminally misused against me, which they commenced before the year was out.

Burning United Airlines DC-8 at Denver, another in a long series of fatal airline crashes associated with hard-core corruption.

CHAPTER SIX

ATTACKING THE WHISTLEBLOWER

My escalating exposure actions threatened many powerful people. I had published the 1978 and 1980 printings of *Unfriendly Skies*. I appeared as guest on hundreds of radio and television appearances. I filed federal lawsuits against the FAA and NTSB, which were getting unpublicized attention. The people and groups threatened by my exposure activities included officials within the Federal Aviation Administration; the National Transportation Safety Board; U.S. Department of Transportation; members of Congress; federal judges, including the Justices of the U.S. Supreme Court; and management at United Airlines. Those who could do the greatest harm to me, however, were Justice Department officials and federal judges, and their influence with state law firms and judges.

INADVERTENTLY GIVING THE CLUE

I inadvertently gave my adversaries the clue as to how to stop my exposure activities. During several radio and television appearances the hosts asked me, "Aren't you afraid of what they might do to you?" The question implied physical harm, but I sidestepped it, saying, "As long as they can't get to my money, I'm OK." I felt there was *no way* that my adversaries could get the assets which funded my exposure activities.

At the beginning of the 1980s, the market value of my real estate properties was close to ten million dollars, and my net worth was over six million dollars. Foolishly, instead of just enjoying life and these assets, I continued my air safety activist activities trying to expose the government corruption that continued to play a role in air tragedies. I was the only person with the evidence and the willingness to fight the powerful thugs involved in this scandal, and foolishly felt I had an obligation as a citizen.

JUDICIAL ATTACK ON ACTIVIST

It took money to continue the activist activities, and I had already inadvertently given the clue to my adversaries. A bizarre scheme commenced in late 1982 to silence me via a sham lawsuit. Those who carried out the scheme had to have assurances, either specifically or from knowledge of widespread corruption in the judicial branch, that every check and balance in the California and federal courts would protect the scheme. The judicially centered scheme commenced with a sham lawsuit that required repeated violations of blocks of California and federal statutory and case law, and basic constitutional protections. The intent was to strip me of the assets that funded my exposure activities.

There are two basic ways to judicially strip a person of his or her assets almost immediately. One is through probate proceedings, but this requires that the person be dead. The other way is through divorce proceedings, seizing the assets on the basis that they are community property. I had been divorced since 1966, and five divorce judgments established that fact.[36] In California where I resided, the 1966 judgment had been entered as a local judgment in the Superior Court, Contra Costa County. Under California and federal law, the judgments were final and conclusive of our divorced status and property rights. The California and 1966 judgments were entered as local judgments in the courts of Nevada, Oklahoma, and Texas. In addition, my former wife, residing in Texas, had been declaring herself divorced for the past two decades, buying and selling real estate as a divorced woman. She applied for higher Social Security payments on the basis of the 1966 divorce judgment, which the federal government recognized when they raised her Social Security benefits. It was safe to say that I was legally divorced.

THE BIZARRE JUDICIAL SCHEME

In December 1992, several months after the Supreme Court Justices dismissed my action against the NTSB, I was served with a dissolution of marriage action,[37] even though I had been legally divorced for the past two decades. The San Francisco law firm of Friedman, Sloan and Ross[38] filed the action in Superior Court, Solano County, Fairfield, California. The lawsuit alleged that I was married to Friedman's Texas client and that she wanted a termination of that marriage (which in Texas she had declared was terminated in 1966). Using the pretense of the marital relationship, the Friedman law firm claimed that my assets were community property. On that basis the law firm filed dozens of lis pendens upon them, which halted important segments of my real estate activities and inflicted serious financial harm upon me.

The Friedman law firm claimed that all of my properties were community property, even though they had been acquired years after the 1964 Colorado separation and acquired after the 1966 divorce, which adjudicated all property rights. Under law, these properties were not community. Even if there had been a marriage, property acquired after separation is separate property and

---

[36] It is common practice, and provided by law (Uniform Divorce Judgment Recognition Act), for original divorce judgments to be entered as local judgments in subsequent states of residence to establish personal and property rights when exercising the constitutional right to change residence and have previously adjudicated rights recognized by the new state of residence.

[37] Number 83472.

[38] I later learned they carried out covert activities for the Justice Department and Central Intelligence Agency, and were members of the ADL and the ACLU.

California judges lacked jurisdiction over such property in a dissolution of marriage action. Building upon the sham divorce action, the Friedman law firm filed lis pendens on all of my properties, which prevented real estate activities, including refinancing loans coming due on various properties.

MASSIVE AND UNPRECEDENTED VIOLATIONS OF LAW

The lawsuit was filed under the California Family Law Act, which is a limited jurisdiction Act, and prohibits attacks upon prior divorce judgments.[39] Orders rendered by a judge who lacks personal or subject matter jurisdiction are void, and also subjects the judge to lawsuits under the Civil Rights Act.[40] For the next eight years, commencing in 1982, California judges rendered orders lacking jurisdiction for the cause of action filed against me, on the basis of California law. Absence of jurisdiction also arose from other sources.

CALIFORNIA LAW PROHIBITED THE LAWSUIT

Technically, jurisdiction could have been obtained to file a lawsuit under declaratory judgment statutes to determine whether the parties were married or not.[41] But to have done that would have prevented immediate seizure of my assets which can be done in a real divorce action on the basis of community property.

In addition, California statutory law prohibits collateral attacks upon *any* prior divorce judgment in any cause of action. The statutes and related case law[42] require mandatory recognition of each of the prior divorce judgments. California Supreme Court decisions prohibited attacks upon prior divorce

---

[39] Rules of Court 1201(c) (limits jurisdiction to three causes of action—dissolution of existing marriage, legal separation from existing marriage, nullity of marriage); Rule 1211 (limited to parties that are married to each other); Rule 1212 (prohibiting stating cause of action or claim for relief other than that provided by Rules of Court, including causes especially stated in Rule 1281 petition for dissolution of marriage form); Rule 1215 (limiting pleadings to those stated in Rule 1281, which does not state attacks upon prior judgments or previously litigated personal and property rights); Rule 1222 (jurisdiction limited to altering existing marital status); Rule 1229 (jurisdiction limited to the causes of action in Rule 1281 petition form and Rule 1282 answer form, which does not list the causes of action attacking prior divorce judgments or relitigating the exercise of jurisdiction basis); Rule 1230(a)(2) (addresses, with C.C.P. § 418.10(a)(1) the court's absence of personal jurisdiction under the Family law Act when there is a prior divorce judgment).

[40] Title 42 U.S.C. §§ 1983-1986. *Dennis v. Sparks* (1980) 449 U.S. 24.

[41] Code of Civil Procedure § 1060. To Ascertain Status or Construe Writing. "Any person ... who desires a declaration of his rights or duties with respect to another, or in respect to, in, over or upon property, ... may, in case of actual controversy relating to the legal rights and duties of the respective parties, bring an original action in the superior court for a declaration of his rights ...

[42] Mandatory divorce judgment recognition statutes (Civil Code §§ 4554, 5004, 5164; Code of Civil Procedure §§ 1699(b), 1713.3, 1908, 1913, 1915 (effective when the 1966 judgment was rendered and for nine years thereafter); Evidence Code §§ 666, 665, 622; (statute of limitations, Civil Code §§ 880.020, 880.250; Code of Civil Procedure §§ 318, 338, 343; Statute of limitations: Code of Civil Procedure 318, 338, 343; Civil Code §§ 880.020, 880.250; mandatory requirement to recognize that the prior court acted in the lawful exercise of its jurisdiction when the judgment is under attack two decades after its exercise of jurisdiction, and the acceptance of the benefits by both parties: Evidence Code §§ 666, 665, 622.

judgments.[43]

Attorneys[44] for the Friedman law firm argued that all five divorce judgments were void on the basis that I did not intend to reside forever in the jurisdiction that rendered the 1966 divorce judgment. But that argument had been declared unconstitutional by the U.S. Supreme Court in the 1940s. The Friedman attorneys spent months arguing what my mental thoughts must have been about permanently residing in the 1966 court's jurisdiction. A person getting a divorce does not have to pledge that he or she will reside forever in that jurisdiction. This is the lie that I had to fight during six years of litigation in California courts. Further, the statute of limitations prohibited an attack upon prior judgments three years after they are rendered. Any one of these dozens of state protections barred the action, in addition to the absence of jurisdiction under California law.

VIOLATING FEDERAL AND CALIFORNIA LAW

In addition to California law barring the sham action, overriding federal law barred the action. Federal statutory and case law, and constitutional safeguards, protect people who change their state of residence from having their prior divorce judgments and personal and property rights voided by a judge in some another state court. The constitution provides that a person cannot suffer loss of previously adjudicated or acquired personal and property rights when the person changes residence to another state. Federally protected rights barred the refusal to recognize residence as a basis for exercising personal jurisdiction in a divorce action. This was settled almost fifty years ago by the U.S. Supreme Court when California judges refused to recognize Nevada divorce judgments obtained after six weeks residence.[45]

Federal law, especially the constitutional and statutory Full Faith and Credit doctrine, requires state judges to recognize the judicial acts of another

---

[43] Prohibiting attacks upon prior divorce judgments on refusal to recognize residence, or for any other basis: *Rediker v. Rediker* (1950) 35 Cal.2d 796 ("it must be presumed that the foreign court had jurisdiction and that its recital thereof is true ... is not subject to collateral attack on a showing of error in the exercise of that jurisdiction ... The validity of a divorce decree cannot be contested by a party who ... aided another to procure the decree."; *Scott v. Scott* (1958) 51 C.2d 249 ("There should be no implication ... that would preclude contacts with the foreign country other than domicile as a basis of jurisdiction. ... Section 1915 of the Code of Civil Procedure provides: "A final judgment of any other tribunal of a foreign country have jurisdiction, according to the laws of such country, to pronounce the judgment, shall have the same effect as in the country where rendered, and also the same effect as final judgments rendered in this state [which are final and conclusive of the rights and obligations of the parties--C.C. § 4554]"; *Spellens v. Spellens* (1957) 498 C.2d 210 ("The principle of estoppel is applicable [when] the divorce decree was alleged to be invalid for lack of jurisdiction ... The validity of a divorce decree cannot be contested by a party ... who aided another to procure the decree ..."); *Whealton v. Whealton* (1967) 67 C.2d 656 ("When both parties to a divorce action are before the court ... it is questionable whether domicile is an indispensable prerequisite for jurisdiction. ... the prerequisite of domicile may be easily avoided at the trial by parties wishing to invoke the jurisdiction of a court, with little fear in most instances that the judgment will be less effective than if a valid domicile in fact existed.").

[44] Jeffrey S. Ross; Lawrence A. Gibbs; Neil Popovic; Carolyn E. Moore; Christopher A. Goelz.

[45] *Vanderbilt v. Vanderbilt* (1957) 354 U.S. 416 (requiring the recognition of *ex parte* divorce judgments; *Estin v. Estin* 334 U.S. 541 (1948)(requiring the recognition of prior divorce judgments; *Sherrer v. Sherrer* (1948) 334 U.S. 343; *Coe v. Coe* (1948) 334 U.S. 378 (requiring the recognition of prior divorce judgments); *Perrin v. Perrin*, 408 F.2d 107 (3rd Cir. 1969) (prohibiting denying recognition to prior judgments when exercised on residence, including one day's residence).

state. This requirement applied to the prior divorce judgments and the property settlement. [46][47]California statutes also have a full faith and credit mandatory recognition requirement.[48] These protections required that the California judges recognize the California, Nevada, Oklahoma, and Texas divorce judgments. The sham lawsuit also violated fundamental constitutional rights and protections.[49]

REMARRYING LONG-DIVORCED PERSONS

The California judges held that they had the right to remarry people who had been divorced for decades; to invalidate subsequent marriages; to void prior property settlements adjudicated in other states and jurisdictions; and to order property acquired years after a prior divorce to be community property with the prior spouse. Three judges[50] in the California Court of Appeals upheld these decisions, as did the judges in the California Supreme Court. Their published decision established the right of California judges to void divorce judgments and property rights adjudicated decades earlier, contrary to federal and state statutory and constitutional protections. The person initiating these attacks need not even reside in California, as long as a former spouse resides in the state. Using the published decision as precedence, California judges can order the former spouse to pay your attorney fees for a new "divorce," and pay support at the same time. At the present time, until that published decision is overturned, the same scenario that happened to me can happen to anyone who has been previously divorced.

SUSPENDING APPELLATE REMEDIES

The appellate court remedy for a judge's refusal to dismiss an action following a motion to quash is to file a petition for writ of mandamus with the California Court of Appeal. Then, if denied, file a petition for hearing with the California Supreme Court.[51] If the lower court lacks jurisdiction, the upper court *must* grant the petition.[52] Even though the lower court judges clearly lacked jurisdiction, the California court of appeal judges denied the petition for relief. The California Supreme Court justices also upheld the violations of state and federal laws and constitutional protections.

The remedy under California law to vacate an order to pay money is by appeal, and I appealed. The appeal was heard by Court of Appeal judges, Donald King, Harry Low, and Zerne Hanning, appointed by former California governor Jerry Brown. Media articles reported the judges paid bribe money for the judicial appointment. These judges rendered a published

---

[46] Article IV, Section 1.

[47] Title 28 United States Code Section 1738.

[48] Civil Code Section 5004.

[49] Right to unabridged interstate travel, arising in the Privileges and Immunities Clause, Article IV, Section 2, and in the Fourteenth Amendment (right to change residence without losing rights adjudicated and acquired in prior jurisdictions); Fourteenth Amendment, relating to due process and equal protection, giving all persons the right to obtain a divorce, and adjudication of personal and property rights; laws respecting property rights.

[50] Judges Harry W. Low; Donald B. King; Zerne P. Haning.

[51] California Code of Civil Procedure § 418.10(b).

[52] Code of Civil Procedure Section 1086.

decision[53] upholding the violations of state and federal law. That decision was published, and is case law in the State of California today. I appealed that decision to the California Supreme Court, and when the violations were approved, I appealed to the U.S. Supreme Court. The issues were of utmost importance to thousands of people who were subjected to the same constitutional outrages inflicted upon me. None provided any relief.

This was a major constitutional set-back, something like returning to the fifties when blacks were required to sit in the back of buses in the South. But it was upheld by the California Court of Appeal and the California Supreme Court. The decision was unconstitutional. As long as that decision stands, others risk the same fate I suffered. This little-noticed decision affects everyone who exercise a constitutionally protected right to change residence to California, making them fair game for losing their personal and property rights; making their wives adulteresses; making their children bastards.

RETALIATION[54] FOR EXERCISING LEGAL DEFENSES

The Court of Appeal judges held in their published decision that it was frivolous for me to exercise my remedies under California law (motion to quash, petition for writ, and appeal). The decision held that I should have willingly submitted to the jurisdiction of the California judges (who under law had no jurisdiction under the Family Law Act to attack prior divorce judgments); that I should have agreed to be remarried; that I should have agreed to undergo another divorce proceeding, and have the properties and assets I acquired during two decades of divorced status divided with Friedman's Texas client and the Friedman law firm (on the basis of the contingency agreement between Friedman and their client).

Based upon this published decision and the holding that it was frivolous for me to object, the three appellate judges ordered me to pay $50,000 attorney fees and financial sanctions. This order was shortly followed by another order that I pay $170,000 attorney fees to the Friedman law firm.

"They can't do that!"

Many attorneys stated to me that the California judges couldn't do what they were doing. I agreed, but they were doing it anyhow. I had not yet recognized that the California lawsuit was a scheme involving federal and state personnel to strip me of the assets I relied upon to fund my exposure activities.

DOZENS OF ILLEGAL LIS PENDENS

Using the sham divorce action as authority, the Friedman law firm filed dozens of lis pendens upon my business and other properties, halting my real estate investment business in its tracks, and inflicting heavy losses upon me. Mortgage loans came due, and could not be refinanced because of the lis

---

[53] *In re Marriage of Stich*, 164 Cal. App. 64 (1985).

[54] **Title 18 U.S.C. § 241. Conspiracy against rights of citizens**
  If two or more persons conspire to injure, oppress, threaten, or intimidate any citizen in the free exercise or enjoyment of any right or privilege secured to him by the Constitution or laws of the United States, or because of his having so exercised the same; ... They shall be fined ... or imprisoned ... or both;

pendens. Valuable property was lost, including my mountain-top home that had over a quarter-million-dollar equity in it. Everything I worked for was being lost. Even on the eve of losing valuable properties due to mortgage foreclosures caused by the lis pendens, the Friedman firm and their attorneys refused to allow the existing loans to be refinanced.

Initially, I had legal counsel,[55] but they were as incompetent as the attorney I hired for the Denver FAA safety grievance hearing. I had to terminate them and proceed in pro se status, representing myself. None of my legal counsel argued current California law. They argued fifty-year-old case law, from the days of segregated bussing, toilets, and eating establishments. None of them knew federal law, which under the Federal Supremacy Clause of the United States Constitution takes precedence over state law. To get the law argued, I had to file my own briefs. But in pro per status, due process almost always goes out the window, as state and federal judges side with their attorney cohorts.

While under constant judicial attack, and suffering severe personal and financial losses due to the sham action, my doctor advised that I must immediately undergo open-heart surgery, which I did, receiving six coronary bypasses. (April 1985.) Before I left for surgery, I notified the California Court of Appeal judges, King, Low, and Haning, of the hospitalization, and requested they delay their decision on the appeal of the May 10, 1983 order until after I got out of intensive care. Otherwise, I would not have time to request a rehearing from the California Supreme Court judges for the expected unfavorable decision.

I was barely out of intensive care, and had just arrived home, when the Court of Appeal judges rendered their decision. Several attorney friends described the decision as the closest thing to a poison-pen letter that they had ever seen. I rushed to prepare a petition for hearing to the California Supreme Court. But the Supreme Court judges had protected the judicial civil right violations since 1983. There wasn't much hope, as the judicial Ponzi scheme protected the renegade judges.

The published decision fabricated facts out of whole cloth. It refused to address any of the California or federal laws that I raised in defense. The decision upheld the right of California judges to void prior divorce judgments of any party moving to California, to remarry the parties so as to support the "divorce" action and to seize properties and businesses, and convey half of it to a former spouse (even if remarried). They held they had the power to destroy, in this bizarre fashion, the personal lives and possessions of innocent people.

The published decision eulogized the Friedman law firm who filed the action that was prohibited by law. The decision eulogized my ex-wife who openly committed fraud and perjury by simultaneously declaring herself married to me in the California action while declaring herself divorced from me in her resident state of Texas. The published decision approved the

---

[55] Douglas Page; Maurice Moyal;

rendering of orders inflicting great harm upon people, without having jurisdiction under California law to even conduct hearings once the prior divorce judgments were presented to them.

Despite the absence of jurisdiction, the absence of any marriage, the absence of any contact between the former spouses for many years, despite the blocks of state and federal law barring the action, California judges continued to render orders based upon there being an existing marriage. These unlawful orders, rendered without jurisdiction, devastated my personal life, causing loss of valuable property.

Appellate judges used all types of schemes to block my defenses. They refused to receive my appeal briefs; they misstated the facts and the law; they ordered me to pay huge fines for filing appeals and oppositions; they threatened to impose additional fines if I exercised any of the judicial remedies available under law. They ordered me to pay over $250,000 in fines for having objected to the proceedings via legal appeals and oppositions. The California judges were openly engaged in dirty legal tactics. It could take a book just to describe the sordid tricks these California judges inflicted upon me.

BENCH WARRANT FOR MY ARREST

The judicial outrages didn't stop. Judge William Jensen ordered me to pay to the Friedman law firm $170,000 attorney fees. When I could not pay them he sentenced me to jail, even though it was the judicial lis pendens placed on my properties that denied me access to my own funds. My income had been halted. Another judge did the same, Judge William Peterson (who was later promoted by California governor George Deukmejian to an appellate judgeship).

Despite the unconstitutionality of the cause of action, its prohibition under California statutory law, despite the absence of jurisdiction under the Family Law Act, California judges[56] repeatedly protected and rewarded the Friedman law firm. The California judges blocked every attempt to defend against the bizarre action. Something was radically wrong. To support the violations of blocks of law, the California judges blocked every procedural defense.

RETALIATION FOR EXERCISING FEDERAL REMEDIES

Another scheme was concocted to put me in jail. Jensen ordered me to appear in court on May 9, 1986, a date that he knew I was calendared to be in federal court at Sacramento. That action was a Civil Rights action I filed against Jensen on the basis of violating my rights under state and federal laws and causing me harm. Jensen retaliated me for my exercising these rights by ordering me to appear in court to answer why I should not be held in contempt for failure to pay the judgments, which he knew I couldn't pay. I was repeatedly in Catch-22 situations.

I filed papers in the Solano County court notifying Jensen that I physically could not appear on that date (which he already knew). I also stated my inability to pay the money orders since the Friedman law firm, with his help,

---

[56] Judges Dwight Ely, Michael McInnis, William Jensen, John DeRonde, Richard Harris, William Peterson.

had tied up all my funds with the lis pendens upon my properties and assets. I again reminded him of the absence of jurisdiction and the wholesale numbers of California and federal laws that barred the attack upon the five prior judgments. I also advised Jensen that an attorney would appear for me at that hearing, and that met the requirements of California law.

Despite all this, Jensen held me in contempt of court for not being present, and issued a bench warrant for my arrest. Since I resided in Nevada, this bench warrant kept me from appearing in California for the next year and a half. Seeking relief from the bench warrant, I submitted petitions for relief to the California Court of Appeals and the California Supreme Court. The Ponzi-like scheme of judge-protecting-judge continued, and relief was denied.

SHAM DIVORCE JUDGMENT

Without my knowledge, the Friedman law firm and California Judge Dennis Bunting conducted a hearing on July 28, 1988, to terminate the non-existing marriage and order the taking of my properties. During the hearing Judge Bunting rendered a judgment that described the cause of action as a dissolution of marriage action (even though there hadn't been a marriage for over twenty years, depriving the judge of jurisdiction under the Family Law Act proceeding). Having "established" that Friedman's Texas client was married to me, Bunting then rendered an order holding that all my assets were community properties. All of my properties met the legal definition of separate properties since they were acquired years after the 1964 separation and 1966 divorce. Properties acquired after marital separation are separate properties.

The same order required me to pay $2500 monthly spousal support for the remainder of my life (contradicting the five existing divorce judgments showing there was no spousal support obligations).

There were now six divorce judgments. Five showed me divorced since 1966; showed all properties were separate; and held that neither party had any spousal support rights or obligations. Then we had the sixth judgment, rendered twenty-two years later, by California judges lacking jurisdiction under California law; lacking jurisdiction under federal law; lacking jurisdiction over properties legally classified as separate; violating dozens of California and federal statutes, constitutional protections, and other laws; in a cause of action barred by forty-five years of U.S. Supreme Court decisions.

Federal statutes provide that a person can obtain a declaratory judgment from a federal judge, declaring his personal and property rights, and the validity of the five prior divorce judgments, when these rights are under attack. There is no other place to go but into federal court when judgments from another state are attacked by a state judge. But to render a decision would unravel the scheme concocted against me, and expose the civil and constitutional violations, and the criminal conspiracy under which they were perpetrated. To this day, my constitutional and statutory rights to have a ruling holding these judgments and the related personal and property rights valid, have been refused to me by at least a dozen federal judges.

I filed a notice of appeal with the California Court of Appeals at San Francisco, and had the appeal heard by the same justices that had aided and abetted these gross violations of law for the past seven years; Justices Donald King, Harry Low, and Zerne Haning. On July 22, 1990, they handed down a decision upholding the judgment rendered without jurisdiction due to removal and which violated the many other state and federal protections.

They approved the judgment that under law was a void judgment, and which violated numerous federal protections, such as the Civil Rights Act. Worse, they placed a frivolous label on my appeal, ordered me to pay $65,000 sanctions to the Friedman law firm for filing the appeal, and ordered me to pay $20,000 sanctions to the State of California! I then filed an appeal with the California Supreme Court, which also had protected the massive judicial violations since 1983. The entire court approved these judicial violations.

It was several years before I recognized what was behind the sham California action. Once the judicial scheme started rendering the unlawful orders it became necessary for each succeeding judge to enlarge on the violations so as to protect the prior acts, and protect those involved in the scheme.

CHAPTER SEVEN

The Little Pawn

One of my daughters, Linda, then a resident of Texas, and one of her sons, became a target of the Friedman law firm. Linda and her son were expendable in the scheme to silence me. This required the cooperation of the Friedman law firm, a Texas law firm, judges in Texas, California and Nevada, and the help of Justice Department attorneys and federal judges. To carry out the scheme the woman residing in Texas, from whom I was divorced two decades earlier, had to be placated. The Friedman law firm used her as a catalyst in the sham divorce action, and the woman knowingly participated in the scheme. When it was over, Linda lost custody of one of her sons who was sacrificed to please the Texas resident.

Linda was the only daughter in touch with her mother, and this woman received considerable joy out of baby-sitting Linda's five-year-old son, Heath. For convenience, Linda often left the child in her care almost daily. But Linda grew tired of the hatred generated by my her mother's participation in the sham divorce scheme, and in 1986 suddenly moved to California with her two sons, five-year-old Heath, and one-year-old Dustin. As the catalyst for Friedman's attacks upon me, this woman's cooperation was essential. Linda's mother was on the verge of ordering the Friedman law firm to drop the California action because she was distraught after Linda moved from California. She wanted Linda's son, Heath, back in Texas, having become dependent upon Heath's companionship.

After Linda left Texas, her mother decided to call an end to the sham divorce action, threatening to collapse the scheme carried out by the Friedman law firm. Friedman warned my former wife that she owed them tens of thousands of dollars, and could not pull out. The Friedman group promised that if she continued with the California action they would obtain legal custody of Heath for her.

The Friedman law firm[57] hired a Texas attorney, Gayle Oler, to submit a petition and affidavit to a Dallas court, obtaining an order granting custody of five-year-old Heath to the nearly seventy-year old grandmother. The attorneys fraudulently declared under oath that Linda was guilty of contempt of court, that Linda's mother had legal custody of the boy, and that the boy was unlawfully taken out of Texas. The affidavit stated that Heath was in great danger, and that Linda was an unfit mother. Actually, Heath was having the time of his life living at Lake Tahoe, where Linda took up residence and sought employment.

The affidavit claiming Linda was an unfit mother made no reference to the welfare of Linda's two-year-old son, Dustin. Linda's mother only wanted Heath. The attorney's affidavit falsely stated that they did not know Linda's whereabouts, and thus could not give her notice of the hearing. But the Friedman group knew where Linda resided, and that Reno attorney Jonathan King was representing her. At least, he was supposed to.

TEXAS JUSTICE!

Without any evidence other than the self-serving statements of an attorney, and without giving Linda a chance to defend herself and her little boy, Judge Hartman of the Dallas Municipal Court rendered an order taking Heath from Linda. He granted custody to Linda's aged mother. That order was rushed by the Friedman law firm to California Superior Court Judge William Jensen at Fairfield, California, where a closed-door hearing was conducted without Linda's knowledge. A California order was rendered by Jensen, who played a major role in the sham action taken against me. That California order ordered the seizure of the little boy. Reno Judge Charles McGee recognized the order as valid. He either did not know about the scheme, or he willingly participated in it.[58]

Friedman planned the seizure of the little boy with the precision of a drug bust. The Friedman law firm flew my former wife to California from Texas, collaborating with the Washoe County Sheriff's Office in Reno. At a predetermined time, the group went into the residence occupied by Linda and her two sons at Lake Tahoe.

"They're taking Heath!"

It was 10:30 a.m. when Linda frantically called me. (February 18, 1987.) "They're taking Heath," Linda cried. She said the house was full of people, and the sheriff's deputies were taking Heath out the front door. The deputy then turned the frightened boy over to Friedman's Texas client, and the attorneys rushed the boy to Reno Airport for an immediate flight to Dallas, before I could obtain a court order stopping them. I tried to get immediate help from Reno attorney Jonathan King, who had been hired earlier to protect Linda's interest, but he was as useless as other attorneys I had obtained.

FRIGHTENED, AND OFF INTO A BLIZZARD

Linda panicked when her son was taken from her. The legal papers served

---

[57] And especially attorneys Larry Gibbs and Ross.

[58] He refused to respond to a letter requesting an explanation, or deny that he knowingly played a role in the boy's seizure.

upon her advised that a hearing to determine Heath's custody would take place in Dallas in thirty-six hours. She frantically packed her belongings, her son Dustin, and her German Shepherd, driving off into the night during a raging winter snow storm, heading for Texas.

Linda drove all night in blizzard conditions, over the desolate mountainous roads of Nevada, seeking to reach Texas in time for the custody hearing. She failed to realize the extreme dangers of driving in the mountains during a blizzard, and that she could not possibly reach Dallas in time for the hearing. Linda became snowbound in the Nevada mountains. Fortunately, she and the children escaped the fate experienced in December 1992, under similar conditions, by the Stolpa family, stuck in a Nevada blizzard. Jim and Jennifer Stolpa lost toes and part of their feet due to severe frostbite. Extensive press coverage and a 1994 TV movie described their plight.

My oldest daughter, Stephanie Stadtler, quickly caught a plane for Texas, and appeared in court on Linda's behalf. Stephanie advised the court that Linda would not be there in time for the appearance, and obtained a continuance of the hearing.

REFUSING TO ACCEPT EVIDENCE

Like much of the public, unaware of the human right outrages that occur in court, Linda was confident the court could not take Heath from her. She was unaware of the dirty judicial politics taking place daily in state and federal courts. She naively thought the law protected her. I didn't want to frighten Linda and have her worry unnecessarily. But I wanted her to realize she was facing a formidable legal and judicial group that has stopped at nothing to carry out their scheme. Ruining her life and that of her five-year-old son meant nothing to them.

I warned Linda we were dealing with the ruthless Justice Department and federal judges who can control state judges. Friedman's plan required the cooperation of Linda's mother and if this required taking Linda's child they would not hesitate for a moment to do so. Unless they could deliver the boy to the woman who was the catalyst for the sham action against me in the California courts, their scheme was in danger of going up in smoke, exposing them in the process.

"Linda, federal judges and the justice department are already involved in your case," I said. "The Texas judges can be manipulated, and they aren't going to let you have your son back. There is too much at stake!"

I told Linda to fight, but also to realize what she was up against. U.S. District Judge Milton Schwartz[59] and Justice Department attorneys had already cited the Texas custody case[60] in a lawsuit I filed against the judge because of his violation of my civil rights.[61] Judge Schwartz and Justice

---

[59] Eastern District of California.

[60] No. 82-9280-V. *In the Interest of Heath Ashley Mulvey.*

[61] District of Columbia Nr. C-87-2214; March 1987. The suit sought declaratory and injunctive relief against the federal judges under the *Bivens* doctrine. That Supreme Court decision called the Bivens doctrine applies the protections of the Civil Rights Act, which is limited to those acting under color of state law, to those who act under color of federal law.

Department attorneys cited the custody case and stated I had lost that case, implying I was on the losing side.

I wasn't involved at all in the custody battle, but found in the past that truth is of little concern to federal judges and Justice Department attorneys. The Dallas custody decision hadn't even been rendered yet, and Schwartz argued that Linda lost custody of her boy! I would later discover that state and federal judges repeatedly coordinated their activities despite the illegality of the practice. The purpose of citing the custody case was to imply that *I* had filed the action taking Linda's boy from her, and that the case was decided adversely to me, showing a pattern of dismissed actions.

REFUSING FAVORABLE TESTIMONY

Dallas Judge Hartman conducted a custody hearing[62] at which I testified, along with my three daughters. We tried to introduce evidence in the form of pictures, videos, and testimony, showing that Linda and her two boys had a loving and pleasant home life in Nevada. Judge Hartman refused to accept the testimony, the video, or the still pictures, turning a deaf ear to our testimony, obstructing entry of any evidence favorable to Linda. The Texas courts hadn't changed from their corrupt practices that I discovered when I left Dallas years earlier. In **every** court proceeding, California, federal, and now Texas, we were totally gridlocked from the protections of law.

The Texas case worker, without any knowledge of Linda's Nevada housing accommodations, recommended that the 68-year-old grandmother be granted custody of the five-year-old child, emphasizing that the grandmother had a brick home. California parents and their stucco houses wouldn't stand a chance in a Texas custody battle!

DESTROYING LINDA'S FAMILY

Based on the self-serving arguments of an attorney from the Friedman law firm and Friedman's Texas client (Linda's mother), Judge Hartman ruled that Linda was unfit to have custody of the five-year-old child, implying that she was fit, however, to have custody of the younger boy that Friedman's client did not want. He gave no consideration to Linda being the boy's natural mother, or to the testimony of Linda's two sisters, myself, and the evidence that the boys were happy.

Heath became a pawn in this intrigue. But as I found out over the next few years, the harm inflicted upon Linda and her son was minor compared to the harm the judicial system and federal prosecutors inflict upon thousands of people. Often, the harm is inflicted to silence them about knowledge of government corruption. Hartman granted custody of the five-year-old boy to the woman who was a key participant in a conspiracy directed against me, and the conspiracy to silence me.

A LEGACY OF SUICIDE AND HATE

Linda had her share of hard times. Most of her problems arose from her failure to break the ties with her domineering mother. After Linda gave birth to her first child, Shawn, her mother developed a fondness for the child, like

---

[62] March 1987.

a new doll. She wanted Shawn, and schemed to get the child. Linda and her husband lived in San Antonio, where he was in the Air Force. Linda's mother missed the child and pressured Linda to leave her husband, which she foolishly did, and moved back home with her mother. My former wife acquired the first of her play toys: Shawn.

I had met Linda's first husband before their marital breakup during one of my frequent trips to visit the children in Dallas. At that time I had a Navion Rangemaster airplane and would take them flying to various Texas destinations. He was a caring individual, deeply in love with Linda.

After Linda left her husband, he became despondent over their separation. Every attempt at reconciliation was thwarted by Linda's mother. One night he wrote a suicide note, parked his car behind the place where Linda worked, then, with the engine running, lay under the exhaust pipe, breathing the fumes. Linda found him dead when she left work. Linda's mother succeeded in that scheme, obtaining the companionship of Linda's first child. Now, with the help of Justice Department attorneys, federal, California and Texas judges, Linda lost her second child.

The suicide distressed Linda, and ironically, she became more dependent upon the person most responsible for the death and for her grief. Many times Linda's mother would accuse Linda, in front of her children, of causing the death of Linda's husband.

SCHEMING TO GET LEGAL CUSTODY OF SHAWN

After obtaining physical care of Shawn, Linda's mother schemed to get legal custody, which brought with it survivor's pension paid by the government because the boy's father, a GI, was dead. She accomplished this by having Linda sign documents allegedly enrolling Shawn in the local school district. After obtaining Linda's signature, she applied to the court for legal custody, arguing that Linda was an unfit mother, was on drugs, and that Linda had voluntarily signed over custody. Without requiring Linda's presence, Texas Judge Hartman, ordered custody given to Linda's mother.

Linda didn't learn that she had lost custody of her son until her sister, Patty, living in Waxahachie, Texas, told her what happened. Without money, and depressed, Linda didn't know what to do. Foolishly, or stupidly, Linda clung even more to her mother.

Linda's mother applied to the government to have the monthly survivor's check changed from Linda's name to hers, and got the added benefit of this money. When Shawn became older, and was no longer the cute little boy, his grandmother lost interest in him, and he became embroiled frequently with the law, showing contempt for his own natural mother.

It was ironic that after scheming to take Linda's first child, Linda's mother schemed with the Friedman law firm to take Linda's second child. Department of Justice attorneys and federal judges assisted in the scheme. Texas Judge Hartman knew about the fraudulent taking of Linda's first child, and of the fraudulent affidavit granting temporary custody of Linda's second child to Linda's mother. I would discover several years later that the Friedman law firm was a front for the Justice Department and the CIA.

CHAPTER EIGHT

COMPLICITY BY
FEDERAL JUDGES

Under our form of government the only place to obtain relief when state judges violate a person's civil and constitutional rights is in federal court, as provided by federal statutes. Any one of the many violations of California and federal law inflicted upon me in the sham California action invoked mandatory federal court jurisdiction. The California judges and the Friedman law firm violated my civil and constitutional rights for six years straight, repeatedly invoking federal court jurisdiction and declaratory and injunctive relief remedies, along with financial damages.

In their positions of trust federal judges are paid, and have the mandatory duty, to provide this federal court access and relief.[63] In addition to the statutory right to federal court access and relief the First Amendment to the Constitution[64] provides additional safeguards so that no one goes through what I went through (and am still going through).

I exercised these rights. For instance, when a divorced person exercises his or her constitutional right to change residence, his or her previously adjudicated personal and property rights in a divorce must be recognized by judges in another state. He or she cannot be subjected to another divorce twenty or thirty years later, invalidating subsequent marriages and bastardizing children, as was done to me in the sham California action. In the bizarre action taken against me, one of the remedies arose under the Declaratory

---

[63] **Title 28 U.S.C. § 1331. Federal question.** "The federal courts **shall** have original jurisdiction of all civil actions arising under the Constitution, laws, or treaties of the United States."

[64] The First Amendment to the Constitution provides That "Congress shall make no law ... abridging the [the right] to petition the Government for a redress of grievances."

Judgment Act and statutes. These remedies required [65]a federal judge to declare the validity of each of the five prior divorce judgments, and the validity of my divorced status and property rights.

When a California judge refuses to recognize any of the prior judgments entered in five different states (including California), and refuses to recognize the divorced status and property rights, federal courts are the only remedy. In my case, to declare these rights, the U.S. District Judge must first apply federal law that requires recognition of the judgments, and then secondarily apply state law if it conforms to federal law. In my case, any one of over a dozen state and federal doctrines of law, constitutional rights, and statutes, required the California judges to recognize the rights established in the five judgments.

Because the state judges inflicted great harm upon me while violating my civil and constitutional rights, there were additional federal statutes insuring that I have access to federal court. These remedies also provided jurisdiction to obtain financial damages against the state judges and the Friedman law firm. This relief arises under the Civil Rights Act, among other statutes, which is embodied in Title 42 Section 1983.[66]

When two or more people act to do a certain thing it is called a conspiracy. It was obvious that the various attorneys in the Friedman, Sloan and Ross law firm and the California judges were acting together to violate the law, inflicting great harm upon me. This conspiracy violated another section of the Civil Rights Act, Title 42 U.S.C. § 1985.[67]

If any person knows that your civil rights are being violated, and they have the power to prevent or aid in the prevention of these violations, and they don't do so, other federal statutes provide federal court jurisdiction and relief.

---

[65] Title 28 U.S.C. Section 2201 to declare federally protected rights.

[66] Title 42 U.S.C. Section 1983: Every person who, under color or any statute, ordinance, regulation, custom or usage, of any State or Territory, subjects ... any citizen of the United States ... to the deprivation of any rights, privileges or immunities secured by the Constitution and laws, shall be liable to the party injured in an action at law, suit in equity, or other proper proceeding for redress."

[67] Title 42 U.S.C. Section 1985 Conspiracy to interfere with civil rights–Preventing officer from performing duties.

(1) If two or more persons ... conspire to prevent ... any person from accepting or holding any office, trust, or place of confidence under the United States, or from discharging any duties thereof; or to injure him in his person or property on account of his lawful discharge of the duties of his office, or while engaged in the lawful discharge thereof, or to injure his property so as to molest, interrupt, hinder, or impede him in the discharge of his official duties.

(2) If two or more persons conspire ... for the purpose of depriving, either directly or indirectly, any person ... of the equal protection of the laws, or of equal privileges and immunities under the laws ...in any case of conspiracy set forth in this section, if one or more persons engaged therein do, or cause to be done, any act in furtherance of the object of such conspiracy, whereby another is injured in his person or property, or deprived of having and exercising any right or privilege of a citizen of the United States, the party so injured or deprived may have an action for the recovery of damages occasioned by such injury or deprivation, against any one or more of the conspirators.

This cause of action arises under Title 42 U.S.C. Section 1986[68] and Title 28 U.S.C. Section 1343.[69]

Under certain conditions this conspiracy creates still another federal cause of action under the RICO statutes (Racketeer Influenced and Corruption Organization Act)[70].

When federal officials violate a person's civil rights, they are said to be acting under color of federal law. They can be sued. These federal personnel include federal judges, federal trustees, or other federal employees. The authority is the *Bivens* doctrine,[71] which is federal case law applying the Civil Rights Act to violations by federal personnel.

MANDATORY DUTY TO PROVIDE RELIEF

I filed the first federal action (January 10, 1984) in the United States District Court in the Eastern District of California at Sacramento.[72] Although I had years of legal experience working with attorneys and in filing federal actions against the FAA and NTSB, and could have filed this lawsuit in pro se, I hired Sacramento attorney James Reed to file the action. He had experience with civil rights as a law school teacher at McGeorge School of Law in Sacramento.

---

[68] **Title 42 U.S.C. Section 1986. Action for neglect to prevent conspiracy**

Every person who, having knowledge that any of the wrongs conspired to be done, and mentioned in the preceding section [42 USCS § 1985], are about to be committed, and having power to prevent or aid in preventing the commission of the same, neglects or refuses to do so, if such wrongful act be committed, shall be liable to the party injured, or his legal representatives, for all damages caused by such wrongful act, which such person by reasonable diligence could have prevented; and such damages may be recovered in an action on the case; and any number of persons guilty of such wrongful neglect or refusal may be joined as defendants in the action, and if the death of any party be caused by any such wrongful act and neglect, the legal representatives of the deceased shall have such action therefor, and may recover not exceeding five thousand dollars damages therein, for the benefit of the widow of the deceased, if there be one, and if there be no widow, then for the benefit of the next of kin of the deceased. But no action under the provisions of this section shall be sustained which is not commenced within one year after the cause of action has accrued.

[69] **Title 28 U.S.C. Section 1343**

(a) The district court shall have original jurisdiction of any civil action　authorized by law to be commenced by any person:

(1) To recover damages for injury to his person or property, or because of the deprivation of any right or privilege of a citizen of the United States, by any act done in furtherance of any conspiracy mentioned in section 1985 of Title 42;

(2) To recover damages from any person who fails to prevent or to aid in preventing any wrongs mentioned in section 1985 of Title 42 which he had knowledge were about to occur and power to prevent;

(3) To redress the deprivation, under color of any State law, statute, ordinance, regulation, custom or usage, of any right, privilege or immunity secured by the Constitution of the United States or by any Act of Congress providing for equal rights of citizens or of all persons within the jurisdiction of the United States;

(4) To recover damages or to secure equitable or other relief under any Act of Congress providing for the protection of civil rights, including the right to vote.

[70] Title 18 United States Code Sections 1961 and 1962.

[71] *Bivens v. Six Unknown Agents*, 403 U.S. 388 (1971).

[72] January 10, 1984. *Stich v. California Superior Court; Dwight Ely, Judge; Friedman, Sloan and Ross*, C-84-0048 RAR.

The lawsuit sought (a) a declaratory judgment to declare my divorced status and property rights, as established in the five divorce judgments and under federal and state law; (b) injunctive relief to halt the orders rendered by the California judges who were acting without jurisdiction under California law, and violating blocks of state and federal law; and (c) financial damages.

The federal lawsuit raised issues that had been settled in the 1940s by the U.S. Supreme Court. It sought to declare my constitutional right[73] to change residence without being remarried to a person from whom I was divorced decades earlier. It sought to protect the considerable real estate that I had acquired since the 1966 divorce, and which was the primary target of the sham action. The lawsuit sought financial damages against the California judges and the Friedman law firm. In the same year, the U.S. Supreme Court clarified the right to sue state judges who violate state or federal law, or who act without jurisdiction.[74] The court clerk assigned the lawsuit to Judge Raul Ramirez.

THE START OF THE FEDERAL DUE PROCESS GRIDLOCK

The Friedman law firm and California Judge Dwight Ely filed a motion to dismiss the federal declaratory judgment and civil rights action on the grounds that the California action was a divorce action, and therefore the federal courts must abstain. The mere fact that I was subject to a divorce action when federal law established that I was already divorced constituted violations of federally protected rights, and invoked mandatory federal court jurisdiction. Further, numerous federal laws, and over two dozen California statutes and Rules of Court had been violated, constituting major federal causes of action. Further, even if I had been legally married, federal court jurisdiction does not cease when federally protected rights are violated.

REPETITION OF THE FRIVOLOUS TACTIC

The standard tactic used by the California judges when I exercised my legal remedies was to place a frivolous label on it and call me a vexatious litigant for exercising lawful defenses against the massive violations of law. The frivolous labels were then used to order me to pay huge financial sanctions to the Friedman law firm, who initiated the civil right violations.

U.S. District Judge Raul Ramirez unlawfully dismissed my action, refusing to address the validity of the five divorce judgments or my personal

---

[73] Under Title 28 U.S.C. §§ 2201, 2202. Among the constitutional rights violated were the rights and protections in the Fourteenth Amendment due process, equal protection, property, liberty, freedom rights; Privileges and Immunity Clause rights under Article IV, § 1, and under the 14th Amendment (depriving right to obtain divorce on universally recognized residence basis, and right to change residence); right to unabridged interstate travel, without losing rights and privileges acquired in prior jurisdictions of residence; Article IV, § 1 (Full Faith and Credit Clause, and Title 28 U.S.C. § 1738, requiring recognition of the personal and property rights in the California divorce judgment, its entry for recognition as local judgments in the courts of Nevada, Oklahoma, and Texas.

[74] *Pulliam v. Allen*, 104 S.Ct 1970 (1984). Followed by other federal decisions: *Harlow v. Fitzgerald*, 457 U.S. 800 (1982); *Dykes v. Hoseman*, 743 F.2d 1488 (11th Cir. 1984). In *Dykes v. Hoseman*, 743 F.2d 1488 (11th Cir. 1984), the Eleventh Circuit federal district court held that a state judge could be sued for money damages when he renders orders without either personal or subject matter jurisdiction.

and property rights, even though he was paid to perform these acts. In addition, he ordered me to pay the Friedman law firm $10,000 for having sought declaratory and injunctive relief remedies. Further, it is not the client, but the attorney, who is usually ordered to pay sanctions when a court declares a lawsuit frivolous.

It is a federal crime to inflict harm upon anyone for having exercised rights and protections under the laws and Constitution of the United States.[75]

DEFINITION OF A FRIVOLOUS ACTION

The United States Supreme Court and other federal decisions defined the term frivolous as any complaint, appeal, or any other motion, for which there is not an arguable point. The U.S. Supreme Court held that they are not frivolous if *"any of the legal points [are] arguable on their merits ... "* *Haines v. Kerner* 404 U.S. 519, 521-522 (1972). Obviously, my federal complaint exercising the right to have my personal and property status declared under federal and state law was not frivolous. Nor was it frivolous to seek injunctive relief against the repeated violations of state and federal law by California judges acting without jurisdiction under California law. This judicial charade was repeated time and time again, as the pack of renegade federal judges engaged in a Ponzi-like scheme protecting the scheme and the perpetrators.

PROTECTION AGAINST WRONGFUL DISMISSAL

Federal law prohibits dismissing an action if the complaint states a single federal cause of action. The law requires that the allegations stated in the complaint be recognized as true for the purpose of determining whether a federal cause of action is stated.[76] If any *single* federal cause of action is *alleged*, the case cannot be dismissed and the District Judge must exercise his duty to provide a federal court forum.

These and many other protections to which all Americans are entitled were repeatedly violated during a ten-year-period by a daisy chain of federal judges, up to and including the Justices of the U.S. Supreme Court.

District Judge Raul Ramirez sought to support his order of dismissal on the basis that the California action was a domestic relations action for which federal courts should abstain. That was a bald-face misstatement. First, the Civil Rights Act protections apply to all actions regardless of the label placed upon the suit. Second, I was exercising my rights under the Declaratory Judgment Act to have a federal court declare as valid the prior divorce judgments and the personal and property rights stated in them. Federal law, in addition to state law, required that these judgments and these rights be

---

[75] **Title 18 U.S.C. § 241. Conspiracy against rights of citizens**
If two or more persons conspire to injure, oppress, threaten, or intimidate any citizen in the free exercise or enjoyment of any right or privilege secured to him by the Constitution or laws of the United States, or because of his having so exercised the same; ... They shall be fined ... or imprisoned ... or both.

[76] *Dennis v. Sparks* 449 U.S. 24 (1980)("a section 1983 complaint should not be dismissed unless it appears that the plaintiff can prove no set of facts which would entitle him to relief ... For the purposes of testing sufficiency of the complaint, the allegations of the complaint must be accepted as true."); *Gardener v. Toilet Goods Assn.*, 387 U.S. 167, 172 (1967). (An action, "especially under the Civil Rights Act, should not be dismissed at the pleadings stage unless it appears to a certainty that plaintiffs are entitled to no relief under any state of the facts, which could be proved in support of their claims."

recognized. Third, the divorce label was a farce as I had been legally divorced for the past two decades. Instead of placing a marriage dissolution label on the action it could just as well have been a probate action, disregarding the fact that I was still alive.

SUSPENSION OF APPEAL REMEDIES

In response to Ramirez's dismissal, I filed a timely notice of appeal with the U.S. Court of Appeals at San Francisco. This was the same appellate court that had wrongfully dismissed my lawsuits against the FAA and NTSB in 1974 and 1980. These unlawful dismissals continued the practices that played key roles in subsequent air disasters. In those earlier actions I exercised the mandatory responsibilities under federal criminal statutes to report safety and criminal violations to a federal court. By their refusal to receive my testimony and evidence these same federal judges blocked the reporting of serious crimes, and became co-conspirators in the criminal acts I sought to expose.

Federal appellate law requires the Court of Appeals to vacate the order of dismissal, and the frivolous holding, if the complaint alleges at least one federal cause of action for which federal courts can grant relief. And the allegations stated in the complaint far exceeded that test. For the purpose of this test, all allegations must be accepted as true.[77]

The Court of Appeals judges denied my appeal, upholding the violations by the U.S. District Court Judge and upholding the pattern of civil and constitutional violations in the state court. They also upheld the $10,000 financial sanctions ordered by Judge Ramirez[78] that retaliated against me for exercising rights guaranteed under the Constitution and laws of the United States. I then sought relief by filing petitions for writ of certiorari with the Justices of the United States Supreme Court. Even they had been implicated in the judicial coverup and the offenses associated with the air safety corruption.

The Ninth Circuit Court of Appeals and the U.S. Supreme Court dismissed my federal actions seeking relief. Their acts approved the unlawful denial of a federal court forum, the denial of the protections of federal law, the unlawful dismissal of the action, and the obvious conspiracy to commit these acts. These higher federal courts gave the California judges and the Friedman law firm carte blanche approval to escalate their attacks upon me, which then occurred. The *lis pendens* that were placed upon all of my properties prevented the normal replacement of mortgages when they came due, and I lost valuable properties. My personal life and my business were in shambles.

California Judge J. Clinton Peterson[79] sentenced me to jail for five days in 1987 for contempt of court when I failed to pay a money judgment to the

---

[77] "In our view, a decision to give less than full independent de novo review to the state law determinations of the district courts would be an abdication of our appellate responsibility. Every party is entitled to a full, considered, and impartial review of the decision of the trial court. *Matter of McLinn*, 739 F.2d 1395 (9th Cir 1983).

[78] Ramirez left the federal bench in 1992 and is now with a Sacramento law firm.

[79] Superior Court located at Fairfield, California. He was later promoted to a Court of Appeal judge.

Friedman law firm. That same judge had tied up all my assets, leaving me without funds to pay any judgment, valid or not.

REPEATEDLY SEEKING RELIEF

As the California judges rendered additional orders, inflicting greater harm upon me, which were new federal causes of action, I filed additional federal lawsuits to avoid waiving my right to relief and seeking to halt the resulting harm. A continuing series of judge-protect-judge dismissals continued. Other federal judges joined the daisy-chain pattern of violating every protection in law, while simultaneously protecting those committing the offenses.[80] I filed numerous petitions with the Justices of the U.S. Supreme Court, making the Justices aware of the pattern of judicially inflicted civil and constitutional violations.

SHAM OATHS

All federal judges, including the justices of the U.S. Supreme Court, take an oath to uphold the laws and Constitution of the United States. The oath is as follows:

I, [name of judge], do solemnly swear (or affirm) that I will support and defend the Constitution of the United States against all enemies, foreign and domestic, that I will bear true faith and allegiance to the same, that I take this obligation freely, without any mental reservations or purpose of evasion, and that I will well and faithfully discharge the duties of the office on which I am about to enter. So help me God.

They would be impeached, and sent to federal prison, If the law was applied as written. But the system has broken down and been thoroughly corrupted.

RECOGNIZING THE JUDICIAL CONSPIRACY

I had been too close to the trees to see the forest. I recognized the pattern of judicial misconduct, but had not associated it with a scheme to silence my reporting of the government corruption. Suddenly it became clear. The California lawsuit was engineered by powerful interests in the federal branches of government, using the Friedman law firm as a front, and obtaining the cooperation of California judges in the conspiracy. It was apparently never anticipated, when the scheme was hatched, that I would exercise federal remedies. And when I did, federal judges had to protect the scheme, and the attorneys and judges carrying it out.

Once I recognized this relationship, I identified it in my federal briefs, and simultaneously identified the criminal activities that I first discovered as a federal investigator. I filed a federal action combining the causes of action relating to the ongoing California action, and simultaneously demanded that I be allowed to present testimony and evidence relating to the criminal activities. This action, filed in the U.S. District Court at Sacramento,[81] was assigned to Judge Milton Schwartz.

"Mr. Stich, these allegations are very serious."

During the first hearing before Judge Milton Schwartz on May 9, 1986,

---

[80] Federal Judges Marilyn Petal, Samuel Conti, Charles Legge.
[81] E.D. Cal. Nr. C 86-0210 MLS.

Schwartz admitted the gravity of the allegations. "Mr. Stich," he stated, "these allegations are very serious. If you wish, I will continue the hearing and give you time to hire legal counsel." But no legal counsel would touch the case; it was too sensitive. Besides, the cost to pursue the case against powerful federal personnel who have the unlimited federal funds of the U.S. Treasury behind them, would run into the hundreds of thousands of dollars. And my adversaries would be the judges and Justice Department attorneys who control access to justice. Also, as I would later learn, virtually no attorney would sacrifice his legal career by exposing the misconduct in the courts and the Justice Department.

RAPID CHANGES IN POSITION

Within a month after Judge Schwartz admitted the gravity of the allegations stated in the complaint, the Friedman law firm and the California judges filed a motion to dismiss the complaint. Despite the multiple federal causes of actions alleged in the complaint, despite the gravity of the criminal acts, which Schwartz admitted during the previous hearing, Schwartz ordered my lawsuit dismissed, and ordered me to pay financial sanctions for having exercised these federal rights.

The dismissal openly violated federal law which bars dismissing lawsuits which state a federal cause of action. Mine stated many causes of actions. Further, I was reporting federal crimes to a federal court, and Judge Schwartz lacked jurisdiction to block these reports.

Judge Schwartz continued the judicial practice of the California and federal courts, ordering me to pay financial sanctions to the Friedman law firm, for having sought to report the federal crimes and for seeking declaratory and injunctive relief.

The total financial sanctions that federal judges ordered me to pay the Friedman law firm now exceeded $150,000. At this stage I had not yet learned that the Friedman law firm was a covert Justice Department and CIA front. (More about this in later pages.)

Schwartz compounded his unlawful actions by rendering an order forever barring me access to the federal court and forever voiding for me the protections in federal statutes.[82] He had no authority to suspend the protections under our form of government.

---

[82] The May 30, 1986 injunctive order stated in part:
IT IS HEREBY ORDERED that plaintiff, Rodney F. Stich, is *barred from filing any action or actions in any United States District Court, or in any state court*, until his current state court action, Solano County Superior Court No. 83472, becomes final and he has exhausted all his state court appellate remedies, against defendants Emma W. Stich, Friedman, Sloan & Ross, P.C., or any attorneys or employees of Friedman, Sloan & Ross, P.C., Lawrence A. Gibbs, Jeffrey S. Ross, the judges of the Superior Court of the County of Solano, State of California, Judge William Jensen, Neil Crawford, Clerk, Solano County, or the Superior Court of the County of Solano, State of California, which in any way relates to issues raised in *Stich v. Stich*, No. CIVS-84-0048 RAR, *In re the Marriage of Stich*, Superior Court of the State of California in and for the County of Solano, No. 83472, and *Stich v. California Court of Appeal*, United States District Court, Northern District of California, Action No. C-85-3600-MHP, or in the instant case. ... after the judgment in that state court action has become final and all appellate processes have been exhausted, this bar to further actions shall still apply to any and all claims precluded by the doctrines of res judicata and/or collateral estoppel.

THE LEGAL BASIS FOR AN INJUNCTIVE ORDER

Federal authority for rendering injunctive orders is to protect a party during litigation who is suffering great and irreparable harm. But the injunctive order rendered by Judge Schwartz protected the parties *committing* the harm, and deprived me, the victim, of protection provided by federal law.

I filed a timely notice of appeal of the dismissal and the injunctive order with the Ninth Circuit Court of Appeals at San Francisco. Instead of vacating the dismissal and injunctive order, the Court of Appeal upheld the right of a federal judge to block the reporting of federal crimes, upheld the suspension of constitutional and statutory protections, and upheld the civil rights violations inflicted upon me. Again I sought relief from the Justices of the Supreme Court via emergency petitions and petition for writ of certiorari, and again they upheld the unconstitutional acts by the judges over whom they had supervisory responsibilities.

In response to these new attacks I filed federal actions against the judges of the California Supreme Court and the California Court of Appeal. The basis for this filing was that they aided and abetted the civil rights violations committed against me. Concurrently, I again sought to have my rights declared in the five judgments which were being violated, as well as demanding that my testimony be received concerning the criminal activities I discovered. The action was assigned to U.S. District Judge Marilyn Patel,[83] who promptly dismissed it, *sua sponte*, without any hearing (March 5, 1987), violating still other federal laws. She ordered me to pay financial sanctions, and then rendered an order barring me for life from federal court access. Therefore, for all practical purposes, the judges were voiding, for me, the rights and protections under our form of government, and making possible the continued judicial attacks upon my freedoms and possessions. This obviously unlawful and unconstitutional judicial order was necessary to protect the state and federal judges who now comprised a conspiracy that joined the underlying criminality that I sought to expose. Patel ordered the court clerk to refuse any filing that I submitted.

With every dismissal by a federal judge and the Supreme Court justices the Friedman law firm and the California judges increased the frequency and severity of their violations against me, inflicting immense personal and property harm. I had to do something, and under our form of government I had rights that these renegade judges could not void.

PRIMA FACIE EVIDENCE BREAKDOWN OF RIGHTS

These acts were prima facie evidence of the destruction of constitutional rights and the criminalizing of the federal courts by renegade judges. The involvement of many federal judges, including the entire Ninth Circuit Court of Appeals, and the Justices of the U.S. Supreme Court, revealed the enormity of the judicial corruption and its deep entrenchment in the United States.

If any individual citizen can suffer these outrages, can lose their U.S. Constitutional rights and protections, all U.S. Citizens can suffer the same.

---

[83] N.D. Cal. Nr. C-86-6046 MHP.

If any federal judge can inflict such great harm upon one individual, in clear violation of law, they are capable of inflicting the harm upon anyone else targeted by either that judge or the system of which he is a part.

Remember, what the corrupt federal judges did to me is only one example out of thousands. It can happen to you, or someone you know.

CHAPTER NINE

CHAPTER 11 RETALIATION

The sham California lawsuit and the refusal by California and federal judges to provide relief from the judicial civil right violations were inflicting serious financial harm upon my real estate business. Mortgage loans that periodically came due could not be refinanced because of the lis pendens that the Friedman law firm had placed on my properties. Valuable properties with hundreds of thousands of dollars in equities were lost, including my mountain-top home near Fairfield, California. Other loans were coming due, and I had to do something to circumvent the vast judicial scheme that misused the courts to destroy me financially, while simultaneously violating the blocks of state and federal statutory and constitutional protections. The Friedman law firm refused to allow the existing loans to be replaced with comparable loans, even though the properties they claimed their Texas client owned with me as community property would be lost. Their intent was to financially destroy me.

EXERCISING CHAPTER 11 REMEDIES
FOR CIVIL RIGHT VIOLATIONS

Chapter 11 is intended to provide time for people with net worth to pay a particular financial obligation, and to remain in control of their business and other assets. I had no financial problems. My problems consisted of the deluge of civil right violations judicially inflicted and the concurrent voiding, for me, the state and federal protections that would have halted the attacks in their track. Taking the plain language of Chapter 11 at its word, I exercised Chapter 11 protections for these violations, which was probably the only time in history this was done. This approach was unorthodox, exercising Chapter 11 courts to force federal judges to provide declaratory and injunctive relief to which I was entitled and long overdue. I filed two cases in May of 1987. One was a *personal* Chapter 11 filing and the other was for my *corporation*, Western Diablo Enterprises.

My plan was to bring the block of civil right violations to the attention of the Chapter 11 judges and have the lis pendens associated with the sham

California action dismissed. The idea had merit, but unknown to me at that time, the judicial corruption didn't stop at the state level, or at the federal district and appellate levels. It was even worse in the Chapter 11 courts. I discovered an entirely new area of corruption that has a devastating influence upon thousands of innocent American citizens who fell victim to tentacles of the same corruption that I uncovered.

I had no warning of the endemic corruption in the Chapter 11 courts, thanks to the media coverup. I hired a San Francisco area attorney to file the two Chapter 11 cases for me, and he in turn hired Las Vegas attorney, Joshua Landish.[84] The cases were filed in Las Vegas.

The intent of filing the two Chapter 11 cases was to have federal judges declare my personal and property rights legally established in the five divorce judgments, applying federal law; and to have the related lis pendens removed. The cases were assigned to federal Judge Robert Jones. Instead of providing relief, Judge Jones protected the Friedman law firm and the California judges who committed the civil right violations that Jones was duty-bound to correct. Jones duplicated the tactics of the U.S. District Judges, and refused to address the violations of my federally protected rights.

However, Judge Jones did provide some relief, initially. During a September 11, 1987, hearing he rendered an order refusing to accept jurisdiction over the two Chapter 11 cases, ordered the removal of the lis pendens, and stated he was dismissing the two Chapter 11 filings. He delayed executing the order dismissing the cases for sixty days, permitting me time to refinance the buildings on which mortgages had come due.   On the basis of the verbal order lifting the lis pendens, I obtained a firm refinancing commitment to pay off the $550,000 in mortgages that had come due,[85] and felt a sigh of relief that part of my problems were now addressed. But my relief was short lived. Someone apparently got to Judge Jones after his September 11 decision.

SABOTAGE BY MY OWN ATTORNEYS

Las Vegas attorney Joshua Landish, hired to protect my assets, proceeded to sabotage me. He did not notify me that there was a court hearing on September 28, 1987, for the **personal** bankruptcy case. This hearing was on a motion by attorney Estelle Mannis (Oakland, CA) for mortgage holder, Robil, Inc., and Superior Home Loans, of Hayward, California, to obtain relief from the automatic stay so they could foreclose on several of my properties.[86] They filed this motion immediately after Judge Jones rendered a decision refusing to accept jurisdiction and ordering removal of the lis pendens, which permitted me to refinance the mortgage and pay it off.

Disregarding these obstacles, by law, that hearing to remove the automatic stay had to be limited to *that issue*, and to the *personal* Chapter 11 case, which contained only a small part of the $10 million in assets. Nothing could be addressed concerning the *corporate* filing that contained most of the $10

---

[84] Joshua Landish of Las Vegas, Nevada. I also hired Las Vegas attorney Earl Hawley for another corporation, and his conduct was almost as bad as that of Landish.
[85] Superior Home Loans-Robil, Inc., Hayward, California.
[86] Held by Superior Home Loans and Robil, Inc. of Hayward, California.

million in assets. Further, Judge Jones rendered a decision at the prior hearing refusing to accept jurisdiction, and that decision had not been reversed. Therefore, there was no jurisdiction to render any further order, except to carry out the dismissal. Robil knew that I would be able to refinance and pay off the mortgage loan due to them. They apparently wanted to foreclose and gain the benefit of the large equities behind the mortgage loans that they had on the properties.

Unknown to me, the attorney that I hired to protect my interests, Joshua Landish, met secretly with my adversaries, and planned to request Judge Jones to order seizure of my assets and subsequent fire sale liquidation. In this way Landish's legal fees would be much higher than if he simply acted to protect my interests.

The official video tapes and transcript of the court proceedings showed that immediately upon the start of the September 28, 1987 hearing, Landish requested Judge Jones to vacate his earlier order providing me relief. Attorney Landish requested that Judge Jones order seizure of my business, my home, my assets, in both the personal and the corporate cases. This request was gross misconduct, and obviously part of a conspiracy with my adversaries. It also violated my rights to a hearing to defend against the seizure of my life's assets.

UNLAWFULLY SEIZING MY ASSETS

Federal statutory law[87] requires certain safeguards before judges can strip a person of his or her assets. There must be a noticed hearing to permit the party to defend against the taking of his or her property. There must be a legally recognized reason for taking and destroying the assets. Due process rights must be protected. Each of these requirements was openly violated, and approved by every appellate court up to and including the U.S. Supreme Court.

Chapter 11 law provides that the only authority for seizing a person's properties through appointment of a trustee are (a) gross mismanagement; or (b) major dishonesty, and (c) that creditors must be at risk. There are other protections against seizure, but these are the main ones. Creditors must be at risk. But in my case all creditors were secured by mortgages on the properties that were worth far more than the loan balances. The request for appointment of a trustee must be made by a creditor. My attorney was not a creditor.

I couldn't be accused of mismanagement. It was my hard work and efforts that caused the assets to grow from starting capital of five hundred dollars twenty years earlier to ten million dollars at the time of filing for Chapter 11 relief. There was no dishonesty, and none was alleged. None of the creditors requested the appointment of a trustee; it was my own attorney.

"Stich is going to be very unhappy when he hears about this."

Disregarding the numerous protections under the Constitution and federal law, Judge Jones rendered two orders seizing my life's assets. One order seized the Chapter 11 assets in the personal Chapter 11 case (which was on the

---

[87] Title 11 U.S.C. Section 1104.

calendar solely on a motion to remove the automatic stay on several mortgages). The second order seized the assets in the corporate Chapter 11 case, which wasn't on the court calendar and for which there was no notice given. They were both rendered after a prior order refusing to accept jurisdiction was announced. Under federal law these were void or voidable orders. The manner in which it was done met federal case law definition of a conspiracy, between Judge Jones, the attorneys, and the trustee. The official court audio tape and reporter's transcript show Judge Robert Jones remarking after ordering the seizure of my assets: "Mr. Stich is going to be very unhappy when he hears about this."

Immediately after rendering the order seizing my assets, Judge Jones was confronted with another problem. The five attorneys who were my adversaries at that hearing (including Landish) presented him with the written order of abstention that Jones rendered at the previous September 11th hearing. He now had to sign an order refusing to accept jurisdiction *after* he had just verbally rendered an order seizing the assets.

Judge Jones got around this problem by signing the abstention order and then signing the orders seizing my assets on October 8, 1987, stating on the orders that there was a hearing on that date. But there was no hearing on that date. The clerk's docket sheet, the reporter's transcript, and other court records proved that there was no hearing on that date. Judge Jones was lying to protect the corrupt seizure of my assets.

Attorney Landish withheld from me knowledge that Judge Jones ordered the seizure of my assets, including my business, my home, my many properties in California and Nevada, and my bank accounts. Unless notices of appeal were filed within ten days, I would lose an important right. When I accidentally discovered that Judge Jones had rendered the order, but unaware that it was Landish who requested the seizure, I instructed the attorney to file a notice of appeal. Landish agreed to do so, but never did it. Finally, I filed my own notice, and discharged Landish on November 10, 1987, for sabotaging my case.

Even though Friedman had no claim to my assets, in response to a motion by the Friedman group, Judge Jones transferred the Chapter 11 cases from Las Vegas to Oakland, California.

TURNING ASSETS OVER TO A KNOWN EMBEZZLER

Before Judge Jones transferred the cases to Oakland, he appointed trustee Charles Duck to seize my assets. Duck had been repeatedly charged by other victims of Chapter 11 courts as having looted their assets after federal judges appointed him trustee. Duck ordered me off my business properties, which I had founded and developed over the past twenty years. He stopped making mortgage payments on most of the ten million dollars in properties and canceled my refinancing commitments, which would have corrected the problem for which I had sought Chapter 11 relief. Duck diverted the $60,000 per month income to his own use, cancelled 30-year mortgages and replaced them with 3-year mortgages, incurring huge fees for churning the loans. Over one million dollars disappeared almost immediately, with no trace of the missing money.

United States Trustee Anthony Sousa and United States Attorney Joseph Russoniello, both of whom headed divisions of the Justice Department, with offices at San Francisco, refused to investigate Duck's embezzlement and looting of my assets.

Duck refused to make mortgage payments on the properties, causing dozens of the mortgages to be foreclosed, losing the properties I had acquired over the years.

EXPANDING JUDICIAL DUE PROCESS VIOLATIONS

After my assets were seized, and while the looting of assets escalated, Judge Jellen rendered orders, starting in 1988, barring me from filing appeals or oppositions. These orders forced me to remain mute while my life's assets were criminally seized and destroyed. Jellen had no more authority than the district judges to void the rights and protections under the Constitution and laws of the United States. I filed appeals, and I filed oppositions. Without authority, Judge Jellen ordered the court clerk to *unfile* them.

Even though attorney Landish had sabotaged my defenses and had committed acts justifying disbarment, Judge Jellen took my assets to pay him a large legal fee. Every party who played a role in the corrupt seizure and looting of my assets was judicially protected and rewarded through liquidation of my assets. Any claim against me was automatically approved and my objections ignored.

The actions of the Friedman law firm that caused me years of grief, the judgments of the California courts that were rendered without jurisdiction and in violation of law in the sham divorce action, were approved and paid. Even my ex-wife, who played a key role in the criminal conspiracy, was paid huge amounts out of the assets. I myself was forced to live on $1000 a month while millions were looted.

The remedy in law for these corrupt acts was to file federal actions, but these had to be filed in the same federal courts that perpetrated the gross civil right violations.

Many victims of Chapter 11 corruption reported the judicial crimes to higher federal courts, to the U.S. Attorney in San Francisco, to members of the Senate and House, with no success. United States Trustee Anthony Sousa—an employee of the same Justice Department who protected and misused the Chapter 11 racketeering activities—arrived in the San Francisco area in 1988 with the duty to prevent Chapter 11 corruption. I brought to his attention the specifics of the corruption in my case which easily revealed the pattern of criminality. He also refused to perform his duty and protected the enormously profitable racketeering enterprise.

Gregg Eichler, assistant U.S. Trustee in the San Francisco area, tried to expose the corruption in Chapter 11 courts. Eichler discovered massive looting of assets by judge-appointed trustee Charles Duck, the same person whom I reported these corrupt acts to the U.S. District and Appellate Courts in the Ninth Circuit and then to the U.S. Supreme Court Justices. Eichler also discovered that federal judges were implicated in the corruption.

Going after Duck threatened to expose the judicial involvement in the epidemic corruption and threatened to expose the nationwide aspect of this corruption in Chapter 11 courts.

Assistant U.S. Trustee Gregg Eichler discovered that Duck had embezzled over two million dollars in just the few cases investigated, and there were hundreds more to go, including mine, in which the losses exceeded that amount. Tens of millions of dollars of assets were destroyed and the people, stripped of these assets by the gang of Justice Department and judicial officers, were put into a state of poverty.

"Largest embezzlement ever ..."

After Eichler examined only a few of the cases handled by Duck, he prepared a report to U.S. Trustee Anthony Sousa, who had known of the misconduct and did nothing. Director of the U.S. Trustee program, Thomas Stanton, stated in a press release: "We believe this is the largest embezzlement ever charged against a court-appointed bankruptcy trustee." Stanton feigned shock at the publicity over Chapter 11 corruption, that was partly of his own making. But the evaluation of the enormity of the corruption was made after only three of the hundreds of cases handled by Duck were examined. They never got to mine, and judicial actions were taken to be sure this never occurred.

Duck's corruption was known for years to the federal judges, to Justice Department attorneys, and to the establishment media. They all protected him, and the system. Duck could not have operated without the aid and protection of these people, and especially the federal judges who assisted and financially benefitted from the scheme.

SLAPPING THE WRIST IN THE NATION'S
WORST REPORTED CHAPTER 11 CORRUPTION

Duck had looted hundreds of cases that he handled over the years, but was only charged with two counts of fraud out of possibly thousands. The arrest and imprisonment of Duck seemingly justified ending all further investigations into chapter 11 corruption. But Assistant U.S. Trustee Gregg Eichler was intent on continuing his investigation, and filing charges against federal judges. This threat was eliminated when the Justice Department fired the investigator in late 1991. The investigations stopped, and the system escaped another threat of exposure.

For almost two years prior to Duck's admission that he embezzled huge sums of money, I reported via petitions and appeals to every level of the federal courts up to and including the Supreme Court, that criminal acts by officers of the court existed. I sought relief, and instead, discovered these judges to be protecting the multi-billion-dollar-a-year racketeering enterprise misusing federal courts. I reported the corrupt seizure and looting of my assets and the many other civil, constitutional, and criminal violations that were rampant in Chapter 11 courts. No one acted.

Some of Duck's Chapter 11 cases were turned over to another trustee, June Haley of Santa Rosa, who was charged with similar embezzlement within two years. After U.S. Trustee Sousa was forced to remove Duck from my Chapter 11 cases, he appointed another trustee, Jerome Robertson, who continued the looting started by Duck.

U.S. Attorney Russoniello stated to the press on September 25, 1989, Justice Department approval of a plea bargain with Duck and his attorney. Duck's attorney, Peter Robinson, informed the press[88] that Duck agreed to cooperate with authorities as part of a plea bargain to include his guilty pleas. In exchange, federal prosecutors would seek a short jail term for Duck.

Duck, who embezzled tens of millions of dollars from thousands of people who had exercised the statutory protections of Chapter 11 and 13, was sentenced on January 18, 1990 by District Judge William Swarzer to a lenient sentence. Duck was ordered to pay only a $5,000 fine and sentenced to twenty-seven months in the jail of his choice, the federal correctional camp at Sheridan, Oregon. Duck moved his family to nearby Lake Oswego, to reduce the inconvenience to himself.

The two charges filed against Duck for embezzlement were for over $2,000,000 embezzled from estates, which was only a fraction of what he stole. He embezzled that much from my assets alone, plus what he looted out of the hundreds of other cases.

After Duck was charged with embezzlement, U.S. Trustee Sousa instructed him to turn over the records on my cases to the next trustee. But Duck refused to do so, and no effort was made to make him comply. At that stage there appeared to be at least a million dollars missing from my cases, and nothing was done to charge Duck with theft. Duck refused to turn over the records, claiming a Fifth Amendment right to avoid self-incrimination.[89] The Justice Department protected his position, and did nothing to prosecute Duck for looting my estates.

The same assistant U.S. Attorney who had protected Duck during his many years of responsibility to do so, Peter Robinson, resigned from the Justice Department and entered private practice, taking as one of his first clients Charles Duck. Robinson was an Assistant U.S. Attorney in the San Francisco office from 1984 through 1988, when Duck's fraudulent activities were repeatedly brought to the U.S. Attorney's attention. Although Duck refused to turn over the records, his attorney, Peter Robinson, argued before U.S. District Judge Stanley Wiegel[90] that his client cooperated extensively with the U.S. trustee.

Duck paid Robinson an initial legal fee of $175,000, much or all of which came from the assets of my estates. The former assistant U.S. Attorney, Robinson, who had done nothing to prosecute Duck when dozens of people sought relief from the U.S. Attorney's office, was now defending Duck.

Duck's looting of my assets, following the unlawful seizure of the two estates, raised serious federal causes of actions. A year before Duck had ever been charged with embezzlement, I filed actions against him in federal court, describing the criminal activities by Duck and Chapter 11 judges. Just as they had done for the prior fifteen years, Justice Department attorneys moved to dismiss each of my actions, seeking to protect Duck and the multi-billion-

---

[88] *San Ramon Times*, September 28, 1989.

[89] *The Recorder*, May 15, 1989.

[90] One of the judges covering up for the FAA and NTSB misconduct in my early federal cases.

dollar-a-year racketeering enterprise. These motions to dismiss occurred even after Duck admitted his embezzlement. If the Justice Department had not obtained dismissal of my cases against Duck, the risk existed that other Chapter 11 corruption would have been exposed.

Immediately after the U.S. Attorney announced the plea bargain, Duck and his attorney made unusual efforts in statements to the press that no one else was involved, apparently seeking to protect the judges and the system itself. These repeated assurances were quoted in the press:

No one else really knew what he was doing. Duck was on his own on this. He offered to take a polygraph test because the FBI had questions about others being involved. They're satisfied no one else was involved.

Entering a plea bargain before completing the investigation into Duck's criminal acts had several results. It protected Duck from further criminal charges and it served as a tenuous excuse to call off further investigation into the epidemic Chapter 11 judicial corruption.

In early 1990, Justice Department officials in Washington reduced the funding for the United States Trustee at San Francisco, causing Eichler to be fired on January 24, 1990. Eichler was about to expose the involvement of federal judges in the Chapter 11 corruption, and this action prevented exposing what was one of America's biggest racketeering enterprise.

Just as in the savings and loan debacle, the Justice Department and the United States Trustee made no effort to look for the multi-million dollar theft from my estates or the others. They made no effort to get the records of my estate from Duck. They ignored the criminal acts committed by Chapter 11 judges. They protected Duck against the criminal acts committed in my estate. As is revealed in later pages, Chapter 11 courts are a major racketeering enterprise, looting billions of dollars a year from the assets of people exercising the statutory protections of Chapters 11 or 13.

REVOLVING DOOR AND OBSTRUCTION OF JUSTICE

Justice Department attorneys knew for years of the criminality in Chapters 11 and 13 proceedings. They not only refused to protect the victims, but they acted to aid and abet the perpetrators, and especially Charles Duck. Instead of prosecuting Duck, Justice Department attorneys misused the Justice Department's power to shield Duck, and the corrupt system. Russoniello resigned on April 1, 1990, returning to his former San Francisco law firm of Cooley, Goddard, Castro, Huddleson and Tatum, the firm who represented the government, including Charles Duck, in previous actions filed against them by defrauded citizens. This relationship appears to be *another* reason Russoniello refused to take any significant action against Duck and the corruption in Chapter 11 while Russoniello was U.S. Attorney.

SEEKING RELIEF FROM SUPREME COURT JUSTICES

Seeking relief, a year prior to the exposure of Duck's embezzlement, I brought the judicial corruption by this "officer of the court" to the attention of the U.S. Supreme Court Justices. They had supervisory responsibilities over the federal judges and the attorneys engaging in the corruption. This practice could not exist if the Justices exercised their duties and responsibilities. Supreme Court Rule 17 (changed to Rule 10 in 1990) states that the Supreme Court Justices **will assume jurisdiction** of a petition brought to the Court when the acts of a lower court requires. Rule 17/10 articulates the Supreme Court's supervision responsibilities. The Rules say in part: "[intervention is required when necessary to] exercise this Court's **power of supervision.**"

The petition for writ of certiorari exposed a pattern of corruption by federal judges and officers of the court who were under the supervisory responsibilities of the Justices in the U.S. Supreme Court. In every case they either stonewalled me, refused to file the petition, or refused to provide relief. I even accompanied my petition with a demand under the federal crime reporting statute, Title 18 U.S.C. Section 4, demanding to report to a federal judge the criminal acts that I discovered. As a former federal investigator holding federal authority to make these determinations, my charges had extra validity. I explained that the criminal acts were perpetrated by federal judges over whom they had supervisory responsibilities. The responsibility to receive this testimony and evidence was even violated by the Justices of the U.S. Supreme Court.

The allegations of judicial corruption were so serious that the Justices of the Supreme Court had responsibility to act regardless of how the message was conveyed. Federal criminal statute Title 18 U.S.C. Section 4 requires that a party learning of federal offenses report them to a federal judge, or other official. Many times I followed this procedure in my petitions to the Supreme Court Justices. Each time they blocked me from reporting the crimes inflicting great harm upon the United States by refusing to receive my supporting evidence. They compounded this obstruction of justice by refusing to provide relief from the harm I was experiencing as a result of the criminal acts of federal judges over whom they had responsibilities. The Supreme Court Justices also had vicarious liability responsibilities over the corrupt actions of the judges under them, and the Justices share criminal responsibility for the criminal acts that could only occur with their complicity.

JUSTICE DEPARTMENT ATTORNEYS PROTECTED EVERY SEGMENT OF THE CRIMINAL ACTIVITIES

I filed several federal lawsuits against Duck and the law firm of Goldberg, Stinnett, & Macdonald[91] (whose assistance made Duck's activities possible), and against the subsequent trustee, Jerome Robertson, who continued to loot my estates. The civil action addressed criminal acts that Duck already admitted, seeking damages from him and the government on the basis of these acts, as well as injunctive relief for the return of my assets. Federal judges dismissed every action I filed. In one action,[92] U.S. District Judge Eugene Lynch ordered on October 3, 1989 that the action I filed be unfiled, without the lawful requirement of a hearing, and in defiance of Constitutional and statutory rights and protections. This judicial dismissal protected Duck and

---

[91] Changed in late 1993 to Goldberg, Stinnett, Meyers & Davis.

[92] *Stich v. Charles Duck, Trustee, Merle C. Meyers, Goldberg, Stinnett & McDonald, Does 1 through 100, Defendants.* C-89-150-Misc EFL

the corrupt Chapter 11 court system, of which he was a part.

**PREVENTING EXPOSURE OF
A MAJOR CRIMINAL ENTERPRISE**

In another action filed in the U.S. District Court in the District of Columbia (No. C 89-2974) Judge Stanley Sporkin dismissed the action against Duck without a hearing, again protecting Duck and the system of judicial corruption of which he was a part. Sporkin's dismissal had an interesting aspect to it. Sporkin was formerly counsel for the Central Intelligence Agency, and as later pages will show, the CIA was heavily involved in Chapter 11 corruption, benefitting from the looting of assets.

Department of Justice attorneys and officials also intervened to protect Duck and the system by filing motions with the court to dismiss my actions. An action that I filed against Duck in the Superior Court of the State of California in Alameda County at Oakland, California, was wrongfully dismissed by Judge Edward Jellen of Oakland, without a hearing. He had a sordid history of protecting the criminality exposed in these pages. The entire federal judicial system and Justice Department attorneys were protecting Duck whenever the need arose.

After Duck admitted his embezzlement, Judge Jellen ordered that over $100,000 of my assets be paid to Duck and his San Francisco law firm of Goldberg, Stinnett and McDonald, for services that consisted of looting the assets. By March 1990 Judge Jellen ordered over a quarter million dollars taken from my assets to pay legal fees solely to protect the trustees and their law firm involved in the seizure and looting of my assets. Simultaneously, Judge Jellen deprived me of funds from my own assets to pay for legal assistance, dental and medical bills. While six million of my equity assets were corruptly seized and looted, Judge Jellen forced me to live on $12,000 a year, for housing, food, and the other necessities.

Further, Jellen refused to provide money for me to hire legal counsel, while he simultaneously authorized hundreds of thousands of dollars to be taken from my assets to pay attorney fees for the Friedman law firm, and for the woman in Texas who falsely claimed she was my wife. Additionally, Jellen rendered an order barring me from filing appeals and oppositions, stating that this could only be done by an attorney. His withholding of money to pay an attorney insured that I would not have one.

These are only a few of the outrages. Throughout these pages there are cited only examples, and by no means the full amount of judicial corruption that I endured.

When Duck was removed as trustee, his cases were assigned to Jerome Robertson, who accelerated the looting of my estate. Other cases belonging to Duck were assigned to trustee June Haley of Santa Rosa. Within a year she also was charged with looting assets from Chapter 11 cases, a fact that was obvious all along to the judges.

DECADES OF CHAPTER 11 CORRUPTION

Public pressure forced Congress to change the Chapter 11 statutes for greater protection of the public against judicial corruption, and Congress passed the Bankruptcy Reform Act of 1978, creating the office of the U.S.

Trustee. The trustee was charged with the responsibility of preventing fraud and corruption. But the changes that provided protection in law were openly violated in spirit and specifics by Chapter 11 judges, with the cooperation of higher federal courts. These U.S. Trustees, arms of the Justice Department, usually attorneys, protected the system instead of the people. Justice Department officials routinely forced people into Chapter 7, 11, or 13, as part of schemes to silence whistleblowers, as will be seen in later pages.

The public outrage and pleas for help continued. Except for minor investigations and refusal to take corrective actions, Congress again refused to investigate the corruption. When the public pressure again reached a crescendo, Congress went through the motions and changed the law, passing the Bankruptcy Act of 1986.[93] The legislative history of that Act addressed the past judicial misconduct in guarded terms, and gave the impression that the new legislation addressed the corruption. The legislative history[94] reemphasized that the U.S. Trustee was to prevent corruption:

The U.S. Trustees were given important oversight and watchdog responsibilities to ensure honesty and fairness in the administration of bankruptcy cases and to prevent and ferret out fraud. ... in carrying out critical watchdog responsibilities, such as preventing fraud and other abuses and in monitoring debtors-in-possession in Chapter 11 reorganization cases.

Congress knew that the rampant Chapter 11 judicial corruption was known to the Department of Justice; that the Justice Department attorneys protected those committing the multi-billion-dollar-a-year racketeering enterprise. Congress knew that Justice Department officials misused Chapter 11 proceedings through their control over the U.S. Trustees. The Chapter 11 judicial racketeering activities continued as before. The media kept the lid on the scandal, insuring its continuation, and insuring that their readers pay the price.

By law, the U.S. Trustee had the responsibility to *prevent* corruption. Just as the Civil Rights Division of the Justice Department should prevent the civil rights violations inflicted upon me by the Justice Department attorneys and their cohorts on the federal bench. For two years I made U.S. Trustee Anthony Sousa aware of the corruption that continued without letup. If anything changed, it was for the worse. After Duck was imprisoned in November 1989, Sousa appointed attorney Jerome Robertson as trustee over my two estates, seeking authority in the unlawful order seizing my assets. That order seizing my assets was void, but the U.S. Trustee acted upon it as if it was a lawful order rendered under lawful conditions.

Robertson immediately accelerated the harm done to my estates that Duck had started. Within a few months Robertson and his retained law firm of Murray and Murray had requested and obtained court approval to take over $250,000 from my assets for legal fees to do things that I routinely did when I controlled my business.

[93] Public Law 99-554.
[94] House Report No. 99-764.

When the U.S. Trustee refused to prevent these corrupt acts, I filed a lawsuit against him—and his boss, the Department of Justice, in the U.S. District Court, District of Columbia.[95] Again, federal judges protected the system of which they were a part. District of Columbia judge Stanley Sporkin dismissed the action on January 17, 1990, without a hearing, and despite the law barring dismissal when the complaint stated federal cause of actions.

EXAMPLES OF OTHER VICTIMS

In one case the Department of Justice forced a publishing company into bankruptcy. The company was set up for the purpose of spreading political ideas, and the Justice Department attorneys did not like the exposures. Presidential candidate Lyndon LaRouche informed the public of corruption by federal officials via the publications, *Campaigner Publications*, *Caucus Distributors*, and *Fushion Energy Foundation*.

The Justice Department obtained an ex parte order, without a hearing, forcing the company into bankruptcy. The company argued that the law required three parties to force a person or company into bankruptcy, and sought to have the seizure overturned, without success. The Justice Department used its United States Trustee Division and its control over private trustees and federal judges to force the company into a Chapter 7 liquidation.

Then Justice Department officials secured indictments against LaRouche and six associates for mail fraud on the basis that the companies did not repay earlier loans. LaRouche argued that the loans could not be paid back because Justice Department officials forced the company into bankruptcy. The Justice Department attorneys obtained a fifteen-year prison term for the 67-year-old LaRouche.

Fortunately, LaRouche had friends outside of prison willing to fight for him. While LaRouche and his associates were in prison, District Judge Martin Bostetter ruled in a 106-page decision on October 25, 1989, that the Justice Department's seizure of the assets and the involuntary bankruptcy action were illegal and a fraud upon the court.

In another case, the husband-and-wife publishing house of *Stein & Day* was induced by attorneys to seek relief in Chapter 11 when a major customer refused to pay a large bill owed to them. Their 26-year-old business had run a small but respectable operation that published about 100 books a year. Their business was good and they were otherwise financially strong. Seeking a time delay in paying pending bills, the primary reason for Chapter 11, owner Sol Stein filed Chapter 11 on the advice of his attorney.

Following the standard script, instead of providing time to pay bills, the Chapter 11 judge seized and then looted the assets of this once profitable company. The husband-and-wife team experienced corruption by the bankruptcy courts that if committed by an ordinary citizen would result in criminal prosecution and imprisonment. Stein lost everything he accumulated for the past three decades. Incensed, he wrote about the judicial Chapter 11 corruption in the book, *A Feast for Lawyers*, subtitled *Inside Chapter 11: An*

---

[95] *Stich v. Stanton; U.S. Trustee Anthony Sousa; Richard Thornburgh; United States of America.*

Exposé. Even though Stein recognized only a small part of the criminality in Chapter 11 and 13 courts, he described the these courts as inhabited by hacks, vultures and scoundrels, who feed on productive companies and people.

In another of thousands of examples, Chapter 11 judges and officers of the court (trustees) stripped San Diego resident Samuel Shen of millions of dollars of assets he acquired from hard work after immigrating from Hong Kong in 1959. Shen was so badly affected by the trauma inflicted upon him that he was committed to a mental institution for thirty days. As other victims had done, with many succeeding, Shen tried to commit suicide several times. He lost his family, who didn't have the character to support him during these troubling times.[96]

Shen's 1982 Chapter 11 filing showed assets of ten million dollars with liabilities of two and a half millions. Everything was almost free and clear. The Chapters 11 and 13 racketeering activities, protected by every level of the federal judiciary, including the U.S. Supreme Court justices, financially destroyed him. Over seven million dollars in assets were looted by the judge-appointed trustee, the trustee's law firm, and whatever hidden interests that Judge Herbert Katz may have had in dummy corporations. There were some who claim Katz was part of a Jewish Mafia that had stolen hundreds of millions of dollars of assets from people who naively sought relief in Chapter 11.

Real estate investor Jay Sobrinia of San Diego was another typical case. He encountered a sudden cancellation of a verbal permanent loan commitment from his bank. When the bank construction loan came due, the same bank that had promised permanent financing commenced foreclosure on the expensive house. If the bank had been successful, it would have made a windfall profit. This was a common tactic with Bank of America during the depression years and in recent times.

Sobrinia's attorney, who had close ties to the Chapter 11 courts, advised him to file Chapter 11 and get a stay of the foreclosure to permit him time to obtain permanent financing. On the lawyer's assurance, Sobrinia then put his entire one million equity estate into Chapter 11. Despite federal statutory law barring seizure of the assets (except when dishonesty or gross mismanagement exists), the Chapter 11 judge ordered Sobrinia's assets seized and turned over to a trustee. The routine destruction of the assets then began, enriching the attorneys, law firms, and corporations that are part of this racketeering enterprise. Sobrinia's million-dollar-equity estate was stolen.

These sad tales can be repeated thousands of times, reflecting the theft of billions of dollars a year, perpetrated by pious-appearing federal judges that have stolen more money than many organized criminal enterprises.

The legal and judicial fraternities at every level are a part of the Chapters 11 and 13 racketeering activities. They include federal judges, Justices of the U.S. Supreme Court, attorneys and officials in the Justice Department, trustees, and law firms. In addition, those who aid and abet these crimes by

---

[96] *San Diego Tribune*, July 10, 1989.

their duplicity of silence include members of Congress and the establishment media. Their victims include many older people who are left destitute, and who were no match for this gang of thugs.

ONE OF MANY TEXAS VICTIMS

Another victim who told me of the experiences he had with crooked federal judges, trustees and law firms was John Hamilton of Cuero, Texas. He owned a 1,800 acre ranch until he was targeted by the bankruptcy club, and then financially destroyed. Earlier, he had been invited to White House functions as a result of his charitable work.

Hamilton and his wife had obtained a loan of $475,000 on their ranch which was worth almost $4 million, the proceeds of which had been used to build a commercial building. For the next ten years the Hamiltons made payments on the loan, which had a ten-year due data. They expected the bank to renew the loan when its term was up, as is standard practice. Over $300,000 had been paid on the $475,000 loan during the ten years, leaving a balance due of $184,000. Instead of renewing the note, the bank[97] called the loan. Under advice of legal counsel, the Hamiltons filed Chapter 12[98] to gain time to refinance the loan that was only about one twentieth of the property value.

These are the types of filings that are targeted by the "bankruptcy club" members consisting of judges, trustees and law firms. By law, the Hamiltons should have kept control of their assets. But if the law was followed, the assets could not be seized and looted. As is widespread throughout the country, the practice then was for an unlawful seizure of the assets and subsequent liquidation, enriching the criminal enterprise.

U.S. Bankruptcy Judge Richard Schmidt ordered the seizure of the Hamilton's ranch and placed Trustee Gary Knostman in control of the assets, a kiss of death for their life's assets. The trustee hired a closely aligned law firm, and between them and their coterie managed to financially destroy the Hamiltons, showing the consequences of trusting the statutory protections to the crooked federal judges and their bank of thieves.

With the seizure of the Hamilton's assets, there was no money to pay for legal counsel, and they had to appear without an attorney, insuring the rapid loss of their life's assets. Eventually the Hamiltons did obtain attorneys, all of whom assisted in the loss of the assets. Today the Hamiltons are destitute, their life's assets stolen from them.

These are only a few of the thousands of cases every year in which honest Americans are stripped of their assets after exercising in good faith the protections of Chapter 11 or 12. They trusted their government, unaware that epidemic corruption of the highest level has taken over many of the federal offices, including the federal courts. Their plight, and the thriving criminality in bankruptcy courts, are well known to members of Congress who have oversight responsibilities; to the media, with its obligation to report criminality in government, that financially destroys many of their own readers; to the

---

[97] Bank of Victoria.

[98] Chapter 12 Farmers and Ranchers Bankruptcy.

checks and balances, every one of which aid and abet the ongoing racketeering enterprise.

Congressman Jack Brooks (D-TX), chairman of the House Economic and Commercial Law Subcommittee, knew about the rampant criminality as a result of receiving reports from hundreds of victims in Congressional hearings, and from my reports. Brooks stated:[99]

I would tell members, if you've gone broke, go into bankruptcy. But if you've got any money at all, don't take bankruptcy, fight it out. They'll take it all.

But the statutes provide that American citizens can file under Chapter 11, 12, or 13, to get a time delay in paying their debts, and that they will remain in control of their assets. Brooks admitted that the assets are taken, and he certainly knew the rampant criminality by federal judges, trustees, and law firms. He protected the system of crooks that prey upon the American public.

A bankruptcy attorney, Lawrence A. Beck of San Antonio, said[100] what many attorneys have admitted or known:

Unfortunately, most individual debtors who enter bankruptcy with significant assets eventually conclude that they have become trapped in a crooked, dishonest system which is run for the benefit of the panel trustee and his hand-picked attorney, and which is supervised by [crooked] bureaucrats.

This is the type of criminality that creates the epidemic criminal mindset in the United States. The trustee program was established by Congress in 1986 and is run by the U.S. Department of Justice, to insure honesty in the trustee program and the courts. Before the last page is reached in this book, the criminality by Justice Department attorneys in almost any Justice Department activity should be obvious.

STANDARD SILENCING TACTIC PROTECTING CORRUPT FEDERAL JUDGES AND SYSTEM

Hamilton described the killing of two attorneys who had knowledge of the criminal activities in Texas Chapter 11 courts. He described the death of a bankruptcy trustee, Jane Ford, in June 1993, by a shotgun blast to her head. Her death left behind a twelve-year-old son. Ford reportedly played a key role in bankruptcy criminality, but eventually the massive theft from bankruptcy estates, carried out with judicial approval and complicity, and citizen outrage, caused indictments to be handed down against her. Seeking to reduce her prison sentence, she announced her intention to expose the criminal enterprise in the Texas bankruptcy courts. This was similar to others who announced their intentions to expose federal officials and judges. She ended in the same condition that other many other whistleblowers did, including those who blow the whistle on judicial corruption in the bankruptcy courts: dead. And in a scenario similar to others, the local police and coroner ruled her death a suicide.

---

[99] *Houston Chronicle*, Nov. 7, 1991.
[100] *Houston Chronicle*, Nov. 7, 1991.

Hamilton described another bankruptcy-related killing, in which attorney John Scott was murdered as his charges of bankruptcy corruption started to threaten the established racketeering enterprise and the involved federal judges, trustees and law firms. Someone killed Scott near Austin, Texas.

GIVING THEMSELVES IMMUNITY FROM THEIR CRIMES

Federal judges of the Ninth Circuit[101] held that the private trustees, including embezzler Charles Duck, who committed the nation's worst Chapter 11 corruption, were officers of the court, and were therefore immune from liability! Federal judges, therefore, held that a citizen has no claim against an officer of the court (i.e., trustee, attorney, judge, or one of their employees) arising from the criminal acts of that federal official, even though the acts are criminal and inflict enormous harm upon an innocent person. They held in effect that officers of the court could inflict any type of outrage upon the public, and the public has no remedy!

One of the many people victimized by the judicial corruption was Thomas Read of Connecticut. Read had not sought relief in Chapter 11, but was affected by Charles Duck, and the federal judges seeking to protect the admitted embezzler. Read obtained a Connecticut judgment against Duck. Bankruptcy Judge Alan Jaroslovsky of Santa Rosa, who had protected Duck's criminal activities, issued an injunction forever barring Read from enforcing the judgment. Read argued that the injunctive order exceeded the judge's authority. Read filed an appeal with the Ninth Circuit Bankruptcy Appellate Panel (composed of Chapter 11 judges!. The appellate panel rendered a published decision:[102]

Federal judges, seeking to protect these criminal acts and themselves, have rendered decisions holding *that "judicial immunity not only protects judges against suit from acts done within their jurisdiction, but also spreads outward to shield related public servants, including trustees in bankruptcy."*

This circuit has adopted a ... rationale stating that a trustee or an official acting under the authority of the bankruptcy judge is entitled to derived judicial immunity because he is performing an integral part of the judicial process. ... a trustee, who obtains court approval for actions under the supervision of the bankruptcy judge, is entitled to derived immunity.

It is well settled that the trustee in bankruptcy is an officer of the appointing court. Courts other than the appointing court have no jurisdiction to entertain suits against the trustee, without leave from the appointing court, for acts done in an official capacity and within his authority as an officer of the court. ... It is ... axiomatic that the Trustee, "as a trustee in bankruptcy [and] as an official acting under the authority of the bankruptcy judge, is entitled to derived judicial immunity because he is performing an integral part of the judicial process."

---

[101] Ninth Circuit Bankruptcy Appellate Panel.
[102] September 27, 1989.

*Sound policy also mandates immunizing the trustee. The possibili-
ty that we would hold trustees personally liable for judgments
rendered against them in their representative capacity would invariably lessen the vigor with which trustees pursue their obligations.
Immunity is essential because, as Judge Learned Hand noted, "to
submit all officials, the innocent as well as the guilty, to the burden of
a trial and to the inevitable danger of its outcome, would dampen the
ardor of all but the most resolute, or the most irresponsible, in the
unflinching discharge of their duties.... Accordingly, we hold that the
trustee [Charles Duck], acting under the authority of the court, is
entitled to derived judicial immunity.*

As the judicial involvement in the Chapter 11 corruption surfaced, the Ninth
Circuit Court of Appeals rendered a judgment[103] protecting judges against
responsibility for their criminal acts. The Ninth Circuit rendered the decision
holding that regardless of any criminal conduct committed against the public
or an individual by a judge or person acting on his behalf, such as a trustee,
the public had no remedy against the judges, or anyone acting with the judges.
The need for these self-protective and unconstitutional decisions is rapidly
increasing as federal judges are heavily implicated in some of the worst
criminal activities ever exposed in the history of the United States. Worse
judicial corruption has yet to be described.

Justices of the U.S. Supreme Court enlarged upon the protection against
their own criminal acts (and they may need this protection shortly). The
Supreme Court Justices held in *Stump v. Sparkman*[104] that a judge could
deliberately commit unlawful, unconstitutional, and corrupt acts upon a
citizen, destroy personal and property rights, and be immune from financial
liability. This decision was repeatedly stated by U.S. District Judge Marilyn
Patel, San Francisco, as I sought relief against California and federal judges.

The Constitution and statutes disagree with judge-made law. federal civil
rights statutes and constitutional rights to seek relief clearly do not provide
immunity to federal judges when they violate clear and settled civil and constitutional rights, or against corrupt or criminal acts, and who inflict harm upon
any member of the American public.

In *Stump v. Sparkman* the judge entered into a conspiracy, ordering a
young girl permanently sterilized. The Supreme Court held that the girl had
no remedy against the judge, as the public's welfare requires that a judge be
free to exercise his duties without fear of the consequences. That is a farce,
and the public's welfare isn't protected by protecting crooked judges.

THE SYSTEM PROTECTS ITS OWN

I filed an administrative claim with the Administrative Office of the
United States Courts, addressing the judicial misconduct (necessary before
filing a lawsuit against the United States government under the federal Tort
Claims Act). The claim was based upon the looting of my assets by trustee
Charley Duck. The Justice Department denied my claim on October 17, 1989,

[103] *Ashelman v. Pope*, 793 F.2d 1072 (9th Cir. 1986).
[104] 435 U.S. at 362.

stating the "claim may not be settled under authority of the Federal Tort Claims Act because that act specifically excludes claims arising from the performance of a discretionary function." In the mindset of Justice Department attorneys and federal judges, Duck's criminal activities were a "discretionary function!"

SECRET JUSTICE DEPARTMENT MEMORANDUM

An assistant U.S. Attorney in the San Francisco office, Michael Howard, wrote a July 11, 1990, report describing the rampant criminal corruption by federal officials in Chapter 11 courts in the Northern District of California, stating in part:

Subject: Alan Jaroslovsky, bankruptcy judge; Charles Duck, former trustee in bankruptcy, convicted; Philip Arnot, Harvey Hoffman, Timothy J. Walsh, Malcolm Biserka, Ruth Harrell, attorneys for numerous trustees in bankruptcy; Susan Euker, Jeff Walk, trustees in bankruptcy; Goldberg, Stinnett and McDonald, law firm that specializes in bankruptcies, primarily Carol Stinnett; David McKim, attorney at law; San Francisco attorney Monseur, first name unknown; Robert and Harrison, law firm in many bankruptcy cases, and primarily Mr. Cook, Esquire; William Kelly, Esquire, attorney for Graham and James law firm in San Francisco; Peter Robinson, private attorney, former Assistant U.S. Attorney.

Why Referral to Public Integrity Section: U.S. Attorney's manual, Chapter 3, ... states in part, most government corruption cases are both sensitive and of intense public interest. It is particularly important that the appearance of fairness and impartiality always be present [by prosecuting such cases].

Considering the possible involvement of bankruptcy court judges, a former U.S. Attorney, and the magnitude of the investigation necessary, it is possible that the U.S. Attorney's office does not have the resources available to investigate the widespread corruption and cronyism which presently exist in the bankruptcy courts. To thoroughly investigate the present quagmire, there is the need for a virtual full-time prosecutor to clean up the system.

Main justice would probably have the resources to provide the prosecutors and the investigators necessary to fulfill the present need to clean up the system. I don't believe we have any criminal assistants who have the time to take on such a case as this, for such investigation. Offenses indicated so far: Information provided to me to date indicates that one or more of the above-named subjects have engaged in one or more of the following felonies: (A) Perjury. Submitted false, forged, or altered documents to the courts. (B) Obstruction of justice; (C) Churning of Chapter 11 estates for the exclusive financial advantage of the trustees and the trustees' attorneys. (D) Failure to provide accurate financial accounts and reports to the courts. Most of the problems appear to arise in Chapter 11 [where there are assets].

Justice Department officials sequestered the report, took no action on the judicial corruption, and reprimanded the Assistant U.S. Attorney who wrote it. Justice Department investigators faced the same problem that FAA inspectors faced.

California Representative Don Edwards, who was instrumental in writing the bankruptcy act, never responded to my reporting of the federal crimes in his Chapter 11 area of responsibilities, or to the many other people who complained to him seeking relief. Nor did Edwards respond to the fifteen years of reports on the air safety and criminal violations related to the ongoing airline crashes that I brought to his attention. Edwards also kept the lid on the Inslaw scandal (which has yet to be described), and sought to block a Congressional or Independent Prosecutor investigation into the serious matter.

Representative Jack Brooks of Texas had the role of Chapter 11 Congressional oversight after Edwards moved to another Congressional assignment. He also protected the multi-billion-dollar Chapter 11 racketeering enterprise[105] that richly rewarded his fellow attorneys.

MEDIA COVERUP

The media was fully aware of the gravity of the Chapter 11 corruption, its nationwide extent, and the pattern of criminality that made many of their own readers victims. The media either didn't report any of the findings by its investigative reporters or, as in most cases, reported the peripheral and minor aspects of the corruption, portraying the acts in a more innocent manner. The San Francisco Daily Journal wrote in an October 4, 1990, article that Haley's "pattern of alleged wrongdoing is strikingly similar to that uncovered against her friend and mentor, Charles Duck, who has admitted embezzling $2.5 million from bankruptcy estates under his control."

Occasionally the media hinted at the problem, but never identified it in a way that the public would react in outrage. The Journal had months of articles describing the Chapter 11 corruption, using such headlines as Bankruptcy Courts, A System in Crisis; The Bankruptcy Club; A System in Crisis; The Road to Ruin. It avoided the heart of the matter: the epidemic pattern of crooked federal judges, trustees, and powerful law firms, and the coverup by Justice Department officials.

The few newspapers that addressed Chapter 11 corruption described Duck's embezzlement as the worst by a trustee in the nation's history. And this assessment was given without considering the total amount of what he actually did embezzle. Obviously Duck did not operate in a vacuum, and needed the protection of federal judges to commit his dirty work. I notified over a dozen magazines and newspapers[106] of the misconduct from 1988 through 1990, a year and a half before signs of Chapter 11 corruption was exposed.

Reporter Linda Martin of the San Francisco Examiner spent over two months investigating the corruption, interviewing many of those victimized by the "bankruptcy club." During the end of January 1990 Martin revealed to Mrs. McCullough, a California resident and activist against corrupt government, that the Examiner refused to print the main part of the judicial

---

[105] Brooks also kept the lid on the air disaster felonies.
[106] Wall Street Journal; San Francisco Examiner; San Francisco Chronicle; Business Week; Newsweek;

corruption, causing her to quit the *Examiner*.

While several San Francisco Bay Area newspapers publicized the Chapter 11 corruption, the mass-media papers kept the lid on the scandal. Reporter Bill Wallace for the *San Francisco Chronicle* explained to one inquirer, Virginia McCullough (September 4, 1990), that the reason they had not contacted me on the Chapter 11 corruption was that I incorporated other areas of government corruption into the discussion. A corollary to that would be a reporter ignoring an informant's description of a murder that took place because the informant also told about another murder. Another reporter for the *Chronicle* gave a different excuse to another inquirer months earlier in answer to a question as to why the *Chronicle* did not print anything about the air safety corruption that I charged existed. He replied, "Stich wouldn't give us any facts."

Reporters Bill Wallace and Jeff Paline came to my home, looked at the volumes of material I had, and went to the federal district courts at Sacramento and San Francisco, examining the papers that I filed describing the corruption in detail. I gave them copies of my earlier book, which explained the serious corruption in detail. All questions presented to me were answered. Nothing was withheld. It was my belief they were under instructions to sequester any mention of the matter in their news stories.

It took a determined effort to keep the scandal hidden, not only in the San Francisco area, but throughout the United States. The number of people financially destroyed by blatant corruption, outright violations of federal statutory and case law, the number of complaints to the Justice Department, to higher federal courts, to members of Congress, reached epidemic proportions. Yet, every major government and non-government check and balance keep the lid on ongoing criminal activities.

Most of the mass media knew of the corruption, and refused to report it. A scandal effecting thousands of people a year could not have escaped the media's attention. By their coverup the media deceived their readers, some of whom lost their life's assets by being unaware of the judicial racketeering activities. Members of the U.S. Senate and House knew of the corruption, as their constituents pleaded with them to investigate and to provide help. The legal fraternity in Congress protected the legal fraternity in the Chapter 11 corruption, and made possible the financial destruction of their own constituents.

There were a few exceptions. The *Indianapolis Star* published numerous reports on the Chapter 11 racketeering enterprises, commencing in 1987. The articles described the judicial corruption that most newspapers kept quiet. In an April 19, 1987, article the system was described as follows:

The [Chapter 11] court system is burdened with cronyism, political favors and conflicts of interest while a "club" of bankruptcy attorneys reaps the largest fees. ... Critics—including other lawyers—use the harshest terms. One described the system as incestuous. ... subverts the judicial system. ... Direct and indirect financial relationships between three judges and lawyers or others to whom they award fees. ... Forged, fraudulent or misleading documents ... fraud ... At stake

*is the fate of thousands of economically distressed companies and
people, as well as the financial interests of hundreds of thousands of
companies and individuals.*

CONGRESS BELATEDLY FEIGNS AN INTEREST

As a result of the exposures, one Chapter 11 judge in Indianapolis was
sentenced to prison, very possibly to diffuse further investigation. However,
the system continued and flourished, and the maverick U.S. Trustee whose
effort put the judge into prison was terminated by the Justice Department.
Two small-town papers near San Francisco, the *Napa Sentinel* and the *Santa
Rosa Press Democrat*, ran articles on the Chapter 11 corruption. But the
major newspapers, including the *San Francisco Chronicle*, the *Wall Street
Journal*, and others, kept the scheme going by not reporting it to their readers.

The articles by the *Napa Sentinel* and the *Santa Rosa Press Democrat*
linked the Chapter 11 corruption with numerous drug enterprises, to federal
judges, judge-appointed trustees, the Department of Justice, and to the CIA.
This book doesn't go into those areas, but makes reference to these
tantalizing issues, especially in light of the revelations of government-
protected drug activities by the CIA.

For years, constituents of California Congressman Don Edwards had
pleaded with him for help, as they were victimized and financially destroyed
by the Chapter 11 racketeering activities. Edwards was known as the "father
of the Bankruptcy Code." Attorneys in the Chapter 11 club praised Edwards
for the law that so enriched their lives. Edwards had Congressional oversight
jurisdiction over the scandal-plagued system, and he also chaired the House
Judiciary Committee's subcommittee on, would you believe, Civil and
Constitutional rights. The Chapter 11 corruption obviously violated these civil
and constitutional rights.

I had repeatedly reported to Congressman Edwards, since 1965, the
federal air safety and criminal violations related to a series of airline crashes,
the corruption by federal officials, including the Justice Department. From
1988 through 1990 I repeatedly made Edwards aware of the rampant
corruption, the specific criminal acts, by Chapter 11 judges and their closely-
knit trustees, law firms, and corporations. I reported the shocking pattern of
civil and constitutional violations committed for over five years by federal
judges and Justice Department attorneys and asked him to help. Instead, he
aided and abetted the acts by covering up. Never once did he respond.

In recent years Congressional jurisdiction over Chapter 11 was transferred
from Edward's subcommittee to Representative Jack Brooks of Texas. The
same coverup tactics protecting Edwards also protected Brooks. I had
repeatedly notified of the hard-core criminal activities that I had discovered,
starting in the mid-1960s, and then the Chapter 11 corruption, followed by an
exposure of the criminal activities found in the remainder of these pages.

Brooks did criticize President Bush and the Justice Department[107] for not
appointing an executive director to head the U.S. trustee system, which had

---

[107] San Francisco *Daily Journal*, November 2, 1990.

been vacant for a year at that time. My subsequent 18-page petition to every
United States senator by certified mail on April 1, 1991, detailed and
documented the ongoing criminal acts, which were crimes against the United
States and the American people. Not a single senator made a meaningful
response. Several years later, Congressman Brooks was still "investigating"
Chapter 11 corruption, while thousands of American citizens were defrauded
of their life's assets.

ONE OF MANY MURDERS

Throughout these pages appear the names of some who threatened to
expose the criminal activities implicating federal officials, and who conveniently ended up dead. One of those victims was San Francisco attorney
Dexter Jacobson. Jacobson was preparing to file several lawsuits against key
law firms implicated in the Chapter 11 corruption in the San Francisco area.
The San Francisco legal paper, *Daily Journal*, had publicized Jacobson's
impending filings, along with the evidence he intended to present to the San
Francisco office of the Federal Bureau of Investigation on Monday and
Tuesday, August 20 and 21, 1990. His evidence implicated Chapter 11
judges, trustees, powerful law firms, and powerful corporations, including
Bank of America.

Jacobson and I had exchanged information on the corruption in the
Chapter 11 courts several months earlier. He didn't know about the Justice
Department involvement in the Chapter 11 corruption, and I did not have time
to bring this to his attention.

Two days prior to Jacobson's meeting scheduled with the FBI, his body
was found in nearby Sausalito, with a bullet hole in his head. Jacobson's death
acted to protect Justice Department officials, federal judges, powerful law
firms made rich by the Chapter 11 looting, and other members of the
"bankruptcy club."

Several Northern California newspapers[108] linked Jacobson's death to
the corruption in Chapter 11 courts. Jacobson was the only attorney willing
to speak out, as the others either took advantage of the system or kept the lid
on it, protecting the legal fraternity from public scrutiny. Many of the
attorneys feared retaliation from the judges and trustees who can withhold
hefty legal fees. Trustees appoint attorneys to "represent" the estates, and
favored attorneys who play the game can be handsomely rewarded.

Jacobson did not practice in the Chapter 11 courts, and therefore did not
risk the financial retaliation faced by attorneys who specialize in those courts.
He specialized in real estate and business law, mostly in California and federal
district courts. Jacobson's murder now silenced his lips.

SOME PAPERS REPORTED THE PROBLEMS

Typical of the media stories after Jacobson's killing included that of the
McClatchy News Service (November 24, 1990):

"Everybody around here is 100 percent convinced that it was a hit,"
[quoting Santa Rosa bankruptcy attorney David Chandler]. Jacobson

---

[108] San Francisco's legal newspaper, *Daily Journal*, *Napa Sentinel*, *Santa Rosa Press Democrat*.

was about to drop a bombshell lawsuit into the burgeoning Northern
California bankruptcy court scandal, naming trustees and high-
powered lawyers, and was about to take his evidence to the FBI and
the Justice Department. ... "We both talked about the safety of the
documents and we both talked about the safety of each other," recalls
Sosnowsksi [referring to his meeting with attorney Dexter Jacobson
who was representing the formerly defrauded Chapter 11 party]. "We
are dealing with some very tough people. They're making big money."
... The killing sent a shudder of apprehension through the legal
profession. ... When an examiner concluded in 1988 that Duck had
engaged in serious misconduct in the Sosnowski case, and suggested
further investigation, Santa Rosa Bankruptcy Judge Alan Jaroslovsky
ordered the 49-page report sealed.

The January 1991 issue of *California Lawyer* magazine ran a nine-page article
entitled, "Who Killed Dexter Jacobson?" Reference was made to key parts of
the Chapter 11 corruption that had appeared in other publications, including:

Jacobson planned to file a civil complaint ... that would charge some
of San Francisco's top attorneys with involvement in the nation's most
costly bankruptcy trustee fraud and embezzlement scandal. ....
Jacobson's secretary, Ginny Morrison, recalls her boss saying shortly
before his death that filing the suit was a "dangerous" move. ... "He
said he was going up against some powerful people, and that this
would be on the front page of every newspaper in the country." ...
attorneys in ... tightly knit bankruptcy community were aware of
Duck's schemes, and probably had participated in them. Dexter
Jacobson was one of the first people willing to investigate that
possibility. ... The final drafts of [Jacobson's] lawsuits have disap-
peared from Jacobson's house, his office, his car, and from the hard
drive of his computer. ... On the day of his death, Jacobson had
planned to meet with FBI Agent Eddie Freyer, ... Jacobson was over-
whelming his opponents with his meticulous research and questioning.
"There is not much doubt in my mind it's tied in with this bankruptcy
stuff," one federal source says.

COVERUP BY LOCAL POLICE

The Sausalito police department and the FBI refused to contact me when
I advised them in 1990 that Jacobson and I had exchanged information on the
Chapter 11 corruption shortly before he was killed. My information may or
may not have been helpful, but an investigation into Jacobson's murder
demanded that I be contacted to determine what was discussed between
Jacobson and myself. But to bring me into the investigation risked exposing
a still bigger scandal.

Another attorney was murdered as he was trying to expose the Chapter 11
corruption. Attorney Gary Ray Pinnell, who had been vocal in fighting the
corruption within the Chapter 11 system in Texas, was slain in San Antonio,
Texas, on February 11, 1991. The San Antonio *Texas Express* (March 14,
1991) reported that Pinnell was preparing to turn evidence over to the FBI,
but was killed before he was able to do so. In both cases Justice Department

officials, including the FBI, would have been exposed if these attorneys had succeeded in getting public attention.

A man was killed in Las Vegas as he was about to testify about an alleged scheme taking the properties of Karin Huffer and her husband, implicating Valley Bank of Nevada (now Bank of America), and the same Chapter 11 judge who corruptly seized my assets, Judge Robert Jones. None of these who died, and who were about to present evidence of Chapter 11 judicial corruption to the FBI, realized their evidence threatened Justice Department officials and federal judges, up to and including the Justices of the U.S. Supreme Court.

While these deaths were occurring, the same Justice Department officials and federal judges, who would be implicated by an exposure, were seeking to silence me by repeatedly charging me with criminal contempt of court[109] for seeking to report the criminal activities through federal filings. More about this later.

CHARGING ME WITH CRIMINAL
CONTEMPT OF COURT FOR REPORTING THE CRIMES

I had been vocal in exposing the criminality in Chapter 11 courts, and especially that of trustee Charles Duck. In an attempt to silence me, federal Judge Edward Jellen, Oakland, charged me with criminal contempt for filing appeals and oppositions to the seizure and looting of my assets. Jellen denied me the right to testify in my defense, denied me a jury trial, denied me legal counsel, and then sentenced me to prison for objecting to the seizure of my assets. U.S. District Judge Samuel Conti approved the prison sentence, and it was sent to U.S. Attorney Russoniello for prosecution.

Several months after federal judges seized my assets and started liquidating them, other federal judges sentenced me to prison for having filed notices of appeal and oppositions to the seizure and looting of my life's assets. These acts were criminal in nature, violating specific criminal statutes.[110] While I was in prison, federal Judge Edward Jellen (Oakland, California) ordered fire-sale liquidation of my assets. While I was in prison, trustee Charles Duck unlawfully ordered my mail diverted to his office and opened.[111] Postmaster Dennis Hughes in Alamo, California, where I resided, stated to me (after I was released from prison on the first contempt of court charge) that many federal officials came to the post office checking on my mail, and that he expected to be subpoenaed because of the serious irregularities.

The reason for rendering these unlawful orders barring me access to the federal courts was that I had numerous claims against federal officials and judges (and the California judges who cooperated in the scheme to silence me). If federal relief remedies were not denied to me, the escalating corruption and the judicial and legal participants in the scheme, would be exposed.

---

[109] Charges were filed on December 10, 1990 in the U.S. District Court, San Francisco, number CR 90-0636 VRW.

[110] Including Title 18 U.S.C. § 241 and §§ 1512, 1513.

[111] Title 18 U.S.C. §§ 1702, 1703.

When the initial scheme involving the sham California action backfired, and federal judges involved themselves in the complicity when I exercised federal protections, the number of judicial and legal personnel implicated in the attacks upon me greatly escalated. With each escalation there were new federal causes of action permitting me to sue for damages. The only way to stop that was to render orders, unlawful of course, voiding for me the protections under our form of government, being the right to court access and the right to relief. More about this in later pages.

In later pages a more complex web of intrigue is presented, showing other reasons why Justice Department attorneys and federal judges blocked all defenses exercised by the victims, and showing how the CIA has infiltrated all segments of U.S. society, misusing government offices, defrauding American citizens and the United States as a whole. Numerous trustees and judges have been identified to me by deep cover CIA operatives as being deeply involved in corrupt CIA activities, especially Charles Duck and Judge Robert Jones, both of whom brought about the destruction of my life's assets.

DISCOVERY OF ADDITIONAL CRIMINAL ACTIVITIES THROUGHOUT CHAPTER 11 COURTS

From 1987 to the present I discovered, both in my own case and from reports I received from CIA sources and other victims, that the criminal seizure and looting of assets in bankruptcy courts was epidemic. The criminal acts involved the federal judiciary, including federal judges, trustees, attorneys, law firms, Justice Department attorneys, and CIA personnel. They were all part of the scheme stripping unsuspecting and innocent Americans of their life's assets.

DEMANDING BRIBES TO GET OUT OF CHAPTER 7

As my knowledge broadened of this corruption I discovered other versions of enriching the participants. In Chapter 11 proceedings, for instance, as was earlier described, the incentive was to steal the assets that exceeded the liabilities. But I later discovered from victims that even when there is no equity in a person's Chapter 7 filing, that money is extracted to discharge the case and allow the person to resume a normal life.

Pat Class of Denver and attorney Andrew Quiat described to me another form of extortion. The law provides that a person with liabilities exceeding their assets may file Chapter 7 to completely wipe out their indebtedness, allowing them to basically start all over again. The pattern of court duplicity touches upon every possible source of money, and in Chapter 7 proceedings, where the debtor has the potential of making sizeable income in port-Chapter 7 proceedings, the trustees and judges often demand hidden money to be discharged, even though all issues have been adjudicated. Pat Class, for instance, described how she was forced into Chapter 7 in the Denver-area HUD and savings and loan related corruption, and then a discharge refused unless she paid the trustee money under the table.

Pat, and attorney Quiat, told me of a case in the Denver courts where the trustee demanded, and received $1.5 million under the table, before a Chapter 7 discharge was granted by the judge.

A CIA contact who had extensive dealings with federal judges in several circuits throughout the United States gave me specific data on the corruption in the San Francisco and Chicago-area bankruptcy courts. More is said about this in later pages. It became clear that the bankruptcy courts serve as one of America's biggest financial frauds inflicted upon the American public, made possible by media coverup.

CHAPTER TEN

REPORT CRIMES OF FEDERAL OFFICIALS–GO TO PRISON

On top of everything else done to silence me, federal judges and Justice Department attorneys commenced charging me in early 1987 with criminal contempt of court in retaliation for seeking to report the criminal acts I had discovered, and for seeking relief. They sought to put me in prison for exercising federal crime-reporting responsibilities and for exercising federal defenses against the judicial and Justice Department scheme to silence me. To this day I face imprisonment in a continuing series of charges of contempt of court for filing federal actions seeking to halt the civil right and criminal violations judicially inflicted upon me, and for reporting the escalating criminal activities that I discovered.

The sham California lawsuit to silence me had not gone as planned. My exercise of federal remedies was unanticipated, and federal judges had to openly protect the scheme and the participants by unlawfully dismissing the actions. These judicial acts raised additional federal causes of actions, for which additional federal remedies existed. It was a literal perpetual motion scenario, as federal judges violated federal law, blocking my exercise of federal remedies, and thereby raising additional causes of action.

The method used by this daisy-chain of judicial obstruction of justice was to render a pattern of unlawful and unconstitutional orders barring me from federal court access and voiding for me the constitutional and statutory protections under our form of government. Although this was unlawful and unconstitutional, the crisis was now so bad that not much more could be lost by a pattern of overt judicial suspension of the constitution and laws upon which I relied.

Several months earlier, in late 1987, this same group seized my life's assets, including my real estate investments (motels, apartments, land, rental houses, and my home). The first of a series of orders was rendered, making me a man without a country insofar as the protections of law and Constitution were concerned. Judge Milton Schwartz rendered the first of many orders blocking my access to federal court. This order barred me from reporting federal crimes to a federal court, as required to be reported by federal crime-reporting statutes such as Title 18 U.S.C. Section 4. If I did not report the criminal activities to a federal court or other federal tribunal I would be guilty of a federal crime. Since I obviously couldn't report the crimes to the same Justice Department officials who had been deeply involved in the criminality, the only avenue open was to report the crimes to a federal court. As a citizen concerned about criminality in government, I also had the *right*, in addition to the responsibility, to make the reports to a federal court.

To this day I haven't had my day in court on any of the issues raised in any of the federal filings, since 1974. Every federal judge who received my federal filings blocked my right to have a federal court declare the validity of the five judgments and the important personal and property rights established by those judgments. I was suffering greatly by their refusal to make the declaration and by the acts of the renegade California judges. I was suffering the effects of the continuing hard-core civil and constitutional violations, and I was entitled, like any other citizen, to relief that only federal judges could provide.

In 1986 U.S. District Judge Milton Schwartz at Sacramento rendered an order dismissing my attempts to obtain the declaratory judgment and to obtain relief from the ongoing pattern of civil right violations. In that order, he barred me from ever filing any federal action seeking relief or reporting the federal crimes, which was then followed by an escalation of previous acts by California judges and the Friedman law firm.

Exercising rights and responsibilities under our form of government, I filed two lawsuits in the United States District Court in the District of Columbia,[112] naming as defendants the FAA, NTSB, the Justice Department, and Judge Milton Schwartz. In these lawsuits I sought to give testimony and evidence about the criminal acts I had uncovered; to obtain an order halting the violations of federally protected rights; to declare my rights in the five judgments; and declaring as void the order barring me from federal court access. Each of these issues constituted a major federal cause of action requiring the U.S. District Judge to perform his duty.

U.S. Attorney David Levi and U.S. District Judge Milton Schwartz retaliated against me for having exercised these rights and responsibilities belonging to every citizen in the United States. Schwartz issued a March 1987 Order-To-Show-Cause (OSC) for me to appear in federal court at Sacramento on April 23, 1987, to explain why I should not be held in civil contempt for filing the federal lawsuits. Schwartz argued that I was in contempt of court for filing the federal action when his May 30, 1986, injunctive order permanently barred me from federal court access.

---

[112] No. 86-2523; 86-2214.

Two days before I was to appear, Judge Schwartz's senior law clerk, Jo Anne Speers, telephoned me at my Nevada residence, and spent fifteen minutes convincing me not to personally appear, but to appear by legal counsel. "But the order requires that I personally appear," I stated. Ms. Speers answered, "I talked to Judge Schwartz, and it was decided that you do not have to personally appear." She was lying.

I told Speers that I didn't have an attorney, and she replied I should get any attorney to appear and that he didn't have to know anything about the case. I thought that statement to be strange.

The reason for avoiding a personal appearance was that California Judge William Jensen had issued a bench warrant for my arrest, which was still in effect. Every time there was an appearance calendared for me, the Friedman group alerted the Solano County sheriff's office and sheriff deputies waited to arrest me.

"They're setting you up!"

I stated to a friend in Reno, Laura Link (who formerly practiced law in California), what Judge Schwartz's law clerk had stated. "They're setting you up," Laura stated. "Oh, come on," I responded, "I know they're a bunch of bastards, but they wouldn't do anything that obvious." Like most of the public, I was naive about the dirty tricks of federal judges and Justice Department attorneys.

I made some quick phone calls and Sacramento attorney Joel Pegg agreed to appear for me. But when Pegg appeared on April 23rd, as Judge Schwartz's law clerk suggested, Judge Schwartz already had a multi-page order prepared, charging me with *criminal* contempt for not personally appearing. Schwartz and his law clerk had set me up. Schwartz then ordered me to appear in federal court on May 7, 1987, on a charge of *criminal* contempt, and warned that if I did not appear, a federal bench warrant would be issued for my arrest.

ARRAIGNED ON CRIMINAL CONTEMPT OF COURT CHARGES

I appeared on May 7th with attorney Joel Pegg, and was promptly arraigned, based on a criminal information filed by U.S. Attorney David Levi. The Justice Department charged me with a three-count criminal indictment; one for each of the lawsuits in which I sought to report, via federal filings as provided by Title 18 U.S.C. § 4, the criminal activities I discovered, and for seeking relief from the judicial acts taken to silence me.

Federal marshals marched me to magistrate Esther Hix, where I was officially charged with the purported offense of criminal contempt of court. I hadn't realized that reporting federal crimes was an imprisonable offense. Justice Department attorneys sought to have me imprisoned in the federal penitentiary for 18 months. These acts were federal crimes. They inflicted harm upon me for having exercised rights and protections under the Constitution and laws of the United States and for having sought to report federal crimes committed by federal personnel.

HIGH FLIGHT RISK?

Assistant United States attorney Peter Nowinski sought to deny me my freedom pending trial, arguing that my offenses made me a high flight risk, and that I had a record of not appearing in court. Magistrate Esther Hix asked why I was considered "a flight risk."

"He failed to appear before Judge Schwartz on April 23rd, 1987," replied assistant U.S. Attorney Novinski. This was the hearing at which Judge Schwartz's law clerk stressed I should not personally appear, and at which I appeared by legal counsel. The assistant U. S. Attorney then argued that I failed to appear before California Judge William Jensen in Fairfield, on May 9, 1986. That was the date when I appeared before Judge Schwartz, and physically could not be in two places at the same time, and had an attorney appear for me.

The United States Attorney continued his lying to the court: "The government also has information that Mr. Stich kidnapped a grandchild from Texas and threatened his wife, with whom he was litigating, that she would never see the child again, if she did not terminate the litigation."

That was a fabrication which is explained elsewhere. One of my three daughters, Linda, moved to California from Texas, taking her two children with her. It was those children that I was supposed to have kidnapped. I had not communicated in any manner with my former wife for years, and certainly made no threats. Nor did I know my daughter was moving from Texas until she arrived. I would discover as years went by that it is normal practice for Justice Department attorneys to fabricate whatever lie is necessary to obtain a conviction and to support whatever order they want rendered.

Magistrate Esther Hix read my rights to me, as if I were a criminal, and warned me of the consequences if I tried to flee. For the prior fifteen years I had tried to appear before federal courts to present evidence. To now imply I might flee was a preposterous statement that only someone in the legal fraternity could utter.

I was treated like a hard-core criminal in retaliation for reporting the crimes in which federal judges and Justice Department officials were implicated. After arraignment, and after signing a stipulation agreeing to a trial before a U.S. Magistrate, I was released on bail. I had to post a $25,000 bond to insure that I would appear in court. I was then booked, my fingerprints and pictures taken, like a common criminal. Unknown to me, there was still more trouble waiting.

FRIEDMAN ALERTED THE CALIFORNIA AUTHORITIES

Waiting to arrest me and take me to Solano County jail were two sheriff's deputies from Solano County, with a bench warrant for my arrest, rendered by California Judge William Jensen. Fortunately I had bail money handy, which I paid to the deputies. The deputies were apparently alerted either by the Friedman law firm, California Judge William Jensen, U.S. District Judge Milton Schwartz, or all of them together. At another time during a 1987 hearing in the California action the Friedman law firm notified the Solano County sheriff's office that I would appear carrying a gun. This was part of the pattern of dirty tricks pulled throughout the eight years of litigation by the Friedman law firm. I was frisked for concealed weapons when I appeared in court.

Trying to retain some semblance of sanity, I had to joke about all of this occasionally. Because the Friedman law firm was heavily Jewish, as were most of the federal judges and Justice Department prosecutors that I encountered, I asked Laura Link: "Do you suppose if I told these bastards I was not of German descent, but of Austrian descent, they would pull back?" She responded, "That won't do any good. Austria was once part of Germany." This conversation was in a light vein, but as I discovered other patterns of corruption far beyond what I had discovered up to this date, I found an inordinate involvement of Jewish attorneys and the Mossad. As shown in later pages, the Mossad is involved in many of the criminal activities inflicting great harm upon the American people.

KANGAROO TRIAL

To avoid a Kangaroo Court trial it was important that I receive a jury trial on the criminal contempt charge. Otherwise, I would be prosecuted by the Justice Department and tried by federal judges, who were the two groups most threatened by my exposure activities. The constitutional right to an unbiased tribunal would obviously be lacking.

During my initial arraignment, attorney Pegg instructed me to sign a waiver to permit a trial before a U.S. Magistrate instead of a district court judge. That was a dumb thing to do, as the part-time federal magistrate was employed, and retained, only so long as he pleased my adversaries in the Justice Department and the federal judges. The saving grace was that the waiver contained a stipulation that I would receive a jury trial.

The Sixth and Seventh Amendments to the U.S. Constitution guarantee the right to a jury trial, and also a trial before a fair and impartial jury. But federal judges have ignored this constitutional protection for years, and the U.S. Supreme Court Justices have held that in federal court the right to a jury does not exist if incarceration does not exceed six months. Federal judges euphemistically call this long incarceration a petty offense. There is nothing petty about six months in prison, especially while a person's business, properties, home, assets, and maybe family, are lost.

U.S. Attorney David Levi sought to have me imprisoned for 18 months; six months for each of the three federal actions that were filed. Before the start of the trial, my attorney reminded Magistrate John Moulds that a jury trial was stipulated earlier. Assistant U.S. Attorney David Flynn responded that I wasn't entitled to a jury trial on the basis that he was lowering his requested prison term to six months from the originally requested 18 months. But that reduction in prison sentence had nothing to do with the written stipulation for a jury trial, which arose when I signed a waiver to proceed before a U.S. Magistrate.

Like every other right to which I was entitled during the past several years, that right was violated. Magistrate Moulds denied me a jury trial, and the trial commenced without a jury. (September 16, 1987.) I had notified several of the news services and numerous radio and television stations in the San Francisco and Sacramento area of the government attempt to railroad me to prison for reporting the criminal activities that I had uncovered. Not a single one showed up.

Attorney Pegg raised arguments that held I couldn't be found guilty, but omitted the hard-core constitutional violations associated with Judge Schwartz's injunctive order; the set-up by Judge Schwartz and his law clerk that converted the civil contempt into criminal contempt; the felonious[113] nature of inflicting harm upon a person for exercising rights and protections under law; and the felonious nature[114] of inflicting harm upon a person for attempting to report federal crimes.

"I find you guilty"!

Magistrate Moulds concluded the trial by declaring I was guilty as charged, setting a November 4, 1987, sentencing date. Attorney Pegg then abandoned me, making no effort to submit briefs for reconsideration as provided by law,[115] or for filing notice of appeals and appeal briefs. I felt that he did not wish to offend federal judges or the Justice Department, people with whom he would deal throughout his legal career.

Several months earlier, I was forced to seek refuge in Chapter 11 to protect my assets against the events taking place in the California courts, and this matter has been addressed in a previous chapter. When Magistrate Moulds held me guilty of criminal contempt of court, Judge Robert Jones used this decision as the basis for seizing my assets of $10 million. While in prison, these assets were looted and destroyed. My world was tumbling down upon me, a terrible price to pay for having exerted efforts to expose the escalating corruption within the federal government. I often thought that if I had never taken the United Airlines assignment my entire life would have been very different.

RAMPANT CONSTITUTIONAL VIOLATIONS

My attorney, Joel Pegg, abandoned me immediately after the decision was rendered.[116] I filed post-trial motions in *pro se* status, raising numerous defenses, none of which attorney Pegg had raised, including:

1. The underlying injunctive order, voiding for me access to federal court and the statutory and Constitutional protections, was unlawful and unconstitutional.

---

[113] **Title 18 U.S.C. § 241. Conspiracy against rights of citizens.**

[114] **Title 18 U.S.C. § 1512. Tampering with a witness, victim, or an informant —**

(b) Whoever knowingly uses intimidation or physical force, or threatens another person, or attempts to do so, or engages in misleading conduct toward another person, with intent to

(1) influence, delay or prevent the testimony of any person in an official proceeding:

shall be fined ... or imprisoned ... or both. [1988 amended reading]"

Title 18 U.S.C. § 1513. Retaliating against a witness, victim, or an informant. (a) Whoever knowingly engages in any conduct and thereby causes bodily injury to another person or damages the tangible property of another person, or threatens to do so, with intent to retaliate against any person for–(1) the attendance of a witness or party at an official proceeding, or any testimony given or any record, document, or other object produced by a witness in an official proceeding; or (2) any information relating to the commission or possible commission of a Federal offense ..."

[115] Motion to alter or amend, Federal Rule of Criminal Procedure 60.

[116] While Pegg was abandoning me, my other attorney, Joshua Landish, was sabotaging me in Chapter 11 courts by secretly dealing with my adversaries and then requesting the court to seize my assets and begin their fire sale liquidation.

2. It constitutes a federal crime to retaliate against a citizen for having exercised the right to federal court access, seeking declaratory and injunctive relief from the pattern of civil right violations judicially inflicted. The prosecution and judgment holding me guilty constituted a criminal act under Title 18 U.S.C. § 241.

3. It constitutes federal crimes under Title 18 U.S.C. §§ 1512 and 1513 to prosecute and hold a person guilty of an imprisonable offense in retaliation for having reported federal crimes or having sought to do so.

4. I would have been guilty of a federal crime, under Title 18 U.S.C. § 4, if I had not reported the federal crimes, which I sought to report through the federal filings which were used as the basis for the criminal contempt of court charges.

5. The injunctive order barring me from federal court reversed the federal criteria for rendering such an order, which is intended to protect a person suffering great and irreparable harm, and not to deprive the person suffering this harm the relief available under law.

6. The underlying injunctive order fraudulently sought support by placing a "frivolous label" on the underlying lawsuit (86-0210 MLS). The major federal causes of actions stated in that action couldn't possibly meet the legal definition of a "frivolous action."

7. Federal case law provides that a person cannot be charged with criminal contempt for exercising a right that would otherwise be lost, and that if I did not file the action I would lose my right to relief.

8. A federal judge lacks authority to force a person who knows of federal crimes to violate federal crime-reporting statutes by remaining silent.

9. A party cannot be punished for contempt when the injunctive order is on appeal. Judge Schwartz admitted this fact in an order he rendered on November 13, 1987:

This court lacks jurisdiction to entertain the motion for contempt since the underlying judgment in this case rendered by this Court is currently on appeal. The Ninth Circuit follows the general rule with some exceptions not relevant here, that the filing of a proper and timely notice of appeal divests the district court of jurisdiction over those matters that are not on appeal or subject to the appeal.

Making reference to the verbal order, Judge Schwartz made a written order on December 9, 1987, making reference to the applicable federal law,[117] stating in part:

The Court denies the Motion of Defendants, Jensen and Superior Court of Solano County for an Order Adjudging Plaintiff in Contempt, ... because it is this Court's conclusion that it lacks jurisdiction to entertain the motion since the underlying judgment in this case rendered by this Court is currently on appeal.

This holding and the law cited made the contempt proceedings before magistrate Moulds illegal, and without jurisdiction. But Moulds continued the

---

[117] *Donovan v. Mazaola*, 761 F.2d 1411, 1414, 1415 (9th Cir. 1985; *Matter of Thorp*, 655 F.2d 997, 999 (9th Cir. 1981).

contempt proceedings and ordered me incarcerated on November 4, 1987. Under federal law I had a statutory *right* to a stay of imprisonment pending appeal if the appeal raised any arguable issues of fact or law.[118] I obviously had many arguable issues.

But Moulds refused to grant me bail, arguing that he did not think the Court of Appeals would vacate his judgment. Federal case law[119] made it plain that bail cannot be denied on the belief by the judge who rendered the judgment that his decision would be upheld. Otherwise, granting bail would depend upon the judge rendering the judgment believing that his judgment would be overturned on appeal.

I filed a motion for stay of prison sentence with District Judge Raul Ramirez, pending appeal of the judgment and sentence. Ironically, it was Judge Ramirez's unlawful dismissal of the first federal action seeking relief, in 1984, that made possible the escalation of the judicial civil right violations against me. Ramirez also denied bail, holding that he didn't think the judgment would be overturned.

SUPREME COURT JUSTICE
ANTHONY KENNEDY AS CO-CONSPIRATOR

Shortly before Christmas 1989, the Ninth Circuit Court of Appeals at San Francisco turned down my appeal of the prison sentence. The three judges, James R. Browning, Alex Kozinski, and Pamela Rymer, turned down my appeal without addressing a single one of the many defenses that I raised. Incredibly, they approved each and every judicial violation inflicted upon me by the California and federal judges. They approved the judicial voiding of all federal remedies. They approved the imprisonment that constituted prima facie evidence of felony retaliation for trying to report the federal crimes that I had discovered. They approved the obstruction of justice tactics, and the many other wrongful judicial acts. The implications of this judicial mindset were extremely serious. Without addressing a single issue that I raised in the appeal briefs, which they should have done, the Court of Appeals judges simply stated: "The judgment is affirmed."

I quickly filed a petition for writ of certiorari with the United States Supreme Court. In my written arguments I raised the pattern of judicial suspension of civil rights and the criminal implications by Ninth Circuit judges, their obstruction of justice, their felony persecution of whistleblowers, and reminded them of their supervisory responsibilities over these judges. Aiding and abetting these acts by judges over whom they had supervisory responsibilities, the Supreme Court Justices upheld this conduct, becoming co-conspirators with the criminal acts that I sought to expose.

I was ordered to turn myself in on January 14, 1988; I had to act fast. Over the Christmas holidays I prepared a petition to Ninth Circuit Court of Appeals Justice Anthony Kennedy (before he became a Justice of the United States Supreme Court). I worked feverishly on Christmas Day to finish the petition for submission to Kennedy the following Monday. Kennedy had

---

[118] Title 28 United States Code section 3143.
[119] *U.S. v. Hurst*, 424 F.Supp. 318 (9th Cir. 1978).

testified at great lengths during his televised Senate confirmation hearing for appointment to the Supreme Court, expressing repeated concerns for due process, constitutional safeguards, respect for privacy. Kennedy denied me relief. His conduct represented numerous criminal acts, including obstruction of justice, aiding and abetting, accessory before and after the fact, misprision of felonies, fraud, conspiracy, and other crimes. The same applies to the other judges described within these pages.

Judge Kennedy was already involved in the corruption I sought to expose. He was on the appellate panel that heard my appeal of the district court's dismissal of the 1974 federal action against the Federal Aviation Administration. Kennedy knew the consequences of coverup as several major air tragedies associated with the air safety corruption followed his decision upholding the district court's dismissal of my action. That action sought to report to a federal court the federal crimes I discovered at United Airlines and within the FAA that were associated with a series of air disasters.

After Justice Anthony Kennedy denied the emergency request, I filed a second motion for stay-pending-appeal with Judge Ramirez. When I appeared before Ramirez on February 16, 1988, on the motion, he delayed rendering a decision, continuing the matter until March 4th, 1988, the date I was to be imprisoned. I asked Ramirez to grant a continuance of the incarceration date, to permit me to request a stay of the prison sentence pending appeal from the United States Court of Appeals if he denied my motion. Ramirez assured me that I could request a stay from him on March 4th, implying that he would stay the sentence.

I was at a serious disadvantage appearing without legal counsel. The Justice Department and federal judges seized all my assets (as discussed in earlier pages), and I was without funds to hire legal counsel. I was entitled to appointment of legal counsel, which I requested. Judge Ramirez appointed federal public defender Carl Larson to represent me. But instead of representing me, Larson acted as damage control for the corrupt judges and Justice Department. Every action he took was to protect the system of corrupt judges and corrupt Justice Department attorneys, and defeat my remedies in law. I discovered over the next five years that this type of legal representation (protection of government corruption) occurs in almost every instance.

Larson made no effort to prepare a defense to the multitude of issues that made the guilty verdict a gross miscarriage of justice. He took the position that I was guilty, advising me to prepare for prison. He refused to request a stay of prison sentence pending appeal, a statutory right in federal law. He refused to file any post-conviction motions or to file an appeal. He protected the corrupt system and became criminally implicated.

When Larson learned that I was to appear as a guest on a talk show on government corruption, he became furious, and ordered me not to appear. I, of course, ignored him. I finally dismissed Larson and appeared in pro se status so as to file my own briefs and raise the important defense issues.

"Bailiff, do your job!"

I appeared before Judge Ramirez at the March 4, 1988, hearing without benefit of legal counsel, expecting to receive a stay of the prison sentence pending appeal. Instead, Ramirez denied my request and ordered, "Bailiff, do your job." Two husky marshals seized me and led me to a dirty prison cell in the basement of the federal building, where I was stripped of all my belongings. Handcuffs and leg irons were put on me.

The U.S. Marshals led me to a van in leg irons and handcuffs, and transported me to a county jail at Yuba City, California, in what would be one of several prisons for the next two months. Driving up to Yuba City, I passed the motel that I owned, Tahitian Gardens. Staying at the motel was my friend Edith Armstrong, whom I hadn't been able to visit for the past two years because of California Judge William Jensen's bench warrant for my arrest. (Edith appears in an earlier chapter entitled, The Imposters.)

No matter how bad life became, it always seemed to get worse, at least for the first month of my imprisonment. Twenty-four hours a day you sit, eat, sleep on a thin, filthy mattress, if you are lucky to have one, and eat under filthy conditions. Life becomes meaningless. I was shocked that this could be happening in America, but things always got worse.

There was also another possible reason for my incarceration. I was recovering from open-heart surgery in which I received six coronary bypasses, and any stress could constrict them and result in a heart attack and possibly death. My death would seemingly end the threat of exposure to those implicated in the various segments of the criminal activities described within these pages. There was no one else with the evidence and the willingness to continue the fight.

While I was in prison and unable to defend myself, the Friedman law firm and California judges rendered orders laying claim to my multi-million dollar estate. They rendered a sham divorce judgment on July 28, 1988, and transferred title to my property, even though there was no marriage to support the divorce judgment.

DEBATE WITH ACLU WHILE IN PRISON

My contact with the outside world while in the Sutter County jail was by mail and a telephone in the crowded cell-block. Each prisoner was limited to a scheduled fifteen-minute call. During a late evening phone call from the prison cell, a friend advised that she arranged an appearance for me on radio station KOH in Reno, hosted by Fred Taft. I was to phone the station collect the following morning, and would be on the air for an hour.

In the meantime Taft arranged that the executive director of the Nevada ACLU, Shelley Chase, would be on the show. On an earlier show, my friend revealed how the ACLU had refused to help me defend against the onslaught of civil right violations, while soliciting money from the public to uphold these protections. Ironically, the Friedman law firm was a key member of the San Francisco ACLU.

I told my friend that it was highly questionable whether I could be on the talk show since I was confined in prison, in a crowded cell, with 16 other prisoners, and limited to a single 15 minute telephone conversation. I explained the situation to the other prisoners, some of whom were bank robbers and drug dealers, explaining that I had the opportunity to debate with the ACLU. The prisoners encouraged me to get on the show. Everyone waived their telephone schedule so I could make the one-hour talk show possible. Of course, the prison officials knew nothing about it. If they had, they would have put an immediate stop to it.

There were some unusual sounds during the show. Clanking of cell-block doors, screaming of prisoners, and a fight ensuing a few feet from the telephone. During this talk show, ACLU Executive Director Shelley Chase, defended and upheld the outrageous civil right violations perpetrated by Justice Department attorneys and the California and federal judges. This is the same ACLU to whom I brought information for the prior twenty years of the ongoing criminal activities that were implicated in a series of air disasters.

Host Fred Taft expressed outrage over the government conduct on two prior shows, relating the government abuse of his cousin by the IRS and his subsequent imprisonment on a tax charge. But during this show Taft changed his colors. He upheld the ACLU's position, causing me to wonder if the station had been pressured by government officials to support the acts taken against me.

START OF DIESEL THERAPY

After spending several weeks in the bleak conditions of the Sutter County jail I went on the "Diesel therapy" route, being transferred from prison to prison. I was transferred to the infamous old Sacramento County jail, where filth, overcrowding, and inhuman conditions took on a new meaning. I wondered how it compared to the infamous Devil's Island Prison. During the frequent changes in prison, I once found myself in a cell with 12 bunks, occupied by over 30 people, with hardly room to sit down. It resembled a cage with animals packed tightly together.

You spend every minute of the day or night sitting or sleeping on the concrete floor, unless you are lucky and have a thin mattress to lie on. The stench of the dirty mattresses is sometimes unbearable. In the Sacramento jail the open toilet was positioned along a glass wall with constant passing of male and female guards, without any screening or privacy. Many of the prisoners looked as if they hadn't washed or changed their clothes in weeks. They resembled something out of a horror story. Food came in unsanitary containers that resembled feeding time in a dog kennel.

SILENCING TECHNIQUES IN PRISON

Diesel therapy is one of many tricks used by the Justice Department to break a prisoner, keep him from his legal counsel, if he had counsel, and keep him from communicating with his family or friends. It is common practice in the federal prison system to move prisoners from prison to prison for weeks at a time, being "lost" for all practical purposes. After Judge Ramirez ordered my incarceration, he sought to keep me in the county jails where there was no access to legal facilities, keeping me from filing legal papers to obtain my release.

BRUTALITY OF PRISON

Prison has its own peculiar sounds. The constant slamming of heavy metal doors, night screams, fights in the cells. Living, eating, and existing like caged animals. Many respond accordingly. There is no privacy. Prisoners sleep in crowded inhuman conditions, often within a few feet of a dirty, seatless toilet, used by dozens of occupants. Modesty doesn't exist.

Anyone who hasn't been in prison doesn't know the degradation, the humiliation that goes with it. The first thing that happens is that you are handcuffed, a chain put around your waist, and connected to leg irons.

Prisoners are stripped of all belongings, including their watch, rings, and identification, and then put into holding cells. The filthy toilet conditions indoctrinate you to what is yet to come. Fingerprints and mug shots are repeatedly taken at every new jail or prison, and you are stripped naked and subjected to embarrassing body-cavity examinations. Smelly and overcrowded prison cells become routine. The smell of urine and god knows what else is overpowering. One's appetite is easily lost.

BROKEN, LONELY, DYING MEN

Under these conditions, broken, lonely, and dying men are found in the medium and high-security prisons. Torn from their families, some for twenty and thirty years, or forever, their lives literally come to an end. There are no hopes, no plans, nothing. In the cases of those framed by the Justice Department attorneys, it is especially pathetic that this could happen in the so-called land of liberty and justice!

I looked at the scribbling on prison walls, made by deranged, dejected, morbid prisoners. Broken men, lonely, and some dying. Despite the overcrowding, it was terribly lonely, and all meaning to life appears lost. For many, all hope was gone. Under these conditions, a day or a week seems forever. It gave me an entirely different perspective of people in prison, and of those who have corrupted our government. Many of these people in prison were railroaded by the misnamed Justice Department, and prosecuted for offenses far less onerous than committed by those charging and sentencing them.

My entire life passed before me. I thought of those I loved, who helped me. I thought of those who didn't seem to care. I thought of the attorneys I hired to defend me, who then conspired with my judicial and Justice Department adversaries. I sometimes wondered what part United Airlines officials played in these events, thinking of how General Motors secretly went after Ralph Nader when he wrote the book, *Unsafe At Any Speed.*

"My God, this can't be!"

Many times I thought to myself: "My God, how can this be happening to me! This can't be!" I couldn't believe that what started out with discovering deadly air safety and criminal violations at United Airlines could have such devastating consequences for me. I thought of people who perished in some of the airline crashes closely connected to the corruption I had first discovered in the aviation arena, and wondered who suffered the most. I was still better off, and had the chance to fight on, while, for them, it was all over.

How could I be in prison for refusing to commit the crime of coverup? Where was the media, the so-called protectors against government tyranny? Where was Congress? I sent out hundreds of flyers before leaving for prison, notifying these parties that had a check and balance responsibility. I appealed to the ACLU, the Ralph Nader group, civil rights groups, and other checks and balances. Every single one refused to help, choosing instead to aid and abet the criminal subversion of our government.

It was all so incomprehensible. I had been financially well off. I had a good life. I had a reputation throughout the United States as an air safety activist, and suddenly I find myself in prison and stripped of the assets I worked for the past twenty years to acquire, all because I felt a sense of responsibility. How stupid I was! I kept thinking this must be a dream, and I'll wake up, and it will all be over. But that never happened.

Prison life is especially hard on older persons. Medical care that exists in theory is incredibly bad in practice. Heart attacks receive virtually no priority, and a dying person suffering a heart attack can linger for hours before being taken to medical facilities. Often it is too late. Older persons have various medical problems which prison life aggravates, and they become prey to young bullying inmates.

ELEMENT THAT ENJOY PRISON

There is a certain element in society that finds prison life, especially in federal prison, satisfactory. They need not worry about housing or food, and have the company of others either like them, or others that they can prey upon. This is the type of individual that will not cease their criminal ways because of the possibility of imprisonment.

SUICIDE

Sometimes I just wanted to die. The strain of all this was getting to me. Flung into prison, things looked bleak. Everything was accumulating. The six years of judicial persecution, the loss of my home, my business, my assets, the humiliation, the character assassination, the loss of privacy, and the hopelessness. There is only so much a person can stand. It caused me to think more than once of ending it all. I had been through World War II as a Navy pilot in the Pacific; I had flown for almost fifty years, experiencing all types of aircraft emergencies; I had been caught in Iranian revolutions. All of these stressful conditions, put together, did not equal the fear that I now experienced. God bless America, where millions of naive Americans recite "with liberty and justice for all," as if it existed!

I looked at the plastic bags used for laundry and other purposes, and thought how peaceful things could suddenly become if one was slipped over one's head and the misery ended. The primary thing preventing me from doing such a thing was the hope that I could expose the corruption in government and somehow motivate the American people to exercise their responsibilities under our form of government. What a dreamer I must have been.

JUSTICE DEPARTMENT CORRUPTION

While in prison I learned about other areas of corruption by Justice Department attorneys and officials, and the harm inflicted upon the American people. I had already seen this misconduct for years, but I discovered areas beyond my earlier comprehension. I found many people in federal prisons who were either falsely convicted or who suffered longer prison terms because of the lying by Justice Department attorneys. Attorneys in the Justice Department are given bonuses for a high conviction rate, motivating this sordid group to send innocent people to prison. Justice means nothing to them, as they seek a high conviction rate, guilty or not.

There are many persons in prison for non-violent crimes who are there because of a lying U.S. Attorney. I got a taste of it several times, as the U.S. Attorney sought to deny me release pending appeal, and to incarcerate me for longer periods of time by making false allegations. I heard many stories from inmates who admitted the crimes they committed, but who described the fraudulent planting of evidence by Justice Department attorneys.

TRAVELING IN CHAINS

From the old Sacramento County jail I was transported in chains to several other prisons. For as long as twelve hours at a time, I was chained and shackled, unable to properly feed myself, or to use the toilet, or any of life's amenities. I ate in the back of crowded prison wagons, stopping at fast-food places for hamburgers. For toilet facilities we stopped at service stations, and were paraded before the public in chains and leg irons. People probably wondered what type of heinous crime we had committed.

Eventually I reached Terminal Island Federal Prison at Long Beach. Approaching the prison, I could see the tourist attractions that I had visited during happier times. I used to visit these same areas when I appeared on radio and television shows as an air safety activist. To stop these activities, the government-funded corruption had me in the same areas, now in chains. How times had changed.

The federal prison at Terminal Island reminded me of pictures I had seen as a child of Sing Sing and Alcatraz. Standing at the bottom of the four story building in unit "J1," all I could see was cell block after cell block, four stories high. It was an eerie feeling.

After a couple of weeks at the harsh Terminal Island prison I was transferred to the Federal Prison Camp at Lompoc, California, where some of the nation's prominent government officials were confined, including former U. S. Attorney General John Mitchell, Wall Street financier Ivan Boesky, and others. Boesky and I worked together on several prison details while I was at Lompoc. The living conditions there were markedly different, but I was still suffering the humiliation, the loss of my liberties, and other protected rights that the public takes for granted.

During these prison stays I met numerous people who were formerly employed by the Central Intelligence Agency as operatives or contract agents who described to me the inner workings of this so-called intelligence-gathering agency. I learned about the CIA's looting of America's financial institutions, about the CIA's drug trafficking within the United States, and other criminal activities. These former CIA people had no ax to grind as they described the work they had been ordered to do, and how they were silenced by Justice Department prosecutors and federal judges. Much more about this in later pages.

At the Lompoc Federal Prison Camp legal supplies were available, making it possible for me to file legal briefs and contact members of Congress. None answered. I should have known. I had reported the air disaster related criminal acts to them for the past twenty-five years with no response.

While I was in prison the court appointed another attorney to represent me, Sacramento attorney Clifford Tedmon. He was as bad as every other one I had. He wouldn't file any papers to obtain my release pending appeal. I filed my own motion for release pending appeal on April 13, 1988, addressed to the Ninth Circuit Court of Appeals at San Francisco.

At the same time, Reno talk show host Fred Taft called in on the nationally syndicated Owen Spann show in San Francisco, and reported my predicament. It is very possible that this talk show was heard by the federal judges heading my motion. The next day (April 16, 1988) the Court of Appeals ordered me released pending a decision on my appeal.

But the Justice Department's Bureau of Prisons refused to release me. I didn't even know of the release order until four days later, when I called Tedmon from inside the prison camp at Lompoc and he was surprised that I had not been released. I then went to the prison authorities and they stated they couldn't find me. Can you comprehend a prison, with checks of the occupants occurring seven times a day, and unable to find me!

Immediately after the Court of Appeals rendered the order for my release, Justice Department attorneys submitted a motion seeking to bar my release. The Justice Department attorneys again misstated the law, arguing that the Court of Appeals lacked jurisdiction to order my release. They argued that I had not filed a notice of appeal of the March 4, 1988, order by Judge Ramirez denying my motion for release pending appeal, and that the court lacked jurisdiction to release me. But the law clearly stated that only one appeal need be filed of the sentence holding me guilty, which I did file. With that filing, the Court of Appeals had jurisdiction to render any order associated with the appeal, including an order releasing me. Justice Department attorneys were apparently desperate to keep me in prison, because I posed a threat if I were free to appear on talk shows and generate public support.

WARM LETTERS FROM CONCERNED CITIZENS

Waiting for me at home was a letter, similar to many others I had received over the years, that was heart warming. Oddly enough, it was from a former United Airlines management official. The letter stated in part: "Many times I've thought about Rodney Stich and his identification with John the Baptist crying in the desert, but you do make a difference and without you whistle blowers our world gets completely out of synch, so don't ever give up, because you do make a tremendous difference!"

CONSTANT BAD NEWS

The freedom didn't last long. On February 26, 1990, I received a notice from the Ninth Circuit Court of Appeals turning down my appeal, upholding each of the outrageously unlawful and unconstitutional acts that I brought to their attention. I quickly filed a petition for rehearing with each and every judge in the U.S. Court of Appeals in the Ninth Circuit, called an *en banc* request, and each and every one of them denied my petition. These judicial decisions had ominous implications of the extreme lawlessness of those in control of the federal judiciary.

DANGEROUS MINDSET

These acts reflected the mindset and *de facto* destruction of the basic safeguards under our form of government. Despite the gravity and implication of these acts, not a single media source, nor any government or non-government check and balance, intervened.

SEEKING RELIEF FROM SUPREME COURT

I quickly filed a petition for writ of certiorari with the U.S. Supreme Court, seeking to halt my imprisonment. And again these nine Justices of the U.S. Supreme Court gave tacit approval to the pattern of corrupt activities perpetrated by those judges who look to them for guidance.

BACK TO PRISON ON JULY 22, 1990

On July 22, 1990, I again appeared before U.S. District Judge Raul Ramirez for a hearing. I attempted to discover the nature of the hearing from Ramirez's law clerk, but was told they didn't know, which was a lie. When I appeared before Ramirez he ordered the U.S. Marshal to seize me. The Marshal put handcuffs and leg irons on me and transported me first to the Sacramento County jail, followed by several weeks of transfer from prison to prison in the western part of the United States.

THE JACOBSON MURDER

Immediately prior to this second incarceration, a San Francisco attorney, Dexter Jacobson, with whom I had previously discussed the Chapter 11 corruption, was killed. Jacobson was to present evidence to FBI agents at San Francisco on August 20, 1990, relating to corruption that he had discovered among Chapter 11 judges, trustees, and law firms. This is discussed in more detail in other pages.

SOLITARY CONFINEMENT

An activist in the San Francisco Bay Area, Virginia McCullough, notified the California prison authorities that I might be at a similar risk to that faced by Jacobson. This warning caused me to be placed in solitary confinement for six weeks. It is difficult to convey to someone who had never been imprisoned how difficult it is to be in solitary confinement for weeks at a time.

Solitary confinement is being locked into a small dimly-lit cell, unable to talk to anyone for days at a time, with your meals slipped into a slot in the door. Rarely is there any reading material. A person in these conditions must sit and stare, for hours and days at a time. In my case this was particularly distressing. I had a full life, I was a multi-millionaire, had two airplanes, a luxurious home, a house on Lake Tahoe. This horror perpetrated by the entire U.S. system entrusted with preventing such outrages, openly retaliated against me for reporting patterns of criminal activities against the United States, and for defending myself.

The same group of judges and Justice Department attorneys who caused me to be in prison were concurrently looting my life's assets, converting me from a multi-millionaire to a state of poverty. My business, my home, my assets, were all being distributed among those who helped inflict upon me the pattern of government-financed civil right and criminal violations. This horror, and the criminal misconduct that it represented, were possible because of the criminal aiding and abetting by the Justices of the Supreme Court, the entire Senate, much of the House, and the establishment media.

During this second period of imprisonment I was eventually transferred to the Federal Prison Camp at Boron, California, where I met several former CIA contract agents who made me aware of a much larger pattern of criminal activities in areas of government to which I had not been exposed. If my efforts ever succeed in waking up the American public and motivating them to act, then this imprisonment may have a redeeming value.

Hundreds of hours of face-to-face conversations with these former CIA people provided information about epidemic corruption within the government of the United States that enlarged upon what I found as a federal investigator. Without the benefit of these CIA contacts I would never have discovered the links between the various criminal enterprises run by federal officials. These contacts helped explain the corruption that I had discovered in the federal courts and in the Justice Department, as the various criminal activities were all interrelated.

I was to have been released on November 23, 1990, after serving out the six-month prison sentence. But Justice Department prosecutors and federal judges had not finished their dirty work on me. Two weeks before I was to be released, U.S. District Judge Marilyn Patel, in San Francisco, signed an order keeping me in prison and transporting me to the federal prison at Pleasanton, California. The charge? I had filed a federal action[120] in Chicago seeking relief from the corrupt seizure of my assets by Ninth Circuit judges and trustees, and reporting the criminal activities I discovered in Ninth Circuit Chapter 11 courts.

I had named Chapter 11 embezzler Charles Duck as one of the defendants. Patel held that the exercise of these federally protected rights constituted criminal contempt of court and had me incarcerated, without a hearing. Patel had no jurisdiction over me. She sought jurisdiction on the basis of a civil action that I had filed against California court of appeal judges in 1986, which she unlawfully dismissed in 1987. Once an action is dismissed the judge has no jurisdiction over the parties. But this didn't bother Patel any more than the other judicial outrages bothered the Ninth Circuit Court of Appeal judges or the numerous District Judges that had become implicated in the criminal activities.

A FORTUITOUS ENCOUNTER THAT
BACKFIRED ON MY ADVERSARIES

Leaving Lompoc in chains, I was again on the prison circuit, going from prison to prison, until I eventually ended up at the Federal Correctional Center at Dublin, California. I arrived at Dublin at the same time as a high-ranking deep-cover CIA operative, Gunther Russbacher, and a relationship started that would make possible exposing to the American people unprecedented crimes by federal personnel against the United States. [During the next few years I was to discovered crimes by federal personnel far exceeding what I had discovered to that date.]

---

[120] U.S. District Court, Chicago, CV 90-2548.

Russbacher held a very high covert position within the Central Intelligence Agency and was a warehouse full of insider information about corruption that is beyond the wildest imagination of the average uninformed American citizen. Russbacher and I hit it off well, possibly because we were both pilots, and both of us had received our Navy wings at Pensacola, Florida. Much more will be stated of this fortuitous encounter in later pages.

On December 10, 1990, I appeared in U.S. District Court at San Francisco, and was charged by U.S. Attorney Anthony Russoniello with criminal contempt of court,[121] based upon the charges initiated by Judge Patel, and arising from the action I filed in Chicago. An attorney practicing in Berkeley California, was assigned to defend me. He promptly proceeded to sabotage my defenses, and refused to file any papers in my defense. He refused to return any phone calls, and all the usual tactics protecting the judicial system and the Justice Department. The case was assigned to Judge Vaughn Walker, whose conduct was clearly to protect the criminal activities that I had uncovered, protect the criminal activities of the federal judges and Justice Department attorneys, and make my life miserable.

I was released on bail, but limited in my travels to a small section of the state of California and Reno, Nevada. To this date I am still confined to this little area, while waiting a non-jury trial on the charge of criminal contempt of court for having filed a federal lawsuit in early 1990 seeking to expose the corruption I discovered in Chapter 11 courts.

In May 1991, after discovering a great amount of additional government corruption, described in the following pages, I filed a declaration in my action putting the court on notice of these criminal activities. I attached to my declaration partial transcripts of sworn declarations given to me by deep-cover CIA operative Gunther Russbacher, describing the criminal activities related to a scandal known as October Surprise, which has yet to be described. All activities seeking to put me in prison halted thereafter. It is now almost three years since I have been charged with criminal contempt, and not a single word out of the Justice Department or the federal courts.

CALIFORNIA ATTORNEYS TOOK ADVANTAGE OF THE JUDICIAL ATTACKS UPON ME

California attorneys, aware of the suspension of my legal rights, zeroed in like vultures to strip my assets clean. Two California attorneys, Maurice Moyal and Edward Weiss, and California Judge Edward Flier,[122] took advantage of the judicial attacks and judicial suspension of protections in law. Knowing that I was to be incarcerated on July 22, 1990, the attorneys calendared a hearing in the Superior Court, Contra Costa County, to have my cross-complaint against them dismissed and to obtain a default judgment against me for $500,000. They knew I could not appear to defend.

After I was released I filed a complaint against the attorneys and the judge, for fraud and other causes of action, and sought to have the default judgment vacated. The developing judicial scandal was known throughout the

---

[121] *USA v. Stich*, N.D. Cal. No. 90-0636 VRW.
[122] From Concord and Walnut Creek, California.

California judicial system, and it was important that I never prevail in the courts. Otherwise, it is possible that the lid on this can of worms would be pried open. Further, Moyal and Weiss had played a role in helping to inflict financial and other harms upon me, and any attorney assisting in the underlying attacks upon me were protected by the system composed of state and federal judges and the legal fraternity. Contra Costa County Judge Ellen James at Martinez, dismissed my action, continuing the ten-year-pattern of judicial gridlock. I filed an appeal, and it was assigned to the same three judges in the California Court of Appeals who played a key role throughout the corruption in the California courts.

But this wasn't all. Without any hearing, U.S. District Judge Vaughn Walker, playing a key role in the latest attempt to have me imprisoned for exposing the escalating criminal activities, rendered an order[123] in a federal case that he opened on his own initiative. In this order, Walker ordered me to pay financial sanctions to the attorneys who had assisted in the attacks against me, Moyal and Weiss, and then entered an order barring the clerk of the court from filing any federal actions presented by me, until such actions met the approval of "a Judge of this court: the United States, the State of California, the County of Contra Costa, Maurice Moyal, Edward Weiss, Edward Weiss, a Professional Corporation, the National Transportation Safety Board, the United States Department of Transportation, United Airlines, any United States Judge, and any California State Judge."

Anyone can do anything to me that they want, in gross violation of state or federal law, and I am totally stripped of the defenses under our form of government. Anyone who thinks these corrupt judicial acts do not effect them, should awaken to reality. The U.S. Department of Justice has a Civil Rights Division whose responsibilities are to uphold and protect the civil rights as articulated in the Constitution and laws of the United States. Obviously, they have corrupted their role, misused their power, to cover up for epidemic corruption within the government of the United States.

Federal judges have a sworn duty to uphold the laws and Constitution of the United States. Their actions, as described in these pages, are clearly to destroy these protections. If they can do this to me, they can do it to you, and they are doing it to many other people. They get away with it because of the orchestrated coverup and disinformation of the establishment media. There isn't much time left, for the American public to wake up and rebel against this judicial and Justice Department tyranny.

MAN WITHOUT A COUNTRY

In the fictional story written by Edward Everett Hale, *The Man Without A County*, the fictional Philip Nolan was stripped of his constitutional rights and protections. An army colonel, acting as a military court, sentenced him to banishment from the United States, imprisoning him for life on a naval ves-

---

[123] *Rodney F. Stich v. State of California*, C-93-0027- MISC-VRW.

sel.[124] The suspension of my civil and constitutional rights—in the effort to silence me—was perhaps even worse than that suffered by Nolan.

I lost every relevant right and protection under the laws and Constitution of the United States, and of the state of California. I was viciously persecuted by those paid and entrusted to uphold the law. I was stripped of my life's assets, my ability to earn income—and my ability to expose the sordid government-funded misconduct that played a key role in many air tragedies.

After each violation of my protected rights occurred I exercised the remedies provided by law, seeking relief. Each time I did, federal judges dismissed my actions without a hearing or trial, in gross violations of constitutional due process and equal protection, and in gross violations of specific statutory and case law. Every time I sought relief from destruction of my personal and property rights arising from some violation of law, federal judges called me a frivolous and vexatious litigant for objecting to the outrages committed by the litany of attorneys from the Justice Department, and federal judges. Thereafter the previous frivolous and vexatious decisions were used to dismiss subsequent actions.

---

[124] The fictional Philip Nolan, an army officer, was tried with numerous other officers for cooperating with the unauthorized military exploits of military commander Aaron Burr. Before sentencing, each officer was asked to make a statement. Nolan, tired of the military life and dirty politics, stated: "Damn the United States! I wish I may never hear of the United States again." The military officer acting as judge (fictional Colonel Morgan) ordered Nolan placed on a U.S. Navy ship, never to see or set foot on the United States again, or to hear the words, "United States." Constitutional freedoms and protections were ignored during this fictional novel. The officers in charge of him during fifty years knew him as "the man without a country."

CHAPTER ELEVEN

VARIOUS FEDERAL ACTIONS

I was judicially gridlocked. But I felt that I had to make a judicial record by filing federal actions against those from whom federal law gave me a cause of action. I also filed the actions on the basis that federal filings are examined by the media, and in this way there was a chance that exposure of the criminal activities could result from the filings.

Federal law provides that any person in the United States can file a federal lawsuit seeking declaratory judgment to establish his personal and property rights under federal law, and under the federal Constitution. Federal law provides that a person can file a lawsuit seeking injunctive relief to halt actions taken under color of state or federal law that violate federally-protected rights. Federal law provides that lawsuits can be filed seeking damages against others who violated these federally-protected rights.[125] To avoid being guilty of a federal crime, federal criminal law requires a person to report federal offenses to a federal court.

Every action I filed contained many serious federal causes of action involving violations of rights protected under the Constitution and laws of the United States. Any one of these violated rights invoked mandatory federal court jurisdiction. But the judicial gridlock was everywhere.

IMAGINATIVE USE OF LAW

Realizing that I may never recover from the persecution, I sought to put on notice those who had responsibilities to prevent the criminal activities, including members of Congress who had a duty to act, and who, instead, engaged in various forms of criminal coverup and obstruction of justice.

---

[125] Federal statutes Title 28 U.S.C. Sections 1331, 1343, 2201, 2202; Title 18 U.S.C. Sections 1961 and 1962, the RICO Act; directly under the U.S. Constitution, including the First, Fifth and Fourteenth Amendments; as a *Biven's* claim; and Title 42 U.S.C. Sections 1983, 1985, 1986.

One federal statute that is little known but which has very clear language, is Title 28 U.S.C. Section 1343, which permits any person who has suffered harm due to violation of his civil rights to sue another person who knew about the violations and who could have prevented or assisted in their prevention and the related harm. Members of Congress, for instance, knew about the violations and the harms, and under the clear wording of the statute they were liable.

I filed two lawsuits against certain members of the U.S. Senate and House[126] on the basis of section 1343, and which I filed to draw attention to the corruption I sought to expose. The defendants knew of the violations of my civil and constitutional rights. They had a far greater responsibility than that of an ordinary citizen to prevent and report the criminal activities. Under federal law they incurred liability for themselves, and those who were federal employees incurred liability on the part of the federal government, under the Federal Tort Claims Act. Another purpose of the lawsuits was to put into a judicial record their responses to the charges I made against them.

THEY ADMITTED THEIR COVERUP

In response to the filing of these actions, the Senate legal counsel filed a motion to dismiss my complaint on February 27, 1989. The motion to dismiss *admitted* that the defendant senators and representatives knew of my allegations and knew of the consequences of the criminal acts I brought to their attention. Under federal pleading practice, any allegation in the complaint that is not denied is deemed admitted as true.[127] The defendants admitted the truth of the charges in my complaint concerning government corruption and that they had knowledge of my charges.

These members of Congress based their defense on one issue: that regardless of any wrong they may have committed, they were immune from the consequences of their acts under the Speech or Debate Clause of the United States Constitution. Put this response in perspective. Visualize an air disaster scene and the corruption that led to a series of airline crashes; that these members of Congress knew about the criminal acts making the crashes possible; that they had a duty to act and refused to do so, making possible other crashes.

Their only defense was that they are immune from the consequences. The same set of conditions exist with every pattern of criminality stated within these pages. Members of Congress knew about the ongoing criminal and

---

[126] In U.S. District Court in District of Columbia: No. 89-0170 SS. *Stich v. [Senators] Edward Kennedy, Strom Thurmond, Ernest Hollings, Albert Gore, Pete Wilson; [Representatives] Joseph Biden, Jack Brooks, John Conyers, Peter Rodino, Harley Staggers, and Henry Gonzalez;* In District Court at Reno: *Stich v. U.S. Senator Alan Cranston from California, and U.S. Representatives George Miller, Fortney Stark, Norman Mineta, Don Edwards, and Daniel Lundgren,* No. 89-85. February 10, 1989. U.S. District Court at Reno, Nevada, under the provisions of Title 28 U.S.C. Sections 1331, and 1343, and Title 42 U.S.C. Sections 1983, 1985, 1986.

[127] Federal Rule of Civil Procedure 8(d):

    (d) **Effect of Failure to Deny.** Averments in a pleading to which a responsive pleading is required, other than those as to the amount of damages, are admitted when not denied in the responsive pleading. Averments in a pleading to which no responsive pleading is required or permitted shall be taken as denied or avoided.

treasonous acts from my petitions to them and from other sources. They knew the harm suffered by many people from the ongoing corruption. Their only defense, as stated in their legal brief, was that they were immune from the consequences of their refusal to perform a duty.

The mentality of these members of Congress, many of whom are attorneys, is comparable to the self-protective case law rendered by Supreme court and other federal judges who hold themselves immune from the consequences of their acts, regardless of how criminal, unconstitutional and outrageous that they may be. These are the mentalities that permit inflicting upon the public the outrages described in these pages, and much worse is yet to come.

IMPLICATIONS OF CONGRESSIONAL POSITION

The response of the senators and congressmen had serious implications. No longer could these members of the Senate and House argue they did not know of my allegations of the corruption that I brought to their attention and for which I sought to produce testimony and evidence. All they could now argue was that regardless of their inactions—which made possible the consequences of the criminal activities I made known to them—they could not be sued. They filed a motion to dismiss, which I of course opposed.

I opposed the motion to dismiss by stating case law showing that the immunity of the Speech or Debate Clause only applied to actions taken on the floor of the Senate and House relating to passage or non-passage of legislation. I recited case law[128] that held the clause did not protect illegal or unconstitutional conduct. I also argued law prohibiting dismissal of lawsuits that state federal causes of action, and that the allegations in the complaint must be accepted as true for the purpose of determining whether federal causes of action were stated in the complaint.

UNPRECEDENTED SECRECY

In addition to seeking dismissal of the action that I filed, the defendant senators and representatives requested that the judge **remove all evidence from the court records that the lawsuit was ever filed.** The intent of this motion was to prevent the American public from learning about the complaint and about their response.

This request was unprecedented, and also barred by law. The court filings were public records, protected by the public's right to know. Their destruction would violate federal law. Further, federal law, including Rule of Civil Procedure 60, permits a party to file a motion, years later, to reinstate an action. This right, however, becomes valueless if the record is destroyed.

Even though I raised federal causes of action which under federal rules of court, case law, statutory law, constitutional due process, prevented dismissal, U.S. District Judge Stanley Sporkin rendered an order on May 8, 1989, granting the motion to dismiss, and to destroy all evidence of the filing:

On consideration of the motion of defendants to dismiss plaintiff's amended complaint, the entire record, and this court's opinion in this

---

[128] *Miller v. Transamerican Press,* 709 F.2d 524 (9th Cir. 1983); *Kilbourn v. Thompson,* 103 U.S. 168, 204 (1881); *Eastland v. United States Servicemen's Fund* 421 U.S. 491, 502. (1975).

case, it is ORDERED that the defendants' motion be and hereby is granted and the amended complaint is dismissed with prejudice.

I immediately filed a Notice of Appeal of that order. (Appeal No. 89-00170.) The senators and representatives then filed a motion with the Court of Appeals requesting that my appeal be dismissed without allowing me to present appeal briefs. The Court of Appeals judges promptly came to their rescue, and granted the request. The decision stated in part:

United States Court of Appeals
For the District of Columbia

No. 89-5163

Rodney F. Stich
Appellant
v.
Edward Kennedy, et al.,
Appellees

On Appeal From the United States District Court
For the District of Columbia

Motion of Senate Appellees For Summary Affirmance

The six senators named as defendants in this action, Edward M. Kennedy, Strom Thurmond, Ernest F. Hollings, Albert Gore, Jr., Pete Wilson, and Joseph R. Biden, Jr., move for summary affirmance of the district court's order of May 8, 1989 (Tab A), dismissing the amended complaint in this case with prejudice. ...

Plaintiff alleges that the Congressional defendants[129] "have responsibilities and the power to prevent and aid in the prevention, of violations of these rights and privileges ...." Id., par 6, at 3. He states that he "notified members of the Senate and the House of the constitutional violations, and submitted petitions under the First Amendment and other safeguards for relief." Id., § 27, at 12. He asserts that "defendants misused their positions of trust and power, refusing to provide the relief to prevent the violation of rights and privileges suffered by plaintiff," id., par 34, at 14, and that the defendants

---

[129] In addition to the six Senate defendants, plaintiff named as defendants in this action five present or former Members of the House of Representatives: Jack Brooks, John Conyers, Jr., Peter W. Rodino, Jr., Harley Staggers, Jr., and Henry B. Gonzalez.

"actually joined the conspiracy by remaining silent, " id., par 36, at 14.[130]

In a Memorandum Opinion filed on March 29, 1989, (Tab B), the district court dismissed plaintiff's complaint with prejudice. The court first held that the suit was barred by the Speech or Debate Clause, Article I, section 6, clause 1, of the Constitution, because "[t]he acts and omissions complained of by the plaintiff clearly fall within the legitimate legislative sphere protected by the Speech or Debate Clause. " Memorandum Opinion at 3. The court also held that the action failed to state a claim under the First Amendment upon which relief can be granted under Fed.R.Civ.P. 12(b)(6), because "[w]hile the plaintiff's right to petition Congress is guaranteed by the First Amendment, a member of Congress is not required to 'listen or respond to individuals' communications on public issues.' Minnesota State Board for Community Colleges v. Knight, 465 U.S. 271, 285 (1984). " Memorandum Opinion at 3.

****

Judge Stanley Sporkin was one of the judges on the Court of Appeals who rendered that decision. He was formerly general counsel to the Central Intelligence Agency, and directly involved in several of the criminal activities described in later pages.

ADDRESSING THE MEDIA COVERUP

I used the same federal statutes and case law to address the coverup of the corruption by the media. I reported the pattern of corruption to key segments of the media since 1965, including the *Wall Street Journal*, the *Washington Post*, the *New York Times*, and others. They had the ability, and the responsibility, to make these serious charges known to the public.

That action was filed in the United States District Court at San Jose, California,[131] naming these newspapers as defendants, along with the *San Francisco Chronicle*, which became implicated at a later date. The filing of this lawsuit made a judicial record of the charges. This lawsuit was assigned to Judge Robert Aguilar.

Shortly thereafter, Justice Department prosecutors charged Aguilar with using his office as a racketeering enterprise to obstruct justice, on the basis of minor and far-fetched allegations. The specific acts that Aguilar allegedly committed were mild compared to the criminal acts committed by Justice Department personnel as described in these pages. Aguilar had made the mistake of opposing and rendering decisions unfavorable to Justice Department prosecutors in a number of cases.

Many people felt that the Justice Department prosecutors were retaliating against Aguilar because of his opposition, and that Justice Department prosecutors wanted to send a warning to other judges who might become uncooperative.

My lawsuit that included charges of Justice Department misconduct was then removed from Aguilar and assigned to another judge.

---

[130] Plaintiff has also filed a substantially identical action in the District of Nevada against Senator Alan Cranston and several other present or former Members of the House. A motion to dismiss that complaint is currently pending. *Stich v. Cranston, et al.*, CV-N-89-85-ECR.

[131] Number C 89 20262 WAI.

The *Wall Street Journal* and its managing editor, Norman Pearlstein, filed a reply (June 15, 1989), requesting that the federal complaint be dismissed. They responded, as did members of Congress, that they knew of the charges; they did not dispute the relationship between the misconduct and the consequences; but that they were immune from liability, based upon the First Amendment to the United States Constitution. They argued that they did not have to print what any person requested them to print. But I wasn't requesting the news media to print what I wanted printed. I expected them to exercise their responsibilities under federal law to report in whatever fashion they wanted the evidence of government corruption that I brought to their attention. They had a responsibility under federal law[132] to aid in the prevention of the corruption that was brought to their attention. Even though the lawsuit against them was newsworthy, and raised issues of national concern, none of the media printed a single word about it.

The *Wall Street Journal* implied in their response that they should be allowed cover up for corruption, and not be liable to anyone. They implied that the First Amendment freedoms given to the press, which were based upon them reporting government corruption, should make them immune from the action. But misprision of felonies, especially of the serious corruption mentioned in these pages, applies to the media as much as to private citizens, if not more so.

The responsibility of the media under the First Amendment was articulated in a Supreme Court decision relating to the Pentagon Papers and the publication of their contents in the *New York Times*. Supreme Court Justice Hugo Black stated:

> *Only a free and unrestrained press can effectively expose deception in government. And paramount among the responsibilities of a free press is the **duty to prevent any part of the government from deceiving the people** ... The New York Times, the Washington Post and other newspapers should be commended for serving the purpose that the Founding Fathers saw so clearly. In revealing the workings of government ... the newspapers did precisely that which the founders hoped and trusted they would do.*

The district judge dismissed my complaint, without a hearing, and despite the fact it stated numerous federal causes of action. I didn't appeal the complaint as I accomplished the primary goal of making a judicial record of the media's complicity and their responses.

CULPABILITY OF SUPREME COURT JUSTICES

The same laws that made members of Congress and the media liable and culpable under federal statutes applied even more so to the Justices of the United States Supreme Court. The Justices had covered up the pattern of criminal behavior by federal judges, the Chapter 11 judges, and private trustees such as embezzler Charles Duck, all of whom were officers of the

---

[132] They also have a responsibility under Title 28 U.S.C. § 1343 to aid in the prevention of civil right violations that come to their attention. With their ability and responsibility to report federal offenses, they could have aided in the violations of my civil rights, by publishing information on the offenses.

court over whom the Justices had supervisory responsibilities.[133] Like a police chief protecting rampant criminal behavior of their police officers committed against citizens, the Supreme Court Justices protected the criminal behavior of those over whom they had responsibilities. Because of their positions of trust, the Justices were more guilty of criminal acts for such crimes as misprision of felonies, coverup, accessory after the fact, conspiracy, obstruction of justice, and others.

Since the Supreme Court justices had the responsibility to prevent the commission of these corrupt acts by judges over whom they had supervisory responsibilities, they were liable. I filed a lawsuit against them[134] in the U.S. District Court in the District of Columbia.[135] They were, of course, employees of the U.S. government, acting under color of federal law, so I also named the government of the United States as a defendant. This was probably the first time in history that Supreme Court Justices were sued for civil, constitutional, and RICO violations. The arguments raised in the complaint were based on solid facts and law. But it was bizarre that a person was forced to resort to suing the Justices of the nation's highest court to report federal crimes and seek relief from judicial violations of federally protected rights.

The truthfulness of the serious allegations made in the complaint could be easily verified by the media. Every major news service monitors the filing of complaints in federal courts. But again, the media kept the lid on this unusual filing and the gravity of the charges made in the complaint.

REFUSING TO RESPOND

Federal law provides for service by certified mail. If the defendants don't respond by returning the acknowledgement of service form, personal service is then required, and the defendants must pay for such personal service. Despite their position as Supreme Court Justices, they refused to return the acknowledgement of service. I then had the Supreme Court justices personally served (June 17, 1989).

I filed a 28-page amended complaint on March 14, 1989, which stated in part:

This suit addresses the wrongful acts and omissions by the defendants, relating to (a) an ongoing, air safety/air disaster scandal, and related air tragedies; (b) upon which has been superimposed a government and judicial scandal of coverup; (c) government and judicial scheme misusing government powers to destroy plaintiff's freedoms, liberties, property rights, privacy, in an effort to halt his exposure activities.

Defendants knew of these wrongdoings, and participated in them. The defendants also had the power to prevent them and refused to do so, aiding and abetting those committing the violations. Defendants

---

[133] Rule 17.1(a) of the U.S. Supreme Court. Responsibility to intervene exists when a lower court "has so far departed from the accepted and usual course of judicial proceedings, or so far sanctioned such a departure by a lower court, as to call for an exercise of this Court's power of supervision."

[134] William Rehnquist; Antonin Scalia; Sandra O'Connor; Anthony Kennedy; Thurgood Marshall; William Brennan; John Stevens; Byron White; Henry Blackmun.

[135] Filed February 17, 1989, No. 89-0470 SS; amended complaint filed March 14, 1989.

knew that plaintiff would suffer great and irreparable harm from massive violations of rights and privileges under the laws and constitution of the United States and of the State of California; and knew that by such refusal to act, the misconduct causing and permitting the prior loss of life in fraud-related air tragedies would continue, with continuing loss of life. The defendants willingly sacrificed the lives that were lost, protecting their own vested interests, their own coverup, and the guilty parties involved in what has become the world's worst air-safety air-disaster scandal, upon which has been superimposed the nation's worst government and judicial scandal.

Defendants are liable to plaintiff as a result of their wrongful acts. (Title 28 U.S.C. § 1343 and 42 U.S.C. § 1986.) Self-proclaimed qualified judicial immunity does not deprive a citizen of the United States of the rights and privileges under the laws and Constitution of these United States, including the right to redress of the harms suffered from judicial misconduct. The federal government has incurred a liability from defendants' wrongful acts.

It is argued that the many persons who perished, and who suffered in airline tragedies caused and made possible by the misconduct of federal officials, have a cause of action against defendants, and against the federal government.

The specifics in subsequent pages of the complaint related to knowledge by the Justices of the government corruption; the repeated violations of civil and constitutional rights in the sham California action; the coverup of the civil and constitutional violations by Ninth Circuit judges; the false imprisonment for exercising constitutionally protected rights; the Chapter 11 racketeering activities; the seizure of my multi-million dollar assets without any hearing, without cause, and under corrupt conditions, that reflected the corrupt mentality in Ninth Circuit courts.

Justice Department attorneys filed a motion to dismiss my complaint (August 17, 1989), admitting that the Justices knew of my allegations and that they failed to act. Their response did not deny the truthfulness of the charges or the resulting harm, and under federal law my charges must then be accepted as true. The primary defense raised in the motion was that the Justices of the U.S. Supreme Court "enjoy absolute immunity from plaintiff's claims."

The motion to dismiss was riddled with false statements of fact and law, and trivial matters. The Justices argued that the complaint should be dismissed because "Rule 8 (a) ... requires that a complaint be a short and plain statement." After arguing that the complaint was too long (there is no page limit in federal complaints), the justices then argued that the allegations were not specific enough! The justices argued that the complaint did not "state facts with particularity in his complaint that demonstrate who did what to whom and why." The complaint stated very clearly what the Supreme Court justices had done. A complaint does not have to *prove* the allegations, but make reference to them so the defendants know the nature of the alleged wrongful acts.

The justices argued that the complaint stated "unbelievable allegations." The charges were certainly unusual, but not unusual to anyone who knows of the covert activities of the Justice Department, the CIA, and everyday shenanigans occurring within the legal process. Under federal law, the allegations made in a complaint must be recognized as true for the purpose of preventing dismissal of the action.

Many of the facts stated in the complaint were supported by taking judicial notice of legal proceedings in the California courts, in federal courts, in Chapter 11 proceedings, and further supported by my voluminous evidence.

The justices sought to have the action dismissed by making reference to the California action, referring to it as a matrimonial action. The very fact that I was in the seventh year of a so-called matrimonial action, when five divorce judgments showed me as divorced for the past twenty-four years, raised serious federal causes of action. The California action was riddled with a pattern of civil and constitutional violations that were major federal causes of action, raising federal court jurisdiction. On the pretext of that sham divorce action my life's assets, used to expose government corruption, were seized.

The justices argued that the statute of limitations prevented lawsuits against them, but never stated how the *ongoing* wrongful acts could have imposed a statute of limitations defense.

The justices then argued that the allegations were already adjudicated and dismissed by other federal courts. Not one of the federal actions had ever been heard on the merits, and never once did I have my day in court. Nothing had ever been adjudicated. Further, the justices were never named in any lawsuit, so obviously the matters could not have been adjudicated. The Supreme Court justices argued:

The nine justices of the Supreme Court are entitled to absolute judicial immunity from plaintiff's claims. A judge will not be deprived of immunity because the action he took was ... done maliciously, or was in excess of his authority.

The criminal statutes, such as misprision of a felony, Civil Rights statutes, do not state a judge is immune when he violates either civil and constitutional rights, or violates criminal statutes. The Supreme Court Justices knew of the pattern of federal offenses committed against me and against the United States, and refused to take any action to halt the criminal acts committed by federal judges and Justice Department attorneys over whom they had supervisory responsibilities.

Under a *Bivens* claim, the rights and protections of the Civil Rights Act relating to wrongful acts taken under color of state law extend to federal officials. The Constitution of the United States provides for redress of wrongdoings by government actors, and says nothing about judges being immune. The Justices were contradicting their own decision in *Pulliam v. Allen* 466 U.S. 522 (1984). The Supreme Court held:

[T]here is little support in the common law for a rule of judicial immunity that prevents injunctive relief against a judge. There is even less support for a conclusion that Congress intended to limit the injunctive relief available under § 1983 in a way that would prevent

federal injunctive relief against a state judge. In Pierson v. Ray, 386 US 547, 18 L Ed 2d 288, 87 S Ct 1213 (1967), the Court found no indication of affirmative Congressional intent to insulate judges from the reach of the remedy Congress provided in § 1983. [N]othing in the legislative history of § 1983 or in this Court's subsequent interpretations of that statute supports a conclusion that Congress intended to insulate judges from prospective collateral injunctive relief.

Congress enacted § 1983 and its predecessor, § 2 of the Civil Rights Act of 1866, 14 Stat 27, to provide an independent avenue for protection of federal constitutional rights. The remedy was considered necessary because "state courts were being used to harass and injure individuals, either because the state courts were powerless to stop deprivations or were in league with those who were bent upon abrogation of federally protected rights." Mitchum v Foster, 407 US 225, 240, ... every member of Congress who spoke to the issue assumed that judges would be liable under § 1983).

Subsequent interpretations of the Civil Rights Acts by this Court acknowledge Congress' intent to reach unconstitutional actions by all state actors, including judges. ... Judicial immunity is no bar to the award of attorney's fees under 42 U.S.C. § 1988.

A primary importance of the lawsuit against the Justices of the United States Supreme Court was that it put them firmly on notice of the serious corruption perpetrated by federal officials, including federal judges, federal trustees, Justice Department attorneys, all of whom look to them for guidance.

District of Columbia Judge Stanley Sporkin came to the Justices' rescue. He rendered a *sua sponte* dismissal (January 17, 1990). Again, he violated federal law barring dismissal of a lawsuit that stated federal causes of action.

HOLDING THEMSELVES IMMUNE
FROM LEGAL LIABILITIES

All of the defendants (members of Congress, news media, Justices of the U.S. Supreme Court) responded in similar fashion, admitting knowing of the charges, doing nothing about the charges, and claiming they were immune from the consequences. Their position was that they could engage in outright criminal acts of coverup, misprision of felonies, obstruction of justice, and be immune from the consequences!

While Ronald Reagan was president, I notified the office of the President of the misconduct described in these pages. No response. In 1988, while Vice President George Bush was campaigning for the presidency, he promised to get tough with criminals. I assumed he included those within government. After Bush became president, and continued to articulate his concern for government ethics and crime, I made him aware of the corruption committed by federal officials over whom he had responsibilities. I sent him a May 1989 certified letter and attachments describing the criminal acts within government, including the Justice Department and the federal judiciary. The White House responded by advising me that the matter was turned over to the Department of Justice, even though I charged the Justice Department with committing many of the criminal acts. So much for that.

Bush and I were both Naval aviators during World War II. We both got our Navy wings at the same time. We both flew in the Pacific theater of operations. He flew single-engine TBF aircraft, while I flew four-engine patrol planes (Privateers and Liberators). Even though his piloting experience was very limited and long outdated, Bush surely recognized the consequences of air safety violations, even though sophisticated air safety matters were not part of single-engine, primarily visual flight rules operations.

When Bush became a junior senator from Texas in the United States Senate, he led a group of junior senators purportedly pushing for ethics in the Congress. The *National Observer* stated of Bush:

A little-noted event that took place on the floor of the House of Repre-
sentatives early last week, two days before the House voted to bar
Adam Clayton Powell from his seat in the 90th Congress. ... With the
House chamber nearly empty, freshman Republicans spent an hour
philosophizing about Congressional ethics. The seminar of sorts had
been organized by a young congressman from Houston, George Bush,
43, ... The discussion was remarkable in that Mr. Bush had quietly
convinced his rookie colleagues of an almost revolutionary proposi-
tion. Although freshmen are traditionally expected to sit back unobtru-
sively while learning from their elders on matters of legislation and
procedure, he contended, the question of ethics is another matter
entirely.

"True, we lack experience in the House," he told his young col-
leagues, "but we bring to this problem a fresh look. We feel totally
uninhibited by tradition in this sensitive [Congressional ethics] area,
because we think we heard the unmistakable clear voice of the people
saying on Nov. 8, 'Go there and do something to restore respect for
the House.'" Their proposal is so starry-eyed in its idealism that it
looks as if it could have come out of a political-science class on good
government. ... Mr. Powell's [denial of his House seat and] fate was
decided by an Ivy League Texan and a freshman philosophy class.

Bush seems to have forgotten his professed idealism, or else it was a farce. Later pages will show Bush involved with the CIA in major scandals of enormous consequences to the United States. If these offenses are true, it is obvious why Bush did not respond to my reports of corruption that were related to the corruption in which he was involved.

These bizarre and convoluted scandals took me into uncharted waters. My imaginative use of the law was proper, but it was bizarre that the conditions existed that made the unorthodox lawsuits necessary. The fact that the media kept the lid on each of them is another indication of how the media censor the news to protect some of the worst scandals in the United States.

CHAPTER TWELVE

HUD

My persistence and determination to bring some semblance of justice to government, especially the sordid legal and judicial fraternities, caused me to discover patterns of criminality in other areas that enlarged upon what I had already discovered while a federal and private investigator. The preceding pages were an introduction to racketeering activities involving corrupt government personnel misusing offices of the United States for criminal activities against the American people.

My knowledge of these criminal activities arose from a combination of personal discoveries while a federal and private investigator, administrative and judicial records, and being a victim. Commencing in 1990 I became a confidant to almost a dozen former deep-cover CIA and DEA people, former FBI and state law-enforcement personnel, and other insiders, who wanted to blow the whistle on the criminal activities involving federal officials that they observed or in which they participated. These discoveries indicate a systematic plan to defraud the American people that took substantial root in the 1970s, and then escalated in the 1980s and 1990s. The following pages enlarge upon what you have already read.

A scheme that defrauded the American public of many billions of dollars had its roots in the Department of Housing and Urban Development (HUD). This scheme involved influence-peddling and self-dealing by government officials, bribes by corporations, over-billing, political payoffs, fraud, favoritism, kickbacks, and work that was never performed. This area of criminality cost the American taxpayer many billions of dollars in the 1970s and 1980s. Former regulators were hired for their insider connections to obtain contracts that could otherwise not be obtained. The *Wall Street Journal* called the corruption a "system of spoils and favoritism." That was the HUD scandal. Much of the money that the public must pay in taxes can be traced, and probably taken back.

The HUD program was legislated to fund the rehabilitation of housing, especially for the elderly. Hundreds of millions of dollars, if not billions, were looted through the HUD program. In the 1980s, during the Reagan-Bush administrations, the fraud in the HUD program was epidemic, and is continuing to some extent today. The American taxpayers must pay billions of dollars to support the criminal activities in the HUD program that were well known to many government and non-government checks and balances.

A major segment of the HUD fraud was centered in the Denver area, and committed by a group of closely related people and companies, who had close ties to the Reagan and Bush administrations. Numerous HUD officials left government to work for the Denver group that defrauded the American people of billions of dollars, much of which is hidden away in either off-shore financial institutions or in secret locations throughout the United States. Philip Winn was one of the kingpins in the Denver group. He was a former HUD Assistant Secretary who joined the MDC group in Denver, and became a key player in the HUD and savings and loan scandals.

Numerous HUD officials left government service and received high paying jobs with an interrelated group in Denver. This group included, among others: MDC Holdings; Richmond Homes; Silverado Bank Savings & Loan; Aurora Bank; M & L Business Machines; Leonard Millman; Larry Mizel; David Mandarich (president of M.D.C. Holdings); Ken Good; Bill Walters; Neil Bush; Silverado's President Michael Wise; James Metz, major stockholder in Silverado; and dozens of subsidiaries and related companies, limited partnerships, trusts.

Federal regulators involved in the HUD scam included HUD Secretary Samuel Pierce, former Assistant Secretary Thomas Demery; Deborah Gore Dean and Lance Wilson, former executive assistants to Pierce. All except Pierce have been indicted. A number of former HUD officials pleaded guilty to various federal crimes. Dean, an executive assistant to the Reagan Administration's Housing Secretary, was indicted on 13 criminal charges of fraud, perjury, submitting false statements to Congress, and conspiring to steer valuable housing grants to favored developers and consultants.

The group made huge financial contributions to various politicians, including the Reagan-Bush team and the Bill Clinton group. One of the key participants in the fraud, Philip Winn, used part of the money looted from the HUD and savings and loan programs to bribe politicians, especially in the Reagan-Bush presidencies. In return, Winn was appointed U.S. Ambassador to Switzerland, and got the protection of the Justice Department through U.S. Attorney Michael Norton, who had secret participation in several of the Denver area real estate projects.

Justice Department officials, with their thousands of investigators throughout the United States, knew of the corruption, and did very little. What little they did was usually to prosecute either innocent people or those who played a minor role in the massive criminality. Attorneys, developers, banks, members of the Senate and House were the recipients of the money defrauded from HUD. Consultants, for instance, with political connections, reaped huge fees of as much as $400,000 for a few phone calls or visits to

HUD officials, or phone calls to powerful members of Congress.

Rampant political favoritism and influence-peddling were part of the HUD scandal, combined with payment of millions of dollars for improvements that were never made. Former HUD personnel acted in collusion with present HUD officials in the fraudulent activities. One of the schemes was buying HUD properties for no-money-down, placing second loans on them for improvements that were never made, and then defaulting on the loans while receiving the rental income.

In 1982 the HUD inspector general made a report to Congress that insiders, including former HUD officials, were defrauding HUD of hundreds of millions of dollars, especially in the Section-Eight program, and particularly sections 224D, 223F, and 202 elderly housing. Congress did not act until six years later when media publicity forced Congress to conduct an investigation. In 1988 Arlen Adams was appointed Special Prosecutor for HUD, and during subsequent investigations confirmed that developers with the aid of present and former HUD officials, were receiving Section 8 rehabilitation units, grossly overcharging the government, and often billing for work that was never accomplished. Simultaneously, the group bilking the government was contributing heavily to the Reagan-Bush team.

In March 1989 HUD hearings were triggered by exposure of huge financial donations by the Winn Group and Richmond Homes in Denver. A key director was Philip Winn, whose heavy financial payments to the Reagan-Bush team paid for an ambassador appointment to Switzerland. It was learned that Leonard Millman, Larry Mizel, and Philip Winn, all members of the ADL, were partners in these schemes. Philip Winn, President Ronald Reagan's appointment to fill the post of Ambassador to Switzerland, and Philip Abrams, former HUD under-secretaries, were part of the scheme.

TURNING PROSECUTION OVER TO THE BAD GUYS

In November 1989 Congress asked U.S. Attorney General Richard Thornburgh to recommend to the Court of Appeals in Washington the appointment of a Special Prosecutor, stalling until March 1990, when Congressional pressure forced him to act. Thornburgh had already blocked the appointment of a Special Prosecutor into Inslaw, October Surprise, and eventually BCCI and BNL. U.S. Attorney Generals Edwin Meese, Richard Thornburgh, and Richard Barr, knew about each of the criminal activities described within these pages, and either aided and abetted them directly, or indirectly, by blocking investigation and prosecution. A corollary to that would be the Mafia controlling the highest law enforcement agency in the United States.

STATUTE OF LIMITATIONS

One of the reasons for stalling prosecution was to allow the statute of limitations to expire, protecting the widespread criminality in the Denver area HUD and savings and loan corruption, and in turn protecting the part played by the Justice Department, the CIA, and many federal and White House officials.

In another investigation a report was issued by the Committee on government Operations, stating that "The Winn Group did not obtain units from HUD on merit alone, but rather from inside favoritism at HUD."

Private investigator Stewart Webb reported that he found that the Winn and MDC group owned over 10,000 units in Colorado, Utah, Nevada, Oklahoma, South Dakota, North Dakota, and another 10,000 units in the area controlled by the Texas regional office of HUD.

Webb and IRS agent Walker in the Denver office frequently exchanged information that they found in the HUD criminality. In June 1991 Walker said to Webb that he could no longer talk to him about the matter, and when Webb asked, "Is [President] Bush covering this thing up," Walker replied, "yes," and then hung up.

Webb stated that his investigation showed that U.S. Attorney Michael Norton was connected to Larry Mizel, a major player in the Denver-area HUD and savings and loan corruption, and that Mizel was Finance Chairman for Norton's unsuccessful Congressional campaign.

Without success, Webb tried to have a Colorado District Attorney in Denver and the U.S. Attorney in Colorado receive his evidence, but they refused.

U.S. Attorney Michael Norton had earlier received hundreds of thousands of dollars in financial contributions running for a U.S. Senate seat from the group he was now supposedly investigating. Although the voters did not send him to Congress, the Reagan-Bush team appointed Norton U.S. Attorney, which served to protect White House and other federal officials from investigation and prosecution in the HUD corruption.

POLITICAL PAYOFFS

Key figures in the Denver-based HUD and savings and loan group were Winn and Mizel, who contributed heavily to California Congressman's Tom Lantos' Congressional race in 1982. (I had repeatedly reported the corruption that I found to Congressman Lantos, and he never once responded; is it any wonder!)

PART OF THE TAXPAYER LIABILITIES

Congressional staff investigators discovered thousands of apartments were obtained by the group for rehabilitation, costing the American taxpayer over $100,000 each, when the cost for comparable privately financed units would be approximately $20,000. Congressional investigators discovered that U.S. Attorney Michael Norton owned five large apartment complexes with the Winn Group being investigated.

It was discovered that former FBI Special Agent in charge, Bob Pence, who retired in 1992, had been receiving bribes, along with U.S. Attorney Michael Norton and the head of the Internal Revenue Service's CID unit. Some of these bribes were laundered through the M&L Business Machine Company in Denver.

HOTBED OF CORRUPTION

CIA whistleblowers and other insiders described to me how a group of Denver area businessmen, with close ties to the CIA and criminal elements, defrauded the United States of billions of dollars in HUD program.

This Denver group reportedly paid huge bribes to members of Congress, and hired former HUD officials to carry out the schemes that defrauded the federal government. Also involved in looting of HUD money were covert CIA operatives and corporations, funneling hundreds of millions of dollars unlawfully obtained from HUD projects into offshore financial institutions.

USUAL COVERUPS

When the scandal exposed California Congressman Tony Coelho and Texas Congressman Jim Wright, they took early retirement to defuse the pending investigations. The media and the public did not address the huge losses inflicted upon the American taxpayer. Instead, after key Congressmen such as Wright of Texas and Cohelo of California were forced to resign to halt further investigation, their constituents showed little concern about the criminality and huge financial losses to be paid by the American taxpayer; their concern was the loss of a powerful Congressman who produced pork barrel benefits for their constituents. Little was said of the huge multi-billion dollar debt inflicted upon the public. If it had been left to the constituents of Congressmen Jim Wright or Coelho, the enormous financial losses would be ignored as long as the voters received benefits from their corrupt Congressmen.

California Representative Tom Lantos (D-Cal.) led a Congressional investigation into the HUD matter, calling it

Influence-peddling of the tawdriest kind. The scandal at HUD is one of the most complex national scandals that we have seen in decades. There is a degree of mismanagement, fraud, abuse, waste, influence-peddling that we have just barely begun to touch.

Representative Charles Schumer, a subcommittee member, said: "Like picking up a large stone only to discover that bugs and slime have grown in the darkness. This investigation has exposed the corruption which flourished unchecked under Secretary Pierce's HUD."

In addition to causing Wright and Coelho to resign (with liberal retirement benefits), Congress tried to stonewall an investigation into HUD by blocking confirmation of HUD appointees expressing an intent to expose the HUD scandal. After Jack Kemp took over HUD and stated his intent to prosecute those involved, Congress blocked confirmation of Kemp's management team. When the Department of Justice started an investigation into HUD, members of Congress then investigated the Justice Department, threatening to cut back its funding. The Justice Department investigation stopped.

Referring to Congressman Wright's blocking of an investigation into HUD corruption, a *Wall Street Journal* editorial (April 17, 1989) stated:

What is most disturbing ... is the obvious pattern of so many violations extending over so many years. ... the brazenness is amazing. Obviously, Mr. Wright felt assured there was no prospect that he ever would be called to account for his actions. ... When Congress is so powerful it can intimidate the Justice Department from another Abscam case, who should be surprised at corruption?

SHADES OF THE SAVINGS AND LOAN DEBACLE

Investigations showed that House speaker Jim Wright obstructed investigation of the HUD corruption while accepting $145,000 in unreported gifts. The House Committee investigating Wright's dealings with the HUD scandal quickly dropped the investigation after some House members reminded them that an investigation would implicate many other members of Congress. After pressuring Jim Wright to resign on the relatively minor charge of ethics violations, the media attention to the HUD scandal ended. The guilty parties went free; the missing billions of dollars of looted money was never found; and the stage was set for more looting of the American taxpayer.

JUSTICE DEPARTMENT STONEWALLING

The House Judiciary Committee requested (November 2, 1989) that the Department of Justice appoint an independent prosecutor to investigate the HUD scandal. Attorney General Richard Thornburgh refused to do so, just as the Attorney General refused to request an independent prosecutor to investigate the criminal activities by federal officials in other scandals yet to be described. To have done so would have implicated White House officials who appointed the Attorney General. Thornburgh accused the committee of introducing partisan politics into the HUD investigations. Representative Charles Schumer of New York replied at a news conference:

There's ample evidence of wrongdoing at HUD, but there's stonewalling at the top. And the only way to get to the bottom of the mess at HUD is through the appointment of an independent counsel. Instead of attacking us, the Attorney General should be focusing on making sure that high-ranking officials at HUD don't get away with breaking the law.

Representative Schumer characterized the attorney general's objections as a "political response." A more correct characterization would probably be felony coverup, obstruction of justice, misprision of felonies.

Another time-honored way that Congress (and the Justice Department) stonewalls sensitive investigations is to withhold funding needed to conduct the investigation. Congress threatens to withhold funding from the Justice Department to dissuade members of Congress from investigating sensitive matters. It was done by Justice Department officials to stonewall investigation of Chapter 11 judicial corruption. It was done to halt further FBI investigations of Congressional wrongdoings in Abscam. As the FBI's continuing investigations into the conduct of Congressmen became too threatening, members of Congress responded by dragging Justice Department officials in for gruelling oversight hearings. It became clear to Justice Department officials that the budget for the Justice Department was in danger if the probes into Congressional wrongdoings did not cease.

CONGRESS FINALLY CONDUCTED
AN "INVESTIGATION"

Eventually, Congress was forced to conduct an "investigation." A House committee stated in a report that the Department of Housing and Urban Development was "enveloped by influence-peddling, favoritism, abuse, greed, fraud, embezzlement and theft."

Samuel Pierce, Secretary of HUD from 1981 to 1988, refused to cooperate in the HUD investigation, repeatedly invoking his Fifth Amendment privilege against self-incrimination. The House Committee report stated that Pierce gave misleading testimony, and that he probably "lied and committed perjury during his testimony on May 25, 1989."

APPOINTING AN INDEPENDENT PROSECUTOR

After Congress covered up the HUD scandal, an independent prosecutor was appointed, who then had to set up an office and hire attorneys to investigate, many of whom had no investigative experience.

The Independent Prosecutor found that HUD officials unlawfully directed federal funds to developers and consultants with whom they had private financial relations, receiving bribes, and other favors. Silvio J. DeBartolomeis, a former deputy Assistant Secretary of HUD, pleaded guilty to three criminal charges,[136] including conspiring to mislead Congress and HUD's own regional offices concerning a HUD rent subsidy program; to receiving an illegal salary supplement consisting of a $20,000 loan arranged by developer Phillip Winn. DeBartolomeis was charged with defrauding HUD's Section 8 rehabilitation program, which enriched the developers based in the Denver area.

INDICTING THE SMALL FRY

Media attention forced Justice Department prosecutors to file charges in the HUD corruption, years after the criminal acts were known. But the indictments were selective. The power brokers with whom U.S. Attorney Michael Norton was in partnership escaped prosecution, or were charged with minor offenses, and evidence was conveniently lost. Federal judges dismissed charges on some before the jury could begin deliberation.

The indictments omitted charging the Denver area developers who donated large sums of money to political figures, who had close ties with the CIA (and this is explained in later pages), and who contributed large financial contributions or bribes to White House officials and other politicians.

Among the HUD officials who were directly involved in the looting of HUD was HUD Deputy Assistant Secretary, DuBois Gilliam, who pleaded guilty (May 1989) to receiving over $100,000 in payoffs and gifts to approve HUD grants for various developers.

During the investigation it was disclosed that HUD Secretary Samuel Pierce received over 1,700 formal requests from Congressmen and senators requesting support for specific projects. These same members of Congress were receiving political contributions from those for whom they sought HUD favoritism.

Winn's political contributions to the Reagan-Bush team bought him appointment as U.S. Ambassador to Switzerland.[137] Winn also pleaded guilty to preparing a false receipt for another HUD official that was submitted to HUD investigators. But these charges were chicken-feed compared to what Winn and his buddies actually perpetrated. My inside informants stated that over $167 million paid by HUD to the Winn group for rehabilitating HUD housing was never spent for that purpose, and sequestered in secret locations.

---

[136] *Oakland Tribune,* October 15, 1992,

[137] Philip Winn was appointed ambassador to Switzerland in the late 1980s after contributing large amounts to the Reagan-Bush team.

A nine-count felony indictment was made against a former assistant to ex-Senator Edward Brooke[138] for allegedly lying to the FBI and a federal grand jury, who were looking into Brooke's role in the HUD influence-peddling scandal. Charges against Deborah Gore Dean included improperly steering funds to clients of former Attorney General John Mitchell after Mitchell was released from his Watergate prison term.

A federal jury in Washington, D.C., on October 26, 1993, convicted former HUD aide Deborah Dean, a central figure in the HUD scandal, of being instrumental in funneling millions of dollars to housing projects that enriched politically-connected Republicans.

Another power broker in Denver, Leonard Millman, and his group, were also key players in the looting of HUD (and the savings and loans). They also hid billions of their ill-gotten gains in secret financial instruments and locations.

GROUP OF HUD WHISTLEBLOWERS

I became a confidant to several former CIA operatives, private investigators, and insiders, who were heavily involved in the Denver-area operations, and through them discovered some of the inner workings of the corrupt operations. One of the investigators and insiders, Stewart Webb, was a former son-in-law of Leonard Millman. During four years of marriage from 1981 to 1985, Webb became privy to many of the procedures used to loot billions of dollars from the HUD and savings and loan programs in the Denver area.

Following the divorce, Webb expanded on what he had learned as an insider. Through aggressive investigations, Webb discovered the paper trail of the looted money, including thousands of documents he obtained in recorders' offices throughout the United States. Webb was able to document major schemes implicating the Denver group in various financial scandals. Webb discovered the trail to offshore bank accounts and trusts, and their secret locations.

Describing some of the key players in the schemes against HUD and the savings and loans operating out of the Denver area, Webb stated that among the top players were nationally known and politically connected powerhouses such as Carl Lindner, Larry Mizel, Philip Winn, Albert Rose, George Riter and many others. He described how many HUD officials left Washington and joined the Denver-based group, and how their prior Washington connections made the looting possible.

Additional data was given to me by other insiders, including high-ranking covert CIA personnel. Gunther Russbacher, for instance, operated numerous CIA proprietaries having secret dealings with the Denver group, including money laundering, looting of the HUD and savings and loan programs, and other activities. Hundreds of hours of questioning of different and unrelated informants confirmed the truth of what they stated.

Webb initially contacted me on September 17, 1991, advising me of what he stated were corrupt dealings in the HUD and savings and loan program by

---

[138] Brooke was a lawyer and consultant for businessmen seeking help with HUD on federally subsidized housing projects in the 1980s.

his former father-in-law and many of the people and groups that worked with him, including M.D.C. Holdings and dozens of limited partnerships, trusts, and subsidiaries. Webb told me about the large numbers of federal officials who were in the schemes.

Webb appeared as guest on numerous radio shows, some with investigative reporter Margie Sloan, describing what he discovered, naming the corporations, the complex paper trial, and the individuals involved. He discovered that U.S. Attorney in Denver, Michael Norton, was deeply implicated with the group, sharing secret ownership of valuable properties. Webb discovered that the corrupt Denver group gave large financial contributions to Norton when Norton ran for Congress in the early 1980s. This discovery helped explain one of the reasons why Justice Department officials never prosecuted the key figures in the HUD and savings and loan debacle.

JUSTICE DEPARTMENT SILENCING
OF ANOTHER WHISTLEBLOWER

These talk shows were causing concern in the Justice Department and the Denver area. Working with Webb's former father-in-law, U.S. Attorney Michael Norton charged Webb with making harassing and threatening phone calls to his former father-in-law, Leonard Millman. Although the language could have been cleaner, the threats were nothing more than a determination to expose the HUD and savings and loan corruption in which his former father-in-law was involved, which threatened to expose the U.S. Attorney's involvement in the criminal activities.

After Webb heard of the warrant for his arrest he went underground for the next year, surfacing only to appear as a guest on radio shows in Denver and throughout the United States. For some of the shows he called me collect, and I would then relay his call to the radio station. I had no knowledge of where Webb was, and didn't want to know.

In September 1992, shortly after Webb had talked to Ross Perot by phone and revealed his location in Houston, the FBI arrested Webb. Justice Department prosecutors demanded that Webb be denied release pending trial, an almost unheard of demand in a case involving harassing phone calls. Justice Department officials were trying to silence Webb and keep him off talk shows, especially before the 1992 presidential elections.

Webb was arrested, and the U.S. District Judge refused to release him pending trial. I advised Webb that he had the opportunity to get additional information on the HUD and savings and loan scandal by talking to other inmates at the federal prison who were former CIA operatives and insiders in the HUD and savings and loan scandal. It was and is standard practice of Justice Department officials to cause the imprisonment of these people to silence or discredit them. By entering prison a writer or investigator has an inside track to information that he would not otherwise get. Sure enough, Webb did discover numerous inmates who gave him additional information, helping to fill in the gaps. While detained in the Federal Correctional Institution at Littleton, near Denver, Webb made contact with a group of former CIA contract agents who were deeply involved with the Denver area

group.
OTHER KEY INFORMANTS
One of these contacts was a former high-level CIA operative named Trenton Parker, who played key roles in numerous covert CIA operations from 1964 until he fell out of grace in the late 1980s. Webb and Trenton shared a prison cell together in December 1992, until Parker was released pending trial, which was to start in April 1993. Parker had seen some of the material I had sent to Webb and contacted me after being released. This relationship produced extraordinarily secret and sensitive material and added to the mosaic establishing the complex intrigue and corruption described in these pages.

The confidential status report establishing Trenton's highly secret status in the intelligence community prevented Justice Department and CIA personnel from denying his high rank and status. Additionally, Parker gave me information including briefs that he filed in the U.S. District Court in Denver that depicted widespread criminal activities by the CIA against the United States. More about this in later pages.

Another insider who contacted me in February 1993 was one of the fall-guys in the HUD scandal, Don Austin. He gave me insider information on the role played by federal officials and the Denver group in looting the HUD program. Austin headed groups of investors buying HUD properties, and operated under the name of Nitusa.

Austin described to me how the Justice Department protected present and former HUD officials who were self-dealing in violation of federal law, and who were involved in massive fraud, especially in the Denver area. He described how people associated with the savings and loan industry, and who had done no wrong, were being prosecuted to make it appear to the public that the Justice Department was punishing those responsible for the huge HUD fraud.

Austin described how his assets were seized by Justice Department prosecutors under the forfeiture laws, depriving him of money to hire legal counsel to defend against the charges brought by the Justice Department. He described how his court-appointed attorney was incompetent in the complex area involved in the charges. Austin described how in desperation he discharged the attorney and appeared in pro se, representing himself, and was then overwhelmed by the top guns of the Justice Department.

Austin was a successful real estate investor who worked with the HUD Administration to rehabilitate and sell hundreds of HUD properties. Justice Department officials, under U.S. Attorney Michael Norton, charged Austin with federal offenses and obtained a twenty-one year prison sentence against him. While Norton was covering up for the multi-billion dollar looting of the HUD and savings and loan people with whom he had been financially involved in Denver, he charged Austin with falsifying HUD applications. The alleged falsification of HUD purchase and loan agreements consisted of minor technicalities, such as showing in the cash-down block the value of notes and deeds of trust. It was standard practice to do this, and then on an accompanying HUD form and title company closing documents the actual form of the down payment was shown.

On the form there was no other way to show the down payment other than as cash. Actually, cash is almost never given, as the standard practice is to give checks, money orders, other properties, or notes and deeds of trust, as down payment.

HUD officials and companies acting on their behalf approved the purchase applications submitted by Austin, knew the form of down payment being made, and approved the form of payment on behalf of HUD. But when it came time to prosecute HUD related corruption, U.S. Attorney Michael Norton protected the king-pins of the racketeering enterprise. He selected scapegoats, and Austin was one of them.

Justice Department attorneys wanted to indict Austin because former and present HUD officials, who had purchased many of the properties through Austin, had defaulted on almost all of the units after bleeding them dry. These HUD officials were involved with others implicated in huge HUD and savings and loan fraud. To indict those guilty of this fraud risked blowing the lid on the multi-billion-dollar racket that implicated people like Neil Bush, George Bush, powerful Denver area and Washington politicians and powerful money figures who routinely bribed the politicians.

Don Austin discovered there was a grant from HUD awarding Justice Department attorneys bonuses for the number of criminal counts filed against defendants, encouraging false charges to be filed. There was reportedly a financial grant specifically to target Austin and have him blamed for much of the HUD corruption, removing attention from present and former HUD officials and the kingpins in the Denver area HUD and savings and loan corruption.

ATTORNEY SABOTAGE

Austin related to me the practice of attorneys demanding huge sums of money up front to defend him. After receiving the money, they sabotaged his case. This scenario had been told to me countless times, and I experienced it myself many times. It appears to be standard practice by the attorneys, preying upon people who are unaware of these corrupt practices. Every CIA whistleblower whom I had contacted, including Gunther Russbacher, Ron Rewald, Michael Riconosciuto, the HUD whistleblower Stewart Webb, and others, encountered the same scenario. Every one of them had strong words describing the sordid conduct of the attorneys that they encountered.

Don Austin's sophisticated lady friend, Pat Class, described the ugly nature of the attorneys she encountered while trying to help Austin. She described the many instances she paid ten, twenty, and thirty thousand dollars to attorneys up front, who then never performed.

In telephone conversations and writings, Austin described the mechanics of what he had discovered in the HUD fraud. Austin operated a company called Nitsua, dealing in purchasing and reselling HUD properties. He described how he and others purchased and paid for HUD insurance, which was kept by the HUD representatives and not applied to their accounts. He described the self-dealing by HUD personnel, including Grady Maples, Regional Director for HUD, and by Gail Calhoon, head of the Denver HUD office. Maples had a major ownership interest in Falcon Development, which in turn acquired the properties that were subsequently looted.

Don Austin described how drug forfeiture and other forfeiture money was being distributed to federal judges and Justice Department prosecutors, something like the Chapter 11 operations. Even the U.S. Marshals were implicated as they were involved in the seizure of assets.

Austin described one of many transactions in which the Maples Group purchased an apartment complex, and then placed secondary financing on it through Greenwood Industrial Bank, owned by a close associate, Bob Hard, one of Maples partners. Rents were collected but no payments were made on the HUD and Greenwood loans.

Also indicted with Austin was James Grandgeorge, who reportedly had been wrongfully convicted but who had offered to pay U.S. Attorney Michael Norton money under the table to get his conviction or his sentence vacated. This plan went haywire after U.S. Attorney General Janet Reno fired Norton in April 1993.

PROTECTING THE OPERATION AND THE HIERARCHY

Following the pattern in other scandals involving federal officials, Justice Department prosecutors fabricated charges against innocent people such as Austin. In this way Justice Department attorneys shifted the blame from those involved in the corruption, including federal officials, former federal officials, and powerful financial figures who orchestrated devastating financial harms upon the American people. Several examples follow, as the information was given to me by people who came to me for help.

During Austin's trial, the Justice Department prosecutor withheld information about the HUD self-dealing, the failure of HUD officers to apply the mortgage insurance money paid by Austin and others, and many other wrongful acts. If the jury had heard this information it would have helped prove Austin's innocence.

Another person set up by Justice Department prosecutors was Paul Jenkins from Utah. Jenkins was one of the owners of six savings and loans in Texas who experienced problems with loans that went bad when the Texas economy slumped in the late 1980s. He arranged with U.S. Homes to purchase all the notes held by the savings and loans that had been taken over by the government at full face value, which would have kept anyone from losing money. But government personnel refused to allow this for several reasons. One, it would diminish the justification for seizing some of the savings and loans, and eliminate the criminal charges filed against some of the lower echelon people being prosecuted in the savings and loan debacle.

During the first trial, Jensen was cleared of the charges against him. Justice Department prosecutors then filed new charges. Jenkins paid over a half million dollars up front to a Texas attorney, Barefoot Sanders, only to have this attorney abandon him the next day, and keeping the money for himself. Justice Department attorneys seized Jensen's assets, leaving him without funds to hire competent legal counsel. He was convicted during the second trial of the federal charges and sentenced to many years in federal prison.

Jenkins joined the long line of people victimized by their attorneys. He paid $1 million up front to Texas attorney Racehorse Haines to represent and defend him against all charges that might be filed against him. During the second trial, Haines abandoned his client, causing Jenkins, without money, to rely upon a federal defender. These federal "defenders" have a history of protecting their cohorts in the Justice Department and on the federal bench.

An irony was that most of the victims of Justice Department and government corruption were nice, honest, sincere people. The biggest crooks were those in control of key government offices, including Justice Department attorneys, federal judges, CIA officials, and members of Congress, especially those who are attorneys.

POLITICAL CONTRIBUTIONS

Michael Norton was the recipient of considerable illegal political contributions, primarily when he ran unsuccessfully for Congress in 1982. The Denver group funded most of his campaign expenses, extorting money from suppliers and their employees, reimbursing them through fraudulent billings later paid by HUD in the rehabilitation program. When these political contributions were publicized, and prosecution commenced, Norton had to recuse himself as federal prosecutor. He covered his rear by appointing a special prosecutor, U.S. Attorney Marvin Collins, from Texas, for damage control. Federal judges cooperated in keeping the lid on the scandals and protecting key players from prosecution.

Those who paid the heaviest for political contributions were the contractors and suppliers to the Denver group, including MDC Holdings, Richmond Homes, and other subsidiaries, who were forced to make illegal political contributions to Michael Norton. The higher-ups, who demanded the contributions, were either not charged, or after being charged, the charges were either dropped or favorable plea bargains were made. The kingpins responsible for the illegal contributions, Leonard Millman, Larry Mizel, and others, went unpunished.

Ironically, Norton lost the election for which the political contributions were made. But the Denver group, heavy financial contributors to the Reagan-Bush team, got Norton appointed U.S. Attorney in Denver, insuring protection against criminal prosecution for the massive fraud in which they were all involved.

The group involved in the HUD scandal was also involved in the massive fraud involving the new Denver airport, the savings and loan fiasco, and much more. Each of these scandals involved the theft of billions of dollars, defrauding the American taxpayer of billions of dollars they will be paying well into the twenty-first century. In each of the criminal enterprises against the United States, in which Justice Department officials were involved, Justice Department officials criminally protected the guilty. Worse, they often caused innocent people to be imprisoned for years, protecting the guilty, which often included themselves.

CIA INVOLVEMENT

As is described in later pages, the CIA, using code names for various operations, had numerous financial companies that played key roles in looting of the HUD, savings and loan institutions. Different CIA divisions or directorates ran parallel operations, using code names for the HUD and savings and loan operations. These code names included Operation Cyclops, and Operation Gold Bug.

DENVER AIRPORT

My CIA contacts operating covert CIA corporations in the United States described the massive fraud involving the new Denver International Airport. They described the tactics involved in the promotion and development of the airport, including influence-peddling, pay-offs, phony billings, phony land-swaps, sham loans, and other forms of fraud. Denver Mayor Federico Pena reportedly received a large bribe for promoting the airport. He was reported by my CIA contacts as conspiring with the key players in the Denver-area HUD and savings and loan corruption, including James Metz (Silverado's Chairman); Michael Wise (Silverado's President); Charles Keating (who cooperated in phony land-swaps and sham loans); Bill Walters and Ken Good (who defaulted on tens of millions of dollars in loans obtained through the help of Neil Bush); Phil Winn (indicted for bribing HUD officials); Larry Mizel; Norman Brownstein (attorney for Mizel and the MDC crowd and Pena's law partner).

Brownstein allegedly helped hide hundreds of millions of dollars of money looted from various fraudulent schemes of this group, some of the money hidden in trusts filed in remote locations, described in later pages. Brownstein was described by Senator Ted Kennedy (D-MA) as "the Senate's 101st member." Brownstein sat on the board of MDC Holdings and represented companies run by some of the biggest crooks in the HUD and savings and loan areas.

PAYMENT OF BRIBE MONEY

Former CIA operative Trenton Parker told me what other CIA informants had told me, that former Denver Mayor Federico Pena, was paid $1.5 million by Leonard Millman to get voter approval for the new Denver Airport. Parker stated that Mayor Pena's office was bugged by the CIA Pegasus group, and that the audio tape shows Millman walking into Pena's office and stating: "Ok, here's the million and a half god-damn dollars; now we want the f......... airport to go through. Now, get off your butts and get this thing going."

As in every other known pattern of criminality involving federal officials, hard-core criminality related to the HUD scandals was ignored. For instance, investigator Stewart Webb discovered that thousands of remodeled units and homes owned by the government were secretly removed from government records by the group consisting of former HUD officials and then sold, making it very profitable for those involved.

CHAPTER THIRTEEN

SAVINGS AND LOANS

Congress and the Reagan Administration deregulated the savings and loan industry through the Garn-St Germain Act of 1982, which was signed into law by President Ronald Reagan on October 15, 1982. As he signed the far-reaching bill, Reagan announced that it was "the most important legislation for financial institutions in 50 years." He added: "I think we've hit the jackpot." If he meant the jackpot reference for the Mafia, the CIA, and a host of crooks, he was absolutely right. Even the famous bank robber, Willie Sutton, never envisioned such riches.

I had considerable real estate at that time, including motels, hotels, truck stops, golf courses, apartments, and land, and knew the financial frauds that would follow deregulation. It didn't take any great expertise to predict the consequences, and surely members of Congress and the industry recognized that fact, even sooner than I.

Developers, Mafia figures, and crooks started buying small savings and loans in out-of-the-way-places. In that manner they gained access to the Treasury of the United States, permitting them to engage in self-dealings, sham transactions, and massive fraud against the American taxpayer. Deregulation and the concurrent fraud were financially fabulous for many people, fueling massive growth in the real estate industry during the 1980s. The price tab was picked up by the public in the 1990s, and they would pay, for decades, well into the next century. The losses, much of which were outright theft, exceeded the cost of World War II. Never in the history of the United States had such a massive financial debacle occurred, making the American taxpayer the victim of the biggest scam in the nation's history.

The crooks acquiring savings and loans immediately gave themselves fabulous salaries and expense accounts. They made loans to themselves or corporations they owned or controlled, and had a fabulous lifestyle that couldn't possibly be supported by the income of the savings and loan they acquired.

Many sordid details of the savings and loan debacle have never been revealed by the mass media. Crooks, with the help of politicians, Justice Department officials and CIA renegades, stripped the American people of hundreds of billions of dollars. The American economy has been badly crippled by this theft, adversely affecting the same American people whose failure to speak out helped bring about their own financial problems.

WARNING FLAGS PRESAGING DEREGULATION

It was no secret to members of Congress what would happen if the savings and loans were deregulated. The consequences of relaxing safeguards were seen elsewhere. For instance, the danger of brokered deposits were evident when serious problems arose in California during the 1960s when these deposits were allowed to reach a high percentage of a financial institution's deposits, threatening its solvency. Sudden withdrawal of such large sums of money deposited as a block could easily make the institution insolvent. To correct this problem, regulators ordered a cap of five percent of an institution's total brokered deposits. This restriction remained from 1963 until the limits on brokered deposits were removed in 1982 by the Depository Institutions Deregulation Committee, chaired by Treasury Secretary Donald Regan. This change was enormously profitable to financial institutions dealing in such deposits, such as Regan's prior employer before joining the Reagan administration.

Brokered deposits consisted of blocks of $100,000 deposits from individual depositors, which was the limit for federal insurance guarantees.[139] By dealing in brokered deposits the bank was able to build its capital and engage in huge fraudulent schemes. The danger arose from the high interest rates and fees needed to acquire them, and these costs were greater than what could be earned by lending the money to safe real estate investments.

Just prior to voting for deregulating the savings and loans, the nation's worst bank failure occurred, caused by eliminating safeguards and permitting brokered deposits. The Oklahoma City financial institution, Penn Square Bank, failed in 1982, and brought giant Continental Illinois National Bank and Trust Company in Chicago to the brink of failure, as well as other lending institutions that had placed large sums of money into Penn Square Bank.

The American taxpayers had to bail out Continental Illinois to the tune of $4.5 billion (plus the interest that is still being paid on the payout). This amount was in addition to the payments made to the insured depositors at Penn Square. It was the largest federal bailout in the nation's history, and showed the dangers of deregulation and brokered deposits, and what could be expected with the subsequent signing of the deregulation act.

Penn Square offered the deposit brokers higher interest rates and substantial brokerage commissions for funds placed with the financial institution, causing brokers to place millions of dollars into the bank on any given day. But the rates and the fees that Penn Square had to pay for these deposits

---

[139] Over strong protests from people who knew what would happen, the federal deposit guarantee was raised from the previous $5,000.

required making loans on high-risk investments and in a Ponzi-scheme. Further, the continual losses due to high costs of the funds and the inadequacy of returns on these funds required a continuing infusion of money to continue the scheme.

Common sense, and the history of failures, made obvious what would happen, when Congress voted for deregulation. But many of those who voted for deregulating the savings and loans were recipients of large financial contributions (i.e., bribes).

With brokered deposits there was no money available to make normal home loans; the spread was too much between the rate that homeowners could pay and the rate the savings and loans had to pay for brokered deposits.

The primary problem of deregulation came when the lending institution engaged in self-dealing, land-flips, sham loans, and many other devices used to carry out the massive fraud. All this was obvious to anyone close to the industry, as were members of Congress. But the immediate financial benefits to those voting for deregulation, the law firms and public relations firms, easily took precedence over the harm inflicted upon the United States and the American people, and this attitude prevails throughout these pages.

EVERY COMMON-SENSE WARNING SIGN IGNORED

Some of the practices that could be expected to occur, and which did occur after deregulation, included:

1. Inflating the value of properties through land flips, whereby a parcel of land was "resold" numerous times, sometimes on the same day. Each time the new "buyer" paid a higher price. In that way, a borrower could indicate the land was worth far more than it actually was, and obtain a larger loan than the property was worth.

2. Making a loan to a controlled corporation, or a dummy corporation, far beyond the value of the property, then let the loan go into default and the property taken back.

3. Making a loan that was not intended to be repaid, to a controlled corporation. Then when the loan and interest payments are due, making a larger loan on the property to "pay off" the prior loan and accumulated interest, showing a sham profit. The loan would be shown as a performing loan on the books rather than a loan in default.

4. Swapping bad loans between cooperating financial institutions, and showing the loans as performing loans on the books.

5. Land flips. Selling land several times over in fraudulent sales, showing a continuing higher "purchase" price, and then obtaining a loan based upon the latest purchase price, which could be five or more times the actual market value. No payments would be made on the loan after receiving the loan proceeds, and the property was allowed to go into foreclosure. The borrower then walked away with the difference between the purchase price of the property and the loan proceeds. In many cases this constituted millions of dollars.

6. Spending lavishly on aircraft, vacation homes, trips, and other lavish life styles, and charging it to business expenses. An honestly operated business would not incur such charges when the business was operating in the

red..

7. Paying inordinately high salaries to themselves, and providing themselves with bonuses when bad non-performing loans are renewed or traded for other bad loans with cooperating institutions.

8. Making sham loans on greatly overvalued real estate owned or controlled by the lending institution, with borrowers never intending to repay the loans.

10. Hiring former federal regulators at exorbitant salaries for their influence-peddling abilities and knowledge, to circumvent regulatory protections.

11. Paying many millions of dollars in bribes to members of Congress to block actions by federal regulators, and block corrective legislation.

TYPICAL LAND FLIP

A typical example of the fraud associated with land flips was a track of property northeast of Denver where the new Denver airport was supposed to be located. The original parcel of land, called the Little Buckeroo Ranch, was purchased for $1 million, and then flipped over several times in dummy land sales, fraudulently showing its value as $5 million. The Denver group involved in this scam obtained a $5 million non-recourse loan on the property and then defaulted when it was discovered the airport would be built elsewhere. They made a $4 million profit on the deal. People involved in that one example were heavily involved in the HUD and savings and loan fraud in the Denver area, and had close ties to the Central Intelligence Agency.

FINANCING THE LOOTING

To generate the hundreds of millions of dollars to fund these scams, the parties operating savings and loans needed a steady supply of money, far more than could be expected from local depositors. The answer was in brokered deposits. Money brokers pooled $100,000 deposits from different sources and deposited the funds into whatever savings and loan offered the highest interest and paying the highest brokerage fee.

The deposited funds would either be used for high-risk loans, or, as was often the case, to fund sham transactions in which there was no intention to repay the loans. The loss of several hundred **billion** dollars that will be paid by the American taxpayer, plus interest that may double or triple that amount, required more than simply poor judgment. There was no risk to the con-artists, as the American taxpayers were insuring the money.

Brokers would often offer deposits to a savings and loan on condition that the institution make one or more loans on a given piece of real estate. The loan amount would often be made in excess of the value of the property used for security, or made without any security. The institution making the loan may or may not realize that the loan would never be repaid.

There were many variations of these scams. All could be foreseen, and all had occurred in isolated cases the decade before deregulation. Members of Congress and Reagan Administration officials, who pushed for deregulation, recognized these problems and what would surely happen throughout the industry when deregulation occurred.

THE EXPECTED COMMENCED IMMEDIATELY

The expected started happening immediately. Among the first was Vernon Savings and Loan in Texas, which failed in 1984, involving brokered deposits, land flips, inflated mortgages, and huge personal expenses billed to the financial institutions. Loans that would never have been made with the former safeguards were made to insiders and friends who scratched each other's backs as they made themselves rich.

Ed Gray was sworn in on May 1, 1983, to head the Federal Home Loan Bank Board (FHLBB), and promptly discovered the seriousness of the massive fraud. He tried correcting the problem by returning the restriction on brokered deposits to the previous five percent, thereby halting the primary problem. But those who used the brokered deposits descended upon Congress, handing out money insured by the American taxpayer. succeeding in blocking this change. Treasury Secretary Regan, whose former employer profited by the brokered deposits, and many others sought to discredit Gray as some sort of wacky.

Finally the discrediting campaign succeeded, and Gray was replaced by Danny Wall, an aide to Senator Jake Garn, Chairman of the Senate Banking Committee. Wall then obstructed corrective action to keep the massive fraud scheme in operation, while simultaneously keeping the money flowing to members of Congress that kept federal investigators at bay. Wall protected Lincoln Savings and Loan from the San Francisco regulatory board which had planned to shut down the corruption-plagued institution, removing Lincoln from the jurisdiction of the regulators who had uncovered the corruption.

In an unprecedented action, Wall transferred regulatory jurisdiction of Lincoln to Washington, and Lincoln continued its corrupt practices of looting assets of U.S. taxpayers and individual investors. One act was to offer bonds of bankrupted American Continental Corporation, Lincoln's parent corporation, to its depositors, falsely claiming they were government-protected. Thousands of elderly people with no other source of income lost their life's savings through this scheme, made possible by Washington and California politicians. These tactics also increased the immediate cost to the American taxpayer to approximately $2 billion, plus the triple or so amount that will be paid in interest before the debt is paid off, if it ever is.

Virtually everyone who played the game, looked the other way, or blocked corrective action, profited. Members of Congress, including the Keating-Five, received bribes for blocking corrective action by federal inspectors. The media received advertising dollars from large numbers of real estate developments built under a cloud of fraud. The crooks in the savings and loans and others acting with them , profited. Everyone involved knew the American taxpayer would foot the bills, and that they would remain indifferent, like cattle going up the ramp to slaughter.

Simultaneously, [140]Lincoln's President, Charles Keating, paid $839,000 of taxpayer's money to various election committees to reelect Cranston,[141] and hundreds of thousands more to the other senators known as the "Keating Five": Senators Alan Cranston (D-CA), senior member on the House Banking Committee; Dennis DeConcini (R-AZ); John McCain (R-AZ); John Glenn (D-OH); and Donald Riegle (D-MI). I had notified each of them of the criminal activities I discovered and demanded they receive testimony and evidence that my CIA and DEA whistleblowers and I were ready to present. They all refused my demand.

Members of Congress sought to continue the coverup to the end. In June 1989, Congress quietly rejected a request for $36.8 million to hire investigators to accelerate the investigation and prosecution of corrupt savings and loan officials.

In 1986 the Keating-Five senators applied pressure upon Washington regulators to halt government investigators from taking actions against Keating's Lincoln Savings and Loan (after the group received huge financial donations from Keating). This Congressional obstruction of the regulatory function of the U.S. government increased the costs to taxpayers for the Lincoln Savings and Loan debacle far in excess of *six hundred billion* dollars for the entire industry. The taxpayers also must pay for the bribes paid to politicians on the California and federal levels, and to the former government officials who became high salaried employees of Lincoln.

California's Senator Alan Cranston obstructed the actions of the regulators who sought to prevent others from losing money, including elderly and retired people who invested in the uninsured bonds issued by Keating's enterprises. This obstructive action interrupted the regulatory process, delaying the government takeover of Lincoln Savings and Loan, as it continued selling worthless, uninsured securities to the public.

Even Alan Greenspan, then a private consultant and later chairman of the Federal Reserve Board, sent a letter seeking to block corrective actions, falsely claiming Lincoln was in good financial shape and had good lending practices. This was preposterous. Lincoln's primary assets were grossly inflated desert land. Lincoln had a practice of lending money to closely related investors or their own real estate enterprises, often without any credit check and without collateral.

Eventually the losses were too great to ignore. A new agency was formed to clean up the mess, and the same parties who blocked prior corrective action wanted Wall installed as its head, fighting to retain the head of the regulatory agency who helped continue the escalating corruption. Senator Cranston and Representative Donald Riegle fought hard to have Danny Wall confirmed as head of the new agency without a confirmation hearing, avoiding senate

---

[140] Charlie Keating was chairman of American Continental Corporation, a major land developer in Arizona. American Continental acquired Lincoln Savings & Loan Association of Irvine, California. Keating became its chief executive officer. Lincoln was then used as a private bank for Keating's own investments, many of them highly questionable.

[141] *San Francisco Examiner*, October 8, 1989.

questioning of the debacle that unfolded while he held responsibility to take corrective actions.

Congress' response to the nation's greatest financial debacle consisted of carefully avoiding charging any of their members, including the Keating-Five, with any crimes. They wrung their hands trying to decide whether any of the senators who received huge amounts of money from the crooks, and who blocked corrective attempts by federal regulators, violated ethics. Using this standard on many people sent to federal prison for far less federal offenses would greatly reduce the prison population.

YOU RAT ON ME AND I'LL RAT ON YOU

Cranston had earlier warned the entire United States Senate that if the Ethics Committee moved to censure him for his role in the savings and loan scandal he would blow the whistle on the role played by other senators in the savings and loan matter. As the "investigating" committee considered whether to censor Cranston for ethics violations, Senator Jeff Bingaman disqualified himself, requiring appointment of another senator, which in turn required weeks for the replacement to review the evidence. Bingaman had disqualified himself after "suddenly" discovering, after three years, that a conflict of interest existed: his wife worked for a law firm that once represented two of Cranston's staff members whose legal bill had not been paid. That move took the heat off the ethics committee until media attention focused elsewhere.

Congress repeatedly refused to provide money to shut down the hemorrhaging savings and loans, which then permitted the looting to go on, as well as continuing the political contributions from the insolvent institutions. Congressman Gonzalez stated[142] that the White House and federal officials could simply have placed the looted and failed "institutions under government conservatorship." But Congressman Gonzalez complained to federal regulators in late 1992 that "Regulators can put failing institutions under government conservatorship now, with or without any new funding. This should save the taxpayers the costs of further depletion of the institutions' assets." The refusal to shut down the fraud-racked savings and loans escalated the losses.

USUAL COVERUPS

Investigators, trying to blow the whistle on rampant corruption, testified to the House Banking Committee in October 1989 that Washington officials repeatedly overruled or restricted their investigation of corruption-riddled Lincoln Savings and Loan (as they had done after I started exposing hard-core government corruption in the aviation field starting in the mid-1960s).

ADMITTING TO PAYING FOR INFLUENCE

Keating admitted giving over five million dollars in political contributions to influence members of the U.S. House and the Senate, and state politicians in California and Arizona. Cranston and the four other senators pressured regulators to back off from shutting down Lincoln Savings and Loan, inflicting even greater losses upon the American taxpayer.

---

[142] *Wall Street Journal*, October 26, 1992, letter to the editor by Congressman Gonzalez.

Keating wasn't hesitant about stating the effects he expected when he paid bribes to members of Congress, stating several times to the press:

One question, among many raised in recent weeks, had to do with whether my financial support in any way influenced several political figures to take up my cause. I want to say in the most forceful way I can; I certainly hope so.[143]

Despite the huge losses incurred by these practices, Keating paid himself and his family over $34 million in the three years before its demise, even though losses during this time were destroying the corporation.

Representative Henry Gonzalez of Texas initially protected the system by using his post as chairman of the House Banking Committee to obstruct an investigation into questionable banking practices in his home district. Gonzalez pushed an amendment to protect First National Bank of San Antonio and other financial subsidiaries from the regulatory actions of the Federal Deposit Insurance Corporation. But as the savings and loan scandal shot out from under the media blackout, Gonzalez, head of the House committee[144] with oversight responsibilities for the savings and loan industry under the Office of Thrift Supervision (OTS),[145] focused attention on the savings and loan problems.

"Honesty doesn't pay."

The *Dallas Morning News* reported a conversation by an anonymous Texas state legislator, who stated that he had to take bribes from the HUD and savings and loan crowd because he needed the money to maintain his life style on a legislator's salary. He reportedly stated: "It's hard to be pious because in all honesty I could use the money. Honesty doesn't pay."

My CIA contacts described a well-publicized area of the savings and loan corruption in Dallas apartment units along Interstate 30, running east to Lake Ray Hubbard. Hundreds of apartments were built for which there was no demand, no rentals, and no sales. Money was made through "land flips" and shoddy construction. Some apartment buildings were shown as completed even though the plumbing and other necessities had not been installed. Covert CIA proprietary operations were involved in this scheme that defrauded the American public.

CALIFORNIA INVOLVEMENT IN THE
GREATEST FINANCIAL DEBACLE EVER PERPETRATED

Corrupt California politics made the Lincoln debacle possible. The California General Services Department (and the California Department of Savings and Loans) obstructed the investigation of Lincoln's corrupt practices, rendering administrative decisions resulting in the loss of almost a quarter billion dollars in savings of the elderly.

---

[143] *New York Times* November 9, 1989.

[144] Gonzalez moved up to the chairmanship of the House Banking Committee in 1989 after his predecessor, Fernand St. Germain (Rhode Island) lost his re-election bid because of investigations into his cozy deals with Savings and Loan lobbyists.

[145] Successor agency to the Federal Home Loan Bank Board (FHLBB).

In California, Chapter 11[146] judicial corruption was especially acute. California was the state producing numerous attorneys and prosecutors that played a key role in some of the scandals described within these pages. The Justice Department's scheme to silence me used California attorneys, law firms, and state judges, augmented by California-based U.S. district court judges and justices. In this way they joined the conspiracy of criminality I sought to expose.

Many on the Reagan-Bush team were from California, including Earl Brian (of Inslaw fame), Edwin Meese (the U.S. Attorney involved in many of the scandals described within these pages), J. Lowell Jensen (part of the Inslaw scandal yet to be described), and Senator Alan Cranston.

Numerous California officials and friends of California Governor George Deukmejian, mostly attorneys, were heavily involved in these scandals. A Keating enterprise, TCS, made political contributions totaling $48,000 to Deukmejian's campaigns. Keating paid over $189,000 to Deukmejian, in addition to the nearly one million given to California Senator Cranston's interests. Over 23,000 California investors were seriously harmed, as they purchased $250 million in uninsured bonds (most investors thought they were government insured) after California regulators approved their sales, knowing the corporation was insolvent. Many of these elderly people lost their life savings and their sole means of financial support.

In November 1984, Lawrence Taggart—while a California Savings and Loan Commissioner—became a director of TCS, rendering official decisions allowing Lincoln to continue their fraudulent schemes, causing thousands of investors to lose their life savings. On December 7, 1984, three days before a crucial deadline that nobody was supposed to know about except highest-level federal regulators, Taggart gave Lincoln approval to move almost a billion dollars to its subsidiaries.

Records showed Taggart was already hired by TCS at that time. On January 1, 1985, Taggart left his California position, responsible for regulating savings and loans, to work full-time as TCS's highest salaried executive. Additionally, he was to receive half of the after-tax profits earned by the consulting department he headed, and other perks. Three weeks later, Lincoln bought $2.89 million worth of TCS common stock.[147]

Barbara Thomas, a former SEC commissioner, reportedly called the SEC to act as a character witness for Keating during its investigation. Gonzalez said his staff's investigation revealed that Ms. Thomas had received a $250,000 loan from Mr. Keating with unusual payback provisions, suggesting a *quid pro quo* arrangement.

Jack Atchison, of the auditing firm of Arthur Young & Company, was primarily responsible for auditing Lincoln Savings and Loan, and submitting the reports to the government. Atchison sent several letters to three senators

---

[146] Reference to Chapter 11 should be considered reference to other bankruptcy chapters, especially Chapter 13.

[147] TCS was losing $70,000 a month and was basically insolvent, paying $2.89 million for a 24 percent ownership of a company with less than $100,000 of solvency.

saying that Lincoln was a sound institution, and that federal regulators were harassing Lincoln executives. Atchison then left his employment with the accounting firm and went to work for Lincoln at a salary exceeding $900,000 a year. The salary far exceeded what the position justified. It was surely another of hundreds of *quid pro quo* agreements in exchange for the sham report showing Lincoln as being solvent and in good financial condition, when actually it was insolvent.

A California Department of Corporations lawyer-regulator issued a strong warning about uninsured bonds sold in Lincoln's offices. But California officials kept the warning quiet, making possible the sale of worthless bonds to thousands of California investors.

California Assemblyman Patrick Nolan received large financial contributions from Keating, after Nolan sponsored legislation removing investment restrictions on state-chartered institutions. California politics made possible the continuation of the scandals and the obstruction of justice. Starting in 1983, I notified Governor Deukmejian, California Attorney General Van De Camp, and numerous state legislators, of the involvement of state judges in seeking to silence my exposure of criminal activities. Instead of investigating the charges and taking corrective action, they protected the judges after I filed civil rights action against them in federal court.

California officials denied state examiners and legislative investigators access to records, stating there was high danger of asbestos contamination where the records were stored. Possibly twenty years residence in the building might constitute a danger, but certainly not ten minutes to pick up the files! The building owner denied there was any danger:[148] "They [the records] could have been picked up any time in the last 200 days. They knew there was no problem [of asbestos]."

Assemblywoman Delaine Eastin of the California House Banking Committee stated that subpoenas would be necessary in the Lincoln case to get the records from the California Department of Corporations and the California Department of Savings and Loans. Officials under Governor Deukmejian refused to turn over the records, knowing that they contained evidence of California politicians' involvement in the savings and loan scandal. California and Arizona committees conducted interim hearings dealing mostly in trivia, and in that way protecting California officials implicated in the savings and loan scandal.

Both U.S. senators from California, Alan Cranston and Pete Wilson, received money from Keating to block the actions by federal regulators. Wilson received over $75,000 from Keating and received large financial contributions within two months of his election to the U.S. Senate, holding the record for the amount of political contributions in 1990, according to the *San Francisco Chronicle* and *San Francisco Examiner*.

Part of the money paid to U.S. senators and representatives to protect the crooks came from the life's savings of many elderly, retired people after

---

[148] *San Francisco Chronicle* November 1, 1989.

California and federal officials blocked the closure of Lincoln Savings and Loan. Widows, retired persons, many of them elderly, testified before a House Banking Committee on November 14, 1989, that they lost their entire life's savings, blaming California Senator Alan Cranston, and other members of Congress, for their losses. Many, unaware they were uninsured, invested their life's savings in the over $300 million in junk bonds after Cranston and other members of Congress blocked the actions of government inspectors and regulators.

What should have been golden years for thousands of retirees, especially in California, turned into abject poverty, compliments of California regulators and members of Congress, who took bribes to prevent exposure and closure of the corrupt practices of Lincoln Savings and Loan, Keating, and others.

A FEW EXCEPTIONS

There were a few members of Congress who spoke out on the rampant criminality in the deregulated savings and loan scandal. Representative Jim Leach told a panel of journalists (May 1989), "You have the opportunity to hold your Legislative Branch accountable, and perhaps bring it down." Referring to the coverup by the government regulatory agency that permitted the corruption to continue, Leach stated: "This Bank Board did the opposite of making timely warnings. It tried to put people to sleep while a fire was raging."

Attorney Joseph Cotchett of Burlingame, California, representing many of the elderly who were swindled in the Lincoln bonds, described the obstructionist tactics by California officials: "And now we have reached the 1,000th coincidence in this case."

CAN THE MONEY BE RECOVERED?

Federal Deposit Insurance Corporation's Chairman, L. William Seidman, described the hopelessness of recovering the huge losses. He warned that the amount of money recovered from anyone found guilty of self-dealing and other insider abuses would be small. "The money is long gone, spent," Mr. Seidman said. "We cannot expect any substantial recovery from criminal abuse."

But it could be traced if they wanted to, as I found through CIA and other informants where many of the trusts were located. Whatever the actual immediate figure is, $250 to $500 billion, these figures exceed many times the total amount looted from publicized savings and loans.

My CIA and other contacts, who had key roles in the HUD and savings and loan scandals, and some yet to be exposed, helped move the money to secret offshore and domestic banks, trusts, limited partnerships and other financial vehicles. They told me where some of the funds could be located. In later pages some of these locations are identified.

HEAVY CIA INVOLVEMENT

Several well-documented books[149] have been written of the savings and loan debacle. One thing that most of them missed, which I would not have

---

[149] *Inside Job*, Stephen Pizzo, Paul Muolo & Mary Fricker; *Daisy Chain*, James O'Shea.

known except for becoming a confidant to several CIA operatives, was the major role played by the CIA in the looting of America's financial institutions. Among the CIA-related savings and loans listed in these books as being part of the looting, but not identified as CIA proprietaries, were Silverado Bank Savings & Loan (Denver); Aurora Bank (Denver); Indian Springs State Bank (Kansas City, Mo); Red Hill Savings and Loan and Hill Financial in Red Hill, Pennsylvania. These authors also failed to discover that many of the other savings and loans were often cutouts for the CIA. More about this in later pages.

SILVERADO BANK SAVINGS & LOAN

Much has been written about Denver's Silverado Bank Savings & Loan, and its most prominent director, Neil Bush, the son of George Bush. But much has remained secret about Silverado. One of the best-kept secrets was that Silverado was a covert CIA operation; that it funded many covert CIA assets; and that many of the huge financial losses were the direct result of CIA activities. It is ironical that Silverado, a CIA proprietary, had as one of its directors the son of former director of the CIA, George Bush. Because of heavy CIA involvement in Silverado, and for other reasons to be covered, Justice Department prosecutors protected the Silverado gang against meaningful prosecution.

Neil Bush played a key role in looting Silverado, receiving only a token reaction from government agencies that kept a lid on Silverado's criminal activities. The original $2 billion looted from Silverado may easily cost the taxpayer $6 billion by sometime in the twenty-first century if these debts are ever paid off. It required over two hundred sham loans of one million dollars each, not repaid, for these losses to occur. Neil Bush, like Oliver North, displayed a look of innocence when questioned about his role in this horrendous fraud.

Neil Bush, while in a position of trust on the board of directors, borrowed over $2 Million from Silverado, part of which went into a dry hole drilling for oil in an unlikely location. Most of the money went for his salary and personal expenses. He was not so stupid as not to realize the money would never be repaid if that hole did not produce oil. He drilled this hole where it was known there was no oil. But the drilling served as justification for paying himself a large salary and lots of perks, which the ever-benevolent American taxpayers now must pay well into the next century. Bush made no payments on the money he borrowed, and no charges were filed by the Justice Department beholden to his father, President George Bush. It paid to have Justice Department personnel in your back pocket.

Two borrowers from Silverado who were partners with Neil Bush, Ken Good and Bill Walters, got away with $130 million in loans from Silverado that were never repaid. Some of this money went to Michael Norton, who later protected them from prosecution when Norton became U.S. Attorney. The Mafia never had it so good.

When the lending institution failed, the taxpayers were stuck with the tab, plus associated costs, including interest on the money borrowed to finance this portion of the national debt. The borrowers in the sham transaction, who had good political connections, often purchased the property at pennies on the dollar from the government after the savings and loans were taken over. Before the taxpayer finishes paying, the cost will probably triple. The infamous Silverado Bank Savings & Loan in Denver was one of the key lending institutions involved in these types of scams.

MEDIA COVERUP

Investigative reporters for the establishment media in the United States knew, for years, about the financial debacle, but kept the lid on the scandal. To have removed the lid would have affected them financially, as major advertisers would have been affected financially. In Denver, for example, three newspapers received considerable income from the advertisements of the group heavily involved in the HUD and savings and loan fraud: *Rocky Mountain News*; *Denver Post*; and *Westword*.

TAXPAYERS'S BILL: OVER $600,000,000,000

The greatest financial debacle ever inflicted in the history of civilization is causing American taxpayers to be saddled with a debt that has been estimated as high as 600 *billion* dollars, an amount far exceeding America's cost of fighting World War II. Probably, this large indebtedness will never be paid off. The interest paid while paying off this indebtedness will take the total figure over the $1 trillion mark. And this is only the savings and loan fraud. Many other corrupt financial scams are pulled on the American public, including HUD, Chapter 11, and others described in these pages. This fraud, and the missing money which no one has sought, are what required the American people to pay huge tax increases, which will continue for decades, and result in severe economic and social harms.

WHERE WERE THE FBI, JUSTICE DEPARTMENT AND OTHER FEDERAL CHECKS AND BALANCES?

A good question would be: Where were the hundreds of FBI and Justice Department investigators during this massive fraud inflicted upon the American people? The criminal activities were too extensive for them not to know of their existence. With its many connections within the United States, one could also ask where the CIA was during all this? The fact is, they did know. Later pages will help to explain how these criminal enterprises are linked together, and how people in control of our checks and balances were implicated in them.

A California banking investigator, Richard Newsom, testified that he went to the FBI in July 1988, after he found evidence of serious criminal activities in the savings and loan industry. He testified that he had found that the parent company of Lincoln Savings and Loan funneled over $800,000 to Senator Alan Cranston, and that "the stuff was too hot." The FBI and Department of Justice refused to take any action on the reported corruption. As is shown throughout these pages, the Justice Department's gang of attorneys, including their FBI Division, are most noted among insiders as being heavily involved in hard-core obstruction of justice when federal officials are implicated.

JUSTICE DEPARTMENT PROTECTION OF KINGPINS AND WRIST SLAPPING OF THEIR UNDERLINGS

James Metz, listed as a majority owner of Silverado Savings & Loan, pled guilty (October 16, 1992) to taking $100,000 of savings and loan funds for personal use, and received a six-month sentence in a half-way house. This sentence permitted him to work as president of Richmond Homes and be home during the day, requiring only that he sleeps at the location at Colfax and Fillmore Streets in Denver. This token judgment ignored the two billion dollars looted with his help from Silverado. My CIA contacts stated Metz was one of many CIA assets in the Denver area.

David Mandarich was indicted for illegal contributions, of which Michael Norton, U.S. Attorney in Denver, was the major recipient. Since Norton was the primary recipient of the money, he had to "stand aside" and have Marvin Collins, U.S. Attorney from Texas, act as special prosecutor (directed by Norton) to prosecute the case. Mandarich took the fall for the many other big names, but was protected by U.S. Attorney Collins, who deliberately presented a weak case to the jury. U.S. District Judge Richard Matsch then assisted in the coverup by dismissing the charges.

Justice Department prosecutors waited until the statute of limitations had run out for charging Neil Bush and others of the Denver gang before filing nominal charges against Silverado's James Metz and Michael Wise. Corruption and coverup in the Denver area was orchestrated by U.S. Attorney Michael Norton and Assistant U.S. Attorney Gregory Graff in Denver. Investigation of key players would have implicated the CIA and risked exposing White House and other politicians involved in the savings and loan crimes (among others yet to be described).

COMING DOWN HARD ON SCAPEGOATS

Many of those charged and prosecuted by Justice Department attorneys in the savings and loan fraud were outside directors of savings and loans, in honorary positions, with no knowledge of, or control in the institution's activities. By seeking to put these people in prison, Justice Department prosecutors were protecting the kingpins that continued to inflict great financial harm upon the American public. By indicting these people, the prosecutors mislead the public into thinking that Justice was being done.

THE FRAUD DIDN'T STOP

The fraud by the Denver group inflicted billions of dollars in direct losses upon the American people. But it didn't end there. The same Denver group and others, who brought about the collapse of the savings and loan industry by their corrupt activities, used their Washington influence to buy back properties and other assets from Resolution Trust Corporation at ten and twenty cents on the dollar. They made money bringing down the savings and loans, and made money buying the assets back, with the help of the same Washington gang. MDC bought from the RTC $750 million in loans that they had obtained from Silverado, for $150 million, making a $600 million profit, defrauding Silverado out of $600 million. This was not mentioned in the "investigation" of that savings and loan.

CENTRAL INTELLIGENCE AGENCY INVOLVEMENT

An article in *Penthouse*[150] described the CIA involvement in fleecing financial institutions. Entitled: *The Banks and the CIA, Cash and Carry*, it carried the subtitle, "How Agency rogues fleeced financial institutions to help create one of the greatest scandals in U.S. History." The article, describing the looting of banks and savings and loans by companies fronting for the Central Intelligence Agency, stated in part:

> *Agency rogues fleeced financial institutions to help create one of the greatest scandals in U.S. history. ... freelance C.I.A. operatives—in the course of carrying out covert operations, fleeced America's financial institutions. ... The C.I.A., it was claimed, sanctioned ... pulling money out of federally insured financial institutions to fund covert activities, particularly arms deals.*

The article described how Congress had shut off funding needed by the CIA for its covert operations, and how the CIA underground smuggled drugs into the country and looted banks and savings and loans. It further described how the CIA covert operations went underground when President Jimmy Carter ordered disbanding of its covert operations in the late 1970s. The article described how President Reagan's 1981 inauguration reinvigorated the covert CIA operations. Denied funds by Congress, the covert CIA network carried out unlawful and clandestine activities throughout the United States and overseas. These activities violated the CIA charter and were criminal acts.

The *Houston Post* started a series of articles in 1991 revealing connections between the CIA, organized crime, and the savings and loan scandal. Investigative reporter Pete Brewton left the *Houston Post* after pressure was put upon him to withhold key facts. In October 1992 his book was published: *The Mafia, the CIA, and George Bush–The Untold Story of America's Greatest Financial Debacle.*

My investigative activities brought me into contact with deep-cover intelligence agency personnel who revealed to me the part played by the CIA in looting the savings and loans, and other financial institutions. In the following pages this relationship is explored.

SECRET CRIMES BY THE CIA AGAINST AMERICA

As described in detail in subsequent pages, I became a confidant to nearly a dozen deep-cover CIA whistleblowers, commencing in 1990. One of these was Gunther Russbacher, whose father was a former German intelligence officer during World War II. Russbacher held many sensitive positions within the covert segment of the Central Intelligence Agency, and was involved in deep cover operations. More is said about Russbacher in later pages, but reference is made to him and some of the CIA activities that he described to me in detail over a four year period.

Russbacher's key covert position within the CIA took him far beyond the limited knowledge many CIA personnel have of CIA operations. The Agency tries to limit knowledge of overall operations by compartmentalizing

---

[150] September 1989.

operations and limiting the knowledge that any one participant has of the overall game plan. But Russbacher's high position within the Agency made him privy to a vast number of secret CIA operations.

Russbacher revealed to me the role played by the CIA in the savings and loan and HUD scandals. He had been with the CIA for over two decades, and had been trained by the CIA to operate covert financial operations under various CIA programs, including Operation Cyclops. As he developed knowledge and expertise, the CIA had him organize and operate many CIA proprietary financial institutions.

Russbacher, and later other CIA informants, gave me innermost CIA secrets of how the CIA looted America's financial institutions, how the money was laundered, the criminal elements with whom the CIA acted, and where some of the money ended up. These CIA operatives stated how the operations worked, and the names of some of the covert CIA financial institutions, fronts, and cutouts. They gave me blank checks, letterheads, copies of corporate filings, and other writings supporting these statements.

For the next few years I conducted hundreds of hours of questioning with Russbacher and other CIA and insider contacts, receiving details of the most secret CIA operations in which he participated during the last three decades. He gave sworn statements during the three years before the first publication of this book. His credibility as a CIA operative was checked and cross-checked with other CIA informants, and most, if not all of what he stated, I believe to be true.

Some banks and savings and loans became fronts for CIA covert operations and often made phony loans, phony appraisals, and phony sales, generating enormous sums of money for clandestine CIA activities.

Russbacher stated to me that the CIA had given him over forty aliases. During the first two years of his affiliation he was a contract employee of the CIA. Then, in 1965, he entered the United States Navy, assigned to the Office of Naval Intelligence (ONI). During all but three years of his CIA affiliation, he was in Covert Operations, Consular Operations, and other branches of covert government service. He did two tours of duty in Vietnam and Laos and was an unofficial prisoner during the second tour of duty in Southeast Asia. The U.S. government didn't list its covert personnel.[151]

In a December 6, 1992 sworn declaration, Russbacher described to me part of the CIA operations in which he was involved:

It is my intent to clarify, once and for all, how the Intelligence Services of the United States of America, have used the savings and loan (Thrift Institutions) to fund their respective covert operations, both within the United States, and abroad. The scheme creating an unlimited money supply was devised after the inside knowledge of how the Federal Reserve operated became known to operatives and case officers.

---

[151] His military numbers included 54 329 963; and his various Social Security numbers included 440-40-1417, 471-50-1578, 441-44-1417, and 447-42-0007.

A monetary growth medium had to be found which would enable the Agency (CIA) to have access to an unlimited supply of funds with which covert operations might be funded. The key was ... "How to utilize/capitalize on the Federal Credit Programs." Careful analysis and study of the Federal Credit Act provided the proper forum.

It was decided that small to medium businesses of the Proprietary Operations Unit would be well on line to provide these expert services. Soon, various businesses, owned and operated by either the Agency or utilizing a front directorship, began to deposit funds (legal tender and bogus bearer bonds) into the selected Thrifts. The loading of these institutions was always accomplished with the help of inside information, gained and acquired by and through information garnered by the FSLIC and their respective service members.

It was decided that various front organizations would deposit millions of dollars into these selected thrifts, and that such deposits would permit the depositors to make collateral loans for eight-five percent (85%) of the deposit value. The disparity of deposit and secured loan was the carrot for the ailing financial institution. The Agency, through its Proprietary Operations Division, was quick to recognize the Fed. Lending to Deposit Rate for Thrifts, which in turn stated that every dollar taken in on deposit would permit the Thrift to borrow up to seven dollars from the Federal Reserve. It was a lucrative enticement to Agency Operations. The loaned funds were soon gathered from all regional affiliates, and channeled to fund the Charters for our own Thrift institutions. The stage was set. It was merely a question of time until we began re-investing our portfolio.

Over a period of approximately 3 years, more than 35 federally insured "Agency Thrifts" were brought on line. Each of the financial institutions was funded in part by Certificates of Deposit (from our own front companies), and various other instruments of financial obligation. Sometimes, bogus (duplicate) Bearer Bonds were used to insure sufficient start-up capital. Slowly, these institutions began making large loans to other Agency front businesses. Many of them flourished regardless of the initial intent to strip them systematically of their assets. Those which failed to provide an unending "money funnel" were soon brought to Court, pursuant to Chapter 11, of the United States Bankruptcy Laws. Prior to permitting entry into such proceedings all visual assets were stripped and/or removed from the insolvent companies.

The United States Bankruptcy Courts, as well as the assigned United States Trustees, would permit us to re-channel the obvious assets prior to satisfying the demands of the legal creditors. It must be stated that in the initial stages of such operations there were no legal creditors as the entire operation was an "in-house operation," and subsequently not issues or obligations traded on the open market. Such practices were soon discarded as the volume of the operation was not able to keep out private and corporate investors. Many of the removed assets were sold to other agency operations, which in turn sold said assets to other linked dealers.

Brokerage companies of dubious repute were soon spin-offs of the mega industry. In order to provide continuity as well as expert disclosure, I shall reference the history of the funding of Hill Financial, as well as Red Hill Savings and Loan; the establishment of the National Brokerage Companies; the creation of National Financial Services Corporation; National Leasing Corporation; National Realty Corporation; Crystal Shores Development Corporation; Crystal Shores Financial Corporation, and Clayton Financial Planning Corporation. It is imperative that the continuity and creation are uninterrupted.

During my time of service within the Proprietary Operations Division of the Central Intelligence Agency, I was approached while using the assigned name of Robert Andrew Walker to initiate contact with a nationally prominent brokerage house. (It must be noted that I had been a part of such brokerage facility under another alias/code name.) I followed the order and began a transfer study, which in turn was to initiate and facilitate the founding of a new savings and loan facility in Red Hill, Pennsylvania. All transfer studies were accurate and the new S&L was soon brought on line. It was funded with corporate paper, other private and corporate bonds/certificates, and other financial obligations.

The founding fathers of Hill Financial were Donald Lutz and Robert A. Walker, a/k/a/ Gunther Karl Russbacher. The financial package of the S&L was born from funds derived from SBF Corporation. The new S&L flourished, making numerous loans to the economically depressed local and regional area. These notes were in part non-secured, and no payoff was anticipated from these local trades. We began to diversify, using the Federal Credit Act to gain and secure additional federal funds, by securing other deposits from Agency Operations. Our deposit portfolio was extended on a ratio of 4.3 to 1 and thereby provided considerable additional loan coverage to other more open and more lucrative markets. We began to explore bringing on line additional feeder organizations which could/would add to our real deposit base. The decision for such action was taken after I received orders to charter a brokerage company in the state of Missouri. We, the directors of Red Hill S&L held a closed meeting, wherein it was decided that I would become Chairman of the Board, and elevating Donald Lutz to the presidency. Pledging my continued assistance, I was permitted, nay ordered, to set up shop in St. Louis, Missouri, where I dropped the name Robert A. Walker, and became Emery J. Peden.

Within three months I was a registered broker of the Prudential Insurance Company of America. Soon after learning the business, I resigned my position and began a long term relationship with Connecticut Mutual Life Insurance Company. I had an office in

Clayton, Missouri, and soon made a significant impact on the financial and insurance industry.
END OF SEGMENT ONE (1) of the deposition of Gunther K. Russbacher.
I do certify the information contained in this segment of my deposition to be true and correct. Such certification is given under the penalty of perjury. Further, affiant/deponent sayeth not.

Gunther Karl Russbacher, deponent in cause.

Dated: December 6, 1992.

Russbacher incorporated and operated a number of covert CIA proprietaries in the United States from the late 1970s to 1986. His main headquarters was in Missouri, but his CIA proprietaries had offices throughout the United States, with heavy involvement in Dallas and Denver, where much of the HUD and savings and loan looting took place.

Russbacher identified as CIA proprietaries or assets numerous savings and loans, including Aurora Bank in the Denver area, Silverado Bank Savings & Loan, Red Hill Savings and Loan, Hill Financial, Indian Springs State Bank, and many others. He described the flow of money from, for instance, Silverado Bank Savings & Loan to start up Hill Financial and Red Hill Savings and Loan. Much of the data that he and other deep-cover CIA operatives gave me still have to be analyzed.

Russbacher made reference to CIA contract agents he encountered, including Heinrich Rupp and Richard Brenneke who worked with the CIA at Aurora Bank in Denver and elsewhere, and Anthony Russo at Indian Springs State Bank in Kansas City.

Russbacher described the links between CIA proprietaries and organized crime, and how the CIA worked with the group in Denver, looting the HUD program and savings and loans of billions of dollars. He described the corrupt practices of groups in the Denver area, such as MDC Holdings, Richmond Homes, Mizel Development, and their nearly one hundred subsidiaries, partnerships and other legal entities.

Describing his role in two of the savings and loans, Russbacher stated: "I held the position of Chairman of the Board [Of Red Hill Savings & Loan and Hill Financial]. Let's back up here, and erase that last thing. Robert Andrew Walker[152] held the position of Chairman of the Board.Russbacher used the CIA-provided-alias of Walker for those positions."

Russbacher described the massive corruption associated with the new Denver International Airport, including bribes, land flips, and sham loans. Promoting the Denver Airport, and allegedly receiving a bribe of over a million dollars, was Federico Pena, whom President Bill Clinton appointed to be Secretary of the Department of Transportation in 1993.

---

[152] One of the aliases provided to Gunther Russbacher by the CIA.

TYPICAL CIA PROPRIETARY OPERATION

An example of how the CIA operated secret companies in the United States is seen from the companies that Russbacher operated for the CIA. Similar to many CIA proprietaries, Russbacher incorporated and operated many CIA proprietaries, with the ownership hidden through stock ownership by CIA-related personnel. At the top of the group of companies that Russbacher operated for the CIA was National Brokerage Companies, a general partnership located in Missouri. Under National Brokerage Companies were a number of other general partnerships and corporations. The stock in these corporations was held in several names, including Gunther Russbacher and his CIA-provided aliases, Emery Peden and Robert A. Walker. The various companies and corporations were controlled by covert CIA personnel installed as directors. In 1986 the NBC name was changed to National Brokerage Companies International (NBCI).

A general flow chart of some of the CIA companies operated by Russbacher went along the following lines: the parent company was National Brokerage Companies International. Its initial funding for NBC came from Silverado Bank Savings & Loan in Denver, via Red Hill Savings and Loan and Hill Financial in Red Hill, Pennsylvania, all CIA proprietaries. Under the parent company of National Brokerage Companies were the following companies and corporations:

* NBC, Inc., a Missouri Corporation, incorporated in Missouri in 1980. (Most of the stock was owned by Russbacher under various aliases).

* Crystal Shores Development.

* Crystal Shores Financial Services, under Crystal Shores Development.

* Under Crystal Shores Financial Services were two groups, including Crystal Shores Financial.

* Under MGM were several European holdings, including Shalimar Perfumes, Shalimar Arms, and Shalimar Chemical Laboratories.

* Under Shalimar Armaments was R & B Weapons Systems International, Incorporated.

* Under R & B were two companies: Pratislaja Brenneke Munitions Amalgam, and R.B. Weapons Delivery Systems.

ANOTHER LINE OF COMPANIES

Another line of companies owned by National Brokerage Companies included:

* Clayton Financial Planning, which had several divisions. One of these was Agean Lines, Europa Link, under which it owned W.P.R. Petroleum International, which used leased oil tankers for delivery of oil to major refineries.

* A division under Clayton Financial Planning was Commercial Federal Savings and Loan, which had connections to National Fiduciary Trust Companies, Inc.

* A division under Clayton Financial Planning was Corondolet Savings and Loan, which also had financial connections to National Fiduciary Trust Companies, Inc.

NATIONAL FINANCIAL SERVICES

Directly under National Brokerage Companies was National Financial Services, Inc.

* National Leasing and National Fiduciary Trust Companies were divisions or holdings of National Financial Services.

* National Realty, Incorporated, was under National Leasing, Inc.

* National Fiduciary Trust Companies, Inc., was a division of National Financial Services, Inc.

UNDER NATIONAL FIDUCIARY TRUST COMPANIES, INC.

* Badner Bank.

* International Commerce Bank Holding Company.

* Under Badner Bank were various airlines, including Zantop Airlines; Tower Airlines; Southern Air Transport; Apollo Air; Virgin Air; RAW World Service.

* Under International Commerce Bank Holding Company the following companies were owned: Baja Enterprises; property at Cabo San Lucas; Hotel Cabo San Lucas; and Cabo Airport.

Russbacher described the practice of the CIA having their own banks as proprietaries, and named, among others, Commerce Bank of Missouri, and particularly the one in Clayton, naming as a CIA asset the manager, John Bittlecomb.

REMOVING HUGE SUMS OF MONEY OVERSEAS

Russbacher described how the CIA moved large quantities of money from U.S. financial proprietaries during the last few years to off-shore corporations and banks, including those in the Antilles and the Cayman Islands. "The Agency is deadly afraid of exposure within the United States," Russbacher said, "and they have begun to siphon off large and tremendous sums of money to foreign accounts. It must be borne in mind that in the last three years there has been a systematic removal of funds and capital assets from these [CIA] corporations."

Russbacher described how the CIA used the savings and loan institutions to fund their covert operations in the United States and abroad and add to the massive amount of funds secreted in foreign financial institutions. Parallel operations were run by different CIA divisions and directorates, using code names to identify the various operations. Included in the operations affecting financial institutions were Operation Gold Bug, Operation Cyclops, Operation Interlink, Operation Woodsman, Operation Fountain Pen, Operation Thunder, Operation Blue Thunder, and Operation Moth.

OPERATION WOODSMAN

Operation Woodsman was a CIA operation that targeted specific companies, forcing the owners out, and taking over the assets. Russbacher described several of these operations in which he himself was directly involved. Information used to carry out Operation Woodsman, such as the financial condition of targeted companies, could be obtained by the CIA through a data base called the Black Flag file, which is located on a Cray computer in Washington, and which is accessed through a government Sentry Terminal (government-secure computer). The Cray computer also contains a list of federal judges, trustees, law firms, and attorneys, who covertly work to carry out Justice Department and CIA activities; (such as the San Francisco law firm used against me in the sham California action).

REFERRING TO JUDICIAL INVOLVEMENT

Russbacher repeated what he had described to me during the past few years about the role of federal judges in the corruption: "More than fifty percent of the judges are compromised through secret bribes or retainers." The bribes take many forms. Sometimes through gambling chips at Atlantic City and Las Vegas casinos, in the form of gratuities, sometimes through second and third parties, inheritances, anything that will whitewash the funds in the property that is given to the judges or trustees. Russbacher stated that these funds are often hidden in offshore financial accounts. He added:

> *Let's say it is property or stock certificates. We'll have phony documentation set up and put in place and show where the stock certificates or the property or the legacy came from. Even if we have to create our own trust with which to do it. It's not like we don't have legally capable counsel available. Now understand this too: these judges received this heavy money regardless of the fact that they have cases pending or not. They get paid whether they do something for us or not.*

Russbacher described the procedure for gaining access to the Cray computer in Washington, stating how the identification number is first entered and then the security code.

Russbacher stated that he learned about Operation Woodsman when he was assigned to CIA headquarters at Langley, Virginia. "Every damn thing, every crooked thing that the DOJ has done," he said, "involving any and all law firms, is registered under the code name that I have given you."

Russbacher continued:

> *Our intent was to take over the tangible assets of the operating license and licenses, we go through the predetermination hearing with the judge, trustee and the simple debtors, and then we buy time to reorganize the lines, and transport capabilities. In other words, we use them for ourselves, these little feeder airlines, we try to keep them alive anywhere from six months to a year and a half. Slowly we set our operations and leverage to where the existing financial records are changed to reflect prior debt encumbrance. We falsify the records. We take an existing carrier, their routes, their equipment, push our schedule and freight manifest through their licenses, and then we .. we have no interest in developing a good business or making a go of it, out of the indentured one that we have taken over.*

Russbacher described how the system uses attorney spotters throughout the United States to identify companies that have large equities but have cash problems. CIA proprietaries buy up the company's receivables and indebtedness, and force the company to sign papers making them susceptible to immediate takeover if their financial situation deteriorates. The CIA proprietary then acts to make this happen, after which the owners lose control. Chapter 11 would be included in Operation Woodsman.

The CIA may loot the company and then put it into Chapter 7 or 11 bankruptcy courts, where several options are available to make off with the assets, or to have the indebtedness discharged. Russbacher described how the CIA has about seventy percent of the trustees and many of the federal judges in bankruptcy courts on retainer. He described the practice known as "drop-offs" that force companies into Chapter 11, involving companies with valuable assets that have a cash crunch.

Russbacher described some of the company takeovers in which he was directly involved, naming Midway Airlines, Southern Air Transport, and Frontier Airlines. In some cases, the targeted company would be liquidated and, as in the case of Frontier Airlines, the aircraft would go to a CIA proprietary. In Frontier's example, most of the aircraft went to the CIA proprietary, Southwest Airlines. In the case of Southern Air Transport, the targeted corporation was kept as a CIA proprietary.

Describing the CIA takeover of Chicago-based Midway Airlines during the last year of its existence, Russbacher said that Midway Airlines was first targeted in 1986 because it had a high debt-to-asset ratio, making the airline vulnerable to the takeover scheme of Operation Woodsman. CIA assets started purchasing Midway's debt with the intention of taking over the company and then liquidating the assets in Chapter 7.

Russbacher described how Midway tried to get absorbed by another carrier, Northwest, and that the CIA blocked it, as it wanted Midway's aircraft. The CIA got Justice Department attorneys and the IRS to take actions against the airline through criminal and tax proceedings through mostly bogus criminal and contempt charges. He explained:

We put together a bunch of phony allegations, mismanagement of funds, possible fraud. Ninety-five percent of it is totally untrue and unfounded, but the five percent that does remain true and factual are at the forefront, and you push those. Some of the directorships on the Board of Directors were subverted and suborned to CIA tactics.

The plan by Northwest Airlines to absorb Midway fell through after both Midway and Northwest were pressured by government agencies acting on behalf of the CIA. This scheme caused Midway to go out of business, so the airline's Boeing 737 aircraft went to another covert CIA operation: Southwest Airlines.

Russbacher described similar CIA takeovers which developed into larger companies instead of being liquidated for their assets. These included Southern Air Transport (which started out as Savannah Charter Airlines); Central Airlines of Fort Worth; Allegheny Airlines; and others.

Russbacher explained that some of the directors had their own businesses and that it was easy for the CIA with its control of other government agencies to put pressure on them, adding: "They were not influenced; they were dictated to."

I asked: "How could they be dictated to?" Russbacher replied: "The director, who has other business interests, and probably a business of his own, suddenly finds himself in a financial quandary, due to various tactics used by the CIA. We put him under our thumb." "If he decides not to play ball we threaten him with criminal charges."

He stated that Justice Department attorneys worked hand in hand with the CIA in Operation Woodsman and other schemes, and that the Agency not only has its own private attorneys but "government attorneys on staff as well as the judges. It's a fixed deck all the way across."

Russbacher described another CIA takeover: "We did the same thing with hotels," describing how the CIA took over the Intercontinental Hotels (IH) chain from Pan American Corporation through its CIA front, Global Hotel Management out of Basel, Switzerland.

Among the airlines that were liquidated after acquisition were Central Airlines out of Fort Worth (the agency's first airline acquisition under Operation Woodsman), and Frontier Airlines of Denver. Russbacher described how the CIA created so much friction between Frontier and United Airlines, who had proposed taking over Frontier, that the deal fell through. These problems included union and other problems. The Boeing 737s then went to another CIA proprietary, Southwest Airlines.

Russbacher stated that one reason Southwest Airlines was making money (when all the other airlines were losing money) was that the airline has significant income from CIA-generated business that shows as income on its records, but the source of the income was bogus.

SAMPLING OF CIA PROPRIETARIES

Russbacher gave me the names of many financial institutions that were CIA proprietaries, including Red Hill Savings & Loan and Hill Financial in Red Hill, Pennsylvania, whose start-up was funded from looting Silverado Bank Savings & Loan. He described the CIA operation known as Valley Bank in Phoenix, which played a key role in moving money for the October Surprise operation (and described by former Mossad agent Ari Ben-Menashe in his book, *Profits of War*).

Other CIA proprietary financial institutions described by Russbacher were Badner Bank, which funded Germania Savings and Loan; Commerce Bank of Missouri; Carondolet Savings and Loan in St Louis; Mega Bank Group which owned First State System which operates in about eighteen states; National Fiduciary Trust Company, Inc.; National Financial Services, Incorporated; Crystal Shores Development; Clayton Financial Planning; Shalimar Perfumes; Shalimar Armaments; Shalimar Chemical Laboratories; R & B Weapons Systems International, Inc.; Pratislaja Brenneke Munitions Amalgam; KRB Weapons Delivery System; National Realty, Inc.; and others.

CONNECTIONS BETWEEN THE CIA AND THOSE
LOOTING AMERICA'S FINANCIAL INSTITUTIONS

Russbacher described the relationship between the CIA proprietaries and the Keating group, adding, "The Keating group is a very small group. There is a much larger group that we [CIA] dealt with, of which Keating was only a part." In response to my question as to why the Keating group would work with the CIA Russbacher stated, "To keep the heat off their backs for one. And number two, some of the companies that were involved were actually proprietary operations."

Russbacher made reference to Anthony Russo, an officer in Indian Springs State Bank, who had financial interest in a CIA proprietary airline, Global International Airways. In 1982, the airline owned by Farhad Azima, an Iranian-born naturalized U.S. citizen, had a fleet of 14 jetliners, making flights to remote airstrips in Central America, carrying military equipment outbound from the United States and often carrying drugs on the return flights. Global flew shipments for CIA operative Edwin Wilson and his company, Egyptian-American Transport and Services Corporation (Eatsco). Well-known national figures involved with Global included Thomas Clines, Theodore Shackley, Richard Secord, Hussein Salem, and others.

BOGUS BEARER BONDS

Russbacher described another ongoing CIA operation inflicting hundreds of millions of dollars of losses upon U.S. financial institutions. In this operation CIA proprietaries obtained loans from various financial institutions on the basis of pledged bearer bonds, all of which were bogus. After obtaining the loans some CIA proprietaries looted the assets and then filed Chapter 7 or 11 in federal courts where they had control over bankruptcy judges and trustees and were represented by covert Justice Department and/or CIA law firms or fronts.

Russbacher was cautious in divulging the secrets of CIA operations, even though he was trying to blow the whistle on some of its worst and most damaging activities against the United States. As time passed, and with my constant probing into different areas of CIA activities, and as Russbacher discovered that other CIA operatives gave me information which he had withheld from me, he gradually gave me more data. In early 1993, as I learned the operational names of many of the CIA operations from other informants, including Colonel Trenton Parker, a deep-cover CIA operative and Michael Riconosciuto, a deep-cover CIA contract agent, Russbacher opened up and gave me code names and data. He stated that different divisions or groups within the CIA ran parallel operations, and had different names for similar activities, a description of some of them follows:

OPERATION INTERLINK

Operation Interlink (IL) was the code name for an operation involving financial institutions, with the goal of raising money for covert CIA activities, and laundering the funds into secret CIA offshore bank accounts.

OPERATION CYCLOPS

Operation Cyclops was the name used by the Pegasus unit of the CIA, and was an overview over most other Pegasus operations. It included all types of covert financial operations including proprietaries involved in the HUD and the savings and loan programs, bogus bearer bonds.

OPERATION MOTH (MH)

Operation Moth was one of the Agency's name for the operation involved in savings and loan fraud.

OPERATION GOLD BUG (GB)

Operation Gold Bug involved the overall scheme of generating money through various financial activities. Under Operation Gold Bug were a number of other operations. Operation Gold Bug was the development of national and international financial programs to develop sources of income which would be available on a regular basis to support and carry out covert CIA activities domestically and internationally.

Russbacher incorporated and operated over a dozen CIA proprietaries, and the tactics used to loot companies of their assets. When used against savings and loans, Russbacher's section of the CIA gave it the name of Operation Moth. The highly secret Pegasus group within the CIA gave this program the name of Operation Gold Bug. The intent of both groups and operations was to loot the assets of targeted financial or other institutions and wealthy people. The overall operation that targeted other companies was called Operation Gold Finger.

OPERATION THUNDER (TD)

Operation Thunder was another name for a CIA covert operation, and included the HUD and savings and loan fraud, bogus bearer bonds, and other financial schemes. Russbacher stated that the home base for Operation Thunder was New Orleans, and was initially located in a private CIA proprietary. He stated that today the cover for the operation is Telemark Communications, one of the biggest companies in the United States, and a CIA proprietary. As with other CIA proprietaries, the top management consisted of Agency people, who had liaison with CIA field people who were contract officers or agents, and particularly attorneys and law firms.

Russbacher described the heading sheet on correspondence pertaining to Operation Thunder. On the very top of the sheet would be the words:

Operations Memorandum.
Classification: Top Secret: SOG-SI/6
Copy Number: 4 [or whatever number of copies were authorized]
SOG/ALPHA/-DETACHMENT TS-TS-Q/SOG-D/F: 701
FP399689
Staging Area: New Orleans, Louisiana

OPERATION BLUE THUNDER (BT)

Operation Blue Thunder related to the destruction of institutions, including taking them over or forcing them into Chapters 7 and 11. After taking them over, the CIA would take over the corporation's license rights. Basically, it destroyed companies and picked up the assets at fire sale prices.

OPERATION FOUNTAIN PEN (FP)

Operation Fountain Pen started with Bank of Zaire, a CIA proprietary, buying banks, corporations and other financial institutions with bogus bearer bonds, treasury bonds, or duplicate issues.

BOGUS BEARER BONDS

Several of the covert CIA operations used bogus bearer bonds, that had a twenty or twenty-five year due date, and were used as collateral for multi-million-dollar loans. After obtaining the loans and laundering the money into other secret proprietaries or offshore financial vehicles, the companies would often file Chapter 7 or Chapter 11. The lender would then think it was covered by the bonds given as collateral, which they would not discover as bogus until many years later. In some cases the CIA proprietary would make interest payments on the loans secured by the phony bonds. The primary criminal act in those cases would be using forged certificates to obtain a loan.

AIDING AND ABETTING BY STATE OFFICIALS

Russbacher stated that in 1986 some of the CIA financial institutions he operated were compromised, that connections between the secret proprietaries and members of Congress were in danger of being exposed, and the decision was made to shut them down. He described how Justice Department and CIA personnel conspired with Missouri officials to remove all traces from the state records that the CIA corporations had been incorporated as Missouri Corporations.

Referring to the shutdown of several CIA proprietaries linked to the 1986 downing of a CIA aircraft over Nicaragua, the famous "Hasenfus" flight, Russbacher stated: "All records that were available to the Department of State or to the [state's] Attorney General's office have been seized, or closed, to where the public cannot get hold of them."

MONEY-PATH FOR BRIBING FEDERAL JUDGES, TRUSTEES, LAW FIRMS

I was prompted to ask Russbacher about payoffs to federal judges after private investigator Stewart Webb heard of a bribe connection between U.S. District Judge Sherman Finesilver in Denver and a corporation in Ireland. After he passed the information along to me I questioned some of my CIA contacts to determine if they knew anything of it.

In response to my questions, Russbacher explained the path of money for bribing federal judges, trustees, law firms, and attorneys. Russbacher stated that the money for these payoffs came from a company located in Dublin and incorporated in Ireland, called Shamrock Overseas Disbursement Corporation. Its telephone is listed as Shamrock Overseas Courier Service. The function of this company was to place money at regular intervals into numbered bank accounts for the recipients to draw upon. Russbacher chuckled as he stated that the Chief Executive Officer at Shamrock Overseas Disbursement was the same person with whom he had worked at other CIA proprietaries: Donald Lutz.

Russbacher and Lutz were on the management staff of various CIA proprietaries, including Red Hill Savings and Loan and Hill Financial, at Red Hill, Pennsylvania, and at Silverado Bank Savings & Loan.

Russbacher stated that the routing of the money funded by Shamrock was "from the Netherlands Antilles. And in turn comes from Grand Caymon. That in turn comes from the Southern Bank in Florida. And that in turn comes from Southern Savings and Loan in Illinois. Which in turn comes from NBC; National Brokerage Company."

"Where does the money originally come from? Is it from stolen Chapter 11 assets," I asked. Russbacher replied, "That's part of it. It is a conglomeration of funds. It is what we call an all-purpose account. Arms shipments, the other stuff [drugs, weapons] that we were transporting back and forth. It is what we call the divisible surplus."

I asked if the federal judges he referred to as recipients of these funds were only Bankruptcy Court Judges, to which Russbacher replied, "No, that's not true. You have to include the DCs [U.S. District Judges] too."

"How is it determined the amount that each judge will get, and what judges are paid off?" I asked. Russbacher replied: "It is predetermined. If you will remember from one of my earlier tapes I told you that the judges receive their funds regardless of whether they have heard a case in six months or not."

"How do they determine which judges are recipients, what qualifies them to be on the payroll?" Russbacher replied, "The fact that they work hand-in-hand with the trustees, and they grant us full power to basically do what we [CIA] want in Chapter eleven, thirteen, and seven proceedings."

"Are there any other similar corporations in the United States like Shamrock?"

"No, Rodney, they are all funded from Shamrock. In other words, if you pull the plug on Shamrock, you have it all."

Russbacher explained how the recipients pick up the money. "They can get it overseas and pick it up, or they can go to Toronto and pick it up there, at the Royal Bank of Canada." Russbacher stated, "when they go in to make a withdrawal, they request to see the President or Chief Account officer." Russbacher explained that this scheme is part of Operation Woodsman, explained in earlier pages.

Russbacher explained that the recipient's available funds will be found on the bank's terminal screen, and that "all they have to have is the account number. No ID is required. Just give them the account number and the four-digit identification number." Russbacher stated that Royal Bank of Canada, Manufacturers Hanover Bank in New York, and Valley Bank in Arizona, cooperate in this scheme.

Russbacher repeated what he had told me in the past: that funds would also be disbursed to the recipient judges, trustees, or law firms, at gambling casinos, including MGM, Harrah's and Resort in Atlantic City, and Frontier, Stardust, and Horseshoe in Las Vegas. The CIA gave the money to the casino, who in turn gave gambling chips to the recipients when they arrived, after which the chips are cashed in for money. In some cases the casinos report the money as winnings and income tax withheld.

"Would your knowledge of this operation be because you were with NBC [National Brokerage Company],"[153] I asked. "Yes, because we made deposits and withdrawals through that route," he said.

BLACK FLAG FILE

Russbacher stated that he had seen the list of recipients in this scheme on the computer data base while he was at the CIA headquarters at Langley, explaining that the data base is called the Black Flag Files (BFF). He stated that the data base is on a Cray computer, accessed from any government Sentry terminal by typing in an identification entry number, and after a flag

---

[153] Russbacher was President of NBC, using the alias of Emery J. Peden, and his former wife, Peggy J. Russbacher, was Executive Vice President. There was a National Brokerage, Incorporated, a National Brokerage Company, and numerous other divisions operated by Russbacher.

shows up the screen, typing in the access code: 3A46915W.

I often asked Russbacher to accompany these statements with a declaration as to their truthfulness, and I did during this questioning. Russbacher replied: "Sure. All the information that we have discussed on this date, May 17, 1993, from approximately 2020 hours Central Daylight Time, the declaration made to area code 510-944-1930, Rodney Stich, by Gunther Karl Russbacher, 44840417, Captain USN, is true and correct as to the best of my knowledge and belief."

WHERE IS THE MONEY?

Losses of approximately half a **trillion** dollars have been the estimated direct cost of just the savings and loan debacle. But where did the money go? It has never been sought, or located. The theft of $2 billion by Lincoln, or $2 billion by Silverado, is a long way from $200 to $500 billion. Neither Congress nor the Justice Department has made any attempt to determine where this money went. Finding it would relieve the American public of a debt load that is affecting the American economy, resulting in a reduction in benefits to individual Americans, and causing a staggering tax burden. There is no way that such a huge sum simply evaporated without a trace.

My CIA informants tell me that many of the funds looted by the CIA, organized crime, and such groups as the Denver group, have been hidden in offshore financial institutions. Some of the funds that have gone overseas have returned to the United States through foreign shell corporations, buying up vast quantities of U.S. real estate and assets.

ONE OF THE PLACES WHERE THE MONEY
IS REPORTEDLY HIDDEN

Investigator Stewart Webb heard from one of his sources that hundreds of trusts are filed with the county recorder in a small town located in southeast Colorado, in Baca County. His source told him that huge sums of money looted from the HUD and savings and loan are hidden in these trusts. In seeking further information, I asked other CIA contacts if they knew anything about this. I hit pay-dirt when I asked Russbacher, "Do you know anything about the Baca trusts?" He replied, "How in the hell did you find out about those?"

Russbacher was especially well informed. He told me that many of the trusts were set up by Denver attorney Norman Brownstein, a key member of the Denver group involved in the HUD and savings and loan scandals. Most of the actual funds associated with these trusts are located outside the United States. He said that he himself had filed trusts in Baca County for his children. Russbacher said that the location of the money covered by these trusts, which he stated amounted to billions of dollars, were located in offshore financial institutions.

This money includes the billions of dollars stolen from the HUD and savings and loan programs, the billions looted every year from Chapter 11 assets, drug profits, and the other dirty schemes involving the characters listed within these pages. If this information is correct, and if the sources of hidden money divulged to me by my CIA informants were traced, possibly large amounts of the huge losses inflicted upon the American people could be recovered.

BILLIONS OF HIDDEN TAXPAYERS' MONEY

Russbacher had several times stated in response to my questions that many billions of dollars of money obtained by CIA proprietaries from the American public were hidden in offshore financial institutions. In the remote town of Springfield, Colorado, at the Baca County Recorder's Office, are located well over a thousand trusts, hiding many billions of dollars looted from the American public. Many of these trusts were prepared by Denver attorney Norman Brownstein, working with the Denver gang, including Larry Mizel, Leonard Millman, MDC Holdings, Richmond Homes, and hundreds of other related legal holdings.

CHAPTER FOURTEEN

OCTOBER SURPRISE

"October Surprise" is the name of a scheme that corrupted the 1980 presidential elections. It included payment of bribes to enemies of the United States who were holding 52 American hostages as prisoners, seized at the American Embassy in Teheran on November 4, 1979. Shiite Muslim militants attacked and seized the Embassy in Teheran, taking the Americans hostage. The attack upon the American Embassy occurred several months after the Shah of Iran was overthrown and power seized by the Ayatollah Khomeini. The American hostages were subjected to 444 days of brutal conditions, including mock executions. If this scheme had not been carried out, the Americans would have been released months earlier.

The intent of the scheme was to alter the presidential elections to bring about the defeat of President Jimmy Carter, and to elect presidential nominee Ronald Reagan. This was accomplished by blocking the release of the American hostages, causing many Americans to be displeased with President Carter, increasing the chances that Carter would be defeated at the polls.

Months of negotiations to affect the release of these hostages went on between the government of the United States, under President Jimmy Carter, and the government of Iran. Early in 1980 the U.S. tried a military mission called Operation Desert One to free the hostages, but it failed miserably in the Iranian desert, resulting in the deaths of eight Americans. While the U.S. military was preparing another rescue try, simultaneously negotiating to obtain the hostages' release, the Reagan-Bush team sabotaged the efforts by making public the hostage-rescue plans and warning the American people that Carter was preparing to exchange arms for hostages. One effect of these tactics that were part of October Surprise was the dispersal of the American prisoners throughout Iran, making rescue all but impossible.

LOSING THE ELECTION IF THE HOSTAGES WERE FREED

The American public was becoming increasingly disenchanted with

Carter, affecting the outcome of the 1980 presidential elections. Analysts in the Reagan-Bush team estimated they would lose the election to President Jimmy Carter if the American hostages were released prior to the November 11, 1980 election.

After the military rescue mission failed, the United States renewed negotiations for release of the 52 American hostages. The Iranians demanded that President Carter release U.S. military equipment that had been ordered and paid for by the Shah of Iran, before Iran would release the hostages.

Despite pressures against an arms-for-hostages swap, in mid-1980 President Carter secretly agreed to Iran's terms. Carter agreed to exchange $150 million in previously ordered and prepaid military equipment in exchange for the release of the hostages. Iran desperately needed the military equipment after Iraqi President Saddam Hussein attacked Iran in September 1980.

SABOTAGING THE UNITED STATES OF AMERICA

While Reagan and his camp were charging Carter with an arms-for-hostages negotiations, the Reagan team, headed by former OSS officer William Casey, entered into secret negotiations with Iranian factions. Casey and other members of the Reagan-Bush team met secretly with Iranian factions, offering bribes in the form of money and U.S. arms if the Iranians *continued* the imprisonment of the American hostages until after the November 11, 1980 elections.

A series of secret meetings were held between the Reagan-Bush team and the Iranian factions in European cities, with the final meeting occurring on the October 19, 1980, weekend in Paris. The Iranians demanded that either Ronald Reagan or George Bush personally appear in Paris to sign the final agreement. Carrying out this scheme required secrecy and massive coverups by many in the United States and in France.

VARIOUS INTERESTS WANTED CARTER OUT

There were special-interest groups wanting President Carter removed from office. Among them was the Central Intelligence Agency, which suffered serious losses to its clandestine operations when Carter ordered the dismissal of large numbers of CIA operatives in 1977. This wholesale firing of Agency employees became known as the "October Massacre."

George Bush, who had CIA connections since the late 1950s, had been Director of the Central Intelligence Agency in 1976, until Carter assumed the presidency and replaced him with Stansfield Turner.

The Reagan-Bush team promised the Iranians billions of dollars of U.S. military equipment and $40 million in bribes to individual Iranians involved in the scheme. The Reagan-Bush team promised to include arms merchants in the lucrative deal, and to include Israel as intermediary in the profitable arms sales.

Carter had refused to deal through arms merchants. He limited the shipment of arms to what had already been purchased. Israel was not included in the sales. The secret and treasonous deal offered by the Reagan-Bush team profited everyone, it seemed. The only people who suffered were the 52 American hostages, held captive months longer, and the American people, who felt the fallout in many ways.

Included in Reagan campaign rhetoric was his promise to get tough with the Iranians, saying he would never negotiate with terrorists. Simultaneously, he and his group were bribing the Iranians to continue the imprisonment of the hostages.

The plan worked. The American public believed the uttering of the Reagan-Bush team. Americans, kept ignorant about the truth, dissatisfied with Carter's inability to get the prisoners released, and elected a president and vice president who had engaged in subversive and criminal activities.

Within an hour of Reagan's inauguration on January 20, 1981, the Iranians allowed an aircraft to leave Teheran Airport with all but one of the 52 American hostages on board. The flight was prearranged to take off immediately after the Iranians knew that Reagan and Bush had taken their oaths of office.

Many participants in this scheme were rewarded with key positions in the U.S. government, and engineered or became part of other major scandals. The October Surprise plot was the genesis to the Iran and Contra affairs, and indirectly to the Inslaw, BNL, and Iraqgate scandals, which have yet to be described.

"The deal is off."

When a White House aide told President Reagan that one of the hostages had not been released, Reagan was heard[154] to respond: "Tell the Iranians that the deal is off if that hostage is not freed."

President Ronald Reagan and Vice President George Bush held widely televised home-coming celebrations for the American hostages, saying all the right things about the sufferings the hostages endured. Reagan never divulged that he and his team were responsible for many months of additional imprisonment and suffering. Neither the hostages, nor the American people, knew about the Reagan-Bush team conspiracy.

It took the cooperation of many people in the United States and Europe to carry out the scheme. Israel's Mossad, acting as a well-paid middle man in the transfer of the arms from U.S. military warehouses to Iran via Israel, played a major role. Without their cooperation, the scheme probably would not have worked.

It also required the cooperation of the French Secret Service and the government of France, who provided security for the secret Paris meetings. It required the cooperation of officials and people in the Central Intelligence Agency; the U.S. Department of Justice, including the FBI, Secret Service, U.S. Attorneys; the Department of State; many members of Congress; among others. It also required the media to cover up.

My CIA sources said that the $40 million bribe money came from the Committee to Reelect the President (CREEP).

DAMAGE CONTROL

To protect the incoming Reagan-Bush team and the many federal officials

---

[154] This response was heard by Barbara Honegger, a member of Reagan's White House staff.

and others who took part in October Surprise, the Reagan-Bush team placed people, including those implicated in the activities, in control of key federal agencies and the federal courts. Some, like attorneys Stanley Sporkin, Lawrence Silberman, and Lowell Jensen, were appointed to the federal bench, defusing any litigation arising from October Surprise or its many tentacles. Attorney William Casey was appointed director of the Central Intelligence Agency. Attorney Edwin Meese, Reagan's campaign manager, was appointed to the highest law-enforcement office in the United States, U.S. Attorney General, insuring that there would be no prosecution of the group. Organized crime never had it so good.

THE FACTS SLOWLY SURFACED

Although the details of the secret agreement were known throughout Europe, the establishment media in the United States kept the lid on the scandal. But the facts started coming out. A *Miami Herald* article[155] described statements made by CIA operative, Alfonso Chardy, describing a secret meeting in early October 1980 between Robert Allen, Lawrence Silberman, Robert McFarlane, and Iranian factions. Robert Allen was foreign policy adviser to President Reagan, and Robert McFarlane was an aide to Senator John Tower on the Senate Armed Services Committee.

In 1987, Abol Hassan Bani-Sadr, the President of Iran during the hostage negotiations, wrote a book published in Europe,[156] describing his knowledge of the October Surprise scheme. The information he had received as President disclosed the secret agreement with the Americans, even though he was kept out of the loop by Hashemi Rafsanjani, one of Khomeini's chief lieutenants and later Speaker of the Iranian Parliament.

In 1988, *Playboy* magazine published an in-depth article on the October Surprise scheme. In what would become a pattern of killings that coincidentally protected high U.S. officials, one of the authors, Abbie Hoffman, was killed shortly after bringing the article to *Playboy*. The eight-page article, "An Election Held Hostage," detailed many of the events surrounding the scheme, as did a ten-page *Esquire* article entitled "October Surprise."

A former member of the Reagan-Bush election team, later a member of the White House staff, Barbara Honegger, authored the 1989 book, *October Surprise*,[157] based upon knowledge she gained as a White House insider and subsequent investigator. Honegger left the Reagan camp when she became disillusioned with certain practices. Living in Monterey, California, she and a friend, Rayelan Dyer, worked together researching the October Surprise story.

Rayelan was the widow of a former professor and dean of the physics department at the Naval Postgraduate School in Monterey, California. She later married a deep-cover, high ranking officer in the Office of Naval Intelligence, Gunther Russbacher, who was assigned to the Central Intelligence Agency. Unknown to her at the time, her new husband played a key

[155] April 1987.
[156] European publisher *Eagleburger*.
[157] *October Surprise*, Tudor Publishing Company.

role in the October Surprise operation. Ironically, she initially found out from me about her new husband's role in the matter she and her friend, Honegger, had investigated. More about this in later pages.

In 1991 Bani-Sadr authored another book describing the October Surprise operation, this time published in the United States: *My Turn To Speak*. On April 15, 1991, *Frontline* aired a television show addressing the October Surprise, which was followed the next day by an article in the Op-Ed section of the *New York Times*, written by Gary Sick, describing his knowledge of October Surprise. Sick authored a book published in 1991 that copied Barbara Honegger's title, *October Surprise*.[158] Both *October Surprise* books relied upon statements made by dozens of people who were part of the operation, or witnesses to it, and who had nothing to gain and much to lose by disclosing what they knew.

Ari Ben-Menashe, a former member of Israel's secret intelligence agency, the Mossad, described in his 1991 book, *Profits of War*, the agency role he and the Mossad played in October Surprise, including meetings he attended in Madrid, Barcelona, and Paris.

Ben-Menashe was heavily involved in various secret activities with the Mossad and the CIA, and was one of the first to expose the Iran-Contra activities, for which October Surprise served as the genesis. Ben-Menashe stated that he was a member of the Mossad's advance team working with the French government, which arranged meetings between William Casey, George Bush, and the Iranian factions, including the meetings on the October 19, 1980, weekend in Paris.

Ben-Menashe related that he and others on the Israeli team stayed at the Paris Hilton Hotel, meeting with various members of the Iranian factions, while waiting for George Bush to arrive from the United States. He stated that on Sunday, October 19, at approximately 11 a.m., the Ayatollah Mehdi Karrubi and his body guards appeared in a room on the upper floor of the Hotel Ritz, where Israeli and French intelligence agencies were waiting for Bush to arrive. They were followed several minutes later by George Bush and William Casey. The meeting lasted about ninety minutes, and a final agreement was reached, whereby the Iranians were to be given $40 million bribe money, and large quantities of arms would be sold to them, in exchange for the Iranians continuing to hold the 52 Americans imprisoned until after the November 1980 presidential election and the January 1981 inauguration.

JUSTICE DEPARTMENT OBSTRUCTION OF JUSTICE

CIA contract agent Richard Brenneke testified in U.S. District Court at Denver in 1988 on behalf of another CIA contract agent, Heinrich Rupp. The purpose of the testimony was to show that Brenneke's friend, Rupp, was a CIA contract agent (as was Brenneke), and that the offenses for which Rupp was being charged were offenses committed under orders of the CIA. Justice Department prosecutors had charged Rupp with money offenses at Aurora Bank in the Denver area.

---

[158] Random House.

During Brenneke's testimony, he described other CIA activities, including his role in the October 19, 1980, weekend flights to Paris, in which both Brenneke and Rupp took part. Brenneke testified that he saw George Bush and Donald Gregg in Paris on the October 19, 1980, weekend. Brenneke had nothing to gain by revealing the October Surprise scheme, and much to lose if he was lying. Justice Department officials already knew of the October Surprise activities. U.S. Attorney General Edwin Meese had been on the Reagan-Bush presidential campaign and knew of the criminal activities. Now he held the top law enforcement spot in the United States. Instead of performing his duty, he engaged in many criminal acts, including coverup, aiding and abetting, misprision of felonies, obstruction of justice, subornation of perjury, and others. He then compounded these crimes by falsely prosecuting an informant to silence and discredit him, and compounded the earlier obstruction of justice.

Instead of prosecuting the guilty people in the October Surprise scheme, Justice Department officials and prosecutors responded to Brenneke's testimony by charging him with perjury for making the statements to the court. This false charge made Justice Department attorneys guilty of felony persecution of an informant under federal criminal statutes,[159] felony coverup, and obstruction of justice.

JUSTICE DEPARTMENT SUBORNATION OF PERJURY

The perjury trial was conducted in Portland, Oregon, where Brenneke resided. Justice Department prosecutors brought Donald Gregg, then Ambassador to South Korea, to testify that he was not in Paris on the October 19, 1980, weekend, even though the prosecutors knew Brenneke was telling the truth and that Gregg was lying. They encouraged Gregg to lie under oath, testifying that he was swimming at a beach in Maryland with his family on that weekend. Justice Department prosecutors produced pictures of Gregg and his family, in bathing suits, on the beach in bright sunshine. They knew the snapshots they were submitting to the court were not taken on that cold October 19th weekend. Encouraging someone to commit perjury is the crime of subornation of perjury.

Brenneke's attorney called a witness from the weather bureau who testified that the sky was overcast during that entire weekend.

Justice Department prosecutors produced two Secret Service agents,[160] to have them testify that Bush never left the Washington area during the October 19, 1980, weekend. But they were vague in their testimony, and failed to produce the Secret Service logs showing Bush's activities during a 21-hour period from Saturday afternoon to Sunday evening. The Secret Service agents could not state where Bush was from 9:25 p.m. on Saturday, October 18, until Sunday at 7:57 p.m. My CIA informants stated to me, as described in later pages, that several Secret Service agents were on board the BAC 111 aircraft that flew vice presidential nominee George Bush to Paris during the missing twenty-one hours.

---

[159] Including Title 18 U.S.C. §§ 1512 and 1513.
[160] Who worked under the control of the U.S. Department of Justice.

Secret Service records, if they are accurate, indicate that Bush gave a speech at 8:40 p.m. on Saturday, October 18, 1980, at Widener University in Delaware County, Pennsylvania, and then do not show where Bush was until Sunday night, October 19, 1980, when Bush gave a speech to the Zionist Organization of America at the Capitol Hilton Hotel, arriving an hour late for his 7:30 p.m. scheduled appearance. I obtained sequestered Secret Service documents showing Bush flying into Washington National Airport at 7:35 p.m. Sunday evening.

PERJURY BY THE SECRET SERVICE?

In addition to lying about Bush's whereabouts, the Secret Service agents testifying in Brenneke's trial withheld the fact that several Secret Service agents were on the plane that carried Bush to Paris during that October 19, 1980 weekend.

October Surprise was a coup against the United States, involving high federal officials, including the Secret Service, Justice Department and other officials. More is stated about these secret activities in later pages.

BLACKMAIL OF THE UNITED STATES

As could be expected, when the Reagan-Bush team took office they were then subject to blackmail by Iran, Iraq, Israel, and anyone who had knowledge of October Surprise.

After Reagan and Bush took office, the Iranians received huge quantities of military equipment, many times more than they could have received had they completed the agreement with the United States government under President Carter. In 1982 the Reagan-Bush team took Iraq off the list of terrorist states, despite the strong protests of intelligence organizations in the United States and Europe. Israel received huge quantities of military supplies and aid, much of it unknown to the American public, who will be paying the bill for years.

October Surprise also adversely effected the military preparedness of the United States and its European allies. To obtain the arms for Iran promised at Paris, military equipment was stolen from U.S. warehouses in Europe, and sent to Iran via Israel.

CIA INFORMANTS

In later pages I describe how I met the CIA informants who gave me many of the specific details of the October Surprise scheme. Briefly, they told me in their sworn declarations that October Surprise was primarily a CIA operation, engineered and carried out with CIA personnel and funds. William Casey, a private citizen and covert CIA operative, met several times with Iranians at different European locations in 1980.

One of the key meetings occurred at the Pepsico International Headquarters building in Barcelona, Spain, in late July 1980. One of my CIA informants was present with Casey at that meeting, arranging for procurement and shipment of the arms from various European locations to Iran via Israel. The final meeting occurred in Paris on the October 19, 1980, weekend. The Iranians wanted either presidential nominee Ronald Reagan or vice presidential nominee George Bush to finalize the agreement.

Vice presidential candidate George Bush, with extensive CIA connections since approximately 1960, flew to Paris from the United States on October 18, 1980, on a BAC 111 owned by a member of the Saudi Arabian family. My CIA contacts have said that the pilots on that flight were Gunther Russbacher, Richard Brenneke, and an Air Force Major.

The BAC 111 reportedly departed Washington National Airport for nearby Andrews Air Force Base on Saturday evening, October 18, 1980. It then departed Andrews at approximately 19:00 pm EST (0000 GMT)[161] for White Plains Airport on Long Island in the New York City area, arriving there at 19:45 p.m. (0045). The BAC 111 landed shortly before the arrival of a Gulfstream jet owned by Unocal, from which William Casey deplaned. Casey then joined the passengers on the BAC 111 for the flight to Paris.

The BAC 111 departed Mitchell at 20:00 p.m, (0100 GMT) for Gander, Newfoundland, arriving there at 21:20 p.m. (EST) (22:20 Atlantic Time; 0220 GMT), where it refueled for the flight over the North Atlantic. It departed Gander at 21:40 p.m. EST (22:40 Atlantic Time; 0240 GMT) for Paris, arriving at Le Bourget Airport at 03:40 EST (9:40 a.m., European time; 0840 GMT).

The passengers on the BAC 111 on the flight from Gander to Paris included William Casey (who would be appointed Director of the CIA); Donald Gregg (who at that time was a member of President Carter's National Security Council); Robert McFarlane (member of President Carter's National Security Council); Senators John Tower and John Heinz; Congressman Dan Rostenkowski; George Bush; Jennifer Fitzgerald;[162] four Secret Service agents; George Cave (former CIA Iran expert and translator); and others.

Unocal's Gulfstream flew non-stop from Mitchell Field to Paris, and was waiting at the airport in London when the BAC 111 arrived. Heinrich Rupp was one of the pilots on the Unocal Gulfstream.

At Paris, the plane was met by a fleet of limousines to carry the passengers to their destinations. George Bush and William Casey went straight to the meetings then in progress. At the Paris meetings were numerous Iranians and members of Israel's Mossad, including Ari Ben-Menashe.

A $40 million bank draft on a Luxembourg bank was given to the Iranians as bribe money and a showing of good faith. CIA operative Michael Riconosciuto played a key role in arranging for the wire transfer of these funds.

Because it was necessary for Bush to return to the United States quickly in order to attend a late Sunday evening speech at the Washington Hilton

---

[161] Greenwich Mean Time.

[162] Some years ago Barbara Walters stated on 20/20 that Jennifer Fitzgerald was George Bush's alleged mistress for many years. My CIA contacts state the same relationship existed, and that she and Bush were in China in the 1970s, that a child resulted from that relationship, which was put up for adoption by an American church with contacts in China. My CIA contacts state that she was a passenger on the BAC 111 flight to Paris on October 18, 1980.

Hotel, the CIA provided an SR-71 aircraft. This plane departed from a military field near Paris at approximately 1450 European time (8:50 a.m. EST; 1350 GMT) and took approximately one hour and forty-four minutes to McGuire Air Force Base in New Jersey, arriving there at approximately 11:50 a.m. EST (1550 GMT).

Later that day Bush boarded the same BAC 111 that had taken him to Paris, and then flew into Washington National Airport. The Secret Service reports that I obtained showed Bush arriving at Washington National at 6:37 p.m., in the BAC 111, and then proceeding with Secret Service escort to the Washington Hilton Hotel, where he gave a speech.

CIA CODE NAME FOR OCTOBER SURPRISE

As will be explained more fully in later pages, most CIA operations have code names, and the code name for the CIA October Surprise scheme was Operation Eurovan (EV).

STRONG CIRCUMSTANTIAL EVIDENCE
SHOWING OCTOBER SURPRISE EXISTED

Even discounting testimony from the many people who were involved in one way or another with October Surprise, the circumstantial evidence is far in excess of that used by federal and state prosecutors to convict a person of a crime, or to sentence the person to death. The facts exposed by investigative media articles and books were of sufficient magnitude to make President Nixon's Watergate coverup child's play.

The factors indicating that October Surprise did in fact occur include:

1. Statements by former president of Iran, Bani-Sadr, whose 1987 and 1991 books described the secret agreement between Iranian factions and the Reagan-Bush team.

2. Statements of numerous people given to Barbara Honegger and quoted in her 1989 *October Surprise*, enlarging upon what she learned as part of the Reagan-Bush team.

3. Statements of numerous people given to Gary Sick and quoted in his 1991 *October Surprise.*

4. Sworn testimony by CIA contract personnel Richard Brenneke and Heinrich Rupp in the U.S. District Court at Denver in 1988.

5. Statements of numerous people given to the authors of various newspaper and magazine articles.

6. Statements made to the press by Ari Ben-Menashe, a former high-ranking Mossad staff officer, who was present at several of the secret October Surprise meetings.

7. Circumstantial evidence in the sequence of events that occurred, including the sudden withdrawal of Iran from further discussions when the United States under President Carter agreed to the terms proposed by Iran; the release of the American hostages within minutes of President Reagan's inauguration.

8. The implications of guilt by the pattern of coverups.

This is not the end of the October Surprise matter; more follows.

CHAPTER FIFTEEN

CIA WHISTLEBLOWERS

Commencing in 1990 I discovered a number of deep-cover whistleblowers formerly employed by various U.S. intelligence agencies, and other witnesses, some of whom had been silenced by Justice Department prosecutors and federal judges. During the past four years, during over a thousand hours of deposition-like questioning of these people, they divulged government corruption beyond the wildest imagination of the average American. They divulged to me the specifics of deep-cover criminal activities that were and are inflicting unprecedented harm upon the United States and the American people. Despite my knowledge of corruption by federal officials I would probably not have believed what I was told if such a great amount of time had not been expended obtaining specifics and confirmation from other informants, much of it supported by highly documented exposé books and articles.

Ironically, it was the corrupt actions by renegade Justice Department attorneys and federal judges in the Ninth Circuit federal judicial district[231] that brought me into contact with these people, and which made possible the exposures found within these pages.

One of the standard tactics employed to keep the lid on the various scandals and to silence or discredit whistleblowers is to falsely charge the person with a federal crime. This is usually followed by seizing his or her assets, depriving the person of funds for legal defenses. Court appointed attorneys are then furnished, who routinely provide a weak defense so as to protect those in power.

JUSTICE DEPARTMENT PERSECUTION BACKFIRED

As described in earlier pages, Justice Department prosecutors and federal

---

[231] Ninth Circuit comprises the States of California, Oregon, Washington, Nevada, and Hawaii, and is the largest judicial district in the United States.

judges tried to silence me by the sham judicial action in the California courts and the voiding of all state and federal protections needed to defend against the scheme. When I sought to protect myself, the coalition of corrupt Justice Department prosecutors and federal judges sentenced me to prison, just as they did when I sought to expose the criminal activities in which they were involved. There is a certain risk to sending a citizen to prison who is determined to blow the lid on these subversive and criminal acts who is also an author.

Virtually nothing has been written about whistleblowers or concerned citizens who blow the whistle on hard-core criminal acts by federal personnel, especially federal judges and their legal cohorts in the Justice Department. All whistleblowers fare poorly, but none fare as badly as those who blow the whistle on the powerful Justice Department and federal judiciary.

It was in prison that many former CIA contract agents educated me about corrupt CIA and Justice Department activities. I met people in prison who, incarcerated for various political reasons, were former CIA operatives or assets, operating covert CIA proprietaries, including airlines, banks, and savings and loans. Either their CIA cover was exposed, and the CIA and Justice Department chose to make them scapegoats, or the imprisonment was to silence potential informants or whistleblowers.

Whatever the reason, CIA and Justice Department officials acted in unison with federal judges, eliminating people who constituted a threat of exposure. The standard tactic is to charge the targeted individual with a federal offense for some act they were ordered to perform by their CIA handlers, deny them adequate legal counsel, deny them the right to have CIA witnesses testify on their behalf, and deny to them the right to present CIA documents. A standard and sham excuse for denying these defenses is that they are not relevant to the immediate charge, when the matter of who gave the person his or her orders is absolutely relevant.

From 200 to 300 former CIA operatives or contract agents had been sentenced to prison by Justice Department prosecutors during the 1980s, on charges arising out of the covert activities they were ordered to perform by their CIA bosses. It was their unanimous belief that the prosecution of these CIA operatives was either to silence them or to discredit them if they talked about the operations.

It was in prison that I first met Gunther Russbacher, a CIA deep-cover high-ranking operative. The hundreds of hours of statements given to me by Russbacher and my exposure activities, brought me into contact with other deep-cover CIA and DEA people, concerned law-enforcement personnel and private investigators. The thousand and more hours of information gathered during the last four years showed a web of intrigue that is bizarre, and irrefutable.

COMPOUNDING THE JUDICIAL PERSECUTION

If the facts in these pages ever motivate enough people to rebel and throw out the crooks, a tongue-in-check gratitude should be given to the crooked judges and Justice Department attorneys that sent me and others to prison to silence us. And these should especially include U.S. District Judge Marilyn

Patel at San Francisco, one of the most corrupt judges I have ever encountered. It was her retaliation against me for having sought to report the criminal activities in Chapter 11 that made it possible for Russbacher and me to meet.

GUNTHER KARL RUSSBACHER

Russbacher's parents were members of the Hapsburg group of Austria, and his father was an Austrian in German intelligence during World War II. In 1950 the U.S. government offered many of these intelligence officers the choice of either being prosecuted for war crimes or going to the United States into various U.S. intelligence agencies. Russbacher's parents were among those who accepted the move to America. In 1950, the Russbacher family moved to the United States, living in Oklahoma City, Oklahoma, and then in Fallon, Nevada.

When Russbacher reached the age of seventeen he entered the U.S. Army, later joining the U.S. Navy, and in 1967 received his Navy pilot wings at Pensacola. He then went on to the Naval air Station at Jacksonville, Florida. (I also received my Navy wings at Pensacola and then went on to Jacksonville, where I became a Navy flight instructor.) Approximately a year later Russbacher received pilot training in the SR-71 at Beale Air Force Base and flew many SR-71 missions for the CIA.

In 1969 Russbacher was attached to the Office of Naval Intelligence and "sheepdipped"[232] into the Central Intelligence Agency. He had two tours of duty in Vietnam; during his first tour, as a fighter pilot, he was shot down and returned to Fitzsimmons Hospital in Denver for extensive hospitalization. Upon his discharge from the hospital, the CIA sent Russbacher back to Vietnam, where he engaged in various covert activities, including attempting to rescue prisoners of war. During one of these attempts he was caught and spent about a year in a North Vietnam prison camp, until he escaped. During his CIA activities he was given numerous aliases and service and Social Security numbers.

The CIA sent Russbacher to Afghanistan in the early 1970s, helping the Afghan fighters against the Russian-backed Kabul government. During this period he helped transfer CIA funds to the newly created Bank of Credit and Commerce International (BCCI). These CIA funds, and those supplied by Bank of America, were a significant source of capital for that bank, and more is said about that bank's operation in later pages.

The CIA then put Russbacher into the financial field, starting in Operation Cyclops, a program where CIA operatives are placed into financial institutions to learn the business. He subsequently started up and operated during the late 1970s and 1980s several covert CIA proprietaries in the United States, including savings and loans, mortgage companies, and investment companies, dealing in money laundering and other covert CIA activities.

---

[232] "Sheepdipped" is the term used to describe the transfer of military personnel to the CIA, in which records are falsified showing the person discharged from the respective military organization, and who then works with the CIA in a clandestine position, where the CIA can deny any relationship to the party doing CIA work.

During over two decades of CIA operations the CIA had given him over thirty aliases for different covert operations. He also had various nicknames including "Gunsel" and "Gunslinger." When undergoing flight training in the SR-71, including at Beale Air Force Base, he used the alias, Robert Behler, and the rank of an Air Force Lt. Colonel. When operating covert financial institutions his usual alias was Emery J. Peden, with occasional use of Robert Andrew Walker, or both. When he wanted to control two positions within a company, he would use two different aliases. With Red Hill Savings & Loan and Hill Financial, he used Emery J. Peden for his role as Chairman of the Board and Robert A. Walker as Chief Executive Officer. He also used his real name, Gunther Russbacher.

Russbacher and I spent hundreds of hours dissecting the mechanics of CIA operations during the past four years, some of it sworn declarations when I thought to ask, and I received numerous written declarations from him. Russbacher described some of the CIA affiliated companies or fronts that he operated, and their covert business activities. He described moving money from Silverado Bank Savings & Loan in Denver to start up other covert CIA operations, including Red Hill Savings and Loan and Hill Financial in Red Hill, Pennsylvania.

Russbacher described other CIA proprietaries that he operated, including National Brokerage, Inc.; National Brokerage Companies, Inc. in Missouri,[233] and its many subsidiaries, including National Brokerage Company; Clayton Financial Planning Group, Inc.[234] (dealing with high-level private enterprise in the international marketplace); Crystal Shores Development Corporation;[235] Crystal Shores Financial Services, Inc; Crystal Shores Estates, Inc.; National Financial Services, Inc.; National Leasing Services, Inc.; National Realty, Inc.; National Realty Services, Inc.; National Commercial Properties, Inc.; Shalimar Management Corporation; Adams Land Company, Inc.; National Fiduciary Trust, Inc.; Badner Bank; International Bank Commerce Holding Company; W.A.R. Petroleum, International (operating under Aegean Lines and Clayton Financial); and Southwest Latex Supply. European corporations that he had an interest in were reportedly Shalimar Perfumes;[236] Shalimar Arms;[237] Shalimar Chemical Laboratories; R & B Weapons Systems, International, Inc.; Pratislaja Brenneke Munitions Amalgam.

Several times during the years Russbacher expressed sorrow to me for having committed some of the things that he was ordered to do by his CIA

---

[233] 7711 Bonhomme Street, Suite 405, Clayton, Missouri. Shared space with Connecticut Mutual Companies, Inc., parent of National Brokerage Company.

[234] Consisting of Herbert Smith and Gunther Russbacher as major directors.

[235] Chartered in the State of Missouri, with home office in Clayton, Missouri and offices in Honor, Michigan, a development corporation that bought land and then subdivided and developed it. Mortgage loans came from Hill Financial through NBC, Michigan National Bank, Traverse City, Michigan.

[236] With offices throughout Europe and the Middle East, and dealt not only with perfume but also with chemical weapons, and buying and selling arms.

[237] With offices in Missouri and Paris.

bosses, including his role in assassinations, both in foreign countries and in the United States. As I became a confidant to other deep-cover high-ranking CIA/ONI operatives I discovered that assassination teams were part of their activities and not simply done by rogue elements.

Russbacher described the various factions operating within the CIA, each with its own agenda and often running similar parallel operations. He fell out of grace with the CIA in the late 1980s for various reasons. Because of Russbacher's role in many CIA activities implicating high federal officials, and his knowledge of serious criminal activities against the United by the CIA, federal judges, Justice Department officials, and others, Russbacher posed a serious threat to those in control of key segments of the federal government. He was the smoking gun in many national scandals, the exposure of which could create a national emergency.

SEQUENCE OF SHAM CHARGES

In late 1986 the State of Missouri filed charges against Russbacher for allegedly writing checks to an alias, upon an account that had inadvertently closed; for allegedly defrauding several people out of $20,000, when the money had actually been returned to them; and for allegedly selling unregistered securities (from one CIA proprietary to another). These alleged offenses occurred while he was operating a CIA proprietary known as National Brokerage Company in Clayton, Missouri and Southwest Latex Supply. Russbacher stated that no one ever lost any money as the amount of money claimed was returned to the people. The charges were not pressed and Russbacher was not arrested.

In August 1989 Russbacher used a CIA Learjet based at Hayward Airport in California to fly his prospective bride from Seattle to Reno, where they were married, and then back to Seattle. Personal use of government aircraft is not exactly an unknown event, but in this case Justice Department prosecutors, representing Faction One of the Central Intelligence Agency (Russbacher was Faction Two), chose to charge him with misuse of government aircraft and fuel.

Another reason for charging Russbacher with an offense was that he married shortly after signing his latest CIA secrecy agreement in which he agreed not to marry for the next two years. On August 30, 1989, Russbacher married Rayelan Dyer, the widow of a former professor[238] at the Naval Postgraduate School in Monterey. Among the Naval personnel that Rayelan had met at the school while her husband was alive was Gunther Russbacher, having first met him in 1982. Several weeks before the marriage, Russbacher requested of his superiors permission to marry. Permission was necessitated by his CIA secrecy agreement barring him from marrying for two years after its latest signing. Russbacher was verbally advised that this approval would probably not be forthcoming because Rayelan was an activist of the 1960s and had sought to expose the October Surprise operation in collaboration with Barbara Honegger, the author of the first book bearing the title *October*

---

[238] Dean of Science and Engineering.

Surprise.

In August 1989 Rayelan accidentally met Russbacher in the State of Washington, while she was traveling with her mother, Bess Smith, in Oregon. Several days later Russbacher called and proposed marriage. After she accepted, Russbacher called the crew of a CIA proprietary aircraft charter operation, Jet Charter International, based at Hayward, California, instructing them to pick him up at Sacramento Municipal Airport and fly him to Boeing Field in Seattle. After the plane was serviced by Flightcraft in Seattle, the Learjet departed for Reno with Russbacher and Rayelan on board. After arriving in Reno they got married, and immediately flew back to Seattle. From Seattle the Learjet pilots, Don LaKava and Jan Pierson, both of whom had served with Russbacher in Central America activities, flew to Modesto, California. They then drove to Bess Smith's home in Newman, California.

Within days after the marriage, FBI agents burst into Bess Smith's home (September 1, 1989) in Newman, arresting Russbacher, falsely charging that he kidnapped his wife's niece, Jennifer Smith.[239] The FBI agents told Rayelan and her mother that Russbacher was a con artist, marrying women all over the country and then taking their money. The FBI agents stated that Russbacher was committing all types of fraud throughout the United States. They stated he had no association with the government and was a pathological liar. The FBI agents were so convincing in their lies that they almost had Rayelan convinced.

The kidnapping charges were dropped on December 1, 1989, but the State of Missouri took custody of Russbacher on the 1986 charges that he had misappropriated $20,000 through bad checks, and sold securities without registering the transaction with the State. Russbacher was denied bail. During trial, the judge declared a mistrial. Waiting for the next trial, which was repeatedly delayed, Russbacher remained in the harsh surroundings of St. Charles county jail in Missouri. His attorney, Timothy Farrell, and the Missouri County Prosecutor, John P. Zimmerman, pressured Russbacher to sign a plea agreement, claiming it would put all of the charges behind him. Russbacher verbally agreed to an "Alford" agreement, or nolo contendere, wherein Russbacher did not plead guilty, but agreed to certain conditions to avoid trial.

Russbacher's attorney appeared more interested in appeasing the judge and the prosecutor, and failed to provide the defenses expected of even a half-baked attorney.

When Russbacher entered the court room on July 16, 1990, the terms in the written plea agreement, which he had never seen before, were very different from what his attorney and the prosecutor had stated earlier. Russbacher was pressured to sign the agreement, stating he would then be set free. The pressure of a year in a county jail, and the promise of a return to his

---

[239] Rayelen's mother received a telephone call from her granddaughter living near Seattle asking that she be allowed to stay in California until the girl's parents recovered from their drug and alcohol problems. Russbacher called the CIA's Learjet to fly him, Rayelan and her mother, to Seattle, where twelve-year-old Jennifer Smith resided. Jennifer's mother agreed to let the daughter go to California.

CIA status, caused Russbacher to sign. During questioning by Judge Lester Duggan, Jr., Russbacher told the judge that he was not pleading guilty but exercising an "alford" plea. But the judge entered into court records that Russbacher pled guilty to the offenses.

UNAWARE OF THE PITFALLS OF PROBATION

The wording of the plea agreement was such that he could be incarcerated again whenever it suited Missouri prosecutors, who were working hand in hand with Justice Department and CIA personnel. Russbacher either did not realize it at the time, or he was desperate to get out of jail.

The terms of the plea agreement required Russbacher to remain silent as to any criminal activities he had discovered or that he would eventually discover. (This was similar to orders rendered against me by federal judges in the San Francisco area, when they barred me from reporting any criminal activities to a federal court).

Under the terms of the probation agreement, Russbacher could be returned to prison, without a trial on the original charges, for 21 years, if he violated any of the terms of the plea agreement. Almost anything he did for the CIA violated the conditions of the plea agreement, including trips outside of the St. Charles area and failure to report regularly to his probation officer.

NO SNITCHING

One paragraph of the plea agreement was obviously meant to keep Russbacher from testifying at any Congressional or other government inquiry. Paragraph number five read:

That the defendant enter into no agreements with any governmental or other agency to provide information concerning crimes or bad acts. No snitching for anyone.

This agreement was signed by the Missouri Assistant Prosecuting Attorney, John P. Zimmerman; by Russbacher's attorney, Timothy Farrell; and St. Charles, Missouri Judge Lester Duggan, Jr. This was another version of the tactic that federal judges and Justice Department prosecutors inflicted upon me, seeking to silence my exposure activities.

The terms of the plea agreement were also spelled out in a July 2, 1990, letter by St. Charles County Assistant Prosecuting Attorney John P. Zimmerman to Russbacher's attorney, repeating the exact words in the plea agreement. There was a determined effort to silence Russbacher, using state officials to carry out the intent of federal officials.

Item number seven provided that Russbacher "not leave the St. Louis area without written permission from his probation officer." But Russbacher's CIA duties required that he immediately leave the area, which he did. The plea agreement also required Russbacher to make weekly reports to the probation officer, which he never did. Nothing was said about it until several years later when Justice Department officials wanted to silence Russbacher.

ULTRA SECRET OPERATION

The CIA had an important task for Russbacher to perform upon leaving prison. He was needed for an ultra-secret project associated with the Bush administration's dealings with Iraq's Saddam Hussein. The signature of Russian President Mikhail Gorbachev was needed on a secret agreement prepared and signed by President George Bush. Russbacher stated that the agreement provided that Russia would not intervene if the United States attacked Iraq in the near future. Russbacher spoke Russian, had been assigned to the U.S. Embassy in Moscow, and knew President Gorbachev personally. The signature and agreement had to remain secret.

Russbacher's handlers instructed him to proceed to Offutt Air Force Base for a top-secret briefing. Immediately upon release from prison at St. Charles, Missouri, on July 16, 1990, Russbacher and his wife drove to Offutt Air Force Base. They arrived there on July 18, where CincPac authorization permitted them to occupy living quarters at this high-security Air Force Base. Russbacher was briefed about the mission in which he was to be involved. Among those present at the meeting were Brent Scowcroft, national security advisor, and CIA Director William Webster.

Gunther Russbacher and his wife departed Offutt on July 21, 1990, driving to Reno, where they stayed at the Western Village Inn and Casino in nearby Sparks, awaiting further orders. Late in the afternoon on July 26, 1990, Russbacher boarded a CIA Learjet at Reno, which took him to Crows Landing Naval Air Station, where four CIA SR-71 aircraft were being readied for a non-stop flight to Moscow, carrying out the plans reached at Offutt.

Russbacher described the inflight refueling of the SR-71's on their transpolar flight to Moscow, with the first one occurring northeast of Seattle and the second refueling by Russian tankers as they approached the USSR. Russbacher identified one of the passengers in the SR-71s as national security advisor Brent Scowcroft.

Russbacher was the only person on the four aircraft who spoke Russian, and had met Gorbachev while assigned to the U.S. Embassy in Moscow during the 1970s and mid-1980s. He described handing the secret agreement to Gorbachev, obtaining Gorbachev's signature on one of the agreements, and then flying back to the United States, along with two of the other CIA aircraft. One SR-71 was left for the Russians, along with a flight crew to check out Russian pilots. It is believed that one of the flight instructors was a former Air Force Chief Flight Instructor from Beale Air Force Base in Marysville, California, reportedly Abe Kardone. (I owned a 60-unit motel in nearby Yuba City and often had Air Force personnel staying there.)

The aircraft refueled twice in the air on the return flight, and the three SR-71s landed at Fallon Naval Air Station on July 26, 1990.

On July 25, 1990, the day before Russbacher obtained Gorbachev's signature, U.S. Ambassador April Glaspie assured Iraq's Saddam Hussein that the United States had no interest in its conflict with Kuwait. These assurances were interpreted by Saddam Hussein as clearance to invade Kuwait, which he did several days later. This sequence of events almost suggests that Saddam Hussein was encouraged to attack Kuwait while the United States waited to retaliate.

Upon landing at Fallon Naval Air Station a Navy Helicopter flew him to Reno and then he took a cab to the motel where his wife was waiting. While at the motel waiting for further instructions from his CIA bosses, Russbacher received telephone instructions on July 28th from Admiral George Raeder, instructing him to report to Castle Air Force Base for a debriefing on the Moscow flight. Raeder further advised Russbacher that he would be promoted from Captain to Rear Admiral, and for Russbacher to get the proper uniform and a Rear Admiral's cap at nearby Fallon Naval Air Station, which he did.

Bizarre as the Moscow flight sounds to people living a normal life, it must be remembered that the CIA deals in the bizarre. I talked to Rayelan, who saw the CIA Learjet and four CIA SR-71s land. She saw Russbacher enter the Learjet, which immediately departed. I talked to Bess Smith, Rayelan's mother, who lived in Hanford, near the Crows Landing Naval Air Station, and who was present at the Navy base during the preparation of the SR-71s. She saw Russbacher get in one of the aircraft. During the debriefing at Castle Air Force Base, she was in one of the adjoining bedrooms and saw the people receiving the debriefing from Russbacher.

The answers Bess Smith gave to my questions showed she wasn't fabricating what she saw. She was a kind, motherly person, who could not fabricate the facts that she witnessed. I also talked to the SR-71 pilot and former instructor at Beale Air Force Base, Abe Kardone of Tacoma, Washington. Kardone, while being circumspect, made statements indicating he was one of the pilots on the flight, and that he was the SR-71 instructor who remained behind in Moscow to check out the Russian flight crews.

The Russbachers arrived at Castle Air Force base on July 29, 1990, and CincPac authorization was again waiting from the navy permitting them to be billeted there for several days. (I have copies of the billeting receipts from both military bases.) Russbacher's CIA handlers debriefed him in his apartment-size accommodations while Rayelan and her mother were sleeping in one of the two adjoining bedrooms. After the debriefing, Russbacher waited to receive his promotion to Rear Admiral. Up to this point he had not worn his Navy uniform, which was hanging in the closet in a protective bag. While Russbacher debriefed his CIA people, Bess Smith walked into the kitchen from her bedroom and exchanged greetings with the people there.

On July 31, 1990, the morning after the late-evening debriefing, FBI agents burst into their living quarters, arrested Russbacher for allegedly impersonating a Naval officer, and had him incarcerated at the Fresno County jail while awaiting trial. Justice Department prosecutors soon dropped the charge, but U.S. Attorney David Levi at Sacramento filed new charges. He alleged that Russbacher misused government aircraft, fuel, military facilities and purchase orders associated with the flights to Seattle and Reno when Russbacher married Rayelan.

During the trial, FBI agent Rich Robley testified that Russbacher had worked for the government, and it looked favorable for an acquittal. Before reaching the jury, U.S. District Judge Leonard Pierce, declared a mistrial, which was followed by months of delaying tactics by Justice Department prosecutors as they prepared for another trial. Meanwhile, Russbacher languished in jail. When Russbacher stated he would fight the charges, U.S. Attorney David Levi threatened to charge Russbacher's wife and mother-in-law with unlawfully trespassing on Offut and Castle Air Force Bases, and request six months in prison for each of them.

Despite the constitutional requirement of a jury trial, federal judges have held that six months imprisonment permits eliminating that constitutional protection, and allowing the federal judge to decide guilt or innocence. In this way a federal judge, who is often a former Justice Department attorney and usually works in unison with the prosecuting attorney, can sentence a person to six months in prison on fabricated charges. This six months imprisonment often destroys a person financially and inflicts great personal harm upon the individual and family. This unconstitutional imprisonment without a jury trial occurs frequently. It was done to me in retaliation for reporting the federal crimes in which federal judges and Justice Department attorneys were implicated.

The U.S. Attorney promised Russbacher that he would receive only a three-month prison sentence if he pled guilty, and Russbacher agreed. However, U.S. District Judge Pierce refused to honor this agreement, and sentenced Russbacher to twenty months in prison. After several months in the county jail, Russbacher was transferred to the federal prison camp at Dublin, California. That is where I met him.

Russbacher and I had a good relationship, possibly due to our prior Navy piloting background. At first, Russbacher was very guarded in what he told me about CIA operations. He described his activities in Central America with the CIA, including Oliver North's involvement, and the disdain that CIA and other people had for North's incompetence and involvement in drug trafficking.

"My life wouldn't be worth a nickel ..."

At first, there were many CIA operations Russbacher wouldn't disclose to me. When I pressed him for details he stated, "My life wouldn't be worth a nickel if I talked about the hush-hush things." A few weeks after we had met, I was released[240] December 10, 1990,[241] and returned to my home in Alamo, California. Russbacher started calling me from prison, and our discussions about CIA and other covert activities continued. Much of the time I asked specific questions about CIA activities and he responded, similar to a deposition. I thought that *I* had discovered major criminal activities while an FAA investigator, but it was child's play compared to what I subsequently discovered. Through my contacts with Russbacher I became acquainted with other deep-cover CIA operatives and contract agents, DEA personnel, and former police and private investigators. This small group had information

---

[240] But the release was only pending still another trial at which the same Justice Department and the same Ninth Circuit judges sought to again send me to federal prison. The FBI and Justice Department again accused me of criminal contempt of court for having filed a federal law suit in the U.S. District Court at Chicago which described additional federal crimes that I had uncovered in Chapter 11 courts, and in which I sought relief from the escalating attacks upon me.

[241] San Francisco U.S. District Judge Marilyn Patel had caused me to be incarcerated without charges, without having personal jurisdiction over me, on the basis that I had filed a federal action in the U.S. District Court at Chicago (No. 90-C-2396), reporting a pattern of federal crimes that I had discovered, and for exercising declaratory and injunctive relief remedies to obtain relief from the Judicial persecution inflicted upon me, that initially commenced from the sham law suit filed by the covert Justice Department law firm, Friedman, Sloan and Ross.

about virtually every dirty covert activity of the CIA. The education was priceless and made possible the exposures described within these pages.

Russbacher's health problems necessitated his transfer to the federal prison at Terminal Island, near Long Beach, California, but our almost daily telephone conversations continued, going further into CIA activities in which he had been involved. Russbacher admitted that, under orders from his CIA superiors, he did things in the past that he wasn't proud of.

Russbacher's CIA status, and his credibility, were proven to me not only by the hundreds of hours of questioning but by the statements given to me by other deep-cover operatives or contract agents, some of whom hadn't seen Russbacher for years.

OCTOBER SURPRISE

In early February 1991, I questioned Russbacher concerning his knowledge of the hostage scandal known as October Surprise. He replied that he was well familiar with the details, that he was part of the operation, but that he would not talk about it except in generalities. But this attitude suddenly changed.

During an early morning telephone conversation on April 30, 1991, Russbacher said that three Office of Naval Intelligence officers were coming to Terminal Island that afternoon and he would be flying with them to Monterey, California, for a special assignment. The flight from Long Beach to Monterey would be in a Learjet, after which a Navy helicopter from the Naval Air Station at Alameda, California, would take them to Fort Ord and then on to Santa Cruz, landing at the college. Russbacher's CIA faction occasionally extracted him from prison for short periods of time. But something happened.

Shortly before midnight my telephone rang. It was Russbacher's wife, Rayelan. She sought my help to determine if her husband was on a helicopter that reportedly crashed several hours earlier at Fort Ord. She had been expecting her husband to arrive at Santa Cruz by Navy helicopter, and when she saw on television that a helicopter had crashed at nearby Fort Ord that evening, she grew worried.

Rayelan had contacted a friend who was CIA Chief of Station at St. Louis, nicknamed the "Rabbit," who in turn phoned an FBI contact in California. The CIA station agent then called Rayelan, advising her that a Navy helicopter at Fort Ord had blown apart in the air, and that there were no survivors. But he didn't know who had been on board when it crashed. Russbacher's wife asked me to call my FAA contacts to find out if her husband was one of the fatalities.

"I've been drugged!"

While Russbacher's wife and I were talking, Russbacher came on the line, calling from federal prison at Terminal Island. He exclaimed, "I've been drugged." Russbacher explained that he had coffee at approximately 2:30 with the Admiral whom he had been expecting. Russbacher stated that the Admiral advised that he would return in about an hour and a half to take him to Santa Cruz.

After drinking coffee with the Admiral, Russbacher suddenly felt drowsy, and went back to his cell and fell sound asleep. Shortly after ten p.m.

Russbacher awoke to the shouts of other prisoners, that he had an emergency phone call from his wife. He called his wife and the call came through as she and I were talking.

Russbacher described what happened, stating that he felt the Navy Admiral deliberately drugged him to prevent him flying back, and may have done so thinking there was a plot to kill Russbacher and in that way protect him.

"Your life may depend on you going public!"

I warned Russbacher that because of the information he possessed that threatened to expose the people involved in October Surprise that his life was in constant danger, and that the sooner he disclosed this information to others, the less would be the danger to him. "Your life may depend on you going public," I added.

It was now about midnight, and Russbacher was still groggy. I suggested that he call me the following morning, when his mind was clear, and give me a sworn declaration of events surrounding the October Surprise operation. I stated that I would record his statements and have the recording transcribed, after which I would send portions of the transcript to members of Congress. (What an optimist!)

REVEALING MAJOR CRIMES AGAINST AMERICA

When Russbacher called the next morning at 8 a.m, I said: "I need to know the specifics on the flight to Europe, including who was on board the aircraft, who stayed at what hotel; where did the flight start from and where did it land enroute?" What he stated on that first questioning session was repeated many times during the next few years as other segments of that and other operations were described. This was the start of years of discoveries, of treasonous, subversive, and criminal acts, implicating many federal officials, enlarging upon the hard-core criminality I had already discovered. A brief extract of that first declaration reads as follows:

"My name is Gunther Russbacher. I am a captain in the United States Navy; my service number is 440-40-1417. My current location is the Federal Correctional Institution, Terminal Island. I am a federal prisoner, awaiting appeal on a charge of misuse and misappropriation of government properties, misuse of government jets, and misuse of government purchase orders, for purchase of fuel. That is my current situation. The date today is May 1, 1991. The time of this interview is 0824. Now that we have the formalities under way, Rodney Stich, we can talk."

"Who were the pilots," I asked.

"On the flight deck were pilots Richard Brenneke, an Air Force pilot, and I was the command pilot."

"Who was in the cabin?"

"In the cabin were George Bush; William Casey; Robert Gates; Donald Gregg, current ambassador to South Korea, and others."

In later sessions I probed more deeply into who the passengers were, and Russbacher presented a more complete list. He stated that other passengers included several Secret Service agents assigned to Vice-Presidential candidate George Bush; Robert Allen; Senators John Tower and John Heinz; Congressman Dan Rostenkowski; Jennifer Fitzgerald of the State Department and reportedly a close lady friend of Bush for many years.

"What type of plane were you flying?" I asked.

"The plane was a BAC 111, and we departed from Andrews Air Force Base, to New York, to Gander, and then on to Paris, landing at Le Bourget."

"At what stage of the flight did you see the passengers?"

"I went back into the cabin after taking off from Gander."

"Where did the crew stay while in Paris?"

"We stayed at the Florida Hotel in Paris."

"How long did Bush stay in Paris?"

"Bush only remained a few hours.

"Did you fly the same plane back?" I asked.

"No I didn't. I flew the man [George Bush] back in the SR71."

"Are you qualified in the 71?"

"Rodney, I flew the 71 for eighteen months."

"Where did the '71 refuel?" recognizing that the SR-71 could not fly from Paris to the United States without refueling.

"The refueling occurred approximately, I would have to say, 1800 to 1900 nautical miles into the Atlantic. We were met by a KC 135."

"Where did you land on the return flight?"

"McGuire," Russbacher replied. [McGuire Air Force Base, New Jersey]

"How long did the flight take?"

"The flight took one hour and forty four minutes."

"What time did you arrive back at McGuire Air Force Base?"

"We arrived at McGuire Air Force Base approximately ten-fifty a.m. the following morning."

"Who were some of the people you saw in Paris?"

"Adnan Khashoggi, Hashemi Rafsanjani. Rafsanjani was the Ayatollah's henchman and the second in command. Please look who is in command now; Rafsanjani."

In response to my probing questions he provided additional data, including rudimentary piloting activities, conversations, airports, and other data, that would be hard to fabricate. Russbacher described the route of flight from Washington to New York, to Gander, and then to Paris. He described specifics that might be meaningless to anyone but a pilot who had been to the airports he described, which provided further confirmation that he was telling me the truth.

After arrival in Paris, Russbacher went to the Hotel Florida, and had been asleep only a short time when he received a call from the CIA station chief in Frankfort, advising him that an SR-71 was being flown to Paris for him to fly back to the United States. The SR-71, with Vice Presidential candidate George Bush as a back-seat passenger and Russbacher at the controls, departed from a military airbase near Paris 2:50 p.m. European Time (13:50 GMT, or 8:50 a.m. EST).

The SR-71 was refueled about 1,800 miles from Paris, over the North Atlantic, by a U.S. Air Force tanker, landing at McGuire Air Force Base in

New Jersey at 10:50 a.m. Eastern Standard Time (6:50 p.m. GMT). After Bush left the aircraft, Russbacher flew the SR-71 to Andrews Air Force Base.

Going back to the October Surprise operation, I asked Russbacher, "What do you know about the first meeting in Madrid between Casey and the Iranians, that reportedly occurred in July of 1980?"

"The Madrid meeting was more of a diversionary tactic. The actual meeting occurred in Barcelona."

"I was in Barcelona at the time of the meetings. I was there at the Pepsico International headquarters building. I gave you the guy's name that was our interface there. V-a-n-T-y-n-e. [Peter Van Tyne]"

"That was approximately what month?" I asked, to make sure we were talking about the same meetings.

"That was in late July of 1980."

"This is the meeting or meetings in which William Casey met with some Iranians?

"That is correct. That was with Hushang Lavi and Rogovin."[242]

"Referring to all of the reports of Casey having been in Madrid, I believe you stated that Casey was never in Madrid?"

"I said that the meetings, the top-level high-speed meetings did not take place in Madrid. The suites and conference rooms and everything were rented and cared for. However, the meetings took place, and the people stayed, at the Hotel Princess Sofia, S-O-F-I-A, in Barcelona."

I responded, "And was this at the same time that he was supposedly in Madrid?"

"Right. It was a little subterfuge upon the part of the government [CIA]. But the actual meetings took place in Barcelona. They took place at the Pepsico International Headquarters building."

"And you were there in town with Peggy [Gunther's wife at the time]?"

"That's right. I was there at the meetings."

"So you know what was stated at the meetings?"

"This is where the first discussions were coming up as to what type of arms and munitions that the Iranians wanted."

"And who was there besides William Casey; was that Robert McFarlane?"

"Yes, it was."

"You previously stated that in Barcelona the meetings were held at the hotel, but then you also mentioned in one place about them being held at the Pepsico plant. Can you explain that?"

"Right. The day's meetings were held over at the Pepsico International Headquarters buildings."

"That was the main meetings then? Did you have any at the hotel that you mentioned?"

"Yes."

---

[242] Mitchell Rogovin, lawyer for Lavi.

"What part did Van Tyne play in the meetings? Did he more or less coordinate the meetings?"

"Facilitator. Yes."

Realizing that Pepsico surfaces in numerous CIA activities, including drug processing in the Far East, I asked Russbacher: "Was Pepsico a CIA proprietary corporation?"

"No, but they have close connections to each other; they work together."

"A few more questions on the Barcelona meeting,[243] just to get clarified in my mind. Why did they have to use Madrid[244] as a diversionary point when they were trying to cover up for the whole operation?"

"There were also high-level meetings going on in the Spanish cabinet at the same time. It would be easier to hide under the cloak of secrecy as to what transpired in Madrid at that time, without going in and having to create a brand new cover for the meeting in Barcelona."

"Can you give me the details on the hour of the day and how long the meetings lasted?"

"I would estimate, according to my recollection, that the meeting began about ten o'clock in the morning, and lasted probably until one o'clock, at which time they broke for lunch, and the meeting reconvened from about three to six pm."

"Was it a one-day meeting?"

"No, two days. The first day was full of meetings, and the second day was only about three hours long."

"What was your role at that meeting?"

"The only part that I took part in was to set up a centralized command in Vienna, which would involve being able to draw large containers and to allow freighting weapon containers, and so on."

"From the reforger stores?"[245]

"From the reforger stores, through Austria and down by rail."

"I would presume, referring to some comments you made about Austria being unhappy, were they to be notified when military shipments went through their country?

"It was a total no-no."[246]

"Even when it is ordered by the United States?"[247]

---

[243] The secret late-July 1980 Barcelona meetings, involving private citizen William Casey, preceded the secret October 19, 1980, weekend meetings held in Paris.

[244] Investigative reporters and writers charge that William Casey met secretly in Madrid with Iranian factions to prevent the release of the 52 American hostages (last week of July 1980). But this is incorrect. The first meeting in Spain was not at Madrid, but at Barcelona.

[245] Reforger stores contain American military weapons and were located in various European locations. To fulfill the Barcelona agreement, US weapons and munitions were fraudulently removed from military warehouses in Austria, Germany, and Italy, commencing in September 1980.

[246] Secretly moving the military shipments through Austria violated the laws and sovereignty of Austria.

[247] Actually, the duly elected government of the United States neither ordered the shipments of military arms, nor knew about the shipments. The removal was unlawfully done through a criminal conspiracy by private citizen William Casey and Central Intelligence Agency factions, in a literal coup against the United States.

"The United States cannot order anything. Austria is a sovereign republic. We made weapon shipments from the early contacts with the Iranians through Switzerland. We railed from Zurich to Vienna, and from Vienna on down."

"You said the people at the meeting were Casey and McFarlane; were there any other Americans there?"

"I think Allen was there for a couple of hours."

"And on the other side there was Hushang Lavi, and I think you mentioned Rogovin?"

"Yes."

"Rogovin was the attorney for Lavi, wasn't he?"

"Yes."

"Was there anyone else there?"

"There were several other people. But the individual I dealt with primarily was Mr. Peter Van Tyne."

"What was his position?"

"Peter Van Tyne was executive vice-president for Pepsico International. I might add that part of the reason I was there was that I was to set up a large production warehouse and production corporation in Vienna. We are talking about an extremely large warehouse where we could hold container shipments until trans-shipment took place. We were withdrawing military weapons and munitions from Switzerland, including Swiss military manufacturer Orlikon. We were drawing stores[248] from Germany. We were also drawing stores up from Italy. The shipments from Italy came up through Brenner Pass in overland containers, at which point they ended up in Innsbruck, Austria. In Innsbruck they were replaced by other containers, that were supposedly at that point moving mineral waters from Innsbruck to Third World areas."

"Mineral water?" I asked.

"That was what the code name was. The code name for it was Seltzer Water."

Describing the route of the arms shipments, Russbacher stated he established "transshipment points from Europe, especially Germany, Italy, and Switzerland. In Italy, up through Brenner Pass; from Germany into Austria. We were buying arms from Orlikon, a corporation, a weapons manufacturer in Switzerland. We had a big warehouse, a huge one. Some went through Yugoslavia. It went through Yugoslavia for transshipment through Macedonia, down through Greece, and then Cyprus, and then across. Hungary was a transship point also. At times it went through Hungary. However, most of the times it went through Yugoslavia.

"Because Austria was a neutral country and Hungary was a communist country, we had a choice of transshipment points. Either first from Vienna to Budapest, where they were then transferred onto trains to Yugoslavia, or directly from Austria to Yugoslavia, and Yugoslavia down into Greece, and then to Cyprus. Most of the time it went through Yugoslavia."

---

[248] Military equipment and supplies.

In a later written response to interrogatories Russbacher replied in a sworn declaration:

I was in attendance during the meetings held in Geneva, Switzerland; the meetings in Barcelona, Spain; the meetings held in Madrid, Spain, and the meeting held in Karachi, Pakistan. I was there as agency supply and logistics person, as well as facilitator for the governments involved.

The initial meeting was held in Geneva, and was held with Ahmed Heidari and Mohammed Hussein Behisti. Mr. Cyrus Hashemi was the arms specialist present at this meeting. In order to be unknown in this field we used the following DOS personnel as cutouts: Mr. Sam Carlton and Peter Merrell. This meeting took place six days after my return from Buenos Aires, Argentina, where a meeting of low echelon state staffers and I talked to the Mossad contact man, Ari Ben-Menashe.

The meeting with Ari Ben-Menashe was held on or about March fourth to the eighth, 1980. The initial meeting with the DOS persons, Hashemi, Heidari, Behisti and myself, was held in Geneva, shortly after our return from Buenos Aires. We met in Geneva on or about 14 March 1980. The discussion centered around another version of the swap for the hostages.

Mr. Adnan Khashoggi permitted us the use of his credit cards for the purpose of purchasing fuel for the aircraft. He indicated that he had specific interest in obtaining a deal for the sale or trade of arms to the government of Iran. We contacted Mr. Behisti and Mr. Heidari (who was the person responsible for coordinating the sale of the arms). Because Mr. Behisti spoke very little English, all conversations were held in either French or German. I was able to function as negotiator and interpreter for several such meetings.

LOOTING UNITED STATES MILITARY WAREHOUSES

During another probing session, Russbacher revealed when the arms and munitions started to flow. The answer was critical, and helped explain how the officially elected government of the United States was rendered helpless by the coup d'etat aspects of the October Surprise conspirators.

"After the [July 1980] Barcelona meeting, how soon did these arms start flowing?"

Russbacher hesitated in answering that question. He replied: "My friend, the arms began flowing, I would say, probably in September."[249]

"Were you over there at that time?"

"Yes, I was."

Since Casey, Ronald Reagan, and George Bush, the principal parties in the

---

[249] The gravity of this is that private citizen William Casey (and others) were able to remove military weapons and munitions from United States stockpiles, that were intended for the defense of Europe, and with the obvious cooperation of CIA factions, ship the arms to Iran via Israel, as part of the treasonous and subversive acts to continue the imprisonment of the 52 American hostages. A coup against the United States had occurred.

October Surprise conspiracy, had not held any government office at that time, and the November 1980 presidential elections had not occurred, the question arose as to who authorized the shipment of arms, especially since there were laws preventing the shipments, and since the shipments undermined the negotiations by President Jimmy Carter seeking to obtain the release of the 52 American hostages.

"Where did the authority come from to move that military equipment, since Casey and the gang held no government positions?"

Russbacher again hesitated, and then answered: "We [CIA] were already in there. The Agency [CIA] was already out on the limb.[250] And bear in mind that Bush was the ex-DCI.[251] Casey had gone back to the days of Wild Bill Donovan. So you are talking about an agency coup that was already in the making at that time.

"What about the military, didn't they have control of those weapons; I mean the US military?"

"Rodney, if I tell you the shenanigans that are pulled, and the shopping that can be done at these reforger stores,[252] you would pull your hair out."

I asked Russbacher who worked with him in procuring the arms and arranging the shipments. "The procurement of them was handled by an associate of mine. The fellow's name was John George Fisher. He is dead."

I asked Russbacher, "What type of paperwork was done to get the U,S. military organizations to release the equipment?"

"It is very simple," Russbacher replied. "All you have to have is a request for transfer; which is commonly referred to as an AF series, duly signed by authorized personnel, or by an authorized officer. And, of course you need a transfer form approved for a transport form. And then you need end-user certificates."

When I asked Russbacher how those in control of the weapon depots allowed the arms to be removed, he referred to the CIA practice of placing CIA people in other government departments: "We [CIA] had already put them in position."[253]

"What about the end user certificate requirements; you had to show an end user, and who was that?"

"We [CIA] had end-user certificates available. That's why all shipments went through Cyprus. By the time the weapons came to Cyprus, new end-user certificates, or the real ones, that were going to be used, then showed up. But the end-user certificates that we always provided would have been countries that were friendly to the United States. Some of them were bogus. A lot of

[250] The CIA arranged for Bush and others to fly to the Paris meetings on the weekend of October 19, 1980, at which the secret agreement was finalized (Paying $40 million bribe money and promising billions of dollars in military equipment and munitions, in exchange for continuing the imprisonment of the 52 American hostages).

[251] Director of Central Intelligence.

[252] Term applied to US military warehouses in Europe.

[253] It is a standard practice of the CIA to install CIA personnel through the federal government, into state governments, and throughout industry, including the media.

them went down to an entity in Spain. We had some sympathetic people."

Continuing, Russbacher stated, "We had embassies in Madrid that provided us end-user certificates. A lot of them were embassies from North African countries, West African countries, including Liberia."

Russbacher referred to the key role played by Israel in the operation, stating, "We worked hand in hand with the Mossad."[254]

During the next few years I repeatedly questioned Russbacher about operations in which he had been directly involved, or of which he had specific details due to the nature of his work. Russbacher repeated details of the various CIA operations that we had previously discussed, often times expanding on what he had earlier described to me.

ISRAELI PARTICIPATION

"Were there any Israel people at the Barcelona meeting?"

"I knew there was a discussion that there were some present."

"Was Karrubi there? [Mehdi Karrubi, presently Iranian Parliamentary Speaker.]" Russbacher replied, "Yes."

In Ari Ben-Menashe's book, *Profits of War*, and in conversations with him, Ben-Menashe stated that he was present at the Barcelona meeting.

Referring to the $40 million bribe money that was reportedly given to the Iranian factions at the subsequent Paris meetings on the October 19, 1980, weekend, I asked: "Do you know anything about the routing of the reported forty-million-dollar bank draft that was given to the Iranians during the Paris meetings?"

"Michael Riconosciuto would be the best one to answer that."

THE HELICOPTER CRASH

I asked details surrounding the helicopter crash that occurred the night before. "Were the Naval officers that you had coffee with [at Terminal Island Federal Prison], on the helicopter?" I asked.

"Yes," he replied, "I had coffee with one of them."

"What was his name?"

"The first guy's name was Samuel Walters."

"And he was Navy?"

"And that's his true name too."[referring to the alias frequently used; Gunther used the alias of Robert A. Walker.]

"What was his rank?"

"He was a captain."

"Did you meet the other two guys that were on it?"

"Yes, one of them was a Rear Admiral. John D. Burkhardt. He was in defense logistics."

"Office of Naval Intelligence?"

---

[254] Israel played a key role in carrying out the secret activities, including participation/attendance at the Barcelona and Paris meetings, the stealing of the arms from US warehouses, and the secret shipment of arms to Iran. Israel obviously knew that the scheme and activities were treasonous, subversive, and harmful to the United States; and also recognized that they could thereafter blackmail the United States while Reagan and Bush were in the White House.

"Yes. And his present job was that he was very strongly implicated in NASA and the SDI initiative." Russbacher continued, "Raye called the Chief of Stations at St. Louis, who is a friend of ours. He made some checks and found out who was on board."

"Were they the ones who were to have gone back with you?"

"Yes."

"Tricky business, Rodney, I don't know if you want to get into this. If I had been on that helicopter, I would be dead."

Describing what his CIA handlers told him, Russbacher said:

"The helicopter took off yesterday carrying a rear admiral, two Navy captains, and it should also have carried myself. Everybody here, including the D of J [Department of Justice], was under the impression that I was going to be on that airplane. The aircraft took off from Fort Ord with a flight to Monterey, and from Monterey they were going to discharge one of the crew who was going to stay at the FBO at Monterey. And then the aircraft was going on to Santa Cruz, and land back behind the university grounds. The incident occurred about 6:18 p.m,. The original incident, as it was described by the radio at Santa Cruz, was that a helicopter exploded about 200 feet above the ground. No pieces. Just general wreckage. What came out about an hour later was that a helicopter went down with two FBI agents on board. There **were** two FBI agents on board, although they suffered serious injuries, they were ok. One of them suffered very serious head injuries. Somehow or other they were able to cover up for the initial flight. Rodney, they are after every one that has anything to do with these activities."

Russbacher continued, "Someone saved my butt last night. I don't know how many more times in the future they are going to be able to do it."

"You felt that something was put in the coffee. Did it just make you groggy?"

"I went right to sleep, and slept until twenty minutes of ten."

"So after you drank the coffee you were supposed to leave right then and there?"

"Within an hour and a half."

"Then you went back to your cell and went to sleep, expecting them to call you?"

"They never called."

"They never tried to wake you up?"

"As far as I know, no one tried to wake me up. The first inclination I had that it was time to wake up was at twenty minutes of ten, people were screaming at me, that I had an emergency call from the [prison] Control Center, and that I needed to call home immediately."

"I'm surprised the prison officials gave you that personal service."

"Well, you have to also bear in mind that [my status is] a little different."

"Well, the fact that you can get to a phone that is not monitored indicates that you are in a different category than most prisoners."

"Within four minutes of being awakened I was on the phone talking to Raye and hearing your voice in the background."

I asked Russbacher how he ended up in prison. He replied, "That could be a book by itself. It dealt with repatriating some of the arms from Central America back to the United States."

Referring to what was done to silence me, Russbacher stated: "Your case is different. It does not address a single issue. Your case addresses multi-issues. If you create sufficient fires, it is extremely difficult to determine where the fires are and how best to put them out. "You pose a significant threat. You pose as much of a threat to their little game as I do to the total administration. You pose a significant embarrassment to the federal government. It isn't quite so easy to shut these people down."

CONFIRMATION OF THE HELICOPTER CRASH AND THE DEATH OF A DEEP-COVER NAVY ADMIRAL

The existence of the Navy helicopter crash was kept secret by the government, as though it never happened. The absence of any report caused me to withhold further mention of it, fearing that reference to a non-reported helicopter crash would discredit the other information Russbacher gave me. However, during a conversation with *St. Louis Post Dispatch* reporter Phil Linsalata, I described the helicopter crash and qualified the information with the statement that I had no evidence to support its occurrence; that I hadn't told anyone else about it, because of lack of evidence. Linsalata said that the *Post Dispatch* had a reliable CIA source, and that they would contact him for possibly confirming the crash.

Linsalata contacted me several days later, on May 4, 1991, advising that the CIA contact confirmed the helicopter crash, and that a Navy admiral was killed. Linsalata stated that the CIA contact expressed surprise that the *Post Dispatch* knew of the crash and the death of the Navy admiral. During another conversation on May 20, 1991, Linsalata again made reference to the statements made by the CIA informant concerning the death of the Navy admiral in the helicopter crash. In response to my questions, Linsalata stated:

The guy (CIA informant) seemed shocked that I had access to this information. His shock seemed sincere. You judge the truth of what a person is saying, such as by the tone of voice. He seemed quite shocked that I had access to this information. He also made a comment that he personally knew who the ranking officer was, the brass, the admiral, and that he knew the guy. He was personally shocked that he [the Admiral] had been killed, and that he was a nice guy. He said the Admiral didn't deserve what happened. The things that he said to me made it impossible to rule out that he was simply offering the information that I gave him. The new information was given to me on his own. I didn't flush it out of him in any way. He just made comments reflecting that he knew what he was talking about. He seemed to be sincere.

COVERUP BY ST. LOUIS POST DISPATCH

Harry Martin,[255] publisher of the *Napa Sentinel*,[256] called me (July 8,

---

[255] *Napa Sentinel*, Napa, California.

1991), stating that he had just received a call from Phil Linsalata of the *St. Louis Post Dispatch*, denying that he had ever talked to any CIA contact about any helicopter crash at Napa. Martin said that Linsalata sounded very nervous, as if he was under pressure to make that call. It appeared that the intent of the call was to dissuade Martin from making any reference to the statements Linsalata made to me that confirmed the existence of the crash and the death of the Admiral.

Martin had been one of the first media sources to respond (May 1, 1991) to the notices that I had a tape and transcript of a CIA operative who had been part of the October Surprise scandal. His subsequent articles were copied by numerous other papers, and members of Congress requested copies of Martin's articles. There was danger of exposing the October Surprise scandal if Martin printed the statements made to me by the *St. Louis Post Dispatch* reporter. Possibly to prevent this from happening, Linsalata's publisher ordered Linsalata to call Martin and deny that he had ever talked to me or to anyone else about the helicopter crash. Martin asked if I had a tape of the conversation, and I replied that I did, of both the May 4 and May 20, 1991, telephone conversations. During these telephone conversations Linsalata went into great detail about what his confidential CIA source stated about the crash and the Admiral.

WARNINGS TO FORGET THE HELICOPTER CRASH

Several days after the helicopter crash, Gunther and his wife warned me to totally forget about it, warning me that my life would be in danger if I made any reference to it, or even made any inquiries. As I started to make reference to the crash during a subsequent conversation Russbacher stopped me: "No Rodney, don't bring that up. Don't touch that with a ten-foot pole."

"Because there is so much coverup in that crash!"

Russbacher said:

Rodney, don't even talk about it. I'm telling you. Because there is so much coverup in that crash. Listen to me. Listen closely. And be very guarded. When Raye got a call, she called St. Louis. St. Louis in turn made a phone call and then called her back. There were three people on board and they are all dead. You got that? Stay away from that as far as you can.

I replied, "It would be important to know the details." Russbacher answered, "This is not the time to know. For your own life. I'm talking about personal safety." At a later date I discovered additional evidence supporting the existence of that crash, and that it was an all-too-common assassination operation.

NOTIFYING THE MEDIA

After I notified various media contacts that I had declarations of a CIA operative concerning the October Surprise operation, journalists from all parts of the United States were calling me for further information. When these journalists contacted Justice Department and White House officials, they were

---

[256] The *Napa Sentinel* had been at the forefront in exposing government scandals, including Inslaw, October Surprise, and other stories.

told that Russbacher was a con artist, that he had a long rap sheet, and was not believable. This followed the standard line when CIA whistleblowers go public.

Shortly after Russbacher supplied me with his first declaration on May 1, 1991, I mailed partial transcripts to members of Congress,[257] along with a petition demanding that our testimony and evidence be received. I reminded them I was exercising rights[258] and responsibilities[259] under federal law and that they had a responsibility under these same laws and under federal criminal statutes to receive our testimony and evidence. I explained that I was a former federal investigator who held federal authority to make these determinations and that I hadn't lost any of my abilities to do that since leaving government.

I mailed certified letters and transcripts to Independent Prosecutor Lawrence Walsh, who had the duty to investigate all aspects of the Iran-Contra affair, which started with the October Surprise scheme. I reminded Walsh of his responsibilities under federal criminal statutes to receive my testimony and evidence, and that of the CIA whistleblowers.

Despite hundreds of certified mailings, each containing over fifty pages of data, no one responded. The non-response was one of the most amazing examples of mass coverup that I had ever witnessed. But it happened time and again. My letters raised very serious charges that, if only a small fraction of them were true, would inflict enormous harm upon the United States. Ignoring these charges from a person or people who could be expected to know, was similar to ignoring a report of a bomb on a Boeing 747 that was scheduled to depart shortly.

As Russbacher provided me with further information, and other CIA informants gave me supporting data, I sent additional petitions to members of Congress, demanding that they receive the testimony and evidence from a **group** of concerned CIA whistleblowers on criminal activities against the United States. I described specific facts that would be revealed. Every senator received at least three certified mailings from me between May 1991 and December 1992, as did the members of the House Judiciary Committee, Foreign Affairs Committee, Oversight and Investigations, government Operations, and Aviation. Not a single reply was received.

As a result of publicity generated by my transcripts and reference to Russbacher on my talk show appearances, Russbacher was asked to appear on numerous radio and television talk shows, which he did, from prison. Despite all this, the public remained passive, and none of those in government wanted to disturb the status quo.

---

[257] Every Senator in the United States Senate and to about 250 Representatives.

[258] Right to petition government relating to criminal acts by federal officials, including the First Amendment right to petition government and Title 28 U.S.C. § 1361, the right to judicial halting of corrupt acts by federal officials.

[259] Federal crime reporting statutes, including Title 18 U.S.C. § 4.

ESCALATING MEDIA AND
CONGRESSIONAL DISINFORMATION

Shortly after I had first publicized Russbacher's sworn statements, the disinformation commenced, trying to discredit him. Even author Barbara Honegger, who authored the first *October Surprise* book, tried to discredit Russbacher, fabricating facts that I had to address by sending out information identifying the apparent deliberate misstatements. Her tactics tended to discredit the existence of the very scandal that her earlier book sought to expose. It was as if she was being rewarded in some way to discredit the smoking gun in the October Surprise conspiracy.

The charges by Justice Department officials, commencing in 1986, were to discredit Russbacher and minimize the danger to White House and other officials. Russbacher had earlier described the three factions in the CIA as often fighting each other. Faction-One was controlled by the Justice Department and the White House under George Bush. Faction-Two was controlled by the Office of Naval Intelligence, often at odds with Faction One. And Faction-Three was a small number of former Office of Strategic Services (OSS) personnel.

"They are deporting Russ!"

Russbacher's appearances on radio and television from his prison environment threatened many people. Justice Department officials addressed this threat by seeking to deport him. Once, upon answering the phone,[260] Russbacher's wife exclaimed, "Gunther isn't in Terminal Island. He is on a flight to Oakdale, Louisiana, a federal prison where prisoners to be deported are sent."

In an attempt to prevent the deportation, I phoned talk-show host Tom Valentine with Radio Free America; senior White House reporter Sarah McClendon; Independent Prosecutor Lawrence Walsh; and appeared on numerous talk shows describing the latest attempt to sequester evidence relating to October Surprise.

"I need more information!"

Despite the gravity of criminal activities I listed in the petitions that I sent to Congress, the recipients did nothing. I felt that I needed more information about additional CIA crimes, that would force members of Congress to respond. I told Russbacher, "I need more information!" Russbacher went into other areas of CIA activities, and additional information continues to this very day.

Russbacher detailed the involvement by CIA factions in the looting of savings and loan institutions and insurance companies; the CIA's role in drug trafficking throughout the United States; and much more. He furnished me with blank checks, letterheads, and incorporation papers of some of the covert CIA proprietaries he operated for the CIA, which dealt in unlawful activities.

The information Russbacher gave was detailed, and presented in a way that I had no reason to question its accuracy. The answers to very specific

---

[260] October 13, 1991.

questions, requiring a very detailed answer, came without hesitation. In those cases when he didn't know, he didn't hesitate to say so, even though he could have fabricated an answer. There were some areas of CIA activity he would not discuss, and information on these areas would often come to me from other informants. Russbacher did back down from refusing to answer questions about a certain area when another source described it to me. Then Russbacher would enlarge upon the information in a manner indicating he was well familiar with the operation.

To confirm his answers, I approached the subject from a different direction, many months later, and the precise detailed facts would rarely waver. His precise knowledge of people and events in many areas of intrigue was unprecedented, and checked out with facts that I obtained from other informants. I was convinced that he was not a con man. He simply could not make up the vast amount of data he gave me in response to questions that covered a broad spectrum. As other CIA whistleblowers came to me I was able to obtain further confirmation of Russbacher's CIA status and of many of the events that he described to me.

Even when I told him information given to me by others, such as former Mossad agent Ari Ben-Menashe, Russbacher often responded with additional information on the person that checked out, and which had never appeared in print. It wasn't Russbacher who sought attention. I was the one that repeatedly told Russbacher to give me information of CIA corruption so that I could force Congress and the media to meet their responsibilities.

Russbacher described how the CIA was part of the looting of Chapter 11 assets, and how the CIA used crooked federal judges, trustees, and law firms to accomplish this, and how the CIA covered up for some of its looted proprietaries by placing the companies into Chapter 7 or 11 where the CIA had control of the judges. He named judges, trustees, law firms and their attorneys, who were present at CIA drug and arms transshipment points in Central and South America, and especially trustee Charles Duck, who looted much of my multi-million in assets. At a later date Russbacher gave me the name of the overseas corporation that paid the bribe money to the judges, trustees and law firms beholden to the CIA and Justice Department gang.

Russbacher described the interrelationships between the CIA and people looting the savings and loans. He described how Keating-controlled corporations hid over $300 million of depositors' money in Colorado through secret trusts and other financial mechanisms. When I quizzed Russbacher about the CIA's role with Charles Keating he responded: "It wasn't just Keating. Bear in mind that we are not talking about strictly Keating-controlled corporations. We are talking about a multitude of corporations that were controlled by outside forces. Keating just happened to be one of them."

REMOVAL OF MONEY FROM THE UNITED STATES

Describing the huge outflow of funds generated by CIA proprietaries through various financial scams and drug money laundering, Russbacher stated: "It is a systematic removal of funds from U.S. bank accounts. And these accounts that held large amounts of funds were then channeled to off-shore bank accounts and off-shore investment companies."

I asked, "How are these funds identified, I'm talking about who would be identified as the owner of these funds? Would it be numbered accounts?" Russbacher replied, "It would be numbered or designated accounts, where you have a primary person that is allowed to make transactions. That doesn't necessarily mean that person is the only one."

"I presume that the CIA has numerous operatives who are authorized to place or remove funds from these accounts?"

"There are only ten or twelve people in the whole agency that are permitted to do that. Let's say, no more than two dozen people."

"Are you one of those?"

"Yes, I am. Or I was."

Russbacher's statements as shown in these pages are but a minute fraction of the in-depth discussions between him and myself. These statements were made during late 1990 and up to the date of this book's publication. Much of the details were unknown to the general public and had not been in print. Many people confirmed to me Russbacher's CIA position, and statements made to me by Russbacher were often confirmed by statements made by others, including Ari Ben-Menashe, Michael Riconosciuto, Ronald Rewald, and other CIA related people.

Many hours were spent on what he saw first hand as a CIA operative in Chapter 11 courts. Russbacher described the CIA practice of using Chapter 11 courts for two primary purposes. One was to cover up for its looting of CIA proprietaries. The other was to loot the assets of small to medium size companies and individuals who filed Chapter 11 seeking time to pay their debts, and who had large equities.

PATTERN OF JUDICIAL CORRUPTION IN CHAPTER 11

Many of the victims didn't understand the blatant illegality of how the racketeering enterprise stripped them of their life's assets. The scheme follows a standard pattern, violating federal statutes and constitutional protections. The Chapter 11 judge, who almost always is a direct participant in the vast enterprise, orders the assets seized, in clear violation of law, and then appoints a trustee who knows nothing about the business, and who promptly proceeds to loot the assets, forcing the Chapter 11 case into a Chapter 7 liquidation.

During liquidation, the trustee, his law firm and attorneys, and others who work together, sell the properties at a fraction of their market value. The person who sought relief in Chapter 11 then becomes the victim of one of the most outrageous racketeering enterprises in the United States.

Russbacher gave me details of this racket as seen from his CIA perspective, that dovetailed with what I had discovered as a victim and an investigator.

I asked Russbacher if during his CIA activities he encountered the people who played a major role in seizing and looting my assets, and his reply was startling. The federal judge who corruptly seized my assets was Las Vegas Chapter 11 Judge Robert Jones. Russbacher described how the CIA arranged transportation to Atlantic City for this federal judge, where letters of credit would be waiting at different casinos for him to obtain tens of thousands of dollars in gambling chips. Russbacher described other federal judges that he knew were present at CIA arms and drug or other operations, including Judge Alan Jaroslovsky, a key judge in the Northern District of California, who had repeatedly protected trustee Charles Duck from his accusers. Russbacher later stated that he was a CIA-asset and was on a secret financial arrangement.

I asked Russbacher if there could be any legitimate basis for the appearances of federal judges, trustees and law firms at the secret CIA arms and drug trafficking locations in Central America. He confirmed that there was no lawful reason for their appearances at these locations.

Russbacher described flying down to Central America CIA sites in CIA aircraft, accompanied by such people as trustee Charles Duck; the law firms of Friedman, Sloan and Ross (who filed the sham divorce action against me); Goldberg, Stinnett and McDonald[261] (who seized and looted my assets in conjunction with Duck and Judge Robert Jones); and Murray and Murray (who took over after Duck was sent to prison).

Russbacher described being at CIA meetings in Central America with Duck, at John Hull's ranch, and at Tegucigalpa,[262] as well as other locations. Referring to Duck, Russbacher described his presence in 1987: "The last time, be apprised of the fact that there were actually three times that I had dealings with him, or came close to having dealings with him. Two times, shall we say, he was there in the hotel room with me."

FUNDING CIA THROUGH SEIZURE OF CHAPTER 11 ASSETS

Russbacher stated that Charley Duck bragged about how he looted the assets of Chapter 11 parties. Referring to Duck and the CIA looting of Chapter 11 assets, Russbacher stated: "Duck has basically siphoned off large sums of money from his assigned cases. He appeared in different areas where we [CIA] were involved. This is the nexus I have been getting across to you, between the bankruptcy issues, and Agency [CIA] operations. It is one of the funding vehicles for the Company [CIA]."

Russbacher stated that the worst Chapter 11 corruption was in federal courts located in the San Francisco, Los Angeles, Chicago, and St. Louis areas. Russbacher added, "Let me tell you like this. St. Louis is notorious on Chapter 11. What it amounts to is: one of the bankruptcy judges in each one of the districts gets definite remuneration from the CIA."

TYPICAL START-UP OF CIA PROPRIETARY

Describing one of the ways in which the CIA proprietaries generate money, Russbacher stated:

Most of them were limited partnerships. The funds would have been from the CIA to start with.[263] What they did, they allegedly put a private offering together, and the subscribers for the private offerings were already in place, before the offering was even written up. Each

---

[261] Name was changed in 1993 to Goldberg, Stinnett, Meyers & Davis, located at 44 Montgomery Street, San Francisco, California

[262] Capital of Honduras.

[263] To establish a net worth from which to seek large loans that were never repaid and never intended to be repaid. The funds were diverted to covert CIA domestic and international uses.

one of these people who subscribed to the offering brought in Agency funds.
Russbacher stated, "The corporation or limited partnership would issue corporate paper, or whatever, and that's how more funds were created. They used the initial funds for the funding of the LTD partnership, strictly as a collateral vehicle for large scale loans." He continued:

If we go in, for instance, with a million or half a million dollars each, on a limited partnership, and there are ten of us, let's say we have anywhere from five to ten million dollars in capital assets, in the limited partnership, that, along with a good financial statement, and what we planned to do with the limited partnership, can earn us the right to a thirty, forty, fifty million dollar loan. Do you see what I am saying?

Russbacher described what usually happened after obtaining multi-million-dollar loans. The people default on the non-recourse loans after the money is pulled out. Russbacher stated, "Generally it was strictly default. We pulled money back out and we would end up with thirty, forty million." Russbacher added, "That particular company would file Chapter 11 in courts where we had control of the judges."

OTHER CIA INFORMANTS

Initially, Russbacher was my best and primary source of information. As I became known in the relatively small intelligence community, other concerned intelligence agency operatives came to me, describing the corrupt activities they had observed or been ordered to participate in. These activities are described throughout these pages, as are the various informants.

MOSSAD-CIA CROSS-CHECK

Adding to the large amount of information supporting Russbacher's statements was an interesting dialogue between a former Mossad agent, Ari Ben-Menashe, and Russbacher. I arranged for several conference calls between these two former intelligence officers and encouraged them to exchange experiences. In one instance, Russbacher told Ben-Menashe of his friendship with the Mossad's station chief in Vienna, Heinz Toch, a name that would be known to very few people, and then primarily the Mossad. This was one example of Russbacher's intimate knowledge of covert activities. He would not have known this unless he was not only the CIA operative he said he was, but an operative in the higher echelon of CIA covert activities.

I talked for many hours to the wives of several operatives who stated facts to me as seen from their perspective, further confirming the truthfulness of what their husbands told me. I had frequent conversations and written communications with other CIA-operatives and contract agents, including Michael Riconosciuto;[264] Russell Bowen;[265] Trenton Parker;[266] Ronald

---

[264] Riconosciuto was a CIA contract agent for many years who was involved in the October Surprise operation, Inslaw, and other activities.

Rewald;[267] Basil Abbott;[268] Chuck Hayes;[269] Edwin Wilson;[270] and others. I was in contact with law enforcement people whose investigative functions brought them in contact with CIA activities, and especially CIA drug trafficking. These included Jim Rothstein;[271] Ted Gunderson;[272] and others. This vast amount of data, plus what I discovered, developed into a mosaic-like depiction of sordid intrigue, deception, and murder, portraying the worst pattern of criminal activities ever reported against the American people.

My phone was used for hundreds of hours of three-way conference calls between CIA and DEA personnel, their wives, a Mossad agent, and even Ross Perot. Often the conversations were of the nature of one pilot describing to another, events that they experienced, each one knowing that any fabrication would be recognized by the other. My position was like a secret mole inside covert CIA activities, adding to the discoveries I made while a federal investigator and while being victimized in one of the many criminal enterprises.

As a former federal investigator holding federal authority to reach conclusions based upon the facts uncovered, based upon the fifteen years of book publishing, and based upon what I had personally observed, the evidence was overwhelming. The American people are being systematically defrauded by a well entrenched group in the federal government.

CONTINUAL JUSTICE DEPARTMENT ATTEMPTS TO SILENCE RUSSBACHER

Russbacher was scheduled to be released December 23, 1991. At that time he would pose a greater threat of exposing October Surprise, Inslaw, and numerous other major criminal enterprises implicating White House and federal officials and ongoing criminal operations.

Justice Department prosecutors used another tactic to keep Russbacher in prison. Shortly before Russbacher was scheduled for release, Justice Department attorneys notified Missouri authorities that he had been charged with impersonating a Naval officer at Castle Air Force Base. The attorneys induced them to revoke Russbacher's parole arising from the sham charges for

---

[265] Bowen was a member of the OSS during World War II and then continued with a small group of OSS people as moles inside the CIA after OSS was disbanded. He was heavily involved in CIA and Mossad drug trafficking and other intelligence agency operations in Europe, the Middle East, and Central and South America.

[266] Long-time deep-cover CIA operative.

[267] Rewald was placed by the CIA head of the Agency proprietary, Bishop, Baldwin, Rewald, Dillingham and Wong (BBRDW).

[268] DEA pilot who flew drugs from Central and South America to the United States.

[269] CIA operative who played key roles in the Central America drug trafficking.

[270] Heavily involved in CIA activities in Southeast Asia, Europe, and the Middle East, who worked with key figures in the Iran-Contra affair, and who was made the fall guy and was sent to prison.

[271] Rothstein was on the New York City vice-squad for many years. He arrested Frank Sturgis when Sturgis arrived in New York to kill a former girl-friend of Fidel Castro. Rothstein had considerable street knowledge of CIA drug trafficking commencing in the 1950s.

[272] Former FBI agent heavily involved in exposing pedophilia.

which Russbacher had never had a trial and for which he was induced to enter an Alford plea. (U.S. Attorney David Levi in Sacramento had dropped the impersonating-a-Navy-officer charge shortly after it was made in 1990.)

Russbacher was transported to St. Charles, Missouri, for a February 7, 1992 hearing on revocation of his parole on the charge of impersonating a Navy officer. Missouri Judge Donald E. Dalton refused to allow him to call CIA personnel that could attest to his being a covert CIA operative on assignment from the Office of Naval Intelligence. However, he did allow Russbacher to call witnesses from Offutt and Castle Air Force Base, who testified that Russbacher and his wife were billeted there, and that the authorization came from Navy CincPac (Commander in Chief, Pacific). The witnesses provided the authorization numbers. This testimony and the Air Force records were strong evidence that Russbacher was on official duty with the United States Navy.

Dalton disregarded the evidence that Russbacher was a covert intelligence officer. He ignored the fact that there had never been a trial on the underlying money offense charge, and that there was no evidence presented to show that Russbacher had committed any of the acts charged, or that anyone suffered any financial loss. (Several of the charges arose from Russbacher's transfer of stock from one CIA proprietary to another, without registering with the State of Missouri. Several charges arose from Russbacher writing checks on a CIA proprietary that he owned, to one of his aliases.)

The judge revoked Russbacher's probation and ordered him to start serving the 21-year sentence that had been rendered in 1990 when Russbacher was encouraged to enter an Alford plea (not admitting any guilt but settling for probation).

Russbacher and I continued our almost daily telephone conversations discussing the specifics of CIA operations in which he was involved. As he became more discouraged he loosened up and gave me more information about CIA/ONI covert (and subversive) activities, most of which were continuing, and inflicting enormous harm upon the United States and the American people.

Russbacher's health was failing due to an urgent need for coronary bypass surgery. Rayelan, his wife, and I, and other people, worked for his release. I rushed to get the first printing of *Defrauding America* published, with the intent of using the book as the basis for appearing on radio and television shows. In this way publicity would be focused on Russbacher and other CIA scapegoats. The primary interest was to make the American people aware of the well-orchestrated criminality involving government personnel, and to motivate them to take action to bring a halt to the destruction of the United States and the values that American people *think* exists.

```
8:32:24 am   Wednesday   February 5, 1992        Offutt Air Force Base

              * SCREEN ONE *
Name: RUSSBACHER , GUNTHER      Grade: CAPT      Arriving: 980719 / 2400
CITY LEDGER   Room/Bed: 3208   Sex: M  Override N   Paygrade: 06 Override N
                                                    Last updated by: HCG
SSAN: 441 40 1617   Distinguished Visitor: N   Special Services Required: N   State: WA
Branch: NAVY   Org: PACIFIC COMAND   Base: QCARVER        / N/A
ZIP/APO: 11111 1111   Contact Name/Phone: SAME
Messages:

Purpose of Visit: TDY-MRD                  Priority: 1    Shift:
Nr of Nights: 4   Room Type: SPCLF   Daily Rate: 15.00    Monthly Rate: .00
Shared Room: N   Number of Persons: 1                     Number of Rooms: 1
Fund Code:       Hotel ID:        S7O Hotel Room:         Guest Days for CQ: N
Non-Availability Promised: N   Confirmed by phone: Y   Confirmed in writing: N
Comments:

Pay by: CASH   Credit Card Number/Name:
Billing Agency #/Name:                 Group Billing:   Group #:
Billing Address:
                                                         hrosvch2

ENTER: More Data              PF3: Next Record           PF16: Exit
```

Copy of official records from Offut Air Force Base showing Russbacher's status as captain, captain's pay grade as Grade 6, assigned to ONI, with authorization from Commander in Chief, Pacific.

CHAPTER SIXTEEN

OCTOBER SURPRISE COVERUP

The mainstream media in the United States kept the lid on the October Surprise operation and the other corrupt activities associated with it through a pattern of disinformation and withholding evidence. The establishment media sought to discredit the CIA whistleblowers who could prove the existence of the October Surprise operation. They fabricated reasons to discredit a group of former CIA and Mossad intelligence agency personnel, who were personally involved in the operation, who had nothing to gain by giving testimony, and had much to lose, including criminal prosecution. These informants were willing to risk their safety and freedom to expose the corruption against the American people.

The "investigating" committees and the establishment media gave absolute credibility to the statements of those who were part of the treasonous and criminal activities, and who faced impeachment and prison terms if the charges were proven. In this way, as a matter of law, members of Congress and the media became co-conspirators.

The *Village Voice* discredited the testimony of CIA contract agent Richard Brenneke because it found ten-year-old credit card slips for Brenneke that were made in Portland, Oregon, on October 18, 1980. These credit card slips were found by Peggy Robahm, who reportedly went to Portland, where Brenneke resided, from her home state of Connecticut, for the sole purpose of becoming involved with Brenneke. Later, she was hired by the House October Surprise Committee to "investigate" the October Surprise allegations.

My CIA sources state that the signatures on the credit cards were not Brenneke's signature, and that it is standard practice for CIA people engaging in covert operations to cause a record to be established showing them to be elsewhere. CIA contract agent, Michael Riconosciuto, a close friend of

Brenneke, both of whom resided in the Portland area, stated to me[273] that "Brenneke's credit card was used by a friend during that weekend."

The same mainstream media discredited CIA operative Gunther Russbacher, the pilot who reportedly flew George Bush and others to Paris on the October 19, 1980 weekend, and flew Bush back in an SR-71. Former, and probably, current, CIA asset Frank Snepp, wrote an article in the *Village Voice* stating that Russbacher didn't even know how to start the engines of an SR-71. This article was then repeated over and over again by the media, until the lie was taken as truth.

I had obtained a copy of the formerly secret SR-71 manual, studied its 1000-plus pages, and quizzed Russbacher on the operation of the aircraft, including the starting procedures for the engines. I was qualified to determine his competency in this area since it was my job for many years to conduct pilot competency checks for airline pilots on jet aircraft. Russbacher certainly knew how to start the engines on the SR-71. The start-up procedures are quite different than other jet aircraft, but amazingly simple.

A *Newsweek* article[274] fabricated facts to discredit the October Surprise charges, stating on its cover: "The October Surprise Charge: Treason; Myth." It misstated and omitted facts so as to support the front page cover. The magazine sought to discredit the testimony of former Mossad agent Ari Ben-Menashe, who was present at the Madrid, Barcelona, and Paris meetings.

Authors of several books and many magazine and newspaper articles found Ben-Menashe credible, and quoted him in their writings. Gary Sick quoted him numerous times in his 1992 *October Surprise* book, as did Seymour Hersh in *The Samson Option*.[275] Russbacher stated to me many times that he saw Ben-Menashe at the Barcelona meetings. The establishment media sought to discredit Ben-Menashe by stating he was only a low-level file clerk who never left Israel.

Denying the existence of the October Surprise operation required discrediting these whistleblowers and informants who were present, who had nothing to gain and much to lose, including their lives. *Newsweek* described Ben-Menashe as a "shadowy, Israeli exile, a former translator for the Israeli government, ... does not seem to check out." Perhaps they expected an espionage agent to live the life of a nun!

Time magazine also joined the disinformation tactics. Its October 28, 1991, issue called Ben-Menashe a "veteran spinner of stunning-if-true-but yarns," and a "fabricator." An eleven-page deceptive article in *The New Republic*[276] was entitled "The Conspiracy That Wasn't," with the subtitle, "The hunt for the October Surprise." The deceptive article, written by Steven Emerson and Jesse Furman, stated in part:

---

[273] During a phone call with Riconosciuto and attorney Jim Vassilos on October 27, 1992.

[274] November 11, 1991.

[275] Described Israel's nuclear program and the part played by Robert Maxwell in various forms of skullduggery.

[276] November 18, 1991.

The conspiracy as currently postulated is a total fabrication. ...
Almost every source cited by Sick or Frontline has been indicted or
was the subject of a federal investigation prior to claiming to be a
participant in the October Surprise.

Ben-Menashe authored the 1992 publication of *Profits of War*,[277] subtitled,
"Inside the Secret U.S.–Israeli Arms Network," which contained copies of
Israeli government documents showing Ben-Menashe as a high-level staff
officer for Israel's Mossad and military agencies.

THE CIA'S MEDIA WURLITZER

The CIA has many media personnel on its payroll to plant stories or
discredit charges against the CIA. It pays out large sums of money for articles
and books to be written on the CIA's behalf. Its control over the media is like
a Wurlitzer, orchestrating and manipulating all segments of the written or
broadcast media. It must be remembered that the CIA has iron-clad control
over the establishment media in the United States, and spends money
supporting journalists and the media.

SERIOUS IMPLICATIONS

The evidence supporting the October Surprise charges required impeach-
ing President George Bush, and filing criminal charges against key officials
in the executive, legislative, and judicial branches of the federal government.
Never in the history of the United States was there such a serious criminal
conspiracy inflicted upon the United States by people in control of the White
House and government. There was no comparison between the relatively
minor coverup of Watergate and the hard crimes associated with October
Surprise. The media exaggeration of Watergate inflicted immense harms upon
the United States. The media **coverup** of October Surprise inflicted far greater
harm upon the United States, but in a form not recognized by the uninformed
American public.

The coverup of October Surprise permitted and caused great harm to the
United States, including a criminal and subversive mindset by people in
control of the three branches of government, and placing into federal office
people who were geared for committing continuing harm against the
American people.

October Surprise was many times more serious, involving people
scattered throughout the three branches of the federal government. Failure to
deny the existence of October Surprise could cause mass impeachments,
criminal prosecution, and awaken the American public to the criminality in
government. The fallout would effect both political parties.

Consider the difference between the political turmoil associated with
exposing the October Surprise crimes and the seeming tranquility following
its coverup. The surface tranquility, however, hid the hard-core corruption
and harm that continued to be inflicted upon the American people in ways not
recognized by the public.

---

[277] *Profits of War*, Sheridan Square Press.

"We couldn't stand another disgraced presidency."

The coverup by some of the media was for reasons other than protecting the guilty or vested interests. Several syndicated columnists, including Jim Fain of *Cox News Service*, explained the reason for the October Surprise coverup in an April 23, 1991, column: "A consensus grew that we couldn't stand another disgraced presidency. Democrats in the bungled Congressional hearings said as much."

One of the tactics used to discredit October Surprise and other scandals was to discredit and make a mockery of those who describe the criminal acts and who use the word conspiracy. This tactic plays upon the ignorance of the public as to what constitutes a conspiracy. A conspiracy exists in almost any type of crime, and consists of two or people agreeing to do one or more acts. There is obviously no shortage of conspiracies anywhere, even though the standard disinformation tactic is to ridicule anyone who makes reference to a conspiracy.

Another coverup tactic is to discredit statements or charges made by someone accused of a federal offense, calling him or her a felon and a person whose statements cannot be believed. Many CIA operations have been unlawful and outside of the law, making it easy for Justice Department officials to silence any potential CIA whistleblower by charging them with committing a crime. Using this argument, the only witness that could be considered reliable would be someone of the order of a nun, who couldn't possibly have access to information about criminal activities.

However, when the shoe is on the other foot, and Justice Department prosecutors are trying to sentence a person to prison, they not only use the testimony of felons but even reward them for their often-fabricated testimony. Paid testimony comes in the form of pardons from earlier convictions, dropping of pending charges, money, including supporting the witness for years in the witness protection program.

If witnesses didn't testify as Justice Department prosecutors wanted, they would face long prison terms or other consequences. In addition, they didn't have to worry about prosecution for perjury. The only law enforcement agency holding authority to prosecute them wanted them to commit perjury. In the criminal trial against Mafia figures Gotti and Thomas Gambino, long prison sentences were based upon the testimony of other felons, who were rewarded for their testimony through sentence and charge reductions.

GREAT PRETENSE

President George Bush, speaking (August 14, 1991) before an audience of nearly 3,000 delegates to the national convention of the Fraternal Order of Police, the nation's major police labor organization, stated:

The time has come to show less compassion for the architects of crime and more compassion for its victims. Our citizens want and deserve to feel safe. We must remember that the first obligation of a penal system is to punish those who break our laws. You can't turn bad people into saints.

So much for hypocrisy. The initial media attention to October Surprise forced the Senate and House to form committees supposedly investigating the charges. But the Republican members of the House and Senate vigorously opposed any investigation, afraid of what would be revealed. When continuing media pressure forced an investigation, safeguards were installed, including bringing people from other government agencies that could be counted upon to insure a coverup. These "investigators" then barred witnesses who would expose what was being investigated. They conducted closed-door hearings of witnesses, preventing the public from making their own decision as to the truthfulness of what was stated. They misstated the facts in the final report.

Another tactic is to label key witnesses as unreliable or discredited, as was done with U.S. and Israeli intelligence agency witnesses: Mossad agent Ari Ben-Menashe; CIA contract agent Richard Brenneke, and deep-cover CIA operative Gunther Russbacher. These witnesses had no reason to lie. They were not at risk because of the role they played in the October Surprise scheme. Instead, they risked persecution by Justice Department prosecutors if they testified falsely. They knew that they faced false prosecution from Justice Department attorneys even if they testified truthfully. Brenneke discovered this when he testified to Bush's and Gregg's Paris trip which Justice Department attorneys sought to cover up.

TROJAN HORSES

In 1991 the Senate refused to conduct an investigation into the October Surprise charges, but the Senate Foreign Relations Committee conducted a small-scale investigation with virtually no staff and very little funding. The Senate Committee selected attorney Reid Weingarten[278] to be Special Counsel, controlling the investigation. He was formerly employed by the U.S. Department of Justice, and could be expected to protect the Justice Department's coverup and involvement in the October Surprise operation. Immediately after Weingarten was named Special Counsel, I sent to him portions of the transcript of Russbacher's sworn declarations describing details of the October Surprise operation. They now had Brenneke's sworn statements in the Denver U.S. District Court and Russbacher's declarations. The committee refused to respond to my petition and refused to receive Russbacher's and Brenneke's testimony.

A key member of the Senate committee was Cecilia Porter, on loan from the GAO's Office of special investigations. Her previous "investigation" into October Surprise discredited key witnesses, including Richard Brenneke (without obtaining his testimony), and then she helped write a report claiming that the October Surprise scheme did not exist.

The chief investigator on the Senate October Surprise Committee was an agent from the Treasury Department's Secret Service, a federal entity that played a major coverup role in the October Surprise operation. The chairman of the Senate October Surprise Committee, Senator Terry Sanford, was formerly the attorney for Earl Brian, one of the principal participants in the October Surprise scheme. Brian was a CIA asset involved in numerous

---

[278] Special Counsel Weingarten was appointed on December 16, 1991.

corrupt CIA and Justice Department activities, including the Inslaw affair. That is described elsewhere.

BLOCKING THE INVESTIGATION

The senators on the committee placed numerous restrictions on the investigation, which were admitted in their final report:

* Imposed travel restrictions, barring the investigators from traveling to Europe, the travel necessary to obtain the testimony of numerous people identified with the October Surprise operation. The report stated that "Senator Jesse Helms, Ranking Minority Member of the Committee, served notice to Chairman Claiborne Pell that he would not authorize any such foreign travel [barring testimony from key witnesses]." The report stated that "Special Counsel was denied authority to travel abroad, thereby precluding the possibility of interviewing Iranian exiles in Europe, Israeli public officials and intelligence operatives, international arms dealers, and prominent Iranian political figures, such as Hashemi Rafsanjani and Mehdi Karrubi, who may have knowledge relating to the allegations at issue."

* Denied subpoena power to the investigators that was needed to compel the attendance of witnesses or the production of documents. The investigators had to submit their request for subpoenas to the full committee of senators and obtain majority approval for the Chairman of the Committee to sign the subpoenas. The Republicans on the committee were primarily responsible for this restriction. This awkward restriction was further compounded by the senators refusing to approve many of the subpoenas. Out of 47 witnesses and 15 entities for which subpoenas were requested, the senators refused to issue 44 of them. Without subpoenas, many government agencies, directed by Justice Department officials, refused to provide important testimony or evidence.

* Limited the funds and the time for completing the investigation. The Senate October Surprise Committee spent only $75,429 by the time it issued the November 19, 1992 report. In comparison, Iran-Contra Independent Prosecutor Lawrence Walsh spent over $40 million and six years investigating White House personnel to determine who withheld evidence from Congress. Compare the $40 million spent for the relatively minor offenses of determining who withheld evidence, to the $75,000 spent to investigate the treasonous and subversive criminal acts involved in the October Surprise operation.

In June 1991, the committee took the testimony of Ari Ben-Menashe, behind closed doors. Ben-Menashe described his presence at the various October Surprise meetings in Spain and France, including the presence of George Bush at the Paris meetings. His testimony was dynamite, describing in a credible manner the specifics of what he had witnessed in the October Surprise scheme. The American public was deprived of this information. Their massive ignorance and indifference to government misconduct made the sham investigation possible.

The Secret Service refused to allow the committee to question their agents who personally followed Bush during the October 19, 1980 weekend. Instead, they limited the questioning to Secret Service agent Leonard J. Tanis, who had not seen Bush on that October 19, 1980 weekend, and had simply read the agent's reports placed before him. If the reports were altered, his testimony would be based upon the altered documents. Tanis' lack of knowledge was revealed during questions about contradictions in his statements.

Tanis testified: "Evidently, I've either mixed up the date or something." If he was deliberately perjuring himself, and his testimony shown as false, it would be easy to state he had the dates confused. Secret Service officials were covering up. The refusal to allow the Secret Service agents to testify, who were with Bush, could only be to hide his actual whereabouts.

ADDITIONAL CONFIRMATION FROM MOSSAD AGENT

In his book, *Profits of War*, author Ari Ben-Menashe describes his part as a Mossad agent in the transfer of bribe money for Iranians, as part of the October Surprise conspiracy. He describes the diversion of part of these funds to Earl Brian, a friend and business associate of California attorney Edwin Meese, who was rewarded for his treachery in October Surprise by being appointed Attorney General of the United States.

Ben-Menashe described receiving $56 million from the Saudi ambassador in Guatemala and leaving $4 million of this in the CIA-related Valley National Bank of Arizona in a bank account belonging to Earl Brian. Ben-Menashe's boss, Director of Israel Defense Forces/Military Intelligence, Yehoshua Sagi, explained that it was CIA money and that the Saudis helped arranging the banking and transfer. Ben-Menashe wrote that this money came from Central America drug deals involving some Israelis and the CIA. Ben-Menashe described being met by CIA Deputy Director Robert Gates at Miami, and who proceed to Phoenix to insure that Earl Brian got his bribe money.

Ben-Menashe described how Brian was involved in other secret deals involving the CIA and other U.S. agencies. Ben-Menashe wrote that bribe money was given by the CIA to the West Australian Labor Party for allowing Australia to be used in the transfer of arms to Iran following the October Surprise agreement. He stated that Richard Babayan, a CIA contract agent, received a $6 million dollar check from Earl Brian, who was acting on behalf of a CIA "cut-out." Hadron and Earl Brian figured prominently in a later scandal given the name of Inslaw. The CIA connections help explain how they avoided criminal prosecution and how Attorney General Edwin Meese, deeply involved in these criminal activities, protected all parties involved, and misused the Justice Department to persecute and imprison informants.

The Congressional committees "investigating" the serious October Surprise conspiracy received testimony from Ben-Menashe, and as is common with testimony exposing serious misconduct by government officials, the testimony was received behind closed doors, and then discredited in the final reports.

Ben-Menashe also writes about personally seeing George Bush, a Secret Service agent, and two aides, in Paris during the October 19, 1980 weekend meetings.

THE SENATE REPORT

The Senate October Surprise Committee issued its report[279] on November 19, 1992. A good liar, or an attorney, will admit certain things to establish a facade of honesty, and then follow with lies to complete the cover-up. The report properly identified the severity of the charges, a standard practice to give the impression of credibility by admitting one or more facts. The report then proceeded to discredit the witnesses whose testimony proved the existence of the October Surprise scheme, and discredit the witnesses who had much to lose if they testified falsely. The report gave absolute credibility to federal officials who would have been impeached and prosecuted if the charges were proven true. This report was prepared by former Justice Department attorney Reid Weingarten.

ACTIONS MET DEFINITION OF COVERUP

The committee refused to receive the testimony of Gunther Russbacher. They called him an imposter (without questioning him), and refused to address the transcript of his sworn declarations that I sent to them. The report discredited Russbacher by making reference to an attorney friend, Paul Wilcher, who reportedly failed to produce a copy of a video[280] that allegedly existed of an SR-71 flight from Paris to Andrews Air Force Base on the October 19, 1980 weekend. The failure of someone else to produce a copy of a video tape had nothing to do with the importance and credibility of Russbacher's testimony.

Richard Brenneke gave sworn statements to a U.S. District Court in Denver in 1988, describing his role in the Paris October Surprise meetings. His testimony coincided with statements and testimony of other people, none of whom had anything to gain by their statements and much to lose, such as a perjury charge and prison. Without requiring Brenneke to testify, the committee's report discredited the former CIA contract agent on the basis of newspaper articles, primarily those written by former or current CIA operative Frank Snepp. The report said:

> On the basis of these published [media] reports, and on the GAO's inquiry (in which Brenneke declined to cooperate), this investigation determined that it would not be fruitful to devote further resources to pursue evidence originating from Brenneke.

On a matter of such urgency, investigators don't ask a key witness to testify; he is ordered to do so. Brenneke had been threatened, just as CIA contract agent Riconosciuto had been threatened, by Justice Department attorneys, not to testify. More about this in other pages. Under these conditions, Brenneke

---

[279] The Senate October Surprise Committee commenced operation after Senate Majority Leader George J. Mitchell requested that the committee, through the subcommittee, investigate the October Surprise charges. The committee was headed by Senator Terry Sanford, Chairman, and Senator James Jeffords, ranking member, and was a subcommittee on Near Eastern and South Asian Affairs of the Committee on Foreign Relations.

[280] CIA SR-71 aircraft made a continuous video recording of the two seat positions, making a permanent tape recording and simultaneously sending transmissions to a satellite which beams the signals to an earth station. The tape recordings are kept at the National Archives in Camp Mead, Maryland.

had no alternative but to decline a voluntary request for testimony.

The Congressional Committee report also sought to discredit Brenneke on the basis of ten-year-old credit card slips showing that someone made charges on his credit card in Portland, Oregon, on October 18, 1980. It is standard practice for covert CIA operatives to disguise their whereabouts to prove they were not involved in a covert operation that may be exposed later. Obtaining Brenneke's testimony would have clarified the matter of the credit cards.

The General Accounting Office (GAO) had earlier discounted Brenneke because he refused to participate in any meetings. But Brenneke had been threatened by Justice Department officials. He had already been charged with perjury when he did testify about the October Surprise operation during a Denver court hearing. The GAO and every member of Congress had a responsibility to order Brenneke to testify, and to protect him from retaliation by Justice Department personnel.

Brenneke had been a CIA contract agent carrying out CIA covert activities, which included drug trafficking. Any one of these CIA-ordered activities could be used for subsequent prosecution by Justice Department attorneys. He saw what happened to CIA contract agent Michael Riconosciuto, and to many other CIA assets who were sent to prison on trumped-up charges, solely to silence them. Brenneke saw the discrediting tactics by key media sources, and the coverup by the entire media, and by the entire Senate and House. He was certainly smart enough to recognize that the safest move was to say nothing.

Barbara Honegger, author of the first book bearing the title *October Surprise*, reportedly had the signatures on these controversial credit cards examined by a handwriting expert, who stated they did not compare with Brenneke's signature. She reportedly stated this fact to Lawrence Barcella, head counsel of the October Surprise Committee, in December 1992. Honegger also personally questioned the people present at the places covered by the credit card receipts, who knew Brenneke. They stated that Brenneke was not at the places shown by the credit cards.

The Senate report discredited the testimony of Jamshid Hashemi, an arms merchant present at meetings between William Casey and Iranian representatives in Madrid in July 1980. I had obtained secret CIA and State Department documents showing Hashami's involvement in the arms-for-hostages operation, in which government officials expressed confidence in his credibility. Copies of these reports, sent to the Senate and the House October Surprise Committees, were ignored.

The report stated of Mossad agent Ari Ben-Menashe and other witnesses, none of whom had reason to lie, that they "have proven wholly unreliable." This decision was based upon their testimony having contradicted the testimony of those who were part of the October Surprise conspiracy.

I sent the Senate committee copies of Secret Service reports showing Bush flying into Washington National Airport on Sunday evening, October 19, 1980. These reports disputed Secret Service reports furnished to the committee. I had obtained the reports from Russbacher, who had received them while he was assigned to the CIA at Langley in 1981. They had been sent by the Secret Service to the CIA shortly after the events occurred, and before the Secret Service found a need to alter the reports years later.

After discrediting the sworn testimony of people who were innocent participants in the October Surprise operation, after placing irresponsible restrictions on the investigation, and encountering great numbers of people who refused to testify, the Senate committee held there was no such scheme:

The vast weight of all available evidence—including sworn testimony from Secret Service agents assigned to protect Bush, extensive Secret Service records and logs, as well as statements by campaign staff—indicates that Bush did not travel to Paris in October 1980 or, for that matter, at any time during the 1980 presidential campaign.

The committee report referred to former President Reagan's refusal to cooperate, stating that the investigators were "disappointed by President Reagan's declination of the request for an interview. President Reagan's written reply was wholly inadequate to explain his off-hand but apparently relevant comment to a reporter that he had acted in some fashion as a candidate in connection with the hostage crisis." The report identified the refusal of the FBI to cooperate:

The history of the FBI's handling of evidence in this case—from the disappearance and discovery of the "Pottinger Tapes," to the disappearance and discovery of the entire Hashemi electronic surveillance, to the discovery of an eight-day period in which the Hashemi New York wiretaps were apparently discontinued—is a curious one. It is not typical for the FBI to simply "lose" evidence.

Basically, the committee sought to support its coverup decision that there was no October Surprise operation, and that George Bush had not gone to Paris, based upon the following:

* Secret Service reports purporting to show that Bush never left Washington during the October 19, 1980 weekend. But the Secret Service agents were barred from testifying, and Secret Service agents were reportedly on the BAC 111 to Paris and would be implicated in a coup against the United States. October Surprise was a coup. Secret documents that I later obtained indicate these were altered. As a federal investigator, and in later discoveries, it is as common for Justice Department attorneys and the CIA to falsify documents.

* A government Accounting Office (GAO) investigation that concluded there was no evidence of the reported October Surprise operation. I had repeatedly contacted GAO for the past two decades with hard evidence of criminal activities I uncovered, first as a federal investigator, and later as a victim in Chapter 11 proceedings, and who refused to investigate. The GAO refused to question any CIA operatives and contract agents who were part of the October Surprise operation.

* The testimony of White House personnel implicated in the criminal activities, and who faced long prison terms if convicted of the crimes in which they participated. The committee wrote:

No credible evidence has been found to indicate that high-ranking Republican campaign figures or other prominent American political officials—including Bush, Casey, Robert McFarlane, Robert Gates and Robert Allen—attended any October 1980 Paris meetings. Moreover, the Special Counsel has concluded, after a review of Secret Service records and testimony from Secret Service agents, that candidate Bush was in the United States through October 1980.

COVER-YOUR-REAR TACTICS

Should the coverup backfire, the Senate October Surprise Committee sought to cover their rear ends. The report stated that certain obstacles existed to determining the truth of the October Surprise charges: "The investigation was handicapped by several factors which made reaching final conclusions an almost impossible task." There were certainly obstacles, and many of them deliberately put in place by the "investigating" committee. The "CYR" tactics included the following:

* "The investigation was hindered by the unavailability of certain key witnesses."

* Key witnesses who would have implicated themselves refused to cooperate, including Ambassador to South Korea, Donald Gregg (who was on the BAC 111 flight to Paris). The report stated that Gregg "declined to be interviewed by the investigators." The great harm inflicted upon the United States (if the charges were true) demanded ordering him, and every other witness with information, to testify.

* The senators refused to issue a subpoena for the testimony of former President Ronald Reagan. They satisfied themselves with a letter from Reagan's attorney, John A. Mintz, who wrote "that he has no recollection or other information relevant to the issues raised in any of your questions."

* Refusal by the Reagan Presidential Library to produce requested records, until after the investigators had already been reassigned and the investigation completed.

* The report admitted that lack of funds and personnel greatly hindered the investigations, forcing investigators to rely upon other federal agencies to conduct an investigation, even though those agencies were implicated and engaged in a coverup.

* The Treasury Department refused to allow the investigators to question the Secret Service agents who had actually been with Bush during the time in question. There would be no reason for refusing to allow these low-level federal employees to be questioned, other than to cover up.

* The family of former CIA Director William Casey (who died in 1987) impeded the investigation by delaying and refusing to provide his personal and business records, including his diary and passport.

* Failure of Donald Gregg, who was on the flight to Paris on the October 19, 1980, to pass a lie-detector test. The Senate October Surprise Committee gave Gregg a lie-detector test. He failed the test when asked about his role in the October Surprise operation. But rather than call the test a failure, the committee report stated "that Gregg's response was lacking in candor." CIA assets Gunther Russbacher and Richard Brenneke, and Mossad's Ari Ben-Menashe, had stated that Gregg was at

several October Surprise meetings in Europe.

There was far more evidence showing the October Surprise charges to be true than existed in many criminal cases resulting in sentences of death. The testimony of criminals, paid to give testimony wanted by the prosecutors, is sufficient to result in life-long incarceration or death, and accepted by the media, the courts, and the Justice Department. But the testimony of whistle-blowers exposing corruption by federal officials, who risk perjury charges and prison if their courageous testimony is proven false, is not accepted by those interested in coverup.

Criminals who testify falsely, as suborned by Justice Department attorneys, are assured of freedom against perjury charges, while patriotic people willing to risk prison, are assured of criminal charges if their testimony is false, and many times, if the testimony is true. People who falsely testify as Justice Department attorneys want, receive protection from perjury charges, receive reduction in prison sentences, have charges against them dropped, or are financially supported through the witness-protection program. If these people refuse to testify as Justice Department prosecutors want, they suffer consequences that can often destroy their lives. Further, their perjury, suborned by Justice Department attorneys, is routinely protected by the nation's highest law-enforcement agency. They were rewarded if they lied, and punished if they refused to lie.

HOUSE "INVESTIGATIVE" TEAM

In response to media pressure, the House of Representatives on February 5, 1992 created a task force to report on the October Surprise operation. The House committee repeated the age-old practice of staffing the committee with people who would carry out the coverup. Its chief counsel, Lawrence Barcella, Jr., followed the standard practice of former Justice Department attorneys of protecting Justice Department officials who were implicated. He had a history of protecting federal officials who had committed criminal acts against the United States.

Barcella had covered up for a CIA operation that went sour, in which the CIA was secretly supplying Libya with war supplies. Justice Department prosecutors charged CIA operative Edwin Wilson with illegal arms sales to Libya that the CIA had earlier sanctioned. Barcella was the Justice Department prosecutor who prosecuted Wilson and insured that the CIA involvement did not surface.

Barcella was the attorney for Lynn Nofziger, President Ronald Reagan's chief political adviser during the 1980 presidential campaign. He was also a member of former Senator Paul Laxalt's Nevada law firm when Laxalt was Reagan's Campaign Committee Chairman in 1980. If the October Surprise conspiracy did in fact occur, these men could be expected to know about it, and at the very least, be guilty of felony coverup. The same could be said of Barcella.

Barcella was one of the key public relations or coverup men for the corrupt bank, BCCI, and one of its most forceful apologists. Attorneys Clark Clifford and Robert Altman hired him to deceive the American public through aiding and abetting the criminal acts of that rogue bank. Barcella was one of four attorneys who requested Senator Orrin Hatch (R-Utah) to give a speech on the Senate floor in defense of BCCI, seeking to block a Congressional investigation into the criminal activities of the Bank. Barcella was known to be a friend and protector of the U.S. intelligence community while he was a federal prosecutor. The October Surprise charges that Barcella was entrusted to investigate threatened to expose this CIA operation, and the coverup by his former Justice Department bosses.

After the BCCI scandal broke, Barcella was asked about BCCI's compliance with U.S. banking laws, to which he falsely replied: "BCCI's policies and procedures were consistent with industry norms in the countries in which they were operating."[281] This bank inflicted the biggest bank fraud in the world's history. It had long been established that BCCI was engaging in criminal activities: drug-money laundering, financing of terrorists, secret takeover of U.S. banks, and bribing of government officials wherever it operated, including the United States.

Another "investigative" committee member was Richard Pedersen, who was involved in other coverups of government corruption. In early 1992 Pederson threatened Garby Leon (Columbia Pictures) and Rayelan Russbacher during a telephone call, warning them to cease further activity in the October Surprise matter.[282]

Shortly after the House October Surprise Committee was formed, I submitted several petitions to its chairman, Congressman Lee Hamilton (D-IN). I enclosed my declaration and a partial transcript of Russbacher's declarations giving specific details of the October Surprise operation in which Russbacher was involved. Hamilton and the committee repeatedly refused to respond to these petitions.

CIRCUMVENT CONGRESSIONAL COVERUPS

I submitted numerous documents to the House Committee showing that the October Surprise operation existed (along with other documents showing that the Iran-Contra arms and drug trafficking existed long before the publicized 1986 starting date). Several of the copies indicated that the Secret Service was lying about the whereabouts of George Bush on the October 19, 1980 weekend.

One Secret Service report, dated October 30, 1980, stated "Bush arrived Washington National aboard a UAE BAC 111 Charter at 8:25 p.m." Another, dated February 17, 1981, was titled, "Visit of George Bush to Capitol Hilton Hotel, Washington, D.C. on October 19, 1980." A report directed to Stuart Knight, Director, U.S. Secret Service, Washington, D.C., stated:

On October 19, 1980, at 8:00 P.M. nominee Bush arrived via motorcade at the Capitol Hilton Hotel. Nominee Bush attended a dinner in the main ballroom.

NO EVIDENCE, NO WITNESSES CALLED

In July 1992 the Hamilton committee released an interim report stating there was no evidence that Bush was in Paris or that there was any support for

---

[281]*False Profits*, Peter Truell and Larry Gurwin, Houghton Mifflin Company.

[282] Told to the author in conversations with Garby Leon and Rayelan Russbacher.

the October Surprise charges. The Hamilton Committee didn't obtain testimony of any of the parties willing to testify that would prove the existence of the
scheme and Bush's presence at the Paris meetings. The only parties the
committee questioned (not under oath and in private) were two Secret Service
agents who guarded vice presidential candidate Bush when Bush was reportedly in Paris. The agents stated that Bush had not been in Paris during the
October 19, 1980, weekend. In later pages it is shown that Secret Service
agents were on the flight to Paris, and that they lied.

Congressman Hamilton had close ties to President Reagan's aide, Earl
Brian (who was deeply involved in the Inslaw scandal described in other
chapters). Hamilton had close ties to CIA operative John Hull, who operated
an arms and drug transshipment point on his ranch in Costa Rica. Hull is
wanted by Costa Rican authorities on drug and murder charges. He also had
close ties to Dan Quayle while Quayle was a U.S. senator from Indiana. Hull
is being protected in the United States by CIA and Justice Department
officials.

AGAIN PUTTING CONGRESS ON NOTICE

I wrote to Congressman Hamilton on November 27, 1992, enclosing
copies of the Secret Service reports, stating that they "showed vice presidential nominee George Bush arriving in Washington, D.C. on a United Arab
Emirates BAC 111 at approximately 7:38 p.m., and his departure for the
Washington Hilton Hotel." I emphasized the significance of the documents,
stating that they showed Bush and Secret Service agents were lying when they
stated Bush had not left the Washington area on the October 19, 1980
weekend.

Arguably, those Secret reports had less significance as to establishing
Bush's Paris presence than the sworn testimony of CIA operatives Russbacher, Brenneke and Riconosciuto, or former Mossad agent Ari Ben-Menashe.

Treasury Agent Richard Pedersen called me several days later, asking
where I obtained the Secret Service reports. He said those reports were
forgeries, that the date of October 19, 1980 had been altered from the October
18, 1980 date he had on his copies. He stated that the airline identification had
been changed from United Airlines to United Arab Emirates (UAE). I
responded that I would check my source and get back to him. If this was
correct, the committee had a responsibility to look at my documents and
question the person who gave them to me. It is a federal crime to falsify
government documents. If Pedersen actually thought that my copies were
forged he had a duty, and surly would have done so, obtained my testimony
as to where I obtained the documents. They never asked.

I asked Pedersen why the committee didn't call Gunther Russbacher to
testify. He said Russbacher was a phony and an impostor; that he was charged
in Oklahoma City with being mentally unbalanced; that he had been in prison
from 1976 to 1983, and could not have been involved in October Surprise.
Further, that Russbacher's attorney friend, Paul Wilcher, had set up
conditions they could not meet.

Several times I had told Russbacher that Wilcher's demand for immunity
was giving the committee an excuse for not calling him to testify, and that

there was no reason to ask for it. Russbacher didn't need immunity if the questions were limited to the October Surprise flights. Because of his widespread involvement in CIA-directed activities such as money-laundering, drug trafficking, and bank fraud, he was subject to prosecution, especially if the CIA pulled the standard disavowal on him. Russbacher could raise the immunity issue if the questioning went into areas other than October Surprise, which was unlikely. However, Wilcher's request for immunity was no excuse for the October Surprise committee not to obtain Russbacher's testimony. The October Surprise offenses were of such great importance that prejudgment of Russbacher's credibility and refusal to obtain his testimony was out of order, and consistent with the coverup pattern.

I asked Pedersen if he had read Ben-Menashe's recently published *Profits of War*, stating that the book contained copies of Mossad documents showing Ari Ben-Menashe to be a high staff officer with Israel's intelligence agency. Pedersen responded, "Ben-Menashe had been discredited," without providing any support. It was obvious that Pedersen was determined to discredit anything and anyone who supported the October Surprise charges.

I contacted Russbacher for a history of the Secret Service reports he had given me that did not coincide with reports the investigative committee had. He said the Secret Service sent copies of those reports to the CIA at Langley, Virginia, shortly after they were filed, and they were routed through him while he was at CIA headquarters. Russbacher advised that the initials, RAW, in the upper right hand corner of the documents, stood for Robert Andrew Walker, one of his CIA-provided aliases. I sent the following letter to Congressman Hamilton:

December 12, 1992

Congressman Lee Hamilton
October Surprise House Committee
RHOB, Room 2187
Washington, DC 20515   *Certified Mail: P 888 324 843*

Dear Congressman Hamilton:

This letter makes reference to a telephone call that I received from Agent Richard Pedersen who is a member of the House October Surprise "investigation," and who was borrowed from the Treasury Department's Secret Service, and puts you on notice of the following facts:

These comments are in response to Mr. Pedersen's recent phone call to me:

1. Agent Pedersen telephoned me recently in response to the letter I sent to you and the attached copies of Secret Service agent reports showing Vice-President nominee George Bush arriving at Washington National Airport at 18:35 on October 19, 1980, and a motorcade to the Washington Hilton.

The significance of that time and date is that it shows Secret Service Agents and George Bush, among others, lying when they stated that Bush had not left the Washington area on the October 19, 1980 weekend.

2. *Mr. Pedersen stated that the multi-page Secret Service agent reports which I sent to you had been altered. He stated that his copy shows 10/18/80 (Saturday) as the date that Bush flew into Washington National Airport, while my copies show 10/19/80 (Sunday) as the date.*

The significance of this is that the Secret Service and George Bush claim Bush never left the Washington area during the October 19, 1980 weekend, and that if the flight into Washington occurred on 10/19/80, it would show both the Secret Service and George Bush were lying and obstructing justice. Further, even if the flight arrived in Washington on the evening of the 18th, for argument, it appears that this conflicts with the schedule reported by Bush and the Secret Service.

3. *Mr. Pedersen stated that whoever altered the document would be guilty of a federal offense, and he asked me where the documents came from. I had found these Secret Service agent reports several months ago in the inflow of papers that I receive in the mail, by FAX, and sometimes given to me. I don't usually keep track of who has sent or given to me any particular papers. I knew that numerous people have the same copies that I sent to you, and which are the subject of Mr. Pedersen's questions.*

4. *Seeking to establish the history of the documents, I questioned CIA operative Gunther Russbacher about them. He stated that the reports were received by him while he was working as a CIA operative at CIA headquarters in Langley, some time after he had played key roles in the October Surprise operation. He stated to me that he placed the initials of one of his CIA-provided aliases, RAW (Robert Andrew Walker), on the upper right hand corner of several of the Secret Service reports. He acknowledged to me that the dates shown on my reports are the same dates as on the reports that he initialed while in his capacity as a CIA deep-cover operative.*

5. *If your October Surprise Committee was an investigative committee instead of a white-wash committee, the answers could be obtained by having this CIA operative, Gunther Russbacher, testify in open door hearings. That same operative can testify to the details of the October Surprise operation, including where the meetings were held in which he participated; when the shipment of arms commenced; how the arms were stolen from U.S. reforger stores; the part played in the treasonous activities of the CIA and high White House officials, and others. He can also describe other patterns of corrupt activities, including the CIA looting of financial institutions; CIA drug trafficking within the United States; CIA participation in looting of Chapter 11 assets as part of a vicious racketeering enterprise preying upon American citizens and small businesses who exercise Chapter 11 protections; and other racketeering enterprises implicating federal officials. He can also testify to the Secret Service Agents that were part of the October Surprise operation, along with White House officials, people who are now federal judges, members of Congress who participated, including Senators John Tower and John Heinz, among others.*

6. *Sworn declarations given to me by CIA informants indicate that four or five Secret Service Agents accompanied the group of Americans who traveled*

to Paris for the October 19, 1980 weekend meetings that finalized the October Surprise operation. The involvement of the Secret Service, the CIA, members of President Carter's staff, and others, in the subversive acts against the United States may constitute one of the worst criminal conspiracies ever exposed against the United States, and surely constitutes an unpublicized coup. Having a Treasury Department agent play a major role in the October Surprise investigation, when Treasury Department agents assisted in carrying out the coup or scheme, is typical of Congressional "investigations," but hardly meets the definition of an investigation.

7. Mr. Pedersen stated that the Secret Service reports were not confidential or secret but simply not released. However, various news media sources claim they have copies of the reports, and presumably this supports his statement indicating that the reports are not classified. I am requesting copies of the reports that your committee has in its possession, and any other reports commencing from Friday, October 17, 1980 through October 20, 1980, Monday.

SIGNS OF COVERUP BY YOUR COMMITTEE

8. In response to my comment that Ari Ben-Menashe's credibility has been established by the copies of Mossad documents in his recently published book, Profits of War, Mr. Pedersen responded that he was totally discredited. Ari Ben-Menashe testified before Congressional committees that he was present at several of the October Surprise meetings, and saw George Bush, William Casey, Robert McFarlane, Donald Gregg, among others, at these meetings. He knew he would be charged with perjury if he lied, and he had nothing to gain. His recent book, Profits of War, include Mossad documents showing him to be a high staff officer possessing details of the October Surprise operation that dove-tails with the testimony, the testimony offered, and the investigative findings of numerous journalists and authors.

9. In response to my question as to why the testimony of CIA contract agent Richard Brenneke was not accepted, Mr. Pedersen responded that he was totally discredited. But Brenneke knew that he would probably be charged with perjury if he lied. He had nothing to gain by his testimony before a U.S. District Court Judge in Denver in 1988. He was simply trying to show that he, and Rupp who was on trial in the Aurora Bank fraud case, were CIA contract agents. Further, his testimony coincided with other CIA operatives, with dozens of people who described their part in the October Surprise operation to various investigative journalists and authors. They, like Brenneke, had nothing to gain by their statements.

10. In response to my question about why the committee did not accept testimony from CIA contract agent Michael Riconosciuto, Mr. Pedersen totally discredited him. Again, as with Brenneke, Riconosciuto gave sworn testimony concerning the October Surprise operation, and he knew that he faced perjury charges if he gave false testimony. He had no reason to lie. He testified to assisting in the relay of the $40 million bribe money in the October Surprise operation.

11. In response to my question asking why the House October Surprise Committee didn't have CIA operative Gunther Russbacher testify, Mr.

Pedersen justified refusing to allow Russbacher to testify on the basis that Russbacher had been continuously in prison from 1977 to 1983, and thereby couldn't have been part of the October Surprise operation. But Russbacher has given me sworn declarations that he had not been in prison continuously during this time, and only was imprisoned for short periods to provide a background for his covert CIA activities with factions in Europe and the U.S. underworld. Further, Russbacher would not risk further imprisonment from perjury charges and could be expected to testify truthfully. I already have hundreds of sworn statements by Russbacher, describing the specifics of the October Surprise operation, which I have personally checked out with Ari Ben-Menashe, and through contacts with various personnel reportedly implicated in the European meetings associated with the October Surprise operation.

12. Mr. Pedersen stated awareness of the SR-71 video tape described by Paul Wilcher, on the purported flight from Paris in which Gunther Russbacher was reportedly the pilot and George Bush the passenger. Your committee could have proved or disproved the existence of that video tape by requesting the tape from the archives at Camp Mead, Maryland. You never did that.

13. Gunther Russbacher, CIA operative and Captain in the U.S. Navy and Office of Naval Intelligence, has offered to testify under oath to your committee and others, describing his role in the October Surprise operation, knowing that he would be charged with perjury if he lied. Congressman Hamilton and his committee knew he offered to testify and that Russbacher would undoubtedly not risk a prison term to lie, especially when it would not be to his benefit to testify.

14. I provided to your committee a partial transcript of sworn declarations by Gunther Russbacher, describing details of the October Surprise scheme, claiming that he was at several of the meetings, and that he arranged for the procurement and shipment of arms following the Barcelona meeting. I am prepared to testify to what Russbacher stated to me during the past two years concerning his role in the October Surprise (and other corrupt) CIA operation. As a former federal investigator I am quite competent to evaluate the sincerity and truthfulness of almost 300 hours of statements. Russbacher has offered to testify to a Congressional committee, including that chaired by Congressman Hamilton, knowing that he would be charged with perjury if he lied.

15. Your group has ignored the statements made by former Iranian president Bani-Sadr in his two books describing details of the October Surprise operation. Presumably he too is totally discredited.

16. I am a former federal investigator who held federal authority to make certain determinations. I witnessed a pattern of hard-core federal crimes perpetrated by federal officials. I have government documents showing the crimes to exist. I have made judicial records of the criminal activities, and the responses of rogue Justice Department personnel and federal judges constitute additional criminal acts on their word. I have questioned CIA operatives, others, and have uncovered a pattern of criminal activities₁ against the United States that are inter-related with the October Surprise operation. I have seen the criminal obstruction of justice by every government check and balance, including Justice Department personnel and members of Congress, among others. These findings coincide with the crimes charged by Brenneke, Riconosciuto, Russbacher, investigative journalists and authors, and the crimes implied by the felony coverups.

17. Even worse, the conduct of your committee includes threats against those seeking to report the October Surprise crimes. Garby Leon of Columbia Pictures and Rayelan Russbacher stated to me that during an early 1992 telephone conversations with Secret Service agent Pedersen, that he threatened them if they continued with their October Surprise exposure activities.

18. Threats reportedly made by Agent Pedersen of your committee against attorney Paul Wilcher as Wilcher sought to give data to your committee showing details of the October Surprise conspiracy. Wilcher states that he was physically shoved against the wall by Pedersen and warned to halt his exposure activities.

19. Agent Pedersen threatened me for having copies of the Secret Service reports, displaying no interest, obviously, in reaching the truth.

20. Aiding and abetting the coverup by this committee are Justice Department prosecutors and federal judges, seeking to cover up for their own involvement in October Surprise and its many related tentacles, by charging me with federal crimes in retaliation for having reported the crimes to a federal court, and in retaliation for seeking to defend against the felony persecution associated with the obstruction of justice.

21. These threats against informants to keep them from reporting criminal acts are criminal violations.₂ The refusal to receive evidence, the threats against informants, the staffing of your committee with people that have a vested interest in coverup, violate blocks of federal criminal statutes.₃

COMPOSITION OF HOUSE OCTOBER SURPRISE COMMITTEE

The composition of Congressman Hamilton's October Surprise "investigative" Committee parallels many other Congressional investigative committees:

A. Chief counsel Larry Barcella is a former (and probably present) CIA asset. Since October Surprise was a CIA operation he could be expected to block any exposure, and his conduct reflects that approach. Further, Barcella was a Justice Department hatchet man and also represented BCCI, defending their corrupt acts and trying to block their prosecution. His partial success in this respect enabled BCCI to continue their looting of assets in what has become the world's worst bank fraud.

B. Richard Pedersen is an agent with the Treasury Department. The Treasury Department's Secret Service agents were present during Vice-president nominee George Bush's flight to Paris on October 18, 1980. Pedersen's role, and certainly his conduct, has been to block any exposure of the October Surprise treasonous and subversive acts against the United States.

C. Peggy Robahm, one of your "investigators," was reportedly used by the CIA and Justice Department to discredit Richard Brenneke, by tactics that are better described in a fiction book. This same Peggy Robahm was then placed on Congressman Hamilton's October Surprise Committee to discredit the existence of the operation.

The impression I received from Mr. Pedersen was that the House October Surprise Committee's "investigative" report would be released shortly, and reveal that no such event occurred. From what I have observed, starting as a federal investigator and then a private investigator for the past thirty years, what else could be expected! For crimes against the United States, the members of the House October Surprise Committee have met past standards.

With tongue in cheek, I offer my services to expose the crimes involved in October Surprise and the various other associated tentacles. Obviously I don't expect the offer to be taken. If you wish, I will send you a copy of Defrauding America when it is released, which puts these events in the proper perspective.

Sincerely,

Rodney F. Stich

Enclosures:
October 3, 1980 CIA: "Proposal to Exchange Spare Parts With Hostages."
October 9, 1980 Department of State: "Approach on Iranian Spares."
October 21, 1980 Department of State: "Talk with Mitch Regovin."
October 29, 1980: "Two Related Items on Iranian Military supply."
October 1980 Secret Service reports: Bush's security detail.
June 3, 1983(?) CIA: Release of Hostages.
July 5, 1985: "New Developments on Channel to Iran."
August 19, 1985: "Status of Hashemi-Elliot Richardson Contact."

****

ENDNOTES

1. The criminal activities include: (a) pattern of air safety and criminal acts related to a series of fatal airline crashes; (b) CIA scheme known as "October Surprise," in which U.S. military equipment was stolen and given to Iran in exchange for continuing the imprisonment of 52 American hostages held by Iran in 1980; (c) CIA embezzlement and looting of America's financial institutions; (d) criminal misuse of Chapter 11 courts by the CIA/federal judges/federal trustees/law firms, to sequester evidence of the looted CIA proprietaries; (e) criminal misuse of Chapter 11 courts by the same group, to fund covert and corrupt CIA activities (including corrupt seizure and looting of Petitioner's assets in the Oakland Chapter 11 courts, cases Nrs. 487-05974J/05975J); (e) CIA drug smuggling into the United States, enlarging upon its history of drug trafficking in foreign countries; (f) felony coverup and conspiracy to coverup by persons in the U.S. Department of Justice and by federal judges/justices; (g) felony persecution of informants, whistleblowers, and protesting victims, by corrupt federal judges and prosecutors; (h) criminal activities related to the stealing of software belonging to Inslaw, and criminal misuse of the Justice Department and Chapter 11 courts; and other criminal activities.

2. Title 18 U.S.C. § 1512. Tampering with a witness, victim, or an informant—
(b) Whoever knowingly uses intimidation or physical force, or threatens another person, or attempts to do so, or engages in misleading conduct toward another person, with intent to—
(1) influence, delay or prevent the testimony of any person in an official proceeding:
shall be fined ... or imprisoned ... or both. [1988 amended reading]"
Title 18 U.S.C. § 1513. Retaliating against a witness, victim, or an informant. (a) Whoever knowingly engages in any conduct and thereby causes bodily injury to another person or damages the tangible property of another person, or threatens to do so, with intent to retaliate against any person for—(1) the attendance of a witness or party at an official proceeding, or any testimony given or any record, document, or other object produced by a witness in an official proceeding; or (2) any information relating to the commission or possible commission of a federal offense ..."
3. Title 18 U.S.C. § 1505 (obstructing proceedings before federal courts, and earlier, before FAA, NTSB, before federal grand jury, to prevent presenting testimony and evidence of federal offenses); § 1512 (tampering with a witness or informant, and specifically, preventing Stich's communication to a federal court of the federal air safety and criminal offenses, using felonious means to block such federal proceedings); § 1513 (retaliating against a witness, victim, or an informant, and specifically against Stich, to prevent his reporting of the federal crimes by federal officials); §§ 1961-1965 (RICO violations, by conspiring to harm an informant, and adversely affecting interstate and international commerce); § 241 (conspiracy against rights of any citizen, including conspiracy that violated wholesale numbers of federally protected rights); § 371 (conspiracy to commit offense against, or to defraud, the United States); § 1951 (interference with interstate and international air commerce, and specifically the FAA, NTSB, wrongful acts, and blocking and retaliating against Stich for seeking to report federal air safety and criminal acts affecting air safety); § 2 (principal); § 3 (accessory after the fact); § 4 (misprision of felony); § 35 (imparting or conveying false information); § 2071 (Concealment, removal, of official reports); § 34 (changing federal offenses to capital offense when death results); § 111 (impeding FAA inspectors or other federal employees); § 1621 (perjury, at FAA hearing); § 1623 (subornation of perjury, at FAA hearing); § 1623 (false declarations before federal grand jury); 28 U.S.C. § 1343 (Failure to prevent the violations of a person's civil and constitutional rights); Title 42 U.S.C. §§ 1983-1986 (Violating civil and constitutional rights of another, conspiracy to do so, failure to prevent the violations when the ability and responsibility to do so exists); Treason, Art 3 § 3 of US Constitution.

****

I sent another letter to Congressman Hamilton on December 29, 1992, enclosing copies of secret CIA and State Department documents describing arms-for-hostages meetings from 1980 through 1985. The documents clearly showed that the arms flow to Iran started not in 1986, as stated in the Iran-

Contra prosecutions and media reports, but years earlier, commencing in September 1980, as part of the October Surprise operation.

To determine whether the Secret Service report in my possession or the one cited by the House October Surprise Committee was correct, I filed a Freedom of Information (FOI) request with the Secret Service, enclosing a copy of my document showing Bush arriving at Washington National Airport on a UAE BAC 111, and asked for their copy of the document. The Secret Service acknowledged finding their copy but refused to release it to me.

INTERIM REPORT OF THE HOUSE COMMITTEE

On July 1, 1992, the House committee issued an interim report on October Surprise, stating its investigation had not been completed, that a final report would be released in January 1993, and that they believed there was no truth to the charges. Special counsel Lawrence Barcella, Jr., issued the preliminary report. The final report, consisting of 968 pages, was issued on January 3, 1993.

The final report followed the standard Congressional pattern of withholding incriminating evidence, discrediting witnesses who supported the original charges, and giving credibility to those government officials who were implicated in the charges. The report withheld knowledge of the Secret Service reports and Russbacher's declarations that I submitted in November 1992.

A number of factors struck me, in the report, including:

* Most of the investigators consisted of current or former Justice Department and Secret Service personnel.

* Withheld knowledge of the Secret Service documents that I submitted to Congressman Hamilton in November 1992, which contradicted the statements made by Secret Service personnel as to George Bush's location on the October 19, 1980, weekend.

* Withheld knowledge of the 40-plus-page sworn declarations given by former CIA operative Gunther Russbacher and other CIA and Mossad assets.

* Refused to receive my testimony and evidence relating to statements made to me by Russbacher over a two-year span that described many specifics involved in the October Surprise operation.

* Refused to allow Russbacher to testify, giving sham excuses for not doing so.

* Fraudulently discredited the testimony of former Mossad operative Ari Ben-Menashe, who was present at several of the European meetings, including the Paris meetings and meetings at which Russbacher was present. The Task Force report stated:

The Task Force has determined that Ben-Menashe's account of the October Surprise meetings, like his other October Surprise allegations, is a total fabrication.

A September 4, 1987, letter written by Colonel Pesah Melowany in the Israel Defense Forces states of Ben-Menashe:

Mr. Ari Ben-Menashe has served in the Israel Defense Forces External Relations Department in key positions. As such, Mr. Ben-Menashe was responsible for a variety of complex and sensitive assignments

which demanded exceptional analytical and executive capabilities.
IDF Colonel Yoav Dayagi wrote on September 6, 1987:
[Ben-Menashe] served in the IDF External Relations Department in key positions. ... is a person known to keep to his principles, being always guided by a strong sense of duty, justice and common sense.
Ben-Menashe's book had copies of other letters from the Israel Defense Forces attesting to his high level position. There are copies of Telex messages from Ben-Menashe to Iranian president Rafsanjani and other Iranian officials, quoting prices for war material to be shipped by Israel.

* Falsely discredited Ben-Menashe's testimony by stating he was only a low-level translator, even though he presented letters and documentation during a closed hearing showing otherwise. Several of my CIA contacts described encountering Ben-Menashe in Europe, Central and South America, and other locations, engaging in covert activities for Israel.

* Accepting at face value written denials by Israel officials[283] that they were not involved in any of the October Surprise activities. These denials contradicted testimony by former Mossad agent Ben-Menashe and my CIA contacts, including Gunther Russbacher. The disclaimers by Israeli officials were made indirectly to the Task Force, as the Israeli government refused to allow them to be questioned. Obviously they had something to hide! Israel has a strong vested interest to make sure the American people never learn of its complicity in October Surprise.

* Refused to have former CIA operative Richard Brenneke testify, despite his key role in October Surprise.

* Discredited Brenneke on the basis of deceptive credit card charges routinely made on behalf of covert CIA operatives for later use as disclaimers.

* Falsely stated that Paul Wilcher, who made numerous attempts to have the Task Force obtain Russbacher's testimony, was an unlicensed lawyer, when in fact he was admitted to practice in the state of Illinois.

* Referred to witnesses who risked Justice Department retaliation by coming forth with the truth as "utter fabricators." This group included Ari Ben-Menashe; Gunther Russbacher; Richard Brenneke; Michael Riconosciuto; Heinrich Rupp; and Jamshid Hashemi. It accepted without question recanted statements made to journalists by Oswald LeWinter, Admiral Ahmed Madani, and Arif Durrani.

* Accepted as true the self-serving statements and denials by those who would be implicated, including Donald Gregg, McFarlane, and Israel officials. The U.S. personnel would be impeached and charged with major crimes if the truth was admitted.

* Refused to contact the National Archives at Camp Mead, Maryland, to obtain a copy of the video tape showing George Bush and Gunther Russbacher in an SR-71 aircraft on a flight from Paris to McGuire Air Force Base on Sunday, October 19, 1980. This is the tape that the report stated Wilcher did not deliver.

---

[283] David Kimche, Shmuel Moriah, Rafi Eitan.

* Refused to have Riconosciuto testify about the electronic transfer of the $40 million in bribe money given to the Iranians during the October 19, 1980 weekend meetings in Paris.

* Refused to address Donald Gregg's failure to pass a lie detector test given by the government Accounting Office.

* Refused to make reference to the transcript of sworn declarations that I had obtained from Russbacher, while including hearsay statements that denied the existence of October Surprise.

The Task Force report dismissed the charges of an October Surprise scheme as "bizarre claims." The American people have been victimized by the subversive criminal conspiracy and its many tentacles, including the brutality of the Iran-Contra operation. These criminal acts against the American people were then followed up with the coverup.

Aiding in the coverup was the media. A classic example was a January 16, 1993 article in the *Wall Street Journal*, praising the House report, and suggesting that Justice department officials charge the witnesses, who had risked so much, with perjury. Since the mid-1960s I had sent evidence to the *Wall Street Journal* of hard-core criminal acts committed by federal officials. Several of my CIA confidants believe that the *Journal's* preoccupation with protecting Israel was the reason behind their efforts to cover up for the October Surprise operation.

COMPLICITY BY THEIR SILENCE

I sent letters to people who were part of the October Surprise operation or who had evidence of its existence, advising them that I was going to publish in this book their involvement, unless they gave me contrary information. Members of the French Secret Service present during the October 19, 1980, meetings in Paris, would have filed reports on their activities. I mailed a registered letter to French President Francois Mitterrand on April 4, 1992, requesting a copy of the French Secret Service report of the October 19, 1980, October Surprise meetings in Paris. Several of my sources stated that French government agents were present during the meetings, and that reports were made. My letter stated in part:

This letter is a request for information, and copies of official writings, relating to the following:

* * Barcelona meetings that occurred in late July, 1980, at the Pepsico International Headquarters Building, at which William Casey (subsequently Director of the United States Central Intelligence Agency) was present, along with Robert McFarlane, Gunther Russbacher, and Iranian nationals. The intent of this meeting was to provide Iranian factions with bribe money and military equipment and munitions stolen from United States military warehouses, and which started flowing to Iran via Israel in September 1980. These meetings consisted of a criminal conspiracy to defraud the United States.*

* *October 19, 1980 weekend meetings in Paris, furthering the treasonous and subversive acts, in which a scheme was finalized to pay large amounts of money, and billions in secret military equipment and ammunition, from the American conspirators, to Iranian factions, to*

continue the imprisonment of 52 American hostages.

These acts were subversive and treasonous, and required the felony coverup by many people. Until these criminal acts are uncovered, the same people who unlawfully and corruptly gained control of the United States government are continuing to inflict great harms upon the United States, with international implications.

I know that the French secret police knew of these meetings; were present at these meetings; and made reports of them. I also know that you were made aware of them. I therefore request that you send to me copies of these reports, and related writings, so I can take actions to have these American officials impeached and prosecuted.

If you refuse to do so, you should be advised that you, as the head of the government in France, will be aiding and abetting the treasonous, the subversive, the criminal acts, that continue to inflict great harms upon the United States and its people. This letter, and your response, will be included in the nearly completed book describing the criminal cartel that is defrauding the American people.

When the president of France did not respond to that request, I sent another request for documents by registered mail on July 7, 1992. The French government again refused to answer or deny my charges. I had advised that their refusal to respond would be included in this book as support for the charges being true.

A manager at Columbia Pictures in Los Angeles, Garby Leon, told me in early 1992 that he had spoken to ABC's Pierre Salinger, who had admitted to him that he had a copy of the French Secret Service report describing the October Surprise meetings in Paris, and that he would show the report to him if he came to London. I sent a request to Salinger and to ABC's corporate headquarters, by registered mail, requesting a copy of that report. My letter stated in part:

This is a request for information, and a copy of documents in your possession, relating to the activities known as "October Surprise." I have been advised by several sources that you, and American Broadcasting Corporation, have writings supporting the existence of these treasonous and subversive activities which were a CIA operation. I am writing in my book that is nearly completed, and it is being stated ... that ABC has these writings in its possession, and ... that ABC has become, as a matter of federal law, co-conspirators, and liable criminally as principals.

Neither Salinger nor ABC responded.

PEPSICO AS A CIA ASSET

Pepsico International Headquarters in Barcelona was the site of one of the meetings held in Barcelona in July 1980.[284] I sent a registered letter to Wayne Calloway, CEO and Chairman of the Board of Directors of Pepsico, in Purchase, New York, advising that I was describing in my book the part

---

[284] Stated and confirmed by Russbacher, his former wife Peggy, and Ben-Menashe.

they played in the October Surprise operation, unless I heard otherwise from them. The letter stated in part:

> I am in possession of declarations/transcripts showing that the Pepsico Corporation played key roles in the treasonous and subversive acts known as October Surprise.[285] These declarations/transcripts, by a deep cover CIA officer, who was present at the Barcelona meetings in late July 1980, at the Pepsico International Headquarters Building, describes the part played by Pepsico in helping to sabotage the United States by becoming a part of the conspiracy known as October Surprise. Other declarations show the part played by Pepsico in other CIA schemes. The Pepsico official directly involved in the Barcelona caper was Peter Van Tyne.
>
> Pepsico's part in the CIA-related schemes is being described in the nearly completed Defrauding America book, which is a follow-up to my last one, Unfriendly Skies—Saga of Corruption. To fill in areas that are not yet clear, would you kindly provide me with the following information:
>
> 1. The address of Peter Van Tyne, and what his position was with Pepsico in mid-1980.
>
> 2. Peter Van Tyne's present address for receiving correspondence.
>
> 3. Who in the CIA, and any others, arranged with Pepsico for the use of its International Headquarters facilities in the subversive acts associated with October Surprise?
>
> 4. What is the relationship between Pepsico and the Central Intelligence Agency in the United States and overseas?
>
> 5. What other covert relationships existed, and exist, between Pepsico and the CIA?
>
> 6. What are the rewards, financial and otherwise, arising from these relationships?
>
> For your information, copies of the transcripts showing Pepsico's involvement with these very serious crimes against the United States have been attached to federal briefs, and have been sent to many members of Congress (despite its record as the world's most reliable coverup body), and others. Many more will be sent out. Your answer to these questions would be useful in clarifying the covert relationships that helped inflict such great harms upon the United States.
>
> If you don't provide this information, the book will show the implications of what Pepsico has done, and what can be implied by your refusal to respond.

No response and no denial.

Russbacher stated that William Casey boarded the BAC 111 at a New York City area airport after deplaning from a Unocal Gulfstream aircraft. I

---

[285] The conspiracy involved private citizens, renegade federal officials, Central Intelligence Agency personnel (all sabotaging the elected Government of the United States), and Iranian factions who were holding 52 American citizens in Iranian prisons.

contacted Unocal[286] by certified mail on June 7, 1992, advising them of the serious charges associated with the October Surprise operation, in which they were a part, and advising that unless I heard otherwise from them I would describe the part they played in the operation. No response and no denial.

The House October Surprise Committee advised me that my Secret Service report showing George Bush flying into Washington National Airport in a UAE BAC 111 should read United Airlines, and the date should be October 18, 1980. I wrote to United Airlines via certified mail asking for their confirmation of the flight and date. They refused to answer.

The treasonous and subversive October Surprise crimes did in fact occur.

1. Sworn declarations and testimony of CIA operatives, including Gunther Russbacher, Richard Brenneke, and Michael Riconosciuto, who had much to lose.

2. Sworn testimony of Mossad officer Ari Ben-Menashe, who was present at several October Surprise meetings.

3. Secret Service documents disproving the statements of Secret Service agents and George Bush relating to Bush's absence from Washington on the October 19, 1980 weekend.

4. Statements by dozens of people in the United States, Europe and the Middle East, describing their knowledge of the October Surprise operation.

5. Refusal of people to deny the charges that I advised would be made against them if they did not respond to my mailings.

6. Large amount of anecdotal and circumstantial evidence.

7. Many people who were killed or who mysteriously died, who had knowledge of the October Surprise operation, and who were a threat to Iranian and U.S. officials implicated in the scheme.

8. Intense opposition by Republican members of Congress to conduct investigations into the charges.

ENORMOUS CONSEQUENCES IF
THE PUBLIC WAS TOLD THE TRUTH

The resulting consequences of being caught in a coverup was minor compared to the consequences suffered by Washington officials if the October Surprise was admitted. Among the potential consequences of admitting that October Surprise conspiracy occurred:

1. Impeachment and criminal prosecution of many federal officials.

2. Exposing the role played by the CIA, and possibly exposing other criminal activities of this agency.

3. Many Congressmen would be criminally implicated by their coverup, calling for impeachment and criminal prosecution.

4. Federal judges, who gained their positions by having played a role in the October Surprise scheme, would be exposed, undermining public respect for the federal judiciary.

5. Past presidents of the United States would be exposed as guilty of treasonous and criminal activities.

---

[286] Richard Stegemeier, Chief Executive Officer, Unocal Corporation
P.O. Box 7600, Los Angeles, CA 90051; Certified P 790 780 431.

6. Powerful law firms, lobbyists, and many other private interests, with fortunes tied to those in power, would be adversely affected if their benefactors were prosecuted and removed from office.

7. All political parties would suffer as a result of the public's awareness of the level of criminality in government.

RESPONSIBILITIES

Every member of Congress had a responsibility under federal criminal statutes to receive testimony and evidence of the criminal acts described within these pages. The oath states:

*I, [name of Congress person], do solemnly swear (or affirm) that I will support and **defend** the Constitution of the United States against all enemies, foreign and domestic; that I will bear true faith and allegiance to the same; that I take this obligation freely, without any mental reservation or purpose of evasion, and that I will well and faithfully discharge the duties of the office in which I am about to enter. So help me God.*

DISCOVERING CONFIDENTIAL DOCUMENTS
ESTABLISHING RUSSBACHER'S CIA/ONI STATUS

In later pages I have included government documents and statements made by other deep-cover CIA personnel, further proving the existence of the October Surprise conspiracy against the American people.

CHAPTER SEVENTEEN

IRAN-CONTRA

Without the October Surprise operation there could not have been an Iran-Contra scandal. The Iran and the Contra portions of what is known as Iran-Contra are really separate scandals, with relatively minor connections. The media and Congress have joined them together, and have loosely described Iran-Contra as unlawful arms sales to Iran in exchange for American hostages seized in Lebanon and unlawful arms sales to Nicaragua. The Teheran hostage seizure associated with the October Surprise operation showed terrorists the profits to be realized in seizing Americans as hostages.

THE IRAN CONNECTION

U.S. media and congressional publicity on Iran-Contra focused on the illegal arms sales to Iran in the mid-1980s. But these sales commenced long before. They started within a couple of months after the secret Barcelona meeting occurring in late July 1980, as part of October Surprise. Although the arms sales were allegedly to obtain the release of American hostages seized in Lebanon, there was also a profit motive for many of the participants. Sharing in the profits from these arms sales to Iran were arms brokers, Israel, and a private network composed of CIA and National Security Council players. These arms sales to Iran violated U.S. law, and the criminal acts involved the president and vice president of the United States, members of the National Security Council, the CIA, and others.

MOTIVES FOR THE ARMS SALES

The sales occurred partly because huge profits could be made by many participants. The arms would be purchased from U.S. or foreign governments, and then resold to Iran. Profits from these unlawful arms sales were stashed away in secret offshore bank accounts.[287] Ironically, about $10 million was placed in the wrong-numbered Swiss bank account that was

---

[287] One such account was in the name of Lake Resources, number 386-430-22-1.

intended for Air Force Maj. Gen. Richard Secord and his business partner, Albert Hakim.

Another motive for the illegal arms sales was for the CIA and NSC participants to purchase arms through their front companies. The money generated by the Iranian arms sales were not gifts to the Contras, as implied by the Reagan-Bush White House and the media. The profits from the arms sales to Iran were used to purchase additional arms, which were then traded to the Contras for drugs. These drugs constituted a large portion of the huge cocaine trafficking into the United States from Central and South America. The aircraft flying arms to Nicaragua and other Central and South America locations returned to the United States with drugs. This was a giant operation resembling a corporation structure such as General Motors.

NAIVETE OF PAYING FOR HOSTAGES

It can only be guessed if the selling of arms to Iran in exchange for the American hostages seized in Lebanon was the primary intent or simply an excuse for the Iran-Contra operation. It is difficult to believe that intelligence agency renegades thought the hostage situation could be solved by paying for their release, thereby encouraging a continuation of the hostage-taking. It appeared that for every hostage returned upon the payment of money or arms, additional hostages were seized. A "cottage industry" flourished. Its sole purpose was seizing American hostages in Lebanon. American hostages seized in Iran as part of October Surprise showed that profits could be made from hostage-taking, especially if they were Americans.

UGLY SIDE OF THE CONTRA CONNECTION

The ugly side of the Contra connection was carefully kept from the American public by the establishment media and Congress. Oliver North and others involved sought to place a humanitarian cloak over their activities with the Contras. They claimed U.S. involvement in Nicaragua was humanitarian, by helping an oppressed people fight communism. But the CIA, representing the American people, traded arms for drugs, and then using aircraft and surface transportation facilities on the return flights from Central America. This was similar to the CIA use of the Vietnam War to greatly increase the flow of drugs into the United States. Enormous profits resulted, and many CIA operatives became rich.

It wasn't only the Contras to whom the CIA furnished arms. The CIA, joined by Israel, arms merchants, and others, were selling and delivering arms to the opposition Sandanistas. One CIA operative stated to me, "How else could we keep the fighting going!"

Drug trafficking from Central and South America into the United States by the CIA, DEA, and the Mossad, was well underway in the 1960s. The CIA's stirring of the pot in Nicaragua greatly aided this by providing a great increase in aircraft availability, and an excuse for the trafficking. Various code names were given to these arms and drug flights, as described in later pages.

As in any CIA operation, there were terrible brutalities inflicted upon innocent people. The Contra affair funded the intrusion by the CIA, representing the United States and the American people, into the affairs of a foreign country, using the same tactics and excuses as in Vietnam. The CIA prepared an assassination manual on torturing and killing people in Central America, resulting in the deaths of thousands of villagers, similar to the infamous Phoenix program in Vietnam that assassinated over 40,000 South Vietnamese villagers.

Numerous books have been written depicting these atrocities.[288] An October 19, 1992, *New York Times* article showed pictures revealing the 1981 massacre of almost 800 villagers at El Mozote, El Salvador. Reporters from the *Times* and *Washington Post* were in agreement that the killings were perpetrated by groups financed and supplied by the White House gang and the CIA. Searchers found many bodies, including those of children, under the floor of a parish house.

Most of the media discredited these assassination reports when they first came out, even though the media knew the reports to be true. The CIA infiltration of the media and the government's furnishing of much of what passes as news, along with the money dispensed to the media by the CIA, made this cooperation quite easy.

The arms sales to Nicaragua, or any other Central American country, violated U.S. law, and specifically the 1984 Boland Amendment. Those involved in the sale of arms, including the trading of arms for drugs, deliberately continued violating the law. If the arms trafficking stopped, so would much of the drug trafficking into the United States on the return flights.

CONGRESS FORCED TO CONDUCT AN "INVESTIGATION" AFTER CIA PLANE SHOT DOWN

Several events caused the American public to become aware of at least peripheral segments of the Iran and Contra operations. One event was the shooting down of a CIA proprietary aircraft[289] over Nicaragua in 1986. This was the highly-publicized shooting down of the C-123 aircraft with four crewmembers on board, and the survival of one of them: Eugene Hasenfus. Despite instructions for all evidence of CIA involvement removed from the aircraft and in the crew's possession, there was much evidence that the arms-carrying flight was a CIA operation.

Nicaraguan authorities put Hasenfus on television, during which he admitted that he was working for the CIA. As U.S. media stopped publicity on that event, other events occurring in Europe and the Middle East focused attention on the Iran segment of Iran-Contra.

An Iranian politician, incensed about his opponent's participation in the Iranian arms deals, distributed thousands of leaflets in Iran exposing these dealings, followed by an article in the Lebanese newspaper, *Al Shiraa*. Israeli

---

[288] *Dangerous Liaison*, Andrew and Leslie Cockburn; *The Politics of Heroin*, Alfred McCoy; *Cocaine Politics*, Peter Dale Scott and Jonathan Marshall; *Everybody Had His Own Gringo*, Glenn Garvin.

[289] The aircraft was owned by Southern Air, a CIA proprietary. The two pilots were killed after the plane was hit by a ground-to-air missile. The cargo-pusher, Eugene Hasenfaus, whose job was to push the military equipment from the aircraft while airborne, had carried a parachute with him, and parachuted from the falling aircraft. He survived, was captured, and testified to Nicaraguan authorities about his CIA connections.

arms dealers who were taken out of the loop by direct arms sales from U.S. officials to Iran sought to eliminate the American competition, and they caused publicity to be generated.

This combination of publicity forced the U.S. media and Congress to focus on at least the outer fringes of the Iran and Contra affairs. Congress conducted one of their "investigations," and then requested that U.S. Attorney Edwin Meese recommend to the U.S. Court of Appeals in Washington appointment of an Independent Counsel (December 1986) to investigate further.

AUTHORITY FOR INDEPENDENT PROSECUTOR

Authority for the appointment of an independent prosecutor to investigate misconduct, criminal and treasonous activities, of high officials in the executive branch, was granted in 1978, following the Watergate affair. Congress passed the Independent Counsel Act,[290] providing for the appointment of an independent prosecutor to investigate crimes by high federal officials, but exempted themselves from being investigated. The mechanics of the legislation provided that the Judiciary Committee of either the House or Senate must request the U.S. Attorney General to submit a request to three judges on the Washington, D.C. Court of Appeals for the appointment of an Independent Counsel.

The Attorney General then decides whether to comply with the request. If the Attorney General does submit a request to the three-judge panel, the panel then decides what law firm or attorney will conduct the investigation. There are several judges on the Washington Court of Appeals who played key roles in October Surprise and the Iran and Contra operations. One of these judges is Lawrence Silberman.

A disadvantage of the Independent Prosecutor is that the attorney selected may be unqualified and without sufficient experience to conduct a criminal investigation. The attorney selected to act as Independent Prosecutor may be biased, or have hidden interests, and often has profitable ties to the Justice Department, CIA, or other government entity. The attorney will rarely jeopardize these lucrative ties. The attorney selected may be a former Justice Department employee still loyal to the mindset of that agency.

LIMITING THE RISKS

Meese made the request, limiting the investigation to determining which of the people who gave testimony to Congress had either lied or withheld evidence. Meese himself was implicated in the Iran and Contra operations and had a vested interest in insuring coverup of the sordid operation. Court of Appeals judges selected former head of the American Bar Association, Lawrence Walsh, an 80-year-old Oklahoman, to conduct a limited investigation as Independent Counsel. The investigation focused on personnel assigned

---

[290] Legislation was enacted in 1978.

to the White House, the National Security Council, and the CIA.[291]

Walsh eventually filed charges against many of them. Caspar Weinberger was indicted on June 16, 1992, on charges of obstruction of justice and of Congress, perjury, and false statements to Iran-Contra investigators. Duane Clarridge was indicted on November 26, 1991, on charges of perjury and making false statements to Congress. Oliver North was found guilty on May 4, 1989, of altering and destroying government documents, aiding and abetting, and obstruction of Congress. This case was dismissed on the technicality that he was immune against prosecution on the basis of testimony given to Congress.

Claire George was indicted and found guilty on December 9, 1992, of making false statements and perjury before Congress. Elliott Abrams was indicted and pled guilty on October 7, 1991, to withholding information from Congress. Alan Fiers, Jr., pleaded guilty on July 9, 1991, to withholding information from Congress. Robert McFarlane was indicted and pled guilty on March 11, 1988, to withholding information from Congress. Thomas Clines was charged and found guilty on September 18, 1990, to tax-related crimes and sent to prison.

Richard Secord was charged and pled guilty on November 8, 1989, to making false statements to Congress. Albert Hakim was charged and pled guilty on November 21, 1989 to supplementing the salary of Oliver North. Carl Channell pled guilty on April 29, 1987, to conspiracy to defraud the United States. Richard Miller pled guilty on May 8, 1987, to conspiracy to defraud the United States. John Poindexter was found guilty on April 7, 1990, of conspiracy, obstruction of justice, and making false statements to Congress. Joseph Fernandez was charged but the case dismissed on November 24, 1989, after the CIA refused to turn over documents relevant to his defense.

Vice President George Bush denied any knowledge of the Iran-Contra affair until it was made public in the American mainstream media in December 1986, just as he denied his involvement in October Surprise. My CIA contacts described Bush's heavy involvement in Central America operations in which drug trafficking constituted a major role. Testimony and numerous books describe Bush's long-time involvement in the Central America operations. Felix Rodriguez, known to be involved with the entire

---

[291] Among those who were investigated were Caspar Weinberger (Secretary of Defense); George Schultz (Secretary of State); George Bush (Vice President of the United States); Edwin Meese (Attorney General); Donald Regan (White House Chief of Staff); John Poindexter (National Security Advisor); William Casey (CIA Director); Alton Keel (Poindexter's deputy); Robert McFarlane (National Security Advisor); Elliott Abrams (Assistant Secretary of State); Duane Clarridge (CIA Chief of European operations); Clair E. George (CIA); Alan G. Fiers, Jr. (Head of CIA Central American Task Force); Richard V. Secord (retired Air Force Major General); Thomas G. Clines (CIA contract agent); Joseph F. Fernandez (CIA station chief in Costa Rica); Oliver L. North (Marine Corps officer and staff member of the National Security Council); among others.

sordid operation, reported regularly to Bush in the White House.[292] Some of North's notes referred to the drug trafficking, relying upon the drug profits to fund other elements of the operation.

The large-scale smuggling of arms out of the United States to Central America and return flights loaded with drugs surely were not unknown to Justice Department officials, to the CIA, to Customs, or the Drug Enforcement Agency in the Justice Department. My CIA contacts who were part of the operation detailed how they continued in their CIA-related drug trafficking unmolested.

Secord and others ran a private company selling arms to Iran, making huge profits, which they put into private bank accounts in Europe. My CIA contacts state that many in this same group managed CIA drug trafficking operations in Central America and in the Golden Triangle area.[293] Poindexter was charged with obstructing, conspiring to obstruct, and making false statements to Congress. North was convicted of aiding and abetting obstruction of Congress, destroying security council documents and accepting an illegal gift.

Aside from the coverup of the sordid aspects of the so-called Iran-Contra affair, there are some contradictions to the prosecution of these people, arising out of their withholding of information from Congress and false statements. For example:

* Members of Congress have engaged in criminal coverup, misprision of felonies, obstruction of justice, falsification of hearing records, and other crimes, for years, and it is shown throughout these pages.

* Members of Congress have obstructed the reporting of federal crimes against the United States as a standard practice. I repeatedly petitioned Congress to introduce my testimony and evidence and that of our group of CIA and DEA whistleblowers. These were criminal acts.

* Members of Congress routinely cover up for serious crimes discovered during closed-door hearings, and then render decisions that are contradicted by the evidence being withheld.

* These acts violated numerous criminal statutes, including:
    * Misprision of felony (refusing to make known criminal acts against the United States).
    * Obstruction of justice
    * Conspiracy to obstruct justice.

* Many members of Congress already knew of the criminal acts involved in Iran-Contra, including the CIA and DEA drug trafficking that they continued to sequester.

* Conspiracy to commit these crimes and others, and defrauding the United States.

---

[292] Statements made to the media by Americans and Israelis involved with the operation; highly documented books, including *Honored and Betrayed*, by former Air Force Maj. General Richard Secord; Felix Rodriguez, a former CIA operative, was in frequent telephone contact with Bush, and described these contacts.

[293] Burma, Laos, Thailand.

CRIMINAL COVERUP BY INDEPENDENT PROSECUTOR

Walsh spent over $40 million focusing on the relatively minor issues of who knew about the arms for hostages and who withheld information from Congress. Walsh focused for six years on these trivial issues, while covering up for the hard-core drug trafficking into the United States as part of the Contra operation. He also covered up for the genesis of Iran-Contra, the October Surprise scandal. Walsh committed worse acts than the people he charged with federal crimes. He covered up for treasonous and criminal activities against the United States, permitting the infliction of much greater harm upon the American people.

Commencing in early 1992 I sent several petitions to Independent Prosecutor Lawrence Walsh, including transcripts of sworn declarations by some of the CIA and DEA whistleblowers, requesting that he receive our testimony and evidence, which he was required to receive as a matter of law.

The petition and declarations exposed corrupt activities by federal officials, including the Iran and Contra operations, October Surprise, CIA and DEA drug smuggling, looting of savings and loans, Chapter 11 corruption, and the criminal activities in the federal courts where he was once a federal judge and federal prosecutor.

PRESIDENTIAL PARDONS

Caspar Weinberger, former Defense Secretary, was scheduled to stand trial in January 1993, on charges of perjury, making false statements to Congress, and obstructing Congressional investigators. His testimony would implicate President George Bush and other high federal officials. Shortly before the trial was to start, Bush executed a Christmas eve pardon for Weinberger, forestalling that risk. He also pardoned Duane Clarridge; Clair George; Robert McFarlane; Elliott Abrams; and Alan Fiers, Jr.

If Bush had not issued these pardons, the danger existed that the sordid parts of the Contra operation would surface, including the drug trafficking into the United States. Further, former President Ronald Reagan's involvement would probably surface.

After Bush issued his pardon, I sent another certified letter and petition to Walsh, again putting him on notice of the criminal activities described within these pages, attaching additional copies of secret government documents supporting some of the charges. The petition stated in part:

December 27, 1992

Mr. Lawrence Walsh, Independent Prosecutor
Office of Independent Counsel, Suite 701 West
555 Thirteenth Street, NW
Washington, DC 20004 Certified: P 888 324 857

Dear Mr. Walsh:

This letter and the enclosures address the Iran-Contra affair that you were hired and paid to investigate. I had several times offered to present evidence to you concerning the hard-core criminal acts associated with Iran-Contra, and you refused to receive the evidence. In your investigation you chose to limit your investigation, similar to limiting the investigation of Murder Incorporated to parking ticket violations.

While you deserve credit for objecting to President Bush's pardons, you share blame for cover up of the serious Iran-Contra violations of federal law, the arms and drug trafficking into and out of the United States by the network, and of the treasonous and subversive October Surprise operations which you chose to cover up, and which were the genesis of Iran-Contra.

This letter, and the attachments, again puts you on notice and under federal criminal statutes and constitutional right to petition government, demands that you receive the testimony and evidence of myself and the parties who have knowledge of the criminal activities of which Iran-Contra and October Surprise are only a part. (I won't hold my breath waiting for you to meet your duty.)

The enclosed documents include Secret Service agent reports as received by the CIA, prior to their alterations to accommodate the coverup. The information that I have is that the Secret Service reports were routed through deep-cover CIA officer Gunther Russbacher, who then placed the initials of one of his CIA-provided aliases on many of them: RAW, standing for Robert Andrew Walker, who also operated a number of cover CIA financial proprietaries.

The documents not only support the charges that October Surprise did in fact occur, but also provide information on the Iran-Contra affair.

SIGNIFICANCE OF DATES ON THE SECRET SERVICE REPORTS

The correct dates and aircraft have great significance:

1. If Bush arrived by aircraft at Washington National Airport on Sunday, October 19, 1980, it would indicate Secret Service personnel lied (as well as George Bush) when reporting that Bush never left the Washington area on the December 19, 1980 weekend. (Wouldn't the false statements also be shown by an October 18, 1980, arrival by aircraft in the Washington area?)

2. If Bush arrived via a United Arab Emirates BAC 111, and several CIA operatives and contract agents testified (and declared in sworn declarations) that Bush and others departed Washington for Paris in a

UAE BAC 111 on October 18, 1980, it appears that Bush returned to Washington on the same aircraft.

3. It would indicate that the several dozen people who testified before Congress and in federal court; CIA operative Gunther Russbacher who made sworn declarations that I have in my possession; and those who described to investigative journalists and book authors particulars of the October Surprise operation, were truthful about the October Surprise operation.

4. If the hard-core October Surprise conspiracy and its implications were exposed to the public, the consequences would be endless. Other criminal activities arising from the operation would surface. The felony persecution of whistleblowers and informants would be exposed, as well as the perennial coverup and obstruction of justice by members of Congress. Key personnel in all three branches of government would be shown implicated in the October Surprise and related criminal enterprises, culminating in a political disaster of unknown consequences.

DETERMINING THE VALIDITY OF THE DISPUTED REPORTS

It is very important to the United States to determine the truth in this matter. A coverup will simply escalate the criminal mindset that has escalated in the federal government. Numerous people have copies of the Secret Service reports that I sent to you, showing George Bush arriving at Washington National Airport on the evening of October 19, 1980 in a UAE BAC 111. These reports have the initials, RAW, in the upper right hand corner.

My investigation indicates that the initials "RAW" stand for Robert Andrew Walker, an alias provided by the CIA to Gunther Russbacher, reportedly a deep-cover CIA and Office of Naval Intelligence officer. I recently questioned Russbacher about these reports, whether the initials were his, and whether the October 19, 1980 dates and the United Arab Emirates BAC 111 information were the same as when he first initialed the reports. He confirmed that the facts on my reports are the same as when the reports came to him.

Russbacher stated that he placed the initials, RAW, in the upper right hand corner of the Secret Service reports when the reports came to him at the Central Intelligence Agency at Langley, Virginia. Apparently the reason the reports came to him was that he was present at several activities related to the October Surprise operation. I have previously sent to Congressman Hamilton partial transcripts of Russbacher's sworn declarations describing the October Surprise activities in which he participated.

If Secret Service agents were on board that flight, then it would indicate further that a coup against the United States did take place, and that the Secret Service (and many others) are now trying to deny that fact.   The only way to establish which Secret Service reports are correct and which are forgeries is to have Russbacher testify in open hearings before the Senate October Surprise committee. Russbacher has advised me that he is willing to testify how and when he received these Secret Service reports; that the October 19, 1980 date was on these reports when he first saw them at the CIA; and the role that he played in the October Surprise operation.

If the hearings are closed to the public, then the usual Congressional coverup will prevail. If you remember, I'm a former federal investigator who is well familiar with the pattern of coverup, obstruction of justice, altering documents and reports. I have reported these crimes for years, with the felony coverups escalating in frequency and severity. Based upon my knowledge over the past thirty years, lying, perjury, obstruction of justice, are routine practices by many in federal government. I describe these acts in my various books and in prior federal court filings.

RUSSBACHER'S CREDIBILITY

Russbacher's credibility has been established to my satisfaction, and can be established in numerous ways:

* He has given me many hours of sworn declarations in deposition-like questioning relating to the specific October Surprise operation in which he was ordered to participate by his superiors (in addition to other CIA operations that have inflicted great harms upon the United States). During the past two years I have questioned Gunther Russbacher extensively, during a minimum of 200 hours of deposition-like questioning, uncovering facts supporting the criminal activities against the United States.

* Russbacher has tried to give testimony to Congress concerning some of his CIA activities, including the October Surprise operation, and is willing to do so at this time. These efforts have and are being made with full recognition that if he commits perjury the present Justice Department staff and the past three U.S. attorney generals (all of whom are implicated in the crimes) would promptly charge him with criminal perjury. The Senate and House October Surprise committees had a **duty** to obtain his testimony, rather than fabricate excuses for not doing so.

* The tone, the conditions under which Russbacher gave me the sworn declarations, and the specifics in these declarations, strongly suggest the truthfulness of these sworn statements. The sworn declarations contain data on the October Surprise activities that have never before been exposed. The declarations coincide with facts that came out a year and two years later, including those in Gary Sick's October Surprise and Ari Ben-Menashe's Profits of War.

* Locations of meetings that have never before been exposed. Ari Ben-Menashe confirmed the meeting site when I told him of the meeting in Barcelona at both a hotel and the Pepsico International Headquarters building.

It is my belief that most if not all of Russbacher's statements and sworn declarations made during the past two years are true, and coincide with statements made to me by Ari Ben-Menashe and by numerous investigative journalists and authors.

FEDERAL CRIMES AGAINST U.S. REPORTED BY RUSSBACHER

In numerous deposition-like sessions, Gunther Russbacher had declared under oath the following activities related to the October Surprise operation (and much more):

D. *Description of several of the secret October Surprise meetings by a deep-cover CIA officer who was present, including the key Barcelona meetings that have not been publicized before. When I made reference to the Pepsico meeting site it refreshed the memory of Ben-Menashe and he confirmed the meeting site.*

E. *The people who were on board the flight to Paris on the October 19, 1980 weekend were identified as including four or five Secret Service agents,[294] George Bush, William Casey, Donald Gregg, Robert McFarlane, and others.[295] If Secret Service agents were on board that flight, as Russbacher's sworn declarations state, it would be understandable that Treasury Department officials are desperately trying to discredit the Secret Service reports allegedly received at the CIA showing that Bush flew into Washington National Airport on Sunday evening, when he and the Secret Service claim he never left the Washington area.*

PRIMA FACIE EVIDENCE OF
OCTOBER SURPRISE OPERATION

* *Specific statements by dozens of witnesses interviewed by investigative journalists and authors, detailing segments of the October Surprise operation, who have nothing to gain by their statements.*

* *Testimony given to the House and Senate October Surprise committees by people who were in a position to know; who had nothing to gain; and who risk prison through criminal perjury charges if the testimony was false.*

* *Refusal by certain individuals to deny their role in the October Surprise operation when I questioned them in writing. These people and firms include Pepsico International Corporation; Pepsico official Peter Van Tyne; Pierre Salinger, who has copies of the French Secret Service report of the Paris October 19, 1980 meetings; French President Francois Mitterrand, who refused to provide copies of the French Secret Service reports; refusal of members of Congress to receive testimony and evidence offered by me in petitions, relating to the multiple criminal activities.*

* *Outright misstatement of facts by the House and Senate October Surprise committees, and using phony reasons to discredit people testifying to what they saw.*

* *Obstructing a thorough investigation by members of Congress, Justice Department officials, U.S. attorney generals, including threatening and prosecuting informants.*

---

[294] If Secret Service agents were actually on board that flight, the coup against the United States takes on wider dimensions, explaining the discrepancy between the Secret Service reports showing Bush flying into Washington National Airport on the evening of October 19, 1980, in contradiction to Bush's arrival the night before.

[295] The other passengers reportedly on the BAC 111 to Paris included, among others, Senators John Tower (Iran-Contra coverup chairman); John Heinz; Congressman Dan Rostenkowski; Jennifer Fitzgerald.

PATTERN OF FELONY COVERUP

* Pattern of felony persecution[296] of informants and whistleblowers by corrupt Justice Department prosecutors and federal judges, as felony retaliation is inflicted upon people offering testimony. The pattern of felony retaliation by a conspiracy of federal prosecutors and federal judges have been inflicted upon:

* CIA contract agent Richard Brenneke, charged with perjury when he testified to his role in the October Surprise operation and having seen George Bush and Donald Gregg at the Paris meetings.

* CIA contract agent Michael Riconosciuto, threatened by Justice Department officials if he testified before Congress concerning the Inslaw corruption and October Surprise. The threats were then carried out against him and his wife, as threatened. Importing a CIA prosecutor specifically for the purpose, Justice Department personnel prosecuted Riconosciuto and caused him imprisonment. As warned by Justice Department official Videnieks, Riconosciuto's wife lost custody of her three children and she was imprisoned for removing them to a safer location.

* CIA operative Gunther Russbacher, falsely charged with money offenses while operating covert CIA financial proprietaries and given 21 years in prison for a $20,000 offense in which no monetary loss was suffered by anyone, in which he pleaded nolo contender, and in which there was never a trial; 18 months in prison for [misuse of government purchase orders while a CIA operative.] Arrested at Castle Air Force Base for allegedly impersonating a Naval Officer, after debriefing his CIA superiors concerning a secret flight of SR-71s to Moscow on July 26, 1990,

* Informant and whistleblower Rodney Stich, repeatedly threatened and imprisoned since mid-1987, as corrupt federal judges[297] and Justice

---

[296] Title 18 U.S.C. § 1512. Tampering with a witness, victim, or an informant—
(b) Whoever knowingly uses intimidation or physical force, or threatens another person, or attempts to do so, or engages in misleading conduct toward another person, with intent to–
(1) influence, delay or prevent the testimony of any person in an official proceeding:
shall be fined ... or imprisoned ... or both. [1988 amended reading]."
Title 18 U.S.C. § 1513. Retaliating against a witness, victim, or an informant. (a) Whoever knowingly engages in any conduct and thereby causes bodily injury to another person or damages the tangible property of another person, or threatens to do so, with intent to retaliate against any person for—(1) the attendance of a witness or party at an official proceeding, or any testimony given or any record, document, or other object produced by a witness in an official proceeding; or (2) any information relating to the commission or possible commission of a Federal offense ...."
Title 18 U.S.C. § 241. Conspiracy against rights of citizens. If two or more persons conspire to injure, oppress, threaten, or intimidate any citizen in the free exercise or enjoyment of any right or privilege secured to him by the Constitution or laws of the United States, or because of his having so exercised the same; ... They shall be fined ... or imprisoned ... or both.
[297] Including District court judges David Levi; Milton Schwartz; Raul Ramirez; Garcia; Marilyn Patel; Samuel Conti; the entire Ninth Circuit Federal Court of Appeals; Justices of the U.S. Supreme Court who knew and aided and abetted the corrupt and criminal acts of the judges over whom they have supervisory responsibilities and duty to act.

Department prosecutors retaliated against me for filing federal actions reporting the federal crimes (in which their group and they were implicated).

* Ari Ben-Menashe, high-ranking officer in the Mossad, possessing information concerning the October Surprise operation and other corrupt acts against the United States in which present federal officials were implicated. He was falsely charged by Justice Department officials in an attempt to silence and discredit him.

The criminal mindset of those now in control of the Justice Department, and in control of the federal judiciary, is reflected by these repeated prison sentences inflicted upon informants and whistleblowers, in retaliation for reporting the criminal activities previously brought to your attention, to Congressman Hamilton's attention, and to every senator in the U.S. Senate. Since 1987, and continuing at this very moment,[298] corrupt federal judges and Justice Department prosecutors are threatening to put me in federal prison in retaliation for filing a federal action reporting certain segments of the criminal activities that I have repeatedly brought to the attention of your committee and others via petitions.

MY CREDIBILITY

My findings and determinations have considerable credibility:

* Former federal investigator holding federal authority to make such determinations, possessing evidence supporting many of my charges, including judicial records which establish the felony persecution of informants and victims by Justice Department prosecutors and federal judges.

* Private investigator for many years expanding my investigations into other and related areas of criminal activities against the United States and its citizens.

* Author of several books exposing government corruption through specific examples, based upon hard evidence and judicial records, having devoted thousands of hours and many years of investigations to this cause.

* Victim of the criminal activities seeking to obstruct justice, as rogue Justice Department personnel, federal judges, cooperating law firms and attorneys, targeted me for the past decade, misusing the judicial process, blocking my reporting of the crimes, and retaliating against me for exposing the criminal activities of which they were a part. These crimes were committed while a majority of the U.S. Senate and House withheld their duty to act, and thereby became accomplices.

* Statements and sworn declarations given to me by deep-cover CIA operatives and contract agents, describing the pattern of criminal activities that I have made reference to in prior petitions to members of Congress and which I have entered into judicial proceedings.

---

[298] U.S. District Court, N.D. Cal. Nr. 90-0636 VRW.

Over 1,800 radio and television appearances since 1978, in which my reports of corruption have been given major credibility.

Judicial records confirm many of my charges, especially relating to criminal acts related to a series of airline crashes; the pattern of corruption in Chapter 11 courts; the pattern of felony coverup and felony persecution of informants by Justice Department personnel and federal judges.

OBSTRUCTING JUSTICE AND MISSTATING THE FACTS

Federal crime reporting statutes make it a federal offense if any person, knowing of a federal crime, does not promptly report it.[299] *Justice Department personnel and federal judges have perverted this requirement by retaliating against informants, whistleblowers and victims who seek to report aspects of these various criminal activities.*

It is a federal crime if anyone retaliates against an informant or victim, as Justice Department prosecutors and federal judges have done. It is a federal crime for a federal officer, such as a member of Congress or a Congressional committee, to refuse to receive evidence offered by an informant or victim.

It is a federal crime to refuse to provide relief to an informant or victim who is suffering such retaliation, especially when the retaliation is perpetrated by a federal employee and agency over whom members of Congress have oversight responsibilities.

It is a federal crime to misstate the facts in a federal report, and this includes Congressional committees, and that includes the House and Senate October Surprise Committees. As a former federal investigator, it is obvious that these Committees are engaging in a felony coverup, withholding of evidence, misstating the evidence.

DETERMINATION OF WHICH SECRET
SERVICE REPORT IS CORRECT

As part of the long-time effort to expose the escalating pattern of criminal activities against the United States by corrupt federal officials, I have repeatedly discovered federal officials falsifying documents, covering up for documents, misstating the facts, showing that perjury by federal personnel and falsified federal documents are normal coverup tactics. In evaluating whether Congressmen Hamilton's copy of the Secret Service reports, or my CIA related Secret Service reports, are accurate, the following actions should be taken:

Obtain the testimony of Gunther Russbacher concerning these reports, in open hearings, and giving the media access to him before and after his testimony.

Allow the CIA operatives to testify,[300] *and compare their testimony, as it relates to October Surprise and peripheral activities.*

Obtain the sworn testimony of the Secret Service agents who were

---

[299] Title 18 U.S.C. § 4 (misprision of felony). "Whoever, having knowledge of the actual commission of a felony cognizable by a court of the United States, conceals and does not as soon as possible make known the same to some judge or other person in civil or military authority under the United States, shall be fined not more than $500 or imprisoned not more than three years, or both."

[300] Gunther Russbacher; Michael Riconosciuto; Richard Brenneke.

with Bush from October 18 through October 20, 1980, in open hearings, making it clear that the Justice Department (in the next administration) and an independent prosecutor (if the statute is renewed) will prosecute for criminal perjury if the statements are false.

* Consider the overwhelming pressures upon Secret Service agents (and others), to lie, concerning their observation of Bush's activities from October 18, 1980 to October 20, 1980, and their knowledge of the October 19, 1980 report date.

* Obtain CIA records and testimony relating to the routing of the Secret Service report that Russbacher initialed.

OBSTRUCTION OF JUSTICE BY THE
HOUSE "INVESTIGATIVE" COMMITTEE

It is my evaluation that Congressman Hamilton's October Surprise Committee will continue to cover up and obstruct justice in relation to the October Surprise matter:

* Agent Pedersen, on loan from the Treasury Department, seeks to protect the Secret Service's involvement in the October Surprise operation.

* Credible witnesses such as former Mossad staff officer Ari Ben-Menashe, CIA contract agents Richard Brenneke and Michael Riconosciuto, who testified under risk of criminal perjury charges, were dismissed by simply calling them not creditable, and giving sham reasons that only a gullible public could swallow.

* Credible deep-cover CIA whistleblowers, such as Gunther Russbacher, are not given the opportunity to testify, eliminating one of the primary sources of establishing the existence of the October Surprise operation and its many tentacles.

* Conducting closed hearings to prevent the public discovering the crimes against the United States on the basis of testimony offered, or the refusal to ask questions that would result in the answers establishing the crimes. This is a standard Congressional tactic of many years.

* Aiding and abetting the felony persecution of informants by corrupt Justice Department officials and federal judges, as a part of the pattern of felony obstruction of justice by Congressional "investigative" committees.

* Refusing to receive testimony and evidence relating to the petition that I submitted, including the declarations of Russbacher and myself, describing the criminal activities that both of us discovered while we were federal employees.

OBSTRUCTION OF JUSTICE BY THE
SENATE "INVESTIGATIVE" COMMITTEE

As a former federal investigator my evaluation of the November 19, 1992 Senate October Surprise report is that it is a blatant and felonious coverup, misstating the facts, omitting key facts, refusing to have key witnesses testify, for the purpose of cover up and of course, obstructing justice.

The report discredits the many witnesses who testified to what they witnessed in their participation in the October Surprise operation. They had nothing to gain by their testimony and risked imprisonment on charges of perjury. Many knew the fate of Richard Brenneke and Michael Riconosciuto when they testified, and yet they had the courage to come forward. Deep-cover CIA officer Gunther Russbacher is suffering greatly from his attempts to report the great crimes committed against the United States in the October Surprise and other criminal activities. I have been stripped of my multi-million dollar assets and have been subjected repeatedly, and at this time, to criminal contempt of court in retaliation for seeking to report the crimes that you coverup, and for seeking relief from the great harms inflicted upon me by criminal misuse of the agencies over which you have oversight responsibilities. These criminal acts and outrages reflect the subversive activities rampant in the United States and made possible by your coverup.

My book describes the felony coverup by members of Congress, Justice Department personnel, others, including Independent Prosecutor Walsh, and describes the criminal aiding and abetting of activities that are destroying the United States form of government from within.

RESPONSIBILITIES OF MEMBERS OF THE COMMITTEE

* Obtain Russbacher's testimony in open hearings. He has repeatedly stated, and reconfirmed it today, December 26, 1992, that he is ready to testify concerning:

* The CIA origin of the Secret Service reports that I mailed to Congressman Hamilton;

* The specific details of the October Surprise operation in which Russbacher was ordered to participate by his CIA superiors, including meetings in Barcelona and Paris; the shipment of arms after the Barcelona meetings; where the arms were obtained; how they were shipped; names of people involved in the shipping of the arms; names of those on the BAC 111 to Paris on the October 19, 1980 weekend.

* With immunity, he would be willing to testify to other activities in which he was ordered to participate, that have inflicted great harms upon the United States. These activities include looting of financial institutions (many of the participants still escape prosecution because of CIA and Justice Department involvement, and especially in the Denver area, involving the many financial institutions related to Metropolitan Development Corporation); CIA drug trafficking in the United States (and the coverup of these activities at Mena, Arkansas, by president-elect Bill Clinton); the CIA role in the BCCI banking scandal; and others.

* Obtain my testimony and evidence in open hearings, relating to the direct and indirect knowledge that I have of these criminal activities.

* Obtain the testimony of other CIA operatives, whose testimony would reinforce that of other informants.

* Include as part of your "investigation" the contents of my manuscript which shows the intricate relationship between the various criminal activities.

This is a request that you include in the final report of your October Surprise "investigation" the comments made in this and earlier letters.

Sincerely,

Rodney Stich

Enclosures:
    October 3, 1980 CIA: "Proposal to Exchange Spare Parts With Hostages."
    October 9, 1980 Department of State: "Approach on Iranian Spares."
    October 21, 1980 Department of State: "Talk with Mitch Regovin."
    October 29, 1980: "Two Related Items on Iranian Military supply."
    October 1980 Secret Service reports: Bush's security detail.
    June 3, 1983(?) CIA: Release of Hostages.
    July 5, 1985: "New Developments on Channel to Iran."
    August 19, 1985: "Status of Hashemi-Elliot Richardson Contact."

Walsh refused to receive my testimony and evidence and that of Gunther Russbacher.

SILENCING THE CHRISTIC INSTITUTE

The public-service-oriented Christic Institute, based in Washington, D.C., investigated the atrocities associated with CIA activities in Central America, and filed a federal lawsuit against White House officials who were implicated. Their complaint stated numerous federal causes of actions, invoking mandatory federal court jurisdiction. But the Christic Institute encountered the same judicial obstruction of justice that I encountered, and similar retaliatory actions. The U.S. District Judge unlawfully dismissed the case, and then ordered the Christic Institute to pay one million dollars damages for having exercised their constitutional and statutory right to file the action and report the criminal activities. The Christic Institute filed an appeal, and was ordered to pay additional sanctions for exercising that right. The Justices of the U.S. Supreme Court approved this judicial misconduct by refusing to provide relief, just as the Supreme Court Justices had done to me.

ELIMINATING THE INDEPENDENT PROSECUTOR

Toward the end of 1992, as the number of crimes directly involving federal officials escalated to an unprecedented number, threatening Justice Department and White House officials, as well as members of Congress. The Independent Prosecutor authority was allowed to expire on December 15, 1992. Congress refused to renew it. Republicans were under great threat of exposure from a decade-long pattern of corruption, and they threatened to filibuster if a vote was taken to renew the legislation. Democrats were also threatened for their role in numerous scandals, and didn't press the matter. Further, the legislation carried a provision that members of Congress could also be investigated by an independent prosecutor.

FINAL REPORT BY INDEPENDENT PROSECUTOR WALSH

The final report by Independent Prosecutor Walsh was sent on August 5, 1993 to a special tribunal of the federal appeals court in Washington, D.C. Copies of the report were sent to the parties named in the report, with an opportunity to object. The special tribunal, headed by Judge David B. Sentelle, gave these parties until December 3, 1993 to raise objections to Walsh's findings.

Walsh's report, avoiding the ugly nature of the ongoing criminality, did identify some of the parties. The report stated that President Reagan, former

Attorney General Edwin Meese, former Defense Secretary Caspar Weinberg-er, engaged in a "broad conspiracy" to conceal the criminal activities. A conspiracy is a federal crime, and in this case, far worse than the after-the-fact coverup of the two-bit break-in associated with Watergate, that was pushed out of proportion by the media, led by the *Washington Post*.

Walsh avoided revealing to the American people the ugly side of the Iran-Contra affair, including the massive drug trafficking into the United States by U.S. intelligence agencies and the Mossad. This massive crime against the American people results in the worse crime wave American has ever experienced.

DOCUMENT SHOWING RUSSBACHER'S CIA STATUS

Several documents of great significance were sent to me by my CIA contacts. They established that Gunther Russbacher was a Navy captain assigned to the Office of Naval Intelligence (ONI) and the CIA. The documents described the unlawful arms-for-hostages scheme, including names of White House officials and others who took part in the arms-for-hostages conspiracy. The documents revealed that George Bush and Ronald Reagan repeatedly lied about their lack of knowledge of the conspiracy.

FAR WORSE THAN WATERGATE

President Richard Nixon's attempt to cover up for the two-bit Watergate break-in was minuscule in seriousness and implications in relation to Reagan and Bush's coverup, and participation, in the Iran and Contra affairs (without even addressing the October Surprise criminal conspiracy).

DOCUMENTATION RELATING TO OPERATION MAGG PIE

The secret, unlawful arms-for-hostages conspiracy carried the code name, Operation Magg Pie. One CIA document, dated May 20, 1986, signed by CIA Director Bill Casey, related to a flight from Tel Aviv to Teheran which received considerable Congressional attention. This was the flight carrying a cake and dueling pistols for Iranian officials. A key reference was to the two pilots who would fly the plane from Israel's Ben-Gurion Airport to Teheran. These two pilots were John Robert Segal (CIA) and Gunther Karl Russbacher (ONI). The memorandum, written six months before the U.S. press publicized the Iran-Contra activities, showed George Bush as receiving a copy. Bush repeatedly denied knowing anything about the arms-for-hostages until after the November 1986 media publicity. He was of course lying.

Another document, from the National Security Agency, dated May 30, 1986, relating to Operation Magg Pie, written by Oliver North to Admiral John Poindexter, NSA, showed Vice President George Bush being advised of the operation.

Still another document, this one from the Israeli government, identified Gunther Russbacher as one of the pilots on Operation Magg Pie. The Israeli letter listed the names of U.S. personnel who were at Tel Aviv's Ben-Gurion Airport in May, 1986.

An official record from Offutt Air Force Base at Omaha, Nebraska, dated February 5, 1992, described Russbacher's stay at that high-security base, listing him as captain in the U.S. Navy; stated the authorizing government agency, Cincpac; and his serial number, 441 40 1417.

Almost all these documents, showing Russbacher as a key officer with the Office of Naval Intelligence, were known to members of Congress who stated Russbacher was a phony. They were known to the prosecutors and officials in the U.S. Department of Justice, who continued to prosecute Russbacher. I brought them to the attention of state officials in Missouri who had caused Russbacher's imprisonment on the sham charge that he was impersonating a naval officer. The establishment press knew about the documents, and maintained their usual duplicity of silence.

NATIONAL SECURITY AGENCY
CENTRAL SECURITY SERVICE
FORT GEORGE G. MEADE, MARYLAND 20755-6000

August 22, 1985

Robert C. McFarlane
National Security Advisor
Old Executive Office Bldg. Rm. 306
Washington, D.C. 20506

CONFIDENTIAL

Re: MAGG PIE

Dear Mr. McFarlane:

The first transaction on August 17, 1985 involved the sale of 100 TOW missiles. In return for the release of an undetermined number of United States citizens held hostage in Lebanon. The missiles were to be provided from the weapons stock of the Israeli Defense Forces.

We have agreed to replenish the Israeli weapons stock after the transaction with Iran is completed.

As of August 20, 1985, our DC-8 transport aircraft, piloted by Gunther K. Russbacher (ONI) and John R. Segal (CIA), along with Robert Hunt (ONI), Oliver North (NSC) and George Cave (CIA), flew from Israel to Iran loaded with 96 TOW missiles. (Rather than the agreed upon 100).

Contrary to the agreement as you know, none of the hostages were released.

Manucher Ghorbanifer contended that the TOWS were mistakenly delivered to the commander of the Iranian Revolutionary Guard rather than to the Iranian faction for whom they were intended.

Please respond to any clarifications.

Yours truly,

John M. Poindexter
Deputy Director
National Security Council

cc: V-P Bush
    William Casey

JMP/sv

August 22, 1985 document from National Security Agency's John Poindexter, to Robert McFarlane, referring to the sale of missiles to Iran. Gunther Russbacher and Robert Hunt, two of my contacts, are named in the document. A copy was sent to Vice President Bush, who assured the American public while vice president and president that he knew nothing about the arms-for-hostages conspiracy.

NATIONAL SECURITY AGENCY
CENTRAL SECURITY SERVICE
FORT GEORGE G. MEADE, MARYLAND 20755-6000

September 20, 1985

Robert C. McFarlane
National Security Advisor
Old Executive Office Bldg. Rm. 306
Washington, D.C. 20506   CONFIDENTIAL

      Re: MAGG PIE

Dear Mr. McFarlane:

     Despite the failure of the first arms transaction, the Iran Initiative
was continued. Our negotiators agreed, the United States, through Israel, would
provide Iran with 400 TOW missiles. In return, the Iranians would arrange for the
release of any U.S. hostage, except for Buckley.

     The transaction was to take place in the same manner as the first. Israel
would provide the missiles and the U.S. would later replenish the Israeli supply.

     Lt. Col. Oliver North and Ltjg. Robert Hunt, on staff to the National Sec-
urity Council, who in their official capacity were to make the necessary arrangements
to receive any hostages who might be released.

     On September 15, 1985, a DC-8, piloted by Gunther K. Russbacher (ONI) and
John R. Segal (CIA) along with Oliver North (NSC) and Robert Hunt (ONI), Howard
Teicher (CIA), flew to Tabriz, Iran, loaded with 408 TOWS. ON the same day, American hostage Benjamin Weir was released in Beirut on information and belief this
transaction was effected to demonstrate the ability of the negotiators on each side
to deliver by providing TOW missiles and releasing a hostage respectively.

     On September 17, 1985, Manucher Ghorbanifer paid $290,000 to the Israeli
intermediary to cover the costs of transporting the TOWS. The following day,
Iran paid $5 million into Ghorbanifer's Swiss bank account at Credit Swiss, No.
913-216-83-7.

     Any further clarifications or changes should be acknowledged.

                     Sincerely,

                     John M. Poindexter
                     Deputy Director
                     National Security Council

CC: V-P BUSH
     WILLIAM CASEY

JMP/sv

September 20, 1985 document describing the arms-for-hostages scheme,
showing Israeli involvement; identifying as ONI, Gunther Russbacher and
Robert Hunt; and informing Vice President Bush of the scheme.

UNITED STATES GOVERNMENT

memorandum

DATE: 20 May 1986

REPLY TO ATTN OF: Bill Casey HQ. CIA.

SUBJECT: Russbacher Karl Gunther ONI. Segal Robert John CIA.

TO:
John Poindexter NSA.
RE. Operation MAGG PIE.

Please be advised these men will meet with agents Robert Hunt ONI.
Bud McFarlane NSA. Oliver North NSA. George Cave CIA. and Howard Teicher
also CIA. They will give complete briefing at TelAviv Ben Gurion airport.
Pilot selection is now finale. If you have any questions please call me
soon. We leave Sunday the 25. Im keeping my fingers crossed.

Good Luck.

Bill Casey CIA.

CC.
VP. Bush

OPTIONAL FORM NO. 10
(REV. 1-80)
GSA FPMR (41 CFR) 101-11.6
8010-114

May 20, 1986 document from CIA Director Casey to Admiral Poindexter,
listing the names of intelligence personnel involved in the arms-for-hostages
scheme, including Gunther Russbacher and Robert Hunt, and showing copy
sent to Vice President George Bush.

UNITED STATES GOVERNMENT

memorandum

DATE: 22 May, 1986

REPLY TO
ATTN OF: John M. Poindexter (NSA)

SUBJECT: MAGG PIE   PROFS: 31305B 89

TO: William J. Casey, Hq. CIA

Bill:

This is a note for the funds that Oliver North (NSC) and Robert Hunt (ONI) have worked out on behalf of the Iranians to deposit $15 million into an Enterprise bank account, and an additional deposit of $1.46 million was made to the Enterprise account to cover 508 additional TOWS which were to be provided to Israel as replenishment for the previous Israeli TOW shipments.

Of the approximate $16.5 million, the Enterprise received for this hardware, the agents caused only $6.5 million to be paid to the United States to cover the cost of the HAWK spares parts and the 508 TOWS, leaving a profit for the Enterprise of almost $10 million. If you have any questions, please call me at the executive office building.

Yours truly,

John Poindexter

John Poindexter

cc: V-P Bush
    O. North

OPTIONAL FORM NO. 10
(REV. 1-80)
GSA FPMR (41 CFR) 101-11
5010-118

May 22, 1986 document from Poindexter (NSA) to CIA Director William Casey, describing receipt of money from the sale of missiles to Iran, the profits, and the deposit of funds by Oliver North (NSC) and Robert Hunt (ONI) into a private bank account.

UNITED STATES GOVERNMENT

memorandum

DATE: 27 May, 1986

REPLY TO
ATTN OF: Mr. John M. Poindexter, NSA

SUBJECT: MAGG PIE   PROFS: 31305B 90

TO: William J. Casey, Hq. CIA

> Bill:
>   Several days after the last of Khashoggi's payment was deposited
> in Lake Resources account - number 386-430-22-1, Agents Robert Hunt (ONI) and
> Oliver North (NSC) worked on Albon Valves - a shell company for additional fund-
> ing. They deposited $26,490 to an account named "Korel." Four days later,
> Hyde Park Square, another account dispensed $200,000 as capital for the Button
> Account set up for Robert Hunt, Oliver North, George Cave, Howart Teicher, Gun-
> ther Russbacher and John Segal and their families. We considered the personal
> benefits of these agents. These accounts must be kept confidential for security
> reasons.

>   Yours truly,
>
>   *John Poindexter*
>   John Poindexter

cc: VP Bush
     O. North

May 27, 1986 document from Bill Casey to John Poindexter, listing a bank account number of a CIA proprietary; and money expended for arms. Also listed were some of the author's contacts and their CIA/ONI status, including Gunther Russbacher and Robert Hunt. Further, the documents show Vice President Bush being kept informed of the operation (that Bush repeatedly denied while vice president and president, knowledge of the unlawful scheme, and while being an accomplice to the unlawful actions).

UNITED STATES GOVERNMENT

memorandum

DATE: 30 May, 1986

REPLY TO
ATTN OF: Oliver L. North   NSA.

SUBJECT: MAGG PIE.   PROFS: 31305B86

TO: John M. Poindexter.   NSA.

— Admiral

Their has been a problem in negotiations in Tehran. Manucher Ghorbanifar had
assured us that we would be meeting with Hashemi Rafsanjani and president Ali
Khamenei on this trip. Instead we met with Dr. No. and the Australian. During
this meeting we were told that our pilots Russbacher Gunther Karl and Segal
John Robert were being brought to our hotel. Agents Hunt Robert and Cave George
had spoken to Robert McFarlane and had decided to cancel negotiations due to
security and nature of this trip. Please get back to me on this as soon as
possible. I will call you in the morning.

Semper Fidelis,

Oliver L. North

— CC:
    VP. G. BUSH
    CIA. W. Casey

May 30, 1986 document from Oliver North to Admiral Poindexter, showing
Gunther Russbacher to be a part of ONI, with copy to George Bush.
Significance is that Russbacher is who he said he is, and that Bush lied, while
vice president and president, when he stated he did not know about the arms-
for-hostages scheme.

OFFICE OF THE VICE PRESIDENT
WASHINGTON

June 16, 1986

Mr. John M. Poindexter
National Security Advisor   CONFIDENTIAL
Old Executive Office Building
Washongton, D.C. 20506

Dear Admiral Poindexter:

        I would like to take this time to offer my gratitude and
appreciation for your hard work and assistance in Operation MAGG PIE.

        Your negotiations on our behalf have proven to be quite eff-
ective in obtaining the release of United States Citizens held hostage in Lebanon.

        I would like you to personally thank Robert McFarlane for
his willingness, daring and efforts in meeting with Iranian factions.

        I would also like you to thank the Staff of the National Secur-
ity Council, including Agents, Lt. Col. Oliver North (USMC), and Lt.
Robert Hunt (USN) for their dangerous assistance and diligence, without which Operation MAGG PIE would never have been successful.

        Finally, you must offer my gratitude to the C.I.A. and their
Agents, George Cave, Howard Teicher, John Segal and Gunther Russbacher.
These men are dedicated and blessed with the gift of courage. They
to truely believe in the pursuit of freedom for all mankind. May God
bless you all.

                                Respectfully,

                                George Bush

                                George Bush

GB/fr
cc: R. Reagan
    W. Casey

June 16, 1986 letter from Vice President George Bush to John Poindexter,
referring to the arms-for-hostages scheme. Both Ronald Reagan and George
Bush are shown as being sent a copy of this document describing part of the
arms-for-hostages scheme. Reagan and Bush repeatedly stated they knew
nothing about the arms-for-hostages scheme until after the November 1986
shoot-down of a CIA aircraft in Nicaragua. This lying was many times worse
than Richard Nixon's coverup of the watergate break-in.

GREAT SIGNIFICANCE OF THE GOVERNMENT DOCUMENTS

Watergate has been cited as one of the biggest scandals in the United States government by the CIA-protective *Washington Post* and members of Congress. But Watergate was a two-bit burglary by CIA and White House personnel, which President Richard Nixon sought to cover up after learning about it. It took months and months of drum-beating by the *Washington Post* and related hyperbole as to its seriousness, to bring down a president who was hostile to the CIA. Either the Iran or the Contra portions of the Iran-Contra scandal were many times more serious than the Watergate affair.

Not only did Ronald Reagan and George Bush cover up for these criminal activities, but they participated in them as the operations developed (unlike Watergate where Nixon did not learn about the break-in until after the fact). Tens of thousands of people died as a result of the U.S. arming of Iran. The Contra operation included CIA-funded assassination squads, intruding into the affairs of a foreign country, and massive drug trafficking into the United States. Where was the *Washington Post* and the many other newspapers that exaggerated the Watergate affair? Where were members of Congress who piously condemned President Nixon? They were engaging in felony coverup and obstruction of justice, and the public has paid and is paying the price for the crimes of their leaders.

CHAPTER EIGHTEEN

CIA AND DEA DRUG TRAFFICKING

The CIA's role in drug trafficking into the United States has been the subject of many magazine and newspaper articles, books, testimony given to Congressional committees in closed-door hearings, and work-place conversation among CIA personnel. Movies and television documentaries have been made on the subject, and many books and articles have been written describing some particular phase of the operation. Yet, most Americans are oblivious to this serious misconduct or its far-flung implications. The DEA's drug trafficking has received little attention.

One of the first books linking the CIA to drug trafficking was Alfred McCoy's[301] *The Politics of Heroin in Southeast Asia,*[302] published in 1972, and his heavily documented 1991 update, *The Politics of Heroin—CIA Complicity in the Global Drug Trade.*[303] The author is a professor of Southeast Asian history at the University of Wisconsin, at Madison. Some of the books written about CIA drug trafficking were written by people who were part of the operation, including pilots.

Professor McCoy started investigating the drug trafficking in the 1950s, questioning people in all phases of the drug culture from the growers to the end users. He spent considerable time in Southeast Asia and throughout the world obtaining first-hand knowledge of the drug trade. He describes how CIA helicopters, supposedly fighting communists in Vietnam, were hauling drugs from the fields to distribution points, including drugs for the American

---

[301] Professor, University of Wisconsin.
[302] Harper & Row.
[303] Lawrence Hill Books.

Gis. He described the role of the Pepsi-Cola bottling plant in the drug trafficking, and how the U.S. media kept the lid on the mushrooming operation.

McCoy describes the pressure put upon the media by the CIA to halt his book. He describes the many people who testified in closed-door congressional hearings for the past twenty years, leaving no doubt that the CIA was involved and primarily responsible for the drug scourge in the United States.

McCoy described giving testimony **in 1972** to congressional committees, including Senator William Proxmire, about the CIA role in the developing global narcotic trade. He describes how members of Congress enthusiastically accepted the CIA's denial of any role in drug trafficking, despite the overwhelming evidence of its existence.

Terry Reed, a CIA asset, and co-author John Cummings, wrote an excellent book in 1994 on drug trafficking and the CIA's role in it: *Compromised: Clinton, Bush and the CIA*.[304] Reed, a former U.S. Air Force Intelligence Officer, a successful businessman specializing in advanced computer-controlled manufacturing, was recruited by the CIA to start up a CIA proprietary in Mexico. The business was to be a high technology trading and consulting firm, but developed into a CIA gun-running and drug operation.

Reed worked closely with key figures in the National Security Council and Central Intelligence Agency, including Oliver North and Felix Rodriguez, unaware of their involvement in a massive drug trafficking operation. Reed discovered that the CIA was misusing the company that he set up in Mexico as a CIA proprietary. In July 1987 he discovered the CIA was shipping large quantities of drugs through the company, and he wanted out. Fearing for the safety of his wife and three sons, and himself, Reed notified his CIA handlers that he was returning to Arkansas. The CIA saw him as a threat.

Using typical attorney tactics, the CIA, through the Justice Department and its control over state police agencies, in this case Governor Bill Clinton's Arkansas, charged the Reeds with engaging in drug trafficking, when in fact it was the CIA.

WORKING WITH GOVERNOR BILL CLINTON'S DRUG COVERUP GROUP

Working in unison with prosecutors and officials in the United States Department of Justice and with police agencies in Arkansas (while Bill Clinton was governor), sham charges were filed against Reed, claiming that he had fraudulently reported his plane as having been stolen. He was charged with mail fraud, an all-encompassing criminal statute. The prosecutors charged Reed's wife, Janis, with conspiracy, seeking to force Reed to plead guilty, at which time he would go to prison and charges would be dropped against her.

For three years the Reeds had to fight Justice Department attorneys and Governor Bill Clinton's police agencies and chief of security, Raymond Young. Clinton's state police officials engaged in a steady pattern of lies, forged documents, perjured testimony, seeking to put Terry and Janis Reed

---

[304] Authored by Terry Reed and John Cummings.

in prison, thereby silencing or discrediting their knowledge of CIA drug trafficking. Massed against the Reeds were the FBI, the CIA, Governor Bill Clinton's law enforcement agencies. and especially Clinton's close associate, Raymond Young. The perjurers had government-granted immunity for their lying under oath.

Reed describes how U.S. District Judge Frank Theis blocked their defenses, and dismissed evidence showing the sham nature of the charges as irrelevant.

OBSTRUCTION OF JUSTICE BY TIME MAGAZINE

In his book, Reed described the role played by George Bush and Bill Clinton in the drug trafficking. Reed describes the coverup and disinformation by *Time* magazine. (I also discovered the coverup (i.e., obstruction of justice) by *Time* and other magazines and newspapers.)

ANOTHER DEA WHISTLEBLOWER

Another DEA whistleblower exposed the DEA and CIA role in America's drug crisis. A twenty-five-year veteran of the Drug Enforcement Administration (and prior drug agencies), Michael Levine, authored a 1993 book[305] exposing the drug trafficking sanctioned by federal officials throughout the federal government. The former DEA agent wrote that the so-called war on drugs is the "biggest, whitest, and deadliest lie ever perpetrated on U.S. citizens by their government." He described how the CIA, the DEA, and other "intelligence" agencies, blocked investigations and prosecution of high-level drug traffickers. Levine described how the CIA was primarily responsible for the drug epidemic as seen from his perspective.

False charges were filed by DEA management against Levine when he persisted in reporting the drug trafficking, reminding me of what I went through as a federal investigator determined to expose the corruption that I found in the Federal Aviation Administration. In the FAA, when I reported the air safety corruption (as other inspectors had done) that played a major role in a series of brutal air disasters, and which exposed the criminality of United Airlines and FAA personnel, a series of petty retaliatory acts were taken against me. DEA management did the same to Levine when he persisted in reporting the drug trafficking by high-level drug traffickers, which exposed the CIA role in this activity.

Levine repeatedly discovered CIA links to the drug trafficking while he was a DEA agent, enlarging upon the evidence of drug trafficking that I had discovered during the past forty years. He discovered that the CIA was primarily responsible for the burgeoning drug activity from Central and South America into the United States, and that the biggest drug dealers are CIA assets. He described how federal judges and Justice Department prosecutors dramatically drop the amount of bail for high-level drug traffickers who are CIA assets and who have been accidentally charged, with the traffickers then fleeing the United States.

---

[305] *The Big White Lie*, by Michael Levine and Lauri Kavanau-Levine.

Levine described how the CIA supported drug traffickers who then seized control of the government of Bolivia. Levine writes that U.S. officials are "afraid the world would find out there wouldn't be a cocaine government in Bolivia if it wasn't for the CIA." He described how high DEA and Justice Department officials "intentionally destroy drug cases" and put conscientious DEA agents at risk, even causing their deaths. Levine described how major drug cases involving CIA assets receive little or no media publicity, thereby protecting the vast criminal activities that are inflicting such enormous harm upon the American people.

HUGE PROFITS FOR CIA AND CIA PERSONNEL IN DRUGS

CIA operatives in the Far East, including such well-known CIA personnel as Michael Hand, General Jack Singlaub, and Theodore Shackley, discovered early during the Vietnam war the huge profits to be made from drug trafficking. My CIA, OSS, and DEA informants described their roles in the intelligence agency drug trafficking starting in the late 1940s and early 1950s. One contact, formerly with the OSS, described his drug trafficking in the Middle East, flying from Kabul to Teheran and then to Beirut, flying C-46 aircraft. Ironically, I was flying the same type of aircraft in the Middle East during part of this time, and learned from his source, Russell Bowen, that one of the management people with my airline, Transocean Airlines, was a CIA operative, receiving drugs arriving in Beirut.

The CIA has stimulated drug trafficking in the Far East, Central and South America, the Middle East, and Africa. These unlawful operations escalated the drug crisis in the United States to epidemic proportions, generating huge profits for the U.S. intelligence agencies and many of those who participate in it.

Possibly the largest CIA drug operation, primarily heroin, was carried out in the Far East in the Golden Triangle area. I learned of this while I was an airline pilot flying into Tokyo for Transocean Airlines and for Japan Airlines, in the 1950s. This drug trafficking greatly increased as the CIA took over from the French in Indochina. The CIA-generated conflicts escalated into the Vietnam war, and became especially profitable for the CIA.

The question arises as to why thousands of Customs and DEA agents, and other law enforcement agencies, have been unable to reduce the huge flow of drugs into the United States. Until I became a confidant to many CIA and DEA personnel, I didn't have the answer. These same agencies responsible for halting the drugs were either shipping them into the United States or aiding and abetting the shipments.

This fact is difficult for the average American to comprehend, especially in light of the media coverup of the activities. Few Americans can believe that the people in control of the CIA, DEA, and other intelligence agencies, would commit these criminal acts that inflict such great harm upon the American people. It also takes the concurrent coverup by many others in the three branches of the federal government to make such a vast operation possible. These include the attorney general, the Department of Justice, the Treasury Department, Customs, Drug Enforcement Administration, and many others.

Sham drug busts occasionally occur to give the public the impression that drug enforcement agencies are carrying out their drug-interdiction responsibilities. One sham drug bust occurred in Miami in the early 1980s to justify hiring more federal personnel, and to reflect favorably on the newly appointed drug czar, Vice President George Bush. Another huge drug bust was set up in the Los Angeles area in 1989, at Sylmar, in which twenty tons of cocaine were seized. The purpose of this drug bust was two-fold. One was for public relations, indicating to the American public that the huge amount of money and taking of constitutional rights were justified. The second purpose was to reduce the amount of drugs in circulation. The drug prices were plunging due to an oversupply, and restricting the CIA's income from its drug trade.

Some drug busts are made to eliminate competition from drug traffickers not connected with the intelligence agencies. Another reason is to bust a CIA drug trafficker who may be getting out of line or who knows too much.

Many informants described to me the drug trafficking they personally witnessed, or in which they were involved while working for the CIA or DEA. CIA operative Gunther Russbacher, working at higher levels, described how he was present at numerous drug operations and how he was opposed to this activity. He described meetings between individual drug dealers in Columbia, at which the CIA caused them to form into groups which are now called the Medellin and Cali cartels.

SOUTHEAST ASIA DRUG TRAFFICKING

For decades the British and the French controlled the huge drug operations in Southeast Asia, which was taken over by the United States through the CIA in the 1950s. The CIA's intervention in Vietnam escalated into the Vietnam War which greatly escalated the drug trafficking and profit for this portion of the CIA operation.

Many Americans, brainwashed to believe that the Vietnam war was in the interest of freedom and to fight communism, sacrificed the lives of 58,000 American Gis who were killed, and the far greater number who were painfully injured and sometimes maimed for life.

EVEN IN DEATH THE GI's WERE USED

The CIA drug trafficking required large numbers of drug addicts, and the endemic drug addiction among American Gis became highly profitable. Even in death the Gis became unwitting participant in the drug trafficking. Plastic-wrapped drugs were shipped into the United States in the bottom of caskets and in body cavities. Upon arrival at West Coast Air Force bases, and especially Travis Air Force Base in California, the drugs would be removed from the caskets and bodies, that were identified by secret codes.

Many articles have been written about this sordid practice in the alternative press, but withheld by the mass media. In one instance, an officer from the army's Criminal Investigation Division uncovered a large-scale heroin smuggling scheme using the bodies of dead Gis who perished in the CIA-originated Vietnam War. His group filed reports with the Pentagon describing how the bodies were cut open, gutted, and filled with sacks of heroin. Approximately fifty pounds of heroin with multi-million-dollar street value were stuffed into each body. The investigators discovered that the documents relating to the heroin-stuffed bodies were coded so that they could be identified at Air Force Bases in the United Stated and the drugs removed.

In typical fashion, revealed throughout these pages, the military hierarchy reacted to the report by disbanding the investigative team. Other reports, plus those given to me by my CIA contacts, provide further confirmation of this sordid practice. This coverup made possible the continued drug smuggling, and constituted criminal coverup.

Crates returning to the United States from Vietnam on military aircraft often contained bags of heroin, and the coded labels labeled some form of military supplies. The coverup in the military, in the CIA, in the Justice Department, wasn't only isolated rogue acts; it was epidemic. Any time an investigator reported the problem, he or she was ordered to stop.

These aspects of the CIA-initiated and direct Vietnam War and the debauchery of the American Gis are never brought up at Memorial Day ceremonies, where the American public is led to believe that the hundreds of thousands of dead, maimed, or injured Americans suffered for an honorable cause. This is not to discredit those who endured the fighting, but to bring reality into the picture.

CIA DRUG TRAFFICKING UNKNOWN
ONLY TO THE AMERICAN PUBLIC

Many highly documented books have been written about the CIA drug trafficking. Hundreds of witnesses have testified before Congress[306] about their direct knowledge and/or participation in this drug trafficking. Many television shows have addressed this fact, with witnesses who were part of it. The criminal elements are aware of it. Those connected with the intelligence agencies are aware of it. Numerous articles appear in newsletters pertaining to these agencies describing the drug trafficking. The media, with its awareness of these facts certainly know about it. But, as usual, many Americans are still ignorant about it.

OPERATION CODE NAMES

The CIA drug trafficking is handled in an organized manner as if it was a large corporation such as General Motors. Different geographical areas and different types or levels of operations are given code names. In the Golden Triangle area of Southeast Asia the code names included Operation Short Flight; Operation Burma Road; Operation Morning Gold; and Operation Triangle.

The CIA transferred some of its operatives who developed the drug trafficking in the Golden Triangle area of Southeast Asia to develop and operate drug trafficking into the United States from Central and South America. They reportedly included Theodore Shackley (who now lives in Medellin, Colombia, a good friend of George Bush); Edwin Wilson (who is

---

[306] Senator John Kerry's office released on October 14, 1986 a classified report describing the testimony of over four dozen witnesses before the committee that he headed, described the drug trafficking into the United States by the CIA and other government agencies and personnel. Thirteen of these witnesses were among the defendants in the Christic Institute's lawsuit. No actions were taken by any of the government law enforcement agencies, as if they were themselves involved. They were involved, of course.

in federal prison); and Frank Terpil. In Central and South America the code names for CIA drug trafficking included Operation Snow Cone, Operation Toilet Seat, and Operation Watch Tower.

Operation Snow Cone was the agency identification for the drug trafficking operation in Central and South America, under which other drug operations were located. One was called Operation Watch Tower. Its function was to aid the pilots of the drug-laden aircraft to fly from Central America to Panama without getting lost on their near-sea-level flight altitude and to avoid detection by the high-flying U.S. drug interdiction aircraft.

Operation Watch Tower consisted of secret radio beacons at remote locations between Colombia and Panama. Because of the extremely low altitude that these drug-laden aircraft fly, often at only five hundred feet, they could not receive the line-of-sight radio signals ordinarily used. Low-frequency radio beacons permitted the aircraft to home in on the signals, and to reach their destination at Albrook Army Airfield in Panama. Radio signals from an aircraft on a particular frequency actuated a relay at the radio beacon site that started up the gasoline-engine-powered generators and the radio transmitters.

The CIA utilized the Army Intelligence Agency in Operation Watch Tower, which started in the mid-1970s. U.S. Army Colonel A.J. Baker was ordered to oversee part of Operation Watchtower and turned the operation over to Army Colonel Edward P. Cutolo, who also commanded the 10th Special Forces based at Ft. Devens, Massachusetts. Cutolo had supervised Operation Orwell for the intelligence agencies. This operation spied on political figures for the purpose of blackmail.

OPERATION TOILET SEAT

The CIA used Boeing 727 and C-130 type aircraft, hauling drugs from Central and South America, to bring drug loads to offshore locations in the United States, throwing the drugs out the rear ramp into the ocean in water-proof containers. The planes were leased or operated by CIA proprietary airlines and flown either by CIA/DIA/DEA crews or by airline pilots supplementing their regular income by becoming contract agents.

One of my informants, Gunther Russbacher, gave me the names of several airline pilots who regularly flew drug operations for the CIA. These included two captains from United Airlines and a retired Pan American pilot. One of the United Airline pilots bragged that he made twice as much money flying illegal cargo as he did on his regular airline job.

FUELING NICARAGUA REVOLUTION
TO PROMOTE DRUG TRAFFICKING

The CIA-initiated Vietnam war was duplicated in Nicaragua to stimulate military action, followed by selling and trading arms to both sides of the conflict, and receiving drugs in exchange for the weapons. The CIA-fed media releases claimed that the United States had to fund the Contra for freedom purposes and to combat communism. The real reason appeared to be the profitable drug trafficking. As my CIA contacts stated, the CIA was shipping arms to *both sides*, defending this in a tongue-in-check comment: "How else can the CIA keep the war going!"

The CIA sought support from Congress for its Contra operation by reporting that the Sandinistas were trafficking in drugs and that the Contras were not doing the same. Actually, U.S. intelligence agencies were selling arms to both the Contras and the Sandinistas and taking drugs as part payment. The drugs were then shipped back to the United States in the same aircraft used for shipping the arms.

To stimulate Congressional and public support for continuing to support the Contras, the CIA installed video cameras in an aircraft flown by CIA pilot Barry Seal, and secretly video-recorded the placement of drugs on board the aircraft at a Central America arms and drug transshipment point. The White House stated that the drugs were loaded by the Sandinistas, making the tapes available to Congress and the media. The White House sought to inflame public opinion against the Sandinistas so that Congress would vote for funding the Contras. The people represented as Sandinistas loading drugs in that video were actually Contras. The scheme worked: Congress voted money for the Contras, and the public generally were oblivious to the truth.

All types of aircraft were used for flying arms to Central and South America and returning with drugs. Many CIA aircraft were large airline or military types, landing in the United States at military or general aviation airports.[307] DEA aircraft used for drug trafficking operations were usually single and twin-engine general aviation aircraft, and usually landed at private airports.[308]

Among the well-known names operating out of Mena Airport was Barry Seal, one of the CIA's drug pilots. He coordinated frequently with Oliver North, who used the drug profits in the Contra arms trafficking. Seal was becoming a threat to the CIA drug operations and was killed. The day Seal was killed, the FBI seized his personal belongings, hiding evidence of his CIA-sanctioned drug operations.

After the drugs were unloaded at drug transshipment points, CIA-affiliated trucking companies transported the drugs throughout the United States.[309]

CIA DRUG MONEY LAUNDERING

The CIA laundered some of the money obtained from drug trafficking in the Far East through covert CIA financial institutions and other banks that

---

[307] Almost all military bases became drug transshipment points, and especially Homestead (Florida); Davis-Monahan (Arizona); Luke (New Mexico); McGuire (New Jersey); McClellan and Travis (California).

[308] Frequently mentioned airports include Mena Airport and others in the vicinity (Arkansas); Angel Fire Airport (New Mexico); Marana Airport (Arizona); Spirit of St. Louis Airport (Missouri); McMinnville Airport (Oregon); Coolidge Airport (Phoenix); Midland-Odessa (Texas); Lakeside Airport (Chicago); Addison Airport (Denton, Texas); Shamrock Airport (Houston); Pietra Negro (Black Rock), northeast of El Paso; and Redbird Airport in Dallas, (where I had once taught aviation flight and ground training). The airport at Mena, Arkansas, was a well-known CIA arms and drug transshipment point, and was featured on two television shows, *Frontline* and *Now It Can Be Told*, and in numerous newspaper stories.

[309] CIA contacts identify some of the CIA-related drug haulers: MNX Trucking; Jayes' Truck Driver Training School; Jiffey Truck Driver Training School; and Zapata Trucking Company, a division of the Zapata Corporation in Houston.

knowingly accepted the funds. These included Nugan Hand Bank (described elsewhere); Bishop, Baldwin, Rewald, Dillingham and Wong (also described elsewhere); the Vatican Bank; Bank of Lavoro; and Bank of Credit and Commerce International (BCCI).

OPERATION BACK BITER

A code name identifies the situation where a CIA or DEA drug pilot is set up and sacrificed: Operation Back Biter. Targeted CIA or DEA drug pilots are routinely set up by top echelon people. Customs and DEA officials are told about the arrival of a targeted pilot at a certain airport, and he is arrested upon arrival. The pilots are charged and prosecuted, denied the right to have CIA or DEA personnel testify in their behalf, and refused the right to obtain government documents on the basis of national security.

AIDING AND ABETTING BY FUTURE PRESIDENT

In 1989, Tom Brown, former leader of the Arkansas Committee,[310] sent a petition to Governor Clinton to convene a special state grand jury. Brown and his committee had obtained considerable information showing that the CIA was using Mena Airport in Arkansas as a major arms and drug transfer point. An Arkansas state prosecutor, Charles Black, requested in 1988 that Governor Bill Clinton provide state money to investigate the drug activities with international that were beyond the financial ability of the small Mena police force. They knew drug trafficking was rampant, but they needed state or federal funds to probe into the international aspects of the operation.

Arkansas papers carried stories of the CIA arms and drug trafficking in the Mena Airport vicinity. The *Arkansas Times* carried a front page story on May 21, 1992, including three pictures showing CIA contract agent and drug pilot Barry Seal, drug trafficker Jorge Luis Ochoa, and George Bush. Below their picture was the title, BAD COMPANY. A subheading read: "Arkansas's most notorious drug smuggler testified about his links to Colombia. His ties to Washington have yet to be explained." The article brought together the CIA's Mena operations; the drug smuggling; the shooting down of a CIA C-123 over Nicaragua; Lt. Col. Oliver North's arm shipments to Central America, and drug shipments back to the United States.

Winston Bryant, later a State Attorney General, turned over the state files involving drug trafficking at Mena Airport to Iran-Contra special prosecutor Lawrence Walsh in 1991. Walsh refused to intervene even though the drug trafficking was a key part of the Contra operation in the Iran-Contra affair.

The criminal activities surrounding the CIA arms and drug trafficking at Mena Airport were well known to local residents, the local police, the Arkansas State Police, and the media. The local *Arkansas Gazette* published numerous investigative articles describing the criminal activities and the coverup by the State Attorney General and Governor Bill Clinton.

Despite many drug trafficking reports by local citizens and police around Mena, the U.S. Attorney in Little Rock refused to conduct an investigation. The Arkansas Highway Patrol received hundreds of citizen reports detailing

---

[310]Student group at the University of Arkansas.

the criminal activities, reportedly consisting of several thousand pages in 34 volumes. Governor Bill Clinton was advised of the activity and requested that he order state law enforcement personnel to investigate. Despite the gravity of the reported drug activities, Clinton and the U.S. Attorney[311] refused to conduct an investigation.

Pressure from people in Arkansas increased to where the U.S. Attorney was forced to convene a federal grand jury in December 1987. After the grand jury disbanded, the jurors and grand jury witnesses complained to the media that there was a cover-up by the U.S. Attorney.

As Clinton entered the presidential race in 1992, the Arkansas Committee, located in Little Rock, concerned with the drug trafficking, asked him why he didn't initiate an investigation. Clinton replied: "Well, I authorized $25,000 for a state investigation, and I never heard anything about it." Clinton told the group that he knew about the complaints, and that he authorized an expenditure of $25,000 to investigate.[312] When the Arkansas Committee wrote to Clinton asking for documentation that he authorized the money, a letter came back stating that there was no supporting that statement.

Back in Polk County where the criminal activities were ongoing and where any state investigation would occur, the assistant prosecutor stated he had not heard of any funds being authorized, and ridiculed the funding of only $25,000, remarking that it would be like spitting on a forest fire.

OPERATION WATCH TOWER

One of the CIA drug trafficking operations from Central America was called Operation Watch Tower. It consisted of a series of radio beacons to guide low-flying drug pilots; making available to the pilots the radio frequencies and schedule of drug interdiction aircraft so that the drug pilots could avoid detection; and other aids to undetected drug trafficking. The CIA used military personnel in helping carry out the operation.

Army Colonel Edward P. Cutolo, who had been ordered by the CIA to supervise Operation Watch Tower, grew increasingly concerned about its flagrant illegality, and conducted an investigation in an attempt to bring it to a halt. Fearing he might be killed because of his investigation, he prepared a fifteen-page single-spaced affidavit, dated March 11, 1980, describing the CIA drug trafficking and other activities. Cutolo gave copies of it to several trusted friends,[313] with instructions to release the affidavit to government officials and the media if he was killed or died. He was prophetic. Cutolo was killed, as were several other people working with him to expose the drug trafficking operations. Their deaths, as with dozens of others, protected high U.S. officials and the sordid operations they inflicted upon the United States.

The affidavit described the installation and operation of the radio beacon towers and several of the drug flights in which he participated. The first one occurred in December 1975, headed by Colonel A.J. Baker, under whom Cutolo worked. Cutolo stated in his affidavit that in the February operation,

---

[311] Asa Hutchinson and later Michael Fitzhugh.
[312] *Spotlight*, November 23, 1992.
[313] Colonel A.J. Baker; Hugh B. Pearce; Paul Neri.

"30 high-performance aircraft landed safely at Albrook Air Station," and "the mission was 22 days long."

The affidavit described key people meeting the aircraft, including Colonel Manuel Noriega, who was then Panama's Defense Force Officer assigned to Customs; CIA operatives Edwin Wilson and Frank Terpil; and Mossad operative Michael Harari. Harari worked closely with U.S. intelligence agencies in the drug trafficking operation, sharing the profits for Israel, and sharing the blame for the U.S. drug epidemic and associated crime wave. Harari had authority from the U.S. Army Southern Command in Panama to operate on military bases.

OPERATION ORWELL

The Cutolo affidavit described another unlawful mission, Operation Orwell,[314] which consisted of spying on politicians, judicial figures, state law enforcement agencies, and religious figures. Compromising information was distributed to certain members of the military-industrial complex. Colonel Cutolo stated in his affidavit that the compromising information was needed to silence these people if information on the criminal activities leaked out:

Mr. Edwin Wilson explained that it was considered that operation Watch Tower might be compromised and become known if politicians, judicial figures, police and religious entities were approached or received word that U.S. troops had aided in delivering narcotics from Colombia into Panama. Based on that possibility, intense surveillance was undertaken by my office to ensure that if Watch Tower became known, the United States government and the Army would have advance warnings and could prepare a defense.

This was another way of accomplishing the CIA's "plausible deniability ... to downplay and defend against inquiries." The affidavit listed some of the people against whom the surveillance was directed:

I instituted surveillance against Ted Kennedy, John Kerry, Edward King, Michael Dukakis, Levin H. Campbell, Andrew A. Caffrey, Fred Johnson, Kenneth A. Chandler, Thomas P. O'Neill, to name a few of the targets. Surveillance at my orders was instituted at the Governors residences in Massachusetts, Maine, New York, and New Hampshire. The Catholic cathedrals of New York and Boston were placed under electronic surveillance also. In the area of Fort Devens, all local police and politicians were under some form of surveillance at various times.

I specifically used individuals from the 441st Military Intelligence Detachment and 402 Army Security Agency Detachment assigned to the 10th Special Forces Group to supplement the SATs tasked with carrying out Operation Orwell.

I also recruited a number of local state employees who worked within the ranks of local police and, as court personnel, to assist in this Operation. They were veterans and had previous security

[314] Authority for the Army to become involved in this CIA operation came directly from FORSCOM through CIA operative Edwin Wilson, under Army Regulation 340=18-5 (file number 503-05).

clearances. They were told at the outset that if they were caught they were on their own.

The Cutolo affidavit described the killing of an Army servicewoman, Elaine Tyree, who had knowledge of Operation Watch Tower, described in her diary. To shift attention from the actual killer and his connection to the ongoing drug operation, the military charged Tyree's husband with the killing.

The Cutolo affidavit continued:

It was too risky to allow a military court to review the charges against Pvt. Tyree with Operation Orwell still ongoing and Senator Garn's office requesting a full investigation. Pvt. Tyree therefore had to stand before a civilian court of law on the criminal charges.

At the first military hearing the presiding judge found no reason to bind Pvt. Tyree's husband over for trial for the murder of his wife. This decision risked further investigation and possible exposure of the corrupt operation. Army pressure caused the county prosecutor to indict the husband for murdering his wife, even though the army knew the actual killer was someone else. The Cutolo affidavit stated:

On 29 February 1980, Pvt. Tyree was convicted of murder and will spend the duration of his life incarcerated. I could not disseminate intelligence gathered under Operation Orwell to notify civilian authorities who actually killed Elaine Tyree.

To prevent further investigation into the murder, Army officials conspired with Lieutenant J. Dwyer of the Middlesex District Attorney's Office and the County District Attorney. They went to the Massachusetts Supreme Court and obtained a ruling prohibiting any court but the Massachusetts Supreme Court from ordering the arrest of suspects in the Tyree murder. This was without precedent, as any court in Massachusetts could issue arrest warrants for murder suspects. But the ruling protected the real murderer, who, if charged, would have exposed Operation Watch Tower and Operation Orwell.

The Cutolo affidavit continued: "I have seen other men involved in Operation Watch Tower meet accidental deaths after they were also threatened." It then identified the people who died in strange fashion, and who had posed a danger of exposing the drug trafficking.

Sgt. John Newby received threatening phone calls and then died in a parachuting accident when his chute failed to open. Colonel Robert Bayard was murdered in Atlanta, Georgia, in 1977, as he went to meet Mossad agent Michael Harari.[315] Colonel Cutolo died in a military accident under strange circumstances in 1980, shortly before he was to meet Harari. Colonel Baker died while trying to determine if Harari had killed Colonel Cutolo. Colonel Rowe was assassinated on April 21, 1989, in the Philippines, within three days after Mossad agent Harari arrived in that country. Rowe had been investigating Harari's links to Cutolo's murder and to CIA operatives Edwin

---

[315] Harari had been the station chief for the Mossad in Mexico. He also headed Mossad assassination teams in Europe. He was responsible for assassinating a waiter in Norway in a case of mistaken identity and was sent by the Mossad to Central America.

Wilson and Thomas Clines. Pearce was killed in a helicopter accident in June 1989 under mysterious circumstances. Larkin Smith died in an airplane accident on August 13, 1989.

The affidavit stated that Mossad agents associated with Operation Watch Tower were being protected by CIA Director Stansfield Turner and George Bush, and that Washington military authorities had approved the drug trafficking operation:

> *Harari was a known middleman for matters involving the United States in Latin America [and] acted with the support of a network of Mossad personnel throughout Latin America and worked mainly in the import and export of arms and drug trafficking.*
>
> *Edwin Wilson explained that Operation Watch Tower had to remain secret ... There are similar operations being implemented elsewhere in the world. Wilson named the "Golden Triangle" of Southeast Asia and Pakistan. ... Wilson named several recognized officials of Pakistan, Afghanistan, Burma, Korea, Thailand and Cambodia as being aware and consenting to these arrangements, similar to the ones in Panama.*

Referring to the huge profits received by the CIA from the drug trafficking, the affidavit continued:

> *Edwin Wilson explained that the profit from the sale of narcotics was laundered through a series of banks. Wilson stated that over 70% of the profits were laundered through the banks in Panama. The remaining percentage was funneled through Swiss banks with a small remainder being handled by banks within the United States. I understood that some of the profits in Panamanian banks arrived through Israeli Couriers. I became aware of that fact from normal conversations with some of the embassy personnel assigned to the Embassy in Panama. Wilson also stated that an associate whom I don't know also aided in overseeing the laundering of funds ... Wilson indicated that most of Operation Watch Tower was implemented on the authority of Clines.*

Referring to Operation Orwell, that spied upon politicians for subsequent blackmail:

> *I was notified by Edwin Wilson that the information forwarded to Washington, D.C., was disseminated to private corporations who were developing weapons systems for the Dept. of Defense. Those private corporations were encouraged to use the sensitive information gathered from surveillance of U.S. senators and representatives as leverage [blackmail] to manipulate those Congressmen into approving whatever costs the weapon systems incurred.*
>
> *As of the date of this affidavit, 8,400 police departments, 1,370 churches, and approximately 17,900 citizens have been monitored under Operation Orwell. The major churches targeted have been Catholic and Latter Day Saints. I have stored certain information gathered by Operation Orwell on Fort Devens, and pursuant to instructions from Edwin Wilson have forwarded additional informa-*

tion gathered to Washington, D.C. ... Certain information was collected on suspected members of the Trilateral Commission and the Bilderberg group. Among those that information was collected on were Gerald Ford and President Jimmy Carter. Edwin Wilson indicated that additional surveillance was implemented against former CIA Director George Bush, whom Wilson named as a member of the Trilateral Commission.

It is easy to understand why members of Congress can be blackmailed into covering up for criminal activities involving personnel of intelligence agencies or the Justice Department when information on their personal lives is secretly collected by the FBI and U.S. intelligence agencies for blackmail purposes. The affidavit described some of the weapon manufacturers who received this CIA information:

Edwin Wilson named three weapons systems when he spoke of private corporations receiving information from Operation Orwell. (1) An armored vehicle. (2) An aircraft that is invisible to radar. (3) A weapons system that utilizes kinetic energy. Edwin Wilson indicated to me during our conversation, which entailed the dissemination of Operation Orwell information and the identification of the three weapons systems, that Operation Orwell would be implemented nationwide by 4 July 1980.

The affidavit made reference to classified information and "the activities of the CIA in the United States and in Latin America."

Referring to people working with Edwin Wilson, the affidavit continued:

Each operation had basically the same characters involved ... with Edwin Wilson.... Robert Gates and William J. Casey ...

As Colonel Cutolo suspected, Neri was killed, apparently to silence him. Paul Neri[316] was one of the people that Cutolo entrusted with the affidavit and who had been requested to make the affidavit public upon his death. In distributing the affidavit to members of Congress and the media, Neri wrote:

Both Col. Rowe and Mr. Pearce agreed to go public, after the meeting with Larkin Smith, to call for a full investigation into the events described in Col. Cutolo's affidavit. But both men died prior to the meeting with Smith.

Referring to the Mossad, Neri's cover letter stated:

With the deaths of Col. Cutolo, Col. Baker, Col. Rowe (and Col. Robert Bayard named in Col. Cutolo's affidavit) it is hard to believe the deaths of these men are not the work of the Israeli Mossad. It is equally easy to attribute the death of Col. Cutolo directly to Operation Watch Tower inquiries.

Meeting the same coverup response that I received for the past thirty years from the establishment media, Neri's letter stated:

For your information a copy of the affidavit will be sent to the New York Times, the Washington Post and the Boston Globe. ... The men

---

[316] Neri was an employee of the National Security Agency.

who died so far ... were good men. They attempted to let the public know what really occurred in Latin America, and in the never ending drug flow.

In 1980 Col. Cutolo died in an accident while on a military exercise. Just prior to his death he notified me that he was to meet with Michael Harari, an Israeli Mossad agent. It is my belief, though unsubstantiated, that Harari murdered Col. Cutolo because of the information Col. Cutolo possessed. I believe that Col. Cutolo died in his attempt to [expose] Operation Watch Tower ...

Colonel Baker enlisted the aid of Colonel James N. Rowe, and between Col. Baker, Col. Rowe and myself, we set out to prove that Harari murdered Col. Cutolo, and that Operation Watch Tower ... netted Edwin Wilson and Frank Terpil of the CIA a large sum of tax free dollars.

Prior to getting very far into the investigation, Col. Baker died ... We had no doubt as to the guilt of Thomas Clines, whom we suspect was the master mind behind Operation Watch Tower.

Neri went on to describe how Harari and Col. James Rowe[317] were in the Philippines when Rowe was assassinated, and that "It is my unsubstantiated belief that Harari murdered Col. Rowe, or arranged it." Neri's letter continued: "I believe Harari's motive for murdering Col. Rowe was due to Col. Rowe's inquiries about Harari's movements and relationships to Edwin Wilson, Thomas Clines and Manuel Noriega."

Referring to another death in the small group seeking to expose Operation Watch Tower and the associated deaths, Neri wrote:

In June 1989, Mr. Pearce was killed in a helicopter accident. The accident has a story of its own I am told. Both Col. Rowe and Mr. Pearce agreed to go public, after the meeting with Larkin Smith, to call for a full investigation into the events described in Col. Cutolo's affidavit. But both men died prior to the meeting with Smith.

Paul Neri continued:

Since the Israeli Mossad openly traffics in arms and drugs in Latin America, a theory that Clines, Wilson, Terpil, Harari and Noriega engaged in Operation Watch Tower is very easy to believe at this time, especially following the Libyan situation and the Iran-Contra affair. It all fits, this entire scenario carried over from Operation Watch Tower directly into the Iran-Contra affair with the same characters.

Neri wrote that he was sending a copy of the Cutolo affidavit to the *New York Times*, the *Washington Post*, and the *Boston Globe*. Referring to the deaths associated with the attempted exposure of the CIA's Operation Watch Tower and the Mossad involvement, Neri wrote, "I'm sorry that I am unable to carry the work any further. This is now your Pandora's Box."

Before he was murdered, Colonel Rowe also tried to get CBS's *60 Minutes* interested in the contents of the Cutolo affidavit, the murders, and the

---

[317] Rowe was in the Philippines serving as chief of the Army Advisory Group.

CIA crimes. CBS replied on July 13, 1987, refusing to proceed with the matter. Despite the responsibility of the media to expose government corruption, CBS chose to cover up. This coverup made possible the continuation of the drug trafficking and more murders.

FINALLY THEY GOT NERI

On April 29, 1990, Paul Neri died. An unknown person wrote a short letter that was sent out with the Cutolo affidavit and Paul Neri's accounting of what had happened, writing:

Mr. Paul Neri, of the National Security Agency, died on April 29, 1990. Before his death, he requested that I mail the enclosed affidavit to you. Paul Neri was concerned that he would be killed or lose his security clearance if he revealed the affidavit before he died. According to him, these facts are true. If you investigate and interview the parties named within the affidavit, you will find the information is true. I am simply carrying out the wishes of a good friend, but do not want to get involved any further; therefore, I shall remain anonymous.

INPUT FROM TALKSHOW LISTENERS

It frequently happened during my almost two thousand talkshow appearances that callers would describe what they witnessed, adding to what I had already discovered. During a July 27, 1993 appearance on the syndicated talkshow, *Radio Free America*, hosted by Tom Valentine, a caller from Houston, Texas described his conversations with DEA pilots at a Houston-area airport. The pilots had admitted to him that the crates on board the aircraft contained cocaine from Central America, but that the drugs were being used for sting operations. This of course was a farce, and a standard excuse used to explain to inquisitive pilots the apparent illegality of the drug shipments.

Another called, an Air Force officer, described the many large Air Force aircraft flying into Homestead Air Force Base with large quantities of drugs on board.

The thousands of people involved in drug trafficking in and out of government, including the military, and those who have knowledge of it, affects the mindset of the entire nation. The same goes for the massive corruption in federal agencies, especially the Justice Department and the federal courts, and spreads its venom throughout the fabric of American society.

MOSSAD IN DRUG TRAFFICKING

Several of my CIA and DEA informants, who were directly involved in the drug trafficking, described the Mossad's role in Central and South American drug trafficking. These informants described how the Mossad marked their drug packages in what looked like the Star of David but which were really three inverted triangles taken out of the Star of David emblem. They described how the Mossad shared space on CIA aircraft flying drugs into the United States.

Mossad operatives connected with the drug operations included Michael "Freddy" Harari and David Kimche. Both worked hand-in-hand with the CIA and the drug traffickers, including the Medellin and Cali Cartels. When U.S.

forces invaded Panama to arrest Noriega, Harari was caught in the fighting. Despite the fact that the Mossad's role in drug trafficking was serious and that he was a co-conspirator with Noriega, the U.S. intelligence agencies allowed Harari to escape in an Israeli jet. If Harari had been captured and questioned, Israel's involvement in the drug trafficking could have come out, as well as that of U.S. intelligence agencies.

Former OSS operative Russell Bowen worked with or alongside the Mossad and Harari for many years. He told me that Harari had started his vast Central and South American operations by hauling cigarettes, and then branching out into drugs.

PANAMA INVASION AND THE CIA DRUG TRAFFICKING

In 1990 President Bush ordered the military to invade Panama on the basis that Colonel Manuel Noriega was violating U.S. laws by allowing drug trafficking through Panama. This was bizarre in light of the fact that CIA operative and then Director of the CIA, George Bush, paid Noriega for years for engaging in drug-related activities.

The invasion of Panama caused hundreds of deaths and billions of dollars in damages, on the pretense that Noriega was dealing in drugs and presumably U.S. agencies were not. People in control of U.S. intelligence agencies and were themselves engaging in drug trafficking against their own country. They were guilty of crimes far more serious than any which Noriega had committed.

CIA personnel believe that Noriega was taken out because he knew too much about the involvement of U.S. officials and that he was demanding too high a cut for his part in the CIA drug trafficking. The federal judge barred attorneys supposedly defending Noriega from presenting any information on the CIA's role in drug trafficking, or anything of a political nature. This is standard procedure to insure the conviction of CIA targets and shield CIA involvement from the public.

The U.S. District Judge repeatedly refused to allow CIA documents to be introduced that Noriega needed to defend himself. Noriega's U.S. attorneys limited their defense arguments so as not to expose the CIA involvement in drug trafficking.

To obtain a conviction, Justice Department prosecutors rewarded known drug smugglers with reduced prison terms, protected them against the consequences of their perjury, and compensated them for testifying against Noriega. On July 10, 1992, a federal jury in Miami sentenced Manuel Noriega to 40 years in federal prison for trafficking in drugs.

Russbacher described the frequent visits of Senator Dan Quayle to the CIA's arms and drug transshipment point known as John Hull's Ranch in Costa Rica. He stated that Quayle was deeply involved with the Contra operation and drugs, as well as being closely associated with noted drug trafficker Felix Rodriguez. Russbacher said, "Quayle was one of our bag boys."

ANOTHER KEY CIA OPERATIVE CAME FORWARD

One of the valuable informants who made contact with me and gave me important data on CIA activities was Trenton Parker. Although many CIA operatives and contract agents operate in a compartmentalized environment, limiting the extent of the CIA operations that they observe, Parker had a high position within the CIA and played a key management role in some of the most secret and corrupt activities that CIA had going.

Parker provided me with information on CIA activities that Russbacher knew about but had not told me. Once Parker gave me preliminary information about the operation, in every case Russbacher enlarged upon it. Becoming a confidant to Parker, therefore, had several advantages. I learned about other CIA corruption, and this knowledge prompted Russbacher to reveal even more about very secret and very corrupt Agency activities. In addition, even though neither one of them was in contact with the other, their statements to me confirmed the Agency status of the other, and confirmed what each told me about the CIA activities.

The documents that Parker gave me included a confidential CIA employee status report that made it possible to positively establish his CIA connections and contradict the CIA and Justice Department's denials of such relationships. He had filed this report in a Denver criminal action. I obtained a copy before U.S. Attorney Michael Norton ordered the court to seal the records.

The confidential employee status report showed that Parker was employed by the CIA from December 23, 1964 to May 24, 1992, and his last rank was Colonel in the United States Marine Corp, attached to the Marine-Naval intelligence and to the CIA. His serial number was 553-60-1458, with an additional MSID identification number of 2072458.

That confidential employee status report was firmly established Parker's CIA status, and identified him as a member of the ultra-secret Pegasus group, with headquarters hidden in the U.S. Department of Labor offices in Fairfax, Virginia. The status report listed his alias, Pegasus 222. One of Parker's friends in the CIA at Langley, Virginia, obtained that document and sent it to Parker. The CIA could no longer deny Parker's CIA status.

OFFICIAL ADMISSION OF LYING AS STANDARD PRACTICE

That document undermines the false statements made to the court by Justice Department prosecutors in early 1993 that Parker had no connection to the CIA or any other intelligence agency. A significant part of the confidential CIA report was the statement on the bottom of the page:

DO/DA RECOMMENDATION: –<u>STANDARD DENIAL</u>

By "standard denial," the CIA was instructing other federal personnel to deny that Parker had any connections with the Central Intelligence Agency, including denials in court, which would of course be perjured statements. Those words show the standard pattern of lying by the CIA, showing how ridiculous it is for the press, members of Congress, and others, to accept as true anything stated by the CIA or those who speak on its behalf.

Higher CIA authority informed Mona Alderson of the true facts, and recommend that she openly lie, even though it would permit the imprisonment of a CIA operative. These sacrifices are standard tactics of the utterly corrupt Central Intelligence Agency.

Parker was bitter because the CIA and Justice Department had sacrificed him in 1982 to protect an ongoing secret scheme called Operation Snow Cone.

Parker's problems commenced several years earlier when he was charged by an investigator for the Security Exchange Commission (SEC) with a money laundering operation, which was part of a CIA operation under Operation Interlink and Operation Gold Bug.

It is not unusual for a CIA operation to be accidentally exposed by employees of another government agency who are unaware of the ongoing unlawful operation. In these cases CIA and Justice Department officials in Washington quickly step in, and the charges are dropped. But in this case the SEC charges were filed, and publicized by the media. It was too late for the CIA and Justice Department officials to pressure the SEC to retract the charges.

There was another possible reason for filing charges against Parker, and this is a common way of disposing of CIA assets who refuse to cooperate. Parker's handlers had asked him to be part of an expanding drug operation in Nigeria called Operation Indigo Sky, and Parker refused. He didn't care to get involved in drug trafficking, and living conditions in Nigeria were deplorable.

SACRIFICING PEOPLE

A criminal trial against Parker could expose the secret CIA operation, which would result in serious consequences for the CIA and other government agencies. Justice Department prosecutors and CIA personnel encouraged Parker to plead guilty, assuring him that he would be released as soon as attention to his case no longer existed. Parker pled guilty in 1982. He refused all newspaper interviews. Parker didn't realize that his usefulness to the CIA was compromised by the publicity given to the money laundering operation, and that it would further threaten any CIA operation if he was brought back.

ORIGINAL TRANSMISSION DATE: 3/3/93 - RETRANSMISSION DATE 3/10/93

DOCUMENT CLASSIFICATION STATUS: T O P   S E C R E T

TO: MONA B. ALDERSON,
    LITIGATION DIVISION, OGC,
    CIA/WASHINGTON D.C.   **CONFIDENTIAL**
    PHO: 703-874-3107
    FAX: 703-874-3208

RE: INQUIRY OF 3/3/93
    MR. JOSEPH MACKEY,
    ASST. U.S. ATTORNEY,
    DENVER, COL.
    PHO: 303-844-2081
    FAX: 303-874-3208

NOTICE: PURSUANT TO THE NATIONAL SECURITY ACT OF 1947, 50 USC 401
& 402, ET. SQ. - THE FOLLOWING INFORMATION IS CONSIDERED
INFORMATION OF A CLASSIFIED NATURE INVOLVING NATIQNAL SECURITY AND
SHOULD BE TREATED BY YOU AND YOUR DEPARTMENT/OFFICE ACCORDINGLY.

RE: BACKGROUND INFORMATION AND CURRENT OPPS-STAT ON SUBJECT:
    TRENTON H. PARKER AKA PEGASUS-222 - 2/2/45-COL.USMC/GS18
    ATTACHED MARINE-NAVEL ITLG-SEC/TAD-CIA-12/23/64 TO 5/24/92.
    SECURITY LVL/TOP SECRET/EXP 5/24/92. MSID NO. 2072458.
    SS NO. 553-60-1458. NSA/SPL-DDO/SEC-CHIEF-SP/AG PEGASUS UNIT.
    CONFIRM/REG/CIA/DENVER,CO. SBS/CUR/RES - DENVER, CO.
    ALL OPPS/ASSIGS CLASSIFIED TOP SECRET/UAVAILABLE.
    CUR/SEC/STAT: HIGH RISK. FED/CR/IDC/DENVER-1/27/93.

NO ADDITIONAL RECORDS OR BACKGROUND INFORMATION AVAILABLE FOR
RELEASE TO YOUR OFFICE AT THIS TIME ON SUBJECT DUE TO MATTERS OF
NATIONAL SECURITY AND PRESIDENTIAL DIRECTIVE/G-BUSH 5/24/92.

DO/DA RECOMMENDATION: - STANDARD DENIAL

ANSWER BACK/REF/P-222,
DO/COMM-CTR/3/3/93,   CONFIDENTIAL
FOR/ITL/SEC - DDO/DDA,
DRC/CIA/LANG/VA.

Copy of the CIA confidential document showing Parker's ONI and CIA
status, and showing lying to be the standard practice of the Agency.

Parker was kept in prison for the next four years. To keep him from blowing the whistle to the media, and to keep him from law library access where he could have filed post-conviction remedies, Justice Department officials kept him in solitary confinement for over two years. When that confinement had to be halted, prison officials moved him dozens of times from prison to prison, denying him access to telephones and to facilities for preparing legal briefs.

The opportunity to seek legal relief arose while Parker was in an Arizona prison where he could prepare and file a post-conviction motion, which was heard by U.S. District Judge Marquez in Tucson. At the February 12, 1986, hearing the judge ordered the prison warden and the U.S. Attorney to release Parker immediately. He was released on February 26, 1986.

Parker was now out of prison, but he had lost his wife and family while incarcerated. In addition, Justice Department prosecutors filed other charges seeking to return him to prison. In 1992, U.S. Attorney Michael Norton in Denver, charged Parker with money laundering charges that had been part of his CIA operations.

At his arraignment in Denver, the judge ordered him released pending trial, set for April 1993. Before his release, Parker occupied a cell with Stewart Webb, a private investigator whom I had met earlier, and who was trying to expose the HUD and savings and loan corruption in the Denver area. Webb showed Parker some of my writings, and Parker decided to contact me after he was released.

Parker stated that he had been with the CIA for approximately 30 years and was part of Faction B[318] in the CIA, and was identified as Pegasus 222. Parker described many of the CIA operations in which he was involved. He responded to my questions concerning his involvement in CIA activities, and sent me copies of briefs that he filed in the U.S. District Court at Denver.[319] His statements and his writings added additional confirmation to what other CIA operatives had stated to me, and especially Gunther Russbacher. I suggested that Parker file certain papers with the court, which he did. These papers included a description of CIA operations that would have catastrophic consequences if the public learned of them and understood their significance.

While waiting for trial, Parker filed papers with the court listing the secret CIA operations that he would reveal at his trial. He also filed a list of documents that he would submit, including the confidential status report showing him to be a Colonel in the U.S. Marines, assigned to the Office of Naval Intelligence and to the Central Intelligence Agency.

The status report showed him assigned to Naval Intelligence and to the CIA from 1964 through May 24, 1992, and that he held a top secret clearance. The combination of that confidential status report and his

---

[318] The CIA has three covert factions. Faction One or sometimes referred to as Faction A, appears to be under the control of the Justice Department. Faction Two or B, as it is sometimes called, is under the control of the Office of Naval Intelligence. Faction Three is very small, including former OSS operatives, and reportedly a loose-knit group of rogues.

[319] U.S. District Court, Denver, U.S.A. v. Trenton H. Parker, No. 93-CR-43.

declarations of CIA activities that he intended to disclose threatened to blow the lid off a major segment of the CIA criminality. Without that confidential status report, Parker would probably have ended up in prison, as the CIA and Justice Department would have denied he had any employee relationship to the CIA. This standard practice of lying caused the incarceration of Gunther Russbacher, Ronald Rewald, Michael Riconosciuto, Richard Brenneke, and many other CIA personnel.

Once Parker filed with the court the list containing documents that he planned to submit, CIA and Justice Department officials had a serious problem. An Assistant U.S. Attorney in Denver complained to the Judge that Parker should have filed the documents under seal because they revealed secret CIA activities. Because of those revealing documents, U.S. Attorney Norton dismissed all charges against Parker, which avoided revealing the Agency's dirty linen. Parker called me on March 23, 1993, quickly stating: "All charges have been dropped. I'm going underground. Don't ask any questions." He then hung up.

During subsequent telephone conversations Parker described the presence of two men in the courtroom who waited for him outside the courthouse after the judge ordered him released. Parker felt they were waiting to seize him, with possible fatal consequences. One of the guards in the federal building also recognized the problem and unlocked a rear door, allowing Parker to evade the men.

SHAM AND PROFITABLE DRUG BUST

Parker described how the CIA, with Vice President Bush's approval, set up a sham drug bust in Miami during March 1980, comprising 4,000 pounds of cocaine, the biggest drug bust at that time. The purpose of the seizure was to generate support in the United States for newly appointed drug czar, Vice President George Bush, and to justify the use of the U.S. military in the "war" upon drugs to carry out the drug trafficking into the United States. It worked.

In carrying out the scheme, the CIA coordinated with Jorge Ochoa, a Colombian drug dealer. Ochoa organized many of Colombia's drug dealers to contribute cocaine for a large shipment into the United States, stating there was safety in numbers. Most of the dealers didn't know that this was a planned drug bust and that they would lose whatever cocaine they contributed to the shipment. After the drug dealers contributed their cocaine into Ochoa's warehouse, Ochoa switched large quantities of bad cocaine, that he had accumulated, with good cocaine contributed by other dealers. Later, Ochoa sold the cocaine obtained in the switch for about fifty million dollars.

The 4,000 pounds of cocaine, including the bad cocaine that Ochoa had switched, was then shipped to Miami and seized by U.S. Customs. The plan worked. Bush got good publicity for his role as drug czar, and Ochoa and his insiders made over fifty million dollars by replacing good cocaine with bad cocaine.

Parker stated that Reagan knew nothing about the CIA involvement in the drug trafficking. Parker said, "Bush knew what was going on. He knew because he gave the order to see what we could come up with, and he cleared it. He knew those we were dealing with would eventually be the Medellin cartel."

The sting operation in which Parker participated used an informer to notify DEA agent Phelps in Bogota that the drugs were arriving at Miami International Airport on a particular flight at a given time. Phelps then notified DEA and Customs at Miami, so they could be present at the aircraft's arrival and to seize the drugs.

There were comical elements to this planned drug bust. Parker described what he observed at Miami International Airport when the 4,000 pounds of cocaine arrived on board TAMPA Airlines. Watching the scene from an unobserved distance via binoculars, Parker said that the airplane with the two tons of cocaine arrived at the parking area, but there were no Custom agents there to seize the drugs, despite the considerable planning that went into the operation.

Several people working with Parker were at the aircraft, presenting the appearance of being there to unload the cargo. However, they intended to run off as the DEA and Custom agents appeared. But there were no agents, the pilots wanted the drugs unloaded fast, and they wanted to leave. To avoid losing the drugs intended for the planned seizure, Parker's people unloaded the aircraft and the crates were sitting on the tarmac.

The cocaine was hidden in boxes of Levi jeans, with yellow bands on the boxes containing the real Levi's, and white bands on the boxes containing the cocaine. Parker's people sprayed the boxes containing the cocaine with ether, used in the preparation of cocaine, so that the Custom agents couldn't possibly overlook the presence of drugs.

The absence of the expected DEA and Custom agents presented Parker with a problem. He advised his men by radio to stand by. An hour later, Parker saw through his binoculars a couple of Custom agents, engaging in frivolity, walking slowly toward the boxes, obviously unaware of the presence of drugs. Parker radioed his men to stay clear of the area.

Parker watched through his binoculars as the agents poked holes in the boxes to check for possible drugs. The third box that they poked caused white cocaine powder to escape. Parker then radioed his people to immediately leave the area.

Parker boarded a commercial airline for return to Denver. That night the U.S. media described the drug find as the largest discovery in the nation's history. DEA and Customs officials described the drug find the result of an intensive, coordinated effort between the DEA and Customs.

CIA COMPLICITY IN ESTABLISHING
THE MEDELLIN CARTEL

Parker described how the CIA set up the meetings in which various Colombian drug dealers organized into a drug trafficking cartel. Parker described two preliminary meetings in late 1981, arranged by the CIA, in which the individual drug dealers in Colombia planned to organize into a cartel for shipping drugs to the United States. He stated that the first meeting occurred with twenty of the biggest cocaine dealers in Colombia present. That the second and final meeting was held at the Hotel International in Medellin, attended by about two hundred drug dealers, pushers, and smugglers. The

Medellin Cartel was established in December 1981, and each of the members paid an initial $35,000 fee to fund a security force for the cartel members to protect their drug operation.

Russbacher confirmed to me the meetings that Parker described. He stated there had been a preliminary meeting in September 1981, in Buenaventura, Colombia, which established the format for the subsequent meetings. Russbacher attended the September 1981 meeting, which was initiated by the CIA to facilitate drug trafficking into the United States, permitting the CIA to deal with a group rather than many independent drug dealers.

At least half a dozen former CIA, OSS, and DEA personnel gave me many hours of statements over a three year period concerning Central and South America drug operations in which U.S. intelligence agencies and the Mossad participated.

CIA PLANNING AND FUNDING
THE KIDNAP OF OCHOA'S SISTER

Prior to organizing the Medellin cartel, the CIA created a crisis situation, providing an impetus for the Colombian drug dealers to form the Medellin Cartel. Parker described the CIA operation in early December 1981, that led to the kidnapping of Jorge Ochoa's sister, Leona, from a University outside of Bogota. Parker stated that, acting in his CIA capacity, he paid a group known as M-19, to carry out the kidnapping, and to also kidnap Carlos Lehder. Lehder escaped after he was captured. The CIA paid the M-19 group three million dollars, of which two million dollars was in guns and one million in cash.

Parker said, "We made arrangements with Colonel Noriega, and this was the point where Noriega became involved with the CIA and the drugs." He continued: "The deal was that the meeting between M-19 and Ochoa and Escobar would be held in a neutral point, namely, Panama. During the second week of January, 1982, everything was set up."

Another one of my CIA informants, Russell Bowen, played a role in the kidnapping of Ochoa's sister. He piloted the DC-3 aircraft that flew Ochoa's sister, Leona, to a remote location, where she was held until the ransom was paid and she was released. This flight is described in greater detail elsewhere.

CROSSING OF PATHS

As Parker was describing one of his money-laundering flights, I discovered that his path had crossed that of Gunther Russbacher, adding further confirmation to Russbacher's ONI status. Parker described the purpose of a flight from Dobbins Air Force Base near Marietta, Georgia, in January or February of 1982, including a description of the pilot, a Navy Lt. Commander with the nickname of "Gunsel." Russbacher had told that "Gunsel" and "Gunslinger" were nicknames he used. Parker stated that the pilot was very articulate, which fit Russbacher's description. Russbacher confirmed that he did fly such a flight, and described the route of flight and the name of one of the passengers, which coincided with Parker's description.

Parker described the series of short flights, with the first landing at Grand Cayman Island, where Parker picked up five million dollars in cash from a CIA source. The plane then went to Nassau, where Parker "paid [Lynden]

Pindling,[320] who was the Prime Minister, one million dollars to get rid of a place called Herman's Cay." Parker explained that Herman's Cay was a main drug transshipment point operated by Colombian drug dealer Carlos Lehder, whom he described as one of the five keys of the Medellin Cartel. Parker stated:

> *Lehder was getting way out of line, he was shooting at people, and when he finally shot at Walter Cronkite, who happened to be sailing around in the area, Walter broke the news and a lot of people were saying how can this guy be operating out of Herman's Key, just off the shores of the United States?*

Parker stated that Lehder was then forced to leave Herman's Cay and return to Colombia, where he joined the Medellin Cartel. Parker said that before leaving Nassau he was joined by Robert Vesco (wanted in the United States for money fraud), and then the CIA aircraft flew them to Havana, where they were met at the airport by security guards and Fidel Castro. Parker said:

> *I personally delivered two million dollars to Fidel Castro. And for those two million dollars he was to see that a shipment of arms was to go to M-19, which was a right-wing revolutionary force that we wanted to keep active, so that we could have pressure on the government to bring about certain things that we wanted to do. And we needed pressure from below and pressure from above. He agreed to do that and he did do that.*

Parker continued: "I took the remaining two million dollars and flew into Panama City, Panama, and there I checked into Holiday Inn," where he met with the head of Colombia's M-19. Parker added: "I delivered my one million dollars to him, and then I met with Colonel Noriega and delivered one million dollars to him. That one million dollars was to pay Noriega to act as the neutral party to negotiate the release of Ochoa's sister. Sure enough, Ochoa's sister was released." Parker continued:

> *And then he was also supposed to make an offer that he could and would provide protection for the drugs coming into the United States through the back door, to the midway. And what that was, is that we had already made a move on the cartel to close down some of the small operations. At that time Noriega offered a connection into the Sandinistas, the drug operations. Refinery plants were set up there. And that's what we wanted, as we wanted to show the Sandinistas as being the bad guys and justify U.S. involvement.*
>
> *What we were doing was also financing operations, because a certain group in the CIA was going ahead and flying guns down into Nicaragua, dropping them off by parachutes to the Contras. They then went over to the Sandinistas, picked up drugs, and flew them into the United States, after which the money would be returned to the Sandinistas. In effect we were taking over some of the flying services for the Medellin Cartel. The money from the drugs produced the*

---

[320] Lynden O. Pindling.

money for the guns, and that is how the operation worked, and Bush knew the whole god-dam thing.

Parker explained that after completing that trip, he flew back to Denver where he was to go to trial on charges relating to a CIA operation called Operation Gold Bug. He explained that he was on a one-million-dollar self-recognizance bond, which was rather bizarre, since any offense requiring that large bond would be serious enough to preclude release on one's own recognizance.

Parker thought that charging him was a mistake, unless it was to silence or discredit him. Parker said, "First, my trial was to start on February 2, 1982. Second, when it came up it came up by a pure fluke." He explained how the CIA was to protect him from prosecution. Prior to trial his CIA handlers instructed him to remain silent about the CIA operation as it was ongoing and that any exposure of it would have serious consequences. His handlers stated that he would receive a very light prison sentence or probation and would soon be free.

PEGASUS UNIT

Parker described his role in a highly secret intelligence unit called Pegasus. Russbacher confirmed this group's existence, although he was hesitant to talk about it. Parker stated that Pegasus was set up by former President Harry Truman to spy on other CIA units and report to the President any unlawful activities by the CIA. He said the last president the Pegasus unit was able to report to was John F. Kennedy.

MORE FUEL FOR CHARGES THAT CIA
WAS INVOLVED IN KENNEDY'S ASSASSINATION

He stated that after President Kennedy decided to pull U.S. troops out of the CIA Vietnam operation, that would cause the loss of billions of dollars from the CIA drug trafficking, certain CIA factions decided to assassinate Kennedy. Pegasus people discovered the plot and told Kennedy two weeks before he was assassinated.

These statements by a deep-cover CIA operative and Marine Corps officer certainly raises serious questions and adds further fuel to the speculation and charges that the CIA was involved in Kennedy's assassination. In light of other CIA criminalities, there should be little doubt that the CIA has the mindset to assassinate a president of the United States. In later pages there is additional support for this theory.

Parker stated that after Kennedy's death the Pegasus unit was not able to function as intended, because of the corrupt activities of U.S. presidents after the Kennedy assassination. He named Johnson, Nixon and Bush. He stated that Reagan was not implicated like the others; he was more of a figurehead for powerful factions controlled by former CIA Director Bush.

Parker described the necessity of Pegasus going underground within the CIA because of the inability to report to a president, and that the files on corrupt CIA operations gathered by the Pegasus group were moved to various secret locations. Denver was one of the sites.

Parker said that his Pegasus group secretly gave files on the CIA criminal activities from 1976 to 1982 to a member of the Joint Armed Services Committee, Congressman Larry McDonald. These files revealed corrupt activities by several U.S. presidents, federal officials, the CIA, and other members of government.

Parker stated that McDonald let it be known to the press that he was going to reveal startling evidence upon his return from the Far East, showing that the CIA and certain high-ranking public officials were part of an operation responsible for drug trafficking since 1963 from Southeast Asia. McDonald boarded KAL Flight 007, which was shot down by the Russians.

REFERRING TO THE THREE
NAVAL OFFICERS KILLED AT FORT ORD

Parker had seen one of my petitions to Congress reporting among other matters the crash of a Navy helicopter at Fort Ord on April 30, 1991, and the death of three naval officers from the Office of Naval Intelligence, one of whom was a woman. He was interested in knowing their names and physical descriptions, as two men and a woman disappeared from his Pegasus group at about that time. He thought the crash might explain their sudden disappearance. He added: "The Pegasus units have been systematically exterminated; people have been knocked off." Since the Pegasus unit was collecting evidence of CIA criminality, the members were frequent targets of assassination by other CIA and intelligence groups.

Parker described many of the CIA operations in which he played a role, and his description coincided with information given to me by Gunther Russbacher and other CIA sources.

OPERATION MOTHER GOOSE

Parker described his various assignments in the CIA, from when he first joined the Office of Naval Intelligence. He was involved during 1964, in the CIA scheme called Operation Mother Goose, dealing with joint military selection, recruitment, and training of qualified enlisted men with security ratings. These people were educated and trained in basic covert and undercover activities. After training they were released from active military duty to enroll in colleges and universities under the G.I. Bill. While under CIA supervision, they infiltrated student activities and student movements as it related to the Vietnam War and other political areas. Parker trained at the United States Marine Corps base at Camp Pendleton, California.

OPERATION BACK DRAFT

Parker's next CIA assignment was an enlargement upon Operation Mother Goose, called Operation Back-Draft. This operation provided financial assistance to /students while attending college and trained them to infiltrate and disrupt student activities. Parker participated in this program while attending college and university programs in Southern California.

Another CIA contract agent, Ron Rewald, was used in a similar operation, and was later recruited by the CIA to operate a proprietary in Hawaii known as Bishop, Baldwin, Rewald, Dillingham and Wong (BBRDW), which is described elsewhere.

To qualify Parker for use in financial operations, the CIA obtained employment for him with New York Stock Exchange brokerage firms from 1971 until 1974, in California and Colorado. While in this position he supplied confidential information to the CIA on customer accounts and transactions. Eventually he opened his own brokerage firm as a front for the CIA through the SEC and NASD. (The CIA trained Gunther Russbacher in a similar manner to infiltrate U.S. financial institutions.)

This is similar to the operation described to me by CIA operative Gunther Russbacher, in which Russbacher received training at Mutual Life Insurance Company, and then incorporated and operated a number of CIA financial institutions, headquartered in Missouri, with offices throughout the United States, including Denver, Dallas, Houston, Atlanta, and Traverse City, Michigan.

OPERATION ANACONDA

Another CIA assignment was participation in Operation Anaconda in the mid-1970s, through which CIA personnel ran for state and federal political office. Another purpose of the operation was to swing key elections to a particular candidate, away from one whose interest may be detrimental to the CIA. This was used against Senator Church and Representative Pike after their committees exposed CIA misconduct.

Parker described other operations in which he was involved, dealing with the CIA's secret infiltration of U.S. financial institutions, drug operations in Central and South America and the Nigerian operation known as Indigo Sky.

Parker appeared as guest on several talk shows with Tom Valentine of *Radio Free America*.[321] During one appearance on July 29, 1993, he shared the two-hour program with former CIA employee and author, Fletcher Prouty,[322] and he described the mechanics of the CIA's Operation Interlink. Prouty stated during the show that Parker's revelations "make this one of the most important shows on the CIA that has ever occurred."

AN OSS MOLE INSIDE THE CIA

One of many intelligence agency informants who contacted me, giving me many hours of information and documents concerning his CIA activities, was Russell Bowen. Somewhat ironically, he said he was a mole within the CIA representing a group of about seventy-five people from the former Office of Strategic Services (OSS). During World War II, Bowen was a Lieutenant Colonel in the military and was one of the youngest P-38 fighter pilots during the war. He received the Distinguished Flying Cross, the Distinguished Service Medal, and other decorations for meritorious service.

During World War II he was brought into the OSS by General William Donovan, who was selected by President Franklin Roosevelt to form this intelligence unit. When President Truman disbanded the OSS in 1947, several dozen OSS members secretly maintained their organization under the cover of the CIA, and were known as Faction Three in the Central Intelligence Agency.

After the war, during his OSS/CIA role, Bowen flew for United Nations Secretary General Dag Hammarskjold, the Shah of Iran, and eventually Fulgencio Batista, the former dictator of Cuba. He and I had crossed paths when my piloting duties took me to the Middle East on temporary assignment from my base at Oakland, California.

Bowen was flying DC-3 and C-46 aircraft from Kabul to Beirut via Teheran, and I flew the same type of aircraft in the same general area. Bowen was flying "material" for the CIA, and I was flying Moslem pilgrims to Mecca from throughout the Middle East, including Baghdad, Teheran, Beirut, Jerusalem, Jidda, and Abadan.

Bowen surprised me when he stated that two employees of the same airline that I worked for, Transocean Airlines, were CIA operatives: Allan A. Barrie, General Manager for Iranian Airways in Teheran, and Henry F. "Hank" Maierhoffer. I had flown for Transocean Airlines and had known them when I flew in the Middle East during the early 1950s, but had no idea they were engaged in such activities.

Bowen described how he started up several airlines in South America after the war that served as covers for the CIA. He described knowing a friend of mine, King Parker, who also started several airlines in South America and who occasionally flew with me in the 1980s, in my Beech Twin Bonanza aircraft. Parker has since passed away. Parker had flown PBY aircraft for the Royal Canadian Air Force during World War II while I was a Navy flight instructor in PBY seaplanes at Jacksonville, Florida, in 1944.

CASEY'S UNDERCOVER CIA OPERATIONS

Bowen stated that he reported directly to William Casey in the CIA during the 1960s and 1970s. He indicated that Casey was with the CIA in a covert capacity after World War II, and long before he became its director in 1981. Bowen said that he flew dozens of covert CIA operations in the Middle East and Latin America, under Casey's direction. Bowen described meeting Casey and other handlers on his trips to Washington, at secret places and receiving verbal instructions and suitcases filled with money.

Casey was part of the OSS during World War II, until it was disbanded by President Truman in 1947. He then became a covert operative for the CIA, with no official connection to the Agency until 1981, when President Reagan appointed him Director of the CIA.

"GARBAGE COLLECTOR"

Bowen was known in the CIA as a "garbage collector," a term used to extract CIA operatives from foreign countries, who had been compromised or were wanted by the local police or military. Bowen told me of the time in 1983 when Theodore Shackley ordered him to fly into San Jose, Costa Rica. The purpose was to extract a CIA asset, Sam Cummings, who was hiding in the Piper Aircraft compound. Cummings was using the alias of Mark Clark.

Cummings was the president of the CIA-related Interarms Corporation of Virginia, the largest small-arms company in the world. Cummings had been in Costa Rica on a sensitive CIA mission to provide arms for dissident groups. One of the meetings resulted in two locals being killed and Cummings charged with their murder. Cummings was the brother-in-law of Senator John Tower, who was implicated in the CIA October Surprise operation and other CIA operations in South America.

Extracting Cummings was utmost priority to the CIA, as failure could expose a highly sensitive operation. The CIA had given orders that Cummings was either to be extracted from Costa Rica, or killed to silence him.

Among the people involved in the extraction were William P. Clark, Reagan's National Security Adviser, who was in Costa Rica at that time; Joseph Fernandez, a close friend of George Bush and who later became CIA station chief in Costa Rica; and Felix Rodriguez, who was a veteran of the CIA Bay of Pigs fiasco. Parker stated that another person working with him was Martha Honey, who would later write several books on the CIA involvement in Central America.

Bowen gave me many details about the CIA drug trafficking. He stated that he was in CIA drug trafficking in the Middle East from 1950, then in the Golden Triangle area in the 1960s, and in Central and South America during the 1970s and early 1980s.

The frequent cross-questioning of CIA and DEA personnel confirmed that Bowen was with the CIA and in drug trafficking, and Bowen's statements to me often confirmed the CIA role played by my other confidants. Much of this information was given during question and answer sessions, but also in a pilot-to-pilot manner. No embellishment; but routine conversations concerning routine piloting activities. None tried to impress me. They simply stated facts.

Bowen described his dealings with the Medellin and Cali drug cartels as a CIA operative, and the role played by the Mossad in these dealings. Bowen was a friend of Theordore Shackley, a CIA kingpin in CIA drug activities, working closely with the cartels, eventually making Medellin his permanent residence. Bowen stated that the CIA provided Theodore Shackley the alias of Robert E. "Bob" Haynes. Bowen worked with Shackley from 1979 to 1984, and they occasionally at each other's home: Bowen's home in Miami and Shackley's home in Medellin, Colombia. Early in their relationship Shackley was on board a C-46 aircraft flown by Bowen when an engine failure forced them to crash-land high in the Andes on the eastern side of Venezuela. But since Shackley was deeply involved in Columbian drug trafficking I thought that this call could have undesirable repercussions.

Bowen described one of the CIA proprietaries operated by Shackley, INTERKREDIT, with offices in Medellin, Amsterdam, and Ft. Lauderdale, Florida. Shackley helped manage the extensive CIA drug operations in the Golden Triangle Area and was the executive director of the CIA Phoenix program that murdered over 40,000 Vietnamese civilians.

Shackley directed the CIA's secret war against Laos in the mid-1960s and later became chief of station in Saigon. He directed the operation known as "TRACK II," which led to the overthrow of the Salvador Allende government in Chile in 1973. He directed the transfer of tens of millions if not billions of dollars received from the CIA-promoted heroin trade in the Golden Triangle of Burma, Thailand, and Laos. He was just the man to coordinate the CIA's development of the burgeoning drug trafficking from Central and South America into the United States.

Bowen gave me details of the CIA ties to the Medellin drug cartel that Russbacher and Parker had stated to me earlier. Each gave me details of the formation of the Medellin cartel from another perspective.

Parker had earlier stated to me that Ochoa's sister, Leona, had been kidnapped as part of the CIA's plan to bring together the various drug traffickers in Columbia into a single group, thinking that her kidnapping would bring Ochoa to the bargaining table. Parker gave Columbia's M-19 group three million dollars to carry out the kidnapping. Bowen said that he flew the DC-3 aircraft that flew Ochoa's sister, from a small dirt airstrip near Bogota, Columbia (after Leona was kidnapped), to a dirt strip at Ipiales, in the southwestern part of Colombia, near Paso. After she deplaned, Bowen flew to a dirt airstrip at Paso. Ironically, several years later, Leona married Shackley, and Bowen was a frequent visitor to their home in Medellin. I asked, "Isn't it awkward to visit the home of a woman that you helped kidnap?" Bowen shrugged off this strange situation, stating "kidnapping is an accepted practice in Columbia."

UNUSUAL ATTEMPT TO EXPOSE
CIA DRUG TRAFFICKING

Bowen, like many other CIA operatives, became disenchanted with the CIA drug trafficking. In 1981 he wrote anonymous letters to U.S. Customs in Miami, reporting the details of the drug operation in the hope that it would be stopped. Nothing happened. During a flight in 1982 he tried another way to get publicity, which backfired on him. Bowen said that he was requested by CIA operative Henry Meierhoffer[323] to fly a trip to Medellin, Colombia, carrying a government undercover agent, and to return with another agent. But when Bowen arrived in Medellin, Shackley placed eight hundred pounds of cocaine on board the return flight, including two hundred pounds belonging to the Mossad, in bags imprinted with the Mossad's triangles resembling the Star of David.

On the return flight to the United States with the cocaine, he decided to land at an airport that had intensive surveillance for drug trafficking, Sylvania Airport in Georgia. His intent was to alert the authorities to the cocaine load, and in his way of thinking, cause the local police to take action against the CIA. This was rather naive, but his heart was in the right place. Bowen was blowing the whistle on the huge international drug operation involving some of the highest officials in the U.S. government. The plan backfired.

Bowen was arrested and charged by Justice Department prosecutors with drug trafficking. Before the trial started in November 1984, Justice Department officials transferred Bowen to the U.S. prison hospital at Springfield, Missouri, where he was frequently injected with Procan, which caused memory loss.

STANDARD SILENCING TACTIC (i.e., felony coverup)

Bowen stated that at his trial in 1985 the U.S. District Judge refused to allow him to have his CIA handlers, including Meierhoffer, appear as

---

[323] On March 2, 1984. Interestingly, Meierhoffer had been an employee of Transocean Airlines in Beirut during the time I was a captain for the airline.

witnesses. The Judge refused to allow him to produce records and testimony showing that he was carrying out CIA activities. My conversations with many CIA and DEA people who were made scapegoats, showed that it is a standard practice by federal judges and Justice Department prosecutors to protect government corruption by denying the accused the witnesses and the evidence needed to show that they were carrying out covert and corrupt government activities.

CIA AND MOSSAD DRUG PRODUCTS

During Bowen's trial, Justice Department prosecutors and the Judge protected the Mossad's role in the drug trafficking by withholding from evidence the two hundred pounds of cocaine with the Mossad's identification on it. If those bags of cocaine were presented as evidence, with the triangles representing the Star of David, serious questions would have been raised, and Bowen's testimony would have taken on a degree of credibility.

The denial of evidence by federal judges is a pattern to cover up for the criminal CIA and DEA activities. Without realizing the pattern, every CIA and DEA person with whom I have talked, and who has been imprisoned, experienced this, and didn't realize it was a pattern. This silencing tactic was inflicted upon Russbacher, Rewald, Riconosciuto, Wilson, and others, some of whom will be identified in later pages.

The court-appointed defender for Bowen displayed the usual lack of aggressiveness, with no desire to make a meaningful attack upon the Justice Department's position. It is probable that the jury felt that Justice Department prosecutors surely would not lie, or bring false charges against an innocent citizen, and convicted Bowen. He was convicted and sentenced to ten years in prison, during which he was sent to Springfield federal prison hospital where he was repeatedly injected with Procan. The prisoners refer to this forced drug injection as "Russian lobotomy," because it reportedly destroys the memory.

Bowen described to me how he was forcibly injected with Procan prior to his trial, which caused memory problems. He described being injected with Procan and other drugs for two and a half years after he was put in prison following the 1985 conviction, in an attempt to destroy his memory and his sanity. I asked, "What happens if you resist taking the shots?" He replied: "Burly guards come in and hold you down, while another prison attendant shoots the drug into you."

ANOTHER DEA CONNECTION

Another one of my informants was a former DEA pilot, Basil Abbott, who had flown drugs from Central and South America for the DEA in DEA aircraft since 1973. Abbott was in federal prison, charged with a parole violation. The parole "violation" consisted of failure to convince the DEA agents that he was not doing anything to violate his parole. The real reason for his arrest was that Abbott had tried to interest the media in his charges that the DEA routinely engages in drug trafficking into the United States.

Abbott gave me a chronology of his DEA employment, starting in 1973. He described receiving pilot training from the DEA's Chief Pilot Bill Coller at the FAA Academy in Oklahoma City, including training for short runway

CIA AND DEA DRUG TRAFFICKING

operations on dirt strips, preparing him to fly drugs in and out of short dirt strips in Central and South America. Classroom training was given, explaining how to avoid radar detection, routes to fly and the hours to fly them to avoid detection by drug interdiction aircraft. Coller trained Abbott in numerous aircraft, including the Cessna 180, 185, 206, 210 and 310; and Piper Aztec, Aerostar and Navajo. Ground training was given on how to survive if forced down in the jungle, and how to ditch the aircraft in the water. He received a DEA flight manual, written by Coller, describing the technique for landing and taking off from unpaved and short runways, as found in Central America.

In addition to English, Abbott spoke Spanish, Swedish, Norwegian, and Danish. He circulated in prominent Central America society, and socialized with well-known personalities, including Alfredo Stroessner in Paraguay.

During Abbott's DEA employment he worked out of DEA offices in Denver and Charleston, and was transferred in 1978 to the DEA facility at Addison Airport, north of Dallas. Coller also operated out of Addison Airport, and was responsible for scheduling DEA flights.

Abbott named other DEA pilots who, acting under DEA orders, flew drug-laden aircraft from Central America to the United States. These included Cesar Rodriguez, Daniel Miranda, and George Phillips, among others. One of his DEA contacts in Panama was Tom Reed, who relayed instructions on drug pickups and related matters. Abbott described a Bolivian 707 that regularly hauled drugs into Panama, with the DEA's knowledge. When Abbott asked his DEA handlers about it, they told him to forget it.

Abbott was ordered by the DEA to fly arms to numerous Central America locations, and in 1982 he flew arms into a dirt strip near Bluefields, Nicaragua, to Miskito Indians. From there he flew to a strip known as B2E, where drugs were loaded, and he returned to the United States, landing at a small airfield near Memphis, Tennessee.

Abbott described DEA pilots flying arms to the M-19 group in Colombia, some of whom were assassinated during these flights. The frequency of drug trafficking flights was revealed by Abbott as he described the large number of aircraft arriving and departing: "It was like Grand Central Station at some airstrips in Belize and Nicaragua."

These flights were profitable for everyone involved, including the pilots. In addition to their government salary, DEA pilots received additional money or perks. Abbott received $60,000 and fifty pounds of pot for this one week of flying to the Miskito Indians.

Abbott described how he and other DEA personnel flew to Santa Cruz, Bolivia, in a Convair 340, setting a trap for the son of the Israeli Ambassador, Sam Weisgal, involving a large shipment of cocaine to the United States. He described flying drug loads out of small landing strips in Nicaragua, Antigua, Honduras, Costa Rica, Salvador, Guatemala, and Mexico. He set up fuel supplies and ground facilities, and regularly bribed local politicians.

When the drug bust occurred several people were killed. The DEA seized the drugs and then reshipped them as if they were DEA loads. Weisgal escaped the drug bust but was later captured. However, he was soon released when Israel complained.

SHADES OF INSLAW

Abbott described a flight to Panama with DEA agent George Phillips.[324] While stopped for fuel at Belize, Phillips opened an aluminum suitcase that held rolls of tapes and disks marked Inslaw. Phillips stated to Abbott that the tapes were money records of a fake company used by a group of drug dealers. This software, called PROMIS, was initially stolen from the Inslaw people by Justice Department officials and their business associates, and then sold to foreign governments and drug cartels.

Abbott described how Justice Department prosecutors kept him from testifying in a sensitive trial by notifying prison authorities that there was a contract out on his life, causing prison officials to put him into isolation, where he was unavailable to give testimony.

Abbott described his frequent contacts with DEA Central America Bureau Chief, Sante Bario, and how the DEA silenced Bario to keep the operations from the public. It is routine to periodically silence CIA and DEA agents every few years after they have learned too much about the drug operations. Bario was one of the victims of this pattern. DEA and Justice Department attorneys charged Bario with federal drug offenses, causing his imprisonment. Bario scheduled many of the DEA drug flights from the DEA facility at Addison Airport near Dallas, and posed a major threat of exposing the operation that could bring down many government officials in the United States.

When brought before U.S. District Judge Fred Shannon in San Antonio, Bario tried to describe his DEA duties and the DEA and CIA drug trafficking. But Justice Department attorneys and the judge blocked him from proceeding. After being returned to his jail cell, a prison guard gave him a strychnine-laced peanut-butter sandwich, causing almost immediate painful convulsions. He died a week later. The official autopsy report covered up for this murder, reporting that Bario died of asphyxiation.

Abbott was also on the list to be silenced. On one flight to Cancun, Mexico, he was seized by Mexican police, jailed, and then interrogated by DEA agents Richard Arnzie, Terry Schultz, Jerry Carter, and Assistant U.S. Attorney (AUSA) John Murphy. When Abbott wouldn't answer the questions, Arnzie had the Mexican police severely beat him, requiring months of hospitalization and care. The DEA and Justice Department charged Abbott with drug trafficking, despite the fact that he carried out the operations under the directions of his DEA handlers, and primarily out of Addison Airport near Dallas.

After his arrest, Abbott pleaded guilty to the charges against him. District Judge Shannon asked him why he pled guilty, knowing that Abbott was a DEA pilot. Abbott replied that he didn't want to end up dead, as DEA pilot Sante Bario. Abbott was afraid that a similar fate would occur to him if he raised the defense of hauling drugs under DEA orders.

---

[324] Phillips was a CIA contract agent assigned to the DEA.

ASSASSINATING ABBOTT'S WIFE

Abbott described acquiring a common-law wife in Sweden, who later bore their child. She moved to the United States and started an import business bringing sweaters into the United States from Norway and Iceland. Abbott feared for the safety of his wife and daughter after the DEA targeted him, and he sent them back to Sweden. While he was in federal prison at Bastrop, near San Antonio, his wife, in Sweden, tried to get media attention on the DEA drug trafficking by talking to Swedish newspapers. She thought that this would focus on how the DEA and Justice Department set up her husband, and possibly bring about his release. Instead, she joined the long list of those who were assassinated, and whose death protected U.S. officials and protected the corruption from being exposed.

After his release on probation, Abbott tried to tell his story of DEA drug trafficking to various network shows, including the Larry King Show, but all refused to allow him to appear. This is the same complicity of silence that other whistleblowers and I encountered, making possible the continuation of the massive financial and social devastation upon the American people. Almost every government and non-government check and balance that had a duty to receive our evidence prevented us from doing it. Put another way, they were guilty of federal crimes, including complicity and felony coverup.

One source did respond to Abbott's efforts: the DEA, FBI, and Department of Justice. They fabricated a reason for arresting Abbott while on probation, stating that he failed to convince them that he was not violating his parole conditions. This time Abbott was going to raise the defense that resulted in Bario's death. Abbott was going to testify about the DEA drug activities. Justice Department officials addressed this issue by having their psychologists report that Abbott was not mentally competent to stand trial, which then permitted the Justice Department gang to incarcerate him indefinitely.

Abbott sent me many letters detailing the DEA drug operations, including maps of landing sites, people he contacted, and other DEA pilots. His grief over his wife's assassination, and the constant attempts to silence him, made him determined to expose the operation.

OPERATION BUY BACK (BB)

Abbott described an operation, which Russbacher enlarged upon, involving smuggling drugs in frozen shrimp, using a CIA front company, Pacific Seafood Transportation Company. Russbacher and other CIA operatives confirmed the drug trafficking by Pacific Seafood. Russbacher stated that shrimp containers "were filled with ice, and everything but shrimp." He stated that it was a joint DEA-CIA operation called Operation Buy Back (BB).

Russbacher also confirmed what Abbott had said, that the operation involved stolen aircraft. They described how the stolen aircraft were repainted and new serial numbers applied, after which they were flown to Central and South American with loads of arms. Abbott said that he flew several of these planes to Central America on orders of his DEA handlers out of Addison Airport.

ENLARGEMENT ON EARLIER DISCOVERIES

The large number of CIA and DEA informants, and private investigators, that contacted me, made it possible to enlarge upon what earlier informants had said, and also confirm the information. Russbacher enlarged upon Operation Indigo which Parker had told me and which was described in Parker's court filings.[325] Referring to Operation Indigo, He said that the full name was Operation Indigo Sky, and confirmed that it had been in operation since approximately 1976. Russbacher stated that the operation consists of producing heroin in poppy fields in Nigeria and processing in the capital city of Lagos, along with transportation to Europe and the United States.

Russbacher stated that the intent of Operation Indigo Sky was to get an alternate source of supply for heroin coming from the Golden Triangle area and the Indian subcontinent. The operation started with the 1976 purchase of the Star Brewery in Lagos and its subsequent multi-million-dollar upgrade into a heroin processing facility. The brewery's name was changed to Star of Nigeria and then to Red Star. The transportation of the drugs from Lagos was initially by the CIA and DEA and then changed to contract operators. Most of the processed drugs in Operation Indigo Sky went from Lagos to Amsterdam, where it was further packaged and then shipped to European and United States destinations.

Russbacher described different ways the drugs are shipped into the United States, including in sealed containers leased from Phillips Electronics. He described ways of circumventing customs inspections in the United States, and those incidents in which Customs and the DEA protected the drug shipments. He described the swapping of sealed containers at bonded warehouses in Hoboken, New Jersey, and other locations, and the secret unloading of drugs at airfields throughout the United States, including Boeing Field in Seattle.

CRUEL HOAX UPON THE AMERICAN PEOPLE

On Memorial Day the nation honors the 58,000 Gis killed in the CIA-initiated and directed Vietnam War. The mass media says virtually nothing about the ugly side of that war, in which Gis were cannon-fodder, and used to protect and escalate the drug trafficking into the United States.

Even in death Gis were used by the CIA. An officer heading a group of investigators from the army's Criminal Investigation Division uncovered a large-scale heroin smuggling scheme. The group filed reports with the Pentagon, describing how the bodies of dead Gis were gutted, and filled with sacks of heroin. Approximately fifty pounds of heroin with a multi-million-dollar street value were stuffed into each body. Documents accompanying the drug-filled corpses were coded so that people at Air Force Bases in the United Stated, including Travis and Norton, could remove the drugs upon arrival in California.

In typical fashion, revealed throughout these pages, the military hierarchy reacted to the report by disbanding the investigative team. Other reports, plus those given to me by my CIA contacts, provide further confirmation of this

---

[325] U.S. District Court, Denver, United States of America vs. Trenton H. Parker, No. 93-CR-43.

sordid practice. This coverup made possible the continued drug smuggling, and constituted criminal coverup.

Crates returning to the United States from Vietnam on military aircraft often contained bags of heroin, and the coded labels falsely indicated the contents were military supplies. The coverup by the military, the CIA, and the Justice Department, were part of the overall epidemic.

These aspects of the CIA-initiated and directed Vietnam War, and the debauchery of American Gis, were never addressed at Memorial Day ceremonies. Instead, the American public was led to believe that the hundreds of thousands of dead, maimed, and injured Americans suffered for an honorable cause, protecting the United States.

Even the heads of veteran organizations, including the Veterans of Foreign Wars and the American Legion, withheld this information from their members.

This is not to discredit those brave men and women who were ordered into battle and who endured such terrible fear, injury, and death. But the American public must wake up, to realize that the extreme losses in human life and dignity were a farce perpetrated upon them.

FURTHER CONFIRMATION OF CUSTOMS
INVOLVEMENT IN DRUG TRAFFICKING

Further support for the DEA and CIA informants who reported cooperation by U.S. Customs agents in drug trafficking was provided by an Associated Press (AP) story on May 3, 1993. The article described an eight-volume file prepared in December 1990, that disappeared from a final Washington report in 1991. The missing files described "Customs Service drug smuggling" and reported a pattern of drug trafficking by Customs inspectors. This report was sent to Washington, and then removed from government files.

Most newspapers refused to print the AP story. It appeared in the *Oakland Tribune*. Former New York City vice-squad investigator Jim Rothstein, sent me a copy of the report.

It was obvious to me that the drug trafficking by government personnel was overwhelming in size. It was obvious that the media and Congress were covering up for the multi-billion-dollar a year criminal enterprise, as they ignored and covered up for the hundreds of reports by informants.

REFERENCE TO JUSTICE DEPARTMENT
CRIMINALITY IN POLITE TERMS

Larry Smith, chairman of the House Task Force on International Narcotics control said: "I personally am convinced that the Justice Department is against the best interests of the United States in terms of stopping drugs."

DEATH OF A MARINE CORPS WHISTLEBLOWER

There were exceptions to the media coverup of the epidemic drug trafficking involving federal agencies. But these were usually brief and totally incomplete portrayals. A June 17, 1993 television show, Connie Chung's premier *Eye To Eye*, addressed the matter of assassination of an informant and drug trafficking into the United States in military aircraft. The show focused initially on a Marine Corps pilot, Colonel James Sabow, assassinated in his on-base housing several days before exposing large-scale CIA drug trafficking using military aircraft. He was shot in the mouth.

One of the guests, a pilot and former Army captain, Tosh Plumlee, admitted he flew many flights loaded with cocaine from Central America into Air Force bases. Some of these military bases were named by my CIA contacts: Homestead Air Force Base; China Lake; Twenty-nine Palms. He stated that he flew civilian and military aircraft into these bases, and flew for the CIA and other government agencies.

Plumlee said that he testified to senate investigators in closed-door sessions. Numerous pilots had done the same over the years, establishing beyond doubt that drug trafficking directed by federal officials did in fact exist. In every case members of the House and Senate covered up this pattern of criminality that, if exposed by Congress, would topple many in control of the federal government, and adversely affect thousands of people and companies that thrive on the racketeering enterprises.

He said that the excuse given to the military pilots flying the drugs into the United States was that they were part of a sting operation to capture drug traffickers. But when the operation continued without arrests, some of the pilots wondered if they were being misled.

A private investigator and former military investigator, Gene Wheaton, appeared on the show, confirmed on the broadcast that he had discovered this to be true. He also made reference to the shipment of arms to both sides in the Nicaraguan war.

The military tried to make Sabow's killing look like a suicide, even though there were no fingerprints on the shotgun found next to the body. The victim's brother, Dr. David Sabow, a neurologist, said on the show: "There's no question in my mind that this [killing] was ordered by the military, it was carried out by the military. He was set up by the military and by people he knew very, very well. I will prove it."

MURDERS OF GI INFORMANTS LISTED AS SUICIDES?

It is believed that many military people are listed as suicides when in reality they were reportedly killed after threatening to expose epidemic drug trafficking in the U.S. military. Relatives of U.S. servicemen, who military officials said committed suicide, formed an organization called *Until We Have Answers*, and demanded investigations into the deaths.[326] The number of questionable suicides represented by the families was seventy-two in late 1993. Congressmen David Levy (R-NY) and Frank Pallone (D-NJ) requested that Secretary of Defense Les Aspin direct the Department of Defense to conduct investigations into the deaths. They also added a rider to the Defense Authorization Bill requiring the DOD inspector general to reinvestigate any finding of suicide, if requested by the family.

Air Force Captain Edward Consuegra disappeared in December 1992, after he discovered serious irregularities in a government contract with Unisys Corporation. That contract had been arranged by a former CIA official,

---

[326] *Unclassified*, October-November 1993.

Deputy Director of the CIA, Frank Carlucci.

Unclassified wrote that there were "eerie similarities to the INSLAW case here." They pointed out that in each case there was a major computer contract; large scale corruption involving a government official with intelligence agency connections; and a person who learned too much and who threatened to expose the criminality.

ANOTHER TELEVISION EXPOSÉ

The television show, *60-Minutes*, airing on November 21, 1993, filmed several DEA official and agents describing smuggling of large quantities of cocaine by the CIA into the United States. DEA agent Annabelle Grimm said on the show: "I really take great exception to the fact that 1,000 kilos came [into the United States], funded by U.S. taxpayer money. I found that particularly appalling."

The CIA conspired with Venezuelan officials, including General Ramon Guillen Davila, to bring in the drugs in CIA-controlled aircraft. General Guillen was head of a joint CIA-Venezuelan task force dealing in drug trafficking.

The CIA, made aware of the *60-Minutes* show ahead of time, quickly issued a statement on November 19, implying that the drug shipment was an accident rather than an intentional act.[327] Many people, and much planning, was required to smuggle this huge quantity of nearly pure cocaine into the United States, and bring about its sale. There was nothing accidental about this complex operation.

Making reference to the CIA statement that the CIA smuggling, distribution, and selling of the ton of pure cocaine was an isolated incident, my CIA contacts laughed. They recognized that the ton of cocaine to which the CIA had to make reference was only a small part of the CIA-drug smuggling operation.

The CIA tried to show that it took corrective action when this multi-million-dollar operation was discovered, stating that one CIA officer resigned, and a second had been disciplined. Many people implicated in a drug sale, even as little as one pound, or one ounce, even if the person was only present when others were talking about it, have been sentenced to many years in federal prison. When the same offense is committed by a government official or agent, the offense becomes far worse, and calls for much longer prison sentences. Since Justice Department officials covered up for the drug trafficking, and since they are the only officials under our form of government that can prosecute for federal crimes, the criminal conduct by federal officials go unpunished.

Chief State Department official responsible for overseeing international narcotics matters, Melvin Levitsky, explained that an indictment against General Guillen would require the United States to cut off aid to Venezuela, and therefore no charges should be filed. Much of the world's coca, from which cocaine is obtained, is grown in Bolivia, Peru, and Venezuela, and

---

[327] *New York Times*, November 20, 1993.

constitute a major part of their income. This fact is no secret to the CIA, and the CIA relies upon this source for much of its cocaine smuggling into the United States.

Obviously, great financial and physical harm is inflicted upon the American people by the drug trafficking. A giant hoax is being played upon the American people by the so-called multi-billion-dollar-a-year drug war financed by the U.S. taxpayer. The fact that hundreds of federal officials are involved in the drug trafficking into the United States, including the nation's highest "law-enforcement" agency, indicates the magnitude of the subversive activities against the United States.

Very few newspapers reported anything related to the CIA statement, the charges made on the *60 Minutes* show, or the significance of the serious charges. They covered up.

BIZARRE ASPECT OF U.S.
TAXPAYER-FUNDED DRUG TRAFFICKING

One of the most bizarre aspects of the epidemic drug trafficking into the United States by the CIA and its co-conspirators in other government agencies is the ignorance by the average American of its existence. Many airline pilots, including myself, have been aware of the CIA involvement in the drug trafficking since the early 1950s. Dozens of people directly involved in the drug trafficking have testified to members of Congress (usually in closed-door hearings) of the drug trafficking. Hundreds of letters have been sent to members of Congress by informants describing the specifics of the drug trafficking and the involvement of people in control of the federal government. Dozens of highly documented books have been written about the subject by people who either investigated the subject or who were pilots involved in the drug trafficking. I sent petitions via certified mail to members of Congress since 1991 describing the operation and demanding that they receive the testimony and evidence of our small group of former government investigators or present and former CIA personnel. The only people who don't know about the sinister practice by government personnel, whose criminal conduct they fund as taxpayers, are the majority of the American people.

Another bizarre aspect of the CIA-generated drug epidemic is that the American taxpayers are paying the salaries and government-related costs associated with the drug smuggling. Thousands of American citizens are incarcerated, some for the remainder of their lives, and many of them fraudulently, as a result of the CIA-generated and taxpayers-funded smuggling.

INVADING A FOREIGN COUNTRY AND KILLING ITS
CITIZENS ON THE BASIS OF DRUG TRAFFICKING

President George Bush ordered the invasion of Panama to capture and bring to the United States Manuel Noriega, on the pretense of halting drug trafficking. Noriega did in fact aid in drug trafficking, assisting the CIA, DEA and other U.S. entities, and the Mossad. He assisted Oliver North and his associates, including Vice President Bush, in the unlawful arms flow to Central America and the drug-laden aircraft returning to the United States. Much has been written, and much testimony has been given, removing any doubt of these joint activities. The actual reason for President Bush's invasion of Panama is only speculation at this time. The Panama invasion cost the lives of twenty-six American servicemen and hundreds of Panamanians.

REPLACING NORIEGA WITH A TEAM
HEAVILY INVOLVED IN DRUG ACTIVITIES

The drug trafficking didn't stop with Noriega's kidnapping. The Bush Administration arranged for the new President of Panama to be Guillermo Endura, President of a Panamanian bank extensively used by Columbia's Medellin drug cartel. The formation of this cartel was orchestrated by the CIA. Two of my key informants, Gunther Russbacher and Trenton Parker, played key roles. Picked for vice president was Guillermo Ford, part owner of the Dadeland Bank of Florida. He reportedly was heavily involved in drug-money laundering. Ford was also Chairman of Panama's Banking Commission. Another official selected by the Bush administration was Rogello Cruz to be Attorney General of Panama.

The New York Times said of Michael Harari in a January 2, 1990 article: *An Israeli reputed to be Gen. Manuel Antonio Noriega's closest associate may have eluded capture on the night of the United States invasion because he was warned to flee six hours before the American troops swept into the capital, the deputy commander of Panama's new police force said today ....*"

Harari, working closely with Noriega in the drug trafficking, undoubtedly warned Noriega of the impending attack, which undoubtedly played a role in the casualties suffered by the invaders. Twenty-six American Gis were killed, but this is still small in comparison to the hundreds of innocent people killed in Panama as a result of President Bush's invasion orders. Compounding the harm inflicted upon Panama, the American public will pay over a billion dollars in taxes for aid sent to Panama after the U.S. invasion.

Harari, a Mossad colonel, was well known in Europe and elsewhere as one of Mossad's primary killers. He carried out numerous assassinations in Europe. After killing a waiter by mistake in Sweden, Israel sent him to Central America, where he took control of the Mossad's widespread drug trafficking, collaborating with U.S. personnel in shipments to the United States. Speaking of Israeli control of Panamanian drug activities, the *Washington Jewish Week* stated (December 28, 1989):

[The Israelis in Panama] do not reflect well on Israel or the Panama Jewish community ... They are engaged in contraband and money laundering. In general, they engage in very aggressive and unfair business practices.

The mainstream press has made possible the escalating drug trafficking by the CIA, DEA, the military, and other federal personnel and agencies. The overwhelming amount of testimony and charges made by these people over the years couldn't leave doubt in anyone's mind that these facts were true. The mainstream media kept the lid on this awesome criminality.

Numerous CIA operatives have written about the criminal activities of the CIA. Phillip Agee, for instance, has written books describing the CIA drug trafficking. Agee had been with the CIA for many years. The *Associated Press* printed quotes (January 29, 1990) from Agee's speech at Oregon State University in Corvallis: "Bush is up to his neck in illegal drug running on behalf of the Contras."

Much of the heroin entering the United States comes from Southeast Asia in the Golden Triangle area. A March 26, 1990 *U.S. News & World Report* article stated:

> For more than a decade, Khun Sa, the warlord of opium, has flooded Washington with offers to end the poppy production within his Golden Triangle fiefdom in exchange for financial aid. The U.S. has not responded, and this year the region's crop could double from the levels of just a few years ago. Att. Gen. Dick Thornburgh unsealed an indictment against the man considered responsible for 40 percent of the U.S. heroin supply. But Sa is not likely to be booked soon. In the remote hills of Burma, a private army of thousands protect him.

LARGEST HEROIN SEIZURE IN U.S. HISTORY–
Another CIA Operation

Much of what is written in the media is not what it seems. In May 1991 federal agents seized over 1,000 pounds of heroin in an Oakland, California, warehouse, the largest heroin seizure in the nation's history. Due to the compartmentalization common to intelligence agencies, the arresting agents were unaware that they interrupted a large-scale drug smuggling operation involving the CIA and other government agencies.

Five people were charged with importing heroin, possession with intent to distribute heroin, and conspiracy. A subtitle to a *San Francisco Examiner* article describing the case stated that it was the "largest-ever seizure." Over 1,000 pounds of high-grad "China White" heroin was smuggled into the Port of Oakland from Taiwan.

The 1989 seizure of the largest quantity of China White heroin involved the arrest of two families from Thailand living in Danville, California. The case was assigned to Judge Vaughn Walker,[328] the same judge that was handling the contempt of court case filed against me for having sought to report the criminality that I discovered. His actions and those of the Justice Department attorneys, as the case proceeded, showed evidence of covering up the drug operation. Apparently, they discovered that the drug seizure involved an ongoing CIA drug smuggling operation, and they now had to keep the lid on the drug seizure and avoid a publicity-generating trial.

COMMON PRACTICE OF JUDICIAL AND JUSTICE DEPARTMENT OBSTRUCTION OF JUSTICE

Despite this being the biggest heroin seizure in the nation's history, Justice Department prosecutors and District Judge Vaughn Walker approved a lenient sentence for most of the defendants. Through a plea agreement reached in July 1993, the defendants pled guilty in exchange for probation or a short prison sentence. Several of the defendants pled guilty to knowing a federal crime had been committed and failing to promptly report it to federal authorities. This

---

[328] *USA vs Chen, et al.*, CR 91-2096 VRW.

offense violated federal criminal statute Title 18 U.S.C. Section 4. This plea agreement with its lenient terms eliminated a trial that could have exposed high-level government connections to the heroin operation.

IRONIC CONTRADICTION

Judge Walker was approving the charge of misprision of a felony against several of the drug trafficking participants for failure to report the federal crimes. At the same time, he was holding me under virtual house arrest, since December 1990, while I waited for a trial on a criminal contempt of court charge for having sought to report the federal crimes I had discovered.

U.S. District Judge Marilyn Patel had me arrested in November 1990 on criminal contempt of court charges for complying with federal crime-reporting statutes. Simultaneously, Judge Walker was charging the participants in the nation's largest heroin smuggling operation with misprision of a felony for not reporting the criminal activities in which they were implicated, and then granting them short or no prison sentences.

Aware of the involvement of federal personnel in drug trafficking into the United States, and suspecting this heroin case may be another government-funded drug operation, I asked Russbacher if he knew anything about it. During the late 1980s Russbacher had been assigned by the CIA to coordinate government-related drug trafficking through the West Coast. This involved monitoring and protecting the drug operations coming into the states of California, Oregon, and Nevada. With this knowledge of government-directed and funded drug trafficking I asked Russbacher if he knew anything the heroin seizure. He said he did.

He gave me details about the operation that he would not know unless he was involved in its operation. Even though he was in prison when I asked, Russbacher was in frequent touch with CIA personnel and kept up to date on covert activities.

OPERATION NEW WAVE

Starting on August 23, 1993, Russbacher told me about the operation, that it was a major heroin trafficking operation into the United States, and that the code name for the parent operation was Operation New Wave. A part of that operation was called Operation Backlash.

Russbacher stated that the operation, sanctioned on September 21, 1987, originated in San Francisco, and operated out of the offices of Levi International Imports-Pier 51. He then gave me the names of many key participants in the operation. He said that key personnel from the CIA included David Fuller from Los Angeles; John Beardsley from Mississippi, and Patrick O'Riley from New York City.

He said that those involved from the U.S. Department of Justice included Russ Taylor out of Lincoln, Nebraska; Saul Trattafiore out of Williamsport; and Sandy Weingarten out of St. Louis. Russbacher stated that they were all attorneys, and he believed, also Assistant U.S. Attorneys.

Drug Enforcement Administration participants in the drug operation, according to Russbacher, included Michael Cobb out of Orlando, Florida, and John David Pigg out of Oklahoma City. Pigg was killed in July 1993 in Anadarko, Oklahoma, reportedly for expressing disenchantment with the operation.

Russbacher described Navy Task Force liaison personnel as himself, using his navy alias of Robert Andrew Walker; John A. Woodruff (CIA person using that alias, and who is now deceased); Jason A. Winters (CIA person using that alias).

Referring to Customs, Russbacher identified key participants as David Cohen out of the El Paso office; Precilla Montemajor out of the San Francisco office; Taulyn Weber, also out of the San Francisco office; Brett Sanderson out of the Seattle office.

NAMING MOSSAD AGENTS

During a telephone conversation on September 6, 1993, Russbacher gave me the names of the Mossad personnel implicated in this drug trafficking operation, who handled drug distribution in the San Francisco area.

First name, is Robert Silberman, out of Chicago. Second name is Marta Bleiberg, also out of Chicago. Third name, Simon, last name Goldblatt, he is out of Heifa and attached to New York. Fourth name, Ariel Colderman, San Francisco. Fifth one is Kasam Merchant, out of Los Angeles. Sixth one is David Turner, San Jose. Silberman and Bleiberg work for a company called Edeco.

Goldblatt is a field supervisor on Operation White Elephant.

The next one, the last three, are attached to Operation Lemgolem.

I stated that I would list their names in the next edition of *Defrauding America*, and he warned me about the viciousness of the Mossad and their killing of people in various countries whose statements or conduct displeased them. "I have no use for the Mossad and the harm they've inflicted upon the United States, and I'll take my chances," was my reply.

IMPLICATIONS OF THE MOSSAD'S INVOLVEMENT

The repeated discovery that the intelligence agency of a foreign country, Israel, was heavily involved in several of the drug operations conducted against the American people by America's intelligence agencies was disturbing. Throughout my discoveries I learned of the involvement of Mossad agents and assets in operations inflicting great harm against the United States and the American people. Drug trafficking, October Surprise, the theft of the Inslaw software, looting of Chapter 11 assets, and more.

Examples of corruption given within these pages are only a fraction of what I discovered during thirty years of investigations, whether it be related to aviation fraud or any other segment of criminal activities described within these pages. The involvement of the Mossad and Israeli personnel, including those who became American citizens, repeatedly came to my attention, and much of it has not been identified within these pages because of limited time available.

Russbacher described the intent of the operation: bringing heroin to the United States from the Far East, using freighters, cruise-line transports, and other international lines. The ships would bring heroin from Far East ports through Central America, sometimes through northern South America, and then into the United States. Some of the intermediate points included Acapulco, Mazatlan, Sewantenego, Cabo San Lucas, and Ensenada.

United States ports included San Diego, Los Angeles, San Francisco, and Seattle. At San Diego, a transshipment point, non-military vessels went to the federal port known as O-1, District 00.01. In Los Angeles they used the Long Beach basin.

Also used were tankers, including the Greek tanker line, Orion, which docked at Manhatten Beach, California. The oldest freighters would normally be Pan American or Iberian registry.

Drugs were also transshipped from Columbia, many times in ships of Norwegian registry, until 1989, and these were mostly cruise ships. Russbacher described the method of packing drugs on ships:

On the cruise liners it was generally in the freezers, brought on board inside carcasses of beef. Also in the flour bags, 100 pound bags. They are referred to as flower barrels. On the other types of ships it was either stored in the paint lockers or there was a separate compartment built.

I asked, "What is the remuneration or rewards for the different agencies that are involved in this operation?" Russbacher stated that there is a "split profit sharing" where the profits are divided among various proprietaries or front companies used by the different agencies.

The drug trafficking operation was coded as NW 688-01-B-NSC, and called Operation New Wave. One segment was named Operation Backlash, and coded BL421-D-06. Russbacher stated the operation was still active, but limited to the DEA and Customs involvement. He said the CIA and Department of Justice dropped from active participation in March 1993, except for the criminal prosecutions in San Diego and San Francisco that had to be eliminated.

I asked Russbacher why the Department of Justice filed those charges when the filings might expose involvement of Justice Department personnel. He said that the many individual fiefdoms in the CIA, Justice Department, and other agencies, and the compartmentalizing of information, results in charges being filed by a local office against a person or operation that may be sanctioned by high officials.

Since the defendants in the San Francisco action were from Thailand I asked Russbacher how that country fits into the operation. He said the drug shipper in Thailand was a CIA front called Van Der Bergen International Shippers in Bangkok. "They're the ones that are responsible for gathering [the drugs] out of Southeast Asia," He said.

Russbacher said that Hong Kong was sought as a drug shipment point:

But they [CIA] couldn't get an agreement going with the British out of Hong Kong. The problem was, they wanted a higher percentile participation than our government was prepared to give. Instead of using Hong Kong, we used Macaw. Eighty percent of the morphine block, we are not talking about the liquid, comes out of Macaw, before it becomes morphine sulphate.

Many books have described the decades of British drug trafficking, originally through the British East India Tea Company, which still exists. Russbacher described the large amount of drugs shipped from the Philippines in the operation.

MOSSAD'S ROLE IN THE OPERATION

Russbacher described the role played by the Mossad in the drug trafficking into the United States in Operation New Wave and Operation Back Lash. He stated the Mossad's role was to guard the shipments until they reached the United States, adding that one of his Mossad contacts was Delilah Kaufman, a para-legal with an Italian law firm in the San Francisco Bay Area.

In 1991, part of the operations were suspended due to increased awareness at the southern transshipment ports. More federal funds were allocated for DEA and Customs agents, and smuggling by the DEA and Customs was compromised. Even though the drug trafficking involved personnel from almost every federal agency responsible to prevent such trafficking, the smuggling is compartmentalized. With the addition of new DEA and Customs agents, the danger of discovery increased.

FEDERAL JUDGE RECEIVING BRIBE MONEY?

Because of U.S. District Judge Vaughn Walker's extremely lenient sentences given to most of the Thai defendants charged with the largest known heroin shipment in the nation's history I asked Russbacher: "Do you know where Judge Vaughn Walker fits into this operation?" Russbacher replied: "He is one of the people getting a payoff."

"Through Shamrock [Overseas Disbursement Corporation]?" I asked.

"Through Shamrock, yes."

"And you know this to be a fact? Did you see this on a printout, or did he simply tell you that?"

"Rodney, I was very very strong in this. I basically baby-sat the operation for about four months. I don't want to go into it."

"Did you have any conversations with Walker," I asked?

"No, I did not. But a woman by the name of Denise Stedman, out of the San Francisco [CIA office] had numerous conversations with him. She is the one we used."

Discovering this operation, and discovering another U.S. District Judge reportedly receiving bribe money, fit with the information I had from other CIA personnel. It also fit with what Russbacher had told me during the past several years.

Judge Walker had me under virtual house arrest since December 10, 1990. While I awaited trial on contempt of court charges for having filed a federal action in Chicago seeking to report the federal crimes implicating federal personnel, especially in the Ninth Circuit federal courts, which includes the San Francisco area. Now that I had information linking Walker to the CIA, DEA, Customs, and Justice Department drug operation I decided to file another report under federal crime-reporting statutes.

CROSS-CHECKING AND CONFIRMATION

These new deep-cover intelligence agency people provided confirmation of each other's status and of the statements given to me by others, and this included Gunther Russbacher. Further, as other covert operatives gave me information about the criminal and subversive activities of officials in control of federal agencies and operations, Russbacher loosened up and exposed sensitive and corrupt activities of which he had knowledge.

CIA-ENGINEERED WARS AND DRUG TRAFFICKING

The CIA-engineered Vietnam War provided the logistics making possible massive transportation of drugs from the Golden Triangle area of Asia into the United States. The CIA-engineered conflict in Nicaragua resulted in and made possible massive transportation of drugs from Central and South America into the United States. These developed into multi-billion-dollar-a-year profits for the CIA. Most of the profits were reportedly hidden in off-shore financial institutions. It is no longer far-fetched to consider that the CIA may have deliberately generated these conflicts primarily to develop its drug trafficking operation into the United States. Nor is it far-fetched to consider that these acts and consequences may be part of a scheme to financially and morally destroy the United States.

The mindset within the CIA, including the Phoenix Program that assassinated 40,000 Vietnam villagers, the Vietnam war that killed millions, and the CIA's massive drug trafficking into the United States, is such that deliberate infliction of harm against Americans, and people of other countries, cannot be questioned.

OPERATION AMERAID

After the Vietnam and Contra wars ended, and heavy military traffic not available to smuggle drugs into the United States, the CIA used CIA proprietary and cutout aircraft and ships. This was called Operation Ameraid.

STATE DEPARTMENT & CIA INFORMANT

In late 1993 Navy SEAL Commander Robert Hunt put me in contact with another deep-cover CIA operative and State Department employee, Michael Maholy, whose primary duty was monitoring cable traffic at different CIA locations. Maholy commenced giving me information and a different slant on the role of federal officials in drug trafficking from Central and South America into the United States. At first, Maholy didn't want to talk about these activities, but he was subsequently encouraged to do so by Hunt. (Hunt will be described in later pages.)

Maholy was liaison officer for the U.S. Embassy in Panama and worked for the U.S. State Department and CIA for over two decades. Maholy wrote in one of his letters about his role at the U.S. Embassy, and his frequent contacts with Oliver North and Commander Hunt.

I have spent time in South American countries, providing photos, documents, maps, and all intel. for the U.S. embassies in Central and South America. I first became acquainted with agent Hunt in 1985 in Panama where I was the liaison officer for the U.S. Embassy. He was always accompanied by [Oliver] North and his team. This went on for several years. I recall reading cable traffic where his name came up repeatedly.

Maholy described the drug trafficking involving the CIA and the State Department:

Hunt was on several covert missions and detached to Operation Whale Watch, which involved me buying drugs from Colombians and trading them for arms and ammo. My part in the operation was to provide a

cover or front through the use of offshore oil rigs, so that Hunt, myself, and others, could complete these transactions. These offshore oil-rigs were all CIA offshore geological survey and logistics services.
Other letters followed, and included considerable:

During my contacts with [CIA Director] William Casey I was drafted into the Southern Zone (Central and South American countries) so that we could start operations on spying on Panama, Columbia, and other countries that were making huge amounts of money from drugs. They needed weapons and fire power. We, the CIA, provided them. They in turn sold us drugs. ... many instances of cover-up conspiracies that continue to multiply as we are talking.

On one tour to South America, while working on a CIA-owned oil rig, the company called Rowan International, based in Houston, Texas, is a world-wide drilling exploration company, with very friendly liaisons in Center America and South America, as well as Africa and Middle East. ... While in Balboa Harbor off the coast of Panama, on the rig Rowan Houston, at approximately 2:00 a.m., a helicopter landed on the heliport, and I was monitoring cables and traffic, when our radar also detected a small support group which turned out to be patrol boats, four in all. At this point I thought the rig was going to be overtaken by hostile. But instead I could not believe who was getting out of the chopper: it was Noriega and another man. I contacted the "company man" and he informed me that this meeting was not to be documented and to go back and resume the task of cable and traffic. I found out later that this man with Noriega was [Mossad agent] Michael Harari. I found out later that they were trying to raise money from CIA by selling drugs to plan the destruction of a hydro-electric power plant on the Orinoco River in Venezuela. ... Bob [Hunt] was responsible for saving my life. The government used me until I was used up.

Over a period of many months, Maholy gave me details of CIA and Mossad drug trafficking. He named the companies owning the oil rigs off the coast of the United States, Central and South America, Nigeria, and Angola: Sante Fe; Zapata; and Rowan. He physically saw Evergreen International Airlines and Southern Air Transport hauling drugs, confirmed by cable traffic he handled.

I had repeatedly heard from various investigators and CIA contacts that various divisions of the Zapata Corporation,[329] such as Zapata Petroleum, Zapata Off-Shore, Zapata Cattle Company, were heavily involved in drug trafficking. The oil rigs were used to carry out the drug operations. Drugs would be off-loaded from ships onto the drilling platforms, and then sent into the nearby coastal areas in helicopters that were constantly carrying supplies and personnel. Maholy confirmed that this practice existed, having learned about it from CIA cable traffic and his own observations while on the rigs.

---

[329] Zapata Corporation is based in Houston, is a CIA asset, and the stock is partly owned by George Bush. Zapata Petroleum was organized by George Bush, who reportedly has major interests in various Zapata divisions.

Maholy described how he was transferred from his detachment in Greenland, under Lt. General John W. Carpenter III, U.S.A.F., to Central America, where he learned about the CIA role in drug trafficking. He also became a standard expendable, as the CIA did to him what they do to most CIA-related assets dealing in drugs. When they learn too much about the operation and pose a threat, the CIA, working hand-in-hand with Justice Department prosecutors, charge the person with a drug offense for having carried out CIA orders.

In another letter Maholy wrote in part:

The real mission [of these oil and gas drilling platforms] was to funnel weapons and money to the Nicaraguans, and also to bring illegal drugs into the United States. Being a CIA-funded mission, the rig had Naval SEAL teams diverted through its location. ... Rowan International was a cover for a branch of Zapata Oil. Zapata Oil and Exploration had many land-based operations in Central and South America as well as offshore rigs.

We had access to military cryptographics, such as the KW 135, the KL 16, KL10 and the CW4 to decode and sifter out any cable traffic from transmissions from Guatemala, El Salvador, Costa Rica, and Panama.

Maholy confirmed what other CIA informants had told me about the CIA drug trafficking through Pacific Seafood. He wrote:

This company [Pacific Seafood] used a number of vessels to carry out covert missions to run weapons, drugs and cash from country to country. Not only would their "shrimp" trawlers use the oil rigs for loading, unloading and refueling, but to deliver large sums of money for aid to the Contras. The shrimpers would constantly converge on our rig to convert, store and transport all of the above. The crews were all seasoned pari-military experts in their abilities to search and destroy, CIA trained and specialists in their fields.

It was from one of the shrimp boat captains that I would come to meet Barry Seal's main right-wing contact from Morgan City, La. His name was Russell Abear, and the name on his shrimp boat was Southern Crossing. This boat had state-of-the-art radar, hi-tech navigation systems, extra fuel tanks, and a crew consisting only of "special forces or [Navy] Seals."

Maholy wrote that he remembers Russell Bowen flying onto the rig and then fly two DEA agents to Columbia. I called Bowen, who lived in Winter Haven, Florida at the time, and asked him about this flight. Bowen confirmed that it was him. He also said that he had frequently talked to Barry Seal and knew Seal's contact by the name of Russell. (Bowen didn't remember Russell's Abear last name.)

Russell was often reluctant to talk about a particular operation in which he was involved, but I could get him to open up if I obtained some information about it from another source. I stated to Bowen that Maholy described having seen him at the oil rig, and Bowen then confirmed it, and stated it was part of the operation that extracted Sam Cummings from Costa Rica.

MOSSAD'S DRUG TRAFFICKING
ON CIA AND ZAPATA OIL PLATFORMS

Maholy stated he had seen drugs on the CIA and [330]Zapata Corporation-owned oil platforms with the Mossad's triangles from the Star of David on them. In one letter he wrote: "A shrimp boat arrived with a load of cocaine with the markings of the Mossad's famous 3 triangles that resembled the Star of David."

Maholy described how the drug planes would fly low and proceed from the off-shore oil rigs to the United States at very slow speeds of approximately 120 knots, so that they would appear on radar as helicopters servicing the rigs. He described how the Ochoa drug family used the CIA oil rigs off the coast for drug transshipments.

Maholy described the role of a Venezuelan naval officer by the name of Lizardo Marquez Perez, as in charge of this drug operation. The role of the Venezuelans in CIA-related drug trafficking was revealed in the *60 Minutes* show on November 21, 1993. Perez frequented many of the oil rigs when Maholy was present.

He described the coverup of the drug operation by Chief of the DEA cocaine operations in Washington, Ron Caffrey, Oliver North, CIA official Dewey Clarridge, Army Lieutenant General Paul Gorman (commander of the Panama-based U.S. Southern Command), and others.

Excerpts from some of his letters are informative:

A person I've met on several occasions was in the Columbia Cartel, Carlos Lehder. During Operation Back Door he and several of his soldiers were planning to use CIA oil rigs and the shrimp industries to import drugs into America. Carlos had DEA personnel assigned to work with him hand and foot. I myself have been to his home on Norman's Cay in the Nassau. He had a stash of drugs shipped back and forth to everglade City in the Ten Thousands Islands area of Southern Florida. When the rig Rowen Midland was in Venezuela, Carlos had a regular agent of his as a tool-pusher to oversee all shipments coming and going. The CIA would buy drugs and supply friends of the Colombian government with money and weapons.

OPERATION BACK DOOR

They used the remote mangrove swamps to unload huge loads of pot and cocaine to get it to Miami to distribute. With help from CIA and DEA agents, Carlos would set up a few loads as decoy to make it look good, therefore he could get major shipments into the United States. Operation Back Door had a priority of grave importance. I was to monitor some of the cable and equipment, also scramble transmissions made from his boats and planes, so he could go undetected. Also to make sure his money could be on the rig when he wanted it. Carlos got to be "mouthing." The government set him up and double crossed him. The rig was then moved to Aruba and once again set up a relay

---

[330] Zapata Corporation was headquartered in Houston, Texas.

*station and command center. The M-19 group was also involved in
several covert missions. Members of their right wing force were
actually flown and boated to Florida to recruit forces and promote a
revolution in the U.S. and an invasion of drugs to Southern Florida.
Operation Back Door simply meant the drugs would come to America
via the back door.*

Maholy described his dealings with drug trafficker Barry Seal, a name that
was an alias for Ellis McKenzie. (Seal had been a pilot for TWA Airlines in
the past.) Maholy stated that Seal was involved with the Noriega Cartel in a
top-secret operation. Seal's Miami contact was a person using the name of
"Lito." Maholy described how Seal had a fleet of aircraft hauling drugs that
flew mostly at night, with the pilots using night-vision goggles. They flew
through airspace "windows" when the military radar would ignore the targets.
As the planes approached the oil rigs off the coast of the United States the
planes flew close to the water, avoiding radar detection. From the oil rights
to the coastline of the United States the planes flew slow, so as to resemble the
speed of the helicopters as seen on the radar screens.

Maholy wrote that Seal was paid large amounts of money by CIA
contacts, and that in 1982 and 1983 Seal brought in more than five thousand
kilos of cocaine, grossing over twenty-five million dollars.

Maholy described his role in Operation Screamer which was a mammoth
sting operation aimed at penetrating the network of mercenary pilots that were
flying drugs in competition with the CIA. On this operation Maholy worked
under DEA agent-in-charge Randy Beasley. Maholy described how Seal
offered to turn informant, allegedly implicating high federal officials,
including former Watergate prosecutor Richard Ben-Vensite. Maholy stated
that "This made Beasley and "Screamer" prosecutor uneasy. Why? Because
they themselves were dirty."

Seal had an informant number, SG1-84-0028. That number, or the initials,
CI–cooperating individuals, would be substituted for Seal's name on all
reports in his case file (which was given the number G1-84-0121).

Maholy stated that a Venezuelan naval officer, Lizardo Marquez Perez,
was in charge of the smuggling operations in Miami, and frequently was seen
on the CIA oil rigs on which Maholy was stationed. Maholy added that there
was a major coverup by Ron Caffrey, Chief of DEA cocaine operations in
Washington, was briefing Oliver North and CIA official Dewey Clarridge
about the drug flights from Nicaragua.

OPERATION WHALE WATCH

Operation Whale Watch was one of the CIA's drug trafficking operations
using CIA-affiliated oil rigs off the coast of the United States and Central and
South America. Maholy described how two oil rigs were deliberately
sabotaged when security was breached and the crews on the rig learned about
the drug trafficking, and voiced their displeasure. Maholy wrote:

*I have information on offshore activities involving the sabotage of two
more drilling rigs involving the deaths of more than 82 persons. One
off the coast of the Yucatan Peninsula in Mexico, and the other off of
the coast of Newfoundland. Both rigs were CIA owned and operated.*

Due to leaks in security they were destroyed by our own government officials.

In the case of the "Ranger I" a semi-submergible deep-water drilling rig, off the coast of Halifax, Newfoundland, the sister company of Exon Oil, Shamrock Drilling, was based out of Ireland. Shamrock Drilling was based out of Ireland. The Shamrock Company was funneling money through "Ranger I" to Canada and was detected by a breach in security. Thus they picked a winter storm as a perfect cover to flood the computerized ballast systems, triggering the rig to list to the port side and sink to the bottom of the North Atlantic. This took place in February 1989 at 3:00 am in the morning. All 42 hands lost. No bodies recovered.

Then there was Operation Odessa. This was a jack-up offshore drilling rig that was stationed off the coast of Nicaragua and had to be moved due to civil unrest of that nation. This was a prime rig where command officers of the CIA had communication offices. I've spent many days and nights reading cable traffic and monitoring daily activities. This rig was a mother ship for distribution of drugs, weapons and money for all parties concerned. The rig moved north because of hostile government takeover. Five days after entering Mexican waters, the rig was blown up. This involved [331]Hunt and his strike team.

This information was intercepted during a non-routine check of all com-sac radio transmissions. I believe the reason was that the Mexican government was paid huge sums of money for the cover-up. Reasons released to the media were "offshore oil platform explodes, all 46 aboard dead."

Over a period of time Maholy furnished me with additional information that made clear the CIA's involvement in drug trafficking into the United States, the details of the operations, the Mossad involvement, and other areas of CIA corrupt activities. I received documents and letters showing Maholy's CIA status. A letter written by the Israeli Embassy in Washington dated October 20, 1993, made reference to the CIA-Mossad drug operation, Operation Whale Watch, stating in part: "These agents [involved in Operation Whale Watch] include: C.I.A. Intelligence Officers Michael Maholy, Dewy Claridge, Steven Tucker, along with two National Security Council (NSC) officers, Lt. Col. Oliver North and Lt. Robert Hunt [and Mossad agent] Michael Harari (Retired)."

Another letter dated October 25, 1993 and sent by the National Security Agency identified Operation Whale Watch and confirmed my contacts as being CIA and part of it. The letter stated in part: "Operatives [include] Special Agent-in-Charge, Michael Maholy, C.I.A. ... Due to the sensitive nature of "Operation Whale Watch" we cannot authorize any further information on this <u>Top-Secret</u> mission."

---

[331] Commander Robert Hunt was Executive Officer of Navy SEAL team Six, and Commanding Officer of Navy SEAL team Two. More about Hunt in later pages.

CROSS-CHECK ON NAMES OF DRUG-SMUGGLERS INVOLVED IN OPERATION NEW WAVE

During one of many conversations describing CIA drug trafficking, Commander Robert Hunt read off a list of people involved in Operation New Wave, the heroin operation described to me by Gunther Russbacher. The names given to me by Hunt included almost all the names Russbacher had listed, including David Fuller, Patrick O'Reilly, Michael Cobb, John Woodruff, Brett Sanderson, and Precilla Montemajor. He named Mossad agents whose names appeared in the San Francisco office with the drug trafficking, including Robert Silberman, Simon Goldblatt, Ariel Colderman, Delila Kaufman, and David Turner. Hunt said Goldblatt was a field supervisor assisted by Marta Bleiblatt. The large number of Mossad agents working with the San Francisco CIA office surprised Hunt.

CONCERN FOR SERIOUS CIA CORRUPTION

Several times Hunt expressed to me his concern for the corruption within the intelligence agencies, which he referred to as "The Company." It was this concern that motivated him to tell me about various operations he found repugnant.

STYMIED INVESTIGATORS

During the 1980s federal investigator William Duncan (IRS) and Arkansas state police investigator Russell Welsh investigated the drug trafficking in Arkansas, and especially around the Mena area. They interviewed many people, including drug trafficker Barry Seal, who were involved in drug trafficking, many of whom trafficked for the CIA.

They described how Governor Bill Clinton's administration blocked prosecution of key CIA drug traffickers, a condition others had reported. During a conversation with Welsh in December 1993 he described how he almost died from a murder attempt during the time that he was presenting evidence to Governor Clinton's attorney general at Little Rock.

Special Investigator William Duncan testified before Congress several times concerning the drug trafficking, the coverup by Arkansas authorities under Governor Bill Clinton, the coverup by the U.S. Department of Justice, and the federal courts. During July 24, 1991 House testimony, Duncan stated:

> By the end of 1987 ... thousands of law enforcement man-hours and an enormous amount of evidence of drug smuggling, aiding and abetting drug smugglers, conspiracy, perjury, money laundering ... had gone to waste. Not only were no indictments ever returned on any of the individuals under investigation for their role in the Mena Operation, there was a complete breakdown in the judicial system. The United States Attorney, Western Judicial District of Arkansas, ... refused to issue subpoenas for critical witnesses, interfered in the investigations, misled grand juries about evidence and availability of witnesses, refused to allow investigators to present evidence to the grand jury, and in general made a mockery of the entire investigative and judicial process.

Duncan's testimony described the attempts by Justice Department officials seeking to have Duncan lie to the Congressional committee concerning "a bribe from [drug trafficker] Barry Seal to a high ranking Department of Justice official." Duncan's testimony continued:

> *[Actions of IRS officials were] purely and simply designed to impede the Congress of the United States in their investigation of issues which impact on the very heart of our judicial system, and ultimately the security of this country. Evidence ... indicates that ... the Mena, Arkansas Airport was an important hub/waypoint for transshipment of drugs, weapons .... The evidence details a bizarre mixture of drug smuggling, gun running, money laundering and covert operations by Barry Seal, his associates, and both employees and contract operatives of the United States Intelligence Services. The testimony reveals a scheme whereby massive amounts of cocaine were smuggled into the State of Arkansas, and profits were partially used to fund covert operations. Two witnesses testified that one of the Western District of Arkansas Assistant U.S. Attorneys told them that the U.S. Attorney's Office received a call to shut down the investigations involving [the drug operation].*

DIRTY AND NEAR-FATAL TRICKS OF U.S. INTELLIGENCE OR JUSTICE DEPARTMENT PERSONNEL

Duncan and Welsh made very clear that Arkansas state officials, including Governor Clinton, and the U.S. attorney's office, blocked prosecution of the drug traffickers, making possible the continuation of the U.S. drug epidemic, along with its killings, crime, and other affects.

Welsh said to me that while he was presenting evidence of the massive drug trafficking to Arkansas officials in Little Rock, he suddenly became deathly sick, and was rushed to the hospital. Fortunately for him, the doctors discovered the problem. They told Welsh that he had been sprayed with military-grade Anthrax (similar to what Saddam Hussein had threatened to use in the Persian Gulf War).

E-SYSTEM

One of the many CIA proprietaries heavily involved domestically in drug trafficking is E-Systems, Inc., a company heavily involved in aviation-related activities, based in Greenville, Texas. As with many CIA proprietaries, it is heavily staffed with former or present intelligence agency personnel. Winfred Richards, a former E-Systems employees, stated to me the consequences experienced by employees who threaten to blow the whistle on the company's illicit activities, including drug trafficking. The United States is criss-crossed by dozens of CIA proprietaries, fronts, assets that carry out the massive drug trafficking promulgated by the intelligence agencies.

This criminal enterprise inflicted, upon an uninformed and gullible nation, horrendous financial, physical, and social harm, far beyond any corruption exposed in the history of the United States. And the perpetrators are known to literally every government and non-government check and balance, all of whom have engaged in coverup and obstruction of justice.

CHAPTER NINETEEN

CIA REVIEW

The CIA was legislated into existence in 1947 via the National Security Act while Harry Truman was president. The primary purpose of the legislation was to centralize intelligence material gathered by U.S. intelligence agencies. This need was made obvious by the disaster at Pearl Harbor in 1941. The Pearl Harbor debacle resulted in 2,500 deaths, loss of many ships and aircraft, and allowed Japan to escalate the global conflict that resulted in tens of millions of deaths and atrocities. If White House and military officials had used street-smarts in defending against that Pearl Harbor attack, Japanese aggression could have been prevented or halted. (The author was attached to a PBY squadron at the time of the attack and was in Hawaii with replacement aircraft within two weeks.)

The National Security Act provided for checks and balances that have become meaningless. The Act required that the National Security Council authorize any covert action taken by the CIA. The Council is composed of the president of the United States, the vice president, Secretary of State, and Secretary of Defense. The CIA can lawfully perform only those operations specifically authorized by the National Security Council. In practice, the CIA either does not inform the NSC of its covert operations, or notifies it after the operations have commenced or been completed.

FAILURE TO REPORT CRIMES
AGAINST THE UNITED STATES

If the CIA had not, itself, been involved in many of the corrupt activities, its vast intelligence network should have discovered the criminal activities against America. Other government agencies whose vast investigative powers probably discovered these crimes include the FBI, its parent, the Justice Department, Customs, DEA, and others. How could such vast safeguards not have discovered these crimes? Were they incompetent, or were they either part of the criminal activities, or blocked by the top law enforcement officer, the U.S. Attorney General, from doing so? The answer is, as shown in these pages, the Justice Department has been made into a vast criminal enterprise.

A SECRET GOVERNMENT

Instead of the CIA being primarily an intelligence gathering and coordinating agency, acting under the National Security Council, the CIA has become so powerful that it can destroy any politician who seriously questions its activities. This is especially true when combined with the criminal misuse of power by Justice Department attorneys and federal judges.

The average American is unaware of the gravity of the CIA's criminal activities, thanks to the orchestrated coverup and disinformation by the establishment media. The corrupt mindset has existed for years. Initiating wars, as in Vietnam, and assassination operations, as in Vietnam and Central America, are routine. Engaging in drug trafficking in foreign countries and the United States, a key reason for world-wide proliferation of drugs, is the type of criminal activities this dangerous agency considers proper. It conspires with underworld figures, including the Italian and Jewish Mafia, to carry out all sorts of criminal activities.

Although the CIA is not permitted by law to operate within the United States, it has done so. And in many forms of hard-core criminal activities against the American people. Through fronts, cutouts, and proprietaries, the CIA has defrauded all types of U.S. financial institutions, including savings and loans, banks, and insurance companies. The CIA is a major player in the looting of Chapter 11 assets, making the exercise of Chapter 11 statutory protections a trap for unwary Americans.

The CIA has corrupted the election process in the United States and in foreign countries. The CIA's October Surprise operation corrupted the 1980 presidential elections and placed into office a group that embarked on a barrage of criminal activities. The CIA-related Watergate affair caused removal from office of President Richard Nixon. The JFK assassination, with its strong CIA overtones, removed another president elected by the people.

NATIONAL SECURITY ACT

The National Security Act establishing the CIA authorized and limited the Agency to certain functions. Portions of the Act state:

(d) **Powers and duties.**

For the purpose of coordinating the intelligence activities of the several government departments and agencies in the interest of national security, it shall be the duty of the Agency, under the direction of the National Security Court–

(1) To advise the National Security Council in matters concerning such intelligence activities of the government departments and agencies as relate to national security;

(2) to make recommendations to the National Security Council for the coordination of such intelligence activities of the departments and agencies of the government as relate to the national security;

(3) to correlate and evaluate intelligence relating to the national security, and provide for the appropriate dissemination of such intelligence within the government using, where appropriate, existing agencies

and facilities: *Provided,* That the Agency shall have no police, subpoena, law-enforcement powers, or internal-security functions; *Provided further,* that the departments and other agencies of the government shall continue to collect, evaluate, correlate, and disseminate departmental intelligence: *And provided further,* That the Director of Central Intelligence shall be responsible for protecting intelligence sources and methods from unauthorized disclosure;

(4) To perform, for the benefit of the existing intelligence agencies, such additional services of common concern as the National Security Council determines can be more efficiently accomplished centrally;

(5) to perform such other functions and duties related to intelligence affecting the national security as the National Security Council may from time to time direct.

UNHEEDED WARNINGS

The lawful functions and restraints given the CIA by the statutes have been violated almost from its inception, and warnings about the CIA problems have gone unheeded. President Harry Truman warned the American people of the CIA danger, stating as quoted in the December 21, 1963, *Washington Post*:

For some time I have been disturbed by the way the CIA has been diverted from its original assignment. It has become an operational and at times a policy-making arm of the government. ... I never had any thoughts that when I set up the CIA that it would be injected into peacetime cloak-and-dagger operations. Some of the complication and embarrassment that I think we have experienced are in part attributable to the fact that this quiet intelligence arm of the President has been so removed from its intended role that it is being interpreted as a symbol of sinister and mysterious foreign intrigue and a subject for cold war enemy propaganda.

Truman's warnings were echoed by President Dwight Eisenhower as he was leaving office, warning the American people of the dangers posed by the military-industrial complex, of which the CIA is a part.

U.S. PRESIDENTS WHO INCUR CIA WRATH

Opposing the CIA has been dangerous, possibly even fatal, for presidents of the United States. President Kennedy, recognizing the dangers of the CIA before his assassination in 1962, threatened to muzzle the CIA after the Bay of Pigs fiasco, and stated his intention to pull U.S. personnel out of the CIA's Vietnam operation. There is considerable circumstantial evidence indicating CIA involvement in Kennedy's assassination. When the many ugly acts of the CIA are recognized, assassinating a president of the United States is not far-fetched.

President Richard Nixon, recognizing the dangers of the CIA, stated his intention to rein in the agency. It was the CIA-related Watergate affair, augmented by the panic-generating antics of CIA's friends, including the *Washington Post* and reporter Bob Woodward, that expanded President Nixon's after-the-fact coverup of the relatively minor break-in into a major scandal that brought the U.S. government to a standstill and global disgrace.

Compare the after-the-fact coverup by Nixon with the massive coverups committed by CIA-affiliated President George Bush, and the silence by the same *Washington Post* and Bob Woodward.

Criminal activities by federal officials included, for instance, October Surprise, HUD, savings and loans, Chapter 11, Inslaw, Chapter 11, BCCI, Iraqgate, defrauding U.S. financial institutions, drug trafficking in the United States, and other criminal activities. The coverup of the October Surprise operation required distorting the facts and printing false statements to discredit whistleblowers. When the press is forced to address corruption by powerful politicians, such as October Surprise or Iran-Contra, it focuses on relatively minor, peripheral issues.

President Jimmy Carter suffered at the hands of the CIA after he fired many of its covert operatives in 1976. Carter was a threat to the CIA, and they retaliated against him several years later by engineering the October Surprise scheme, which helped insure Carter's defeat in the November 1980 presidential election.

Ronald Reagan and George Bush, who benefited from the CIA's October Surprise, were the only presidents of the United States since before President Kennedy who were not adversely effected by CIA tactics. Bush was director of the CIA in 1975 and 1976, and reportedly a CIA agent since 1960. Reagan and Bush, and those who aided and abetted these acts, were beneficiaries of the CIA October Surprise operation and other CIA dirty tricks.

NAZI INFLUENCE EFFECTING THE UNITED STATES?

After World War II many former Nazi intelligence officers were brought to the United States and placed into various intelligence agencies, including the Office of Naval Intelligence and the Central Intelligence Agency. Many had been given the choice of being prosecuted for World War II war crimes or joining the U.S. military and intelligence agencies.

These former Nazi officers gained key covert positions in the CIA and other intelligence agencies, engaging in activities that inflicted great harm upon the United States. This Nazi influence could explain the enormous harm inflicted upon the United States by the CIA.

EXPOSÉ BOOKS BY INSIDERS

Many books have been written by former CIA insiders describing the agency's covert activities and misuse of power. In *Secret Team*,[332] written by CIA insider Colonel Fletcher Prouty, he describes what he discovered during many years as Chief of Special Operations (clandestine activities) with the U.S. Joint Chiefs of Staff. Prouty writes: "The CIA is the center of a vast mechanism that specializes in covert operations," which is, of course, obvious to anyone with a basic knowledge of CIA activities. Prouty writes: "The CIA is the willing tool of a higher level Secret Team, or High Cabal, that usually includes representatives of the CIA and other instrumentalities of the government, certain cells of the business and professional world and, almost always, foreign participation."

---

[332] *The Secret Team*, L. Fletcher Prouty, Institute for Historical Review, Costa Mesa, California.

CIA PLANTS EVERYWHERE

Referring to news management that enables the CIA to escape unfavorable publicity, Prouty writes about the media's reliance upon CIA "news" handouts and the infiltration of the media by CIA personnel:

> Leaders of government and of the great pressure centers regularly leak information of all kinds to columnists, television and radio commentators, and to other media masters. ... [fabricated data] will be skillfully leaked to the press and to selected businessmen ... designed especially for "Periscope" in Newsweek, or perhaps for its old favorite, Joe Alsop. ... advance top-level information is a most valuable and saleable commodity.

To defuse any criticism or exposure of the CIA's unlawful activities, the CIA has people widely dispersed throughout the U.S. government and industry. Prouty writes:

> There are CIA men in the Federal Aviation Administration, in State [Department], all over the DOD, and in most other offices where the CIA has wanted to place them. Few top officials, if any, would ever deny the agency such a service, and as the appointive official departed, and his staffs came and went, the whole device would be lost with only the CIA remembering that they were still there. Many of these people have reached positions of great responsibility.

In this way the CIA is able to control other government agencies in carrying out its corrupt, and sometimes treasonous and subversive activities. The CIA infiltrates Customs and other agencies, blocking the checks and balances that could otherwise threaten the various CIA operations.

SILENCING CIA WHISTLEBLOWERS

Many CIA personnel became disenchanted or outraged by the harm inflicted by the Agency's corrupt activities and would like to blow the whistle, but fear the consequences. These include:

* Charging potential CIA whistleblowers with federal offenses for having performed duties ordered by their CIA superiors. This tactic has the cooperation of Justice Department officials.

* With the cooperation of federal judges, strip the targeted person of his defenses, including refusing to allow him to call CIA witnesses; refuse to provide CIA documents; strip him of his assets so he cannot hire attorneys and investigators; assign a court-appointed attorney whose loyalty is to the system.

* Justify the refusal to permit CIA witnesses and documents on the grounds of national security, a catch-all phrase used to block exposure of rampant government criminality.

* Assassinations and mysterious deaths.

HUNDREDS OF THOUSANDS OF DEATHS

Prouty described how the CIA got the United States embroiled in military conflicts, including the Korean and Vietnam Wars. He tells how independently acting CIA groups initiated the conflict leading to the U.S. involvement in Vietnam. Supporting this position was the Asian scholar, Eugene Windchy, in The New Republic: "What steered the nation into Vietnam was a series of tiny but powerful [CIA] cabals."

Prouty wrote, "By the time of the Bay of Pigs operations, the CIA was part of a greater team, which used the Agency and other parts of the government to carry out almost any secret operation it wanted." He continued, "In this unusual business I found rather frequently that the CIA would be well on its way into some operation that would later require military support before the Secretary and the Chiefs had been informed."

Prouty explains that the CIA contains the real power structure in the United States, and how the CIA has infiltrated other government agencies and private enterprises with people loyal to the various CIA hierarchies.

CIA PROPRIETARIES

Included among past or present CIA proprietary airlines or assets were the following: Civil Air Transport (CAT) based in Taiwan; Air America; Southern Air Transport; Global International Airways; St. Lucia Airways; Intermountain Airways; Summit Aviation; Aero Airlines; Apex Aviation at Spirit of St. Louis Airport; Evergreen International Airlines and its related subsidiaries, including Evergreen America Corporation; Race Aviation; Ransom Aircraft; Resorts International; Flying Tiger Line; Response Air; Seagreen Air; Skyways Aviation; International Air Tours; Capital Airlines; Air Asia, and Southwest Airlines.

CHAPTER 11 TIE-IN

Included in CIA corrupt activities is the multi-billion dollar a year looting of assets in Chapter 11 courts, with the assistance of crooked federal judges, trustees, and law firms. This operation is covered in other pages.

ASSASSINATIONS

Assassinations have been a routine part of the CIA mindset. In Vietnam, the CIA Phoenix Program resulted in the assassination of upward of 40,000 people. Numerous books have identified CIA operatives with the assassination of President John F. Kennedy.[333] Congressional hearings had brought out the CIA's plans to assassinate Cuba's Fidel Castro and other heads of state. Leaders of other nations and people considered a threat to the CIA's interests have been assassinated. Many people throughout the world with knowledge of the CIA October Surprise operation have been killed or have mysteriously died. Francis Nugan, who assisted in operating the covert CIA money operation known as Nugan Hand Bank, was killed in Australia after the CIA's cover was blown, keeping him from testifying about the CIA operation.

In trying to comprehend what these CIA-induced deaths mean, and to equate the brutality with the CIA, think of thousands of people disemboweled, decapitated, dismembered while still alive, and other types of brutality that are periodically revealed by the alternative media.[334] If the American public exercised its responsibilities, especially in the misuse of its tax dollars needed to finance these CIA outrages, many of these killings would not have occurred.

---

[333] *Plausible Denial*, Mark Lane; *JFK, The CIA, Vietnam and The Plot To Assassinate John F. Kennedy*, L. Fletcher Prouty; *Act Of Treason*, Mark North; *Crossfire*, Jim Marrs.

[334] National weekly, *Spotlight*.

Entire continents such as Central and South America have been converted to constant and brutal upheavals, with the money and the arms given by the CIA. Death, destruction, horror, follows wherever the CIA goes.

Former Mossad operative Ari Ben-Menashe described in his book the assassinations carried out by the Mossad, many of which required the specific approval of Israel's leaders. He related how Amiram Nir was killed by a CIA asset to keep him from testifying to a Congressional committee investigating the Iran-Contra affair that would have implicated President Reagan, Vice-President Bush, Oliver North, Israel's Mossad, Israeli officials, including Shimon Peres.

As is described in detail in later pages, various CIA factions or fiefdoms have their assassination squads whose victims even include other CIA personnel.

AVOIDING RESPONSIBILITY FOR THEIR ACTS

The CIA uses various methods to avoid responsibility for its actions. One method is to use "cut-outs," acting in place of the CIA. In this way the CIA can distance itself from the operation if its cover is blown. The CIA makes a standard practice of "sheep-dipping" those people carrying out their dirty tricks, including military personnel. The person's records are removed from the military agency and placed in a special intelligence file. Fictitious records are processed showing the military person to have been released from the agency. His or her records are changed, with letters sent to civilian agencies, banks, friends, indicating discharge from the service. The CIA helps the sheep-dipped person to change his credit and employment records, and the many things that a person does when discharged from service. The sheep-dipped people are often eventually returned to military service, and the time spent with the CIA counts toward retirement and other benefits.

The CIA often uses contract employees and mercenaries to carry out acts within the United States and abroad. If the CIA's cover is blown, the standard practice is for the CIA, through Justice Department attorneys, to charge the covert employee with violating federal law, strip him or her of their defenses, and insure that they are sentenced to long prison terms. They will either die in prison or be too old to cause trouble for the Agency.

The CIA's denial of involvement is willingly accepted by Congress and the establishment media over statements made by brave whistleblowers. This, combined with the absence of responsibility by checks and balances, are key reasons why whistleblowers are little known to the American public.

CIA ASSASSINATION TEAMS

The CIA has its own assassination teams, as will be explained in later pages, carrying out their deadly tasks in foreign countries and in the United States. One of my CIA informants, commander of a Navy SEAL Team, described how his group taught methods of assassinations to various intelligence agency personnel. Gunther Russbacher did the same.

It has been reported that CIA covert activities in inciting wars, revolutions, social unrest, throughout the world, has resulted in over six million deaths, including the 58,000 American GIs who perished in the Vietnam War.

LYING AS STANDARD POLICY

Lying to the media, to Congress, in criminal trials to imprison CIA assets, has long been recognized as standard practice. One of the documents shown in later pages, relating to CIA operative Trenton Parker, clearly shows this practice by the statement: STANDARD DENIAL.

REFERENCE TO CIA

Throughout these pages when reference is made to the CIA, it includes all U.S. intelligence agencies. These agencies are referred to by CIA personnel as "The Company," or "The Firm."

CHAPTER TWENTY

NUGAN HAND BANK

A primary CIA money laundering operation in the Pacific area was Nugan Hand Bank, with headquarters in Sydney, Australia, and branch offices throughout the Far East and Europe. One branch office was in Chiang Mai, Thailand, in the heart of the Golden Triangle drug producing area. Its primary function was CIA drug-money laundering. Nugan Hand was a covert CIA financial operation comprised primarily of those with ties to the U.S. intelligence community.

The money-handling activities consisted of laundering CIA funds, much of it obtained from drug trafficking in the Golden Triangle area. These funds were used to fund subversive activities in Southeast Asia after pulling out of Vietnam and other covert activities. Vast amounts of money were hidden in assets and financial holdings throughout the world. Disavowal is the standard CIA tactic to escape blame.

Nugan Hand engaged in all forms of financial fraud and deception, including drug-money laundering, looting assets, fraudulent records, and lies. When the CIA proprietary was exposed, the CIA denied any involvement. Simultaneously, its CIA assets were reassigned to other areas. The same happened in the Hawaiian operation that replaced Nugan Hand. In both cases the CIA immediately looted the assets and transferred them to other CIA proprietaries. Often, hundreds of people are left finally impoverished, some for the remainder of their lives.

EXPOSING NUGAN HAND FRAUD

Nugan Hand's cover was blown on April 11, 1980, by a reporter for *Target*, a Hong Kong financial newsletter, requiring the CIA to shut down the operation and destroy any evidence of its CIA links. Francis Nugan was one of the most visible players in the Nugan Hand operation. He was an alcoholic with a reputation for talking too much, a trait that threatened to expose the

CIA's role in the operation. Assassins killed Nugan,[335] leaving his body in a car outside Sydney, Australia. A bolt-action rifle was found alongside the body, and the scene was made to look like a suicide.

An unspent bullet remained in the chamber, requiring that the bolt action be operated after the last shot was fired. That shot killed Nugan instantly, blowing away much of the skull and scattering it throughout the car. There were no fingerprints on the gun, indicating that whoever fired the fatal bullet wiped the fingerprints from the rifle.

The only identification on Nugan's body was a calling card apparently overlooked by the killers, belonging to William Colby, former Director of the Central Intelligence Agency, with a meeting date written on the back.

Just prior or just after Nugan's death, the CIA removed the funds from the various Nugan Hand offices and laundered them into other CIA operations. Misinformation commenced immediately, blaming Nugan for the missing money. Before Australian authorities started an investigation, Michael Hand disappeared, along with most of the Nugan Hand records. Hand secretly surfaced in Iran, followed by his participation in the huge Central America CIA drug trafficking, working with one of my informants, Trenton Parker.

Like all CIA operations, Nugan Hand relied upon a pattern of fraud and deception. Large amounts of currency were moved in and out of various countries, including Australia and the Golden Triangle areas. The Nugan Hand operation received considerable media attention in Australia, but the establishment media in the United States said virtually nothing about this CIA operation and its implications. Australian authorities conducted numerous investigations but in their final report they white-washed the Nugan Hand affair.

Michael Hand was a Green Beret, a colonel in the U.S. Army, assigned to the CIA. Earlier, Hand was handling the CIA's heroin and opium business, and laundering the money from the Golden Triangle area of Asia. In the 1960s the CIA transferred Hand from the Golden Triangle assignment to Teheran, where he set up the secret police for the Shah of Iran. (I was flying as pilot in Iran at that time.)

One of Nugan Hand's CIA assets was John Fredericks, who was sought for questioning by another CIA contract agent, Michael Riconosciuto, who wanted to question Fredericks about Michael Hand's location. But before this interview could be consummated, Fredericks and his bodyguard were killed (July 28, 1991) in Australia.

Hand disappeared as Australian authorities sought to question him about Nugan's death, the Nugan Hand Bank operation, and the disappearance of approximately one billion dollars from the bank. Hand first went to Thailand under CIA cover and then showed up in Florida and the Caribbean area. One of my deep-cover CIA contacts, Trenton Parker, described how he and Hand had worked together in the early 1980s. Parker's CIA faction was interested in discovering Hand's operation, and Parker met Hand in Jamaica on

[335] January 27, 1980.

February 2, 1980. They then worked together on Operation Interlink and Operation Anacondor.

Parker stated that Hand and Vice President George Bush were in frequent contact after Bush became vice president, and while Australian authorities were searching for Hand. Parker stated that CIA Director William Casey frequently met with Hand in Panama in the early 1980s concerning the arms and drug trafficking. It was obvious that Hand was a deep-cover CIA asset, and that the Director of the CIA and the vice president of the United States were engaging in covert activities with Hand.

Parker stated that he and hand took over one of the drug trafficking operations for the CIA in Central and South America. He said that Hand's experience in developing the Golden Triangle drug operations for the CIA made him useful in expanding the drug operations from Central and South America into the United States.

Investigation by Australian authorities into Nugan Hand revealed the CIA's meddling in Australian affairs, including inciting political unrest, intrusion into Australian elections, deception, invasion of its sovereignty, and other dirty tricks. The Australian investigation sought to determine the location of about one billion dollars. One of my CIA contacts, who later worked with Michael Hand in Florida and the Caribbean, stated the missing funds totaled about three billion dollars.

STAFFED BY THE CIA

Most of the management personnel of Nugan Hand Bank were intelligence community personnel.[336] When Nugan Hand shut down, most of them moved to other CIA operations, including drug trafficking. Nugan Hand Bank was incorporated in 1976 in the Cayman Islands, and it is believed that it was a replacement for Castle Bank & Trust, incorporated in Nassau, Bahamas. After Castle failed, Nugan Hand commenced operation.

The Nugan Hand operation obtained funds from investors. When the

---

[336] Michael Jon Hand, CIA operative, former Green Beret, vice-chairman and part owner of Nugan Hand Bank; General Edwin F. Black ran Nugan Hand's Hawaii office; Paul Helliwell was a CIA asset heavily involved in drug money laundering; General Earle Cocke, Jr., ran the Nugan Hand Washington office and headed the American Legion; William Colby, retired Director of CIA, was the attorney for Nugan Hand; Dale Holmgren headed flight services for several CIA airlines and ran Nugan Hand's Taiwan office; Robert Jantzen, CIA station chief in Thailand, was Nugan Hand's officer in Thailand; General LeRoy Manor, chief of staff for U.S. Pacific Command, ran Nugan Hand's Philippine office; Walter MacDonald, former deputy director of CIA for economic research, was a consultant to Nugan Hand; Theodore G. Shackley, top clandestine officer at the CIA, had numerous dealings with Nugan Hand (now living in Medellin); Admiral Earl Yates, chief of U.S. strategic planning for Asia and the Pacific, was president of Nugan Hand Bank. Yates had been commander of the aircraft carrier, *John F. Kennedy*. He retired, or was sheep-dipped, from the Navy in 1974, and became president of Nugan Hand Bank in 1977; Gordon (Billy) Young, CIA asset, represented Nugan Hand in the Golden Triangle drug zone of Southeast Asia; George Farris was a military intelligence specialist working in the Hong Kong office of Nugan Hand; Guy Pauker was an advisor to Henry Kissinger; Edwin Wilson, a CIA operative, had frequent dealings with Nugan Hand Bank; Thomas Clines, a CIA operative and deputy to Major General Richard Secord in the Iran-Contra arms network, had frequent dealings with Nugan Hand. After Nugan was killed, and before Australian authorities started investigating the bank, Clines rescued Houghton from Australia.

cover was blown, the funds were quickly moved to other CIA proprietaries, inflicting financial losses upon the investors and depositors. The Nugan Hand affair deteriorated the relationship between the United States and Australia.

Many people holding check-and-balance responsibilities covered up for the Nugan Hand scheme. These checks and balances included the oversight agencies in Australia; the Reserve Bank in Australia that had responsibilities over Nugan Hand; Citicorp, who traded securities with Nugan Hand; taxing authorities in Australia, who were familiar with Nugan Hand's operation; the accounting firm that certified the Nugan Hand records; U.S. Consul General in Australia who knew of the CIA operation; the Premier of Australia, who had offices adjacent to Nugan Hand; Irving Trust Company, the correspondent bank for Nugan Hand in the United States; Corporate Affairs Commission in Australia that stonewalled requests for information; prominent Australian attorneys who worked closely with Nugan Hand); Australian Department of Commerce, who had considerable information about Nugan Hand's activities; Australian intelligence agencies that worked with U.S. intelligence agencies, and who knew about the rogue operations; and others.

Some of the key players in the Nugan Hand affair surfaced in the news years later in the Iran-Contra affair. But the sordid aspects were kept from the American people by members of Congress and the establishment media. Virtually nothing was stated about the huge drug trafficking aspects of the Contra operation, or the thousands of assassinations and brutal crimes funded and directed by the CIA.

CHAPTER TWENTY ONE

BBRDW

After Nugan Hand's cover was blown and the operation abandoned, the CIA redirected many of the Nugan Hand operations to another Pacific financial institution based in Hawaii, named Bishop, Baldwin, Rewald, Dillingham and Wong (BBRDW). By the end of 1980, BBRDW started setting up offices in Hong Kong, Taiwan, Indonesia, Singapore, and Australia, all former Nugan Hand locations, staffing the offices with some of the same personnel. As in most CIA-related proprietaries, its key management was comprised of CIA-related personnel.[337]

The CIA placed in charge of its proprietary a Honolulu businessman who had worked for the CIA years earlier while attending Milwaukee Institute of Technology. That CIA college project was called Operation MH Chaos, consisting of a spying operation on college campuses during the mid-1960s. The CIA gave Rewald the alias, Winterdog. Other CIA divisions had parallel programs called Operation Mother Goose and Operation Back Draft.

Rewald left the CIA after college, married, and had five children, living comfortably in a home on Lake Michigan. Business changes caused Rewald to move his family to Hawaii, where he opened an investment consulting company under the name CMI Corporation. It was here in 1978 that the CIA lured Rewald back into the Agency, and used his company as a cover. By 1979, the CIA established another proprietary called Bishop, Baldwin, Rewald, Dillingham, and Wong, headed by Rewald. Rewald's first CIA station chief and handler was Eugene J. Welch, who was later replaced by

---

[337] Including retired Pan American chief pilot, Captain Edwin Avary, reportedly a CIA contract Agent; Sue Wilson, former National Security Agency employee; Jack Kindschi, former CIA Station Chief; Charles Richardson, Chief of Base, Foreign Resources, CIA; John Sager, former Moscow Station Chief; Clarence Gunderson, CIA/Air Force Intelligence Officer; General Hunter Harris, retired four-star Air Force commander; and General Edwin F. Black, former head of Nugan Hand operations based in Hawaii.

Jack Kindschi, followed by Jack W. Rardin, all of whom coached Rewald on CIA operations. Rewald would be the fall-guy when the cover was blown on BBRDW. When the cover *did* blow, several years later, it almost killed Rewald.

The CIA proprietary, BBRDW, used the cover of an international investment company, with 120 employees staffing offices in sixteen countries, including Hong Kong, India, Indonesia, Taiwan, New Zealand, Singapore, London, Paris, Stockholm, Brazil and Chile. CIA personnel opened and operated these far-flung offices.

Rewald became an international polo player, later using BBRDW to purchase the Hawaii Polo Club, which enabled him to cultivate friendships with many influential people throughout the world. These included the Sultan of Brunei, who later transferred seven billion dollars from British banks to U.S. banks.

BBRDW was active in numerous covert CIA activities, including:

* Supplying arms to Taiwan, India, and other countries.

* Setting up banking and trust companies for CIA money laundering.

* Secretly acquiring Japan's secret plans for the Japanese High Speed Surface Transport (HSST), by paying a $27,000 bribe.

* Targeting foreign political, military and business leaders whose funds were placed in accounts alongside money obtained through clandestine CIA operations. Legitimate investors unwittingly commingled their funds with those of the CIA.

* Funded CIA operations worldwide, including assassinations unknown to Rewald.

* During the Falklands War, Rewald traveled to Chile and Argentina, under cover of playing polo, and obtained intelligence information for the CIA.

CIA COVER BLOWN BY TV REPORTER

Honolulu TV reporter Barbara Tanabe drew attention to suspected financial irregularities in BBRDW's operations in July 1983, creating a crisis within the CIA. When a CIA proprietary is investigated by any outside agency, state or federal, the standard practice is for Washington CIA and Justice Department officials to contact the investigative agency to discontinue their investigation, regardless of how many laws may be violated by the CIA operation. This was done on numerous occasions over the years with BBRDW.[338] However, when the cover was blown by a local reporter who thought she had stumbled across a fraudulent operation, it was too late to stop it.

While denying any knowledge of the operation, which of course was a lie, the CIA pulled the assets out of the various bank accounts in Hong Kong, Singapore, London, Switzerland and the Cayman Islands, transferring the money into other CIA proprietaries and off-shore financial institutions. The looted assets consisted not only of CIA money, but also funds invested by

---

[338] Security Exchange Commission, Internal Revenue Service, Banking Commission, and other regulatory agencies.

private citizens residing in Hawaii and California.

Before the cover was blown on BBRDW, millions of dollars of money were received from investors in Hawaii and California by the CIA operation. During a Board of Directors meeting shortly before the cover was blown on the operation, Rewald had ordered these investors to be paid off, and no private investment money taken in. But after the cover was blown, and without Rewald's knowledge, the CIA moved all the funds into other CIA proprietaries, including the money of the private investors. [The CIA did the same with assets deposited in Nugan Hand Bank after the cover was blown.]

The local media in Hawaii focused considerable attention on the BBRDW affair; it was Hawaii's most famous legal case. But little was said by the establishment media on the mainland.

Rewald became depressed by being made the scapegoat, and the lack of any support by his CIA handlers. He checked into room 1632 at the Sheraton Waikiki, with thoughts of committing suicide. Before checking into the hotel, Rewald visited the office of the CIA station chief in the federal building in downtown Honolulu. Finding Jack Rardin out of the office, Rewald left, and placed a message on Rardin's answering machine:[339]

Jack, this is the chairman. I am checking into the Sheraton Waikiki under the name Ronald Imp. Status urgent. Mayday. I'll be waiting for your call.

A bottle of Codeine # 3 sat on the end table alongside the bed, which Rewald contemplated taking, and a Bible. This was not the behavior of a person intentionally engaging in criminal activities, but more of a person who was distraught at being used as Rewald's CIA handlers had done.

Rewald had kept highly sensitive records of key financial transactions in a green-cover book, which the CIA wanted. The book contained information showing BBRDW to be a CIA operation. Among the contents were coded words, account numbers, figures, names, addresses, and phone numbers, banks, including Union Bank of Switzerland, Hong Kong and Shanghai Bank, and Grand Caymans Bank.

In an effort to obtain possession of the valuable book, two CIA agents, Angelo Cancel and Robert Allen, entered Rewald's hotel room, attempting to force Rewald to reveal the location of the book. Rewald was groggy from taking a heavy dose of the Codeine tablets and wasn't responding to their requests. They dragged him into the bathroom, placed him against the tub, and plunged a knife deeply into his arms. Bleeding profusely, Rewald lapsed into unconsciousness. Unable to find the book, the CIA assassins left Rewald to die from loss of blood. Fortuitously, a hotel maid discovered Rewald's bleeding body, and an ambulance rushed him to Honolulu's Queens Hospital, saving his life.

While Rewald was recovering in the hospital, he was warned by his CIA handlers to remain quiet, say nothing, and the CIA would financially support his family. This was never done. The former CIA station chief, Kindschi,

---

[339] Rardin's number was 531-1023.

visited Rewald in the hospital and asked: "Ron, where is the green book?" "It's safe," replied Rewald.

In response to a question from Honolulu detective Lingo, the present CIA station chief, Rardin, claimed he didn't know Rewald, that he didn't know anything about BBRDW except what he read in the papers, and that he had no connection to either. He was of course lying. Rardin socialized frequently with the Rewald family and was in almost daily contact with Rewald as his CIA handler.

Agents Allen and Cancel, who had tried to kill Rewald in the hotel, threatened Rewald's secretaries, Sue Wilson[340] and Jackie Vos, ordering them to leave Hawaii immediately, and never return. This was done to prevent them from testifying about the CIA operation.

As the two women later discussed their problem, Sue told Jackie that if she hadn't heard from her in the next thirty days to call the local police. When Jackie asked Sue if the FBI should be called, Sue responded: "They won't help us. They're all in this together. We might be able to trust the local guys. They're not part of the system."

While these events were taking place, another CIA contract agent and close friend, Thomas Wilhite, of San Rafael, California, became outraged at what was done to Rewald. He said to Rewald:

There's a big coverup going on. They've completely disavowed any knowledge of you. You are being left out to dry, pure and simple. I'm calling a press conference for tomorrow at the ranch. I'm going to tell the media everything. Tell them this is all a CIA coverup and that you were just following orders.

Rewald responded:

Tom, you can't do that. I have an agreement with the agency. They assured me that as long as I keep quiet, Nancy and the children will be taken care of. They will take care of me as soon as all this cools down, so don't do this. It's not necessary.

Wilhite replied:

They're lying to you, Ron. I assure you they are destroying every bit of evidence. They are shutting us all up, transferring others to who knows where. All the bank accounts are being emptied. Believe me, you are being abandoned and set up. You know what plausible deniability is all about.

Before the press conference the following morning, Wilhite took his red aerobatic Pitt Special bi-plane for a morning flight. Taking off from the grass runway on his ranch, the plane climb steeply to 1,000 feet and then suddenly plunged to the ground, killing him. The aircraft had been sabotaged. The primary group who wanted Wilhite dead was the CIA. Wilhite's death wasn't the only one connected to BBRDW. Two attorneys were killed in Washington as they searched for evidence linking President Marcos of the Philippines to the CIA.

---

[340] Wilson had been a semifinalist in the Miss Teenage America pageant, after which she worked with the National Security Agency in Washington and Honolulu, before joining Bishop Baldwin.

A low-level BBRDW employee, Richard Craig Smith, while under cover of BBRDW, had spied on the Russians in Japan. Now, without CIA support, or maybe he was deliberately turned in, he was arrested by police and charged with selling secrets to the Russians.

KING PIN OF CIA OPERATIONS IN THE PACIFIC

After BBRDW's collapse, the British Broadcasting Company (BBC) referred to Rewald as "King Pin of CIA Operations in the Pacific."

Former CIA station chief, Jack Kindschi, a partner in BBRDW, attempted to make Rewald the fall guy by filing charges, accusing Rewald of fraudulently absconding with the funds. These were the funds that the CIA and Kindschi looted while Rewald was hospitalized. Kindschi withdrew $170,000. Rewald was then arrested, and U.S. District Judge Harold M. Fong set bail at ten million dollars, reportedly the highest bail in history for a white-collar crime.

The judge sought to limit the danger to the CIA by issuing gag orders barring Rewald's attorney from repeating what Rewald had told him. Case records, normally available to the public, were sealed from public view. Rewald was ordered not to talk about the CIA. These measures would not have been necessary if the CIA was not deeply involved in BBRDW. The public, especially the investors who lost millions of dollars, had a right to have access to whatever records and testimony applied to the case.

Justice Department officials, seeking to protect the CIA, charged Rewald with defrauding the many investors who put money into the operation, and who lost their investment when the assets were looted. Many of these investors blamed Rewald for their losses, apparently assuming that Justice Department prosecutors were telling the truth.

DENIAL OF DEFENSES

Justice Department prosecutors used the standard procedures to keep the public from learning about this covert CIA operation. These included:

* Charging Rewald with the federal offense of defrauding the investors, while simultaneously protecting those who actually perpetrated the crime.

* Seizing all of Rewald's assets, depriving him of the funds necessary to hire legal counsel.

* Appointing inexperienced legal counsel to represent Rewald. They appointed a young attorney just out of law school who had never tried any case: Brian Tamamaha. He didn't obtain clearance to examine classified documents until shortly before the start of the trial, at which time it was too late to conduct a meaningful examination of the thousands of documents. The judge refused to delay the start of the trial despite the obvious injustice to Rewald. However, the attorney made an effort to defend Rewald, which is more than can be said of many other public defenders who were more interested in maintaining a friendly and eventually profitable relationship with federal judges and Justice Department attorneys.

* Transferring a key attorney, John Peyton, from the CIA to Honolulu, to prosecute the case against Rewald, and insure that CIA witnesses and documents were not available to him. Prior to this transfer,

Peyton was chief of litigation for the Central Intelligence Agency. He took a demotion to Assistant U.S. attorney in order to prosecute Rewald and keep the lid on the scandal.

* Denying Rewald the right to call CIA witnesses and obtain CIA documents. This denial by U.S. District Judge Harold Fong undermined Rewald's defenses and prevented the public from learning about the criminal operations of the CIA.

* Withholding evidence that the CIA looted the assets of BBRDW.

* Denying to Rewald's attorney important documents needed to prepare a proper defense. Justice Department prosecutors refused to allow Rewald's attorney to make copies of most of the documents, barring their introduction into the record.

In the case of White House officials charged with offenses by independent prosecutor Lawrence Walsh, prominent Washington law firms, receiving large retainers from well-heeled defendants, possessed the clout and legal acumen to demand that the documents and witnesses be produced, or that the charges be dismissed. Rewald and other CIA personnel made the scape-goats lacked the protection of big-name Washington attorneys. Without hundreds of thousands of dollars in attorney fees, long prison terms resulted.

While denying that BBRDW was a CIA operation and that Rewald was a CIA agent, Justice Department prosecutors requested the court to seal the records for national security reasons. But how could there be national security concerns if BBRDW was not a CIA operation?

The jury knew that classified documents upon which Rewald's defenses were based had been denied to him. Possibly naive about the criminality in the CIA and Justice Department, the jurors believed the charges filed by Justice Department prosecutors and refused to believe Rewald.

THE VERDICT

The trial started in mid-1985 before a Honolulu federal jury in Hawaii, and a verdict was reached on October 21, 1985. The jury agreed with Justice Department prosecutors, and Rewald was sentenced to eighty years in prison, insuring that he would die in prison, and his knowledge of CIA corrupt activities went to the grave with him.

Making matters worse for Rewald during his remaining life in prison, he had suffered an injury in a polo accident that caused him serious health problems, making imprisonment far more difficult. He had poor control over his bladder and bowel movements and was confined to a wheel chair.

Rewald filed a motion to vacate the sentence, which was heard by the same Judge Fong who had blocked his defenses during trial. The motion was denied in November 1992.

Rewald filed a lawsuit against the CIA, seeking to have the investors who were defrauded by the CIA join in the action. Justice Department attorneys sought to dismiss Rewald's action on the grounds that Rewald "seeks monies based on his intelligence gathering services on behalf of the United States," citing *Totten v. United States*, 92 U.S. 105 (1875).[341] At his criminal trial, the same Justice Department denied Rewald was employed by the intelligence services, but the civil action implied that he was so employed. This "implied admission" by itself should have caused vacating Rewald's conviction and sentence.

A small handful of BBRDW investors also filed a civil suit against the CIA, including Dr. Theodore Frigard. But their suit was dismissed by a U.S. District Judge. Some of the investors obtained fabulous returns on their money. For instance, Napa attorney David Gilbrath invested $390,000 in Korean oil futures and within months received almost $700,000. The profits were so huge that BBRDW planned to pay off the investors and close it to the public. However, blowing the cover changed these plans a month before this termination was to have occurred.

Helping to hide evidence of BBRDW's ties to the CIA, the company was put into bankruptcy in 1983 and turned over to trustee Thomas Hayes. It is standard CIA procedure to conceal evidence of CIA involvement in looted companies by placing them into Chapter 7, 11, or 13 bankruptcy courts. This filing usually occurs where the CIA has control of federal judges and trustees, and have covert Justice Department and CIA law firms do their dirty work.

OUT-OF-PROPORTION PRISON SENTENCES

The prison sentence imposed on Rewald was outrageously out of proportion to the offense charged, even if, for argument, Rewald had been guilty. Judge Fong sentenced a convicted swindler, Richard Garcia of Oahu, Hawaii, to eight years in prison for federal offenses similar to those charged against Rewald by Justice Department officials. Even more disproportionate, a greater number of investors lost more money as a result of Garcia's offenses than in BBRDW. Further, Garcia admitted that he intended to defraud the investors, while Rewald denied culpability.

Another strike against Rewald was that Garcia was a local resident, while Rewald was from out of the area. Under present sentencing guidelines, if Rewald had actually been guilty as charged, the prison sentence would have been limited to a maximum of five years.

During Rewald's trial, Justice Department prosecutors and CIA witnesses denied that Rewald was a CIA employee, which they knew to be a lie. I obtained copies of several CIA documents approving Rewald's security status for CIA operations, including one dated June 8, 1979, which clearly lists him as a "CIA employee." Among dozens of other CIA documents in my possession is a copy of the CIA secrecy agreement signed by Rewald, proving that he was employed by the CIA. The wording of the agreement follows:

---

[341] The denial of compensation for intelligence gathering services during the Civil War were denied because, "The service was secret and to be obtained clandestinely, and communicated privately; the employment and service were to be equally concealed. Both employer and agent must have understood that the lips of the other were to be forever sealed. In sum, any person who allegedly enters into an intelligence gathering agreement must recognize that such an agreement must remain forever secret."

SECRECY AGREEMENT

1. I, Ronald Rewald, hereby agree to accept as a prior condition of my being employed in, or otherwise retained to perform services for, the Central Intelligence Agency, or for staff elements the Office of the Director of Central Intelligence (hereinafter collectively referred to as the Central Intelligence Agency), the obligations contained in this agreement.

2. I understand that in the course of my employment or other service with the Central Intelligence Agency I may be given access to information which is classified with the standards set forth in Executive Order 12065 amended or superseded, or other applicable Executive Order, and other information which, if disclosed in an unauthorized manner, would jeopardize foreign intelligence activities of the United States government. I accept that by being granted access to such information I will be placed in a position of special confidence and trust and become obligated to protect this information from unauthorized disclosure.

3. In consideration for being employed or otherwise retained to provide services to the Central Intelligence Agency I agree that I will never disclose in any form the following categories of information or materials, to any person not authorized by the Central Intelligence Agency to receive them:

a. information which is classified pursuant to Executive Order and which I have obtained during the course of my employment or other service with the Central Intelligence Agency.

b. information, or materials which reveal information, classifiable pursuant to Executive Order and obtained by me in the course of my employment or other service with the Central Intelligence Agency but which because of operational circumstance or oversight, is not formally marked as classified in accordance with such Executive Order, and which I know or have reason to know has not been publicly acknowledged by the Agency.

c. information obtained by me in the course of my employment or other service with the Central Intelligence Agency that identifies any person or organization that presently has or formerly has had a relationship with a United States foreign intelligence organization, which relationship the United States government has taken affirmative measures to conceal.

4. I understand that the burden will be upon me to learn whether information or materials within my control are considered by the Central Intelligence Agency to fit the description set forth in paragraph 3, and whom the Agency has authorized to receive it.

5. As a further condition of the special confidence and trust reposed in me by the Central Intelligence Agency, I hereby agree to submit for review by the Central Intelligence Agency all information or material including works of fiction which contain any mention of intelligence data or activities, or contain data which may be based upon information classified pursuant to Executive Order, which I contemplate disclosing publicly or which I have actually prepared for public disclosure, either during my employment or other service with the Central Intelligence Agency or at any time thereafter prior to discussing it with or showing it to anyone who is not authorized to have access

to it. I further agree that I will not take any steps toward public disclosure until I have received written permission to do so from the Central Intelligence Agency.

6. I understand that the purpose of the review described in paragraph 5 is to give the Central Intelligence Agency the opportunity to determine whether the information or materials which I contemplate disclosing publicly contain any information which I have agreed not to disclose. I further understand that the Agency will act upon the materials I submit and make a response to me within a reasonable time.

7. I understand that all information or materials which I may acquire in the course of my employment or other service with the Central Intelligence Agency which fit the descriptions set out in paragraph 3 of this agreement are and will remain the property of the United States government. I agree to surrender all materials reflecting such information which may have come into my possession or for which I am responsible because of my employment or other service with the Central Intelligence Agency, upon demand by an appropriate official of the Central Intelligence Agency, or upon the conclusion of my employment or other service with the Central Intelligence Agency.

8. I agree to notify the Central Intelligence Agency immediately in the event that I am called upon by judicial or Congressional authorities to testify about, or provide information which I have agreed herein not to disclose.

9. I understand that nothing contained in this agreement prohibits me from reporting intelligence activities which I consider to be unlawful or improper directly to the Intelligence Oversight Board established by the President or to a successor body which the President may establish. I recognize that there are also established procedures for bringing such matters to the attention of the Agency's Inspector General or to the Director of Central Intelligence. I further understand that any information which I may repeat to the Intelligence Oversight Board continues to be subject to this agreement for other purposes and that such reporting does not constitute public disclosure or declassification of that information.

10. I understand that any breach of this agreement by me may result in the Central Intelligence Agency taking administrative action against me, which can include temporary loss of pay or termination of my employment or service with the Central Intelligence Agency. I also understand that if I violate the terms of this agreement, the United States government may institute a civil proceeding to seek compensatory damages or other appropriate relief. I understand that the disclosure of information which I have agreed herein not to disclose can, in some circumstances, constitute a criminal offense.

11. I understand that the United States government may, prior to any unauthorized disclosure which is threatening me, choose to apply to any appropriate court for an order enforcing this agreement. Nothing in this agreement constitutes a waiver on the part of the United States to institute a civil or criminal proceeding for any breach of this agreement. Nothing in this agreement constitutes a waiver on my part of any possible defenses I may have in connection with civil or criminal proceedings which may be brought against me.

12. In addition to any other remedy to which the United States government may become entitled, I hereby assign to the United States government all rights, title, and interest in any and all royalties, remunerations, and emolument that have resulted or will result or may result from any divulgence, publication or revelation of information by me when carried out in breach of paragraph 5 of this agreement or which involves information prohibited from disclosure under terms of this agreement.

13. I understand and accept that, unless I am provided a written release from this agreement or any portion of it by the Director of Central Intelligence or the Director's representative, all the conditions and obligations accepted by me in this agreement apply both during my employment or other service with the Central Intelligence Agency, and at all times thereafter.

14. I understand that the purpose of this agreement is to implement the responsibilities of the Director of Central Intelligence, particularly the responsibility to protect intelligence sources and methods, as specified in the National Security Act of 1947, as amended.

15. In any civil action which may be brought by the United States government for breach of this agreement I understand and agree that the law of the Commonwealth of Virginia shall govern the interpretation of this agreement.

16. Each of the numbered paragraphs and lettered subparagraphs of this agreement is severable, if a court should find any of the paragraphs or subparagraphs of this agreement to be unenforceable. I understand that all remaining provisions will continue in full force.

17. I make this agreement in good faith, and with no purpose of evasion.

_____
Signature

_____
Date

The execution of this agreement was witnessed by the undersigned, who accepted it on behalf of the Central Intelligence Agency as a prior condition of the employment or other service of the person whose signature appears above.

WITNESS AND ACCEPTANCE:

_____
Signature

_____
Printed Name

_____
Date

Among the many CIA documents I acquired were those that listed Kindshi and Rardin with the BBRDW operation. These same CIA station chiefs denied that they were associated with BBRDW or even knew about its operation. Other documents described Rewald's participation in secret CIA operations throughout the Pacific and also in South America.

A cable message marked SECRET referred to the hours of operation for the CIA proprietary, and referred to it as a "cover operation." Another report marked SECRET, dated September 10, 1982, referred to instructions sent to Rewald for coordinating the visit of Philippine President Marcos to President Ronald Reagan.

Other documents from CIA headquarters at Langley, Virginia, described three cover stories that CIA station chief Rardin should provide for Rewald to use in response to IRS questions. The wording in one of these cables from Washington headquarters to CIA chief of station in Honolulu is reprinted here:

SECRET

TOC: 1716347 Jan 83   *1242*
XXXXXXXXXXXXXXXXXXXXXXXXXXXXXXXXXXXXXXXXXXX
SECRET 171625Z Jan 83 STAFF
   CITE DIRECTOR 441183.
   TO: IMMEDIATE DCD/HONOLULU INFO DCD/HEADQUARTERS
   WNINTEL
   SUBJ: LPBURGER CHAIRMAN'S TAX PROBLEMS

REF: DCD/HONOLULU 12288
   1. Regret delay in providing cover guidance for use by L.P. Burger, Chairman (LPC). A cover story based on the limited information available at HQS is tentative at best. We do not know the full scope of transactions he brokered for various CIA elements or his relationship with the accountant. The approach to a cover story could vary if the accountant works full time for LPC, does not work full time but does all LPC bookkeeping, or is only involved in ad hoc tasks such as tax return preparation. Based on interim answers in DCD/FRD, headquarters suggest that the following explanation be discussed with LPC to determine if he is willing to proceed along these lines with his accountant:
    A. LPC established three companies in question for undisclosed foreign clients who needed U.S. government base for certain unspecified business operations; thus LPC is strictly a nominee in all matters pertaining to these companies and has no beneficial interests in the entities.
    B. Client forwarded certain monies to LPC personal account for establishment of companies and other transactions which LPC passed through his personal account to bank accounts of companies (if such existed); alternative is that LPC disbursed monies from personal account in furtherance of business of clients. In brief, all funds involved were clients' funds and not personal income or expenses of LPC.

C. LPC did not file tax returns for companies because it did not know all transactions for which companies use and assumes that clients have taken care of tax filing. (In fact, no such filings have been made.)

Another CIA message (December 1982) from CIA Langley headquarters to the CIA Chief of Station in Hawaii made reference to the arms agreement between Rewald and Rajiv Gandhi. In a letter written to CIA Director William Casey on December 8, 1983, attorney Robert Smith made reference to an arms transaction between the CIA proprietary BBRDW and the Taiwan government in which Rewald participated.

Another CIA cable marked Secret related to Rewald's participation in a search for missing American prisoners of war in Vietnam, noting CIA funding requirements. Reference was made to the disbursement and use of $75,000, and the need for another $75,000. A February 14, 1983, CIA document made reference to Rewald of Bishop, Baldwin, Rewald, Dillingham & Wong, and the transmittal of Japanese HSST plans and material to CIA Langley headquarters. Obviously, Rewald was a contract employee of the Central Intelligence Agency and BBRDW was a CIA proprietary.

Rewald was made the fall guy by CIA and Justice Department officials, to protect renegade CIA officials from their corrupt activities. It was the CIA, whose decision to disavow Rewald and strip the company of its financial assets, that caused investors to lose millions of dollars.

Rewald will die in prison if help doesn't come soon. I offered to prepare and file federal court actions for him, and petition Congress, including:

* Motion to vacate the prison sentence;

* A habeas corpus action to vacate the prison sentence;

* A *Bivens* action against the federal government and certain known and unknown federal employees, which is the equivalent of a Civil Rights Action that is limited to offenses committed under the color of state law. The *Bivens* action would be for damages, for declaratory judgement holding the prison sentence invalid, and for injunctive relief to obtain Rewald's release.

* To file a petition with members of Congress requesting that a bill be introduced in Congress to provide relief to Rewald, using in the petition the sworn declarations given to me by Rewald and attaching government documents showing Rewald to have been a federal employee.

Tragic and outrageous as this conspiracy was, Rewald is only one of dozens who have been criminally victimized by those in control of the CIA and the Justice Department. There are many other examples that I uncovered, some of which are described in other pages.

Even while Rewald was in prison, the CIA attempted to have him assassinated. American Broadcasting Company (ABC) presented a two-part report on *World News Tonight*, on September 19 and 20, 1984, featuring a former CIA contract agent, Scott Barnes, describing a plan in which the CIA hired him to infiltrate the prison where Rewald was an inmate, and check on Rewald's activities. According to Barnes, two CIA agents, John Stein and Gene Wilson, hired him to investigate whether Rewald was blowing the whistle on the CIA's operations. Barnes stated during the ABC show that in November 1984 he met Stein, Wilson, and two Office of Naval Intelligence agents at the Royal Hawaiian Hotel in Waikiki, and that during the meeting Barnes was told: "Rewald is no longer an asset; he is only a liability." Barnes was then directed to kill Rewald. Barnes refused.

CIA THREATENING, AND THEN BUYING, A MAJOR NEWS SOURCE

In November 1984 CIA Director William Casey complained to the Federal Communication Commission about the ABC television network for having aired a show featuring CIA agent Scott Barnes. In the television presentation Barnes said he was asked by two CIA agents in Honolulu to kill Ronald Rewald. This airing had the danger of revealing the CIA role in BBRDW and could lead to endless number of other covert CIA proprietaries and operations. Casey was a founder,[342] major investor, and director, in Capital Cities Corporation, which then took over the ABC television network the following year, in March 1985. As stated in *National Affairs*:

> *The CIA director openly attacks a leading network and threatens its broadcast license, ultimately causing it to issue a retraction of a [highly sensitive] story. Meanwhile, wearing his other hat as an investor, founder and close confidante of the Capital Cities management, Casey also stands to further his private business interests, as well as those of his friends, who were mounting a takeover of ABC.*

The combination of the media being infiltrated by CIA assets, threatening to revoke its government-granted license, and business interests linked to government officials linked with government corruption, are key reasons why the media has engaged in a complicity of silence.

In April 1993 prison officials at Terminal Island placed a block on Rewald's outgoing phone calls so that any calls to me would be automatically blocked. The following November, after the first printing of *Defrauding America* came out with reference to Rewald, prison authorities seized all of his records, preventing him from disclosing to me evidence of CIA-related corruption against the United States.

A SMALL PART OF AN OVERALL PLAN

Nugan Hand and BBRDW were only two out of many other vehicles used by the CIA to defraud innocent people out of large sums of money, as part of a much greater conspiracy and criminal enterprise. During hundreds of hours questioning CIA and DEA whistleblowers and police investigators, I discovered the existence of many other similar operations, and also the mechanics of how they were formed and operated.

REFUSAL OF REWALD TO COOPERATE

Most of what I learned about BBRDW was learned from sources other than Rewald. He provided me with some documents showing him to be connected with the CIA, but he refused to provide me information about the crimes committed by the CIA and key CIA officials. He chose to protect

---

[342] Along with Lowell Thomas and others.

them, knowing that the harm would continue to be inflicted. He sought to justify keeping secret the CIA crimes on the argument that he signed a CIA secrecy agreement. I reminded him several times that the secrecy agreement cannot be used to keep a federal employee from exposing criminal acts by his or her superiors. And especially the subversive and criminal acts that include drug trafficking and drug-money laundering.

Using Rewald's arguments, if he knew of an assassination attempt upon the president of the United States planned by CIA superiors, he would remain silent about it, and allow it to happen.

Other former CIA agents, Heinrich Rupp and Richard Brenneke, refused to cooperate, withholding information about CIA criminal activities that could have been exposed through the publication of *Defrauding America*. Fortunately, there were others who were willing to meet their responsibilities as citizens, who joined our small group seeking to alert the American public to what was being done to them.

CHAPTER TWENTY TWO

INSLAW AND CRIMES AT JUSTICE

The primary importance of the Inslaw affair is to provide additional examples of the criminal mindset of federal officials and attorneys in the highest law-enforcement agency of the United States, which has converted the Department of Justice into a criminal enterprise.

Inslaw is the name of a small computer programming company owned by William and Nancy Hamilton, that was subjected to criminal activities and a conspiracy by high Justice Department officials. By misusing the power of their office, these officials, including the three U.S. attorney generals in the Reagan-Bush administrations, Edwin Meese, Richard Thornburgh, and William Barr, misappropriated, or aided and abetted, the theft of the software called PROMIS. The tactics used by the highest law-enforcement officers in the United States to steal the software forced the small company into Chapter 11, after which Justice Department officials misused the U.S. Trustee division of the Justice Department, and the federal courts, seeking to force the company into a Chapter 7 liquidation.

In 1982 the U.S. Department of Justice signed a $10 million contract with Inslaw to install an enhanced version of software known as PROMIS in 42 U.S. Attorney offices. The Inslaw company went heavily into debt, obtaining a loan, to complete the contract. After the software was installed, and found to be satisfactory, and its value recognized for an upcoming half-billion-dollar government contract, Justice Department officials refused to pay Inslaw, knowing that it would force them into bankruptcy. Once Inslaw filed for bankruptcy, Justice Department officials could force the company into a Chapter 7 liquidation through its U.S. Trustee division and control of the bankruptcy process.

As stated elsewhere in these pages, it is a standard practice for people in control of the CIA and other government agencies to target selected companies and force them into bankruptcy, and then have associates take over the assets.

A close friend of Attorney General Edwin Meese, Earl Brian, had a controlling interest in a software company seeking to obtain the government computer contract: Hadron Incorporated. The company was primarily owned by Earl Brian,[343] who served in the White House as chairman of a task force which reported to Attorney General Edwin Meese. Meese and his wife had a financial interest in Hadron.

Key Justice Department and White House people who were part of the conspiracy included the three U.S. attorney generals (starting with Edwin Meese), Earl Brian, Deputy Attorney General D. Lowell Jensen, among others. All were from California and, except for Brian, they were all California attorneys. Earl Brian and Edwin Meese were from California and in former Governor Ronald Reagan's administration. Brian wanted the Inslaw software, which would subsequently be sold to the Justice Department and other government agencies in a $500 million contract.

Brian expected to obtain the contract through his influence with Meese, whose wife had stock in Hadron. The value of that stock, and the company's profits, would soar into the tens of millions of dollars upon obtaining the rights to Inslaw's Enhanced PROMIS software and the government contract.

Earlier, the chairman of Hadron, Dominic Laiti, attempted to purchase the PROMIS software from Inslaw, but Inslaw refused to sell. Laiti warned Lee Hamilton that Hadron was politically connected to Attorney General Meese, and "We have ways of making you sell." After this threat was made, Justice Department officials refused to pay for the PROMIS software, knowingly forcing the Hamiltons to seek refuge in Chapter 11. Deputy Attorney General Lowell Jensen, another former California attorney, was directly responsible for approving payment to Inslaw, and refused to pay for the installed software. Unable to pay their employees and the bank loan, the Hamiltons sought refuge in Chapter 11.

In what was probably a *quid pro quo* for his cooperation in the scheme against Inslaw, Meese recommended to President Reagan that Jensen be appointed to a U.S. District Judge in San Francisco. Jensen played key roles in the obstruction of justice when I sought to report the federal crimes to federal courts in the San Francisco area. He was one of several October Surprise and Inslaw participants who profited by their role in October Surprise, Inslaw, and other crimes against the United States.

Another federal official involved in the scheme against Inslaw was Edwin Thomas, Assistant Counsel to President Reagan, and a friend of Meese. Thomas loaned Meese's wife, Ursula, $15,000, in early 1981, to buy stock in Infotech (then operating under the name of Biotech Capital Corporation). Thomas was working directly for Meese as Assistant Counsel to the President, and earl Brian loaned him $100,000 in July 1981. Thomas, using his official White House position, made calls to the Small Business Administration to

---

[343] Brian owned United Press International.

have the SBA approve a loan application to a Biotech subsidiary owned by Thomas which was involved in computer software. Biotech hoped to obtain Justice Department software contracts worth an estimated half billion dollars, using the stolen Inslaw software. The insiders to this scheme anticipated they would be multi-millionaires. But the scheme required that Infotech/Biotech/-Hadron obtain the Enhanced PROMIS software from Inslaw, which the owners, Lee and Nancy Hamilton, refused to sell.

After Inslaw sought refuge in Chapter 11, Justice Department officials pressured the IRS to force Inslaw into a Chapter 7 liquidation, hoping to have Hadron acquire the PROMIS software, which would then be offered to the government for the estimated half billion dollars in contracts. In an unusual refusal to cooperate with Justice Department dirty tricks, Chapter 11 Judge George F. Bason blocked that attempt.

SELLING THE STOLEN SOFTWARE

After receiving the leased software from Inslaw, Justice Department officials gave the software to Earl Brian,[344] who then used CIA contract agent Michael Riconosciuto to alter the program at the Wackenhut-operated facilities on the Cabazon Indian Reservation near Indio, California.

The Hamiltons, who owned the Inslaw Company, discovered the unlawful sale of their software by Justice Department officials and Earl Brian to Canada when Canadian government personnel inadvertently contacted Inslaw for information on the software which had been sold to them. The Hamilton's visited the Canadian offices that had requested information, discovering that numerous Canadian offices were using it. After the Hamilton's reported that they had not sold the software to any Canadian offices, and that they were not authorized to use it, Canadian officials falsely claimed that none of their offices were using the software. Canadian authorities covered up for the theft and protected Justice Department officials. Brian and others who worked with him sole the stolen Inslaw software throughout the world for tens of millions of dollars. Crime does pay.

CIVIL SUIT AGAINST JUSTICE DEPARTMENT OFFICIALS

While in Chapter 11 proceedings, the Inslaw Company filed a civil action[345] against the U.S. Department of Justice and the officials who stole the PROMIS software. In court filings, Inslaw and its attorney, former U.S. Attorney General Elliott Richardson, claimed that Inslaw was a victim of a conspiracy by Meese and his friends, who capitalized on their government positions for the purpose of stealing the software and converting it into private use and personal gains.

Justice Department officials sought to block this lawsuit by misusing the power of the Justice Department. The first attorney representing Inslaw against the Justice Department was Leigh Ratiner in the Washington law firm

---

[344] *The Financial Post* August 19, 1991, issue linked Brian to covert operations with the United States and Israeli intelligence communities. He was reportedly involved in the sale of weapons to Iran in the 1980s. He reportedly worked with the CIA. He was reportedly implicated in the many scandals involving Ed Meese.

[345] *Inslaw v. Thornburgh*, Civ. 89-3443.

of Dickstein and Shapiro. As Ratiner discovered, Justice Department officials put pressure upon his bosses, causing them to dismiss him from the law firm. However, they paid him the fabulous sum of $120,000 yearly for the next five years, on the condition that he not practice law during that time.

In this way the attorney could not represent the Inslaw firm in its lawsuit against Justice Department officials, and the Hamiltons, now without funds, would have great difficulty finding a law firm that would take their case. This inability to obtain legal counsel is made worse by attorneys' refusal to take cases against the Justice Department when that powerful agency can retaliate.

Ben-Menashe saw a cable from Israel's Joint Committee[346] to the United States requesting that $600,000 be transferred from the CIA-Israeli slush fund to Hadron. The cable stated that the money would be transferred to the law firm of Dickstein and Shapiro as compensation to remove Inslaw's attorney, Ratiner, from the case. Talk about conspiracies!

TWO FEDERAL JUDGES RULED AGAINST JUSTICE DEPARTMENT

At the end of the civil trial against the Justice Department in the Inslaw case, Judge George Bason ruled in favor of Inslaw and awarded Inslaw $6.8 million. Bason lambasted Justice Department officials, stating they were guilty of deceit, theft and trickery. Justice Department officials appealed the judgement to the U.S. District Court,[347] where U.S. District Judge William Bryant upheld the decision, praising Judge Bason's "attention to detail and mastery of evidence."

That decision was then appealed to the U.S. Court of Appeals in Washington, D.C., where several of the October Surprise participants had received federal judgeships for their loyalty to the conspirators. The decision was reversed, claiming the lower court judges had no jurisdiction to render such a decision.

A practice in federal courts, little understood by the public, is to appoint U.S. Attorneys to the federal judiciary who are loyal to the Justice Department's controlling clique. These insiders then act to protect the dirty business in the Justice Department, the CIA, or any other federal agency. Judges who don't cooperate are sometimes charged with criminal offenses by Justice Department prosecutors for some real or fabricated minor offenses, and removed from the bench.

JUSTICE DEPARTMENT RETALIATION

Bankruptcy court judges must be reappointed every fourteen years, and that reappointment was denied to Judge Bason after the unfavorable ruling against Justice Department officials. Justice Department officials then recommended for appointment to Bason's former position the Justice Department attorney who opposed the Inslaw litigation. Judge Bason later testified to a Congressional committee: "I have come to believe that my non-reappointment as bankruptcy judge was the result of improper influence from

---

[346] Israel's Joint Committee was formed to deal with Iran-Israel relations.
[347] The United States Court of Appeals in Washington vacated the judgment against the Justice Department, ruling that the bankruptcy courts lacked jurisdiction over the matter.

within the Justice Department which the current appointment process failed to prevent."

It is normal for over 90 percent of the incumbent bankruptcy judges who sought reappointment to be reappointed. Bason's replacement had no bankruptcy experience, but could be counted upon to carry out Justice Department wishes.

ALTERING TESTIMONY, A CRIME

In March 1987, Justice Department officials pressured an important witness, a federal judge, to change testimony that he had previously given in the Inslaw matter. A Justice Department attorney also was pressured to recant his previous testimony favorable to Inslaw. For them to recant their earlier testimony and state the opposite, means that they lied the first time they testified, and committed perjury, for which Justice Department prosecutors should file perjury charges. If their earlier testimony had been perjured, the same Justice Department attorneys should have prosecuted them. Actually, Justice Department attorneys were suborning them to perjure themselves by stating the opposite of what they testified earlier, and the opposite of what was the truth.

ALTERING THE PROMIS SOFTWARE

Prior to selling the software to foreign countries for use by their intelligence and military agencies, the CIA and Justice Department altered the PROMIS program to permit the CIA to secretly tap into it and extract information. The alterations were accomplished at the Cabazon Indian Reservation near Indio, California by a group of computer programmers led by CIA contract agent Michael Riconosciuto.

Riconosciuto played a key role in the 1980 October Surprise scheme. He and Earl Brian played a part in the wire transfer of $40 million in bribe money related to the Iranians in Paris during the October 19, 1980 Paris meetings.

Riconosciuto stated to me that the Inslaw PROMIS software was brought to him at the Cabazon Indian Reservation near Indio, California, by Earl Brian while Riconosciuto was a contract agent with the CIA. Riconosciuto was skilled at computer programming and made modifications to the software in order to meet the requirements of the Canadian Mounties and the Canadian Security and Intelligence Service. He reported that it was Brian who sold Inslaw's software to the Canadians.

Another CIA operative knowing of the sale of the PROMIS software was Gunther Russbacher, who carried the software to Australia and provided me with a sworn statement to that effect, which I, in turn, provided to the Hamiltons and their attorney, Elliott Richardson.

Ari Ben-Menashe, a former member of Israel's Mossad, told the Hamiltons that he had obtained the enhanced PROMIS software from Earl Brian and Robert McFarlane (who at that time was Reagan's national security adviser). Documents and CIA statements made to me showed that McFarlane played a role in the 1980 October Surprise scheme and the following Iran-Contra scandal.

Ben-Menashe stated that he was at a meeting in Israel when Brian stated he owned the PROMIS software and was trying to sell it to Israel. Ben-

Menashe stated that Chilean arms dealer Carlos Cardoen told him that "he brokered a deal between Brian and a representative of the Iraqi military intelligence for the use of Promis." Iranian arms dealer Richard Babayan stated in a 1987 affidavit that a member of Iraqi intelligence told him Iraq had acquired PROMIS from Brian on the recommendations of the Libyan government.

YEARS OF SELECTED MEDIA EXPOSURE

An article in *The American Lawyer* (December 1987) referred to the Inslaw affair:

> *No sooner had the Justice Department awarded Inslaw a $10 million contract than things began to go wrong. Hamilton couldn't understand why. Suddenly Inslaw's finances were in shambles. By February 7, 1985, the government had withheld payments on $1.77 million in costs and fees. Inslaw, the market leader, filed for bankruptcy. Hamilton says he was mystified. How could everything he had built fall apart so fast—and with no explanation? [Inslaw said]*
>
> *I think, in a perverse way, I was ... slow to catch on. I feel silly. I wasn't paranoid enough.*
>
> *A story of government conniving and manipulation ... and in Elliot Richardson's words, "complemented and allowed to run its course by ill will at the higher level," meaning former Deputy Attorney General Jensen. [Now a federal judge at San Francisco.]*

SERIES OF KILLINGS PROTECTED FEDERAL OFFICIALS

Following a deadly pattern, many people who posed a threat to U.S. officials because of what they knew turned up dead. The most publicized killing related to Inslaw was free-lance reporter and author, Danny Casolaro, who was investigating criminal activities implicating Justice Department officials and writing a book on the subject. Casolaro was killed at the Sheraton Inn in Martinsburg, West Virginia on August 10, 1991.

A CIA operative had met Casolaro earlier at a restaurant, advising Casolaro that he knew of a person who could give Casolaro additional evidence proving the link between Justice Department officials and the Inslaw scandal.

Shortly before his death, Casolaro met with a former CIA Special Forces operative who had worked for a company involved in the Inslaw case, and who was also a good friend of Justice Department official, Peter Videnieks. Videnieks was the Justice Department official who would later threaten Riconosciuto if he testified before a Congressional committee in the Inslaw investigation or gave affidavits into the Inslaw civil action. The former CIA operative set up a meeting between Casolaro and Videnieks, and it is at this meeting that Casolaro was killed.

Casolaro traveled to Martinsburg, Virginia, about 40 miles from Washington, to meet the informant. The following morning, August 11, 1991, Casolaro was found dead in the bathtub of his room in the Sheraton Hotel, his wrists slashed ten times. His briefcase and all his notes were missing. There were many similarities between Casolaro's killing and the attempted murder of CIA operative Ronald Rewald in Honolulu.

Casolaro had been talking almost daily with CIA contract agent Michael Riconosciuto, and had stayed with Riconosciuto and his wife, Bobbi, at their residence near Tacoma, Washington, obtaining additional evidence. Casolaro's death was one of at least half-a-dozen closely linked to the Inslaw matter. Casolaro's death bred numerous media articles linking Justice Department officials with Inslaw.[348]

Despite identification in Casolaro's personal belongings listing his relatives, the police made no effort to contact Casolaro's family before placing a suicide label on the death and ordering an immediate and unprecedented embalming of the body. No permission was sought from Casolaro's family, and no check was made for incapacitating drugs that may have been given to him. This unusual response destroyed any evidence that might have linked Casolaro's death to others.

Casolaro had suspected his life may be in danger, and said several times to his brother, a medical doctor, that if anything happened to him that looked like an accident, for him not to believe it.

After Casolaro's murder, Inslaw's attorney Elliott Richardson again demanded that the Justice Department conduct an investigation, citing the fact that Casolaro found evidence proving the existence of misconduct by high Justice Department officials over whom the Attorney General had supervisory responsibility. Richardson was in effect asking the U.S. Attorney General to investigate criminal misconduct implicating Attorney General Edwin Meese, and those working under him.

SENATE "INVESTIGATION"

Probably motivated by media attention to the Inslaw matter, the Senate Permanent Subcommittee on Investigations, chaired by Senator Sam Nunn, conducted a typical Congressional investigation in 1989 into the theft of the PROMIS software, and into problems in Chapter 11 courts. Justice Department officials blocked the investigation by refusing to produce documents and refusing to allow Justice Department personnel to be questioned under oath. Attorney General Thornburgh refused to appear before the committee, even though he had a duty to do so. The Senate Committee also had a duty to force the Attorney General and other federal employees to appear. Instead, the Committee disbanded the investigation and issued an incomplete report.

CONFIRMATION BY CIA INFORMANTS

Several CIA operatives and contract agents, including Gunther Russbacher and Michael Riconosciuto, offered to testify before the Congressional committees to provide evidence. Only Riconosciuto was allowed to give testimony, showing that the PROMIS software was stolen by Justice Department officials, given to Earl Brian, and sold to numerous foreign countries, including Canada, Libya, Iran, Iraq,[349] and South Korea.

---

[348] A typical article was entitled, "The Dark World of Danny Casolaro," a four-page article in the October 28, 1991 issue of *The Nation*.

[349] The PROMIS software was reportedly sold to Iraq in 1988, while the Bush Administration was supplying Iraq with billions of dollars in grain subsidies, that were diverted to arms purchases.

The Inslaw contract with the Justice Department to install the PROMIS software did not constitute a sale, like most software purchases. Similar to the purchase of software such as Word Perfect, the buyer of that software only has a license to install and use it, and not to turn around and sell it, as Justice Department officials and their associates in business subsequently did.

THREAT OF PRISON IF THE TESTIMONY WAS FALSE

The Senate report described the stonewalling, stating that its inquiry into Inslaw's charges had been "hampered by the [justice] department's lack of cooperation." The report stated that it had found employees "who desired to speak to the subcommittee, but who chose not to, out of fear of for their jobs." The report addressed not only the Justice Department's misconduct in the Inslaw affair but also its misuse of Chapter 11 through its U.S. Trustee Division. The report concluded that the Justice Department politicized the U.S. Trustee program, forcing the Inslaw company, with whom it did business, into bankruptcy, by refusing to pay for the PROMIS software program.

These were serious charges of misconduct by officials in an agency over whom Congress had oversight responsibilities, requiring Congress to fully investigate the matter and bring it to a satisfactory conclusion. As usual, they engaged in, at best, misfeasance, allowing the criminal and corrupt activities to go unpunished and to continue.

The report agreed with the findings of Judge Bason, who blasted the Department of Justice in his decision. The judge's decision stated in part:

[Justice Department officials] took, converted, stole, [the plaintiff's property] by trickery, fraud and deceit. [made] an institutional decision ... at the highest level simply to ignore serious questions of ethical impropriety, made repeatedly by persons of unquestioned probity and integrity, and this failure constitutes bad faith, vexatiousness, wantonness and oppressiveness. ... engaged in outrageous, deceitful, fraudulent game of cat and mouse, demonstrating contempt for both the law and any principle of fair dealing.

The Senate report included articles appearing in *Barron's*[350] and *The American Lawyer*[351] which went into great details describing the Justice Department and U.S. Trustee misconduct. One article in *Barron's*[352] described the Justice Department's attempts to bankrupt and destroy Inslaw, misusing the U.S. Trustees and the bankruptcy judges to carry out their scheme. The article stated in part:

Justice officials proceeded to purposefully drive the small software company into bankruptcy, and then tried to push it into liquidation, engaging in an "outrageous, deceitful, fraudulent game of cat and mouse, demonstrating contempt for both the law and any principle of fair dealing." ... Ultimately, the series of "willful, wanton, and deceitful acts" led to a cover up. Bason called statements by top

---

[350] March 21, and April 4, 1988.
[351] December 1987.
[352] March 21, 1988.

Justice Department officials "ludicrous ... incredible ... and totally unbelievable."

Some of the evidence against the department came from one of its own. During the course of the litigation, Anthony Pasciuto, Deputy Director of the department's Executive Office for United States Trustees, told ... how the Justice Department had pressured Trustee officers to liquidate [Inslaw]. Later, a superior confirmed Pasciuto's story. But at the trial, a horrified Pasciuto listened while his superior changed his testimony. Close to tears, he, too, recanted.

Judge Bason ... ordered Justice to pay Inslaw about $6.8 million in licensing fees and roughly another $1 million in legal fees. ... In November, Judge Bason rejected a Department of Justice motion to liquidate Inslaw. ... one month later, the Harvard Law School graduate and former law professor discovered that he was not being reappointed.

Describing how government officials hang in until the press drops the subject, and then continue the misconduct, the article stated:

It seemed as if the controversy was winding down. ... It would follow a natural course in the press, and then fade from view. Inslaw would become another shocking event that slinks off into obscurity: Someone occasionally might dimly remember and idly ask, "What ever did happen to Bill Hamilton and those Inslaw people? A real shame ... I heard the judge was back teaching law somewhere...

The *Barron's* article described the efforts of Anthony Pasciuto, a Department of Justice insider, who blew the whistle on the Justice Department's misuse of this powerful federal agency against Inslaw and his small company:

In an interview with Barron's ... Pasciuto explained how the Justice Department blacklisted Inslaw. It was a tale that involved two U.S. trustees, a federal judge who told two versions of the same story, and a Justice Department that routinely refused to pay certain suppliers.

Pattern of harassment [by the Justice Department] that helped drive Inslaw into Chapter 11. ... the Justice Department was trying to starve Inslaw. They didn't just push to bankrupt the software firm, ... they wanted to liquidate it, converting it from Chapter 11 to Chapter 7, as soon as possible. Why?

Tony Pasciuto [said] that his boss, Thomas Stanton, director of the Justice Department's Executive Office for U.S. Trustees, was pressuring the federal trustee overseeing the Inslaw case, William White, to liquidate Inslaw.

Cornelius Blackshear, the U.S. Trustee in New York at the time of Inslaw's Chapter 11 filing, knew all about Stanton's plan. Pasciuto said that Judge Blackshear had repeated this tale of pressure in the presence of United States Court of Appeals Judge Lawrence Pierce in the judge's chambers in Foley Square in New York.

Blackshear met with a Justice Department representative, and signed a sworn affidavit, recanting, and said that he had confused Inslaw with another case—United Press International, which had also been involved in bankruptcy proceedings in Judge Bason's court.

Cornelius Blackshear left his position as United States Trustee and became a United States bankruptcy judge the following fall.[353]

"A LOT DIRTIER THAN WATERGATE"

Ronald LeGrand, Chief Investigator for the Senate Judiciary Committee, told William Hamilton and his attorney that a trusted Justice Department source confided that the Inslaw case was "a lot dirtier for the Department of Justice than Watergate had been, both in its breadth and its depth."

Despite the oversight responsibilities of this Senate group, despite the requirements of federal criminal statutes, the Senate committee refused to take any actions against the criminal acts of federal employees in the U.S. Department of Justice, and did nothing to alleviate the harm inflicted upon the innocent owners of the Inslaw company. In this way they aided and abetted the criminal activities, of which Inslaw was only the tip of the iceberg.

HOUSE "INVESTIGATION"

The Congressional Subcommittee on Economic and Commercial Law of the Committee on the Judiciary, also held hearings concerning the Inslaw matter and the related death of Danny Casolaro. Congressman Jack Brooks (D-Texas) chaired the committee investigation. U.S. Attorney Meese and the Justice Department group stonewalled the House committee just as they had done with the Senate committee, refusing to turn over requested documents, fraudulently stating the key documents had been accidentally destroyed or could not be found. How convenient! At the start of the hearings Congressman Brooks stated:

As incredible as this sounds, federal Bankruptcy Judge George Bason, who will be testifying later, has already found much of the first part of the allegation to be true. In his decision on the Inslaw bankruptcy, Judge Bason ruled that the Department "took, converted and stole" Inslaw's proprietary software using "trickery, fraud and deceit." The judge also severely criticized the decisions by high-level Department officials to "ignore the ethical improprieties" on the part of the Justice Department officials involved in the case.

During the committee hearings, over thirty people testified, revealing how Justice Department officials had stolen the software, schemed to force Inslaw into bankruptcy, and then stole the computer program. Among those who testified before the House committee was former Chapter 11 Judge Bason, who heard the case against the Justice Department. He testified:

The judicial opinions that I rendered reflected my sense of moral outrage that, as the evidence showed and as I held, the Justice Department stole Inslaw's property and tried to drive Inslaw out of business. Those opinions were upheld on appeal by Judge Bryant in a memorandum that noted my attention to detail and mastery of evidence.

---

[353] For those who cooperate with the Justice Department, federal judgeship positions are the carrot.

Revealing Justice Department retaliation for rendering a decision unfavorable to the agency, Judge Bason testified:

> *Very soon after I rendered those opinions, my application for reappointment was turned down. One of the Justice Department attorneys who argued the Inslaw case before me was appointed in my stead. Although over 90 percent of the incumbent bankruptcy judges who sought reappointment were in fact reappointed, I was not among them.*

By placing one of their own as a judge on the federal court system (a common practice), the Justice Department officials expanded their pattern of influence.

Congressman Brooks stated in the final committee report: "Despite the dramatic findings by the two courts, the Department has steadfastly denied any wrongdoing by its officials, claiming that its conflict with Inslaw is nothing more than a simple contract dispute. I find this position a little hard to swallow."

The September 10, 1992, report accused high Justice Department officials of criminal misconduct and recommended appointment of a special prosecutor. The 122 page report stated in part:

> *There appears to be strong evidence, as indicated by the findings in two federal court proceedings, as well as by the committee investigation, that the Department of Justice "acted willfully and fraudulently,"[354] and "took, converted and stole," Inslaw's enhanced PROMIS by "trickery, fraud, and deceit." It appears that these actions against Inslaw were implemented through the project manager from the beginning of the contract and under the direction of high level Justice Department officials.*
>
> *What is strikingly apparent from the testimony and depositions of key witnesses and many documents is that ... [The Department] engaged in an outrageous, deceitful, fraudulent game of cat and mouse, demonstrating contempt for both the law and any principle of fair dealing. ... high level officials at the Department of Justice conspired to drive Inslaw into insolvency and steal the PROMIS software so it could be used by Dr. Earl Brian, a former associate and friend of then Attorney General Edwin Meese. Dr. Brian is a businessman and entrepreneur who owns or controls several businesses including Hadron, Inc., which has contracts with the Justice Department, CIA, and other agencies. ... the circumstances involving the theft of the PROMIS software system constitute a possible criminal conspiracy involving Mr. Meese, Judge Jensen, Dr. Brian, and several current and former officials at the Department of Justice. ... the committee's investigation largely supports the findings of two federal courts that the Department "took, converted, stole" Inslaw's enhanced PROMIS by "trickery, fraud and deceit," and that this misappropriation involved officials at the highest levels of the*

---

[354] *INSLAW, Inc. v. United States*, opinion of U.S. District Court Judge William Bryant, at p. WP.

Department of Justice.

One of the principal reasons the committee could not reach any definitive conclusion about Inslaw's allegations of a high criminal conspiracy at Justice was the lack of cooperation from the Department. Throughout the two Inslaw investigations, the Congress met with restrictions, delays, and outright denials to requests for information and to unobstructed access to records and witnesses since 1988. [fraudulent claims] Some of the documents held by the Department's chief attorney in charge of the Inslaw litigation had been misplaced or accidentally destroyed.

The ultimate goal of the conspiracy was to position Hadron and the other companies owned or controlled by Dr. Brian to take advantage of the nearly 3 billion dollars' worth of automated data processing upgrade contracts planned to be awarded by the Department of Justice during the 1980's.

The enhanced PROMIS software was stolen by high level Justice officials and distributed internationally in order to provide financial gain to Dr. Brian and to further intelligence and foreign policy objectives of the United States.

Numerous potential witnesses refused to cooperate, for the stated reason that they were fearful for their jobs and retaliation by the Justice Department, or that attempts had already been made to intimidate them against cooperating.

The Department's unwillingness to allow Congressional oversight into its affairs, in spite of an alleged coverup of wrongdoing, greatly hindered the committee's investigation of the Inslaw allegations. The committee also encountered serious problems with obtaining cooperation from U.S. intelligence and law enforcement agencies. The committee also encountered virtually no cooperation in its investigation of the Inslaw matter beyond U.S. borders. The government of Canada refused to make its officials available to committee investigators for interviews without strict limitations on the questioning.

Referring to an even worse level of corruption, the committee report stated:

According to LeGrand, a trusted source, described to the Hamiltons as a senior DOJ official with a title, had alleged that the two senior Criminal Division officials were witnesses to much greater malfeasance against Inslaw than that already found by the Bankruptcy Court, malfeasance on a much more serious scale than Watergate. LeGrand told the Hamiltons that D. Lowell Jensen did not merely fail to investigate the malfeasance of Videnieks and Brewer but instead had "engineered" the malfeasance "right from the start" so that Inslaw's software business could be made available to political friends of the Reagan/Bush administration.

Can identify about 300 places where the PROMIS software has been installed illegally by the federal government. Dr. Brian sold PROMIS to the Central Intelligence Agency in 1983 for implementation on computers purchased from Floating Point Systems and what *the CIA called PROMIS "Datapoint." Dr. Brian has sold about $20 million of PROMIS licenses to the federal government. Department officials hinted to CIA officials that they should deny that they are using PROMIS.*

[A DEA agent] reassignment in 1990 to a DEA intelligence position in the State of Washington, prior to Michael Riconosciuto's March 1991 arrest there on drug charges, was more than coincidental. ... the agent was assigned to Riconosciuto's home State to manufacture a case against him. Mr. Coleman stated he believes this was done to prevent Mr. Riconosciuto from becoming a credible witness concerning the U.S. government's covert sale of PROMIS to foreign governments.

The committee encountered numerous situations that pointed to a concerted effort by Department officials to manipulate the litigation of the Inslaw bankruptcy, as alleged by the president of Inslaw. During this controversy, one key Department witness was harassed and ultimately, ...

Unauthorized destruction of government documents ... Department employees were involved in the illegal destruction (shredding) of documents related to the Inslaw case.

Riconosciuto stated that a tape recording of the telephone threat was confiscated by DEA agents at the time of Riconosciuto's arrest. ... the timing of the arrest, coupled with Mr. Riconosciuto's allegations that tapes of a telephone conversation he had with Mr. Videnieks were confiscated by DEA agents, raises serious questions concerning whether the Department's prosecution of Mr. Riconosciuto was related to his cooperation with the committee.

IX. CONCLUSION

Based on the committee's investigation and two separate court rulings, it is clear that high level Department of Justice officials deliberately ignored Inslaw's proprietary rights in the enhanced version of PROMIS and misappropriated this software for use at locations not covered under contract with the company. ... Instead of conducting an investigation into Inslaw's claims that criminal wrongdoing by high level government officials had occurred, Attorney Generals Meese and Thornburgh blocked or restricted Congressional inquiries into the matter, ignored the findings of two courts and refused to ask for the appointment of an independent counsel. These actions were taken in the face of a growing body of evidence that serious wrongdoing had occurred which reached to the highest levels of the Department. The evidence received by the committee during its investigation clearly raises serious concerns about the possibility that a high level conspiracy against Inslaw did exist and that great efforts have been expended by the Department to block any outside investigation into the matter.

Finally, the committee believes that the only way the Inslaw allegations can be adequately and fully investigated is by the appointment of an independent counsel.

X. FINDINGS

... *the Department ignored Inslaw's data rights to its enhanced version of its PROMIS software and misused its prosecutorial and litigative resources to legitimize and coverup its misdeeds.* ... *Several witnesses, including former Attorney General Elliot Richardson, have provided testimony, sworn statements or affidavits linking high level Department officials to a conspiracy to steal Inslaw's PROMIS software and secretly transfer PROMIS to Dr. Brian.* ... *the PROMIS software was subsequently converted for use by domestic and foreign intelligence services. This testimony was provided by individuals who knew that the Justice Department would be inclined to prosecute them for perjury if they lied under oath. No such prosecutions have occurred.*

The reviews of the Inslaw matter by Congress were hampered by Department tactics designed to conceal many significant documents and otherwise interfere with an independent review. The Department actions appear to have been motivated more by an intense desire to defend itself from Inslaw's charges of misconduct rather than investigating possible violations of the law. ... *the Department "stole through trickery, fraud and deceit" Inslaw's PROMIS software.*

13. Further investigation into the circumstances surrounding Daniel Casolaro's death is needed.

14. The following criminal statutes may have been violated by certain high level Justice officials and private individuals:

18 U.S.C. § 371–Conspiracy to commit an offense.

18 U.S.C. § 654–Officer or employee of the United States converting the property of another.

18 U.S.C. § 1341–Fraud.

18 U.S.C. § 1343–Wire fraud.

18 U.S.C. § 1505–Obstruction of proceedings before departments, agencies and committees.

18 U.S.C. § 1512—Tampering with a witness.

18 U.S.C. § 1513—Retaliation against a witness.

18 U.S.C. § 1621—Perjury.

18 U.S.C. § 1951—Interference with commerce by threats or violence (RICO).

18 U.S.C. § 1961 et seq.—Racketeer Influenced and Corrupt Organizations.

18 U.S.C. § 2314—Transportation of stolen goods, securities, moneys.

18 U.S.C. § 2315—Receiving stolen goods.

AIDING AND ABETTING

Every Republican Congressman[355] on the committee voted against the

---

[355] Congressmen Hamilton Fish, Jr.; Carlos J. Moorhead; Henry J. Hyde; F. James Sensenbrenner, Jr.; Bill McCollum; George W. Gekas; Howard Coble; Lamar S. Smith; Craig T. James; Tom Campbell; Steven Schiff; Jim Ramstad; George Allen.

report, claiming there was no support for the findings by the two federal judges and the committee investigators. This coverup tactic duplicated the obstruction of justice in the October Surprise scheme. The Republican block stated in their dissenting report:

Those entrusted with the enforcement of our laws in the Executive Branch are better qualified than Members of Congress to assess the utility of settling a legal controversy on terms favorable to a private litigant.

These Republican Congressmen held that the very same Justice Department officials (committing the criminal acts, including the obstruction of justice, the destruction or withholding of documents, the threatening of informants) should be the only persons permitted to investigate their own misconduct. The Republican Congressmen eulogized the very same Justice Department officials who had been found by two federal courts to have engaged in corrupt acts. The dissenting opinion by the Republicans stated "Fairness to DOJ requires ..." Fairness? Under these bizarre conditions, destruction of documents (a felony), threatening witnesses (a felony), using government agencies to steal the livelihood of innocent citizens (another felony)!

TRAP DOOR ALTERATIONS

Assured that the Congressional investigation would go no further, Justice Department officials and their business associates continued their sale of the stolen PROMIS program. Meese's friend and business associate, Earl Brian, sold copies of Inslaw's software to intelligence agencies all over the world, collecting millions of dollars in the process. Who says crime doesn't pay!

Israel's Mossad, who knew the software was stolen, obtained the PROMIS software from Earl Brian in 1982, through a front company called Degem. The Mossad installed their own "trap-door" into the software, permitting the Mossad to secretly enter the data base after it was sold to other countries, including Nicaragua, Colombia, Chile, and Brazil. In this way the CIA and the Mossad could spy on the countries that bought the program, including friendly nations.

The trap door alteration of the PROMIS program was accomplished for the Mossad through Mossad agent Ben-Menashe, using a computer software company in Chatsworth, California.

The CIA, working with Justice Department officials and Earl Brian, had the trap door changes made by a group headed by CIA contract agent Michael Riconosciuto,[356] working on the Cabazon Indian Reservation near Indio, California. After the trap door changes were made to the software, Brian sold the first program to Jordan via his company, Hadron. The Mossad then secretly entered the computer program without Jordan's knowledge, revealing the success of the trap-door.

The CIA and Mossad approached Robert Maxwell, a British citizen and secret Mossad agent, through Senator John Tower, in 1984, to sell the PROMIS software to East Bloc countries, including Russia. Maxwell's Berlitz

---

[356] Riconosciuto was Director of Research for the Wackenhut Corporation.

language schools, scattered throughout the world, made him an excellent source to carry out the plan. Maxwell also purchased an existing computer company owned by the Mossad, Degem, with offices in several foreign countries, to install the software.

According to Mossad agent Ari Ben-Menashe, by 1989, sales of the stolen PROMIS software brought in $40 million. Not bad for criminal activities using U.S. Department of Justice facilities, with the activities financed by U.S. taxpayers' dollars, and aided and abetted by the highest law enforcement official and agency in the U.S. government.

SOFTWARE FOR DRUGS

Guatemala purchased the PROMIS software, and the vast network of IBM computers needed to operate the program, in 1985, using money obtained from shipping drugs to the United States. Even the drug cartels used the PROMIS software. One of my DEA informants, Basil Abbott, described a flight to Panama via Belize in a small plane, along with DEA agent George Phillips, as passenger. Phillips had the PROMIS software in his suitcase belonging to a drug cartel and used to keep track of drug sales. Phillips was a CIA operative on loan to the DEA.

Unhappy with the U.S.-sanctioned shipment of chemical weapons to Iraq from Cardeon Industries in Chile, Ben-Menashe threatened to expose the sale of PROMIS software, and the hidden trap-door, if the U.S. did not halt the shipments. Justice Department officials retaliated, seeking to silence him by charging Ben-Menashe with selling aircraft to a foreign country. Justice Department prosecutors and a federal judge caused Ben-Menashe to be imprisoned for a year pending trial, until a New York federal jury acquitted him.

SELECTIVE MEDIA COVERAGE

A February 5, 1990 article in the legal newspaper, *The Recorder*, criticized Michael Shaheen, Jr., head of the Justice Department's Office of Professional Responsibility, for "outrageous, deceitful, fraudulent" acts and the coverup of such acts. Professor Bennett Gershman at New York's Pace University School of Law and author of *Prosecutorial Misconduct*, was quoted as stating, "It is a joke to say Justice [Department] polices itself."

The heading in a March 15, 1991 *Miami Journal* article read: "Justice Department perverts justice in Inslaw case." The article stated in part:

In the matter of the Department of Justice and the Inslaw case, a remarkable thing is happening: The stench gets worse. Until recently, it could be said of this shameful affair that it smelled only to high heaven. It is now beginning to smell to outer space. As Attorney General, he ought to be doing his damndest to get to the bottom of this disgraceful matter. Instead, he has stalled; he has stonewalled; he has taken refuge in legalisms; he has obstructed efforts of two Congressional committees to dig out the facts. And this isn't even his scandal. He inherited the mess from Ed Meese.

A *Vancouver Sun* headline on April 5, 1991 stated: "Probe of hot-software charge urged." The article stated in part:

Solicitor-General Pierre Cadieux should go before a parliamentary committee to answer charges the RCMP and CSIS are using stolen computer software, opposition Mps said Thursday. The PROMIS software was allegedly pirated by U.S. Justice Department officials and sold by associates of former president Ronald Reagan to government agencies in Canada, Libya, Iraq,[357] and Israel, according to affidavits filed in U.S. bankruptcy court last week.

An article in the *Financial Times* of London on April 5, 1991 referred to the Inslaw matter:

A BIZARRE series of allegations—including claims of misconduct by Mr. Robert McFarlane, the former National Security Adviser to President Ronald Reagan—have surfaced as a result of a seemingly obscure legal action involving the US Department of Justice and a small Washington computer software company called Inslaw. ... the charge Israeli intelligence forces are using an Inslaw computer software system illegally provided by Mr. McFarlane. ... several members of the Washington establishment and US press reports suggest Inslaw may be only the tip of an iceberg that could have implications for US foreign policy in the Middle East.

An October 25, 1991 *Daily Journal* headline stated: "The Promisgate Plot Thickens," with the subtitle: "Scandal over Justice Department Software Could Run Very Deep." The article revealed that the scheme was to deliver Inslaw's stolen software to a company in which Attorney General Edwin Meese had an interest and then the stolen software would be sold to the Justice Department in a $250 million contract to automate Justice Department litigation divisions.

Syndicated columnist James Kilpatrick headlined his August 29, 1991 article stating, "Odor Of a Situation Needing a Probe." The article stated in part:

Some months ago, writing about the Inslaw case, I said the affair was beginning to stink to high heaven. with the death of Danny Casolaro, a free-lance investigative reporter, the stench grows worse. ... There is reason to believe that Danny Casolaro went to Martinsburg to crack the [Inslaw] case. He had told friends that Inslaw was part of an "octopus" of criminal activities in high places, including the BCCI and the savings and loan scandals.

ORGANIZED CRIME IN THE JUSTICE DEPARTMENT

An October 27, 1991 article written by former U.S. Attorney General Elliot Richardson, appearing in newspapers throughout the United States, stated:

Organized crime in the U.S. Justice Department—The Stench at the U.S. Justice Department. The former Attorney General called for appointment of independent counsel to investigate the alleged corrup-

---

[357] It is believed that Iraq used the PROMIS software during the Persian Gulf war.

tion by Justice Department officials [358] in the Chapter 11 misconduct involving Inslaw. Richardson called for an independent counsel to investigate the Justice Department's misconduct on the basis that the nation's highest law enforcement agency was heavily implicated in Chapter 11 corruption.

OTHER CRIMINALITY SURFACED

Another pattern of corruption surfaced as Congressional investigators questioned Michael Riconosciuto. They learned that he helped arrange the transfer of $40 million bribe money from the Reagan-Bush team to the Iranians during the October 19, 1980 weekend meetings in Paris. This revelation provided further evidence that the October Surprise operation did take place, but the Senate and the House kept the lid on this awesome scandal.

Inslaw's attorney, Elliott Richardson, requested an affidavit from Riconosciuto concerning his knowledge of the Justice Department's role in the Inslaw matter. When Justice Department officials learned of these requests, Peter Videnieks of the Justice Department threatened Riconosciuto during a telephone call. Videnieks warned Riconosciuto that if he gave evidence to the Congressional committee (and a pending Inslaw civil suit against the Justice Department), serious things would happen to him and his wife, Bobbi. Riconosciuto taped this telephone conversation.

Despite Justice Department threats, Riconosciuto submitted testimony to Congress and an affidavit to Inslaw's attorney. The March 21, 1991 affidavit stated:

---

[358] Earl Brian, California health secretary under Governor Ronald Reagan, and a friend of Attorney General Edwin Meese, linked to a scheme to steal Inslaw's computer software used by the Justice Department.

UNITED STATES BANKRUPTCY COURT
FOR THE DISTRICT OF COLUMBIA

IN RE:	)	
	)	*Case No. 85-00070*
INSLAW, INC.,	)	*(Chapter 11)*
	)	
Debtor,	)	
———————————	)	
	)	
INSLAW, INC.,	)	*Adversary Proceeding*
	)	*No. 86-0069*
Plaintiff,	)	
	)	
v.	)	
	)	
UNITED STATES OF AMERICA,	)	
and the UNITED STATES	)	
DEPARTMENT OF JUSTICE,	)	
	)	
Defendants.	)	
———————————	)	

AFFIDAVIT OF MICHAEL J. RICONOSCIUTO

State of Washington	)
	) *ss:*
	)

I, *MICHAEL J. RICONOSCIUTO, being duly sworn, do hereby state as follows:*

1. During the early 1980's, I served as the Director of Research for a joint venture between the Wackenhut Corporation of Coral Gables, Florida, and the Cabazon Bank of Indians of Indio, California. The joint venture was located on the Cabazon Reservation.

2. The Wackenhut-Cabazon joint venture sought to develop and/or manufacture certain materials that are used in military and national security operations, including night vision goggles, machine guns, fuel-air explosives, and biological and chemical warfare weapons.

3. The Cabazon Band of Indians are a sovereign nation. The sovereign immunity that is accorded the Cabazons as a consequence of this fact made it feasible to pursue on the reservation the development and/or manufacture of materials whose development or manufacture would be subject to stringent controls off the reservation. As a minority group, the Cabazon Indians also provided the Wackenhut Corporation with an enhanced ability to obtain federal contracts through the 8A Set Aside Program, and in connection with government-owned contractor-operated (GOCO) facilities.

4. The Wackenhut-Cabazon joint venture was intended to support the needs of a number of foreign governments and forces, including forces and governments in Central America and the Middle East. The Contras in Nicaragua represented one of the most important priorities for the joint venture.

5. The Wackenhut-Cabazon joint venture maintained closed liaison with certain elements of the United States government, including representatives of intelligence, military and law enforcement agencies.

6. Among the frequent visitors to the Wackenhut-Cabazon joint venture were Peter Videnieks of the U.S. Department of Justice in Washington, D.C., and a close associate of Videnieks by the name of Earl W. Brian. Brian is a private businessman who lives in Maryland and who has maintained close business ties with the U.S. intelligence community for many years.

7. In connection with my work for Wackenhut, I engaged in some software development and modification work in 1983 and 1984 on the proprietary PROMIS computer software product. The copy of PROMIS on which I worked came from the U.S. Department of Justice. Earl W. Brian made it available to me through Wackenhut after acquiring it from Peter Videnieks, who was then a Department of Justice contracting official with responsibility for the PROMIS software. I performed the modifications to PROMIS in Indio, California; Silver Springs, Maryland; and Miami, Florida.

8. The purpose of the PROMIS software modifications that I made in 1983 and 1984 was to support a plan for the implementation of PROMIS in law enforcement and intelligence agencies worldwide. Earl W. Brian was spearheading the plan for this worldwide use of the PROMIS computer software.

9. Some of the modifications that I made were specifically designed to facilitate the implementation of PROMIS within two agencies of the government of Canada; the Royal Canadian Mounted Police (RCMP) and the Canadian Security and Intelligence Service (CSIS). Earl W. Brian would check with me from time to time to make certain that the work would be completed in time to satisfy the schedule for the RCMP and CSIS implementations of PROMIS.

10. The proprietary version of PROMIS, as modified by me, was, in fact, implemented in both the RCMP and the CSIS in Canada. It was my understanding that Earl W. Brian had sold this version of PROMIS to the government of Canada.

11. In February 1991, I had a telephone conversation with Peter Videnieks, then still employed by the U.S. Department of Justice. Videnieks attempted during this telephone conversation to persuade me not to cooperate with an independent investigation of the government's piracy of INSLAW's proprietary PROMIS software being conducted by the Committee on the Judiciary of the U.S. House of Representatives.

12. Videnieks stated that I would be rewarded for a decision not to cooperate with the House Judiciary Committee investigation. Videnieks forecasted an immediate and favorable resolution of a protracted child custody dispute being prosecuted against my wife by her former husband, if I were to decide not to cooperate with the House Judiciary Committee investigation.

13. Videnieks also outlined specific punishments that I could expect to receive from the U.S. Department of Justice if I cooperate with the House Judiciary Committee's investigation.

14. One punishment that Videnieks outlined was the future inclusion of me and my father in a criminal prosecution of certain business associates of mine in Orange County, California, in connection with the operation of a savings and loan institution in Orange County. By way of underscoring his power to influence such decisions at the U.S. Department of Justice, Videnieks informed me of the indictment of these business associates prior to the time when that indictment was unsealed and made public.

15. Another punishment that Videnieks threatened against me if I cooperated with the House Judiciary Committee is prosecution by the U.S. Department of Justice for perjury. Videnieks warned me that credible witnesses would come forward to contradict any damaging claims that I made in testimony before the House Judiciary Committee, and that I would subsequently be prosecuted for perjury by the U.S. Department of Justice for my testimony before the House Judiciary Committee.

FURTHER AFFIANT SAYETH NOT.

Michael J. Riconosciuto
Signed and sworn to before me this 21 day of March 1991.

Notary Public

****

Richard Babayan submitted an affidavit dated March 22, 1991 into a federal court proceeding[359] in the District of Columbia, describing the sale of Inslaw's software by Earl Brian to Iraq, Korea, Libya, and Chile. The affidavit follows:

---

[359] Case number 85-0070, U.S. Bankruptcy Court, District of Columbia.

UNITED STATES BANKRUPTCY COURT
FOR THE DISTRICT OF COLUMBIA

IN RE:	)
	) Case No. 85-00070
INSLAW, INC.,	) (Chapter 11)
	)
Debtor,	)
	)
_____	)
	)
INSLAW, INC.,	) Adversary Proceeding
	) No. 86-0069
Plaintiff,	)
	)
v.	)
	)
UNITED STATES OF AMERICA,	)
and the UNITED STATES	)
DEPARTMENT OF JUSTICE,	)
	)
Defendants.	)
_____	)

AFFIDAVIT OF RICHARD H. BABAYAN

State of Florida	)	
	)	ss:
Palm Beach County	)	

I, Richard H. Babayan, being duly sworn, do hereby state as follows:

1. During the past several years, I have acted as a broker of sales of materials and equipment used by foreign governments in their armed forces, intelligence and security organizations.

2. In the capacity described in paragraph # 1, I attended a meeting in Baghdad, Iraq, in October or November, 1987, with Mr. Abu Mohammed of Entezamat, an intelligence and security organ of the government of Iraq. Mr. Abu Mohammed is a senior ranking official of Entezamat and a person with whom I had extensive dealings over the previous three years.

3. During the aforementioned meeting with Mr. Abu Mohammed, I was informed that Dr. Earl W. Brian of the United States had recently completed a sale presentation to the government of Iraq regarding the PROMIS computer software. Furthermore, it is my understanding that others present at Dr. Brian's PROMIS sales presentation were General Richard Secord, of the United States, and Mr. Abu Mohammed.

4. In early to mid-1988, in the course of subsequent visits to Baghdad, Iraq, I was informed that Dr. Earl W. Brian had, in fact, provided the PROMIS computer software to the government of Iraq through a transaction that took place under the umbrella of Mr. Sarkis Saghanollan, an individual who has had extensive business dealings with the government of Iraq since the late 1970/s in the fields of military hardware and software. I was also informed that the government of Iraq acquired the PROMIS software for use primarily in intelligence services, and secondarily in police and law enforcement agencies.

5. During the course of the visits described in paragraph # 4, I also learned from Mr. Abu Mohammed that the government of Libya had acquired the PROMIS computer software prior to its acquisition by the government of Iraq; that the government of Libya had by then made extensive use of PROMIS; and that the government of Libya was highly recommending the PROMIS software to other countries. I was informed that the high quality of the reference for the PROMIS software from the government of Libya was one of the principal reasons for the decision of the government of Iraq to acquire PROMIS.

6. In the capacity described in paragraph # 1, I attended a meeting in early 1988 in Singapore with Mr. Y.H. Nam of the Korea Development Corporation.

7. The Korea Development Corporation is known to be a cutout for the Korean Central Intelligence Agency (KCIA).

8. I learned from Mr. Y.H. Nam during the meeting described in paragraph # 6 that the KCIA had acquired the PROMIS computer software, and that Dr. Earl W. Brian of the United States had been instrumental in the acquisition and implementation of PROMIS by the KCIA.

9. In the capacity described in paragraph # 1, I attended a meeting in Santiago, Chile, in December, 1988, with Mr. Carlos Carduen of Carduen Industries. During this meeting, I was informed by Mr. Carduen that Dr. Earl W. Brian of the United States and Mr. Robert Gates, a senior American Intelligence and national security official, had just completed a meeting in Santiago, Chile, with Mr. Carlos Carduen.

10. I hereby certify that the facts set forth in this Affidavit are true and correct to the best of my knowledge.

FURTHER AFFIANT SAYETH NOT.

_____
Richard A. Babayan

AFFIDAVIT OF FORMER MOSSAD AGENT

Affidavits exposing Justice Department corruption in the Inslaw scandal came from many areas, and from people who had nothing to gain and much to lose. Former Mossad agent Ari Ben-Menashe provided an affidavit to Congress showing that Earl Brian brokered the stolen PROMIS software to Iraq through the office of Carlos Cardoen in Santiago, Chile. Cardeon was a CIA asset selling chemical weapons and arms to Iraq.

Ben-Menashe testified before Congress about the Justice Department's theft of the PROMIS software, and also gave an affidavit into the Inslaw litigation. The affidavit also stated details of the October Surprise operation, including: that there were three meetings in Madrid between the Reagan-Bush campaign group and Iranian factions; that there was a fourth meeting in Barcelona; that he saw Bush, William Casey and key Iranian officials in Paris at the October 1980 meeting; that the head of the French intelligence (SDECE), was at the Paris meetings; that Hamid Nagashian, deputy director of the Iranian Revolutionary Guard, aides to high ranking Iranians, were present in Paris. The affidavit stated that Bush showed the Iranians a check for $40 million made out to them, which was then deposited in a Luxembourg bank.

Former U.S. Attorney General Elliott Richardson, the attorney for the Inslaw company, requested the present U.S. Attorney on October 27, 1991 to request appointment of an Independent Prosecutor to continue the investigation, and to prosecute the involved Justice Department officials. His statements appeared in media articles under the title: "Organized crime in the U.S. Justice Department–The Stench at the U.S. Justice Department." Richardson cited charges made by thirty people supporting the existence of criminal acts by Justice Department officials in the Inslaw case.

SHIFTING RESPONSIBILITIES

The Congressional committees had the power and the responsibilities to commence impeachment proceedings against Justice Department officials, but avoided the fight and the possibility of Justice Department retaliation. Instead of taking meaningful action, it issued a report condemning the Justice Department and let it go at that. The misuse of the U.S. Department of Justice for criminal activities, and the harm suffered by Inslaw, continued as before.

AT BEST, A GROUP OF COWARDS

Not a single member of that Congressional committee, or of any other Congressional committee who knew of the threats and the carrying out of the threats, exercised his or her duty to investigate and provide corrective actions against the ongoing criminal activities. They were like crooked police officials who looked the other way.

The House committee recommended to the Justice Department that it request the Court of Appeals in Washington, D.C., to appoint an Independent Prosecutor to investigate and prosecute the criminal acts by several U.S.

attorney generals and Justice Department officials.[360] Attorney General William Barr[361] refused to do that. What else could be expected? Attorney General William Barr, who was also implicated, refused to do so, just as the attorney generals have refused to appoint an Independent Prosecutor in October Surprise, BCCI, Bank of Lavoro, and other scandals described within these pages.

SPECIAL COUNSEL "INVESTIGATION"

Media publicity forced Barr to do something. He appointed a former Justice Department crony to conduct an "investigation" of the Inslaw matter, and then report back to him. The special counsel would be selected by Barr; would be subservient to him; and would report to him. Barr could then ignore the recommendations if, in the remote possibility the special counsel did not cooperate in the expected coverup. Barr hand-picked Chicago attorneys Nicholas Bua, a former U.S. District Judge, and his law partner, Charles Knight,[362] and five Justice Department prosecutors, to investigate the Justice Department's criminal misconduct. Bua then empaneled a federal grand jury to conduct an "investigation" into the Inslaw affair. Bua's law partner, attorney Charles Knight, controlled the witnesses and questioning before the grand jury in a manner almost guaranteed to avoid a grand jury indictment.

UNLAWFULLY DISMISSING THE GRAND JURY

The first grand jury[363] started listening to the evidence, and giving it credibility. Bua quickly dismissed that jury and empaneled another one, who would rubber-stamp the acts of the special counsel. Grand juries that exercise the independence they are expected to have, and who act contrary to the U.S. Attorney, are called "runaway" grand juries.

A rare example of a runaway grand jury occurred in Denver in November 1992, as the jury received evidence of massive pollution at the Rocky Flats nuclear weapons plant. U.S. Attorney Michael Norton sought to block the investigation, and the jury ignored his attempts. Instead of covering up for large-scale problems at Rocky Flats, the grand jury, under the guidance of a rancher and grand jury foreman, Wes McKinley, prepared a letter for President-elect Bill Clinton to appoint an independent prosecutor to circumvent the Justice Department and investigate whether any federal criminal laws were violated at Rocky Flats.

CITIZEN COMMITTEE CHARGING THE INSLAW
SPECIAL COUNSEL WITH OBSTRUCTION OF JUSTICE

The coverup by the Inslaw special counsel aroused the ire of the Citizens' Committee to Clean Up the Courts,[364] causing them to file a September

---

[360] An independent prosecutor (or counsel) is appointed by a panel of three judges in the U.S. Court of Appeals at Washington, following the recommendation by the U.S. Attorney General.

[361] Former legal counsel with the Central Intelligence Agency, who is deeply involved with the stolen PROMIS software.

[362] Partners in the Chicago law firm of Burke, Bosselman & Weaver.

[363] Chicago, No. 92 GJ 811.

[364] A citizen's group in Chicago that investigates and exposes government corruption, especially that which involves corrupt state and federal judges.

1992 lawsuit in the U.S. District Court[365] at Chicago, naming as defendants, attorneys Nicolas J. Bua[366] and Charles Knight. This lawsuit was in response to the coverup and obstruction of justice by Bua and Knight in the Inslaw investigation.

Two of the plaintiffs[367] in the action, Sherman Skolnick[368] and Mark Sato,[369] had been in Bua's law offices, advising that they were going to circumvent the special counsel and give evidence and testimony to the foreman of the grand jury relating to Justice Department misconduct in the Inslaw matter. According to Skolnick and Sato, Bua stated, referring to the Inslaw investigation: "I do not intend to prosecute anyone. I want the matter behind me." Bua told the Citizens' Committee group that he would block the giving of testimony and evidence to the grand jury, and would hold them in contempt if they tried to give evidence to them.

TRYING TO CIRCUMVENT THE COVERUP

Recognizing the imminent coverup, several members of the Citizens' Committee to Clean Up the Courts[370] advised Bua that they were presenting evidence to the grand jury investigating the Inslaw scandal. Bua angrily responded that he would bring charges against the group, and against any grand jury member who acted on the evidence. Bua warned the group that he wanted to get Inslaw behind him, and that he had no intention of prosecuting anyone in the Justice Department.

The Chicago federal grand jury subpoenaed Riconosciuto in November 1992 to testify concerning the Inslaw affair.[371] On the first day of testimony, Justice Department officials moved Riconosciuto from his jail cell, without advising him that he would be testifying, preventing him from bringing his evidence. Justice Department officials then had Riconosciuto appear before the grand jury in shackles, leg irons, and handcuffs, creating the impression that he was a dangerous criminal, rather than a former CIA asset deeply involved in the Justice Department and CIA theft of the PROMIS software.

Knight sought to discredit Riconosciuto by admonishing him for not having brought any evidence to support his testimony, even though it was the Justice Department that was responsible for that matter. Seeking to influence the jury against Riconosciuto, Knight warned Riconosciuto in a sneering tone that he would be criminally prosecuted if he gave false testimony. (i.e., if he told the truth.)

---

[365] Number 92-C-6217.

[366] Bua was a Federal District Court judge in Chicago until 1991. He then joined the Chicago law firm of Burke, Boggelman & Weaver.

[367] The third plaintiff was Michael Riconosciuto, charged with reportedly trumped-up amphetamine charges shortly after giving testimony to the House committee investigating the Inslaw matter. A week earlier a high Justice Department official, ... Videnieks, warned Riconosciuto that he would suffer the consequences if he gave testimony to Congress. (These threats constituted federal crimes.)

[368] Skolnick is chairman of the Chicago based Citizens Committee to Clean Up the Courts.

[369] Sato is a legal researcher and writer.

[370] 9800 So. Oglesby, Chicago, IL 60617.

[371] Riconosciuto was in federal prison at Terminal Island, California, as a result of the charges filed by Justice Department officials after Riconosciuto testified to the Congressional committee.

Bua kept witnesses from the grand jury investigation who would have revealed the truth of the Justice Department's criminality in the Inslaw matter.

Riconosciuto was already aware of how Justice Department prosecutors charged CIA agent Richard Brenneke with perjury when Brenneke had truthfully testified to being employed by the CIA, and having seen George Bush and Donald Gregg in Paris on the infamous October 19, 1980 weekend. Brenneke had nothing to gain by his testimony. Neither did Riconosciuto. They were both disillusioned with the corruption in the CIA, and sought to exercise their responsibilities under federal crime-reporting statutes and as citizens. As a result, they both suffered from Justice Department retaliation.

ANOTHER JUSTICE DEPARTMENT COVERUP

In June 1993, Nicholas Bua sent his report to his Justice Department employer, exonerating Justice Department officials, stating that there was no truth to any of the charges. The evidence showed otherwise, including the findings of two federal courts, a host of investigators, and the testimony of independent witnesses. Bua's report discredited the testimony of the victims and witnesses who risked Justice Department retaliation by coming forward, and accepted as true the statements made by those implicated in the wrongdoings, and especially those made by Earl Brian. The Bua Report stated facts absolutely contrary to the findings of the U.S. Bankruptcy Court judge, the U.S. District Court judge, and the Congressional investigations.

Former Attorney General Elliott Richardson, the attorney for the Inslaw Company, issued a statement on June 18, 1993:

What I have seen of [the report] is remarkable both for its credulity in accepting at face value denials of complicity in wrongdoings against Inslaw and for its failure to pursue leads making those denials implausible.

Former Attorney General Elliot Richardson and his staff prepared an eighty-page report plus exhibits exposing the errors and falsehoods in the Bua report. Richardson's report referred to the obvious absurdity of Justice Department officials using their own personnel to investigate themselves. The report pointed out the lunacy of the Bua Report taking at face value the statements of those people who were part of the corrupt acts and who had everything to gain by lying, and for discrediting the testimony of those who had no reason to lie and risked perjury charges if they did lie.

The Richardson Report exposed the refusal of the Bua group to obtain the testimony and documentary evidence that would expose the Justice Department misconduct and which would have contradicted the Bua Report findings. The Richardson Report stated in part:

The Bua Report denigrates the findings of the Bankruptcy Court without clearly acknowledging that those findings were affirmed and supplemented by two other entities independent of DOJ, the U.S. District Court and the House Judiciary Committee [including the 44-page opinion by District Judge William B. Bryant, Jr.]

The Bua Report focuses only on those facts that its authors deemed relevant to the conclusions they intended to reach. The report's remarkable credibility toward professions of innocence by the *very individuals heretofore identified as the principal culprits in the theft of the software. To accept the self-serving, long after-the-fact and post hoc rationalizations of these individuals over their testimony at trial, which testimony clearly evidenced their propensity for lying and covering up the truth, as found by two federal courts, is ludicrous. A separate adversarial hearing ensued on this subject, and the bankruptcy court found that DOJ officials had, in fact, secretly attempted in 1985 forcibly to <u>convert</u> INSLAW from a Chapter 11 reorganization into a Chapter 7 liquidation in order to prevent INSLAW from seeking redress in the courts for DOJ's theft of the PROMIS software in April 1983.*

COVERUP BY ATTORNEY GENERAL JANET RENO AND CLINTON ADMINISTRATION

Attorney General Janet Reno then accepted the Bua report as the final word, and stated that she would not conduct any further investigation into the matter. That decision covered up for the criminality related to Inslaw and the criminal mindset in the Justice Department. She also acted to cover up for other criminal activities of federal officials, including BCCI, BNL, and others, as described elsewhere in these pages. The Clinton Administration, through its Attorney General, was continuing the pattern of criminal coverup and related crimes that I had discovered of that Department for the past thirty years.

SIMULTANEOUS MURDERS AND RETALIATION

Riconosciuto sought help from various people to gather supporting documents for this grand jury proceeding. Among those gathering documents were his wife, Bobbi, and CIA contacts, including Ian Spiro, who resided near San Diego with their three children. Spiro had reportedly worked with Riconosciuto and the CIA.

Spiro never provided Riconosciuto with the Inslaw data. Spiro's wife and three children were found murdered in different rooms of their home near San Diego on November 1, 1992. Each of them had been shot in the head. Several days later, police found Ian Spiro's body in a parked car on the Borego Desert east of San Diego. Even though the murders were a state responsibility, the FBI did damage control by intruding into the investigations, stating that Spiro had killed his family and then committed suicide.

LARGE NUMBER OF RELATED MURDERS PROTECTING JUSTICE DEPARTMENT AND OTHER OFFICIALS

Danny Casolaro had evidence that would have assisted Riconosciuto, but he was killed. Earlier legal counsel and others who had worked with Riconosciuto were also killed, including attorneys Alan D. Standorf and Dennis Eisman. Earlier, an investigator hired by Riconosciuto, Larry Guerrin, was killed. The skeletal remains of Riconosciuto's friend, Vali Delahanty, were found on April 12, 1993 in a nearby ravine. Another attorney, John Crawford, who worked with Riconosciuto, died of a reported heart attack in April 1993.

Riconosciuto had relied upon Ian Spiro to obtain evidence needed for his defense, but Spiro and his family were killed. Almost simultaneously, a business and social acquaintance of Spiro was killed. Several months later, attorney Paul Wilcher, who sought to expose the Inslaw and October Surprise scandals, sharing data with me, was found dead. These deaths, and dozens of others, protected key officials in the government of the United States, especially within the U.S. Department of Justice.

CHAPTER TWENTY THREE

BCCI, BANK OF CROOKS AND CRIMINALS

The world's worst banking scandal, inflicting huge financial losses on thousands of people worldwide, surfaced in the media in 1991. This was the Bank of Credit and Commerce International (BCCI). As could be expected, it had heavy ties with the CIA, terrorist organizations, drug traffickers, and any other crooked financial transaction shunned by most other banks. It financed terrorist activities, financed drug trafficking deals, defrauded depositors. Years before it was shut down, Robert Gates referred to BCCI as the Bank of Crooks and Criminals.

Following a standard pattern, Justice Department officials and the various divisions including the FBI, and other government agencies, kept the lid on the worldwide criminal activities of the bank. It wasn't until law enforcement agencies in Europe and a state prosecutor in New York City prepared to file charges that the bank's corrupt operations were shut down in the United States. By that time billions of dollars were lost by thousands of depositors all over the world.

BCCI was a private bank operating in over seventy countries, including the United States. At one time BCCI had over 400 branches in 78 countries, and assets of over $20 billion. Its holding company was based in Luxembourg and its principal operation in London. The primary bank supervisor for BCCI was Luxembourg Monetary Institute, the central bank of Luxembourg.

The BCCI scandal was related to other criminal activities, including BNL; Iraqgate; Iran and its Contra cousin; and others. BCCI and BNL both played a role in the Iraqi armament buildup, in which funds provided by U.S. taxpayers were forwarded by the Atlanta branch of Italy's Banca Nazionale del Lavoro. There were numerous cross-dealings between the banks. BCCI used its international connections to fund loans to BNL, which funded the Iraqi weapon buildups, which then required the U.S. taxpayer to fund much of the Persian Gulf War.

COVERUP OF THE BANK OF CROOKS AND CRIMINALS

Millions of people throughout the world lost billions of dollars, made possible by the coverup actions of people in foreign countries and in the United States. These losses would not have occurred had officials and attorneys in the United States not engaged in the crimes of coverup, misprision of felonies, obstruction of justice, and had they not aided and abetted the criminal activities. Congressional committees, Justice Department personnel, the FBI, and the CIA, all knew about the corrupt operation for years.

SOURCE OF STARTUP FUNDING

BCCI commenced operations in Pakistan in 1972, with much of its funding provided by Bank of America and the CIA.[372] Bank of America claims that it sold its BCCI interest in the early 1980s, but records show that Bank of America continued to control much of BCCI's operation until shortly before BCCI was shut down. In the early 1970s CIA operative Gunther Russbacher transferred sizeable amounts of CIA funds into the bank for the start-up operations.

MADE TO ORDER FOR CIA ACTIVITIES

The CIA knew about BCCI's activities, finding this mindset suitable to its own operations. If, for argument, the CIA was not in partners with the BCCI activities, its world-wide network of operatives and assets should have discovered the BCCI activities that brought about the world's worst banking loss. BCCI was custom-made for the covert and corrupt activities of the CIA, the Mossad, drug dealers, and terrorists. My CIA contacts, including Russbacher, described how CIA operatives used the bank to launder money from CIA enterprises, including drug trafficking proceeds, money from its various financial activities within the United States, including its looting of savings and loans, to fund unlawful arms shipments, finance terrorist operations,[373] undermine foreign governments, and other covert activities.

Three years before the BCCI scandal broke, Robert Gates, Deputy Director of Intelligence Operations at the CIA, stated to another CIA official that BCCI stood for the Bank of Crooks and Criminals!

MANIPULATING U.S. CHECKS AND BALANCES

Investigative reports showed that BCCI was able to simultaneously manipulate the spy agencies of numerous countries, including the U.S., Israel, Pakistan, China, Saudi Arabia, and Pakistan, among others. BCCI was supplying funds for terrorist organizations such as Abu Nidal. BCCI rigged international commodity markets that permitted certain insiders to make hundreds of millions of dollars in profits, offset by the same amount lost by depositors. BCCI was laundering drug money for drug cartels throughout the

---

[372] The author's CIA informants described how they diverted funds from secret CIA bank accounts in Europe to BCCI in 1972. CIA operative Gunther Russbacher informed me that while he was in Afghanistan he placed a large amount of CIA money into BCCI.

[373] The Abu Nidal terrorist group and others obtained funds through BCCI, which helped to bring about the Pan Am 103 tragedy and others.

Americas, Europe, and the Middle East. BCCI eliminated those who threatened the operation. BCCI engaged in pedophile practices, obtaining children for the sexual gratification of clients. My CIA contacts described how the CIA made children available for sexual abuse in the United States as a blackmail device.

BANK OF AMERICA INVOLVEMENT

Bank of America was heavily involved in BCCI from the date of its inception in 1972. It put up an initial cash investment amounting to 25 percent of the stock, which was later increased to 45 percent. (Some argue that Bank of America had a 60 percent interest.) Bank of America and the CIA had a major ownership in BCCI at that time.

Bank of America loaned money to people to buy stock in BCCI, possibly as fronts, making Bank of America's interest considerably higher. Three out of seven members of BCCI's board of directors were former senior executives at Bank of America, some of whom were on leave from BofA.

A class action lawsuit[374] filed in San Francisco courts[375] by a class of defrauded BCCI depositors charged that Bank of America officials had considerable control over BCCI and more knowledge of its illegal operations than previously disclosed. The lawsuit charged that Bank of America had a major ownership interest and control in BCCI, that Bank of America loaned millions of dollars to BCCI front men so that they could unlawfully purchase financial institutions in the United States. The suit charged that five Bank of America officers were either on BCCI's board of directors or helped manage the bank. One of them, P.C. Twitchin, allegedly approved all BCCI loans over $5 million.

The suit charged that in 1978 Bank of America hired the son of Pakistani General Zia for a position, even though he was completely unqualified, solely to bribe important Pakistani officials. The suit charged that through a correspondent banking relationship with BCCI, Bank of America continued to conspire with and aid and abet BCCI activities until the summer of 1991. The suit charged that the wrongful acts of BCCI could not have been accomplished without the active and knowing assistance of Bank of America.

It was alleged in the suit that Bank of America became involved in another scandal when it sold part interest in BCCI in 1979 to help BCCI purchase Washington, D.C.-based Financial General Bankshares Inc. The suit argues that BCCI could not have made that purchase while having a major interest in another U.S. bank holding company. Bank of America's interest, therefore, had to be reduced below fifty percent.

The president of an Atlanta Bank controlled by BCCI was a Bank of America official, adding to the evidence that BofA had heavy interests in the activities that constituted the world's worst banking fraud. Bank of America had a symbiotic relationship with the bank of crooks and criminals, which continued years after the criminal activities became public. Bank of America made large profits from its relationship with the rogue bank. But fearing that

---

[374] Filed by the San Diego law firm of Milberg Weiss Bershad Specthrie & Lerach.

[375] *San Francisco Chronicle*, with the column headed, "Lawsuit Links BofA to BCCI."

its direct ownership in BCCI could be embarrassing, Bank of America officials started selling (1977) its interest in BCCI, loaning money to front men to acquire these interests.

"The mother of all scandals," stated syndicated columnist Jack R. Payton in the *San Francisco Examiner*,[376] as he described the BCCI affair. "Top BofA Alumni Filled Major Posts At BCCI," was another headline in the *San Francisco Chronicle*. The article described how top executives of Bank of America filled high-level positions at BCCI.

Another *San Francisco Chronicle* article was entitled, "BofA, BCCI Dealings Hit $1 Billion-Plus a Day." Bank of America was a crucial repository for large infusions of cash needed by BCCI to keep its worldwide financial empire afloat. The article stated that the transactions continued throughout the 1980s, long after BCCI's corrupt activities were known to thousands of people.

The article stated that Congressional sources found that Bank of America's daily activities with BCCI reached $1.3 billion a day in some years, and that the relationship continued even after the U.S. government indicted two BCCI officers and nine BCCI executives in 1988 on charges of laundering over $32 million in drug money. The article quoted banking sources stating that the level of financial transactions that Bank of America conducted with BCCI was rare for a foreign correspondent bank.

According to a *San Francisco Chronicle* article quoting a Congressional source, Bank of America did not sever ties after BCCI's corrupt activities became common knowledge. The Congressional source added that as late as March, 1990, Bank of America kept two of its accounts open with BCCI's Miami office, two years after the Miami office had been indicted and was widely known for alleged money laundering deals involving drug money for former Panama dictator Manuel Noriega, among many others.

BANK OF AMERICA KEPT BCCI IN BUSINESS

Without these financial transactions from Bank of America, BCCI would have occasionally run out of funds. Bank of America was instrumental in permitting BCCI to continue stealing depositors' money. Without this help the corrupt activities of BCCI would have been discovered years earlier.

The author of numerous books on financial institutions,[377] described the Bank of America $1 billion daily money transfer as strange and unusual. He estimated that the deposits were a "Ponzi game," probably involving letters of credit, which banks use to handle foreign trade payments. Mayer stated that a great deal of BCCI sham activities were in bogus letters of credit.

Bank of America sold some of its stock to a BCCI subsidiary called International Credit and Investment Company Overseas, making a $27 million profit on the transaction. That same company, ICIC, has since been identified as the BCCI entity that handled some of BCCI's most notorious deals. These included fraudulent insider loans that were never repaid.

---

[376] October 9, 1992.
[377] Mayer.

Congressman Frank Riggs (D-Calif) asked the House Committee on Banking, Finance and Urban Affairs to investigate Bank of America's ties to BCCI, stating in a letter to Congressman Henry Gonzalez, chairman of the Committee, that there is "very clear evidence" that Bank of America had links to the scandal ridden BCCI. In his letter to Gonzalez, Riggs stated, "I believe that the links that have already been found between BCCI and BofA are of such far-reaching implications that a hearing is needed now." Riggs continued, "It troubles me that BofA continued to handle as much as $1.3 billion of BCCI deposits per day even after BCCI was indicted for money laundering in 1988."

Riggs pointed out that there exists a close financial relationship between Bank of America and International Credit and Investment Company (ICIC), a BCCI subsidiary in the Cayman Islands. Riggs added, "We know that Bank of America, a founder of BCCI, also provided a start-up loan to ICIC. We also know that BofA later sold its BCCI holdings to ICIC and provided financing to ICIC for the purchase. BofA made more than a 600 percent profit off this transaction."

BANK OF AMERICA MONEY LAUNDERING

Bank of America was fined $7 million in 1986 for 17,000 separate acts of money laundering.[378] Bank of America's name surfaces throughout BCCI's sordid history. Despite the widespread knowledge by U.S. banking and intelligence agency personnel of the BCCI criminal activities during its two decades of corrupt operations, Bank of America officials, who controlled much of the BCCI operation, claimed they knew nothing about the corrupt unlawful activities.

UNLAWFUL ACQUISITION OF U.S. BANKS
AND SAVINGS AND LOANS

BCCI, as represented by Clark Clifford and Robert Altman, tried to convince U.S. regulators in the 1970s to allow BCCI to purchase a bank holding company. When U.S. regulators refused to allow this purchase that was barred by U.S. law, BCCI then loaned money to people who bought shares in American banks, including Financial General Bankshares, Inc.

When BCCI secretly sought to acquire in 1978 Financial General Bankshares, Inc., the stockholders of Financial went to court to block a takeover attempt, citing questionable activities by the BCCI front men. The stockholders requested supporting documents from Bank of America. To keep the BCCI activities from the public, from the stockholders, and from the government, Attorneys Clark Clifford and Robert Altman threatened to sue Bank of America if the bank produced the requested documents.

Bank of America officials then refused to produce documents that would otherwise expose these activities.[379] With the help of powerful U.S. law firms willing to subvert U.S. laws and interests, BCCI was able to violate U.S. banking laws, engaged in a pattern of criminal activities, and inflict billions of dollars of harm to people throughout the United States and other

---

[378] *Time*, October 7, 1991.
[379] *San Francisco Examiner*, September 22, 1991.

countries. But U.S. taxpayers came to the rescue, and are paying now and seemingly forever for these criminal activities made possible by powerful law firms, public relations or influence peddling firms, U.S. officials and members of Congress.

After secretly and unlawfully purchasing Financial General Bankshares, its name was changed to First American Bankshares. Altman was rewarded by being named president of the holding company and given stock that eventually netted him several million dollars profit, in addition to the monthly compensation. Many politicians were also paid off handsomely. When billions are stolen it is possible to pay well for those helping in the scheme. They all played the part of the "amiable dunce," claiming they did not know First American Bankshares was controlled by BCCI or that the criminal activities existed.

These covert ownerships, that were harming U.S. interests were fraudulently hidden by many law firms and attorneys, including Clifford and Altman. Clifford, chairman of First American Bankshares, stated he didn't know of any ties to BCCI, in spite of the fact that the law firm represented BCCI, he was Chairman of BCCI front companies, and was the main U.S. lawyer for BCCI in the late 1970s. There is nothing like the integrity of the American lawyer.

First American Bank in New York was part of the BCCI operation. BCCI secretly acquired First American's parent, First American Bankshares of Washington, D.C., in 1983. Federal law restricted the operations of BCCI's offices, prohibiting BCCI from accepting deposits in the United States. This restriction was violated; a number of depositors reported that BCCI took their deposits.[380] BCCI secretly acquired Independence Bank in Encino, First American, and invested in CenTrust, in complex financial deals difficult to understand. BCCI acquired various U.S. banks including First American Bank in Washington with its many branches; National Bank of Georgia; Independence Bank in Encino, California.

SAUDI ARABIA INVOLVEMENT

The biggest and most prestigious bank in Saudi Arabia, National Commercial Bank, was implicated in the BCCI scandal. The District Attorney of the County of New York brought a fraud indictment against the largest banker in Saudi Arabia, Sheik Khalid bin Mahfouz, charging the Saudi bank with failing to report purchases of stock in Washington's largest bank holding company, First American Bankshares, which was illegally and secretly controlled by BCCI. The purchase of the stock was financed by loans from the Saudi bank to people acting as fronts for BCCI. The Saudi bank loaned money to BCCI in a manner that permitted BCCI's illegal operations to continue.

CANADIAN INVOLVEMENT

Canada politicians were also implicated. When members of Canada's Parliament were forced to investigate BCCI activities, they learned that the former deputy commissioner of the Royal Canadian Mounted Police (RCMP),

---

[380] *San Francisco Examiner*, September 22, 1991.

Henry Jensen, who had supervised the BCCI investigation from 1987 to 1989, had gone to work for BCCI as a paid consultant shortly after his retirement.

Canadian officials refused to cooperate in the Inslaw investigation. Canadian officials have been charged with covering up sensitive facts relating to the Aero Airlines DC-8 crash at Gander that killed 248 American GIs under suspicious circumstances. Aero was a CIA front company.

CONGRESSIONAL HEARINGS

A BCCI insider, Abdur Sakhia, testified at a Senate Foreign Relations Subcommittee on Terrorism, Narcotics and Internal Operations about events that he had seen as a BCCI officer. He described a July 1988 meeting at the Washington offices of Clifford and Warnke, at which Clifford joked to one of the BCCI officers: "Welcome aboard. We will tell more lies now." Sakhia testified to meetings at which Altman and other senior BCCI executives referred to secret agreements under which BCCI retained control of Independence Bank of Encino. Clifford and Altman have consistently denied knowledge of any relationship to BCCI. Sakhia told how the CIA used BCCI for money transfer in the Iran-Contra affair.

Former federal budget director Bert Lance in the Carter Administration testified before Congress (October 23, 1991) that he was convinced the CIA recruited the founder of the Bank of Commerce and Credit International to use the bank for CIA purposes.

Acting director of the CIA, Richard Kerr, testified to the Senate subcommittee (October 26, 1991) that the CIA knew in 1985 that BCCI had secretly gained unlawful control of Washington's largest bank holding company.

SAVINGS AND LOANS AND BCCI

The savings and loan debacle had numerous connections with the BCCI scandal. Savings and loan figure Charles Keating served on the board of a Bahamas-based investment company, Trendinvest Ltd., along with Alfred Hartmann, who was a director of BCCI. Reports given to me by CIA informants state that the Keating group, among others, moved hundreds of millions of dollars into offshore bank accounts and trusts. Attorneys at the law firm of Alvarado, Rus & Worcester, representing over 15,000 investors who were defrauded by the Keating group, stated: "It was clear to us back in 1989 that Mr. Keating had been involved in significant movement of cash offshore."

Two failed savings and loans, CenTrust Savings Bank in Miami and Viking Savings in Santa Monica, California had direct or indirect connections to BCCI. Viking Savings and Loan was secretly acquired through money provided in part by California Democratic State Senator Alan Robbins, who contributed $900,000. Robbins allegedly obtained the money from BCCI Independence Bank of Encino, California. Viking was acquired by Michael Goland, a pro-Israeli candidate. Goland used money to mount a 1984 Senate campaign against Republican Charles Percy, whom Goland felt was anti-Israel.

BCCI had a secret and illegal 28 percent ownership in CenTrust Savings Bank. CenTrust's failure will cost the American taxpayer over $2 billion.

CenTrust was run by David Paul, a major fund raiser for the Democratic Party, and a close friend of Senator Kerry, who investigated the BCCI scandal, and to this day hasn't taken any significant action. Senator Kerry was chairman of a key campaign committee for Senate Democrats in the late 1980s, while Paul was the chairman of the committee's fund-raising arm. Ghaith Pharaon, a Saudi Arabian financier, openly acquired a 28 percent stake in CenTrust, acting as a front man for BCCI.

A BCCI front purchased the Bank of Georgia in 1977, in which Burt Lance had a large financial interest, while Lance's friend, Jimmy Carter, was President of the United States. Saudi businessman Ghaith Pharaon was the front man for the BCCI acquisition of the bank and BCCI's initial penetration into the United States. Pharaon sold the Georgia Bank in 1987 to First American Bankshares, another secretly controlled BCCI operation.

BCCI had tentacles in other criminal activities, including Iraqgate and the bank primarily owned by the Italian government: Banca Nazionale del Lavoro (sometimes referred to as Bank Lavoro, or BNL for short). Both of these scandals implicated high U.S. officials.

BCCI, BUSH, AND CLINTON

One of the men behind the founding of BCCI was Jackson Stephens, who headed Stephens, Inc., located in Little Rock, Arkansas. Stephens, Inc. was a large U.S. investment bank with numerous hidden connections, including one with Harken Energy, to obtain the oil drilling rights off Bahrain. George Bush, Jr., was a consultant and member of the board of directors of Harken before the oil drilling contract was signed. Stephen's firm helped secure a loan from a BCCI affiliated Swiss bank for Harken Energy, in which President Bush's son, George W. Bush, Jr., sat on the board of directors.

Bill Clinton's involvement in the BCCI affair was shown in a February 1992 article[381] under the headline "Clinton and BCCI." The article reported that the Clinton campaign had a $2 million credit line from a bank with connections to BCCI. The credit line was from Worthen National Bank in Little Rock, Arkansas, controlled by Little Rock billionaire Jackson Stephens, and managed by Curt Bradbury. Stevens was involved in the 1970s deals in which BCCI unlawfully acquired Washington's First American Bank.

Stephens' links to BCCI were reported in an *Arkansas Democrat* article (December 1991) titled, "Reports link Stephens to BCCI." The article stated that an employee of Stephens acted as chairman, president, and chief executive officer of Worthen National Bank. The article stated that in 1977, Stephens, Inc. assisted BCCI to unlawfully take over First American Bankshares. Another *Arkansas Gazette* article (August 1991) entitled, "Little Rock on the BCCI route to power," stated in part:

Curt Bradbury, then a financial analyst for Stephens, Inc., and now chairman and chief executive officer of Worthen National Bank of Arkansas, provided [a BCCI officer] research about Financial General, including a copy of its latest annual report. Financial

---

[381] The article first appeared in the *New York Times*, and reported in the *Wall Street Journal*, February 10, 1992.

General was the parent company of the National Bank of Georgia, the bank run by Bert Lance [longtime crony of former President Jimmy Carter]. "

It was the purchase of Financial General and the National Bank of Georgia that evolved into First American Bankshares, operated by attorney Clark Clifford in Washington.

An article in *Spotlight*[382] tied Democratic presidential candidate Clinton to the BCCI scandal and charged that the mainstream press was concentrating on Clinton's extramarital activities and his draft-dodging during the Vietnam war, while ignoring Clinton's involvement in the BCCI scandal. The article referred to *New York Post* writer Mike McAlary's reporting of the connections between Clinton and the BCCI mess. Money allegedly came from Arkansas billionaire Jackson Stephens, who reportedly brokered the transaction that enabled BCCI to gain unlawful and covert control of two U.S. banks, First American Bankshares and the National Bank of Georgia.

Houston oil consultant Michael Ameen, who was on the payroll of the U.S. State Department as a consultant, was highly instrumental in working out the Bahrain deal. Ameen had close contacts with a major BCCI shareholder, Kamal Adham, who was also a former chief of Saudi Arabian Intelligence.

MANY LINKS

Alfred Hartmann, a Swiss banker, was a BCCI director and chairman of its Swiss unit, Banque de Commerce et Placements S.A., or BCP for short. Hartmann was also chairman of BNL's unit in Zurich, Switzerland, known as Lavoro Bank. Hartmann was vice chairman of a joint-venture institution in Geneva called Bank of New York-Inter Maritime Bank. Hartmann was involved in the BCCI and BNL banks, and in the Bank of New York-Inter Maritime Bank. An officer of Bank of New York, Bruce Rappaport, also had close ties to the CIA and the Mossad.

PROFITS FOR SABOTAGING AMERICA'S INTERESTS

Many attorneys, public relations firms, members of Congress, and others, made handsome profits at the expense of the American taxpayers and the thousands of depositors who lost their life's savings. Former budget director during the Carter administration, Bert Lance, sold his shares in National Bank of Georgia to BCCI front man Ghaith Pharaon, who then sold them to First American Bank Holding company in Washington, D.C.

Carter, while President of the United States, owed money to a bank with connections to BCCI, and was bailed out, along with his banker friend, Bert Lance, by Pharaon. Pharaon first loaned $3.5 million to Lance through BCCI and then bought control of Lance's bank for an additional $2.4 million.[383] Several days later President Carter approved the sale of F-15s to Saudi Arabia. BCCI paid for former President Jimmy Carter's trips around the world after he left the White House.

BCCI wrote off a $160,000 loan to an Atlanta consulting firm operated by

---

[382] March 2, 1992.
[383] The Jack Anderson syndicated column.

Andrew Young, former mayor of Atlanta.[384] The loan had been made by National Bank of Georgia, which had been acquired by BCCI front man Ghaith Pharaon. Young, a black, had served as U.S. ambassador to the United Nations during the Carter administration. Enlarging on his many trips to Africa, Young promoted BCCI to individuals and governments in Africa and Central America. Mayor Young received a retainer for introducing Third World leaders to BCCI. A former BCCI official stated that he provided about $11,000 in travel accommodations to Reverend Jesse Jackson.

White House aide and attorney Ed Rogers went to work for a BCCI front man, Kamal Adham, in October 1991. Adham was a front man in the illegal purchase of Washington's First American Bank. In a press conference, President Bush denied knowing Adham, although the facts indicated otherwise. Adham was head of Saudi Arabia's spy agency while Bush was head of the U.S. Central Intelligence Agency. Despite Rogers young age, 33 years, and his lack of legal experience, BCCI offered him $600,000 up front, for two years work, plus expenses, to leave his job as White House aide and assistant to chief of staff John Sununu. Rogers, a young attorney who had never practiced law and had relatively little experience, stated on his application to register as a foreign agent that he was hired for his legal expertise. The two most probable reasons for Rogers to be hired by a mastermind in the BCCI web were (a) either for his influence in the White House, or (b) with the urging of the White House to facilitate the various covert activities between President George Bush, other White House officials, or the CIA.

Abu Dhabi's role takes on political dimensions because the ruling family of Abu Dhabi contracted with a firm operated by President Bush's deputy campaign manager, James Lake, to handle public relations. That firm has been paid over $1 million over a twelve-month period to have the U.S. media define Abu Dhabi as a victim of the scheme. Abu Dhabi was uncooperative in providing documents and refused to allow any of its citizens to testify. Lake was sitting in on White House campaign strategy meetings while simultaneously providing information to Sheik Zaved bin Sultan al-Nayhan,[385] who controlled a major portion of BCCI's shares.

PUBLIC RELATIONS FIRMS SELLOUT OF U.S. INTERESTS

BCCI hired a public relations firm led by prominent Republican Robert Gray and Democrat Frank Mankiewicz, who was paid fees of $50,000 a month while it spread false information to Congress and the public protecting BCCI. The accounting firm responsible for inspecting BCCI, Price Waterhouse, received a $600,000 loan from BCCI.[386] An employee of Price Waterhouse, who audited the financial statements of BCCI and covered up for the irregularities, received over $100,000 from a BCCI affiliate within two years after leaving the accounting firm. The same practice continued as private auditors (hired by those looting the savings and loans, and receiving exorbitant salaries), kept the lid on the corrupt activities.

---

[384] *Wall Street Journal* September 3, 1991.
[385] Sheik Zaved bin Sultan al-Nayhan was president of the United Arab Emirates.
[386] *Wall Street Journal* article by Peter Truell.

San Francisco attorney Henry Fields and the law firm of Morrison & Foerster were used by BCCI front man, Ghaith R. Pharaon, to obtain regulatory approval for the purchase of Independence Bank of Encino, California. Fields assured regulators that Pharaon would be the sole owner of Independence. But Pharaon signed an agreement putting 85 percent ownership of the California bank in the hands of a BCCI subsidiary. Immediately after the California bank changed hands, Pharaon hired another Morrison & Foerster attorney to be on the board of directors of Independence Bank.

ATTORNEYS' SELLOUT OF U.S. INTERESTS

Many attorneys in the United States and overseas were involved in the complex activities of BCCI, and not a single one spoke out, typical of their role in almost every scandal described within these pages.

CIA CONNECTIONS

The CIA provided part of the startup funding for BCCI. I moved large amounts of money through BCCI during its entire operation. Former CIA Director Jesse Helms tried to arrange for the purchase of First American by BCCI, and failed. Clark Clifford then sought to arrange the purchase, using BCCI front men, obtaining U.S. regulatory approval based upon Clifford's false representations.

JEB BUSH

One of President Bush's sons, Jeb Bush, had numerous dealings with BCCI, and was frequently in BCCI's Miami office. Jeb Bush's company invested in real estate with a company controlled by a BCCI customer, who was later sent to prison for defrauding BCCI and other banks.

Bahrain, a small emirate with close ties to Saudi Arabia, gave a lucrative oil drilling contract to Harken, a company with ties to the Bush family and who had never drilled any oil wells in the sea and had virtually no assets.

BRIBERY WAS EVERYWHERE

BCCI had a bribery list of U.S. elected public officials. Reference was made to this list during Congressional testimony (September 13, 1991) before the House Banking Committee, chaired by Representative Henry Gonzalez. One method reported for conveying bribes to members of Congress was through the Chicago Commodity Exchange, Chicago Board of Trade, Chicago Board Options Exchange, and the Chicago Mercantile Exchange. Money was put into commodity exchange accounts overseas under the name of a particular member of Congress. Periodically the Congressman would be informed that there was money in his account, and he was advised how he could withdraw it if he wished. Huge amounts of cash were brought into Chicago to orchestrate this scheme.

BOTH POLITICAL PARTIES IMPLICATED

As in many of the scandals described within these pages, both political parties were implicated, receiving large financial contributions or bribes from the illicitly operated bank. As in the savings and loan scandal, members of Congress were handsomely rewarded for either looking the other way or obstructing any investigations. The key to continuing the corruption and harms inflicted throughout the world by BCCI was bribing U.S. and other officials.

Senator Orrin Hatch (R-Utah), the senior Republican on the Judiciary Committee, was one of hundreds of Congressmen who received money from BCCI officials. He was more openly protective of the BCCI corruption. Senator Hatch issued a glowing endorsement of the Justice Department's plea bargain settlement with BCCI's money-laundering operation in Tampa, Florida, which was a slap-on-the-wrist settlement blocking further investigation into high-level BCCI corruption. It also halted investigation into Hatch's involvement with BCCI.

Although BCCI pled guilty to several dozen felony counts, Senator Hatch said in his Senate floor speech that "There was no systematic money laundering uncovered in the BCCI case." Hatch has extolled "senior management, directors and shareholders of BCCI for the responsible way" they behaved. This probably reflected the mindset of U.S. Congressmen (and Congresswomen).

Senator Hatch's speech had been prepared by the same BCCI cutouts that perpetrated the sham against the American people: Washington attorney Robert Altman and his law office. Immediately after giving the unusual speech, defending the crime-infested bank and those who made the crimes possible, Senator Hatch placed a telephone call to BCCI's chief executive officer, Swaleh Naqvi. Hatch requested a loan for his business associate, Munzer Hourani, a Houston businessman.

In another instance, Senator Hatch's office misused his senate office trying to protect BCCI against drug money laundering charges. When the media exposed this attempt, Hatch sought to divert attention from himself by blaming a former member of his staff, Michael Pillsbury. Pillsbury had represented Senator Hatch by seeking a more favorable outcome in the 1989 money laundering indictment in Florida against BCCI officials. Hatch sought to sidestep blame by asking the Senate Ethics Committee to investigate his former aide.

Senator Hatch was involved with a part owner of BCCI, Mohammed Hammoud, a front man for BCCI in First American Bankshare purchases. Hammoud's loose talk about the BCCI operations threatened politicians and crooks worldwide, possibly causing his May 1990 death under mysterious circumstances in Geneva, Switzerland. The insurance company refused to pay death benefits because the corpse was four inches shorter than shown on Hammoud's last physical examination.

Senator Hatch was one of the senators to whom I sent evidence of these various scandals, and who refused to receive my evidence. It is understandable that a member of Congress already implicated in one or more scandals or criminal activities would refuse to receive evidence of other criminal activities. The same argument can surely be applied to each of the other senators and representatives who refused to receive the testimony and evidence of our group of whistleblowers.

One of the infamous Keating-Five senators from the savings and loan scandal, Senator Alan Cranston (D-Calif.), intervened on behalf of BCCI.[387] Cranston wrote a letter to the Federal Home Loan Bank Board at the request of David Paul, owner of BCCI-related CenTrust Savings Bank[388] of Miami, requesting relief from regulatory actions, while simultaneously receiving political contributions (i.e. bribes). Senator Cranston repeatedly intervened on behalf of the biggest crooks in the savings and loan debacle while refusing to receive my evidence of massive criminal activities as described in these pages. He also intervened on behalf of the crooks in the world's worst banking scandal. That same scenario applied to many other members of the Senate and House.

CONGRESS FORCED TO "INVESTIGATE"

The media attention over BCCI's activities forced Congress to conduct an "investigation." The Senate Foreign Relations' Subcommittee on Terrorism, Narcotics and International Operations, chaired by Senator John Kerry (D-MA), conducted an investigation. Simultaneously, Kerry received financial contributions from BCCI's front man, David Paul, of Florida's CenTrust (a U.S. financial institution unlawfully affiliated with BCCI). CenTrust failed, costing the American taxpayer over two billion dollars. CenTrust Chairman, David Paul, arranged for BCCI to invest $25 million in CenTrust bonds in 1988, and then repurchased the bonds two months later. The intent was to make CenTrust temporarily look healthier that it really was. This temporary financial support further showed the BCCI-CenTrust relationship.

The bribe to Kerry, or whatever one wishes to call it, may be the reason that the Senate Committee did not request the appointment of an Independent Prosecutor, despite the serious corruption uncovered by the committee investigators. Many members of Congress were involved in the scandal, which also helped to eliminate any desire for an Independent Prosecutor.

COVERUP OF VERY SERIOUS CRIMES
IGNORED BY THE SENATE COMMITTEE

Senate investigator Jack Blum unsuccessfully sought to have Congress act on the alarming disclosures that he discovered. When much of the criminality focused on corrupt members of Congress, other U.S. officials refused to delve into those areas. In desperation, Senate Investigator Jack Blum quit his Senate investigative function, and tried to get Justice Department officials to act. After being stonewalled there, Blum sought to interest Manhattan District Attorney Robert Morgenthau in the scandal that had tentacles in New York. The overwhelming evidence that Blum presented resulted in Morgenthau obtaining a grand jury indictment (July 29, 1991) against BCCI and two cutouts, Clark Clifford and Robert Altman. They were charged with engaging in a multi-billion-dollar scheme to defraud depositors, falsify bank records, hide illegal money-laundering, and engage in larceny. Even after the indictment, Justice Department officials refused to produce requested documents. By July 1991 Morganthau had enough evidence to indict Clifford and Altman. They were charged with bank fraud and receiving $40 million in

[387] *Los Angeles Times*, October 7, 1991.
[388] About one fourth of CenTrust's stock was owned by BCCI before it collapsed.

bribes from BCCI, as part of a conspiracy to give BCCI control of several banks in the United States.

THE SENATE REPORT

The committee issued a nearly 800-page report (October 1, 1992), accusing BCCI of using political insiders to commit fraud upon the United States on a global scale. The report stated that there exists "an elaborate corporate spider-web with BCCI's founder, Agha Hasan Abedi and his assistant, Swaleh Naqvi, in the middle." The report stated that BCCI's *modus operandi* throughout the world, including the United States, was bribery and subversion of government officials.

The report stated that BCCI "systematically bribed political figures around the world." Senator Hank Brown, a member of the Senate committee, stated at a news conference, "We found it was BCCI's overpowering use of the nation's political insiders like [former Defense Secretary] Clark Clifford ... that permitted BCCI's secret expansion in the United States."

It described an international operation that would exceed SPECTRE, the fiendish "Special Executive for Counter-intelligence, Terrorism, Revenge and Extortion," found in James Bond novels and movies. Senator Kerry stated that "BCCI constituted international global crime on a level that boggles the mind." The report criticized U.S. bank regulators, the CIA, and the Justice Department, and offered a scathing portrait of political influence, international bribery, and inaction by agencies holding the duty to act, becoming the catalyst for one of the biggest financial frauds in the world's history.

The report describes the financial contributions or bribes paid to various members of the U.S. Congress, including former Senator John Culver (D-Iowa) and Senator Orrin G. Hatch (R-Utah). The report severely criticized two attorneys, Clark M. Clifford, a former Cabinet member and adviser to various Presidents of the United States, and his protege, Robert A. Altman, who have been charged with taking bribes from BCCI in exchange for hiding BCCI's ownership of First American Bankshares, a Washington holding company of which Clifford was the chairman.

Senator Hank Brown (R-CO), who was the subcommittee's ranking minority member, stated BCCI's financial contributions were so extensive that "there was not a single committee of this Congress that wanted to conduct a complete, thorough investigation."

The report stated that while Senator Hatch and Mr. Pillsburg, a former State Department official, worked on behalf of BCCI to halt investigations, Senator Hatch was requesting BCCI to lend $10 million to a business associate with whom the Senator was in partnership.

The report stated that BCCI used political insiders such as former Defense Secretary Clark Clifford and members of Congress to commit fraud on a global scale. It described how BCCI paid members of Congress, lobbyists, and attorneys to obstruct the investigation into its terrorists and drug-money-laundering activities. The report implicated Democrats and Republicans, lawyers and lobbyists, public relations firms, Congressional staffers and former senators.

The report treated with kid gloves Senator Hatch's frequent attempts to protect BCCI, to obstruct criminal investigations, while receiving BCCI money. The report tried to make Senator Hatch's aide the scape goat and recommended that the aide be "investigated" by the Senate Ethics Committee. The activities of attorney and former Senator John Culver (D-Iowa), were addressed, stating in part:

> *Sen. Culver's role in lobbying Congress to assist BCCI was more significant than had been publicly understood, and ... he provided valuable advice to BCCI on how to handle Congressional attempts to investigate the bank.*

Despite the gravity of the crimes depicted in the Senate report, much remained to be discovered when the Senate committee halted its investigation and issued its report.

CIA officials refused to produce hundreds of documents that it had on the BCCI operations, in which the CIA itself was involved.

REFUSAL TO REQUEST INDEPENDENT PROSECUTOR

Despite the many unanswered questions about involvement of U.S. officials, the Senate committee refused to request appointment of an *independent* prosecutor. To have done so would have implicated many members of Congress in both major political parties. When asked by reporters whether he would request appointment of an independent counsel, Senator Kerry replied, "There already is an independent counsel, Bob Morgenthau." That answer was a farce.

A county district attorney has a limited budget, and has neither the funds, nor the authority, nor the responsibility, to investigate a complex scandal with international implications of the magnitude of the BCCI scandal. The authority of a local county prosecutor is obviously inadequate to investigate the national and international aspects of the BCCI scandal. Morgenthau's yearly budget for prosecuting all criminal acts in Manhattan was approximately $50 million. Independent prosecutor Lawrence Walsh, for instance, spent over $40 million just to determine who was lying to Congress in the Iran-Contra affair.

HUNDREDS OF TIPS AND INFORMANTS AND THE USUAL JUSTICE DEPARTMENT OBSTRUCTION OF JUSTICE

Federal agencies received hundreds of tips for over ten years describing BCCI criminal activities. Federal agencies, including the FBI, Justice Department, Drug Enforcement Administration, the Internal Revenue Service, had thousands of investigators, many of whom knew about the corruption for years, and no action was taken. As in every other scandal, Justice Department officials blocked corrective actions.

An initial investigation in 1989 by Justice Department officials into BCCI's secret ownership of First American was abruptly cancelled, protecting the criminal elements within BCCI, powerful Washington law firms, members of Congress, Bank of America, and others.

Former BCCI officers stated to the Senate committee they believed the Justice Department's coverup and failure to properly investigate BCCI was due to BCCI's extensive connections to the CIA and other U.S. intelligence agencies. An investigation would expose the unlawful Iran-Contra arms flow, the drug trafficking into the United States from throughout the world, CIA money laundering from its covert domestic proprietaries, bribing of U.S. officials, especially members of Congress, and God knows what else.

The BCCI scandal would most likely have slowly drifted away and become worse, if it had been left up to those in charge of the U.S. Department of Justice and Congress. It would be one more major scandal kept secret from the American public. But a persistent investigator, Jack Blum, who went to a County Prosecutor in New York when Congress and the Justice Department stonewalled the matter, and convinced a 73-year old County Prosecutor, Robert Morgenthau, to prosecute BCCI and the crooks associated with it. Soon after commencing the investigation, Morgenthau encountered the obstruction of justice tactics by Justice Department attorneys, who wanted to keep the lid on the scandal.

OVER A DECADE OF IGNORING INFORMANTS

Thirteen years before BCCI was seized in 1991, an American bank examiner, Joseph Vaez,[389] warned in a letter that BCCI was rife with bad loans and that the bank used front men to disguise fraudulent transactions. The memo described the incestuous lending and ownership arrangements with affiliate companies in offshore havens, the practice of almost limitless lending to favored customers, and other serious banking irregularities.

The memo referred to the ICIC Group, a Cayman Islands affiliate that the Federal Reserve called BCCI's alter ego, and estimated that it controlled 70 percent of BCCI, and that BCCI's front men operated through ICIC. Vaez testified before a Senate subcommittee[390] concerning the memo, which mysteriously disappeared from the government files. Vaez then produced his copy of the document, and the Senate committee requested the original from the comptroller's office, which refused to produce it. The committee then subpoenaed the document.

Assistant Secretary of Intelligence at the State Department, Douglas Mulholland, testified about another hidden memo on BCCI. In January 1985, while he was special assistant for national security to the Secretary of the Treasury, he received an unusual report from the CIA, relating to BCCI. Mulholland further testified that the CIA forbade him from discussing the memo on the basis of national security.[391]

A 1978 CIA telex message from CIA Director Richard Helms was entered into the Senate hearing record showing the CIA knew of the BCCI activities a decade before the scandal surfaced. The telex related to the wording of an agreement to grant power of attorney to a Washington law firm relative to a transaction involving Financial General Bankshares of Washington, D.C., later renamed First American Bankshares.

HOUSE "INVESTIGATION"

---

[389] Vaez was an examiner for the Office of the Comptroller of the Currency testifying before a Senate subcommittee.

[390] *New York Times*, February 20, 1992.

[391] The "national security" label is routinely used to prevent the disclosure of information on internal misconduct by government officials.

The House also conducted an "investigation" into the BCCI scandal. Representative Charles Schumer chaired the House committee, and the report was, for all practical purposes, a coverup. Congressional investigator and coverup artist Lawrence Barcella helped persuade Senator Orrin Hatch to give a speech on the Senate floor praising BCCI.[392] This is the same Barcella who in 1992 engaged in a coverup of the House October Surprise "investigation." Barcella also helped to cover up a covert CIA operation supplying military equipment to Libya's President Moamer al Kadhafi, after its cover was blown by charging CIA-operative Edwin Wilson with a federal crime for carrying out orders of his CIA superiors.

CIA Deputy Director Robert Gates stated in 1988 to the head of Customs, William von Raab, that BCCI stood for the "Bank of Crooks and Criminals International." But the CIA continued to deposit and launder funds in BCCI, covering up the criminal activities that would defraud people all over the world who had put their money into the bank.

In the 1980s U.S. Customs Commissioner William von Raab unsuccessfully tried to get the Justice Department to act on the serious federal violations committed by BCCI. Raab testified to Senate investigators that in 1988 he told CIA Deputy Director Robert Gates of the drug money laundering at BCCI, and that Gates refused to proceed with the information. Raab did not know, apparently, that the CIA was itself laundering drug and other illicit money through BCCI.

BCCI officer Nazir Chinoy tried to provide information to federal prosecutors about covert arms deals involving BCCI and the CIA.[393] Instead, Justice Department officials indicted Chinoy, and in that manner the CIA drug smuggling was again kept under wraps.

Justice Department officials were put on notice during a 1985 federal heroin investigation that money was being laundered in BCCI's Independence Bank of Encino in California. The Justice Department's DEA and the Treasury Department's Internal Revenue Service discovered the BCCI connection and the drug money laundering, and did nothing about it. To have done so would have exposed the CIA and bribing of federal officials. Tape recordings of a BCCI officer talking to an undercover investigator included the following statement:

Now we are trying to extend our operations into the United States, we have offices in New York, Atlanta, Miami, Houston, San Francisco, also we have acquired some local bank which we take over very shortly.

Kidder, Peabody & Company notified federal regulators from 1978 through 1981 that it was helping BCCI acquire an interest in First American Bankshares, Inc, while First American was telling banking regulators that First American had no connections to BCCI.[394] This information was prepared by Martin Siegel, showing that BCCI was behind the ownership change

---

[392] *Newsweek*, August 26, 1991.
[393] *San Francisco Daily Journal*, November 13, 1991.
[394] *Wall Street Journal*, September 10, 1991.

involving First American, the largest bank holding company in Washington. After the acquisition was approved in 1982, Kidder renewed its registration as an agent for BCCI, working in connection with the acquisition of First American. No reference was made on the application form that Kidder was working with the front men.

Seeking to circumvent the block by Justice Department officials, U.S. Customs officer Robert Mazur wrote to Senator John Kerry (D-Mass.), chairman of the Senate Subcommittee on Terrorism, Narcotics and International Operations, complaining about the coverup within the Justice Department and Customs. Mazur wrote:

> *Tons of documents were not reviewed ... and the CIA put a halt to certain investigative leads into a 1988 Florida inquiry that led to the indictment of BCCI officers in Tampa. We had drug traffickers, money launderers, foreign government involvement, Noriega and allegations of payoffs by BCCI to U.S. government political figures. I will not elaborate on who these U.S. government figures were alleged to be, but I can advise you that you don't have all of the documents. Some were destroyed or misplaced.*

Senator Kerry refused to release the letters written by Mazur, but those who have seen them state they were political dynamite, exposing serious misconduct by many members of Congress. Dozens of members of Congress received political contributions or bribes from BCCI and its unlawful outlets in the United States, including the chairman of the investigating committee, Senator John Kerry, who received the highest reported amount of contributions. Kerry also failed to recommend appointment of an independent prosecutor into the BCCI scandal.

In testifying before the Senate committee,[395] Mazur testified to the following facts: (1) that his group discovered hundreds of leads indicating gross misconduct by BCCI officials; (2) that Justice Department officials refused to send investigators that were needed to follow through on the leads;[396] (3) that the leads indicated large political payoffs in the United States; (4) that BCCI was financing unlawful arms transactions; (5) that BCCI secretly owned U.S. banks, and other federal violations; and (6) that Justice Department officials blocked exposure of these matters in numerous ways, including refusal to provide additional personnel, refusal to grant permission to obtain testimony outside the United States, and by reaching a plea bargain with BCCI before higher-ups were implicated.

Mazur further testified that he resigned from the U.S. Customs Service[397] because of his frustration at the coverup by Justice Department officials and within the Customs Service. He described the discovery of BCCI's money-laundering activities in Tampa, Florida, and the political payoffs, along with the secret ownership of U.S. banks.

JUSTICE AND CIA CAUGHT RED HANDED

---

[395] November 21, 1991.
[396] *Los Angeles Times*, November 22, 1991.
[397] Resigned in April 1990.

Feisty Congressman Henry Gonzalez's (D-TX) persistent investigations and demands for documents exposed the coverup by Justice Department and CIA officials. Each of them had stated to Congressional committees that every document in their files pertaining to BCCI had been released to the Congressional investigative committees. These statements were proven false after the CIA inadvertently released sensitive documents disproving the statements. Media attention and charges of coverup created a crisis situation, each of the two agencies blaming the other for coverup.

Acting CIA Director Richard Kerr testified to the Senate committee on November 11, 1991, revealing that between 1983 and 1985 the CIA had sent several hundred reports to government agencies, including the Justice Department, chronicling BCCI's illegal activities. Justice Department officials had lied to Congress, stating initially they did not have any other documents. Thereafter, Justice Department officials sought to have CIA officials explain the discrepancy by lying, but without success.

RETALIATING AGAINST FBI DIRECTOR

Congress and the media demanded that an independent prosecutor be requested to investigate the Justice Department and the CIA. FBI Director William Sessions assured Senator David Boren (D-OK) that the FBI would investigate the conduct of Justice Department officials. When Boren announced this to the press, Justice Department officials, Session's superiors, announced that there was a criminal investigation of him for having used government telephones for private business, and for allowing his wife to ride on government aircraft. If applied in the same manner, this charge could be leveled at a major segment of the federal and state governments. Senator Boren was among the Congressmen who charged Justice Department officials with trying to obstruct justice by threatening the Director of the FBI with phony charges.[398]

ELIMINATING THE MEDDLESOME FBI DIRECTOR

The FBI Director's statement that he would investigate Justice Department officials was an unprecedented threat to the epidemic corruption in the federal government. Two days after Sessions stated to Senator Boren that he would investigate Justice Department officials, U.S. Attorney General William Barr announced an investigation of Sessions for ethic violations. Strange coincidence. Sessions was charged, through the media, with taking his wife along on government aircraft, on a space available basis, and with installing a security fence at his home to protect government secrets.

It was ironical that while Attorney General William Barr was engaging in widespread coverup and obstruction of justice of many of the crimes described within these pages, he had the audacity to seek the removal of the FBI Director on these sham charges.

PRESIDENT OF THE UNITED STATES ASSISTED IN

---

[398] Very few government employees have not used government phones for private calls. Many government employees, including myself, used government aircraft for flight experience which concurrently had an element of private use attached.

COVERUP AND OBSTRUCTION OF JUSTICE

Clinton had already played a key role in obstruction of justice relating to the vast CIA drug trafficking near Mena, Arkansas, while Clinton was governor of that state. After Bill Clinton became president and appointed Janet Reno as U.S. Attorney General, the two of them carried out Barr's previous plan to remove the Director of the FBI who constituted a threat to government corruption. Without allowing Sessions to defend against the obvious sham charges, Reno and Clinton removed the FBI Director.

The lapdog press eulogized this removal, and said nothing about its relationship with Sessions' intent to investigate Justice Department corruption.

It is estimated that the BCCI corrupt practices cost innocent depositors from $5 to $15 **billion** in losses. Over a million depositors in 69 countries, including the United States, lost all or most of their savings and deposits. Part of BCCI's losses will be paid by the U.S. taxpayer through the losses of secretly owned savings and loans and the stockholders in the U.S. banks secretly owned by BCCI. The Independence Bank of Encino, California,[399] a BCCI bank, caused losses of $130 to $140 million. These losses are insured by the American public, who will pay the tab.

U.S. investors in the bank-holding company secretly acquired by BCCI lost large sums of money. First American Bankshares paid $225 million to acquire National Bank of Georgia in 1985, receiving only $90 million from its 1992 sale after the BCCI scandal broke. The $135 million difference is a loss to the U.S. investors who owned part of the bank holding company.

Central banks and governments of Third World Nations will lose billions. These losses could have been prevented if the CIA or any of the other U.S. officials had performed their duties instead of engaging in felony coverup. And the same goes for the members of Congress who also covered up. Of course, the same goes for each and every one of the other corrupt activities described within these pages.

VATICAN BANK SCANDAL

Similar to the deaths of informants in other scandals such as Inslaw, Chapter 11 corruption, and October Surprise, witnesses and informants to the BCCI scandal were killed or mysteriously died. The 1988 death of a New York City attorney, Cornelius Ahearn, is believed due to the fact that he knew too much about the links between the BCCI scandal and the Vatican Bank scandal[400] of the 1980s.

WHITE HOUSE INVOLVEMENT

The White House had numerous tentacles to the BCCI scandal, and through its control over the Justice Department blocked or greatly reduced action against BCCI for years, despite knowledge of the bank's criminal activities. attorney Ed Rogers, the right-hand assistant to President Bush's Chief of Staff, John Sununu, signed an employment agreement with a BCCI participant, Sheik Kamal Adham, the former chief of Saudi intelligence.

---

[399] Independence Bank had fourteen branches in the Los Angeles area.

[400] The Vatican bank scandal surfaced in 1982, following the collapse of Calvi's Milan-based bank. The Vatican settled law suits for $250 million.

Adham was at the heart of the BCCI bank swindle. Rogers had graduated from the Alabama Law School in 1985, and never practiced law in his life, and obviously wasn't being paid for his legal knowledge but for his political contacts with the Bush Administration. Adham offered to pay Rogers $600,000 to provide legal assistance, when he was totally ignorant in those areas. Adham was buying contacts with the White House and indirectly the Justice Department, who would be prosecuting BCCI.

President Bush's deputy campaign manager, James Lake,[401] simultaneously worked in 1992 for the main owner of scandal-riddled BCCI.[402] Simultaneously, the U.S. Attorney General and his Justice Department were blocking prosecution of BCCI. It was an interesting connection, to have a top-level campaign adviser for President Bush representing a major owner of the corruption-riddled renegade bank.

BRITISH COVERUP

It was the English government that first acted to shut down BCCI in 1992 when the scandal became public. BCCI was chartered in Luxembourg, but actually operated primarily in England, and under British regulators and investigators. The Bank of England and other English checks and balances knew about BCCI corrupt activities for years, and covered up. England's security agencies surely knew what was going on, and did nothing.

British media attention forced an "investigation," conducted by Lord Justice Bingham, who issued a report in October 1992. The report did nothing to prevent another BCCI, and did not delve into those responsible for the world's worst banking scandal. The report described BCCI's performance as "a tragedy of errors, misunderstandings and failures of communication." It wasn't any misunderstanding, nor failure of communication, that permitted BCCI to engage in world-wide money laundering, financing terrorists and drug cartels, threats and murders; it was criminal coverup by every check and balance.

The people sabotaging their own country's interest were not only in the United States. The Bank of England reported (September 28, 1992) that it would seek a probe into allegations revealing that several of its employees took bribes from BCCI. It subsequently issued a white-wash report, stating that no evidence was found of bad faith, duplicity, coverup, or conspiracy, by British subjects in the BCCI corruption. The Bank of England entered into an arrangement with the bank's principal owners, Abu Dhabi, and under this agreement, important records and witnesses were allowed to leave England. In that way, those in England who aided and abetted the BCCI scheme, escaped exposure.

JUSTICE DEPARTMENT COVERUP

"Something fishy is behind this government's reluctance to prosecute aggressively the well-connected predators of BCCI," stated William Safire in his November 1991 syndicated column.

---

[401] Lake worked as a senior communications adviser to the Bush campaign, being promoted on February 27, 1992 to deputy campaign manager for surrogates, advance and scheduling.

[402] *Associated Press*, February 28, 1992.

Until January 1992, high Justice Department officials blocked an investigation into BCCI corruption, according to the testimony of a former U.S. Attorney in Miami, Dexter Lehtinen.[403] He testified that in 1991, when he was building a case against BCCI, Justice Department officials in Washington blocked court orders to obtain documents from foreign countries concerning BCCI corruption. Lehtinen also testified that in late August 1991 he received a phone call from a high Justice Department official who said he was calling on behalf of Acting Attorney General William Barr. The official stated that Barr wanted him not to seek an indictment against BCCI. Congress also assisted in this coverup, by refusing to approve Lehtinen's temporary U.S. Attorney position to a permanent position, causing him to resign.

Members of Congress demanded in 1992 that Attorney General William Barr request the appointment of an Independent Prosecutor to investigate BCCI. Barr refused to do so. He had earlier refused to appoint a Congressionally-requested independent prosecutor in the Inslaw matter, in the Bank of Lavoro matter, and in the Iraqgate matter.

The prosecution of BCCI on the money-laundering charge was not initiated by the Justice Department but on the initiative of local Customs Service agents. Justice Department officials had sought to block that prosecution and when this proved difficult due to media attention, Justice sought to limit the scope of the investigation by reaching a plea agreement allowing BCCI to ensure that the evidence collected during the investigation wouldn't be used against BCCI in any future federal charges.

ONE OF MANY REASONS FOR
JUSTICE DEPARTMENT COVERUP

Before William Barr came to the Justice Department he was an attorney with the Washington law firm of Shaw Pittman Potts & Trowbridge. This law firm represented BCCI for several years. A partner in the law firm, Kenly Webster, was representing a former BCCI chief executive, Swaleh Naqvi, who had been indicted by a Manhattan grand jury on fraud, false accounting, money-laundering and other charges. Naqvi had also been indicted in Tampa, Florida, on similar charges. Barr's former law firm also represented B. Francis Saul II, a director and powerful shareholder in Financial General Bankshares, Inc. Financial later became First American Bankshares, a covert BCCI operation.

Further, Barr had been legal counsel for the CIA, the same agency that was heavily involved with BCCI corrupt activities. He was CIA counsel during the time that George Bush was Director of the CIA. Barr appeared with CIA Director Bush in hearings before Congress.

Miami attorney James F. Dougherty II, representing an insurance group that had sued BCCI, appealed directly to Attorney General Richard Thornburgh (December 1990) when evidence surfaced that BCCI was planning to destroy or move records of its corrupt activities. No response was re-

---

[403] Testified on May 14, 1992, before the Senate Subcommittee on Terrorism, Narcotics and International Operations.

ceived.[404]

Justice Department officials blocked the testimony of two key witnesses before a Senate hearing on BCCI,[405] who would have exposed not only BCCI's criminality, but also the coverup by Justice Department and CIA officials. Robert Mazur, who headed the Customs Service's investigation of BCCI in Tampa, and an assistant U.S. Attorney, Mark Jackowski, had sought to file charges against BCCI, but Washington officials sought to block the investigations.

Justice Department officials shut down an investigation into the BCCI ownership of First American Bankshares in October 1989, allegedly so that it could focus on another probe. But when that probe was completed, Justice Department officials never went back to the far more serious matter of illegal ownership of First American Bank Holding Company. It wasn't until the Manhattan prosecutor started exposing the BCCI corruption, and the Bank of England seized control of BCCI, that Justice Department officials showed signs of life. At that point Justice Department officials had to do something. Some reports state that as many as twenty percent of the members of both houses of Congress received bribes from BCCI.[406]

Although known for years, the corruption surfaced in September 1991. BCCI accomplished its corrupt activities by bribing prominent citizens and high government officials throughout the world, including the United States.

Top law firms and public relation firms in the United States fronted for the rogue bank, secretly enabling it to operate in the United States. Members of Congress, the CIA, Justice Department, and other U.S. government agencies made possible years of these criminal activities. The mentality of BCCI suited to a "t" much of the criminality by U.S. officials described throughout these pages.

BCCI secretly and unlawfully owned several American banks, in violation of federal law. Included in these banks secretly owned by BCCI were First American Bank of the District of Columbia and its 43 branches in New York City.

U.S. authorities knew of BCCI's corruption and looting of deposits for years. Dozens of informants notified Justice Department officials and members of Congress of the corrupt activities. But, as in every other scandal within the federal government, nothing was done to stop BCCI's corrupt activities until the scandal broke (July 1991) in England, causing the bank to be closed.

HUNDREDS OF WARNINGS

Before the bubble burst on this racketeering operation, depositors lost billions of dollars, wiping out the life savings of many people, especially those in undeveloped countries. Insiders, including drug traffickers[407] and the

---

[404] *Daily Journal*, October 21, 1990.
[405] *New York Times* October 2, 1991.
[406] *Spotlight*, October 21, 1991.
[407] *New York Times* October 28, 1991.

CIA,[408] had advance notice of the pending collapse and took out their money before BCCI collapsed. In 1988, the CIA pulled its money out of the bank.

Just prior to the crackdown on the BCCI front in Tampa, by Justice Department prosecutors, drug dealers made a run on the bank, withdrawing over $10 million before Justice Department officials made their arrests.

Front men, such as former Defense Secretary Clark Clifford and Robert Altman, acted as cutouts or front men to cover up for the unlawful BCCI ownership. In 1979, attorneys Clifford and Altman deceptively acted to permit BCCI to unlawfully acquire ownership of First American Bank in Washington, D.C. Clifford was an attorney and veteran power broker in Washington, and he was a pillar of the Washington Beltway establishment.

Other U.S. financial institutions were later acquired through attorneys acting as BCCI front men, or with their connivance. These included Independence Bank in Encino, California, and CenTrust Savings in Miami.

The Atlanta branch of BNL loaned or pledged nearly $5 billion to Iraq between 1985 and the summer of 1989.

Jack Blum, who initially discovered the criminal activities while an investigator for the Senate, believes that both Republicans and Democrats blocked an investigation because members of their own parties were responsible for covering up early warnings of the criminal activities. The same can be stated of the 1980 October Surprise scandal and the others within these pages.

Prominent Washington figures made the BCCI scandal possible. There were numerous members of Congress; prominent attorneys Clifford and Altman; former Treasury Secretary John Connally, who bought a Texas bank with BCCI front man Ghaith Pharaon; former Atlanta Mayor Andrew Young, who borrowed money from BCCI and never paid it back; Ron Brown, chairman of the Democratic Party, of the Washington law firm of Patton, Boggs and Blow, who received $1.3 million in fees from BCCI, joined President Clinton's Washington staff.

In February 1992 a federal grand jury indicted David Paul, the former chairman of CenTrust Savings Bank in Miami, on fraud charges. The charges arose from a $25 million securities deal involving an investor linked to BCCI. Also charged were Ghaith Pharaon, reportedly a front man for BCCI, and William Christopher Berry.

SCANDAL AFTER SCANDAL OF CONGRESSIONAL BRIBING

BCCI penetrated the U.S. financial system through American law firms and attorneys who helped inflict upon the United States and other countries great financial harm and aided and abetted the drug-money laundering, financing of terrorists, and other unlawful activities. They turned their legal expertise against the United States for profit.

CRIMES AIDED BY JURY MEMBERS

The trial of attorney Robert Altman as part of the largest bank fraud in the nation and the world's history, occurred in 1993 in New York City. Altman, with his boyish smile of innocence (similar to Oliver North), was accompa-

---

[408] Statements made to me by CIA informants.

nied throughout the trial by his attractive wife and former television star, Lynda Carter. Her lifestyle was enriched by the money her husband made through his role in the BCCI fraud. She was a popular sideshow to the trial.

The jury, composed of many unsophisticated people, some of whom couldn't be expected to balance their personal check books, were confronted with complex matters, compounded by the usual misrepresentation of legal counsel. On August 14, 1993, the jury acquitted Altman of the charges, proving again that crime pays, especially when cloaked in complex legal activities.

The outcome of a jury trial by unsophisticated jurists is similar to playing a slot machine. There are those jury members who believe everything the prosecutor says, assuming that **surely** an innocent person would not be charged if the facts were not true. There are the jurists who are influenced by legal chicanery that tricks the jury. There are those jurists who are influenced by the look of innocence, such as displayed by Oliver North and Robert Altman.

The BCCI corruption was effectively covered up by the New York jury members, followed by the coverup of President Clinton's Justice Department. It remained for foreign countries to prosecute and punish many of those who played key roles in the BCCI debacle.

INDEPENDENT COUNSEL VERSUS SPECIAL COUNSEL

There are vast differences between an "independent counsel" (or independent prosecutor as they are sometimes called) and a "special counsel." A special counsel is selected by the U.S. Attorney General, working under Justice Department officials, and submitting a report to the Justice Department. If Justice Department officials are implicated, the most obvious expectation is that it will be a coverup. The Attorney General's selection of the special counsel will be almost sure to obtain that result.

An Independent Counsel or Independent Prosecutor, on the other hand, is selected by a panel of three appellate judges in the District of Columbia, following a request by the U.S. Attorney General. The Attorney General considers the request for an independent counsel, following the request by a majority of the House or Senate Judiciary Committees. But even an independent counsel has its limitations. The person appointed by the federal appellate judges is often not an experienced or aggressive investigator, and is often an amateur in that respect. Lawrence Walsh, for instance, fits that definition.

CHAPTER TWENTY FOUR

BANK OF LAVORO
AND IRAQGATE

Another of the many scandals involving high-level federal officials surfaced in the late 1980s, referred to as Iraqgate. It evolved around the Banca Nazionale del Lavoro (BNL), owned primarily by the Italian government. Implicated in the scandal with the bank were White House and Justice Department officials. The details of this scandal first surfaced in the alternate media, as is often the case, and especially in the weekly newspaper, *Spotlight*.[409]

While other members of Congress engaged in the usual coverup of this scandal, Congressman Henry Gonzalez of Texas exposed the BNL corruption in 1991. He had to surmount the coverup by other members of Congress, the CIA, Justice Department personnel, and the White House. BNL first attracted his attention when he discovered that the small Atlanta branch of BNL had made over $5 billion in loans to Iraq.

The scandal made it possible for Iraq's Saddam Hussein to wage war against Kuwait, and caused the U.S. taxpayers to be saddled with over ten billion dollars in debt over the next several decades. Another newspaper that exposed many of the scandals described within these pages was the local *Napa Sentinel* in Napa, California.

BNL was tied in with the Persian Gulf war and President Bush's arming of the Iraqis through loans for which the American taxpayers will be paying for the next few decades.

In November 1989, White House officials guaranteed the payment of loans made by banks to Iraq for the purchase of U.S. farm products under a program run by the U.S. Agriculture Department's Commodity Credit

---

[409] *Spotlight*, 316 Independence Ave, S.E. Washington, DC 20003

Corporation. The approval provided that United States taxpayers would indemnify the banks lending money to Iraq for the purchase of U.S. food supplies, if Iraq defaulted on the loan payments. Iraq had already made a name for itself by defaulting on earlier loans, and its income left little possibility of repayment.

Instead of using the money to purchase U.S. food supplies, Iraq diverted billions of dollars of these farm loans to purchasing military equipment. In some cases Iraq exchanged food shipments for arms, including poison gas and chemicals. When farm products were actually purchased in the United States, the ships supposedly hauling the products to Iraq would be diverted in Europe, and the food supplies traded for military equipment and supplies. These loans, secured by the United States, made possible the war capability for Iraq to invade Kuwait. In effect, the U.S. taxpayers, through their leaders, made possible the terrible bloodshed in the Gulf War.

Many U.S. investigators warned the Bush Administration that Iraq was diverting the money for war purposes. But despite repeated warnings, and proof of the diversion, President Bush pushed to continue the program. This continued funding of Iraq's war-making capabilities resulted in tens of thousands of deaths within a few years, as Iraq invaded Kuwait.

Iraq's invasion of Kuwait on August 2, 1990, caused it to default on its loans to the BNL bank. The loans guaranteed by the U.S. taxpayers to the participating banks then became due. Making matters worse, Iraq had part ownership interest in some of these banks, and stood to gain not only from the five billion dollars originally received, but from part of the funds to be paid to the banks that made the loans. The U.S. taxpayers would pay this tab, and the interest required to finance it, doubling or tripling the amount.

Some of the money furnished by the United States was used to purchase poison gas that was used on Iraqi Kurdish villages,[410] much of it purchased through Cardeon Industries in Chile, a CIA asset. Cardeon supplied considerable war materials to Iraq and other countries under the guidance of the CIA.

The Rome-based Bank of Lavoro, through its Atlanta branch, loaned directly and through other participating banks, over five billion dollars to Iraq under the program. The young manager of the Atlanta branch of BNL, Christopher P. Drogoul, was ordered by his superiors in Rome to fund the loans and falsify the paper work so that U.S. authorities would not discover the fraudulent diversion of funds from farm to military uses. In carrying out the scheme the Bank of Lavoro borrowed money from other banks and then reloaned the money to Iraq at a slightly higher interest rate, relying upon the United States loan guarantees to protect itself from losses.

The scheme required secret telexes, separate sets of books, phony taxes, and other devices to escape detection by bank examiners. The fraudulent program was known to bank employees as "Perugina," the name of an Italian candy factory.

---

[410] *San Francisco Examiner* July 26, 1993.

The thousands of agents in the CIA, the Justice Department, the State Department, and other U.S. agencies, could hardly miss evidence of this massive fraud. But despite the reports about the diversion of funds, the Bush White House continued the scheme that built up Iraq's military. It was as if the White House wanted Iraq to escalate its military might and start a Middle East war.

Britain was also involved in the diversion of funds that made possible the Gulf War. Matrix Churchill, a machine tool company in England, secretly and unlawfully supplied military equipment to Iraq during this period, even while the company knew that Iraq was using poison gas on the Kurds. The only people in the western hemisphere who didn't know about the scam, it appears, were the American people, who were ignorant about the misconduct by their government due to the controlled media.

Two BNL employees reported the scheme to the local U.S. Attorney in Atlanta, causing the local U.S. attorney to raid BNL's Atlanta office and seize incriminating documents. The U.S. attorney discovered that bank officials in BNL's home office in Italy knew of the scheme, directed it, and ordered the local bank manager in Atlanta to carry it out. But Justice Department officials in Washington did not want Italian officials blamed, which would implicate U.S. officials.

To divert attention elsewhere, Justice Department prosecutors charged the young Atlanta bank manager, Christopher P. Drogoul, with defrauding his bank by disbursing the $5 billion in loan proceeds without home office knowledge and approval. The Justice Department's indictment was based upon the charges that the bank manager acted alone, without knowledge and approval of BNL's home office in Italy, and therefore committed fraud. If the home office had known and approved of the scheme, the bank manager and employees could not be charged with defrauding the bank. Further, if home office officials knew of the scheme, it would have serious political implications in Italy. Additionally, if BNL officials in Rome knew of the fraud associated with disbursing the funds guaranteed by the U.S. taxpayers, the liability of U.S. taxpayers to pay the billions of dollars that were fraudulently diverted would not exist.

By fraudulently covering up for the corruption, Justice Department officials and the White House were causing the U.S. taxpayers to pay billions of dollars that may never be repaid as the United States pays the interest on the horrendous national debt.

Following a standard pattern, Drogoul's court-appointed attorney, seeking to protect the Justice Department and other federal officials, urged him to plead guilty, which he did. He faced twenty years in prison. The attorney had falsely assured Drogoul that if he pled guilty he would receive a suspended sentence. But the sentencing judge wasn't going along with the scheme.

In an unusual twist of not going along with Justice Department prosecutors, U.S. District Judge Marvin Shoob demanded that Drogoul explain truthfully at the sentencing hearing what had actually occurred.

Fearing a long prison term instead of the suspended sentence promised to him by his attorney and the federal prosecutor, Drogoul obtained other legal counsel for his appearance at the sentencing hearing. The new attorney, Bobby Lee Cook, moved to have Drogoul's guilty plea rescinded on the basis that the BNL bank manager acted in the multi-billion-dollar scheme with the knowledge and approval of his superiors in Italy. Judge Shoob granted the motion and rescinded the guilty plea, over the protests of Justice Department prosecutors who knew the bank manager was not guilty.

Cook demanded documents from the CIA and Justice Department that showed federal agencies had prior knowledge of the BNL activities and knew that high Italian officials in Rome had fraudulently approved the corrupt activities. At first, Justice Department officials denied having such reports. Congressman Henry Gonzalez, who had been exposing the BNL corruption for months on C-Span, submitted a CIA document to the court showing that Italian officials in Rome had knowledge of the multi-billion-dollar transactions and fraud.

Several days later, CIA officials sent a letter to Justice Department prosecutors, omitting the fact that the CIA had evidence that Rome officials knew of the scheme. CIA officials then accused Justice Department officials of trying to get the CIA to provide U.S. prosecutors and the court with misleading information to support the imprisonment of the young BNL bank manager. As Congressman Gonzalez released more documents, it became obvious that the CIA had numerous documents showing the guilt of Rome officials and that the CIA deliberately withheld this evidence from the court.

It also turned out that federal officials had altered a list of high technology items that were sent to Congress to obtain approval for the shipment to Iraq. The evidence indicated that high federal officials knew about the fraud being perpetrated by BNL and Iraq against the United States, and had not only deliberately covered up for it, but enlarged upon it. Evidence indicated that President Bush was determined to arm Iraq for attack upon its neighbors.

Among the documents that surfaced was one written by Secretary of State James A. Baker, urgently warning the White House that Iraq was secretly using technology provided by the United States to build up its chemical, nuclear, biological and ballistic missile capabilities.

Not only were Justice Department attorneys trying to imprison an innocent bank manager, but were imposing upon the U.S. taxpayers the $5 billion in losses plus the doubling or tripling of that amount from interest payments as the taxpayers sought to pay off that amount for the next few decades. With friends like that in the Department of Justice, the United States and the American public do not need any more enemies.

JUSTICE VS CIA VS FBI

In October 1992, the coverup of the Bank Lavoro scandal started to unravel. Foreign media exposure of the BNL scandal forced Justice Department officials to take some type of action appearing to prosecute the guilty. Instead, to protect key officials in the United States and Italy, Justice Department prosecutors filed criminal charges against Drogoul for reportedly defrauding the Italian bank when the young bank manager disbursed five **billion** dollars in loans to Iraq without knowledge and authorization of bank officials in Rome. Justice Department prosecutors of course knew this to be a lie.

Robert Gates, Director of the CIA, and other agency officials told the House Banking Committee that the CIA knew nothing about the huge loans to Iraq. Congressman Henry Gonzalez, Chairman of that committee, produced evidence showing they were lying.

Common sense indicated that a low-level bank manager in a small bank branch could not loan $5 billion without knowledge and authorization of top officials in the home office. Lending the equivalent of five hundred loans of one million dollars is hardly within the authority or resources of a small local bank manager.

The federal judge in the Drogoul case refused to support the Justice Department's attempts to settle the case by laying the blame on Drogoul. Unable to control the judge (truly a rare occasion), Justice Department prosecutors disqualified him. Justice Department attorneys then went shopping for a judge that it could control, but to no avail, as the judge refused to disqualify himself.

The scenario leading to the rift between Attorney General William Barr and his Justice Department gang, the CIA, and FBI Director William Sessions, followed the following schedule:

* CIA officials submitted a document to an Atlanta district court that contained misleading information, conveying false information that covered up the true facts. The document was intended to deceive,[411] to deny that the CIA had knowledge of the BNL fraudulent loans for several years. The CIA would have been highly incompetent if, with all its agents worldwide, it did not know of the fraud that required participation of many people.

* Senator David Boren, suddenly showing an unusual display of duty, identified the submitted document as containing false information. In response to this public rebuke, the CIA drafted a memorandum to correct the falsified information in the previously submitted document. Justice Department attorneys objected to the CIA correcting the original report, as Justice would then have to explain its own deception.

* The CIA then acquiesced to the Justice Department's demands to continue the coverup. But the next day the CIA prepared a document for Justice Department officials to sign that would protect the CIA's lying. Justice Department officials refused to sign, as it would further show their lies.

* CIA officials then testified in a closed-door Senate Intelligence Committee hearing, describing what happened. The CIA attorneys placed the blame for their coverup on pressures from Justice Department officials.

* Attorney General Barr then told the Senate committee that the Justice Department would investigate the matter of the Justice Department coverup, using its own guilty Justice Department personnel, to conduct the "investigation." This was similar to the "investigation" by Justice Department officials of the criminal misconduct involved in the Inslaw affair, in October Surprise, in Iran-Contra, in Iraqgate, and other scandals.

---

[411] Submitting documents knowingly stating wrong facts and wrong conclusions, or withholding facts that would show a different conclusion, is a crime under federal law.

* During a discussion between Senator Boren and FBI Director Sessions, the Director stated he would have the FBI investigate Justice Department officials, who were his bosses. Boren announced this fact to the media that same day, October 11, 1992.

* The next day, in obvious retaliation, Attorney General Barr announced that the Justice Department was charging FBI Director Sessions with ethics violations for unauthorized use of government vehicles. This was a petty charge made while the FBI was investigating criminal activities involving the CIA, the Justice Department, and the White House.

"Never In the History Of the Republic"

New York Times syndicated columnist William Safire stated (October 12, 1992) that "Never in the history of the Republic ... has the nation's chief law enforcement officer been in such flagrant and sustained violation of the law." Safire was stating in a relatively mild way what we (who knew the Justice Department's conduct first hand) had recognized years earlier.

Where is the American public in all this? They may have to pay not only the five billion in loan guarantees, but also the interests while taxpayers pay off this amount. They must pay the costs involved in the Persian Gulf War. They are effected by the endemic corruption within the U.S. Department of Justice. And much more.

ANOTHER COVERUP COSTING THE AMERICAN PUBLIC BILLIONS OF DOLLARS

If the case against the young bank manager of BNL in Atlanta had gone to trial, the involvement of President George Bush and members of his Administration, and of the government of Italy, would have been exposed. U.S. District Judge Marvin Shoob, after hearing evidence, stated:

[The five defendant employees of BNL] were pawns or bit players in a far larger and wider-ranging sophisticated conspiracy that involved BNL-Rome and possibly large American and foreign corporations and the governments of the United States, England, Italy and Iraq.

Justice Department attorneys lied[412] as they stated to Judge Shoob that the bank employees acted on their own, lending five **billion** dollars to Iraq without knowledge or approval of BNL's home office. Judge Shoob replied:

Based on the information that I have seen and that has been revealed, that kind of conclusion could only come about in never-never land.

During an August 23, 1993 sentencing hearing for the five BNL employees Judge Shoob stated he would not sentence any of them to prison because the Justice Department's contention that they defrauded the parent bank in Rome was too incredible. He added that they were merely "pawns and bit players in a far more wide-ranging conspiracy." Of course, Justice Department officials knew this. Judge Schoob said there were too many circumstances that made it implausible that the conspiracy was a small one involving only the Atlanta bankers, adding: "Smoke is coming out of every window. I have to conclude the building is on fire."

---

[412] *Wall Street Journal*, August 24, 1993.

Congressman Gonzalez had argued for an independent prosecutor to investigate the BNL affair. As in the Inslaw and BCCI case, the Attorney General appointed one of its own to investigate itself, former U.S. District Judge Frederick B. Lacey, to allegedly conduct a Justice Department investigation. Judge Shoob said of the Lacey report: "If Judge Lacey had investigated the Teapot Dome scandal," referring to the 1922 scandal which almost caused removal of President Warren G. Harding, "he would have given out a medal instead of a jail sentence."

Justice Department officials didn't care for this type of honesty and lack of control over the judge, and moved to disqualify him from presiding over the trial for BNL bank manager Drogoul, which was set to start on September 8, 1993. Another judge was then selected to conduct the trial.

Risking exposure of the role played by many people still in office, and especially the Justice Department, former president George Bush was subpoenaed to testify during the trial of bank manager Drogoul. The subpoena was accepted by the Clinton Justice Department, which is responsible for defending the acts of past presidents while they were in office.

STANDARD JUDICIAL COVERUP TACTIC

The new judge, Ernest Tidwell, was more amenable to the Justice Department coverup. Drogoul's attorney, Robert Simels of New York, stated that the judge issued two rulings refusing to allow the bank manager to give testimony and evidence showing that President George Bush and White House officials knew and acted to carry out the fraud. He stated that the judge blocked him from introducing evidence about the role of U.S. intelligence agencies in making the sham loans to Iraq, and the Italian government's efforts and pressures upon the Bush Administration to avoid indicting BNL. Judge Tidwell stated that this evidence was not related to the charges against Drogoul. That was not so.

This judicial strategy is repeatedly used against CIA personnel who for various reasons are charged with criminal offenses for carrying out their orders. The compromised judge renders orders barring the defendant from showing his CIA employment and that he was carrying out orders. They are barred from introducing CIA documents and barred from having CIA personnel appear. It happened to almost every CIA operative named in these pages.

The Drogoul trial was to have been the main stage for exposing the misconduct by the Bush Administration leading up to the Gulf War.

Drogoul wanted to go to trial to clear his name and expose the corruption related to the BNL affair. His attorney convinced him, however, to plead guilty. A week before trial, on September 2, 1993, Drogoul reluctantly pleaded guilty to something that he had not done. This guilty plea avoided the trial that would have exposed much of the U.S. misconduct and that of Italian bank officials.

The losers, as usual, are the U.S. taxpayers, who must now pay the money obtained through fraud, and the interest on that money, which it would not have to pay if the fraud by BNL bank officials had been exposed. This three to five billion dollars will multiple several times over by the time the money borrowed to pay for it will have been paid. This plea agreement insured that the American public would never discover the truth of the corruption preceding the Gulf War.

Again and again, due to its ignorance of corruption by government officials, and especially government corruption, the American public blissfully suffers the consequences of the criminality of its leaders and especially the Justice Department attorneys and officials.

ROLE OF KISSINGER IN THE GULF WAR

Spotlight wrote (November 9, 1992) that as early as 1984 Kissinger Associates were involved in arranging some of the loans from the Banca Nazionale del Lavoro (BNL) to the Iraqi government to finance its arms acquisitions from a little-known subsidiary of Fiat corporation. Referring to a confidential report prepared for the Economic Planning Group of the European Community by the Centre Des Etudes Transatlantiques (CETRA), *Spotlight* described the deal set up by Kissinger Associates involving the secret sale of five million land mines and other war material.

BNL was used for this transaction, funneling over one billion dollars through a small BNL branch in Brescia. At the same time the U.S. taxpayers were saddled with billions of dollars in debt to finance arm sales to both sides in the Iran-Iraqi war. Profiting from these secret deals were U.S. and foreign arms manufacturers, the arms merchants, Israel, and those in the United States who aided and abetted the activities.

Brent Scowcroft and Lawrence Eagleburger were employed by Kissinger Associates. Scowcroft would become President Bush's National Security Adviser and Eagleburger acting Secretary of State.

Spotlight stated: "CETRA's data prove the scheme for financing and supplying Iraq's military purchases was set up by Kissinger Associates long before BNL's Atlanta branch became involved." The article continued: "[It is] time we forgot those scapegoats in Atlanta [and] focus on the real culprit: Kissinger Associates."

Referring to Charles Barletta, a former Justice Department investigator, *Spotlight* wrote:

Barletta added that federal probers had collected dozens of such incriminating case histories about the Kissinger firm. But Henry Kissinger seems to possess a special kind of immunity. I'm not sure how he does it, but Kissinger wields as much power over the Washington national security bureaucracy now as in the days when he was the Nixon administration's foreign policy czar. He gets the payoff; others get the blame. Kissinger will remain unscathed until Congress finds the courage to convene a full-dress investigation of this Teflon power broker.

SOMETHING FISHY OCCURRED

On July 25, 1990, U.S. Ambassador to Iraq, April Glaspie, assured Iraq's Saddam Hussein that the United States was not interested in its dispute with Kuwait. Some reports state that April Glaspie assured Saddam Hussein that if Iraq invaded and seized only the northern part of Kuwait, the United States would not object.

According to CIA operative Gunther Russbacher, several days prior to July 25th, President George Bush and close advisors, including Brent Scowcroft, prepared an agreement to be submitted to President Gorbachev for signing, in which the USSR would not intervene if the United States invaded Iraq. Further, that in exchange for that agreement the United States would provide the USSR with large amounts of financial aid.

DETAILS OF MOSCOW FLIGHT

On July 26, 1990, four CIA SR-71s reportedly flew from Crows Landing Naval Air Station in California to Moscow, carrying an agreement signed by President George Bush and to be signed by Gorbachev.

Russbacher described to me the events that happened. Part of this has already been described, and it will be only briefly repeated here.

Russbacher was first briefed on the Moscow flight at Offutt Air Force Base in Omaha, Nebraska, in mid-July 1990. At this briefing were CIA Director William Webster, Brent Scowcroft, and members of the White House staff. Russbacher and his wife were billeted at this top-secret Air Force Base as authorized by CincPac. (I have seen the copy of the billeting receipts and authorization number.)

Russbacher and his wife then left by car for Reno, where Russbacher waited for further instructions. A CIA Learjet based at Hayward Airport near San Francisco, California, and operating under the CIA cover of International Jet Charter, took Russbacher from Reno's International Airport on July 26, 1990 to Crows Landing Naval Air Station. Four SR-71s were being readied for the flight to Moscow. Within a couple of hours, the flight of four SR-71s departed for Moscow, refueling twice in the air. The first refueling occurred over Canada from Air Force tankers, and the second refueling occurred as the aircraft were approaching the USSR, the refueling conducted by Soviet tankers.

Each of the two-seat SR-71s contained passengers to help carry out the highly secret political mission. Russbacher stated that two of the passengers were Brent Scowcroft and William Webster. Russbacher was the only one of the eight people on the flight who spoke fluent Russian, and he had been assigned to the U.S. Embassy in Moscow during the 1970s and mid-1980s, and had known Gorbachev previously.

Upon landing at Moscow, Russbacher met with Gorbachev, who signed one of the agreements, which was carried back to the United States on the return flight. Russbacher piloted one of the three SR-71s that returned to the United States, all of which landed at Fallon Naval Air Station, east of Reno. The one SR-71 that did not return was given to the USSR, and two former Air Force SR-71 instructors remained behind. One of these instructors was reportedly Abe Kardone, who was chief instructor on the SR-71 program at Beale Air Force Base in Marysville.

After landing at Fallon, Russbacher obtained a helicopter flight to Reno and then caught a cab to the motel where his wife, Rayelan, was waiting for him. Several days later Russbacher and his wife proceeded to Castle Air Force Base in California, where orders from CINCPAC authorized them to remain in an apartment on the base while Russbacher was debriefed on the flight.

What happened next is described elsewhere within these pages.

Seeking further confirmation that a CIA SR-71 was left in Moscow, I contacted two sources in early 1993 that would be most apt to know if this in fact occurred: Jane's All The World Aircraft and Aviation Week. Despite the fact they knew that I was an author, a member of the Aviation Space Writers Group, and that a reply should be sent, neither one of these groups replied. I wondered if they did in fact have knowledge that an SR-71 was left in Moscow, and that they recognized the classified nature of this act and chose to keep it from the American public.

CLINTON'S RHETORIC

While on the campaign trail, Clinton stated he would recommend the appointment of an independent prosecutor to investigate U.S. involvement in the BNL fraud. But upon assuming the presidency, and through Attorney General Janet Reno, who appeared to be more of a figure head for the Justice Department, the position was changed. The Clinton Administration, including the Attorney General, argued that there was no U.S. involvement in the BNL corruption and that the BNL headquarters in Italy and the Italian government were not involved. Attorney General Janet Reno and President Bill Clinton were lying.

CONGRESSIONAL HEARINGS

During Congressional testimony before the House Banking Committee on November 10, 1993, Christopher Drogoul was brought from federal prison to testify about the BNL scandal. He testified that he tried to report the criminal activities involving Iraq, his bank, and U.S. officials, but that the U.S. attorney's office in Atlanta repeatedly barred him from telling the truth. They wanted to protect the U.S. officials, Italian officials, and Iraqi officials, and to blame him for making loans totaling about five-and-a-half billion dollars that were beyond his ability to make.

Drogoul testified, and the facts showed, that he was merely a tool in the scheme involving the United States, Iraq, Italy, Britain, and Germany, to secretly arm Iraq. Not only did this conspiracy result in thousands of needless deaths, but the American public must pay this amount and the interest that will surely triple the original figure before the money is repaid somewhere in the twentieth-first century.

CHAPTER TWENTY FIVE

SILENCING WHISTLEBLOWERS

Every one of the criminal activities within these pages, and the U.S. officials implicated in them, were protected by the deaths and false charges by Justice Department prosecutors of whistleblowers, informants, protesting citizens, and victims. Killing witnesses or informants is nothing new. But these acts have greatly accelerated within the government of the United States as the criminal acts against the American people have accelerated.

Publicity was given to one of the first whistleblowers to be killed, federal inspector Henry Marshall, an employee of the Agricultural Stabilization and Conservation Service. He was killed in June 1961 on a farm in Texas, much to the relief of high federal officials. Marshall had evidence linking a multi-million-dollar commodity fraud to an LBJ aide, and to Lyndon Johnson himself. Alongside Marshall's body was the .22 caliber rifle that had fired the fatal bullets. Texas authorities obligingly ruled Marshall's death a suicide, even though the position of the wounds indicated it would have been physically impossible for them to have been self-inflicted.

An AP article prepared by the *Dallas Times Herald*[413] reported that convicted swindler Billy Sol Estes secretly testified before a grand jury empaneled at Franklin, Texas, relating to the Marshall death. Estes testified that he was present when Lyndon Johnson and two other men discussed having Marshall killed because Marshall knew too much about illegal manipulation of cotton allotments. Johnson reportedly gave the order to have Marshall slain. Estes identified the two men as Clifton Carter and Malcolm Wallace. Carter was once Johnson's top political aide in Texas and later his White House liaison to the Democratic National Committee. Wallace was a former University of Texas student body president.

---

[413] March 24, 1984 article appearing in *Sacramento Bee*, prepared by the *Dallas Times Herald*.

The Marshall killing and its relationship to Lyndon Johnson had been the subject of intense gossip and rumor in Texas political circles for years. Estes, who had aged considerably since Marshall was killed, agreed to testify about the Marshall killing at the urging of U.S. Marshal Clint Peoples of Dallas, who had pursued the case for more than two decades.

Other testimony in the grand jury hearings revealed that Johnson approved the killing out of fear that Marshall would give Attorney General Robert F. Kennedy evidence concerning cotton allotments incriminating LBJ. Kennedy was known to have no respect for Johnson.

The deaths of key people in the alleged murder conspiracy prevented further grand jury investigation. Former President Lyndon Johnson died January 22, 1973, on his ranch near Austin, Texas. Wallace died in a car accident in 1971, and Carter died September 22, 1971. The grand jury came to the conclusion that Marshall was killed, but reached no conclusion as to who may have done it.

"You're Going To Get Killed!"

When FAA inspectors warn another inspector his life is in danger by reporting safety violations and related criminal acts, the public might get the impression FAA inspectors are not going to report safety problems! "You're going to get killed," was the warning I received from several FAA employees as I tried to expose the FAA corruption. If other inspectors feared for their lives if they report safety violations at favored airlines, such as United, they could not be expected to report the misconduct.

The CIA was heavily involved in activities surrounding the John F. Kennedy assassination, and this group, like no other group in the United States, has a long history of assassinations. The death rate of people associated in some way with the JFK assassination was extraordinarily high. A partial list of those who died in the JFK assassination follows, and that list is followed by a *partial* list of those who posed a threat to U.S. officials because of their knowledge of activities described within these pages.

EXAMPLES OF KILLINGS & MYSTERIOUS DEATHS
ASSOCIATED WITH THE JFK ASSASSINATION

David Ferrie, a CIA contract agent, died on February 22, 1967, of a brain hemorrhage. Ferrie was one of Jim Garrison's main witnesses.

Dr. Henry Delaune was murdered on January 26, 1969, by being shot in bed and then set afire.

Dr. Mary Sherman, a close friend of Ferrie, was shot in bed and then set afire.

Aladio del Valle, a prospective witness for Prosecutor Garrison, was killed in Miami on February 22, 1967, within an hour after Ferrie died. He was one of Garrison's witnesses.

Robert Perrin died from arsenic poisoning. His wife, Nancy Perrin Rich, was a key witness, and a former employee of Jack Ruby.

Clyde Johnson was beaten the day he was to give testimony in the Garrison trial and was later murdered. He had knowledge of the close relationship between David Ferrie, Harvey Oswald, Jack Ruby, and Clay Shaw.

David Goldstein, who helped the FBI trace the revolver used in the murder of Officer Tippit, died in 1965.

WP Levens, who operated a burlesque theater in nearby Fort Worth and employed some of the girls working for Jack Ruby, died on November 5, 1965.

Thomas Howard, an attorney for Ruby and who had been at Ruby's apartment the night Ruby shot Oswald, died of a heart attack after acting in a strange manner for several days.

Jim Koethe, who was at Ruby's apartment the night Ruby shot Oswald, was murdered as he came out of his shower in his Dallas apartment on September 21, 1964.

Lee Bowers, Jr. died in a one-car crash near Midlothian, Texas, on August 9, 1966. He had witnessed suspicious activity behind the fence near where Kennedy was shot, and from where some of the shots reportedly originated. The coroner's report stated Bowers had suffered a strange shock at the time of the accident, suggesting that he was under the influence of drugs possibly administered by others.

Bill Hunter, who was at Ruby's apartment the night Ruby shot Oswald, was shot to death in a police station at Long Beach, California, on April 24, 1964.

Nicholas Chetta, the coroner for New Orleans who had key evidence against Clay Shaw, the person charged by prosecutor Jim Garrison with conspiracy regarding Kennedy's murder, died of an apparent heart attack on May 25, 1968.

Thomas Joyce, husband of a woman hired by Ruby, succumbed as the result of throat lacerations in March of 1964. He reportedly told friends he was marked for death because of information he had and that he was tired of running.

Dorothy Kilgallen, columnist and TV personality, attended Jack Ruby's trial. She told friends in late November 1965 that she was going to expose and break open the Kennedy assassination. In less than a week she was dead of unexplained causes, and her death was ruled a suicide.

Mrs. Earl T. Smith died of unexplained causes two days after her close friend, Dorothy Kilgallen died.

Marilyn April Walle, stripper for Jack Ruby, whose testimony a week earlier freed Darrell Wayne Garner, the man accused of shooting Warren Reynolds, was found hanged in her Dallas jail cell within an hour after being booked in February 1964.

Karen Bennett Carlin, one of Ruby's strippers, was shot to death in August, 1964, at Houston, Texas.

Earline Roberts, who rented a room to Oswald and had knowledge of Oswald's activities with Dallas police, died on January 9, 1966, of reported heart failure.

Harold Russell, a witness in Tippit's murder, was killed by a Dallas policeman in February of 1967.

William Whaley, the cab driver who reportedly drove Oswald from the assassination site and could have testified as to what Oswald may have stated to him, died in a suspicious auto accident in December 1965.

James Worrell, who witnessed a person run from the Dallas School Book Depository immediately after President Kennedy was shot, died on November 9, 1966, when his motorcycle was hit by a car.

Richard Carr had seen a man on the sixth floor of the Depository before the Kennedy shooting, and saw two men run from the building and speed away in a station wagon. The FBI warned him to remain quiet about what he knew. The FBI refused to believe his statements, even though they coincided with statements made by others. The FBI didn't want to hear any statements implicating anyone but Oswald. Carr was shot at and received threatening phone calls. Dallas police harassed him and his son. He finally moved to Montana. Shortly before he was to testify in the Garrison trial, his body was blown apart by dynamite wired to the ignition of his car.

Sam Giancana told columnist Jack Anderson that the CIA's plot to kill Castro may have back-fired, resulting in President Kennedy's assassination. He was killed with a .22 caliber pistol, the favorite for intelligence agency assassinations.

John Roselli was killed under the same conditions, as he gave Anderson similar information.

Karyn Kupcinet was overheard by a telephone operator talking about Kennedy's assassination shortly before it happened. She was killed two days after Kennedy was assassinated.

Rose Cherami reportedly told hospital employees of the plot to kill Kennedy. She was killed in a hit-and-run accident in 1965.

Captain Frank Martin, a member of the Dallas Police Department, died of cancer in June of 1966, shortly after he told the Warren Commission he was afraid to talk.

Jack Ruby, who killed Lee Harvey Oswald, suddenly developed cancer and died, on January 3, 1967.

Roger Craig was a Dallas Deputy Sheriff who, with two other persons, discovered the assassination rifle in the Dallas Book Depository, and signed an affidavit stating that it was a Mauser, 7.65 caliber. He testified that he had seen a man run down from the Book Depository and speed off in a car. This testimony contradicted the Warren commission report. Craig had been driven from his job, he had been shot at, he was threatened, and stripped of his ability to obtain employment. Craig was seriously injured from an explosion occurring when he started his car. Craig reportedly killed himself on May 15, 1975.

Hiram Ingram was a member of the Dallas Sheriff's department and a close friend of Dallas deputy Roger Craig. Ingram died suddenly of cancer on April 4, 1968.

George McGann held evidence obtained through his wife, Beverly Oliver, known as the "Babushka Lady." McGann was killed in the house occupied by Ronny Weeden, who knew Charles Harrelson, the person convicted of killing U.S. District Judge John Wood, Jr. McCann's associates included persons close to Jack Ruby.

Warren Reynolds witnessed the shooting of officer Tippit in Oak Cliff, a Dallas suburb. Reynolds had followed the killer and claimed that he was not Oswald. Reynolds was shot in the head in January 1964, but survived.

Edward Benevides, mistaken for his brother, Domingo, who had witnessed the shooting death of Tippit, was killed in February 1964, a suspected case of wrong identity.

Lt. Commander William Pitzer, who had taken pictures of President Kennedy at the autopsy, was shot to death on October 29, 1966, in his office at Bethesda Naval Hospital.

Gary Underhill, a former CIA agent, who had told people that the Kennedy assassination implicated a CIA faction, was shot to death on May 8, 1964.

Antonio Veciana was a key witness before the House Committee investigating Kennedy's death. He was the target of an assassination attempt.

Guy Banister and his partner, Hugh Ward, connected to the Office of Naval Intelligence, played key roles in the JFK investigation. Both were former FBI agents. Their almost simultaneous deaths occurred in 1964 during the Warren Commission hearings. Ward died in a plane crash in Mexico.

Maurice Gatlin, Sr. was involved with CIA activities and was an associate of another CIA asset, Guy Banister. Gatlin fell, or was pushed, from a window to his death in Panama in 1964.

Clay Shaw was a former CIA operative suspected of being in conspiracy to kill JFK. He met death under mysterious circumstances after being indicted by New Orleans District Attorney Jim Garrison for conspiracy in the Kennedy assassination. Shaw's body was embalmed before it could be examined, preventing a determination as to the cause of death.

Regis Kennedy, a former FBI agent, died in 1978 shortly after talking to the Assassination Committee.

William Sullivan, a close assistant to FBI Director J.Edgar Hoover, was shot and killed in 1977, before he could give testimony to the Assassination Committee. A half dozen key FBI figures died within a six-month period in 1977, silencing any testimony that they might have given.

John Martino claimed he had personal knowledge of the plan to kill President Kennedy. He died of a reported heart attack.

William Pawley was involved in the Cuban connection and worked with John Martino. Pawley was shot to death.

Congressman Hale Boggs of Louisiana had been a member of the Warren Commission, and had been critical of the FBI, accusing them of "Gestapo tactics." His plane disappeared in Canada on a flight to Alaska.

Buddy Walthers, a Dallas Deputy Sheriff, had found the bullet on the ground at the Kennedy assassination site and turned it over to an FBI agent. He was shot to death during a police shoot-out in 1969.

Albert Bogard was an employee of the Dallas Lincoln-Mercury dealer where Oswald allegedly test-drove a car. He was found dead in his car in Louisiana on February 14, 1966.

George DeMohrenschildt, with CIA connections, and a close friend of Oswald, was killed on the day that he was to be questioned by several investigators, including a representative of the House Assassination Committee.

Deaths due to heart attacks, strokes, and cancer can be induced and masked by certain drugs, a fact well known to the intelligence community. These drugs, and these tactics, are used routinely by covert operatives.

The *London Sunday Times* estimated that the odds of sudden deaths among approximately three dozen witnesses over such a short time span to be 100,000 trillion to one.

Despite the pattern of killings and mysterious deaths of informants under these unusual conditions, the Warren Commission held that they did not establish any relationship with the Kennedy assassination or constitute a conspiracy to silence opposition to the Warren Commission findings. The pattern of silencing whistleblowers or informants is seen in other scandals described within these pages.

Karen Silkwood, a whistleblower exposing misconduct at the Kerr-McGee plant where she worked, died in an auto accident while driving to a meeting with a reporter for the *New York Times*. Silkwood was to present documentary evidence that Kerr-McGee violated safety measures and quality controls in the plutonium recycling plant where she was employed. Her death has been the subject of many articles, books, a movie, and television.

PATTERN OF RETALIATION COMMENCING
WITH THE SCANDALS OF THE 1980's

The pattern of killings, mysterious deaths, and persecution of informants and whistleblowers continued with the escalating pattern of criminal activities described within these pages. A partial list follows:

Attorney Dexter Jacobson was killed on August 14, 1990, just prior to presenting evidence of rampant Chapter 11 judicial corruption to the FBI. Several months before his death, Jacobson and I had exchanged information on the Chapter 11 corruption each of us had discovered. The conduct of local police constituted a coverup that aided the killers to escape detection.

Attorney Gary Ray Pinnell was killed on February 11, 1991, in San Antonio, Texas, just prior to presenting evidence of Chapter 11 judicial corruption to the FBI. Judge-appointed trustee Marten Seidler was under investigation by the grand jury in Pinnell's murder on the basis that he was associated with Charlie Rummels, a prime suspect in the attorney's death. Many of those who were corruptly stripped of their assets after they exercised the statutory protections of Chapter 11 wanted to testify before the grand jury looking into Pinnell's death, but they were blocked by Justice Department attorneys. Some of those who sought to testify were of Hispanic origin, some coming from as far away as El Paso. When they returned home, they were harassed by Immigration and Naturalization Service personnel.

Danny Casolaro was killed on August 10, 1991, as he was obtaining evidence of corruption linking Justice Department officials to Inslaw, October Surprise, and BCCI. He was a Washington-based freelance reporter, and was killed in the Sheraton Hotel in Martinsburg, West Virginia. After Casolaro was killed, his body was embalmed before the family was notified, violating state and county rules and blocking a thorough autopsy, which might have revealed incapacitating drugs.

Alan D. Standorf was murdered on January 4, 1991, and his body found on January 31, 1991, in the back seat of a car parked at the Washington National Airport. Standorf was a source of information for Casolaro. CIA operative Michael Riconosciuto had introduced Casolaro to Standorf. It is believed that Standorf, an electronic intelligence employee for the National Security Agency, was a key source for some of the information obtained by Danny Casolaro, linking the Justice Department to the various parts of the scandals. Casolaro had previously told a friend, Bill Turner, that a key source of information on the scandals that he was investigating had disappeared (referring to Standorf).

Attorney Dennis Eisman was shot to death in April 1991, twenty-four hours before he was to meet with Michael Riconosciuto, who was involved in numerous CIA activities, including October Surprise and Inslaw. Eisman was building a defense for Riconosciuto against the charges filed by Justice Department prosecutors as they sought to silence him. Shortly before Eisman was killed, he was to meet in Philadelphia with a woman who would deliver to him important evidence of corruption by Justice Department officials.

Attorney John Crawford, one of the attorneys who worked with Riconosciuto, died from a heart attack in Tacoma in April 1993. This death raises questions, since he was one of several attorneys and investigators working with Riconosciuto to die within a relatively short period of time.

Paul Morasca was working with CIA operative Michael Riconosciuto. He opposed, and started to expose, corrupt activities carried out by the CIA and CIA contract agent John P. Nichols, and which included the Wackenhut Corporation, including George Wackenhut. He was killed in January 1982 in the San Francisco condo that he shared with Michael Riconosciuto.

Larry Guerrin, a private investigator, was killed in Mason County, Washington in February 1987, as he conducted an investigation seeking evidence for Michael Riconosciuto relating to the Inslaw scandal.

Alan Michael May was killed in his San Francisco home on June 19, 1991. May was involved with Michael Riconosciuto in the October 1980 movement of $40 million bribe money to Iranian factions. May had requested that Riconosciuto not divulge May's ties with the Iranian hostage scandal out of fear for his life. Within four days after the *Napa Sentinel* published Riconosciuto's description of the October Surprise operation, May was killed. The local coroner's report stated death was due to a heart attack. However, a subsequent autopsy revealed that May had poly pharmaceuticals in his system.

Vali Delahanty disappeared on August 18, 1992 as she was trying to warn Michael Riconosciuto about a plan by DEA and Justice Department officials to set him up on a drug charge. The skeletal remains of her body were discovered in a ravine at Lake Bay, Washington on April 13, 1993. Her disappearance and death prevented her from testifying on behalf of CIA Agent Michael Riconosciuto and against the Justice Department and DEA. She joined the long list of people who were killed, and who posed a threat to Justice Department officials in the Inslaw matter. Delahanty's sister, Debbie

Baker, told me that Vali had called her shortly before her disappearance and stated that she had very sensitive information concerning the Inslaw matter and the DEA and Justice Department's attempt to falsely imprison Riconosciuto. Vali reportedly wrote to Riconosciuto stating that she had information showing the DEA agent Hurley was working with John Munson to set up Riconosciuto. Vali was an alcoholic, living with a Munson. The evidence strongly indicates that Munson collaborated with DEA and Justice Department personnel to frame Riconosciuto on the sham amphetamine-manufacturing charge. Several months before Vali's body was found, Munson reportedly told people at a local bar, while he was under the influence of alcohol, that she was dead. Later discovery of her body proved him correct.

Pete Sandvigen, who resided on Whidbey Island in Washington, was ready to leave from the Navy Air Station on Whidbey Island, as part of further investigation into Inslaw. His body was found on December 2, 1992. The gun that he carried was found without the ammo clip, raising questions. Sandvigen had been part of a 26-man CIA team in Afghanistan during the late 1980s. He tried to help Riconosciuto defend against the Justice Department's amphetamine charges, along with exposing the Inslaw scandal.

Alfred Alvarez and two friends who were part of the Cabazon Indian Reservation, were killed in July 1981. Alvarez opposed the operations and takeover of the Indian reservation by the CIA front, Wackenhut Corporation.

Darlene Novinger, former FBI operative, reportedly discovered during an FBI investigation that Vice President George Bush and two of his sons were using drugs and prostitutes in a Florida hotel while Bush was vice president. She reported her findings to FBI supervisors and then warned not to repeat what she had discovered. Novinger had been requested to infiltrate drug trafficking operations in South America and the United States. She was pressured to quit her FBI position; her husband was beaten to death; and four hours after she appeared on a July 1993 talkshow[414] describing her findings (after she was warned not to appear), her father mysteriously died. A dead white canary was left on his grave as a warning to her. After receiving death threats she went into hiding, from where she occasionally appeared as guest on talk shows, and called me from undisclosed locations.

Ian Stuart Spiro, his wife, and three children were killed on or about November 1, 1992 in the San Diego area. Spiro's wife and three daughters were killed with large-caliber bullets to the head in their home near San Diego. Ian Spiro was found dead in a car parked in the desert, having died from ingesting cyanide. Spiro had connections to the CIA and British intelligence agencies, and had been involved in various CIA operations, including October Surprise, Iran-Contra, and the Lebanese hostage crisis. He was helping Riconosciuto collect documents to present to a federal grand jury conducting hearings into the Inslaw matter when he was killed. The FBI pressured the media to report that Spiro had committed suicide after having killed his family.

---

[414] Tom Valentine, *Radio Free America*.

Spiro had worked with Oliver North in the arms-for-hostages schemes. Some reports link the death of the Spiro family with Israel's Rafi Eitan. The maid who worked part-time for the Spiro family had identified from pictures Rafi Eitan, as having been to the Spiro home several days before the Spiro murders. This doesn't prove that Eitan committed the murders, but his reputation in the intelligence community as a brutal murderer, shared with Mossad agent Michael Harari, is of an assassinator.

A former officer in the U.S. Army Criminal Investigation Division contacted Inslaw president William Hamilton, advising him that his contact in Israel warned that he, Bill Hamilton, and former Mossad agent Ari Ben-Menashe, were slated for assassination by Rafi Eitan. Hamilton made a memorandum of this phone call on dated May 18, 1993, which stated in part:

On Saturday, May 15, 1993, Bill McCoy, a retired Army Criminal Investigation Division officer, told me that his military intelligence sources reported that Rafi Eitan was then in Quebec.

One day earlier, on Friday, May 14, 1993, Ari Ben Menashe had told me that an "ex-colleague in Tel Aviv" had warned him that Rafi Eitan was planning to kill Ari Ben-Menashe and William Hamilton, and that Rafi Eitan had arranged last year for the murder of Ian Spiro and his family in the San Diego, California, area.

Upon hearing from McCoy on Saturday, I, therefore, advised McCoy that Ben-Menashe is currently living in Montreal, Quebec, and may be in danger if the information is true and accurate. I gave McCoy the telephone number for Ben Menashe so that McCoy could contact Ben Menashe directly with his information from U.S. military intelligence about Rafi Eitan's alleged presence in Quebec.

Yesterday, Monday, May 17, 1993, Ben-Menashe claims that he met Rafi Eitan in the lobby of a hotel in Montreal after first speaking with him by telephone on two occasions over the weekend. Ben-Menashe says that Rafi Eitan was accompanied by a bodyguard, possibly from Germany.

According to Ari, the following are highlights of the conversation between Rafi Eitan and Ari Ben-Menashe:

Rafi: *"Ari, you have done enough damage (by publication of Israeli secrets in his book, Profits of War)."*

    "If you testify in England in the Maxwell inquiry, you are finished. [Euphemism for termination.]"

    "Your friend, Hamilton, is perpetuating something very delicate and talking about things that shouldn't be talked about."

Ari: *"It's Hamilton's software."*

Rafi: *"There are greater things to consider."*

    "Fricker's article is very damaging."

On a separate subject, I questioned Ari Ben Menashe about his appearance in Chicago before Judge Bua's federal grand jury on INSLAW. I asked whether Bua or his staff asked any questions about the claim, published in Ben Menashe's book, Profits of War, that Israeli intelligence slush funds were used to finance the termination agreement between Leigh Ratiner and Dickstein, Shapiro and Morin. Ben-Menashe said he was not asked a single question about the subject.

****

I received a letter on October 20, 1993 from Ron Veatch, stating:
I had spoken to Ian Spiro a few days prior to his murder. Ian was working for a CIA cover and he became aware that Jonathan Wise, who was president of the Communications 900-type business was also CIA/NSA federal front. He begged me for help.

Jonathan called me the next day after the murders and missing of Ian, and tried to draw me into their scheme. Ian gave me some CIA/FBI top secret papers to hold and he was murdered by CIA/FBI-directed Mossad.

Veatch stated that Spiro was planning to duplicate a nationwide 900-sexually-orientated business, New Media Telecommunications, located in La Jolla, California, which was run by Jonathan Wise, whose father, John Wise, was a CIA asset. Spiro had become very concerned about the harm being inflicted worldwide by the U.S., British, and Israel intelligence agencies, and started exposing some of their worse secrets.

Russbacher learned through his intelligence agency contacts that the Spiro murders were carried out by Israel's Mossad and Britain's M-5 intelligence agencies.

Russbacher had stated to me in the past that one of the methods the CIA uses to blackmail people, including politicians, was through the promotion of the 900-sexual numbers and pedophile activities. When I quizzed Russbacher about this information he stated that New Media Telecommunications was an CIA operation and that John Wise had been a CIA asset for many years. This discovery added additional intelligence/espionage agency involvement in the death of the Spiro family.

Robert Corson, a business associate of Ian Spiro, was found dead in an El Paso motel room[415] a day before Gail Spiro and her three children were found. Corson reportedly worked for the CIA and in the CIA's drug and arms trafficking.

Jose Aguilar, a tree trimmer who worked occasionally at the Spiro property, reportedly identified a picture of Rafi Eitan as a visitor to Spiro's home shortly before the Spiro family was found dead. Shortly after the Spiro killings, on November 14, 1992, Aguilar was killed by a bullet in the head.[416]

Howard Cerney, attorney from New York City, who represented Ian Spiro on some of Spiro's legal matters, was found dead in July 1993.

Attorney David Mayer was killed by gunshot on February 6, 1989, in the San Francisco Bay Area. On February 7, 1989, he was to have appeared in

---

[415] November 4, 1992.
[416] Valley Center, California.

the U.S. District Court at San Francisco, before Judge Paul Vukasin, Jr.,[417] defending people in drug-related charges that were reportedly tied in with covert CIA drug trafficking activities. Mayer was an activist seeking to expose the contra-drug connection involving the Reagan-Bush administration, the CIA, Justice Department officials, and others. His investigation and files disclosed links between high federal officials and associates, and a number of major federal crimes.

Abbie Hoffman was reportedly killed in his home on April 12, 1989, just prior to delivering a manuscript on the October Surprise operation to *Playboy's* Chicago offices.

Wife of DEA drug pilot Basil Abbott was killed in Sweden in 1982, after talking to European reporters about the DEA drug trafficking operation into the United States. She sought publicity to obtain the release of her husband who had outlived his usefulness to the DEA.

Robert Maxwell died after falling or being thrown off his yacht, shortly after his role in the Inslaw affair was publicized. He had considerable knowledge and/or participation in U.S., Israel, and British intelligence agencies, in Inslaw, and other areas associated with assassinations and mysterious deaths.

Charles McKee and other CIA operatives on Pan Am Flight 103 died when the plane was blown apart over Lockerbie, Scotland. McKee's CIA team was returning to Washington, in defiance of CIA orders, to give testimony to Congress on the CIA's drugs-for-hostages operation by another CIA faction.

Reported assassination of three navy officers on the evening of April 30, 1991, at Fort Ord, California, including Admiral John D. Burkhardt, Captain Samuel J. Walters, and a female Navy officer, whose first name was Marilyn.

John David Pigg, was killed in July 1993 in Anadarko, Oklahoma. He was a CIA agent involved in a major heroin operation going involving several federal agencies[418] through San Francisco and other key U.S. cities, which is discussed in more detail in later pages. He reportedly wanted to get out of the operation and it was suspected that he constituted a threat of exposing the multi-billion-dollar-a-year operation.

William Casey, Director of the CIA, a key participant in the October Surprise operation and its related Iran-Contra arms and drug activities. He experienced seizures on the morning that he was to testify before the Senate Intelligence Committee, and underwent brain surgery. He died several months later, on May 6, 1987. Friends believe that Casey would have told the truth if he had testified, thereby implicating people in high positions. CIA operatives have told me that the rumor within the CIA is that Casey's medical condition was induced by drugs.

---

[417] A friend of Earl Brian, Edwin Meese III, and other parties implicated in October Surprise, Inslaw, Chapter 11 corruption, Justice Department pattern of coverup, are all part of the Reagan-Bush coterie.

[418] Central Intelligence Agency; Drug Enforcement Administration; Customs; U.S. Department of Justice.

Former Senator John Tower was killed in a plane crash at New Brunswick, Georgia, on April 5, 1991, just as the October Surprise scandal was again surfacing. Towers was involved in the October Surprise and Iran-Contra operations, as was his aide, Robert McFarlane.

Granddaughter of CIA station chief found dead In November 1993 the granddaughter of the St. Louis CIA station chief, Bob Peters (alias, the "Rabbit"), was found dead in her car, under mysterious circumstances. The station chief had provided Russbacher with assistance throughout his period of imprisonment since 1990 while high CIA officials sought to silence Russbacher. It is suspected that the young girl's death was a CIA act. It is standard practice in the spook agencies to inflict harm upon a family member as they try to silence or retaliate against someone. Peters grand-daughter was in her teens, and found slumped over in her car parked along the highway. There was no known cause of death, a common finding in assassinations by any of the various spook agencies of the United States or foreign governments.

Paul Wilcher was found dead on July 23, 1993, under mysterious circumstances. He was an investigator and attorney living in Washington, D.C., who was in frequent contact with Gunther Russbacher and myself. He and I shared information together and were in frequent contact with each other. He had recorded sixty tapes of statements made by Russbacher during about six weeks of daily questioning, taking place in the Missouri State Prison at St. Charles, Missouri. These tapes revealed CIA secret operations in which Russbacher was involved. Russbacher warned Wilcher that these tapes were never to be revealed to anyone unless he died. I had a set of them in the event something happened to Wilcher's originals. More about Wilcher's death in later pages.

Shortly before Wilcher's death he wrote a 105-page letter to Attorney General Janet Reno, describing evidence that he allegedly acquired concerning several of the criminal patterns described in these pages. His letter stated that "Bush Administration hold-overs in the Justice Department, along with others tied to the CIA," were blocking exposure of the criminal offenses. The first page of his letter stated in part:

The lives of key participants, other witnesses, and even myself, are now in grave danger as a result of my passing this information on to you. If you let this information fall into the hands of the wrong persons ... some or all of those who know the truth ... could well be silenced (i.e., murdered) in the very near future.

Reno refused to receive Wilcher's evidence, and Wilcher was found dead shortly thereafter.

WHO WERE THE ASSASSINS?

The people or groups responsible for the assassinations, according to my CIA contacts, included teams within the intelligence community and the FBI. Two of my informants who were close to the assassination teams in the CIA were Gunther Russbacher and Commander of Navy SEAL Team Two, Robert Hunt. These activities are described in other pages, and their description of the assassination teams showed that the intelligence agencies have separate fiefdoms (something like I found initially in the FAA), and that some of these fiefdoms had their own assassination groups. They even targeted other CIA personnel.

Several of my CIA contacts described an FBI agent noted for his assassination activities, and how they feared him: Charles "Chuckie" Peters, employed by the Federal Bureau of Investigation in the Chicago area. Other persons connected to the CIA and allegedly involved in assassinations were reported to me as Chuck Hayes and Anthony Russo. Hayes was a former TWA pilot in the 1950s. I have no knowledge to substantiate these claims, other than what had been told to me by several CIA informants.

Russbacher described to me the assassination orders that he had to carry out during his CIA career. He said one of the "termination" operations was called the Omega Plan. Another informant with the ONI and CIA described the assassination operation known as Operation Ringwind. He trained some of these assassinators, and he is described in later pages.

KILLINGS OCCURRING IN FOREIGN COUNTRIES

Francis John Nugan operated a covert CIA proprietary known as Nugan Hand Bank in Australia. After the cover was blown on Nugan Hand by a Hong Kong financial reporter, Nugan was found shot to death, holding a rifle with an unspent bullet in the bolt-action operated chamber. Nugan had information on CIA links to money laundering, drugs, and other criminal activities that threatened to expose a fundamental operational pattern.

Thomas Wilhite threatened to expose the CIA role in Bishop, Baldwin, Rewald, Dillingham, and Wong to newspaper reporters. He died in a plane crash within 24 hours of announcing his intention to blow the whistle. Wilhite was a friend of Ron Rewald, who was the fall guy when its cover was blown by a Honolulu television reporter.

Houshang Lavi worked with Iranian arms dealer Cyrus Hashemi (now deceased) on covert arms sales to Iran. Shortly after trying to obtain documents establishing arms sales between the United States and Iran through Israel, an assassination attempt was made on his life.

Anson Ng was shot to death a month before Casolaro's murder. Ng was in Guatemala working for *Financial Times* to interview Jimmy Hughes, who had important information on misconduct relating to murders occurring on the Cabazon Indian Reservation. Hughes had fled to Central America to escape the fate of other informants who had been killed, or prosecuted by Justice Department officials.

Jonathan Moyle was a journalist investigating the sale of military equipment by arms merchants in Chile to Iraq as part of a CIA operation. Moyle was killed on April 1990, while in Santiago, Chile.

Arnold Raphel was one of several top officials in the Carter Administration participating in the October Surprise operation. He was killed in a plane crash with Pakistani President Mohammed Zia ul-Haq (August 17, 1988), in which sabotage is suspected.

Mohammed Ali Rajai, a former Iranian official, reportedly met with George Bush and William Casey on October 18, 1980, just prior to their flying to Paris to formalize the October Surprise agreement. Rajai was killed in a bomb blast in his Teheran office.

Cyrus Hashemi was a key party in the October Surprise operation, and was killed after stating to a reporter that his arms sales to Iran were part of the October Surprise operation.

Shahpur Bahktiar, an Iranian living near Paris, had evidence proving the existence of the October Surprise operation. He was killed on August 6, 1991.

Mehdi Hashemi was head of Khomeini's office for export of militant Islamic fundamentalism, and a part of the October Surprise operation. He was executed in Iran on September 21, 1987.

Hassan Sabra, chief editor of the Lebanese weekly *Al Shiraa*, who had been exposing the October Surprise and arms-for-hostages operation, was shot on September 21, 1987, the same day that Mehdi Hashemi was executed in Tehran.

Sadegh Ghotbzadeh was foreign minister of Iran during the Iranian hostage crisis. He negotiated with the CIA in the October Surprise operation. Ghotbzadeh encouraged Ayatollah Khomeini to go along with the October Surprise scheme advanced by the Americans. In *October Surprise*, Secretary of State Alexander Haig's aide, Michael Ledeen, tipped off the Khomeini regime to an alleged coup attempt involving Ghotbzadeh, resulting in his death.

Ayatollah Mohammed Beheshti reportedly sent a representative to the October 1980 Paris meeting. Beheshti was killed by a bomb explosion at the Islamic Republic Party headquarters in Iran on June 28, 1981.

Glenn Souham was a business partner of Iranian arms dealer Cyrus Hashemid and Adnan Khashoggi. He was killed, which silenced a possible informant.

Mohammed Zia ul-Hag, President of Pakistan was killed in a sabotaged plane crash on August 17, 1988, following a falling out with the CIA.

John Friedrich was a close ally of Colonel Oliver North and Amiram Nir, and had considerable knowledge of the Iran-Contra operation and the Justice Department's theft of the Inslaw PROMIS software. Friedrich and his body-guard were shot and killed in Sale, Australia. According to CIA-operative Michael Riconosciuto, Friedrich was the third party that he was using to try to set up an interview with Michael Hand of the covert CIA Nugan Hand Bank for an Australian television station. Friedrich owned a company (National Security Council) dealing in search and rescue equipment. Friedrich's real name may have been Haffenberger before he moved to Australia.

Amiram Nir was involved with Colonel Oliver North in various arms sales and the Iran-Contra affair, and was to be a major witness in North's forthcoming trial. If he had appeared, his testimony threatened to expose President Reagan and Vice President Bush, Oliver North, Israel's Prime Minister Peres, the Mossad, and the CIA, among others. He was reportedly writing a book on his experiences. Israel's Mossad investigated Nir's death and determined that he was killed by a woman friend he had met earlier, and who was a CIA contract agent.[419] As described more fully in later pages, Oliver North told one of my CIA contacts that Nir was killed because Nir had secretly tape-recorded Vice-President George Bush during a 1986 meeting in Jerusalem discussing arms-for-hostages and that Nir had planned to go public with the tapes.

MOSSAD ASSASSINATIONS

Dozens of people were assassinated throughout the world by Mossad squads when their activities displeased Israel or its intelligence agency. Even my CIA covert operators feared speaking out against this group. These killings have been described by former Mossad agents in their books,[420] and elsewhere within these pages.

These are only a few of the many people killed, or who mysteriously died, who posed a threat to U.S. officials, including those federal personnel described within these pages.

CIA ASSASSINATIONS

Throughout these pages are descriptions of CIA operatives who were taught to kill by their CIA bosses. Gunther Russbacher participated in numerous assassinations, under orders of his CIA handlers. A Navy SEAL team commander, whose activities are yet to be described, taught assassination techniques, as well as participated in assassinations. The CIA released a report in November 1993 describing its role in assassinations, including in unison with the Mafia, which reflects the mentality of this sinister and criminally-operating agency funded by the U.S. taxpayers.

The 133-page report, dated May 23, 1967, cataloged the riveting details of the CIA planning assassinations of foreign leaders.

PERSECUTION OF INFORMANTS

It is standard practice for Justice Department prosecutors to silence or discredit whistleblowers and informants, especially intelligence agency personnel, by charging them with federal offenses for carrying out what they were ordered to do by their handlers. Their subsequent imprisonment silences them and the felony conviction is used to discredit them.[421] A few examples of this practice follows, but there are hundreds of other instances of this Justice Department persecution.

Gunther Russbacher was repeatedly charged with federal offenses after he posed a threat to high U.S. officials. He was charged with kidnapping, misuse of government purchase orders and fuel, impersonating a naval officer, and other offenses. As with the others who were imprisoned, he constituted a serious threat to many White House officials and to exposing the criminal activities described within these pages.

Ronald H. Rewald, a CIA operative, installed as head of the CIA proprietary known as Bishop, Baldwin, Rewald, Dillingham & Wong (BBRDW). After the cover was blown on the secret CIA operation by a

---

[419] *Profits of War*, Ari Ben-Menashe.

[420] *Profits of War*, Ari Ben-Menashe; *By Way of Deception*, Victor Ostrovsky and Claire Hoy.

[421] Of course, when it suits the Justice Department prosecutors, they use felons and reward them to testify against someone that the Justice Department wants silenced.

Honolulu television reporter, CIA and Justice Department officials charged Rewald with money offenses to shift attention away from the CIA proprietary.

Michael Riconosciuto was a former CIA operative who was directly involved in highly sensitive CIA and Justice Department activities, including October Surprise and Inslaw. Justice Department personnel, including Peter Videnieks, threatened to retaliate against Riconosciuto and his wife if he testified before Congress on the Inslaw matter. Riconosciuto testified, and he was subsequently charged with manufacturing amphetamines.

Bobbi Riconosciuto lost custody of three of her children. She was charged with criminal contempt of court and held for six months in jail on $50,000 bail for alleged child abduction. She had moved from the state of Washington where her former husband had physically assaulted her. While residing in California, a Washington judge rendered an ex parte order changing custody of her three children to her former husband. Michael Riconosciuto was warned by Peter Videnieks of the Justice Department that his wife would lose custody of the children if he testified before Congress in the Inslaw matter. Washington and California judges ordered her jailed under $50,000 bail, on the basis of a judicial order changing child custody, rendered without her knowledge and without her appearance, and while she was a resident of another state.

Richard Brenneke had been a CIA contract agent for many years and was involved in numerous CIA operations, including October Surprise, arms and drug trafficking. Justice Department officials charged him with perjury after he testified in a 1988 U.S. district court hearing on behalf of another CIA operative, Heinrich Rupp, that they had both been CIA contract agents, and that he had seen Vice Presidential nominee George Bush and Donald Gregg in Paris in October 1980.

Stewart Webb was charged by Justice Department prosecutors with making threatening phone calls after he commenced exposing the ties between federal officials and the CIA in the HUD and savings and loan scandals. Justice Department prosecutors and federal judges incarcerated him for nearly a year, waiting to go to trial on the charge of making harassing phone calls to a kingpin in the Denver area HUD and savings and loan scandals.

Heinrich Rupp, a long time CIA contract agent and pilot, flew a Unocal Gulfsteam from New York to Paris as part of the October Surprise operation. He was charged by Justice Department officials with fraud relating to the covert CIA Aurora Bank in Colorado.

Imprisonment of over 300 CIA and DEA personnel who posed a threat of exposure to corrupt CIA activities. During the 1980's and early 1990s Justice Department attorneys charged them with federal crimes for having carried out the orders of their handlers.

Scapegoats for the HUD and savings and loan scandals. Seeking to shift attention from the kingpins in these scandals, and away from the CIA involvement in them, sham charges were filed by Justice Department prosecutors against dozens of innocent people.

Brett C. Kimberlin made known to the media that he sold marijuana to Vice Presidential candidate Dan Quayle from the fall of 1971 through early

1973 while Quayle was a law student in Indiana. Justice Department prosecutors retaliated by cancelling his 1989 parole date and resetting it for 1994, causing him to be imprisoned for an additional five years.

Rayelan Russbacher

Justice Department and DEA personnel tried in April 1993 to set Rayelan Russbacher in a drug sting. This attempt started with a call to Russbacher's wife by a former CIA operative with whom Russbacher worked, Fred Flinter, in the Los Angeles area.[422] Flinter advised Russbacher that he had something very urgent to tell him and that it could not be stated over the phone, but could be stated to Rayelan. Flinter suggested that Russbacher's wife meet him face to face, and that he would relay the information to her. The meeting took place in Denny's at Barstow, California and started out by Flinter attempting to interest Russbacher's wife in a drug operation. There was nothing urgent about the matter, and Rayelan was not the type of person who would mingle with drug traffickers.

Fortunately, Rayelan immediately got up and left, when drugs were mentioned. It was good that she did, as it is standard practice in a sting operation to charge anyone who is present during drug conversations with conspiracy. Unknown to Rayelan at that time, Flinter was wired with a microphone and transmitter, and two DEA agents were nearby listening to the conversation, ready to make an arrest if Rayelan engaged in conversations relating to drug trafficking, which could be called conspiracy to engage in drug trafficking. Justice Department prosecutors have filed conspiracy charges against many innocent people who were merely present when drug sales were discussed and considered.

After marrying Russbacher, and due to the Justice department constant persecution, Rayelan and her mother lost their home, their life's savings, and lived at the poverty level. Before being targeted by the CIA and Justice Department gang, she had enjoyed the amenities that went with the wife of a Dean at the Navy Post Graduate School in Monterey. She had her own home, and a decent way of life. All that changed as the Justice Department attorneys focused the raw power of the U.S. government upon her.

John Cole was sentenced to federal prison in 1992, after he had reported to the FBI and U.S. Attorney in Illinois details of criminal activities that he had discovered while in management with Granite City Steel. This steel company was involved with a group of other companies, some of which were CIA proprietaries, including unlawful arms shipments overseas, drug trafficking, and which included FBI and Justice Department personnel, CIA officials, Japanese Mafia figures, among others.

Lester Coleman fled the United States after the FBI tried to arrest him on trumped up charges of passport irregularities, after Coleman tried to reveal CIA-connected terrorists believed responsible for placing the bomb on Pan Am flight 103. His statements contradicted the U.S. claims that Libya was responsible, rather than Iran and Syria. Coleman had been based in Cyprus

---

[422] 714-854-3335.

as an agent for the Defense Intelligence Agency, a top-secret military intelligence unit reporting directly to the Pentagon in Washington.

THE AUTHOR

I must be included in the list of those persecuted to silence their exposure activities. To silence me, Justice Department prosecutors and federal judges acted in unison, misusing the courts to seize my assets, suspend all constitutional and statutory protections, and then charge me with criminal contempt of court for using the remedies in law to protect myself. When I sought to expose the criminality described within these pages the federal judiciary acted in unison, repeatedly sending me to prison in retaliation for reporting the crimes.

U.S. District Judge Vaughn Walker, acting in unison with Justice Department prosecutors (under Janet Reno), seek to send me to federal prison for having filed a federal action reporting the crimes in the Chapter 11 courts and other criminal activities. I am also waiting to go to prison on a charge of criminal contempt of court for having filed oppositions and appeals of the criminal seizure and looting of my life's assets. Orders have been rendered barring me access to the federal courts, preventing me from defending myself. This criminal misuse of the federal courts and the Justice Department converted me from a multi-millionaire to a state of poverty. My business, my home, my assets, were all destroyed. A half million dollar default judgment was obtained against me when I was incarcerated and unable to defend. I have been barred by federal judges from even filing actions addressing that judgment. For the remainder of my life I cannot acquire any assets, cannot engage in any of my prior investment activities, and cannot defend myself, regardless of the rights in law.

STANDARD TACTICS FOR SILENCING INFORMANTS

Justice Department prosecutors have standard tactics to silence informants who threaten to expose corruption by federal officials:

* Fabricate charges against the person, or simply charge them with offenses that they committed under orders of their CIA handlers.

* Seize all assets, preventing hiring their own legal counsel, and require them to rely on the usually ineffective court-appointed defender.

* Block them from raising matters relating to their CIA activities.

* Block them from subpoenaing CIA people with whom they worked.

* Deny to them access to CIA documents, or bar the introduction of these documents that may be in their possession.

* Have CIA personnel engage in perjury and subornation of perjury as they falsely testify against him or her and deny that the person had any CIA connections.

* Pay informants to testify against the person, either through money, reduction in prison sentence, or vacating prior criminal charges.

* Put all evidence under seal, preventing public access to the testimony and documents.

* Discredit charges made by informants by claiming they are felons and their word cannot be accepted as true. Simultaneously, the same Justice Department buys testimony from hard-core criminals to imprison

targeted informants.

PARTIES WHO BENEFITTED, OR WERE PROTECTED, BY THE DEATHS AND THE PERSECUTIONS

Central Intelligence Agency officials and their criminal operations, including for instance (a) looting America's financial institutions; (b) drug smuggling into the United States; (c) October Surprise; (d) Chapter 11 courts; and many other operations.

Justice Department personnel, who aided and abetted the CIA-related activities and who persecuted those who threatened to expose the criminal activities.

Federal judges, especially those who were directly involved in the Chapter 11 looting and were on secret retainers with the CIA. Also, those who assisted in the persecution of informants and whistleblowers, and those who unlawfully dismissed federal actions that otherwise exposed the corruption described within these pages.

Justices of the U.S. Supreme Court. Every Justice of the U.S. Supreme Court was repeatedly informed of these criminal activities, either by petition or appeal that I filed, or by personal letters sent by certified mail. They had a duty to act, especially when the criminal activities were perpetrated by the federal judges, federal trustees, and Justice Department attorneys over whom they had a direct supervisory responsibility, in addition to other responsibilities under federal criminal and civil rights statutes.[423] Instead of meeting their responsibilities, they aided and abetted the criminal acts, making possible the continuation of the criminal activities described within these pages.

Members of the U.S. Senate and House, who aided and abetted the criminal activities by blocking investigations and blocking the reporting of the federal crimes, many of which occurred in their areas of supervisory responsibilities.

Establishment media, who knew of the government crimes, and, despite First Amendment constitutional responsibilities, refused to report the serious government corruption that inflicted such great harm upon the American people.

State judges, repeatedly used by federal authorities to take judicial or police actions on targeted individuals, or to cover up for them.

EVIDENCE SHOWING SCHEME TO SILENCE RUSSBACHER

Adding to the circumstantial evidence that the charges against Russbacher by Missouri officials was a document I received in August 1993, revealing the scheme to falsely charge Russbacher with criminal activity. The document consisted of a May 14, 1989 letter written by a former Missouri Secretary of State, Roy Blunt, on stationary of the Missouri Secretary of State, to a Missouri prosecutor, Scott Sifferman, prosecuting attorney in Lawrence County. The letter exposed the scheme by state officials, working with a faction of the CIA, to press charges against Southwest Latex Supply and its management, who was Gunther Russbacher, operating the company as a CIA

---

[423] Title 28 U.S.C. § 1343; 42 U.S.C. §§ 1983-1986.

proprietary. The charges were based upon Russbacher's alleged attempt to sell unregistered securities of Southwest Latex Supply Company.[424]

Southwest Latex Supply was one of the CIA proprietaries Russbacher operated while a deep-cover CIA operative.[425] The reference, in the document, to Christian, was to a CIA Deputy Director of Covert Operations (DDCO). Russbacher referred to him as part of the CIA's "Faction One," reportedly under the control of George Bush during Bush's stay in the White House. Russbacher described how the interests of Faction-One often clashed with the Office of Naval Intelligence Faction, known as Faction-Two. Russbacher felt that Christian was attempting to silence and discredit him through the sham charges and subsequent imprisonment, and discredit any disclosures of October Surprise and related operations that threatened George Bush and the many people who were part of the operations.

Gunther said, "You have to understand, we always had to use Roy Blunt, he was our intermediary. Without Roy we couldn't have chartered half of the CIA proprietaries that we did." Russbacher added:

And then he [Blunt] was going to use me [through the sham charges] after I had been sanctioned by the Agency. He was going to use me to put a cap in his head and become the new governor of the State of Missouri. But it didn't work.

I asked, "When you had to pay him off, what was he doing, looking the other way as it related to the CIA proprietaries?" Russbacher responded, "Sure. Absolutely."

Russbacher said to me that Missouri Secretary of State Blunt worked with the CIA in the past in covert activities, and that he and other CIA personnel paid Blunt bribe money to carry out CIA proprietary activities.

One of the significant aspects of the letter was how State Prosecutors and officials criminally misused government offices against private citizens, and brazenly put into writing details of the scheme, confident that no State or federal officials would prosecute. That is what always astounded me through the thirty years of discovering major corruption implicating federal officials: none ever feared prosecution for their crimes.

The letter revealed that the sham charges were return of a favor to a Mr. Christian; and that the Prosecuting Attorney carrying out his part of the conspiracy would be rewarded with a judgeship. The letter, with the official seal of the State of Missouri and on the stationary of the Office of Secretary of State read in part:[426]

---

[424] Southwest Latex Supply was a spinoff from National Financial Services Corporation. National Financial was to buy the stock from Southwest Latex. Because they were not registered, the trade was not outside of Southwest Latex and considered a violation of the "blue-sky" law. National Financial Services provided the money to start up Southwest Latex Supply and it was considered a daughter corporation from NSF.

[425] Russbacher stated that Southwest Latex Supply manufactured the five-gallon buckets used to package the C-4 explosives sold by CIA agent to Libya.

[426] Because of poorer quality of the FAX copy in the author's possession, the exact wording of the letter is duplicated here.

State of Missouri
Office of Secretary of State
Jefferson City, 65102

Roy D. Blunt
Secretary of State

May 14, 1989

To: Scott S. Sifferman
       Prosecuting Attorney
       Lawrence County Courthouse
       Mount Vernon, Missouri 65712

Re: Southwest Latex Supply

Dear Mr. Sifferman:

I have tentatively set my schedule to be in Mount Vernon on June 14, 1989. We will need you, to do the following:

1. Have the charges ready to be filed for selling unregistered securities, fraud, and commingling of funds. Please forward for my review.

2. Schedule Press and Miller People.

3. Itinerary.

As you have seen, we have no grounds for these charges but, I owe one to Christian and, with full press coverage I should pick up some strong support in Webster's stronghold for 1992. I have spoken to the Lawrence County Republican Committee [and] they have assured me you will be recommended for the judgeship after the charges are filed. I will personally make the statements to the press and, they will not have any credibility after that.

Pursuant to our conversation we should set the bond high and you can advise Mr. Tatum. He can then present our scenario. You and John can handle it from there.

Sincerely,

Roy Blunt
Secretary of State

THE REWARDS

The prosecutor who assisted in carrying out the scheme, Scott Sifferman, was later appointed a judge in the State of Missouri, as promised. Russbacher stated that other State officials who participated in this scheme that eventually resulted in his state imprisonment included State Prosecutor Scott Zimmerman, who prosecuted Russbacher knowing the charges to be false; William Webster, a nephew to former FBI and CIA Director William Webster (who was Missouri Attorney General); former Missouri Governor John Ashcroft; former Lt. Governor Mel Carnahan (who became Missouri Governor in 1993).

On August 15, 1993 I sent a copy of the Blunt letter to Missouri's Secretary of State, Judith Moriarty, requesting a clean copy of the letter I sent and which should be in their files. She never responded, and I sent another request on September 3, 1993. Obviously, a letter by a prior Secretary of State outlining a plan to charge a person with a crime, for which that person is currently in prison, and which admits in its contents that the charges are false, isn't the type of letter that a State official wants exposed. No response to either letter.

I sent a letter to Missouri's Governor Mel Carnahan, on October 1, 1993, requesting his assistance in obtaining a copy of the Blunt letter. Carnahan was Lt. Governor of Missouri during the 1989 scheme to incarcerate Russbacher, and was a close friend to the writer of the letter, Roy Blunt. The Governor had a vested interest in preventing exposure of the Blunt letter. The Missouri Governor had the power to pardon Russbacher, and I demanded that he do so.

VACATING PRIOR JUDGMENT AND SENTENCE

In September 1993 Missouri Circuit Judge Michael W. Brown ordered the judgement and sentence that incarcerated Russbacher to be vacated and that Russbacher be remanded to the Trial Court for further proceedings. This judicial order came about as a result of a motion filed a year earlier by State Public Defender Rob Fleming. Missouri Prosecutor Philip Groenweghe ordered Russbacher held for a new trial, and caused bail to be set at nearly half-a-million dollars, $450,000 in cash.

This high bail was extraordinary for such minor alleged offenses, which could be expected to result from the desire of the CIA, Missouri and U.S. officials, to keep Russbacher imprisoned and silenced.

Several of the charges against Russbacher allegedly arose from Russbacher writing checks on one of his CIA proprietary to one of his aliases. No one lost any money in the matter as the checks never cleared: Russbacher's former wife had check-signing authority and had closed out the bank account.

Again facing at least one year in prison while waiting for trial, Russbacher, with the aid of friends in Missouri, filed on September 22, 1993 a federal habeas corpus action[427] seeking a federal court order for Russbacher's release. On that very same day, as if he was waiting for the filing to occur, a

---

[427] CV 002078 JCH.

U.S. District Judge entered a four-page order denying Russbacher's habeas corpus filing.

Simultaneously, the U.S. Immigration and Naturalization service filed a detainer with the Missouri prison, seeking to deport Russbacher on the apparent basis that Russbacher was not a U.S. citizen. CIA documents[428] in my possession identify Russbacher as a captain in the Office of Naval Intelligence, as well as statements made to me by covert CIA personnel who worked with or under Russbacher (and who themselves gave me documents establishing their rank in the ONI and CIA).

Russbacher's imprisonment by Missouri officials was the result of cancelling his suspended sentence based upon the alleged impersonating of a Naval officer while at Castle Air Force Base. In September 1993 I received secret copies of CIA memorandums showing Russbacher to be attached to the Office of Naval Intelligence, and to be a Captain in the U.S. Navy. I sent certified-mail letters on October 21, 1993 to Missouri Governor Mel Carnahan and to U.S. Attorney General Janet Reno, including copies of these documents, demanding that they provide relief for Russbacher. Governor Carnahan had the ability to circumvent the judicial and prosecutor corruption associated with Russbacher's imprisonment. Janet Reno had the ability to vacate the order of deportation. As usual when I sent highly sensitive letters, neither answered.

LETTERS AND EVIDENCE THAT
DEMANDED RUSSBACHER'S RELEASE

Shortly after Russbacher's sentence was vacated and a nearly half-a-million dollar cash bond demanded to secure release pending trial, other CIA contacts started sending me confidential Central Intelligence Agency and National Security Agency documents showing Russbacher to be an officer in the U.S. Navy and assigned to the Office of Naval Intelligence. I then sent letters in September 1993 to several officials that had the power and the duty to obtain Russbacher's release.

On October 21, 1993 I again sent a certified letter to U.S. Attorney General Janet Reno, explaining to her that Russbacher was in a Missouri jail, his freedom taken, on the basis of the sham charges by U.S. Attorney David Levi in Sacramento (now a U.S. District Court judge) that Russbacher was impersonating a Naval officer at Castle Air Force Base. I attached to that letter copies of confidential/secret CIA and NSA documents showing Russbacher to be a Naval officer. I reminded her that she had a duty to correct this sham charge and bring about the release of Russbacher. As in every other letter that I sent to this attorney general, she refused to answer.

At this stage, any state or federal official who exercised their duty and provided relief to Russbacher, or any one of us suffering from the judicial and Justice Department persecution seeking to silence us, risked prying open the lid that could expose some element of the epidemic corruption.

---

[428] May 20, 1986 memorandum from CIA Director Bill Casey to John Poindexter, NSA.

On that same date I sent a certified letter to Missouri Governor Mel Carnahan, along with the CIA/NSA documents, demanding that he step in and bring about Russbacher's release. I explained to him that it was the sham charge of impersonating a Naval officer that caused Missouri Judge Donald Dalton to order Russbacher incarcerated, and that the documents in the letter show that he was a Naval officer doing covert operations for the Office of Naval Intelligence. I explained the corruption in the office of the Missouri Prosecutor at St. Charles, including prosecutors Tim Braun and Phil Groenweghe.

Recognizing that the pattern of corruption was too enormous for anyone to act, I continued to put officials on notice who had a duty to act, so that if *someday* I could reach and motivate sufficient Americans to act, that those who played criminal roles in the scandals could be prosecuted. On October 26, 1993 I sent a certified letter to Missouri Prosecuting Attorney Tim Braun, whose office was responsible for the sham charges against Russbacher and his imprisonment. As with the other letters, I reminded him that Russbacher lost his freedom based upon the sham charges that he was impersonating a Naval officer, and I attached copies of the ONI/NEA documents showing that Russbacher was a Naval officer.

The U.S. Department of Immigration and Naturalization Service (INS) had a detainer filed with the Missouri prison officials to take Russbacher into custody and deport him, on the alleged basis that he was not a U.S. citizen. I wrote to INS Commissioner Doris Meisner on October 26, 1993, explaining the detainer on file, and attached to it copies of confidential/secret CIA and NSA documents showing Russbacher to be a captain in the Office of Naval Intelligence. I demanded that the detainer be vacated, that no further deportation proceedings be taken against Russbacher, and that she notifies me of the action she intended to take, or not take.

CONTINUING IMPRISONMENT ON THE
SHAM CHARGE OF MENTAL INCOMPETENCY

The common practice of Justice Department attorneys causing the continued imprisonment of people threatening to blow the whistle on these various crimes by charging them with mental incompetency threatened two of my informants. Justice Department attorneys charged Stewart Webb with being mentally incompetent to stand trial on the charge of making harassing phone calls to his former father-in-law, Leonard Millman. In July 1993 Webb had already been in prison for a year, without trial, on a charge that if he was guilty, which he wasn't, he would have had a shorter prison sentence. I sent a letter to Judge Richard P. Matsch describing my evaluation of Webb during many hours of telephone conversations, and that there wasn't any question that he was not only mentally competent but a sharp investigator.

Prison psychiatrists at Springfield, Missouri had ruled Webb mentally competent, after which the Denver U.S. Attorney assigned another psychiatrist, with connections to Webb's former father-in-law who made the original charge. That psychiatrist, Erwin Levi, and the attorney that Webb discharged, David Lane, argued that Webb was incompetent to stand trial, which, if upheld by the court, would have resulted in indefinite incarceration for Webb.

I sent a copy of the just-released book, *Defrauding America*, to Judge Richard Matsch, which he acknowledged in a July 14, 1993 letter to the U.S. Attorney, advising the Justice Department that they could view the book in the Judge's chambers. During a hearing on July 22, 1993 requested by Justice Department attorneys seeking to have Webb declared mentally incompetent with indefinite imprisonment, Judge Matsch made reference to my book several times, which he had on his bench, and ordered Webb released immediately. The Judge calendared a hearing to rule on Webb's pro-se motions to have the charges dismissed.

While out of prison waiting for the next hearing, Webb appeared on several radio talk shows, and renewed his many media contacts seeking to get them interested in the corruption that he uncovered. He was a threat to Leonard Millman, the other parties involved in the HUD and savings and loan corruptions, to White House officials, the CIA, and many others. I felt his life was in danger.

Shortly after his release, members of the Millman family sought to find out where Webb was physically located. Men were watching the residence of Webb's parents in Independence, Missouri, apparently seeking to find Webb. The most probable reason for these actions to determine Webb's physical location would be to silence him, and of course, that would probably mean to murder him.

ANOTHER TARGET OF JUSTICE
DEPARTMENT PROSECUTORS

Justice Department attorneys were simultaneously trying to cause the indefinite incarceration of another of my informants, Basil Abbott, by claiming he was delusional because he described his role as a DEA pilot flying arms to Central America and drugs on the return flights. I also sent a letter and book to the Judge hearing his case. Justice Department attorneys take advantage of the public's ignorance relating to the pattern of hard-core corruption in government, and place a sham delusional or paranoid label on anyone blowing the whistle.

Edwin Wilson, a former CIA operative who was made the scape-goat for a CIA operation that was exposed, wrote to me seeking my help to locate three witnesses who falsely testified against him: David Vogel, John Randolph, and Wayne Trimmer. Wilson hopes to have someone contact them, seeking to have them recant their perjured statements given during Wilson's trial, which caused Wilson to be sentenced to life imprisonment. When I brought this matter to Russbacher's attention, he advised that he knew the location of one of the witnesses, that he and his wife were in telephone communication with the wife of the witness, and confirmed that Wilson was indeed set up by Justice Department prosecutors through perjured testimony.

There are hundreds of other victims languishing in prison, their families torn apart, as a result of the misuse of government power. But they are not the only victims; the American public suffers as a group. The 58,000 deaths and many more injuries in Vietnam; the deaths in the Korean debacle; the huge financial losses; the drug epidemic; are all a result of the corruption within the CIA and other government agencies, and the coverup of these crimes.

STANDARD PRACTICE OF FALSE CHARGES OF MENTAL INCOMPETENCY AGAINST CONCERNED CITIZENS

It is standard practice for Justice Department attorneys to charge CIA and other whistleblowers who threaten to expose some aspect of the corruption described within these pages with mental incompetency charges. These charges, made after arresting a defendant and while keeping him in prison pending trial, stop all proceedings, but keep the person in prison indefinitely, and sometimes for years. It is also standard practice to inject the defendant, who had never had a trial, with mind-destroying drugs at the Federal Prison Hospital in Springfield, Missouri.

Justice Department attorneys select cooperating psychiatrists to examine the imprisoned defendants. To "justify" the charges of mental incompetency, these cooperating psychiatrists will render a decision of mental incompetency on the basis that they report specific corrupt acts that they had discovered.

This was done in mid-1993 to two of my informants, Stewart Webb and Basil Abbott. In Webb's case, he was in prison for almost a year, waiting for trial, solely on the charge by his former father-in-law, Leonard Millman, that Webb had made harassing and threatening phone calls. Millman was a kingpin in the Denver-area HUD and savings and loan areas, working closely with the CIA and underworld figures, and a financial backer to U.S. Attorney Michael Norton when Norton ran for Congress in the early 1980s.

Webb was denied release pending trial, and then charged by the U.S. Attorney and his own attorneys with mental incompetency. By doing this, the trial was delayed, preventing Webb's release. The imprisonment and sham psychiatric charges kept Webb from appearing on talk shows exposing the massive corruption that he had discovered. The imprisonment kept Webb from continuing his investigations, and from reporting his findings to his many contacts in the media.

Webb encountered the standard pattern of clients sabotaged by court-appointed legal counsel. His first attorney, Charles Szekeley, refused to raise the defenses that would have exposed the corruption in the Denver area, including that involving Justice Department attorneys. Webb discharged the attorney, who then responded by filing papers recommending that Webb be ordered to undergo a psychiatric/psychological examination.

Webb's next court-appointed attorney, David Lane, had connections to many of the financial figures involved in the Denver-area HUD and savings and loan scandals, and proceeded to sabotage Webb's defenses. Webb responded by dismissing Lane and requesting the court to appoint another attorney. Lane responded to this request by filing papers with the court charging Webb with mental incompetency and recommending that he be sent for psychological examination.

Judge R. Thompson rendered an order sending Webb to Springfield Federal Prison Hospital on April 1, 1993, where the psychiatrist-M.D., Chris Peitz, held that he was mentally competent. Upon returning to Denver, a hearing was held by U.S. District Judge Richard Matsch on May 7, 1993, for a judicial determination of Webb's mental competency to stand trial.

The U.S. Attorney, and Webb's new attorney, Charles Szekely, requested that another mental examination be conducted. The U.S. Attorney then had a psychologist appointed, William Hansen, who was closely connected to Leonard Millman, the powerful financial figure who had filed the charges against Webb. As could be expected in this type of scheme, Hansen reported that Webb was mentally incompetent.

Under these conditions Webb again dismissed the attorney and requested appointment of other legal counsel, which Judge Matsch did order. In the meantime, I sent a copy of *Defrauding America* and my evaluation of Webb's mental competency to the judge, which showed the massive corruption that Webb was trying to expose, including the corruption in the office of the U.S. Attorney in Denver. On July 14, 1993, Judge Matsch sent a letter to the U.S. Attorney in Denver making reference to the book he had received, adding, "This book may be examined by you at any time in my chambers."

At the July 22, 1993 hearing for a judicial determination of Webb's competency, Judge Matsch several times made reference to the book, admonished the U.S. Attorney, and criticized Webb's new attorney, Neil McFarlane for not properly defending his client. Judge Matsch then held that Webb was mentally competent, an obvious conclusion, and ordered Webb immediately released. The judge set a hearing on Webb's *pro se* motions to have all charges dropped.

Psychologist William Hansen was sent to evaluate Webb, who recognized Hansen as connected to his former father-in-law who filed the harassing charges against Webb. Webb refused to cooperate with Hanson. The probation department then sent psychiatrist Erwin Levi to conduct an examination of Webb. Instead of asking questions that would permit an evaluation of Webb's mental competency, the psychiatrist tried to encourage Webb to plead and get released. Webb had to be mentally competent to make such decision. When Webb refused the advice offered by Levi, the psychiatrist wrote in his report that Webb was mentally incompetent. (Based upon what I had seen over a period of years, and as stated to me by some of my psychologist friends, many psychologists are those in the greatest need of psychiatric therapy.)

As all this was going on, I sent a copy of the first edition of *Defrauding America*, along with a statement describing my evaluation of Webb's mental competency, to U.S. District Judge Richard Matsch, on July 12, 1993. At the court hearing on July 22, 1993, the judge held Webb mentally competent, which he obviously was, and ordered him released. Webb spent almost a year in prison, without a trial, solely on the claim by one of the key players in the awesome HUD and savings and loan scandal, that he had received harassing and threatening phone calls from his former son-in-law.

DELUSIONAL LABELS PLACED ON WHISTLEBLOWERS

A similar scenario was occurring with another informant that Webb and I discovered, Basil Abbott, a former DEA pilot. Abbott had been a former DEA pilot flying arms to Central America and hauling drugs back into the United States. He knew too much, and it was necessary to silence him by causing his imprisonment. He was incarcerated for several years and then after he was released he started exposing DEA involvement in drugs. To silence him, DEA agents arrested him, claiming he was violating his probation by failing to prove to them that he wasn't.

While waiting trial, during which he was denied his freedom, Justice Department attorneys charged him with being mentally incompetent, based upon his charges that the DEA was smuggling drugs into the United States. In other words, any citizen who describes misconduct by federal officials that are not known by the most naive in the population is a candidate for mental incompetency charges by Justice Department attorneys, and in many cases, indefinite-term imprisonment and to be forcibly injected with mind-altering drugs.

U.S. District Judge R. Thompson in Montgomery, Alabama, ordered Abbott sent to the Federal Prison Hospital at Springfield, Missouri, for a psychiatric examination. Two prison psychologists rendered a report holding that Abbott was delusional and paranoid because he reported the DEA drug trafficking in which he was ordered to perform for several years. In December 1993 Abbott was still in prison, waiting to receive a trial on his parole revocation.

Returning to the Montgomery jail waiting for a judicial hearing on his mental competency, another psychologist, Guy Renfro, was ordered to evaluate Abbott. Renfro then contacted me for my opinion, during which I spent twenty minutes describing to Renfro my months of phone conversations with Abbott, and the many letters that I had received from him, which indicated to me that he was above-average in intelligence and had good control of himself. I said that he was very naturally concerned about the assassination of his wife when she tried to help him expose the DEA drug trafficking, and the pending forced injections of drugs at the Federal Prison Hospital if the scheme to hold him mentally incompetent succeeds. I followed this conversation with a FAX to Renfro, along with flyers on my last two books, which included highly favorable comments from book reviewers.

Renfro issued a report that Abbott was delusional and paranoid, based upon Abbott's statements of specific drug activities that he had observed. Renfro recommended that Abbott be forcibly subjected to drug therapy for his alleged mental problems. Shortly before that evaluation, Abbott had given testimony in another case at the request of attorney Susan James, who considered Abbott very competent. Renfro was apparently lying, carrying out the scheme that would result in continued business from the court and the Justice Department.

While this scenario was occurring, an investigator with whom Webb and I communicated on a frequent basis, Paul Wilcher, lay dead in his apartment in Washington, D.C.

RECIPIENT OF CONTINUED PERSECUTION

As these events continued to unfold, the Justice Department and federal judges continued to misuse their positions of trust to silence me. U.S. District Judge Vaughn Walker continued my virtual house arrest which was now almost three years in duration. As I was waiting a Kangaroo-Court trial, without a jury, conducted by the same Justice Department prosecutors and federal judges who were implicated in the criminal acts I sought to expose, I was barred from leaving the limited area of Northern California. The charges were fabricated on the basis that I filed a federal action in Chicago in mid-1990, seeking to report the federal crimes I had uncovered up to that date. I simultaneously exercised federal remedies to obtain relief from the onslaught of civil, constitutional and criminal violations judicially inflicted upon me in a obvious conspiracy. These charges against me were ironical–and criminal–in many ways.[429]

---

[429] Obstruction of justice; retaliation against a whistleblower; misprision of felonies; aiding and abetting; becoming a principle; conspiracy; among others.

CHAPTER TWENTY SIX

FEDERAL GOVERNMENT
AS A CRIMINAL ENTERPRISE

Many people in control or in key positions in the three branches of the federal government were either directly involved in the activities described within these pages, or were involved in the coverup. Their dereliction of duty, their aiding and abetting, caused, and made possible, great harm inflicted upon the American people.

As I stated in my 1978, my 1980, my 1990 editions of *Unfriendly Skies*, and more so in *Defrauding America*, at the epicenter of the corruption described within these pages are the attorneys and officials in the U.S. Department of Justice. Without their pattern of hard-core criminal acts[430] none of these criminal activities could have been perpetrated and continued.

ORGANIZED CRIME IN THE U.S. JUSTICE DEPT.

The heading in the Forum section of the *Sacramento Bee*[431] read, "Organized Crime in the U.S. Justice Dept," and accurately reflects the decades of criminality in the most misnamed agency of the federal government. The article stated in part: *"Indications ... point to a widespread conspiracy implicating government officials in the theft of Inslaw's technology."* Inslaw, bad as it was, constitutes only the tip of the iceberg.

For twenty-five years Justice Department attorneys blocked every attempt that I made to report the pattern of hard-core corruption by federal officials. Without their criminal coverup and obstruction of justice the rampant corruption described within these pages could not have occurred. With thousands of investigators in the Department of Justice, the crimes described

---

[430] Obstruction of justice, criminal coverup, persecution of whistleblowers, informants and protesting victims.

[431] October 27, 1991.

in these pages could not have escaped detection.

If my reports of the pattern of criminality had received the reaction in the three branches of the federal government and from the media that a properly functioning government requires, there could not have been the epidemic corruption that now exists in government. Even now, the criminal activity continues, and increases in frequency and severity, as the public concerns itself with such trivia as ball games, a whale trapped in the Arctic ice fields, or an endangered species of cockroach being threatened by much-needed development of natural resources.

Thousands of people have been financially destroyed and their lives made miserable by the coordinated theft of their assets in Chapter 11. Many deaths in fraud-related airline crashes would not have occurred if Justice Department attorneys had not engaged in the coverup. Decades of financial deprivation and financial problems for individuals and the United States itself will result from the savings and loan debacle, made possible by the same coverup.

RESPONSIBILITIES OF JUSTICE DEPARTMENT

Under federal law, the responsibility for ensuring that the laws of the United States are properly enforced falls to the United States Department of Justice, which is under the control of the U.S. Attorney General. He or she is appointed by the President of the United States. In practice, the Attorney General routinely misuses the Justice Department to protect the criminal acts of those who appointed him or her.

History has shown that the office of U.S. Attorney General will routinely obstruct justice, engage in felony persecution of informants, and become involved in criminal acts. Obviously, the structure of government is sadly defective, and has made possible some of the most obscene and damaging harm ever inflicted upon the United States.

RESPONSIBLE FOR PROTECTING THE
CIVIL RIGHTS OF AMERICAN CITIZENS

Within the U.S. Department of Justice are numerous divisions. These include the Federal Bureau of Investigation holding the responsibilities to investigate the crimes that I sought to report with the help of my group of concerned people. There is the U.S. Trustee, who is responsible for preventing the rampant fraud in Chapter 11 courts, and who is part of the Chapter 11 racketeering activities. There is the Drug Enforcement Administration (DEA), responsible for preventing drug violations, and who uses pilots to smuggle drugs into the United States. And there is, would you believe, the division responsible for protecting civil rights. This is the Justice Department that has persecuted me continuously, since mid-1987, retaliating against me for reporting the federal crimes that I uncovered; who retaliated against me for exercising lawful and constitutional protections to halt the barrage of civil and constitutional (and criminal) violations inflicted upon me. Every one of these divisions have been routinely used to commit the federal crimes that they are entrusted to prevent.

SUCCESSION OF CORRUPT ATTORNEY GENERALS

A succession of attorney generals have been implicated in corrupt acts and federal crimes, but have escaped prosecution because they held the highest law enforcement position in the United States. Attorney General John Mitchell, for instance, went to prison for his activities. Subsequent attorney generals have committed federal offenses far more serious crimes, and were never prosecuted or called to task by the checks and balances in government.

Attorney General Edwin Meese, a former California attorney and Alameda County District Attorney, was prominently associated with an escalation of the sleazy and corrupt activities in government. He was implicated in the 1980 October Surprise scheme that helped bring the Reagan-Bush team into power. As a reward, or to protect the Reagan-Bush team from prosecution in that scandal, the Reagan-Bush Administration appointed Meese U.S. Attorney General. Meese was then used to protect Reagan and Bush from the October Surprise scandal and others that followed.

In addition to the October Surprise criminality, Justice Department officials misused this powerful agency to steal the software from the Inslaw people, showing their corrupt mindset. This was followed by protecting the rampant drug trafficking into the United States by the CIA and DEA. In every area of major criminality implicating federal personnel, Justice Department attorneys and officials have engaged in obstruction of justice and other crimes of coverup.

When the stench from Meese's activities forced him to resign, he was replaced by Richard Thornburgh, who continued the criminal activities of Inslaw, the obstruction of justice activities, and the persecution of whistle-blowers and informants. Thornburgh left the Attorney General position in 1991 to run for the Senate seat vacant by the death of Senator John Heinz in a plane crash in Philadelphia. A Pennsylvania newspaper identified Thornburgh as the "Harrisburg Mafia."

President George Bush, who had a long-time relationship with the CIA, then appointed[432] William P. Barr, as U.S. Attorney General. Barr was General Counsel of the CIA while Bush was Director of the Agency. From the very beginning, Barr blocked investigations into the major scandals that were surfacing almost daily, including those that directly involved the Justice Department and the CIA.

Barr blocked an investigation of the part played by Justice Department officials in the Inslaw affair, denying the request by the House Judiciary Committee for an Independent Prosecutor.[433] Barr refused to appoint a special prosecutor to investigate the White House's funding of Iraq's military build-up. Barr refused to appoint an independent prosecutor to investigate the White House's role in the Bank of Lavoro scandal. He refused to appoint an Independent Prosecutor to investigate Inslaw. The House and Senate Judiciary committees had requested the attorney generals to request appointment of an independent prosecutor in each of these matters.

Making matters worse, a large percentage of federal judges are former Justice Department attorneys, whose mindset is to protect the Justice Department mentality. As shown in other pages, many federal judges secretly

---

[432] October 27, 1991.
[433] Sometimes called independent counsel.

receive money to carry out CIA and Justice Department wishes.

PROSECUTING FEDERAL JUDGES
WHO DON'T COOPERATE

Justice Department attorneys, misusing the power of the U.S. government, have tremendous ability to destroy persons who threaten to expose their dirty games. U.S. Attorney Joseph Russoniello at San Francisco, charged U.S. District Judge Aguilar in June 1989 with misusing his judicial position in a racketeering enterprise (RICO) and obstructing justice. What did Aguilar do? He allegedly made false statement to an FBI agent who talked to the judge on the beach at Waikiki during a Hawaiian vacation; he suggested to an attorney the use of a defense in the trial of Aguilar's brother-in-law; and he told his brother-in-law not to phone the judge because the brother-in-law's phone may be tapped.

The real reason for prosecuting Aguilar for these relatively minor offenses, compared to the monumental offenses committed by other federal judges and Justice Department officials, was that Aguilar often disagreed with the Justice Department prosecutors in judicial proceedings. Aguilar halted the deportation of refugees that Justice Department attorneys wanted deported. He also engaged in a heated argument with U.S. Attorney Russoniello in open court, threatening Russoniello with contempt of court.

Unlike the Justice Department and judicial corruption described throughout these pages, no one was harmed by Aguilar's acts and he made no money or profited in any way. Compare the alleged offenses charged against Judge Aguilar with the pattern of obstruction of justice and felony persecution of informants by Justice Department personnel; or the FBI's pattern of lying to grand juries and trial juries.

Another judge charged with a crime by Justice Department officials was former U.S. District Judge Claiborne in the Las Vegas District Court (1986), who was noted for rendering decisions contrary to those wanted by the Justice Department. Claiborne's accountant had failed to list the profit made on one of several real estate transactions on his income tax report. Justice Department prosecutors then charged Claiborne with income tax evasion.

The mere investigation by the FBI arm of the Justice Department can cause a member of the U.S. Senate and House to lose an election. The Justice Department can easily fabricate charges, especially conspiracy or misprision of felony offenses, by stretching facts clearly out of proportion to reality. Possibly the fear of what the Justice Department can do was one of the reasons every member of the U.S. Senate from 1991 to 1993 refused to respond to my multi-page petition to investigate the corruption I brought to their attention. But this was no excuse for them aiding and abetting the criminal activities. They had a duty to perform. When they accepted their position, they assumed the responsibilities that went with the pay, the perks, and the prestige.

PATTERN OF CRIMINAL ACTIVITIES BY
JUSTICE DEPARTMENT ATTORNEYS AND OFFICIALS

For thirty years I have been intimately connected with the criminal acts committed by Justice Department officials and their various divisions. Their misconduct in the 1960s, which I initially discovered while a federal investigator, had devastating consequences in the aviation areas that I brought to their attention. Since then, as these pages reveal, the criminality in the U.S. Department of Justice has increased many times over, very possibly making it the key cog in the pattern of racketeering activities against the American people.

If Justice Department personnel did, in fact, do any of the acts described within these pages, these same personnel would *have* to misuse the power of the federal government and of the Justice Department to block the reporting of these crimes.

These Justice Department attorneys have made it standard practice to misuse Justice Department facilities to falsely charge dozens of informants and whistleblowers with federal offenses to block their reporting of crimes implicating federal officials.

The list is much longer than those mentioned within these pages. They include CIA operative Gunther Russbacher; Trenton Parker, another high-ranking deep-cover CIA operative; Michael Riconosciuto, a CIA contract agent; Ronald Rewald, contract agent; Bobbi Riconosciuto; Richard Brenneke, CIA contract agent; Heinrich Rupp, CIA contract agent; Basil Abbott, DEA pilot hired under the Confidential Informant category; Russell Bowen, OSS and CIA; Stewart Webb, concerned citizen and private investigator.

Compare the prison sentences given to concerned citizens who speak out, or to silence informants, with the hard-core criminal offenses committed by federal officials whose crimes are far more serious because of the positions of trust that they occupy.

PLACING A YOUNG LADY IN PRISON

A federal judge sentenced a young lady to federal prison (1989) for failure to remember details of stock transactions that occurred several years earlier while she was a stock broker for Drexel Burnham Lambert. Lisa Jones, a 24-year-old dropout and runaway who became financially successful at the Wall Street investment firm of Drexel, was one of the first witnesses called by Justice Department attorneys investigating insider trading and other security violations at Drexel. She refused to fabricate testimony requested by Justice Department attorneys, who then retaliated when she could not remember details of the stock transactions. Justice Department attorneys charged her with perjury, and would you believe, Justice Department prosecutors charged *her* with obstruction of justice. Lisa Jones was victimized in the battle between Drexel and Justice Department attorneys, and sentenced to eighteen months in federal prison.

The young woman suffered the indignities accompanying federal imprisonment, including frequent transportation with leg irons, handcuffs, and body cavity searches. Lisa Jones joined the many thousands of citizens who became victims of Justice Department and judicial corruption, and understandably, developed psychological problems.

After all this, Drexel's attorneys sued the young lady for payment of legal fees that Drexel had agreed to pay. In response to Drexel's claim that they would sue Ms. Jones for the amount of money that they had advanced, San

Francisco attorney Daniel Bookin stated: "It is inconceivable to me that Drexel would sue Lisa after all that she's gone through, and in view of her serious psychological problems. All issues of compassion and decency aside, however, one simple fact seems certain: Lisa has virtually no assets; she could not even begin to repay the cost of her legal representation."

SENDING SENIOR CITIZENS TO PRISON

Justice Department prosecutors charged Leona Helmsley with evading income taxes, and sentenced the 72-year-old woman to four years in federal prison, leaving behind her 81-year-old husband, who could be expected to be dead before she would be released.

Helmsley's accountants had claimed as business expenses, charges that Justice Department attorneys considered personal items. Helmsly's income tax forms were made out by professional tax preparers, who determined that the deductions were business related. The accountants who made that determination were never charged with any wrongdoing. Helmsley paid over $4 million federal income taxes in the disputed tax year and the amount owed by the disputed charges was a very small percentage of that amount.

Seeking to show that the Judge who sentenced Helmsley to prison did himself commit a serious federal crime, I mailed to the federal judge on April 25, 1992, a list of the criminal activities that my CIA informants and I were trying to report, and demanded that he receive our testimony and evidence. I reminded him of the mandatory requirements that we give our evidence to a federal court and that the court receives it.[434] He refused to receive our evidence, making possible the continuation of the epidemic corruption that we discovered.

While aiding and abetting, and covering up for the serious crimes described within these pages, and sending informants to prison, Justice Department prosecutors found time on December 15, 1992, to indict[435] Bobby Fisher for playing a chess game in Yugoslavia, charging him with violating the presidential order barring business relations with communist countries.

TEN YEARS FOR A TELEPHONE CONVERSATION

On December 7, 1990, Judge Samuel Conti sentenced a young black girl from Oakland, California, the mother of two infants, to ten years in prison, on a conspiracy charge. The young girl had a telephone conversation with another person concerning the sale of drugs. The conversation never went any further, but federal agents, monitoring the phone call, charged the girl with conspiracy. She was in tears when U.S. Marshals drove her back from the federal court house in San Francisco to the Dublin Federal Detention Center after Judge Samuel Conti sentenced her to ten years in a high security prison. This same judge played a major role in blocking my exposures of the criminal activities and in protecting the many people that were implicated in the attacks

---

[434] Title 18 U.S.C. § 4.

[435] Fisher violated a June, 1992 executive order by President George Bush restricting commercial relations with Yugoslavia. The indictment subjected Fisher to ten years in prison and a fine of as much as $250,000. Is it any wonder the United States has the highest percentage of its citizens in prison?

upon me. He, as with many other federal judges named in these pages, should be impeached and sentenced to a long prison term. But this will never happen, because crooked federal judges and Justice Department attorneys have a strangle-hold on the justice system.

PRISON FOR REFUSING TO COMMIT PERJURY

Justice Department prosecutors charged a Sacramento area real estate developer, Marcel Cordi, with a federal offense for refusing to testify falsely against a bank official whom Justice Department prosecutors wanted to convict. U.S. Attorney David Levi of Sacramento wanted Marcel to testify against a bank official and alter the facts in his testimony. Marcel was willing to testify, but would not commit perjury to enable Justice Department prosecutors to falsely convict the person. In retaliation for refusing to commit perjury, U.S. Attorney Levi charged Marcel with fraud, based upon an incorrect statement on a prior loan application relating to his length of employment.

Levi was the U.S. Attorney who charged me with criminal contempt of court when I filed federal actions reporting the criminal activities implicating federal officials, including his Justice Department employer. In retaliation for reporting the crimes, and for exercising federal defenses, Levi charged me with criminal contempt of court. Levi was appointed in 1992 to a federal judgeship in Sacramento. It is standard practice to appoint Justice Department officials to the federal bench. This plan insures that Justice Department prosecutors are successful in federal court.

Another example of how the public is victimized by the mindset in the Justice Department: A woman in Texas with five children drove her boyfriend's van into Mexico and was arrested at the border when she was returning home, having no idea cocaine had been hidden in her van. The jury, assuming that Justice Department officials would not prosecute an innocent woman, rendered a decision holding her guilty, causing her to receive a 10-year mandatory minimum sentence. She knew nothing about having been used as a "mule."

Making these outrages even worse is the fact that their sufferings are shared by thousands of others who become forgotten victims of corruption by Justice Department attorneys.

Cases have been cited[436] where major criminals are not charged by Justice Department prosecutors on the basis of information that they gave relating to other drug operations, often enabling Justice Department prosecutors to obtain many other convictions of lesser figures. There are hundreds of peripheral drug players in prison, facing long mandatory prison terms, while those guilty of far more serious drug offenses are free, primarily because they were able to snitch on others.

Long prison terms for drug offenses become even more preposterous when it is realized that the CIA and DEA have engaged in large-scale drug trafficking operations into the United States for decades.

---

[436] Including a December 26, 1990 article by Harry Hellerstein, Assistant Federal Public Defender in San Francisco, in the *Wall Street Journal*.

MISPRISION OF FELONY

A frequent charge for sentencing innocent people to prison is charging them with the federal crime, misprision of felony. Anyone who knows of a federal crime and who does not promptly report it to a federal judge or other federal tribunal is guilty of this crime. This statute has no exclusions, and applies to members of Congress, White House officials, Justice Department personnel, the media, all of whom have committed this crime. In practice, punishment for this crime is limited to citizens, and not to those in government who hold a far greater responsibility to act on the crimes described within these pages.

An example of the misuse of this criminal statute occurred when a Memphis aircraft broker sold a used aircraft to a customer, who later used it in drug-related operations. The aircraft broker had no way of knowing how the plane was to be used, nor is he required to become an investigator. Later, when federal authorities were building a case against the suspects, they requested that the aircraft broker fabricate testimony in order to assist in obtaining convictions.

The broker was willing to testify, but refused to lie. Justice Department attorneys then retaliated against him, charging him with misprision of a felony on the basis that he failed to report to federal authorities that the aircraft was to be used in unlawful activities. The aircraft broker was subsequently put on trial with 32 other defendants, who apparently *were* guilty of drug-related offenses. Without competent legal counsel to protect his interests, the unsophisticated jury accepted the prosecutors' charges as true, and held that he was part of the drug trafficking operation. He was then sentenced to five years in federal prison, even though he never committed a single offense.

SUICIDE INDUCED BY
CORRUPT FEDERAL CORRUPTION

Another example of the harms inflicted upon innocent people was related to me by the aircraft broker in the preceding example. The broker was in a county jail near Memphis waiting for trial when he witnessed the fatal consequences of arrogance by federal agents. His cell mate, Mike Scarlett from Texas, had been enticed by federal agents into making the controlled substance "speed."[437] Knowing that Scarlett was having serious financial problems supporting his family, federal agents encouraged him to produce the drug, teaching him how to produce it, financing the operation, and setting him up with the equipment and a location. On the first day Scarlett started to make it, these same federal agents arrested him, charging him with manufacturing amphetamines.

While in prison, Scarlett discovered that his wife was sleeping with one of the federal agents who had set him up. Al told me that his cell-mate, Scarlett, was very distraught-looking after phoning his wife. Al described to me how the inmate wrote what was later discovered to be a suicide note, and

---

[437] Speed had been prescribed for years by doctors for weight reduction, by decreasing a person's appetite. It is now a controlled substance for which prison terms are prescribed for its unlicensed manufacture or sale.

that Scarlett hung a bed sheet over the prison bars, as if he wanted privacy for sleeping, as is often done. Behind the sheet Scarlett stepped onto the rim of the toilet and tied a strip, torn from a bed sheet, to a grill near the ceiling. Scarlett then stepped off of the toilet, and hung himself.

PRISON FOR FILLING IN A
MOSQUITO-BREEDING MUD HOLE

Justice Department prosecutors sent Ellen Kafkaesque to prison for filling in a mosquito-breeding low spot on his 103-acre ranch.[438] He allowed two loads of dirt to be dumped in a low spot as a base for a shed. federal officials then charged him with filling in "wetlands," which has been made a crime by Congressional legislation. Justice Department prosecutors sought to have him imprisoned for 27 to 33 months. When the judge reduced the sentenced to six months in prison, Justice Department prosecutors appealed, seeking to have Kafkaesque imprisoned for almost three years, for filling in a low spot on his 103 acres! Simultaneously, Justice Department prosecutors were protecting CIA assets involved in drug traffickers, looting of financial institutions, were themselves involved in the Inslaw scandal, and looting of Chapter 11 assets, among other crimes.

OUTRAGEOUS PRISON SENTENCES

America reportedly has the greatest percentage of its population in prison of any country in the world. Outrageous prison sentences are imposed for often minor offenses, such as filling in swamps on one's own property, or being found with small quantities of drugs. Minor drug offenders are sentenced to twenty or more years in prison for a one-time offense, while vicious killers are often released in a fraction of the time. Often the drug offender is a person simply filling the demand created by a drug-crazed society that may share a greater blame than the person responding to the demand. A person charged with a hand-full of drugs receives a far longer prison sentences than a person who brutally kills another.

THREATENING AN AGED PARENT
OR WIFE TO GAIN A CONFESSION

A favorite stunt of Justice Department prosecutors is to charge the wife or an aged parent with a crime. They had no part in the offense charged, and an offense may not have even been committed. In this way the brave attorneys in the Justice Department coerce defendants to plead guilty (who may be innocent), or to plead guilty to charges greater than what were committed. Justice Department prosecutors threatened to charge Russbacher's wife with a crime if he did not plead guilty to misusing government fuel and aircraft when he had the CIA Learjet fly him to Seattle and then to Reno in 1989. Numerous inmates described to me how they were forced to plead guilty to something they hadn't done, or to plead guilty to a greater offense than they were guilty of, after Justice Department prosecutors threatened to imprison their parents or wives.

[438] *Wall Street Journal*, November 18, 1992.

BLACKMAILING MEMBERS OF CONGRESS

It is well known that FBI Director J. Edgar Hoover was skilled at obtaining incriminating and embarrassing information on political figures, and had a file on almost every member of Congress. In *From the Secret Files Of J. Edgar Hoover*, by Athan Theoharis, the author describes Hoover's interest and ability in gathering scandalous information about prominent political figures. The book describes FBI reports on John F. Kennedy's affair with Inga Arvad, Robert Kennedy's affair with Marilyn Monroe, Eleanor Roosevelt's affair with Joseph Lash, homosexual activities, and other activities. The CIA does the same thing to exert control over members of Congress. The CIA reportedly threatened Senator Boren in 1981 with exposure of his alleged pedophile activities after Boren initially stated he would not vote for Robert Gates as CIA Director. The book shows that Hoover's activities did not die with him, but continue to this date. Other intelligence agencies have similar activities. The U.S. Army has a surveillance and blackmail program called Operation Orwell, which is described in earlier pages.

BUYING AND SELLING HUMAN LIVES

Judges, prosecutors and attorneys sometimes buy and sell cases and human lives, as if they were commodities. Judges are paid off to rule favorably on particular cases. A clerk can lose a key file or piece of evidence. The court reporter can change the transcript to indicate the reverse of what is actually in the record.

Attorneys often sabotage their own clients, allowing them to be convicted, to satisfy a debt to his adversary's legal counsel, or to placate a judge who may want the other party to prevail. Trading of human life, in court, or in the air safety environment, is like kids trading marbles. Prosecutors will let a defendant go free, in exchange for the life of another man. Criminal attorneys will plead a man guilty just to pay back a prosecutor for not prosecuting another client. Prosecutors will lie to imprison an innocent person, or to cause his incarceration for years longer than the law provides for the offense that was actually committed. Cases are fixed by paying judges, prosecutors, police, and others.

Some Justice Department attorneys justify their lying, using the argument that the defendant lies, so why shouldn't they lie. But a defendant may lie to avoid prison. Prosecutors lie to imprison innocent persons, or to greatly increase the length of sentence for the purpose of making their record look good, regardless of the human tragedy it brings.

The public doesn't perceive this misconduct as a threat to themselves. When the Justice Department prosecutes a party for an alleged crime, the average person, including unsophisticated members of the grand jury, assumes that the party is guilty. Otherwise the accused would not be charged, or so they think. I fell into that trap in the past, until I learned that Justice Department attorneys lie and cheat as a standard tactic. Unfortunately for the victims of this prosecutorial misconduct, as a *Wall Street Journal* article once stated, the grand jury would indict a ham sandwich if the prosecutor told them to do so.

Justice Department attorneys win year-end bonuses and personal-recognition awards for putting people in prison, guilty or not.

DISMISSING INVESTIGATORS WHO
EXPOSE HIGH LEVEL CORRUPTION

A common method for covering up evidence of the ongoing criminal activities described in these pages is to dismiss investigators who report evidence of the crimes. For instance, when the investigative activities of the U.S. Attorney in Philadelphia threatened too many politicians involved in political corruption, President Carter reportedly pressured the Justice Department to remove U.S. Attorney Martson from office.

Speaking before the Washington National Press Club on January 25, 1978, Martson stated:

If a single Congressman can remove his home-town prosecutor who's actively investigating public officials, with a single call to the President—if that can happen, and that's what did happen—our federal criminal-justice system won't work. No amount of rhetoric will ever convince the bagmen and the fixers that they can't pull strings in Washington, because they're sure that strings got pulled in Washington.

The Justice Department—controlled by the United States Attorney General, who is appointed by the President of the United States—investigated President Carter and his political friend, Attorney General Griffin Bell, for possible obstruction of justice. Is it any wonder the Justice Department cleared their boss of any wrongdoing?

The same tactics were used by Justice Department officials against Assistant U.S. Trustee Gregg Eichler in the San Francisco area when his investigations exposed the part played by federal judges and Justice Department officials in the corrupt Chapter 11 courts. I had given Eichler information on the criminal activities I experienced in Chapter 11, implicating federal judges, federal trustees, and law firms. Eichler was dismissed from government service in late 1991 after he had exposed the corruption by CIA-related trustee Charles Duck, and as Eichler was going after the judges.

Justice Department officials fired one of their investigators in retaliation for testifying in the Inslaw affair. Justice Department officials arranged for the removal of Chapter 11 Judge George Bason from the District of Columbia bench after he ruled in favor of Inslaw, and then arranged for the Justice Department's attorney defending against the Inslaw charges to replace Judge Bason. By packing the courts in this manner, corrupt Justice Department officials gain control over the judicial process, wherein they protect themselves.

Investigator Lloyd Monroe quit the Justice Department after he discovered connections between the savings and loan scandal and the CIA-related Southmark Corporation in Dallas.

Justice Department officials reprimanded assistant U.S. Attorney Dave Howard in the San Francisco office after he filed a highly sensitive eleven-page report on July 11, 1990, describing the judicial corruption in Chapter 11. Howard recommended the appointment of a special counsel to investigate the corruption by federal judges and trustees in Ninth Circuit Chapter 11 courts. Instead of acting on the report, Justice Department officials censored Howard for preparing the report.

Jack Blum, on Senator Terry Sanford's committee, was forced to resign when he pursued the investigation of BCCI corruption when the committee wanted to drop it. After Sanford's committee blocked the investigation into BCCI, Blum went to Manhattan's District Attorney Robert Morgenthau with his evidence, resulting in criminal prosecution against powerful attorneys who sold their country down the river for financial wealth. Justice Department officials repeatedly blocked the exposure of the BCCI corruption, just as they blocked the exposure of every other scandal described in these pages.

The FBI has its own way of dealing with whistleblowers. The former head of the Los Angeles FBI office, Ted Gunderson, stated[439] that he had been harassed by the FBI to suppress his reports of drugs smuggled into the United States in the bodies of dead GI's sent back from the Vietnam War. Gunderson retired from the FBI in 1979, becoming a private investigator, during which time he obtained evidence of widespread drug dealings at Fort Bragg, North Carolina. Numerous CIA assets have given me data confirming this sordid practice. Gunderson told the United Press reporters that the FBI and Justice Department had tapped his business phone and smeared his name.

DEATHS OF THOSE EXPOSING
JUSTICE DEPARTMENT CORRUPTION

Mysterious deaths of people exposing Justice Department and CIA corruption have been repeatedly reported throughout these pages. One of the main murders, closely associated with the Justice Department's criminality in the Inslaw matter, was the widely publicized death of Danny Casolaro. The September 10, 1992, Congressional Inslaw report addressed this link, reporting that there was a need for a further investigation into Casolaro's death and the link to the Justice Department officials.

INTERNATIONAL ARROGANCE

The mindset rampant in the Justice Department has no bounds. Justice Department attorneys have sanctioned and ordered the seizure in foreign countries of foreign citizens, who had never been in the United States, for the Justice Department to have jurisdiction over them. In one instance involving a resident of Mexico, Dr. Humberto Machain, Justice Department personnel paid bounty hunters $50,000 to kidnap him, and bring him into the United States to stand trial. He had allegedly assisted in torturing a U.S. DEA agent in Mexico. Civilized international law procedures require that extradition be requested of Mexican officials.

Applying this tactic to other nations, there is far more "justification" for other nations to kidnap American citizens, based upon the crimes inflicted in their country by the CIA and other U.S. dirty-trick squads. Using this reasoning, hundreds of federal officials, especially those in the CIA, could be seized for the crimes that they caused to be inflicted, as they invaded the

---

[439] United Press, February 22, 1986.

sovereignty of foreign countries.

Iranians could justifiably sneak into the United States and abduct American citizens to stand trial in Iran for having committed crimes under Iranian laws, including interference in Iranian governmental activities, or the shooting down of an Iranian airliner by a trigger-happy U.S. Navy crew that had invaded Iranian waters.

The Vietnamese government could sneak into the United States and abduct American officials for their part in causing the deaths of tens of thousands of Vietnamese in the Phoenix program.

The U.S. invades Panama, killing hundreds of Panamanian citizens, to capture the head of a foreign country, who has never committed a crime in the United States, for having trafficked in drugs in Panama. Making the seizure of Manuel Noriega more bizarre, he was formerly on the payroll of the same CIA, engaging in drug trafficking in partnership with the Central Intelligence Agency's sanctioned operations.

SUPREME COURT APPROVAL OF UNLAWFUL SEIZURE

A federal judge in Los Angeles threw out the indictment against the Mexican physician, Dr. Humberto Machain. Entered into the court records were the declarations of a Mexican informant that another doctor, Fidel Kosonoy, was responsible for administering the drugs that kept an American DEA agent, Enrique Camarena, alive so that the agent could be tortured for obtaining additional information. Kosonoy was the personal physician of Rafael Caro Quintero, a Mexican drug trafficker. Justice Department prosecutors withheld this declaration that contradicted their charges against the Mexican doctor.

The Justices of the U.S. Supreme Court upheld the right of Justice Department officials to invade a foreign country and seize their citizens in this manner. This is the same group that upheld the right of Justice Department prosecutors to imprison me in retaliation for reporting federal crimes and in retaliation for exercising constitutional and statutory remedies. There was an exception: Justice John Paul Stevens called the decision "monstrous," which it was. The United States has given federal bounty hunters carte blanche to violate a widely held principle of international law, implying that foreign countries can do the same to U.S. citizens.

Chief Justice William Rehnquist upheld this shocking violation of international law on the basis that "the treaty says nothing about the obligations" of the two countries "to refrain from forcible abductions." Using this rationale, U.S. bounty hunters can kill foreign citizens in foreign countries if the extradition treaty says nothing about that issue.

The Supreme Court Justices held that it was legal for American bounty-hunters to invade the sovereignty of a foreign country, use force if necessary, including killing foreign citizens and police of such foreign country, and kidnap them, bringing them to the United States, before our biased and corrupt system, with Justice Department-appointed "defense" attorneys, to be held for trial. These are the same Justices who have obstructed justice when I repeatedly brought the corruption described within these pages to their attention via petitions, appeals, and letters.

Foreign nations and their media strongly criticized the United States Supreme Court for this position. Chile's most important newspaper, *El Mercurio*, reacted to the Supreme Court's ruling with the heading, "Caramba! they've legalized terrorism." The June 23, 1992, editorial summarized the arrogance:

The decision promotes contempt for the rule of law and the right of due process, violates national sovereignty and opens the door to acts of reprisal among nations. And what happens if U.S. agents—or people cooperating with the U.S.—clash with police in Mexico, Colombia or some other country, with gunfire that may even injure or kill innocent bystanders?

Chilean Socialist leader Marcelo Schilling said of the Supreme Court rule that it was "the law of the jungle in which the weaker countries will lose out." Guatemalan President Jorge Serrano called the Supreme Court's ruling an "unacceptable judicial monstrosity."

When asked what he thought of the kidnapping doctrine, legal adviser to the State Department, Judge Abraham Sofaer, testified before Congress in 1985:

How would we feel if some foreign nation ... came over here and seized some terrorist suspect in New York City, or Boston, or Philadelphia ... because we refused through the normal channels of international, legal communications to extradite that individual?

In 1989 the Assistant Attorney General in charge of the Office of Legal Counsel, William P. Barr, held that the FBI could legally seize suspects in foreign countries, even though they had never been in the United States and had never committed any offense in the United States.

The heading in the Mexico City newspaper *El Financiero* read: "Bush and the Culture of Terrorism." The article described the "new world disorder in which the United States ... can kidnap, torture and assassinate citizens from other nations."

On November 11, 1990, the United Nations Convention Against Illicit Traffic in Narcotic Drugs came into force, and passed a resolution stating in clear text that a treaty party "shall not undertake in the territory of another Party the exercise of jurisdiction and performance of functions which are exclusively reserved for the authorities of that other Party by its domestic laws."

It was the invasion of Mexico under orders of Justice Department officials that required this restatement of international law. The resolution was introduced by Canada and Mexico and approved by the United Nations group. The United States ratified that convention agreement in 1990, and then promptly violated it by seizing a Mexican citizen in Mexico in 1992.

In response to the U.S. kidnapping of a Mexican citizen and the U.S. Supreme Court upholding that act, the Mexican senate approved an amendment to the Mexican criminal code imposing a 40-year sentence on anyone who kidnaps Mexicans on behalf of the United States or any other foreign authority who may wish to duplicate America's invasion of a foreign country's sovereignty to kidnap foreign citizens. So intense was Mexican anger toward the United States that the bill was approved unanimously, and then approved by President Carlos Salinas de Gortari. This new law was Mexico's response to the U.S. Supreme Court ruling in June 1992 that approved the 1990 kidnapping of the Mexican doctor from Mexico.

WEAVER FAMILY AGAINST THE
"BRAVE MEN" OF ATF AND JUSTICE

At an isolated mountain-top home in Idaho, five hundred heavily armed ATF and FBI agents, U.S. marshalls, local law enforcement agencies, military vehicles and tanks, surrounded a small home owned by Randy Weaver, a former Green Beret. Weaver was on the Justice Department's hit list for refusing to cooperate in an undercover operation against a group of local skinheads. Weaver had been asked to infiltrate the group, and after attending a few meetings, Weaver didn't want anything more to do with the plan.

The chance came for ATF and FBI personnel to retaliate against Weaver when he sold a shotgun in which the barrel was allegedly a quarter inch shorter than the law allowed. Justice Department prosecutors charged Weaver with a federal offense and ordered him to appear in federal court at Boise, Idaho. When Weaver failed to appear, due to an error in the reporting date made by the court clerk, six U.S. Marshals in camouflaged clothing sneaked onto Weaver's mountain-top property. Weaver's dog spotted the intruders and started barking, after which a family friend, Kevin Harris, and 14-year-old Samuel Weaver went to investigate.

As the dog approached the intruders they shot and killed the animal. The young boy cried out, "You've killed my dog," and then ran back toward the house, at which time one of the U.S. Marshals shot him in the back, killing him. Harris, who had gone with the young boy to investigate, witnessed the killings and shot back at the strangers, killing one of the marshals. Back at the house, Randy Weaver, who heard the shooting and seeing his son lying on the ground, and not knowing the trespassers were federal agents (and surely not caring at this stage), shot at the intruders.

The remaining U.S. marshals then retreated, returning with a force of over 500 heavily armed, battle-ready, FBI and other federal personnel, bravely massed to do battle against the father, the mother, a daughter, and a friend.[440] Included in this armada against the family under siege were tanks and other weapons of war.

During this siege, the father crept to a storage building adjacent to the house to view the body of his slain son. Huddled in their cabin, frightened by the massive force surrounding their humble home, the mother opened the door and stood in the doorway, holding her infant daughter in her arms. A federal agent shot her with a large caliber rifle, splitting her head apart. Blood spurting from her head, Weaver pulled his wife inside and laid her down on the kitchen floor, as blood drained from the lifeless body. Frightened, Weaver and his children lay on the blood-splattered floor, expecting to die at any

---

[440] *Spotlight*, September 25, 1992.

moment. Outraged neighbors and people from all over the country converged on the site, protesting the slaughter.

Several members from a concerned citizens group in Hawaii arrived, as did people from throughout the state, including Lt Col. James "Bo" Gritz, a candidate for the 1992 presidential election. Their presence may have saved the remaining hostages from annihilation. Gritz arranged for the wounded Weaver to surrender to the federal marshals.

Justice Department prosecutors obtained an indictment against the remaining Weaver family from a rubber-stamp federal grand jury in Boise (September 16, 1992), charging the victims with federal crimes. The indictment against the father, whose son and wife had been killed by federal marshalls, read in part:

Vicki Weaver and other members of the family did unlawfully, willfully, deliberately ... shoot, kill and murder one William F. Degan.

That indictment, as worded, included the infant whose mother had been killed.

A jury eventually cleared Weaver of the murder charge, but held him guilty of the gun charge.

KILLING A NEARLY BLIND RANCHER

Another example of the vicious mindset of ATF and Justice Department agents was the shooting death of a wealthy and nearly blind rancher, Donald Scott, near Malibu, California (October 2, 1992). Federal personnel had tried to buy the ranch to expand the adjacent Santa Monica Mountains National Recreation Area. But Scott, a recluse, partially blinded by recent cataract surgery, didn't want to sell.

A multi-agency drug task force of over two dozen heavily armed California and federal agents[441] mounted a military-type assault upon Scott's home. They were allegedly looking for a field of marijuana they claimed that a federal agent spotted from a plane flying a thousand feet over the 200-acre property in the hills above Malibu, called Trail's End.

Instead of going to the ranch in a peaceful manner with a search warrant, they conducted a commando-type raid, breaking into Scott's home while he was sleeping, killing him as he came out of his bedroom. No marijuana plants or drugs were found on his property.

There was no reason for this commando-type raid, as there was no need for the element of surprise. If Scott had actually been growing fields of marijuana, he could not suddenly dispose of it down the toilet, and the peaceful serving of a search warrant was all that was necessary.

---

[441] The invaders were from the Los Angeles County sheriff's department, the Los Angeles Police Department, the U.S. Drug Enforcement Administration, the National Park Service and the California National Guard.

Investigation showed that the real motive was not a search for drugs, but a desire to seize Scott's ranch under federal forfeiture laws. Scott's wife had been a former user of drugs and if the slightest traces of drugs could have been found on the property, the five million dollar ranch could be seized under the draconian federal forfeiture laws.

Subsequent investigation revealed that federal agents had obtained a property appraisal before invading Scott's home, showing the value of adjoining property, and indicating the desire to seize the property. Federal personnel in charge of the raid advised the attacking agents to look for evidence of drugs so as to justify seizing the property.

ENLARGEMENT ON THE WEAVER TRAGEDY

The Weaver tragedy received very little press coverage, even though it indicated a very dangerous mindset by ATF and Justice Department officials. By ignoring it, as in every other form of corruption implicating federal officials, the pattern continued and worsened. On Sunday morning, February 28, 1993, about one hundred heavily armed Alcohol, Tobacco and Firearms agents (ATF) invaded the residence of a religious group in Waco, Texas, attacking the building with loud shouts as if they were attacking a drug cartel. There were about a hundred people inside the residence, primarily women and children.

The religious group resided in a large building on property known as Mount Carmel, by a religious group known as Branch Davidians. They were a relatively peaceful group, harming no one, wanting to be left alone. As is common in Texas, and to earn extra money, the group frequented gun sales, and had accumulated a large cache of various types of weapons. They also knew about the Weaver tragedy and others, and didn't want the same to happen to them. They were more aware of the government arrogance than most Americans.

Upon hearing the shouting hoard of heavily armed para-military group descending upon them, the religious group locked the doors and braced for an attack. ATF agents broke windows and shot into the residence, killing eight people inside, including a two-year-old girl. As agents started entering the building, the people started defending their home by fighting back, killing four of the assaulting ATF agents. Firing stopped, and the para-military force retreated, followed by a nearly-two-month standoff.

The residents placed bales of hay against the gaping holes in the walls and where the windows were knocked out. Federal agents ordered electricity cut off to the compound, forcing the residents to use kerosene lanterns for illumination, creating a high fire risk. government agents blasted the occupants twenty-four hours a day with loud noises, and shook the building with the movement of huge military tanks. Several of the besieged residents gave up and left the building, at which time they were immediately arrested and charged with conspiracy and murder of the four ATF agents who had invaded their residence.

The ATF agents were joined by FBI agents and National Guard troops, equipped with heavy attack vehicles and tanks, surely the envy of many third-world military leaders. They were brave men, ready to do battle with the frightened religious group consisting mostly of women and children.

If the besieged residents had any hope that public pressure would bring a halt to the siege, they were sadly mistaken. The government's Wurlitzer-like manipulation of the media sought to make the besieged victims the culprits.

The large building in which the occupants were trapped was an old wooden building and highly inflammable. A fire starting inside the structure could be expected to spread rapidly, especially if the winds were blowing hard, as they often do on the Texas prairie. Once fire started inside, escape would be very difficult. In the MGM Hotel fire in Las Vegas many years earlier, the fire in the football-field-size main casino spread so rapidly that people on the far side of the casino from where the fire started were engulfed in flames before they could make their escape.

APOCALYPTIC ASSAULT

Early in the morning on April 19, 1993, while the lanterns burned inside the building, the war-ready heavily-armed military force commenced an attack, using armored vehicles and tanks, knocking down walls that fell inward upon the residents. Inside the building, sections of sheetrock and wood rained upon the frightened occupants, knocking burning lamps onto the piles of hay, causing them to ignite. As if this weren't enough, over 200 tear gas canisters were thrown into the building.

The leader of the religious group rushed through the building handing out gas masks, and instructing the people to put them on immediately. The wind was blowing at over thirty miles an hour, roaring through the holes ripped in the building by the tanks, fanning the flames started by the overturned lanterns. Inside, the residents were trapped and scared, and unable to escape. The blackness of the early morning hours, the heavy smoke, the eye irritation caused by the tear gas, and the piles of debris in the hallways, made escape impossible for most of the residents. Eight managed to flee the searing heat, some of them with their clothes on fire.

Once the fires took hold, they spread in firestorm fashion, insuring the fiery death of everyone inside. Many of the frightened women and children huddled in fear, feeling the effects of the searing heat. Suddenly, as the flames reached the butane fuel escaping from a ruptured tank, an explosion sent flames hundreds of feet into the air, an event seen throughout the world on television screens. Possibly never in the history of the civilized world had such an arrogant attack upon a group of religious people occurred, the horrible consequences watched throughout the world.

OILING UP THE MISINFORMATION MACHINERY

The Waco tragedy had the potential for waking up the American public to the mindset of their leaders. This possibility required oiling up the nationwide misinformation network controlled by various federal agencies. It appeared to work. While the residence was still burning, President Bill Clinton appeared on TV, stating the residents committed suicide and they were to blame for the horrible outcome. Clinton stated government agents and officials weren't responsible because "a group of fanatics tried to kill themselves." U.S. Attorney General Janet Reno echoed his words. Clinton and Reno had other reasons for blaming the victims. The two of them had approved the attack upon the residents before the attack started.

The same federal agents who inflicted this terrible tragedy upon the religious group stated they saw the residents starting the fire, basing that statement upon seeing someone bending over. It is very possible that the person bending over was trying to put out the many fires started when the lanterns were knocked over.

Federal officials stated many of the bodies had bullet holes in them, implying they were shot by the leader of the religious group to prevent them from escaping the flames. Texas coroner Dr. Nizam Peerwani, heading the Tarrant County Coroner's office in Fort Worth, stated: "There is absolutely no evidence of that, as far as we are concerned at this stage." Interviewed on *Good Morning America* on April 23, 1993, the coroner stated that because of the condition of the bodies it would be difficult to determine bullet wounds and that the immense fire left very little of the bodies to examine. He added, "When a corpse is exposed to such intensive heat, the head will often explode."

The bullet theory was important, to shift blame to the victims. Later reports stated that there were bullet holes in many of the bodies. Anything stated by government personnel must be considered suspect in light of the long history of disinformation and outright lies.

The establishment media, which had kept the news of the Weaver tragedy from the American people, couldn't hide the Waco tragedy as they did the Idaho assault. But they did repeat as fact, over and over again, that the group had committed suicide; that the blame for the holocaust was upon them and not upon the attacking military force.

Nine members of the religious group escaped the inferno and were immediately arrested and kept separate from each other. When questioned separately by their attorneys, each of them described what happened inside the building and stated the same facts. The survivors described the chaos in the building as the tanks inflicted heavy damage. They described the knocking over of the kerosene lamps by the tanks and the resulting fires, the difficulty of moving about the building because of debris from the collapse of the second-story walls and due to the heavy smoke and tear gas. The smoke caused total darkness inside the building. "You couldn't see your hand in front of your face," stated attorney Dick Kettler, speaking for one of the religious group members, Remos Avraam.

Attorney Dick DeGuerin stated that his client told him "there was pandemonium, they knew they were trapped. It was difficult to move around even before the fire started because the tank battering had damaged the inside of the compound."

After hearing the facts stated by the survivors, Clinton repeated during an April 23, 1993 press conference what he had stated several days earlier, that the victims were responsible for their deaths. "I do not think the United States government is responsible for the fact that a bunch of fanatics decided to kill themselves." Clinton used the disinformation given by Justice Department agents to support his statements, even though they were contradicted by the independent statements of the survivors, and common sense.

START OF ANOTHER CONGRESSIONAL COVERUP

Appearing on the *Larry King Live* television show within a few days of the holocaust, Senator Dennis DeConcini stated he would head a Senate investigative committee investigating the Waco affair. DeConcini repeated the statements of the Justice Department and President Clinton placing the blame for the deaths on Koresh. This dogmatic statement indicated his pre-judgment of the matter and his determination to protect government personnel who caused the deaths to occur. His statement blaming one of the victims came after there was overwhelming evidence showing Justice Department agents to be lying.

THE "INVESTIGATORS"

Never at a loss to find people willing to assist Justice Department mischief, a team of "investigators" came upon the scene several days later and defended the onslaught, stating the occupants themselves decided to set the building and themselves on fire. The wife of the team's leader, Paul Gray, worked for the same people who started it all, the Bureau of Alcohol, Tobacco and Firearms. Gray taught at the ATF's academy, and had been selected by the ATF to conduct the "investigation." Gray stated that "this fire was intentionally set by persons inside the compound."

SUBSEQUENT REPORT

In response to pressure from groups of concerned citizens, Treasury Secretary Lloyd Bentsen called for an independent review to determine what really happened. In September 1993 the Treasury Department released its report, defending the use of the para-military force on the residence occupied mostly by women and children. The report admitted that there was a pattern of deception by senior officials in the aftermath of the bungled operation. Simultaneously, Department of Justice officials released a report clearing Attorney General Janet Reno and other federal officials (who had given approval to the attack), blaming the tragedy on field personnel.

GUN OWNERS BEWARE

Millions of gun owners who legally purchased guns that were legal at the time of purchase can end up in prison and financially destroyed, solely at the whim of a bureaucrat from the ATF and Justice Department. One gun owner, W.J. Chip Stewart, from Springdale, Arkansas, was charged with a federal offense by the ATF, the same people responsible for the Weaver family and Branch Davidian massacres (and others). ATF and Justice Department attorneys caused him to be sentenced to federal prison for twenty-seven months. As a result of his imprisonment, Stewart lost his business, his wife who didn't wish to be inconvenience, his credit worthiness, and his money.

What did bureaucrats in ATF and Justice Department consider to be a crime? Stewart had legally purchased two semi-automatic handguns, that were legal to own at that time: a small 22 caliber and a 45 caliber semi-automatic pistol from Holmes Firearms Company, similar to those owned by millions of people in the United States.

ATF bureaucrats decided, after many of these guns were sold, that the widely-sold semi-automatic guns could be converted by a gunsmith to become an automatic weapon, and were therefore illegal.

Shortly after ATF agents notified Stewart that the guns that he had legally purchased were now unlawful, he turned the guns over to the ATF. They had gotten his name from the gun manufacturers registration records. Eight months after ATF notified Stewart that his two pistols were put onto the banned list, and after Stewart voluntarily turned the guns over to them, Justice Department prosecutors obtained a grand jury indictment against him. Stewart, who owned an auto wrecking business and a relatively permanent member of the community, could have been served peacefully with the warrant for his arrest. Instead, sixteen heavily armed ATF and FBI agents and local sheriff's department personnel converged upon his home, breaking down the door. Fortunately for Stewart, he wasn't home. Otherwise, he could have met the deadly fate of Scott, the Weavers, the Branch Davidians, or the many others who were killed by the brave men of ATF and FBI.

With this type of mindset almost anyone can be financially destroyed and put in prison, either because of violating some obscure statute, or by being falsely charged.

WIDESPREAD INVOLVEMENT OF FEDERAL JUDGES

The direct and indirect involvement of federal judges in almost every one of the criminal enterprises shown in these pages has already been described. In Chapter 11 courts they were directly involved in the theft of billions of dollars a year. In other pages the mechanism for paying off certain federal judges is described. My impression is that they are as sleazy a group as the attorney group they represent.

Federal judges[442] were repeatedly put on notice through my federal court filings of the criminal activities described within these pages that a group of CIA insiders were ready to testify. They blocked the reporting of federal crimes, which made **them** guilty of federal crimes. I repeatedly appealed and petitioned the Justices of the U.S. Supreme Court to intervene, as they had a duty to do.

SUPREME COURT'S COMPLICITY

None of these criminal enterprises could have continued without the criminal coverup by each of the Justices of the U.S. Supreme Court. In the 1970s I brought the corruption to the attention of the Supreme Court justices as it related to the air safety and criminal violations associated with a series of air disasters and the felony coverup by Justice Department attorneys and federal judges. In the 1980s I brought to their attention the pattern of hard-core civil right violations that were part of the California scheme to silence me and the destruction of federal remedies by a gang of federal judges.

As a matter of law, under Supreme Court procedures as specifically provided by Rules of Court of the Supreme Court, a person has the right to petition an individual Justice for relief. Also, under federal crime-reporting statutes, the law clearly provides that a citizen must report federal crimes to

---

[442] Including, for instance, Ninth Circuit Judges, including Marilyn Patel, Samuel Conti, Milton Schwartz, Edward Garcia, Raul Ramirez, and each of the Justices of the Ninth Circuit Court of Appeals; District of Columbia judges and justices, including Stanley Sporkin, Green, Silberman; Second Circuit judges and Justices at New York City; Fifth Circuit judges at Chicago.

any federal judge. Implied in the law, a federal judge must receive the evidence. Every time that I exercised these rights and responsibilities the Supreme Court Justices blocked me.

Only once did a Justice of the Supreme Court make any type of response, and this was highly unusual. In response to my petition addressed to Justice Byron White, which he refused to grant, he stated in an October 28, 1991, letter:

> As a single Justice I can be of no help to you. I am returning your petition.

White and the other Supreme Court Justices aided and abetted the persecution of whistleblowers and informants who threatened to expose the criminal activities in which they were involved. The charges of organized crimes involving major U.S. agencies that I brought to their attention left no discretion for any federal official to deny me a hearing, especially when the crimes included judges over whom the Justices of the Supreme Court had supervisory responsibilities.

SUPREME COURT'S SOILED RECORD

President Lyndon Johnson relied upon voter fraud to get into the U.S. Senate, as related in the 1964 publication of *A Texan Looks At Johnson* and *Means of Ascent* by Robert Caro, published by Knopf. When Johnson discovered that Texas Governor Coke Stevenson had received 112 votes more then he did, Johnson arranged for a "recanvass," of the records. Lo and behold, an additional 202 suspicious votes appeared, nicely arranged in alphanumerical order, in a district he controlled. When the matter was taken to the federal district court, the court issued an injunction barring Johnson from claiming victory, and setting a hearing to address the voter fraud.

To circumvent the unfavorable evidence being presented in the U.S. District Court in Texas, Johnson's attorney, Abe Fortas (who was later appointed to the U.S. Supreme Court), filed a petition with Justice Hugo Black of the U.S. Supreme Court to block the federal district court in Texas from taking any action. Black ruled in Johnson's favor, without allowing the evidence of voter fraud to be presented. Johnson later rewarded Fortas as he appointed Fortas to the U.S. Supreme Court. But as the saying goes that "a leopard doesn't change its spots," Fortas's conduct on the Supreme Court was sufficiently outrageous that he was later forced to resign rather than face impeachment.

An editorial in the *San Francisco Chronicle*[443] titled, "The pernicious Court," stated the "judiciary is riding roughshod over rights and precedent as it enacts its legislative agenda into law." The editorial stated that "the Supreme Court rode roughshod over traditional constitutional rights, ignoring settled precedents and overturning others that got in its way." If no constitutional outrage was examined other than what federal judges have done to me in retaliation for exercising federal crime reporting requirements and exercising federal defenses, it would be *prima facie* evidence of a criminal mindset in the

---

[443] June 30, 1991.

federal judiciary.

UNCONSTITUTIONAL SEIZURE LAWS,
APPROVED BY SUPREME COURT JUSTICES

The Supreme Court Justices in June 1989 upheld the right of state and federal agents to confiscate the assets of a person possessing drugs, or who committed a crime, even though charges may not have been filed (and maybe never would be), and there had never been a trial. This seizure of assets usually deprived the person of funds needed to hire legal counsel to defend against the charges. The Court's fuzzy argument is that the Sixth Amendment right to appointment of legal counsel will insure proper legal representation. The Supreme Court Justices knew that court-appointed attorneys are usually a farce.

Even if the party is never accused, or he is found innocent, the person is usually unable to obtain his or her seized property. The *Pittsburgh Press* described the seizure laws as a "License to Loot?-Victims lose even if charges aren't filed." These and other articles depict how police in the United States can take a person's assets, including their homes and money to pay for legal defenses, even without being charged with a crime. The police need simply charge the person with an offense, which can easily be fabricated. Supreme Court Justices have rendered decisions making police officers and prosecutors usually immune from liability. It is a stacked deck against the people of the United States, and they don't even recognize it.

To get the property back, if it hasn't already been disposed of, the person has to sue the government, and this takes money for legal fees, which the person usually doesn't have.

Simply because small quantities of drugs were found, large ships, airplanes, and buildings have been seized and forfeited, without any regard to the financial relationship between the amount of drugs and the value of the seized property. The person who put the drugs on the seized property may not even be its owner, while the actual owner may be totally unaware and unable to control the presence of drugs.

Property seizure laws permit taking a person's assets on the mere suspicion that the person violated the law. Justice Department officials either violate the law themselves, or protect those government officials who do.[444] In December 1993, after much public outrage, five of the nine supreme court justices held that there must first be a hearing before property may be seized. Reno's Justice Department replied, "We will continue to use the forfeiture laws vigorously." With the heavy concentration of former Justice Department attorneys on the federal bench, forfeiture will probably continue as before, as targeted citizens must prove a negative, that they did not violate any laws.

SELF-IMMUNITY AGAINST JUDICIALLY-INFLICTED
CIVIL RIGHTS AND CRIMINAL VIOLATIONS

The arrogance of federal judges and justices is reflected by a U.S.

---

[444] Made more preposterous by the CIA and other government agencies involvement in smuggling drugs into the United States in the interest of funding covert CIA activities (many of which terminate in wholesale deaths of Americans such as in the Vietnam conflict), which makes a mockery of the so-called drug wars.

Supreme Court decision in which the Justices of the Supreme Court held that a citizen cannot sue a judge for harms inflicted by the judge, regardless of whether the judge acted in error, maliciously, or in excess of authority. In one instance the Supreme Court Justices ruled that a judge who ordered a young woman sterilized was immune from damages. The US Supreme Court Justices have held in such cases as *Stump v. Sparkman*[445] that the American public has no protection against the renegade judges, over whom the Supreme Court Justices have supervisory responsibilities, who inflict great harms upon a particular targeted person.

This isn't what civil rights statutes read; it is self-made law by judges that violate the statutes and constitutional protections. These self-protective case law decisions conflict with the public's right to seek damages from *anyone* who knowingly inflicts harms through known and deliberate violations of protected rights.

The greatest threat to our constitutional protections is with the present group of judges and Justice Departments attorneys, who are openly destroying the protections under our form of government. The media and every major check and balance have kept the lid on these outrageous acts, as they have done with every major scandal described within these pages. The implications of this are enormous. The loss of civil rights are all around us, but the majority of Americans, kept ignorant of these matters by the mass media, haven't the faintest idea what is actually going on and being done to them.

In 1993 the California Supreme Court held that a citizen could be arrested and held in jail for several days solely on the basis that he or she was not carrying identification. A swimmer walking to the beach could end up in jail, in chains, enduring body-cavity searches, and risking rape, solely because he or she did not have identification suitable to the stopping officer.

THE CRIMES OF CONGRESS

The public has a short memory. Scandal after scandal by members of Congress has surfaced, and rarely has a member of Congress been criminally prosecuted. Simultaneously, thousands of American citizens are charged and put in prison for committing some minor offense, or imprisoned on thumped-up charges. Even in the Savings and Loan scandal, the nation's worst financial debacle that will adversely affect Americans for decades, not a single member of Congress, including those who openly solicited money to block regulators' actions, has been sent to prison.

Members of Congress limited their investigation of the Keating-Five to "ethics" violations, which is comparable to limiting the charges against the Murder Incorporated assassins to ethics violations. Even here, Congress couldn't hold that those who aided and abetted the greatest financial debacle had violated any ethics.

People in the CIA, for instance, have reported to members of Congress for years about the CIA and DEA drug trafficking, during closed-door hearings, by letters, and by petitions as I have sent. In every instance these

---

[445] *Stump v. Sparkman*, 435 US 349 (1978).

members of Congress have kept the lid on the scandals, and are co-conspirators.

CREATING A CRIMINAL MINDSET THAT ESTABLISHES GOVERNMENT AND NON-GOVERNMENT RESPECT FOR LAW AND HUMAN RIGHTS

The conduct by Justice Department attorneys and officials, by federal judges, by the CIA, sets a pattern of lawlessness for the country to follow. The people in the ghettos know about this criminality, while the average middle-class American is uninformed. We cannot halt or reverse the escalating lawlessness in the population while the lawlessness exists. And the system in place is so corrupt that it cannot and will not correct itself.

CHAPTER TWENTY SEVEN

LEGAL FRATERNITY

The common denominator in the entire sordid mess was the legal and judicial fraternities. I wrote of this in the first two printings of *Unfriendly Skies—an Aviation Watergate* in 1978 and 1980, and greatly enlarged upon that in the 1990 *Unfriendly Skies*. This revised *Defrauding America* expands upon the sordid and criminal nature of this legal fraternity group.

It was the legal fraternity within the FAA and NTSB that covered up for the air safety and criminal acts which other federal inspectors and I found at United Airlines and within the FAA. Justice Department attorneys enlarged upon these coverups and obstruction of justice. For the past thirty years Justice Department attorneys have blocked every attempt to report the crimes revealed in these pages.

REPORT A CRIME, GO TO JAIL

After failing to block the exposure of these criminal activities in this manner, Justice Department attorneys then proceeded to destroy me financially through the covert Justice Department and CIA law firm of Friedman, Sloan and Ross. And when that failed to stop me, they proceeded to repeatedly charge me with contempt of court, from 1987 to the present date, in retaliation for reporting the criminal activities against the United States.

Sabotage of my exposure activities in the air safety field commenced with attorneys in the Federal Aviation Administration and the National Transportation Safety Board, especially during the Denver air safety grievance hearing. This was compounded by the Denver attorney whom I hired to assist me in that hearing, J.E. Kuttler. Kuttler either sabotaged my exposure efforts from the very start, or was grossly incompetent.

I sought legal representation to help expose the FAA corruption while residing in Oklahoma City. Several expressed shock at what I told them, and they stated they would get back to me, and then never did. I presume they talked to another attorney in the Justice Department and that ended their interest. I asked Oklahoma City attorney Clyde Watts for help to expose the corruption. He was a former attorney with the Department of Justice in Washington, and stated he would question some of his Justice Department friends when he went to Washington. Watts was defending General Walker, whom the federal government was trying to silence, and who was placed in a federal prison hospital on the argument that he had mental problems. When Watts returned to Oklahoma City, he wouldn't talk to me. When I went to his office to pick up my papers, his associate greeted me, looked at me sadly, and wished me luck. Other attorneys advised that they would check the matter and get back to me. They all then avoided me.

Los Angeles attorney Ned Good contacted me and stated he would use my testimony against United Airlines in a lawsuit against United Airlines concerning a Boeing 727 crash into the Pacific Ocean at Los Angeles (January 18, 1969). The sequence of events suggests that Good simply threatened to use my testimony if United did not agree to a financial settlement dictated by the attorney.

This same problem happened when attorneys contacted me to obtain information on the crew partying and NTSB coverup associated with the PSA San Diego crash (that was the world's worst air disaster at that time). They advised me that they would publicize my evidence, when in reality they simply used it to extract more money from PSA and its insurance carrier.

Some of the largest law firms in Salt Lake City, and the Utah State Bar, sought to block the introduction of my evidence into the trials relating to the United Airlines crash at Salt Lake City. The same occurred in the New York City and Denver crashes when I sought to introduce evidence that I acquired while I was a federal air safety investigator on that very same program at United Airlines.

LACK OF INTEGRITY AT AIR-CRASH TRIALS

The level of integrity at court trials is of the level expected from the legal fraternity. Employing attorneys demand that their expert witnesses slant their testimony in favor of their client, making the expert witnesses nothing more than brokers of disinformation.

AMERICAN CIVIL LIBERTIES UNION

The American Civil Liberties Union, the self-professed protector of civil rights, played a key role in the pattern of hard-core civil right violations judicially inflicted upon me. I repeatedly notified the ACLU of the civil right violations inflicted upon me, why it was being done, and the damage to the judicial system and our constitutional protections. The first contact was in 1965 and continued through 1989. They not only refused to provide help, but they upheld and aided and abetted the escalating civil right violations.

In 1989, the Executive Director of the Nevada ACLU, Shelly Chase, and I appeared on Reno radio station KOA, during which she upheld the right of Justice Department attorneys and federal judges to imprison citizens who report crimes committed by federal officials. She upheld the right of California judges to void divorce judgments rendered years and decades earlier, even though these acts were gross civil and constitutional violations. The Friedman law firm that played a key role in the ten-year-pattern of civil right violations was a key member of the ACLU in the San Francisco area.

The ACLU gets large financial donations from the public on the argument that they protect civil and constitutional rights. While some of their stated motives and actions are meritorious, there are many who question whether their goals enhance the quality of life. The ACLU often protects the most vicious and seamy side of society, often working to inflict harm upon others by protecting the guilty. Despite the fact that people were dying from aircraft hijackings, they opposed using metal detectors to screen passengers for weapons.[446] The ACLU opposed drug testing of transportation employees, even though studies showed that excessive alcohol consumption was a serious problem among railroad employees. They opposed roadblock stopping of cars in an attempt to reduce the high death rate and maiming resulting from excessive drinking. They argued repeatedly to allow brutal murderers to go scot free because of some minor procedural requirement dreamed up by the same U.S. Supreme Court justices described in these pages.

CONGRESSIONAL ATTORNEYS

Without the coverup by members of Congress, most of whom are attorneys, the present number of scandals could not have been possible, and would have been nipped in the bud in their infancy, instead of escalating into the epidemic corruption that now exists. Members of Congress proposed legislation in mid-1989 to authorize federal employees in various government agencies to shoot down private aircraft in the drug-interdiction program, and proposed immunity for those shooting down and killing the occupants of the aircraft. They proposed that aircraft should be shot down if they did not respond to signals from an intercepting Customs or other government agency aircraft. The Senate voted to authorize the Customs Service and other federal agencies in August 1989 to fire upon small planes that do not respond to interception. Entire families can be wiped out by gunfire in this manner.

CALIFORNIA SEGMENT OF LEGAL CORRUPTION

Corruption in the legal fraternity is rampant throughout the United States, but that segment based in California has probably inflicted more damage upon the United States than any other segment. Upon becoming President in 1981, Ronald Reagan brought into the White House many California attorneys, including Edwin Meese (former district attorney from Alameda County near San Francisco), Lowell Jensen, and others. They were all involved in scandal after scandal, using their control of the Justice Department to protect themselves from criminal prosecution.

It was the California legal fraternity who acted as a front in the sham action filed against me in the California courts. It was California judges, up to and including the Judges in the California Supreme Court, who aided and abetted the scheme through a ten-year pattern of outrageous civil and constitutional violations.

---

[446] Between 1968 and 1973, there was an average of over two dozen attempted airplane hijackings a year. But after airports commenced using metal detectors in 1973 to screen passengers for weapons, the hijacking attempts dropped dramatically. ACLU argued that the security devices violated the Fourth Amendment protections against "unreasonable search and seizure."

It was a large group of federal judges in the State of California that enlarged upon the earlier violations, aiding and abetting not only the corrupt judicial actions in the California courts, but blocking the reports of the criminal activities described within these pages. It was federal judges in the State of California and in the largest federal circuit, the Ninth Circuit, who have made it an imprisonable offense to report government crimes, or to exercise federal protections to defend against the civil, constitutional and criminal violations inflicted upon me.

The attorneys that I hired were equally abominable. I finally had to appear without attorney to get the law into the record that barred the actions taken against me. In the sham California action the attorneys refused to raise the defenses in mandatory statutory law and under federal law, arguing instead fifty-year-old case law that permitted judges to do what they please.

My first attorney, Walnut Creek practitioner Douglas Page, jeopardized my defenses by substituting a young attorney right out of law school to argue important matters of law at a critical hearing, contrary to our employment agreement. The substituted attorney knew nothing about the unusual issues arising in the bizarre action filed against me. I fired both attorneys.

I contacted over thirty attorneys during the next few years, seeking legal representation. I knew the law, but recognized that *pro per* defendants, appearing without legal counsel, usually end up on the losing side, due to judicial prejudice. (Refusing to recognize prior divorce judgments and the adjudicated personal and property rights, because the parties did not intend to live forever in the prior court's jurisdiction, was barred by the U.S. Supreme Court in the mid-1940s and barred by state and federal statutes. Most attorneys didn't have any knowledge of the law pertaining to the issues. Or, they were deliberately playing stupid to facilitate the scheme against me. Some attorneys admitted that I faced a judicial gridlock, and that their legal practice would suffer if they raised the legal defenses necessary to halt the sham action.

When I decided it was time to exercise federal remedies for the massive civil and constitutional violations running rampant in the California courts, I engaged Sacramento attorney James Reed, who taught civil and constitutional law in the local law school. He wasn't much on California law relating to the underlying action filed against me by the Friedman law firm, but he used the law I researched on the matter, and got it into his federal briefs. It was necessary to sue state judges to obtain declaratory and injunctive relief, something very few attorneys will do, fearing judicial retaliation.

The first federal lawsuit exercising federal remedies to address the civil right violations named Solano County Judges Dwight Ely and Michael McInnis as defendants, along with the Friedman law firm. It appeared that Reed was pressured to drop the judges as defendants, and over my objections amended the complaint eliminating them. He appeared to panic. This federal action was assigned to U.S. District Judge Raul Ramirez, who quickly dismissed the action, clearly violating many federal statutes and related case law. Reed then changed residence and became county counsel at Mammoth Lakes, causing me to look for another attorney specializing in civil and constitutional rights.

In 1985 I contacted attorney John Moulds who specialized in civil and constitutional law. Moulds, you may remember, was the part-time magistrate who in 1987 sentenced me to prison for filing three federal actions seeking declaratory and injunctive relief, and for reporting the federal corruption I had uncovered. These actions sought a judgment to declare the validity of the five divorce judgments and the personal and property rights established in them. This was a right to which I was entitled, and not up to the whim of any judge. I also sought injunctive relief from the unlawful orders rendered without jurisdiction in the sham California action. After Moulds looked over my papers, he admitted the gravity of the violations committed in the California action, but stated he couldn't represent me in federal court because of his part-time magistrate position. He had known that earlier, and never raised the objection, until he recognized the nature of the problem.

ANOTHER IMPOSTER

I wasn't doing very well in finding attorneys by referrals, or even on blind calls, so I tried a different approach. I advertised in the San Francisco newspapers for an attorney, receiving a telephone call from an attorney who represented himself as Sid Saperstein, with offices supposedly in San Francisco. I resided in Reno then, seeking to escape the worse of the California judicial tactics. Saperstein stated he would come to Reno the next day. I was unable to visit California because California judge William Jensen, Fairfield, rendered a bench warrant for my arrest. This warrant was issued when I had an attorney appear on my behalf during a hearing in Solano County Superior Court, which was necessitated by my appearance in U.S. District Court at Sacramento in a civil rights action, in which that same California judge was a defendant. Even though appearance by attorney was permitted by California law, and he knew I could not physically be in two places at the same time, Jensen issued a bench warrant for my arrest. The Solano County bench warrant for my arrest was still outstanding, and I wanted an attorney to get that removed.

Saperstein came to my Reno residence on January 23, 1987, claiming that he had connections in the courts and could get the bench warrant lifted. He asked for money and I wrote him a check, and asked him for his calling card. He pulled out a hand-written calling card, stating he had changed offices and that his printed cards had not yet arrived. Sounded strange, but possible.

Several days later, Saperstein called and said that he had succeeded in getting the bench warrant lifted. This sounded fishy, as it normally requires a noticed hearing to have the matter heard. I asked him if he had the judge's order in front of him that vacated the bench warrant, and he said that he did. I asked him the name of the judge who signed the order. "Judge Schwartz," he replied. There was no Judge Schwartz in the Solano County courts where the warrant originated, causing me to ask which court issued the order. "The Superior Court in San Francisco," he answered. The San Francisco courts had no authority over the order rendered by the Solano County courts. Saperstein had a scheme going that obviously smelled to high heaven.

I asked Saperstein to read off the exact wording on the order that he stated a few minutes earlier was right in front of him. He couldn't do this because there was no such order. He stated he would call me back shortly. That was the end of Saperstein. I never saw or heard from him again. I sent a certified letter to the address that he gave me as his office, and it came back with a post office notation that the address didn't exist.

What I suspect happened was that the Friedman law firm saw my advertisement for an attorney in the San Francisco legal paper, and got Saperstein–or whoever he was–to contact me for the purpose of giving me false assurance that it was safe to return to California. Then, upon returning to California, Friedman would insure that I was arrested.

I hired a Sacramento attorney, Joel Pegg, to have the bench warrant removed and to file appeal briefs that were due, seeking to vacate the orders rendered in the sham divorce action that had been rendered without jurisdiction and which violated blocks of California and federal law. His services were also needed as U.S. District Judge Milton Schwartz and U.S. Attorney David Levi, Sacramento, charged me with civil contempt of court for filing federal actions to have the validity of the five judgments declared under federal law and seeking relief from the civil right violations. Further, the actions reported the early stages of the federal corruption that I had uncovered up to that time.

Pegg has a prestigious looking office, and a charming picture of Rhonda Fleming, supposedly one of his clients, on his desk. He looked impressive, and said the right words, and I felt confident that I could trust him. I paid Pegg a $20,000 retainer, and from that point he started sabotaging me at every turn, which is a common practice.

It was urgent that the attorney file several appeal briefs with the California Court of Appeals that were coming due, but Pegg repeatedly put off preparing and filing the briefs. I was appealing decisions that would overturn the past three years of illegal and unconstitutional orders by the California judges, and which affected the ownership of ten million dollars of property. The California Court of Appeals had already given me a time extension, and the three judges, Donald King, Harry Low, and Zerne Haning, were anxious to find some excuse to dismiss the appeals.

Forty-eight hours before the filing deadline I forced Pegg to give me an answer about the briefs that he had not even started to prepare, and he answered that he had requested a time extension from the court and the court granted it. By this time my opinion of attorneys was about as low as it could possibly get, so I checked to determine if he was lying. I telephoned the Clerk of the Court of Appeals at San Francisco, asking if an extension of time was requested and if it was granted. The clerk advised me that there was no request for an extension and none was granted. Pegg had lied to me. I wrote Pegg a letter and asked him for an explanation, which he refused to give me.

I then had to quickly prepare and file my own appeal briefs. This didn't take too long as I had already prepared a draft for Pegg. Appeals by people appearing without attorneys are usually denied in California courts, which are openly hostile to those appearing without attorneys. The system protects itself.

The briefs were filed, but the three judges in Division Five, District One, refused to even consider the briefs. They fraudulently said that the decisions being appealed were not appealable orders, repeating the misstatement of facts and law that kept the sham California action going for the past six years. I then sought relief from the Justices of the California Supreme Court, but by this time the judicial corruption had progressed to such an advanced stage that it became necessary for every state and federal judge to protect the earlier judicial conduct.

Joel Pegg was to seek removal of the lis pendens placed upon my dozens of properties in the sham divorce action that halted my business operations, and caused loss of valuable properties. He repeatedly stated he would do so and then never did. His refusal to seek this basic relief forced me to seek relief in Chapter 11.

As stated in earlier pages, U.S. Attorney David Levi and Judge Schwartz converted the civil contempt into a criminal contempt, and I now faced prison for having exercised federal remedies to defend against what was being done in the California courts. Pegg represented me in the defense against the criminal contempt charge, but refused to raise the defenses that would expose the scheme by Justice Department prosecutors and the federal judges. Just before the trial commenced, Pegg notified Magistrate John Moulds that he wanted to withdraw from the case. By that time Pegg had my money, and the Chapter 11 seizure of my assets left me without funds to hire other legal counsel. It also showed Moulds that there would be no attorney to file appeal briefs and other post-conviction defenses.

THE BANKRUPTCY SCENE

In 1987 I sought relief in Chapter 11, and obtained other legal counsel. I hired attorney Vernon Bradley of Sausalito, California, who was to represent me both in the California action and in the Chapter 11 proceedings. He then hired Las Vegas attorney Joshua Landish to handle the filing of the Chapter 11 papers in Las Vegas. Both Bradley and Landish agreed before I hired them that they would seek relief from the federal judge in Chapter 11 from the illegal orders of the California judges. But then when they became attorneys of record, they refused to file the necessary papers to obtain the relief.

I was present at the first hearing on the Chapter 11 cases, on September 11, 1987. The two attorneys made a passionate argument on my behalf, and although they failed to raise the civil and constitutional violations that forced me to seek Chapter 11 relief, they argued in my defense. They praised my management style that built up a multi-million dollar equity estate in twenty years. They argued that the sham California divorce action filed by the Friedman law firm caused me to seek relief in Chapter 11, and if federal law was applied requiring the California judges to recognize the five prior judgments, there would be no reason for my seeking relief in Chapter 11. This was the hearing where federal Judge Robert Jones rendered an order abstaining from hearing the cases, refusing to accept jurisdiction, and ordering that the two cases would be dismissed in 60 days. This was not the full relief I wanted, but it removed the lis pendens and permitted me to pay off the mortgage loans that had come due.

These attorneys then sabotaged my defenses. Attorney John Landish appeared at a hearing limited to the personal Chapter 11 filing and limited to removal of the automatic stay on several mortgages. That hearing took place on September 28, 1987, without my knowledge. The mortgage holder[447] sought to foreclose on the properties for which the mortgages had come due, and which would have been shortly paid off since Judge Jones ordered removal of the state lis pendens that had blocked the refinancing. Landish, whom I had hired specifically to protect my properties, then requested Judge Jones to vacate the earlier order providing me relief; to seize the business, home, and assets on both the personal and corporate Chapter 11 cases via appointment of a trustee; and then to liquidate the assets, leaving me penniless.

I would later learn that this is a common trick used by attorneys after they recommend to their clients that they seek Chapter 11 relief. The attorneys then strip their clients of all assets! In this manner the attorneys and trustees generate huge fees as they plunder the assets. Through their attorneys the Bank of America was famous for jumping the gun to seize the properties of their clients, ever since the 1930 depression days.

Landish kept notice of the seizure from me until after the ten-day period to appeal passed. I discharged Landish, but by that time he had done the damage. I did not learn what occurred at that hearing until several months later, after I obtained taped recordings of the court proceedings.

I hired other legal counsel, and the integrity problems continued. I hired attorney Raymond Goodman of Concord, California, to represent me in the bankruptcy proceedings, and he too agreed to file briefs to remove the illegally appointed trustee. He didn't tell me that the California state bar had suspended his right to practice law. Also, he didn't tell me that he would turn my Chapter 11 cases over to an associate attorney, William Rubendall, whom I had never seen, and who turned out to be a disaster. He failed to file opposition briefs, and refused to file the briefs to remove the illegally appointed trustee as was agreed before I paid the retainer. He refused to return phone calls. Contrary to my instructions, he notified Judge Jellen that my earlier appeals would be withdrawn. And much more.

I then retained attorney Robert Ayers of Walnut Creek, California, and paid him a retainer. After six weeks of failing to file the required briefs, he then stated he was not my attorney. But he kept the money I gave him. I even had trouble getting my files back.

SEIZING MY ASSETS AND THEN
STRIPPING ME OF LEGAL COUNSEL

After attorney Pegg abandoned me, I asked for a public defender to defend me against the false imprisonment. Judge Raul Ramirez appointed Assistant Federal Public Defender Carl Larson, who operated as a puppet for the Department of Justice gang.

---

[447] Robil, Inc., and Superior Home Loans.

Larson refused to perform any of the fundamental legal requirements needed to defend me. He refused to file a motion for stay of my imprisonment pending appeal, which is a right under law. Larson refused to file briefs raising the many fundamental constitutional and statutory defenses that were violated. Larson refused to acknowledge the grotesque violations of law and constitutional safeguards, and supported the actions taken against me.

Larson refused to obtain the hearing transcript or the records required to prepare a defense. He refused to file any briefs on my behalf, arguing that he would give a verbal presentation. That was totally unacceptable. Court rules and proper defense tactics require filing a written brief addressing the dozens of statutory and case laws and constitutional protections. A court hearing of this type is limited to a brief verbal argument, and is totally inadequate and not intended to present the dozens of case laws, constitutional protections, and other complex issues. Larson was protecting his employer, the Justice Department, and the federal judges.

I discharged Larson, and requested another attorney. At first this request was refused and I had to present briefs in pro se status. Finally, federal judges appointed another attorney, Sacramento sole practitioner Clifford Tedmon. He too duplicated the prior counsel misconduct and again I had no alternative but to discharge him. None of them would file motions for my release or raise any of the glaring violations of law. Federal judges appointed still another attorney, Brian DeAmicis, who repeated the tactics of the prior attorneys, refusing to argue the controlling law, and refusing to prepare adequate defenses. It was hopeless to obtain defenses under this pattern of legal misconduct. Finally, I discharged him, and filed my own briefs.

HOW WOULD THEY PROTECT AGAINST MALPRACTICE?

The conduct of these attorneys was hard-core misconduct, and I wondered how they would protect themselves from a malpractice action. I learned later that in judicial and Justice Department corruption of this magnitude the legal system bands together to protect itself.

I filed complaints with the California State Bar Association concerning Pegg and other attorneys, and they held the conduct to be proper. I filed a complaint with the Nevada State Bar and the Governor of Nevada concerning the misconduct of attorney Joshua Landish, who sabotaged me and caused the loss of my ten-million-dollar estate. They held that the attorney conduct was proper. When I filed malpractice actions in the State of California against the attorneys, the judges unlawfully dismissed the actions. I was totally gridlocked in every state and federal court, reflecting the cohesiveness of the legal fraternity.

Nevada Attorneys stated to me that I probably could never find a Nevada attorney to file a malpractice action against Landish, as the attorneys protect each other. I contacted at least half a dozen California malpractice attorneys concerning the misconduct by California attorneys, and none would take the case. Most had already heard about the judicial involvement and wanted no part of it. The legal fraternity had me gridlocked in the California and federal courts while simultaneously using the courts to destroy me financially and take away my freedom.

Eventually the California and federal judges settled on two quick responses to strip me of all defenses. They placed a frivolous label upon anything I filed, and then called me a vexatious litigant for seeking relief. In this way they stripped me of all statutory and constitutional protections and protection the legal and judicial fraternities from the consequences of their actions.

POWER OF THE LEGAL AND JUDICIAL BROTHERHOODS

In *With Justice For None*[448] the author and attorney, Gerry Spence, described the power of the legal and judicial fraternities, and that most judges are the lackeys of big-money interests. Mr. Spence spent much of his life representing insurance companies and government contractors, and later, protecting the rights of people adversely affected by injustice, such as the case of Karen Silkwood against Kerr-McGee. He also sympathized with me when I sought his help in 1988, but refused to help, even though the actions taken against me represented attacks upon fundamental constitutional rights, and revealed a corrupt judiciary.

In *A Feast For Lawyers*[449] the author describes the hacks, vultures and scoundrels in the legal fraternity, and the judges who feed on the public. He describes the mentality of "we against them," the "we" being the legal fraternity, and "them" being the public.

JUDGES FOR SALE

The practice of buying decisions is firmly embedded in the legal fraternity. A typical example was San Francisco Bay Area attorney Suren Toomajian who spent his vacations in Palm Springs and other places, accompanied by California judges whose expenses he paid. In return, the attorney received favorable decisions. One of his clients, a lady friend of mine, described the tactic of cancelling hearing dates until the court clerk assigned the case to a judge which the attorney controlled. Crooked attorneys leave envelopes containing money with particular judges, or the judge's law clerk, in payment for favorable rulings. Often, when the attorney appeared before a judge that he controlled, there would be virtually no arguments raised in support of the decision sought. The decision had been reached in private conversations before the hearing on the matter.

The legal fraternity has no interest in cleaning up the system that benefits attorneys and judges, even though the public is repeatedly victimized. The charade of standing up when the judge enters the court room, the rhetoric of justice, are deceptions to impress the public.

TIES BETWEEN RELATED LAW FIRMS AND
COVERT GOVERNMENT ACTIVITIES

I discovered that the San Francisco law firm of Friedman, Sloan and Ross, who filed the sham California action against me and whom the California and federal judges protected, was a covert Justice Department and CIA law firm, wielding immense control in the courts. The first indication I had of that

---

[448] *Times Books*, Gerry Spence.
[449] *Evans & Company*, by Sol Stein.

relationship was when an attorney in Las Vegas told me about it in early 1991.[450] The following year several of my CIA contacts described the clandestine CIA activities in which attorneys, law firms, trustees, and judges, are paid off.

CIA operative Gunther Russbacher described to me in sworn declarations the role played by law firms and attorneys in covert dealings with the Central Intelligence Agency and the Justice Department. He described how these attorneys do covert legal work for the two government agencies and how they play a key role in the Chapter 11 corruption. Russbacher described numerous covert CIA locations at which he saw members of this group, and how they received payoffs.

Russbacher described seeing Las Vegas federal Judge Robert Jones at Atlantic City gambling casinos and the method of paying off the judge (and others). Russbacher described the presence of Chapter 11 trustee Charles Duck at secret Central America CIA meetings and his related law firm of Goldberg, Stinnett and Macdonald. This entire cast of characters were key players in seizing and looting my assets in Chapter 11.

Russbacher described the role one of his companies, National Brokerage Company, played in the money trail to the overseas company that serves as the payoff center for federal judges, trustees and law firms, which is described in more detail elsewhere. Shamrock Overseas Disbursement Corporation in Dublin, Ireland, receives and disburses funds for these payoffs. The telephone listing is under Shamrock Overseas Courier Service. The same person who was a CIA asset in the CIA-associated Silverado Bank Savings and Loan is reportedly the Chief Executive Officer of Shamrock, Donald Lutz.

LEGAL FRATERNITY IN CHAPTER 11 CORRUPTION

The legal fraternity is deeply implicated in the massive Chapter 11 corruption that is inflicting billions of dollars of fraud upon American citizens every year. Attorneys often encourage their clients to file Chapter 11 to gain a little more time to pay a particular debt that has come due, fraudulently stating that the Chapter 11 court will provide the extra time. This is what the law says. But in practice, the fraud starts immediately. The federal judges order a trustee to seize the person's properties, business, and assets. The owner who built up the business and assets is ordered to vacate. The trustee then proceeds to liquidate the assets at fire-sale prices, incurring huge legal fees and losses that usually destroy the assets. It's all blatantly unlawful, but the entire judicial system, including the Justices of the U.S. Supreme Court, protects the multi-billion-dollar a year racketeering enterprise. It is all part of the vast secret government looting assets of the American people.

After placing their clients in Chapter 11, the attorneys then request the court to appoint a trustee to take over from the person whose competency built up the business. From that point on, fire sale liquidation takes place, and the client usually loses everything. It is a criminal enterprise and one of the best-kept secrets in the United States.

---

[450] January 22, 1991.

LEGAL FRATERNITY IN SAVINGS AND LOAN DEBACLE

The legal fraternity was heavily implicated in the savings and loan debacle. In 1992 numerous law firms were charged by various federal agencies with helping to carry out the looting of the savings and loans. The law firms associated with covert CIA activities, however, escaped the financial penalties. Despite their key role in the hundreds of billions of dollars in fraudulent transactions, I know of no law firm that was criminally prosecuted.

Blasting the role played by attorneys in the fraud involving Lincoln Savings and Loan Association, U.S. District Judge Stanley Sporkin of Washington, D.C., asked: "Where were these professionals? Why didn't any of them speak up?" Sporkin was involved in the 1980 October Surprise scheme, and his judicial appointment was probably his reward by the Reagan-Bush administration for helping to carry it out, and to block any judicial exposure or prosecution activities.

"Thievery by Lawyers Is on the Increase, With Duped Clients Losing Bigger Sums," headlined the *Wall Street Journal* article. (November 26, 1990.) Dozens of articles like this appeared in the legal publications throughout the United States, especially in California. The cases (where attorneys receive large sums of money from estate or litigation settlements and then steal the funds intended for their client) are endless. The *Daily Journal* legal newspaper wrote (January 9, 1992) about the sharp rise in larceny by attorneys against their own clients. Sporkin's role in treasonous and criminal activities makes him the last person to point a finger. But it was good public relations.

ATTORNEY "WATCHDOGS"

Complaining to State Bar Associations about incompetence or outright thievery by attorneys is usually useless. The practice of attorneys stealing money received for their clients is endless, and when this is reported, the bar association often times will refuse to suspend the attorney's license to practice.

LEGAL FRATERNITY IN PROBATE

Even in death, the legal and judicial fraternities continue their sordid conduct. Attorneys have turned the probate field into a system to loot the deceased's assets, depriving widows and orphans of money they would receive if the corruption did not exist. In many states the probate system is a means of plundering estates, dividing up the loot among attorneys, judges, and their fronts. Local party bosses often select probate judges who will continue the system of looting assets of the deceased.

An article in the *Journal of the American Bar Association* described the probate courts as "one of the most viciously corrupt systems ever devised by the inventive minds of the greedy." This is basically true, but the Chapter 11 courts are even worse, and more crooked.

The *New York Times* reported "the probate procedures in many areas border on the scandalous." A leading professional journal involved in probate reporting, *Trusts and Estates*, described the routine nature of probate work as being "cut and dried ... Most of the work is done by the lawyer's secretary ...

very little of the lawyer's own time is consumed." But the fees extracted from probate estates often consume most of the assets, and in some cases, the charges exceed the assets. Attorney fees are astronomical in relation to the time that the attorney spends on the case. In addition, probates that could be quickly settled are dragged out for months and years longer than necessary, to inflate the attorney's already padded charges.

Probate judges and attorneys work hand in hand, cooperating in the looting of assets, often forcing the surviving widow or children to go on welfare while the legal fraternity devours the money intended for the surviving family members.

There are cases where the heirs had to go on welfare, while a million dollars or more of assets were tied up in probate by crooked judges and their attorney cohorts. Even when wills have been made, some judges will find fault with them, declare that the person died intestate, and divide the assets as they see fit, increasing even further the attorney charges and kickbacks to the judge.

Attorney fees come from the assets before the heirs receive their inheritance, even when the attorneys appointed by the judges are unnecessary, and their appointment results in the heirs receiving nothing. What a system! There is virtually nothing a victimized heir can do as the system protects its own, regardless of how corrupt the attorneys and judges may be.

Connecticut attorneys conspired with their attorney friends in the legislature to pass a law taxing inter vivos trusts that were circumventing the probate racket. This law requires a person filing an inheritance tax return due on a probate-exempt trust to pay huge fees to the local probate judge, even though that person performed no services in connection with the trust. The legislatures on the state and federal level are controlled by attorneys, who block almost every effort by the public to protect themselves against these parasites. Like sheep, the public remains unresponsive as it is devastated, financially and otherwise.

It has been said that it costs over one hundred times more to probate an estate in the United States than the same size estate in Britain, and takes over ten times longer to do it.

Often times, as in other legal cases, the attorney absconds with all the assets, leaving the surviving widow or orphans penniless. Attorneys and judges lust after the assets people accumulate in a lifetime of hard work.

The public doesn't understand the gravity of this misconduct. During the 1984 presidential campaign of Vice Presidential candidate Geraldine A. Ferraro, it was revealed that her attorney husband, John Zaccaro, had taken $175,000 from an elderly woman for whom he had been appointed conservator. As if the money was his own, he used part of it as a deposit to purchase property for a client of his real estate company and part of it to pay tax and mortgage payments for another client. Confirming that no one can lie like an attorney, Zaccaro stated to a *New York Times* reporter that no one told him that he couldn't use someone else's money for his own use.

If this was a book on probate it could be filled with horror stories of attorneys and judges stealing money from innocent people through probate fraud that they call legal.

TYPICAL LEGAL SABOTAGE

Another example of how an attorney will sabotage his own client occurred during a trial on drug smuggling charges. A federal judge in San Francisco dismissed charges (November 15, 1991) against a person charged with drug smuggling, on the basis that the defendant's attorney conspired with attorneys for the Justice Department to get him convicted.

The judge blasted the U.S. Attorney's office for "outrageous misconduct" in encouraging the defendant's attorney to set up his client. "The conduct of the Justice Department in the investigation and prosecution of Steven Marshank was so outrageous that it shocked the universal sense of justice," said the U.S. District Judge. The written ruling by the judge said that the defendant's attorney, Ronald Minkin of Los Angeles, supplied information to Justice Department attorneys about his client and other defendants in order to get them convicted. Through this misconduct the attorney was able to collect thousands of dollars in legal fees and stood to gain millions of dollars when the prosecutor seized his client's properties under forfeiture laws.

Outrageous as this is, I experienced this attorney misconduct over and over again, and learned of many other cases similar to this. It is a firmly established mindset and accepted code of conduct of this sordid group.

An article in the *Wall Street Journal* (September 11, 1991) said, "Lawyers Who Tattle On Clients Prompt Concern." The article described the situation in Houston where the attorney became a government informant against his own clients. U.S. District Judge Lynn Hughes held, however, that tape recordings made by the attorney of his client can be used in criminal proceedings against the client.

"The notion of attorneys as informants, particularly as informants against their own clients, is an area that we've seen sporadically over the years," said Neal Sonnett, a Miami criminal-defense lawyer. "We do not condone the government's use of criminal-defense-attorneys as informants against their clients," said a federal appeals court in Atlanta. (1987) However, they allowed the indictment against the victimized client to stand.

Assistant U.S. Attorney Turow in Chicago approved the treachery, saying that the intrusion is justified, "It's obviously a treacherous area for the government to work in, but it's an area that sometimes the government has to work in." Attorneys involved in the profitable sabotage of their own clients have even agreed to keep Justice Department prosecutors informed of their client's *future* crimes. In the case against Manuel Noriega, Justice Department prosecutors obtained the help of an attorney who formerly represented Noriega and who turned government informant, a profitable change for the attorney.

Attorneys have even killed their clients. An example: San Jose, California, attorney Norman R. Sjonborg was charged by Santa Clara County Superior Court Judge with being "one of the most dangerous sociopaths that I have ever seen," for having killed one of his female clients. Attorneys taking advantage of their female clients, demanding sex, is so rampant it is hardly news anymore.

FORCING SEX UPON WOMEN NEEDING LEGAL HELP

A standard practice of attorneys is forcing female clients to have sex with them in order to be represented. This practice was so outrageous that New York and California passed legislation barring sex between an attorney and client. But whether this will stop the abuses is questionable. The routine violations of the canons of ethics by attorneys, and the State Bar refusal to prosecute for such violations, leave no hope for reform.

SEIZING A CLIENT'S PROPERTIES

One of the scams used by attorneys is to take a deed of trust on a person's home or properties to insure payment of legal fees, followed by outrageously excessive fees resulting in loss of the property to the attorney. New York State passed legislation in 1993 preventing this onerous practice.

THOSE UNABLE TO STOMACH IT

In a full page *Newsweek* article (November 4, 1991), a former attorney described why he quit the business of law, repeating what has been written in many other articles. Sam Benson stated in a book he wrote:

I am astounded that I was able to practice law for more than two years of my life. It was not any single event that pushed me over the edge. It was an uneasiness, an uncomfortableness that was always there for me. I was tired of the deceit. I was tired of the chicanery. But most of all, I was tired of the misery my job caused other people.

THE POWERFUL TRIAL LAWYER LOBBY

The Trial Lawyer Lobby is one of the most powerful lobbies in the United States, consisting of over 60,000 trial lawyers. They exert great influence upon politicians through their political contributions or bribes. This lobby has become the Democratic party's most important special interest group, supposedly more powerful than government unions. Congressmen vote against the wishes of this lobby at risk of being targeted for removal.

Two prominent names on the list of financial recipients of the Trial Lawyers Lobby were Senator Howard Metzenbaum (D-OH), and Senator Ernest Hollings (D-SC) who received over $400,000 from members of the Trial Lawyers' Lobby.[451] The bundling of contributions from these attorneys and their family members, and the political-action committee, can buy virtually any Senator's votes. So-called public interest advocate Ralph Nader gets a major share of his contributions from the trial-lawyer groups. Attorneys in the trial lawyer lobby control sufficient Democrats to block any vote in the Senate on changing the liability laws.

Studies have shown that less than 40 cents of every dollar paid to settle litigation goes to the person who suffered the injury. The rest goes to the attorneys.

Election of attorney Bill Clinton to the presidency of the United States, with his attorney wife, didn't help the problem, especially with Clinton's role in scandals such as the CIA and DEA drug trafficking into the United States.

---

[451] *Daily Journal*, September 30, 1992.

PROTECTED BY THE STATE BAR ASSOCIATIONS

In case after case these corrupt practices continued without any corrective actions after people made complaints to the State Bar Associations. My complaints to the California and Nevada Bar Associations relating to the pattern of attorney misconduct resulted in approval of the misconduct.

Major law schools and universities have a responsibility to act when a pattern of judicial activities destroys the rights and protections under our form of government. They have the legal knowledge and the duty to act, but when hard-core corruption is involved that would bring adverse public reaction upon the group, they aid and abet the activities. These legal institutes of learning knew of the criminal activities implicating federal judges and Justice Department attorneys.

I brought these activities to the attention of Professor Ulysses Crockett of the University of California at Berkeley. Crockett had first telephoned me in 1991 when he heard about my contact with CIA operative Gunther Russbacher, and then seemingly took an interest in what I was doing. When I later confronted Crockett with his responsibility to intervene, especially in the nearby San Francisco federal action against me. Instead, he referred me to several law professors in New York and Massachusetts that he stated owed him a favor.

I wrote to these professors and only one responded, expressing a lack of interest. Crockett has been a prosecutor in the same Alameda County District Attorney's office as Edwin Meese, who was deeply involved in most of the scandals described in these pages. I wondered if Ulysses was simply trying to find out how much information we had about the scandals in which his fellow attorneys, such as Edwin Meese, were involved.

WOLVES IN SHEEP'S CLOTHING

From this sordid group come state and federal judges, who try to present to the public a sense of honor, integrity, and justice. Many judges require everyone in the court to stand up when they enter the court room, as if they are someone to be revered. Much of the public is taken in by these charades.

There are thousands of examples of the sordid conduct of state and federal judges. On a lighter vein was the conduct by U.S. District Judge Robert H. Schnacke, to whom I sought to report in 1974 the criminality I uncovered in the aviation environment. Reflecting on Schnacke's personal life, the headline in *The National Educator*[452] stated: "Kindig fights Pan Am and cathouse judge." The article stated in part:

A judge who has a reputation of siding with the big corporations and who, to say the least, is anything but squeaky clean in his own personal life, having been caught up in a police vice squad raid on a house of prostitution on January 25, 1985. One way or the other, the raid, which took place in San Francisco, did not make the news media until the San Francisco Chronicle finally reported it on March 16th. The federal judge, Robert H. Schnacke was in the audience of an adult

---

[452] March 1989.

*theater on Market Street, when the vice squad officers arrested 11
women performers on lewd conduct charges. According to one of the
arresting officers, the judge was more than in the audience; he was
allegedly "performing" by placing Federal Reserve Notes in the
private parts [vagina] of the prostitutes.*

"Months of Lies to the Press."

Famed defense attorney Gerry Spence described during a 90-minute talk
to the Montana Trial Lawyers Association (July 22, 1993)[453] his observations of the lying by Justice Department attorneys in criminal trials. He
exhorted the attorneys to challenge federal prosecutors and not accept as true
anything that they say.

"These are not the good guys," Spence stated, "These are people who do
[lie, fabricate evidence] what they believe is necessary to bring about a
conviction."

Spence had just finished the trial in which Justice Department attorneys
sought to imprison Randy Weaver after they had killed his wife and son as
they stormed their humble cabin. Spence stated to the trial lawyers group:

*The siege against Weaver brought in enough [weapons of war] to take
over a small country for this little man sitting in this little plywood
cabin.*

Spence stated that after killing his wife and son, the Justice Department
attorneys "charged him with conspiracy, ... and they made the entire family
the conspirators. ... The federal government now has the audacity to say that
members of a family are members of a conspiracy, little children are members
of a conspiracy."

**HIGHEST JUDGE IN NEW YORK STATE
SENTENCED TO PRISON**

One of the highest-ranking judges in New York State was sentenced to
prison on September 9, 1993. Former Chief Judge of New York's Court of
Appeals embarked on a two-year pattern of sending vulgar, harassing, and
threatening letters and phone calls to his former mistress and her daughter.
Judge Sol Wachtler, who was married, was upset over the ending of his four-
year secret love affair with Manhattan socialite Joy Silverman. He disguised
his voice while making threatening phone calls to his former mistress,
threatened to kidnap her fourteen-year-old daughter, sent obscene letters and
pictures to the daughter, and other despicable acts. These were obscene and
criminal acts, but the many judges and their co-conspirators that strip innocent
people of their life's assets, or their liberties, commit far greater harm.

**AMAZING THAT MORE ATTORNEYS AND JUDGES
ARE NOT SHOT BY THEIR VICTIMS**

It has always amazed me that more attorneys and judges are not shot by
their victims, some of whom have lost through judicial and legal corruption
their life's assets, and now must face their remaining years in abstract
poverty, along with their families. Often, the victims are unaware of the

[453] Associated Press, July 23, 1993.

mechanics of how they had been financially destroyed.

The individual attorney or judge who gets shot receives little publicity. But in one case the publicity was nation-wide when a client stormed a San Francisco high-rise office building on July 1, 1993, and shot over a dozen people, eight of whom died.

CREATING A DANGEROUS MINDSET NATIONWIDE

The endemic corruption within the legal and judicial fraternities, the abominable integrity, infects government and non-government activities throughout the United States. These two groups are at the center of every corrupt activity within these pages. Their conduct has created a mindset of corruption throughout America, destroying the moral fibre of the United States. And these are the two groups most responsible for upholding the laws and Constitution of the United States, and establishing a guideline for acceptable conduct.

CHAPTER TWENTY EIGHT

ISRAEL,
THE MOSSAD, AND AMERICA

Israeli officials and agencies, and particularly its intelligence agency, the Mossad, aided and abetted many of the criminal activities described within these pages, inflicting great harm upon the American people. Without the assistance of the Israelis, some of the treasonous and subversive acts against the United States would not have been possible, especially the October Surprise operation. Israel was needed to transship the arms to Iran and to act as end-users on the bill-of-lading.

KILLING PEOPLE WHO DISAGREE
WITH ISRAELI POLICIES

Similar to CIA activities, and possibly worse in some respects, the Mossad doesn't hesitate to assassinate people whose lawful conduct irritates the Israelis. Gerald Bull, a Canadian scientist who developed the Super Gun used by Iraq, was killed by the Mossad at his Brussels apartment in March 1990.[454] Israeli assassination squads killed Bull to halt his development of the Supergun project for the Iraqis.

During that same time frame, Israeli agents were assassinating others, as reported by former Mossad officers Ari Ben-Menashe and Victor Ostrovsky in their books.[455] Nineteen people were killed by Israeli agents within several weeks in 1990, including eight German scientists hired by a company in Miami and who were traveling back and forth to Iraq; a German scientist, Hans Mayers, in a car "accident" in Munich; four Iraqi businessmen, and two Pakistani scientists in Britain. A television production aired on June 17, 1993,

---

[454] *Profits of War*, Ari Ben-Menashe.
[455] *Profits of War*, by Ari Ben-Menashe; *By Way of Deception*, by Victor Ostrovsky and Claire Hoy.

focused on the many killings by the Mossad, including the botched killing in Sweden of the wrong person by Mossad operative Michael (Freddy) Harari. One of their favorite stunts was to put a pressure sensitive plastic-explosive bomb in the victim's bed. When the intended victim lay on the bed the bomb went off. Another tactic was to place plastic explosives in a telephone handset, and when the person answered, and the caller identified him as the intended victim, the bomb would be set off by a signal carried over the telephone wire. Although the plastic explosive was small in size, it usually caused fatal injuries.

Victor Ostrovsky detailed the specifics of several of the killings by Israeli agents, describing the composition of the Israeli assassination department inside the Mossad as a small internal unit called *kidon*, divided into three teams consisting of approximately twelve men each.

Ostrovsky described the shooting down of a Boeing 727 operated by Libyan Arab Airlines by two Israeli jets, killing over a hundred people. He told how two Israel agents killed Arab scientist Yahia El Meshad, by slipping into his apartment with a passkey and then cutting his throat while he slept. He also told how the Mossad killed a PLO official in Paris who was preparing to meet with the French Secret Service.

A December 14, 1992, issue of *Spotlight* carried a story about Israeli assassination squads operating in foreign countries under the title, "Foreign Killers Run Loose in U.S." The article related how Israeli-trained assassins, funded by U.S. taxpayers, are entering the United States, often with the help of the CIA, leaving a trail of unsolved and unreported killings. The report explained how the United States is funding Mossad's criminal operations in Third World countries.

Ben-Menashe's book portrays the Mossad's hiring of Arabs who unknowingly carried out terrorist attacks against Americans, inflaming the American public against the Arabs, who didn't know the attacks were planned and directed by the Mossad. He also tells how Mossad agents paid Palestinians to seize the Mediterranean cruise ship, *Achille Lauro* in 1985, which ended in the killing of one of the passengers. Ironically, the passenger was Jewish. Ari Ben-Menashe wrote in his book, *Profits of War*, that the attack upon the cruise ship was financed by Israel, and its intent was "to show what a deadly, cutthroat bunch the Palestinians were." The American public was told that the attack upon the *Achille Lauro* was a Palestinian operation when in fact it was engineered and financed by Israel.

ISRAEL'S ADMISSION OF WORLD-WIDE ASSASSINATIONS

A *London Observer* article carried in the *San Francisco Examiner* on November 24, 1993 was headlined, "Israeli official admits unleashing assassins." The article described the practice of Israel's military-security establishments carrying out assassinations on a global basis, many of them specifically authorized by Israel's prime ministers, including Golda Meir. The article admitted the mistaken assassination of a waiter in the Norwegian town of Lillehammer, thinking the victim was a PLO terrorist, Ali Hasan Salameh. Israeli officials admitted the disclosures by retired Major General Aharon Yariv on state-controlled Israeli Television, but felt that the information

should have remained secret.
SPREADING OPPRESSION
UN official Lt. Col Tren Lagerkrantz said that the U.S.-funded operation carried out by the Mossad has brought "nothing but oppression, cruelty, bloodshed, corruption and ultimately turmoil" to the backward regions where it operated. (The same, of course, applies to U.S. Intelligence Agencies.) The *Spotlight* article quoted Lagerkrantz:

Since Congress has decided to grant the most aid to governments who agree to let Israel train and equip their security troops, it has been precisely those African nations where the Mossad has been most active—Sudan, Zaire, Somalia, Liberia—that have suffered the worst outbreaks of famine, violence and disorder.

AMERICAN VICTIMS
Israel didn't limit their assassinations to Arabs. Israeli forces deliberately machine-gunned and bombed a virtually unarmed U.S. Navy communication ship, the *U.S.S. Liberty*, off the coast of Lebanon on June 8, 1967. The *Liberty* carried clear markings indicating it to be an American ship, and Israel knew that. As the Israeli aircraft approached the *Liberty*, the fighter pilots radioed and protested to their base, "It's an American ship!" Tel Aviv disregarded the pilot's protests, and ordered the fighters to attack. The brutal and bloody assault continued for almost half an hour, during which time missiles, napalm, and torpedoes were used to kill thirty-four U.S. Navy men and injuring 171 others.

The U.S. sailors had intercepted Israeli radio communications relating to a planned attack on Syria which occurred the following day, and Israel felt the Americans would expose the sneak attack.

For damage control, to prevent the American public from learning the truth, the powerful U.S.-funded Israel lobby in the United States sprang into action with disinformation to the media, and pressure on members of Congress who were recipients of their political contributions. (i.e., U.S. taxpayers money.) It worked. The American public never learned the truth. Even White House officials acted to protect Israel, publicly accepting Israel's apology that the attack was an accident. The American service men were expendable, as they were in Vietnam and other CIA operations.

Seeking to evade blame, Israel asserted that they thought the *Liberty* was another ship, the *El Quseir*. They were lying. But that Egyptian supply ship was in Alexandria, a fact known to Israel. The ugly truth of the deliberate killing of U.S. military personnel by Israel was shown through radio messages intercepted by the American embassy in Beirut, which were slowly and belatedly leaked out. In 1991, former U.S. Ambassador, Dwight Porter, revealed the radio communications intercepted by his office in Lebanon on that fateful day in 1967, revealing that Israeli commanders knew the ship was an American ship and that they were killing American sailors.

Porter's revelations are supported by Seth Mintz,[456] a Major in Israel's IDF,[457] who was present in IDF headquarters for several hours before starting the attack on the U.S. communication ship. Shortly after Mintz made these statements he was threatened by Mossad agents, causing him to recant his earlier statements. In a dispatch in Ha'aretz on November 7, 1991, Mintz expressed "grave anxiety over the media interest in him" relating to the *Liberty* affair. He told Ha'aretz, "Everyone is after me now, and that is what I'm afraid of. I don't need the Mossad[458] and Shin Bet[459] knocking on my door." His knowledge of Mossad's assassination squads and their practice of assassinations certainly justified his anxiety.

The orders to attack the U.S. Navy communication ship came from a high Israeli official, reportedly General Yitzhak Rabin, who later became Israel's Laborite Prime Minister. President George Bush's White House staff tried to portray Israel's Rabin as a peacemaker, despite his long history of terrorist activities.

STEALING U.S. MILITARY SECRETS

Secret weapon technology sent to Israel has been repeatedly copied, stolen, and sold to foreign countries, violating agreements with the United States. In *Dangerous Liaison-The Inside Story of the U.S.-Israeli Covert Relationship,* authors Andrew and Leslie Cockburn describe the symbiotic relationship between the United States and Israeli intelligence networks, the stealing of nuclear fuel by Israel from the Nuclear Materials and Equipment Corporation plant at Apollo, Pennsylvania, in 1968; Israeli and CIA involvement with the Medellin drug cartel and Guatemalan death squads; and other treasonous activities. *Dangerous Liaison* describes the coverup of the nuclear fuel theft by U.S. and Israeli officials, abdicating the loyalty to the United States and protecting those inflicting harm. Their book portrays the role played by the CIA and Mossad in drug trafficking, including relations with the Medellin drug cartel, and their role in the Guatemalan death squads.

Reports in the March 15, 1992, *New York Times* and *Wall Street Journal* related the long pattern of illegal sales by Israel of U.S. weapon technology. The articles revealed that Israel does this by either installing the U.S. components in an Israeli weapon system, or disassembling the weapon to discover how it works, and then constructing its own, selling the secret technology to foreign countries who may be hostile to the U.S. interests.

Israel received Patriot missiles worth hundreds of millions of dollars from the United States, and was required to keep the technology secret. Instead, Israel sold the Patriot missiles and their technology to other countries, including China, in clear violation of U.S. law. A State Department

---

[456] Residing in Houlton, Maine. He was a U.S. citizen who went to Israel in 1962, joining the Israeli Army in 1965, and assigned to the IDF war room during the Six-Day War with Syria.

[457] Israel Defense Forces.

[458] Mossad is the Israeli highly secret intelligence service and a worldwide network of agents, much of it funded by the United States.

[459] Shin Bet acts in a similar manner as the Mossad, performing for the military.

report[500] accused Israel of engaging for nearly ten years in a "systematic" pattern of reselling cutting-edge U.S. military technology to Third World countries, some of whom were adversaries to the United States.

The report described how Washington officials protected this unlawful transfer of U.S. technology by ordering U.S. investigators in Israel not to check on the destination of U.S. technology sent to Israel, as is required of all other countries. Israel, using money supplied by U.S. taxpayers, retains powerful Washington law firms and bribes U.S. officials to carry out their dirty work against the United States.

DOTAN AFFAIR

Another example of Israeli attacks upon U.S. interests was the Dotan affair, in which U.S. corporations paid bribes to Israeli officials, the bribes coming from U.S. taxpayers. Over $11 million in bribe money was diverted from General Electric Company through a small New Jersey front company to European bank accounts controlled by Israel Brigadier General Rami Dotan, who was convicted by an Israeli military court of theft and fraud. The case involved bribery, money-laundering, violations of the Foreign Corrupt Practices Act, insider trading, and espionage.

A General Electric official, Herbert Steindler, was considered a partner in the illicit schemes. Both General Electric and Pratt and Whitney knew the United States was being defrauded, but it was profitable for them to remain quiet, to become co-conspirators. Falsified Bills of Lading and shipment of fictitious equipment were all part of the scheme that was paid by U.S. taxpayers. Shell companies were used for facilitating the payoffs.

General Electric agreed to pay $69 million in fines, penalties and damages, and pleaded guilty to defrauding the United States in the sale of military equipment to Israel. Israeli officials impeded the investigation by U.S. officials, despite the fact that U.S. funds were involved.

Duplicating its denial of involvement in the October Surprise affair, the Israeli government claimed itself innocent in the Dotan matter. But the facts speak otherwise. It is believed that the millions of dollars diverted from engine orders of United Technologies and General Electric through front companies were for the purpose of Israeli covert operations.

Most of the diverted money came from U.S. foreign-aid programs destined for Israel. This money-diversion had been known to be standard and unlawful practice for years to members of Congress, its investigative arm, the General Accounting Office, and White House officials.

Congressman and House Energy and Commerce Committee Chairman John Dingell stated that Congress has been reluctant to embarrass Israel politically. This attitude exists because of past retaliatory measures inflicted upon members of Congress by the Israeli lobby when Israel's activities were questioned.

---

[500] *New York Times*, April 4, 1992.

POLLARD AFFAIR

Israeli agents paid a U.S. Navy intelligence analyst, Jonathan Jay Pollard, to steal military secrets, using a Washington apartment owned by attorney Harold Katz. Israel paid Pollard for his treasonous activities from the money given to Israel by the U.S. The seriousness of the spying operation was reflected by the life sentence given to Pollard on June 4, 1986, by Chief District Judge Aubrey Robinson in Washington. But Israel's Zionist lobby in the United States protected Israel from any fallout.

ISRAEL, THE MOSSAD, AND DRUG TRAFFICKING

Several of my CIA informants, some of whom were pilots with me in the Middle East, described to me in minute detail the role they observed which the Mossad played in drug trafficking into the United States. These CIA people described their direct personal and business contacts with the Mossad, relating to the drug trafficking from South and Central America into the United States.

They described how Mossad agents, including Michael Harari and David Kimche, for instance, were present at many of the drug transshipment points and especially in Panama. They described to me the joint shipment of CIA and Mossad drugs in CIA and DEA aircraft, with the Mossad drugs identified by triangles on the drug packages, resulting from dissembling of the Star of David on the bags.

CIA AND THE MOSSAD

The CIA and Mossad have a symbiotic relationship, jointly inflicting great harm upon the United States, from the treasonous activities of October Surprise to the devastating drug epidemic destroying America. Together, they have inflicted unmeasurable financial and other harm upon the American people. Both engaged in assassinations, and while the CIA has by far the record in mass associations going into the tens of thousands, the Mossad has the record for individual assassinations in Europe and the United States.

Several of my CIA contacts have warned me against saying anything unfavorable about the Mossad or Israel in my book, making reference to the pattern of assassinations by the Mossad when they believe their interests are adversely affected.

The treasonous and subversive CIA October Surprise operation could not have occurred without the cooperation of the Mossad and other Israeli officials. They knew the October Surprise operation was defrauding the United States and became co-conspirators. It was profitable for Israel. Israel was then able to blackmail officials in the government of the United States, including Presidents Ronald Reagan and then George Bush. Besides, any member of Congress who dared to investigate and retaliate against Israel faced the prospect of being defeated at the polls as the Zionist lobby routinely funds opposition candidates.

Former Mossad agent Ben-Menashe described Israel's involvement in the October Surprise operation, which conformed with statements made to me by several CIA people with whom I had been in frequent contact for several years, including Russbacher and Riconosciuto. Israeli agents were at the Madrid, Barcelona, and Paris meetings, as related to me by Russbacher and Ari Ben-Menashe. Israel knew the October Surprise operation was an act of treason, and they aided and abetted it.

ENORMOUS POWER OF THE ISRAEL LOBBY

One of the most powerful forces in the United States is the Anti-Defamation League, whose parent is B'nai B'rith. Much of the money used to bribe members of Congress and other federal officials is sent to the United States by Israel, which obtains the money from U.S. loans and grants that are rarely repaid. Through its powerful Zionist group it can fund campaigns to defeat politicians not adhering to Zionist wishes.

ADL blocks any exposure of wrongful activities by Israel and its Mossad. It spends huge sums of money to oppose members of Congress whose interests are not aligned with Israel. Much or all of this money comes from the U.S. taxpayers who provide loans or grants that are not repaid. One tactic used to silence those who report or criticize the Mossad or Israel's conduct is to label them an anti-Semite. It is risky business for a public official to defend U.S. interests when it means confrontation with the Zionists. Apparently anyone who disagrees with Israel is anti-Semitic, and the vast control by Israel over the U.S. media will be sure the American people hear this version.

ADL has been able to defuse any attention focused upon unlawful activities of people connected with Israel or the Mossad. The ADL lauded a major Jewish crime figure, Morris Barney Dalitz of Las Vegas, who regularly donated heavily to the ADL. Dalitz was called Chairman of the Board to such crime figures as Meyer Lansky and Benjamin "Bugsy" Siegel. Lansky and Siegel were members of the original "Murder Incorporated," also known as the Meyer and Bugsy Gang. An ADL[501] chairman, Irv Rubin, was accused in 1992 of plotting a murder-for-hire operation.

In *American Jewish Organizations and Israel*, author Lee O'Brien states of the Anti-Defamation League of B'nai B'rith (ADL):

In later years, ADL has turned to ... aggressive measures. ... outright surveillance of individuals and groups, the results of which are fed into both the Israeli intelligence-gathering apparatus, via their consulates and embassy, and American domestic intelligence, via the FBI. Top ADL officials have admitted the use of clandestine surveillance techniques.

The Anti-Defamation League of B'nai B'rith has been functioning as the action arm of the Israeli Mossad in the United States. In 1993 an ADL spy scandal erupted in San Francisco, after which it was discovered that the ADL had been acting as proxy for the Mossad. The scandal surfaced after it was discovered that San Francisco police inspector Tom Gerard[502] was stealing police intelligence files and selling them to the ADL.

It was learned during the investigation that Roy Bullock was an ADL operative spying on numerous individuals and groups in the United States. According to an April 9, 1993 *Los Angeles Times* article the ADL disguised payments made to Bullock by funneling the money through Beverly Hills attorney Bruce Hochman, who in turn paid Bullock. Hochman was a

---

[501] ADL is a group founded in the late 1960s to fight those opposed to Israel.
[502] *San Francisco Chronicle*, May 8, 1993.

prominent ADL figure, and a member of a panel appointed by Governor Pete Wilson to recommend the names of attorneys for federal judgeships. This helps explain why the inordinately high percentage of federal judges are Jewish.

During a three-hour press interview in the Philippines Gerard revealed that he was a former CIA operative and had evidence that the CIA trained, supported, and encouraged death squads operating in El Salvador, Honduras and Guatemala during the 1980s. The sheer brutality of the carnage was too much for him, and he left the CIA in 1985. "This was not good guys versus bad guys," Gerard said. "This was evil, evil. ... This was something the devil himself was involved in. And I wanted no part of it."

Gerard described how the CIA supported the death squads that tortured and murdered thousands of people in Central America, including political opponents, union members, peasants, clergy, throughout Central America. Gerard stated that the San Francisco police and the FBI have joined forces to discredit him. Following its standard practice of lying, a CIA spokesman denied that Gerard had any relationship with the Agency.

CIVIL RIGHTS UNDER ISRAEL'S GOVERNMENT

Civil rights are largely ignored in Israel. Only those with Jewish mothers have full stature in Israel, a form of apartheid. Christians and Moslem Palestinians are deprived of their basic human rights in Israel, and United States has been subsidizing this Israeli socialism, or Israel's form of apartheid. The Israeli government regulates and controls almost every facet of personal and business endeavors.

In late 1992, Israeli officials deported 415 Palestinians from their homes, forcing them into the mountains, and barring relief supplies that the Red Cross tried to deliver to them. Those deported included doctors, accountants, lawyers, lecturers, and engineers, some of whom were elderly, and some of whom had heart problems or were crippled. They were driven into a no-man's land in the mountains as winter approached.

An Israeli human rights group[503] charged their government with routinely torturing Palestinian political prisoners, reporting that "Violence and ill-treatment have become an expected part of interrogations." The report stated that at least 5,000 of the 25,000 Palestinian prisoners jailed in the previous year had been tortured, while Palestinians stated the percentage was much higher. An April 3, 1993, *New York Times* article was entitled, "Israeli Study Finds Torture Common."

AMERICAN TAXPAYERS FUND THESE ACTIVITIES

Israel depends upon the largesse of the United States government, and its powerful Israel lobby, as well as other Zionist groups, to fund these activities, including paying U.S. lobbyists, public relations firms, and members of Congress. Billions of dollars in loans have been given to Israel that will never be repaid, the cost of which must be borne by the American taxpayer, plus the interest on the money. In 1991 Israel literally demanded that the U.S.

---

[503] Betselem, the Israeli Center of Human Rights in the Occupied Territories.

guarantee $10 billion in loans to build housing for Jews in land taken from Jordan.

Despite the enormous amount of gifts to Israel, their appreciation was reflected in the 1991 statement by Israel's Prime Minister Yitzhak Shamir, as he attempted to lay a guilt trip on the United States, claiming it had an obligation to help settle Soviet Jews in Israel through the guarantee of a $10 billion loan.

In 1991, the United States taxpayers paid over $4.3 billion in aid to Israel. Israel then invested these funds in U.S. savings bonds for which the United States paid Israel over $34 million in interest (on the money that the United States gave to Israel in the first place).

From 1974 to 1989, Israel received $16.4 billion in loans that would never be repaid. The loans were secretly converted to grants, which did not have to be repaid. The reason the White House officials referred to the money transfer as loans in the first place was to avoid U.S. oversight, which is required only of money grants. By this time the money had already been used, and there was no control over how it was used.

If Israel defaults on the $10 billion loan and the American taxpayer is forced to make the payments, interest and principle have been reported to total $116 billion over a 30-year repayment period.[504]

ISRAELI CITIZENS HAVE SIMILAR PROBLEMS WITH CORRUPT GOVERNMENT AND INTELLIGENCE AGENCIES

Government officials in control of Israel's foreign relations, and its intelligence agency, the Mossad, have engaged in a pattern of criminal acts inflicting great harm upon American citizens, including those of Jewish faith. This indictment of those operating under the flag of Israel does not indict the average citizen of Israel any more than the criminal activities by U.S. officials indict the average American.

More inside and secret information on the activities of the Mossad has been described in earlier pages, and more follows.

---

[504] *Spotlight*, August 24, 1992.

CHAPTER TWENTY NINE

EPIDEMIC CORRUPTION

It is probable that if any of dozens of government or non-government checks and balances had performed their legal responsibilities in the 1960s, such as when I first went public with the massive corruption I discovered, the epidemic corruption that is overwhelming the federal government today would not have occurred. In this chapter other scandals of corruption are described which have not been addressed earlier.

DEFENSE AND AVIATION RELATED CORRUPTION

President Eisenhower warned about the military-industrial complex as he was leaving office, but to no avail. Pentagon fraud and bribery, CIA covert operations to protect the interests of powerful U.S. corporations overseas, and aviation-related crimes were some of the many scandals surfacing in the 1980s, creating a well-entrenched mindset that continues to this date. Establishment media coverup plays a key role in the American public's ignorance about corruption in government. Refusal to read the many highly detailed exposé books and articles is another reason why this corruption is able to escalate.

Evidence of aviation and space related frauds by major corporations repeatedly surfaced in the 1980s and the 1990s. An *Aviation Week & Space Technology* article (April 3, 1989) stated in part:

The pattern of corruption that has emerged from the Ill Wind cases involves classic influence peddling. government employees received bribes in return for providing consultants with early notice of upcoming contracts and for helping them devise strategies for winning those contracts. The consultants convinced contractors to hire them based on their access to an inside source.

A bribed government employee like Berlin could use his influence to determine which firms would be eligible for a contract and, in some cases, could help determine the winner by inserting specific criteria in a service's acquisition plan, favoring one contractor over another.

*Berlin did this for Teledyne and Hazeltine. The corrupt official also
could provide confidential bidding information so a favored contractor
could submit a superior best and final offer to win an award.*

Despite the consequences in money, safety and lives, bribing of government
officials exists in the aviation field. Lockheed, Douglas, Northrop, and other
aircraft manufacturers have repeatedly been charged with paying bribes to
generate orders for their product, and to avoid complying with inspections and
design safeguards.

Justice Department prosecutors filed a lawsuit on July 31, 1991, in New
York charging General Electric with defrauding the Pentagon of more than
$30 million on the sale of jet engines and support services to the Israeli Air
Force. Implicated in this fraud was an Israeli Air Force general who pled
guilty to fraud and bribery charges.

Lockheed admitted bribing foreign government officials as an inducement
for them to buy military and commercial aircraft. In one instance, Lockheed
officials resigned after Justice Department prosecutors charged Lockheed with
bribing foreign officials.[505] These corporate officials admitted sanctioning
bribes exceeding $22 million to European and Japanese officials. Lockheed
pled guilty to secret payoffs[506] to Japanese government and business officials
to promote the sale of Lockheed L-1011 aircraft.

Boeing Corporation paid bribes exceeding $3 million for promoting the
sale of Boeing 747s to Middle East Airlines.[507] Northrop Corporation bribed
Korean officials through a fictitious hotel project that served as a conduit for
bribes.[508] American Airlines agreed to pay a civil penalty for making illegal
political contributions.[509]

Bribes were paid to Japanese politicians and firms to obtain aircraft
orders,[510] and government auditors could not account for $3.4 million paid by
Boeing and McDonnell Douglas. Boeing agreed to plead guilty[511] to felony
charges of illegally obtaining classified Pentagon documents from a lobbyist,
Richard Fowler, who illegally obtained the documents from Pentagon
insiders. Many believe Boeing got off with a slap on the wrist as many Boeing
executives were directly involved with the unauthorized handling of military
planning material.

Defense Department investigators reported they were looking at other
major defense companies suspected of trafficking in secret government documents. The Boeing investigation was pursued independent of the massive
Pentagon bribery and influence-peddling probe code-named "Operation Ill
Wind." Fowler was convicted by an Alexandria, Virginia, jury on December
7, 1989, on 39 felony counts related to unlawful acquisition and distribution

---

[505] Dan Haughton and Lockheed President Carl Lotchian resigned. February 13, 1976.

[506] *San Francisco Chronicle* June 2, 1979.

[507] *Wall Street Journal* April 16, 1979.

[508] *Wall Street Journal*, October 27, 1989.

[509] *Wall Street Journal* May 2, 1975.

[510] *Air Line Pilot*, July 1979.

[511] *New York Times* November 7, 1989.

of Pentagon papers.

Loral Corporation, a major electronics-defense contractor, pleaded guilty on December 8, 1989, to federal charges of fraud and obtaining inside information on defense contracts. The defense contractor unlawfully obtained the military documents by paying over half a million dollars to William Galvin.[512]

One of the main officials caught in the defense fraud investigation code named "Ill Wind" was Melvyn Paisley, Assistant Secretary of the United States Navy. While profiting through unlawful activities, he frequently stated: "Every citizen who enjoys the protection of a free government owes not only a portion of his property, but even of his personal service to the defense of it." Paisley was one of several Boeing Company executives appointed by the Reagan administration to top positions in the Department of Defense. Upon leaving Boeing for the government position, Boeing gave the officials a half-million dollars in severance pay, of which Paisley received $183,000. Boeing regularly receives large amounts of military business from the government through orders generated by their former employees.

Several years before Paisley's government appointment, two Boeing executives accused Paisley of bribing military officials and bugging the offices of competitors to help Boeing win government contracts. Despite these charges, Reagan's Defense Secretary, Caspar Weinberger, made Paisley the senior Navy official responsible for research, engineering and systems. As one newspaper reported,[513] "This, it turns out, was like turning a hog loose in a silo." Weinberger was later indicted in the Iran-Contra affair. (And pardoned by President Bush as he was leaving office.)

Whistleblowers forced the Justice Department, in 1987, to investigate the complaints, including those filed by the whistleblowers under the Whistle-blower's Act, after which influence-peddler William Galvin pled guilty. A contract with a small company owned by two Israelis, requiring Paisley's approval, required the company to deposit two million dollars into a Swiss bank account belonging to Galvin and Paisley. The scheme backfired when the military equipment (drone system) was so poorly constructed that the Navy canceled the contract. When Paisley tried to transfer his share of the bribe money, his involvement was discovered by Justice Department investigators. Galvin was the first one sentenced to prison, and Paisley fell next.

The scheme revealed a pattern of fraud and deceit implicating many others and involving far greater amounts of money. Among the corporations implicated with Paisley and Galvin were Unisys Corporation; Martin Marietta Corporation; United Technologies Corporation; Northrop Corporation; General Electric; General Dynamics; and many others.

One of the high-ranking Air Force officials implicated in the widespread corruption in the military procurement system was Victor D. Cohen, formerly Deputy Assistant Secretary of the Air Force in charge of buying communication and computer systems for the federal government. On August 22,

[512] *San Francisco Chronicle* December 9, 1989.
[513] *San Francisco Daily Journal*, November 7, 1991.

1991, Cohen pleaded guilty to conspiracy and bribe-taking during the five-year investigation into the Pentagon procurement scandal dubbed "Operation Ill Wind."

Unisys Corporation, a major defense contractor, agreed to pay a record $190 million in criminal fines and civil recoveries from the Operation Ill Wind investigation of military procurement corruption. Unisys pled guilty September 6, 1991, in federal court in Alexandria, Virginia, to conspiring to defraud the United States, and to bribery, among other counts.

Some FAA inspectors received money or perks from the airlines they inspected, and I often wondered if this was the reason United Airlines and Congress could block inspectors' safety activities. It is believed that bribes played a part in the FAA's refusal to act on such glaring aircraft design defects as the DC-10, Beech V-tail Bonanza, and other defective aviation products that resulted in many hundreds of deaths.

FALSIFIED AIR SAFETY REPORTS

As the 1980s ended, many Eastern Airlines management personnel admitted falsifying maintenance records that fraudulently indicated repair work was done, or inspection accomplished, that had not been performed. Pilots and mechanics at Eastern Airlines repeatedly reported this falsification problem, in the late 1980s, to the company, the FAA, and the media, followed by the usual refusal to act and concurrent coverup.

Some inspectors and management officials resigned, rather than be a part of the fraud affecting air safety. A former Eastern management official, Paul Kilpatrick, stated to me[514] that he resigned his position, giving up 24 years seniority, when Eastern's hierarchy wanted him to sign off for work that was never done. Many of the Eastern Airlines' pilots complained about pressure from top management to fly aircraft that had numerous system malfunctions constituting unsafe conditions. In answer to these complaints, FAA officials stated the reports were not true, and gave Eastern a clean bill of health. They were, of course, lying, a mindset that other inspectors and I had seen for years.

If it were not for the persistence of Eastern employees and former employees, the truth would probably never have surfaced. Their persistence caused a federal grand jury in New York to take evidence, and their findings proved the charges to be true. The grand jury handed down a 60-count indictment in July 1990, charging Eastern officials with falsifying maintenance records to indicate repairs had been made when they had not been made; falsifying documents; and conspiring to impede an investigation. After several Eastern officials entered into plea agreements admitting their crimes, other officials agreed to plead guilty. Justice Department prosecutors did not file any charges against FAA officials who engaged in the coverup.

Causing terrible consequences for hundreds of victims, McDonnell Douglas Aircraft Company at Long Beach falsified records indicating that safety changes had been made on three DC-10s sold to Turkish Airlines, when

---

[514] May 1989.

they had not been made. As a result, 346 people were shredded into little pieces in the Paris DC-10 crash. FAA Western Region officials, whom I had exposed in criminal misconduct, knew the many problems with the DC-10, and ignored the impending consequences.

In 1985, the FBI investigated an alleged cover-up of violations by the FAA at Continental Airlines. Seeking to protect Continental and its own refusal to perform its safety duties, FAA Western Region officials deleted three pages of violations and criticisms prepared by FAA inspectors from a final version sent to Washington.

The leader of the FAA inspection team, Harry Langdon, found significant problems in Continental's pilot checkout and training procedures, reporting: "It shows either a lack of understanding of federal aviation regulations or a disregard for them. Continental does not, in our opinion, presently meet certification standards." The report also criticized FAA officials at Western Region headquarters in Los Angeles, stating that they were "remiss in condoning the situation". Nothing has changed since other inspectors and I made similar reports for the past thirty years.

The NTSB's politically-sensitive Board routinely sequesters evidence uncovered by its investigators, making it a co-contributor to many crashes that it subsequently investigates.

AIRLINES SACRIFICE SAFETY FOR MONEY

The willingness of a few airlines to sacrifice safety has existed for years. The airlines knew the dangers of outward-opening cargo doors; the absence of backups for flight controls; the danger of no fire extinguishing agents in the cargo compartments. Airlines sought to make one of the emergency exits on the 747 inoperative, to save a relatively small amount of money. They knew that in emergency evacuations, lives may be lost by closing off an exit. They knew that eliminating flight engineers from the jets decreases safety. They knew the dangers of the early Boeing 737s when there is wing contamination, and refused to require speed adjustments to offset the problem. These were calculated risks, accepting the occasional mass-fatality crashes as an acceptable part of doing business.

The airlines even opposed legislation requiring a medical kit on board the aircraft to handle heart attacks, asthma, and diabetes emergencies. I noticed in 1951, when I first started flying for the airlines, that the on-board medical kit consisted of nothing more than Band-Aids and Iodine, meaningless for anything other than a slight cut. Numerous inflight emergencies occur where a meaningful first aid kit can mean the difference between life or death. The Air Transport Association (ATA) opposed the legislation requiring the same medical kit required by most foreign airlines. The ATA argued in a statement released on September 15, 1985, that most domestic flights can land within minutes of an on-board emergency to rush injured or ill passengers to hospitals trained to handle medical emergencies. That is not so.

The truth is that there are many personal emergencies where the person perishes before a plane can land and receive medical attention, which in many cases could have been prevented if adequate medical supplies were on board. Congressman Norman Mineta (D-Cal), chairman of the House Aviation

Subcommittee, acknowledged the resistance by airlines to place emergency supplies on the aircraft.[515]

Year after year the perils of air travel are lamented. In 1985 a Congressional panel investigating air safety stated that air travel was less safe; this was the third scathing criticism of the FAA in less than a month. A month earlier another Congressional study said investigators found disturbing gaps in the FAA's airline inspection program. A week later, an internal Transportation Department report found that the FAA had been slow in devising safety regulations and that they enforce them inconsistently. Similar reports were made for the prior 30 years. Nothing changes. In 1989 an internal Boeing report stated that unless major changes are made in crew training, the loss of aircraft would reach crisis proportions.

CHALLENGER DISASTER

Coverup of a serious safety problem preceded the Challenger disaster, which carried seven people to their deaths, including school teacher Christa McAuliffe. Those who had the technical competency to know, wanted the launch scrubbed, because of serious safety problems caused by the cold weather conditions.[516] But this would delay the launch and affect the plans of President Reagan, who had a television appearance that evening, using the Challenger launch to convey a theme in his State of the Union message. Management personnel, sensitive to political and other pressures, overruled the technical personnel and approved the launch. Tragedy followed, as forewarned.

APOLLO COVERUP PRECEDED CHALLENGER

Known safety problems preceded the Apollo tragedy. NASA officials preceded the Challenger irregularities with the Apollo irregularities, where astronauts perished in the oxygen-fueled fire that cremated the unfortunate occupants. The manufacturer of the capsule had warned that bathing the entire capsule with oxygen was dangerous, a warning that was ignored by NASA. Then, when the astronauts perished, NASA tried to hide these warnings and instead, blamed the manufacturer's purported quality defects for the deaths.

HARASSMENT OF NUCLEAR PLANT INSPECTORS

Harassment of company inspectors at a nuclear plant under construction by Brown & Root, Inc., was reported in a *Wall Street Journal* article dated November 7, 1984. The *Journal* reported that the plant, Comanche Peak, was riddled with poor workmanship. When quality-control inspectors refused to pass defective work, the company fired the inspectors. The company falsely claimed the fired inspectors did not follow orders. The Nuclear Regulatory Commission conducted an inquiry to determine whether harassment and

---

[515] *Aviation Week & Space Technology*, October 7, 1985.

[516] Infrared temperature-sensing instruments showed abnormal "cold spots" on the lower part of the right-hand booster, which later failed during launch. The Thiokol engineers were adamant that the launch be delayed. They felt that the O-rings lost some of their resiliency and ability to seat tightly in their grooves, when their temperatures fall below 50 degrees. The O-ring temperatures had fallen to 30 degrees, far below the safe limit. Despite the engineer's protest, NASA officials went ahead with the launch, with fatal results. The company later fired the inspectors who exposed the defects in the Challenger launching.

intimidation of these and other inspectors compromised the plant's safety. Dozens of inspectors around the country complained of pressure to ignore defects, which otherwise would be costly to the companies. The inquiry concluded that the company fired inspectors who adhered to quality control standards required by federal regulations.

The *Wall Street Journal* article described the actual physical threats against inspectors at the Zimmer plant of Cincinnati Gas & Electric Company in Moscow, Ohio. Inspectors were doused with water and with fire extinguisher fluids during inspections. Ultimately, the quality of the plant was in such doubt that the plant converted from nuclear energy to coal. At a nuclear plant built by four utility companies near Bay City, Texas, the Nuclear Regulatory Commission threatened to halt the project in 1980, after it found that supervisors consistently overruled quality-control inspectors in favor of construction workers.

LOSS OF RETIREMENT BENEFITS

Numerous pensioners discovered, and will continue to discover, upon retirement that there was no money in the pension fund, and that they were financially destitute. This problem became evident in the late 1980s and escalated in the 1990s. The media gave very little if any publicity to this scandal, making possible the losses suffered by their readers.

Two government regulatory schemes exist when pension funds are federally regulated: the Employee Retirement Income Security Act of 1974 (ERISA) and the Pension Benefit Guaranty Corporation. The Pension Benefit Guaranty Corporation protects the pension benefits of the 30 million Americans in programs regulated by the federal program. If the pension funds are guaranteed by the government, and are underfunded, the U.S. taxpayers may have to pay many billions of dollars on top of the other horrendous debt. More than $1.6 *trillion* in pension funds is potentially at risk because of poor regulations and failure of the checks and balance systems to enforce federal law, according to the report of the Labor Department's Inspector General, J. Brian Hyland.[517]

The Employee Retirement Income Security Act of 1974 (ERISA) is supposed to protect workers' pension benefits when employers go out of business. The protections are inadequate to insure that the funds are there, and the results are that the taxpayers must pay the pension funds through the Pension Benefit Guaranty Corporation.

Hyland urged Congress to immediately investigate potential abuses and shortfalls of federal pension laws, reporting that existing laws and regulations allow employers and pension-fund managers to hide abuses from the government. Further, that inadequate staffing at the Labor Department leaves the government little chance to catch offenders.

Pension Benefit Guaranty Corporation reported that its 1991 losses were greater than $1 billion, plus many more billions of potential losses. One bankrupt airline by itself, TransWorld Airlines, was short over $1 **billion** on

---

[517] Stated on June 2, 1989 and reported the following day by *Associated Press.*

its pension plan. It is believed that about twenty percent of government insured pension plans are underfunded, the shortage amounting to over $40 billion. There are about 95,000 federally insured pension plans.

The underfunded pension plans of numerous large companies will have to be funded by the taxpayer and include, for instance, CF&I Steel Corporation of Pueblo, Colorado; LTV Corporation; and the former Eastern and Pan American Airlines.

One of the reasons pension funds are underfunded, or funded with near-worthless financial paper, is that corporate raiders seized the cash in many pension funds, replacing it with junk bonds or financial paper issued by potentially insolvent insurance companies. The pension plans are then "guaranteed" by the near-worthless junk-bonds, many of which actually became worthless in the early 1990s.

"Pension disaster is looming," was a headline on an *Associated Press* story of November 14, 1989. The article stated that "Fraud and mismanagement could wipe out the retirement nest eggs of millions of working Americans in private pension programs, and saddle taxpayers with a multibillion-dollar bailout, according to government officials and agency documents." The article stated that the Labor Department Inspector General's office warned that the fraud and mismanagement could dwarf the recent savings and loan financial debacle, adding to the problems that could set the stage for our country's second worst depression of the twentieth century.

The report stated that many of the underfunded pension plans are not insured by the government; that retirees will often get nothing; and that only some of the 107,000 private pension plans were covered by the government's Pension Benefit Guaranty Corporation (PBGC) insurance.

The Director of Pension Rights Center, a public interest group, stated in the article that "It's astonishing how much of the money is being stolen," and referred to some $14 million stolen from two union locals.

A *National Law Journal* article (June 3, 1991) was headlined, "Unfunded Retirement Plan: Ticking Bomb?" A subsequent *National Law Journal* article (December 16, 1991) referred to the continuing savings and loan debacle followed by the growing pension fund problem, stating that the plans are more than $40 billion underfunded. The article stated that the American taxpayer may be burdened with pension fund liabilities almost as great as the savings and loan debacle, and described how seemingly safe pension funds are unsafe because of the intricate involvement with failed or failing savings and loans and insurance companies. "Pensions could be next S&L debacle," was the headline on a 1991 *San Francisco Chronicle* article. "Tension mounts as pension-fund troubles grow in U.S.," was the headline on a February 1992 *Newsday* article.

There were many other articles describing similar problems, including a *Wall Street Journal* article (June 10, 1992) reporting that Chrysler's pension plan was short by $4.4 billion; Bethlehem Steel's pension plan $1.3 billion short; Navistar $500 million short. PBGC had to pay over $1 billion after Pan Am and Eastern Airlines folded, with an estimated liability to pay of over $21 billion. PBGC estimates that if Chrysler went bankrupt its underfunded pension plans would approach $8 billion.

Pan American Airlines filed for Chapter 11 bankruptcy in 1990, and then went out of business in 1992, with its pension fund over one billion dollars short.[518] Pan Am's bankruptcy required the Pension Benefit Guaranty Corporation (PBGC) to pay approximately $1 billion dollars to cover the pension fund shortage, which of course will be paid by the American taxpayer, plus the interest charges.

In one instance involving LTV Corporation, government lawyers stated[519] in a Supreme Court case that the taxpayers were liable for "an open-ended source of industry bailouts" which would probably spark a financial crisis similar to the one facing the government's insurance program for the savings and loan industry.

PRIVATE PENSION FUNDS OR PLANS

There are approximately one million company pension plans that are not guaranteed by the government. These include the popular 401(k) retirement savings plans, employee stock ownership and profit-sharing plans. The federal government considers these to be savings plans and not pension plans. Over 13 million Americans have these non-government insured plans. For the employer they are relatively cheap. They do not promise workers a definite benefit upon retirement, and employers do not pay any insurance costs.

Private pension funds are not guaranteed by the government, relying upon the continued survivability of the company, or the integrity of the bonds or other financial paper that the company provides. In many cases healthy pension funds containing large amounts of cash or liquid assets became the target of corporate takeovers or leveraged buyouts, solely for the purpose of enriching the new owners. The cash would then be replaced with financial paper of questionable value. In some cases the company is the target for a "bustout," in which the sole purpose of acquiring the company is to loot its assets, including the pension funds, and put the company into Chapter 7 bankruptcy. The employees are then left without any retirement funds if it is not a federally insured plan.

INSURANCE COMPANY FAILURES
ADDED TO THE ESCALATING PROBLEMS

Attention was focused in April 1991 on another aspect of the pension fund problem as it related to insolvent insurance companies guaranteeing pension fund payments, when California officials seized Executive Life Insurance Company due to its insolvency. Junk bonds yielding great profits to attorneys and Wall Street firms arranging the funding were key factors in the failure of the insurance company.

The failure of the twelve billion dollar life and health insurer adversely affected over 200,000 policyholders, over 115,000 annuity owners, and hundreds of plundered pension plans. Within days of seizing First Executive's West Coast branch, California insurance regulators on May 14, 1991, were forced to seize another insurance company, First Capital Holding Corpora-

---

[518] *Wall Street Journal*, April 18, 1991.
[519] *The Recorder* October 31, 1989.

tion. The failure of Capital Life Insurance Company in California was billed as the biggest insurance bust in U.S. history.[520] Monarch Life Insurance Company was seized in May 1991 by Massachusetts regulators. New Jersey officials took over the venerable $13.8 billion Mutual Benefit Life Insurance Company, the nation's 18th-largest insurer, in July 1991. Many elderly people lost their pensions, their annuities, their retirement income. As in every major scandal, multiple checks and balances existed in theory and on paper which should have prevented these consequences.

Senator Howard Metzenbaum, head of the Antitrust Subcommittee, stated during Senate hearings that California officials had ignored clear signals of the insolvency years earlier, having allowed the insurance company to continue the practices, guaranteeing heavy losses would be suffered by thousands of people.[521] Speaking of the California regulators, Metzenbaum stated: "It's clear that they knew [several years earlier] that Executive Life was in a precarious position and yet they allowed the company to continue [offering pensions and life policies]."

CALIFORNIA, THE BREEDING GROUNDS FOR SCANDALS

If it were not for the coverup by California officials, the Lincoln Savings and Loan debacle would not have financially destroyed thousands of people. This same group of state officials, and their coverup, resulted in huge losses to thousands of people who relied upon the pensions, annuities, and contracts paid by Executive Life Insurance Company. Corruption was rampant in the California legal fraternity.

There may be other problems for insurance companies that have not received any exposure. In other pages a practice was described in which CIA operatives obtained hundreds of millions of dollars in loans from insurance companies using bogus bearer bonds, including treasury bonds, as security. These bonds had a 20 and 25 year due date, which should start coming due in the mid-1990s. Massive losses will be recognized at that time, unless the bonds are not redeemed.

BANKS

Bank deposits up to $100,000 are guaranteed by the Federal Deposit Insurance Corporation, and losses up to this amount are being paid by the American taxpayer through borrowing and interest paid on the borrowed money. "Bank Bailout Called Near Certainty," was the headline on a *San Francisco Examiner* article,[522] warning that the taxpayers will have to pay over $100 billion to bail out the banks (plus interest on the indebtedness). "Banking on the Brink: The Troubled Future of American Finance," stated the article, quoting Edward W. Hill, a professor at Cleveland State University, and Roger J. Vaughan, economist, of Santa Fe, New Mexico. The article estimated that if the weak or insolvent banks were shut down at that time the cost would be $45 billion to $59 billion and a delay in closing would exceed $75 billion to $95 billion.

[520] *Spotlight*, May 27, 1991.
[521] *Wall Street Journal*, April 26, 1991.
[522] October 6, 1992.

"Another Banking Debacle Feared," was another headline.[523] The article stated that "Wall Street analysts and investors who follow the banking industry are worried that a new financial horror movie is opening in the stock market."

"State's banks ready for more bad times," headlined an *Associated Press* article.[524] The article referred to the unemployment levels in the Los Angeles area as being close to Depression levels, much of it due to the reduction in the military-industrial complex and the depressed economy caused in part by the vast looting of the savings and loans.

The number of problem banks would be increased if they valued the real estate covered by their loans at the current market value rather than at the original value. The problem arises when the real estate on which the loan was based subsequently dropped in value, possibly lower than the mortgage balance.

FDIC regulator L. William Seidman warned that the $70 billion bailout voted by Congress in 1992 would not be enough to cover the expected bank failures in the near future.[525]

There were mixed signals as to the health of the nation's banks. In 1993, by paying very little interest to its depositors and charging high interest for the money loaned, and for credit card balances, the financial health of the banks improved.

WALL STREET SCAMS

Billions of dollars were taken out of the American economy, much of it lost by investors, from the corrupt insider trading, junk bonds, and other acts of Wall Street rogues: Ivan Boesky, Michael Milken, Dennis Levine, Martin Siegel and others. Boesky, responsible for billions of dollars of losses, had a CIA background, including an assignment in Iran.

Typical of how the public gets fleeced was the case of Prudential-Bache, in which hundreds of millions of dollars were fraudulently taken from trusting investors. In an October 1993 settlement offer Prudential agreed to pay nearly half a billion dollars to investors that were swindled out of their investment money.

Prudential had previously argued, before federal and state regulators applied pressure, that none of the investors had a valid claim because they waited beyond the statute of limitation period to file a lawsuit. The settlement barred the defrauded investors out of other forms of compensation, including punitive damages. Prudential, a subsidiary of the Prudential Insurance Company, ran roughshod over the defrauded investors, using a former ex-convict with a crooked real estate record, to carry out the fraud.

CORRUPTION EVERYWHERE

Even a household name like Beech Nut committed fraud when it represented a sugar and water concoction as being "100 percent pure apple juice," and this continued for five years from 1977. The threat to the health of babies and children went uncorrected by government investigators for

---

[523] *San Francisco Chronicle*, July 8, 1991.

[524] October 27, 1992.

[525] *San Francisco Chronicle*, October 17, 1991.

years. Not until a detective from the Processed Apple Institute informed Beech Nut of a lawsuit, did Beech Nut discontinue the deception. Eventually the government was forced to intervene. Former Beech Nut executive John Lavery was convicted of conspiracy and mail fraud selling corn syrup to babies and children as pure apple juice. When Lavery appealed the conviction, the Court of Appeals ruled: "The evidence was ample to permit the jury to infer that Lavery conspired with the suppliers to perpetrate a fraud on the public through the distribution of the adulterated juice."

Corruption exists in the kind of music played on the radio stations via Music-Payola, the catchy term used for bribing radio stations to play certain records. This scandal first came to light in the 1970s, and persisted, despite federal criminal laws prohibiting the practice. The Justice Department's Organized Crime Strike Force charged four people with violating federal payola laws by paying over $300,000 in bribes to radio station executives between 1980 and 1986. Could this have a bearing on the onslaught of junk "music" that traumatizes the entire spectrum of the radio dial?

THE FDA SCANDAL

As the HUD and other scandals surfaced, so did the FDA corruption. The Food and Drug Administration regulates 25 percent of the nation's consumer economy, affecting the entire nation. Evidence revealed that FDA officials engaged in corruption, bribery, and illegal gratuities associated with generic-drug makers. Generic pharmaceutical companies admitted bribing FDA officials, submitting falsified data, and other wrongful acts. Just like FAA officials, the FDA officials treated the industry that it regulated as a partner.

The scandal became known in 1988 when the House Energy and Commerce Committee initiated an investigation following a complaint from Roy McKnight of Pittsburgh-based Mylan Laboratories Inc. By creating an atmosphere of embracing the generic-drug industry as a partner rather than a regulator, the FDA created an atmosphere of lawlessness, said Sidney Wolfe, head of the Public Citizen Health Research Group. "It isn't surprising that the generic companies pulled these shenanigans."

REQUESTING INVESTIGATION OF ITS OWN OFFICIALS

FDA internal regulations prevent the approval of a new generic drug if inspectors find manufacturing problems at the drug company's plant. Officials within the FDA plant inspection department refused to provide inspection reports to other FDA officials reviewing new-drug applications. The FDA's new-drug department had to resort to the Freedom of Information Act to get copies of the FDA's plant inspection reports from its own agency! This unheard-of withholding of information by one part of a government agency from another segment of the same agency prevented the agency from accomplishing its lawful functions. When the documents were finally obtained, important information was blacked out. Who in the hell did these federal employees think they were working for!

COMMON KNOWLEDGE, BUT NO ONE COMPLAINED

Fear of retaliation kept companies who were aware of the FDA corruption from complaining. Clark Research & Development Inc., filed a lawsuit accusing the FDA of losing documents and pursuing a "pattern of harassment" after Clark complained that FDA officials allowed a competitor to make misleading claims.

The impetus for the FDA corruption came from companies scrambling to be the first to win FDA approval for their products as patents expired. High stakes were involved. The first generic company to get FDA approval, and place its product on the market, was often the one who captured the lucrative market.

Middle management at the FDA began receiving reports as early as December 1985 that drug reviewers favored one company over others in return for bribes. FDA officials based drug approval on bribes–either sex, money, or other perks. There was a tip that a woman executive from a drug company exchanged sex with an FDA drug reviewer, and then got quick approval of the company's product. No one investigated the tip.

Two small generic-drug makers[526] had a phenomenal success in obtaining quick FDA drug approval. They received a stunning seventy-seven drug approvals in 1986, almost twice as many as any other company, including those much larger in size.

DRUG APPROVALS BASED ON BRIBES

"We screwed you on this one, so we'll take care of you on the next one," FDA officials stated to H. Lawrence Fox, an attorney for Barr Laboratories, Inc. Fox testified before a Congressional committee, showing the passing out of drug approvals based upon bribes. They sounded like crooked judges and attorneys, making favorable decisions based on quotas, ignoring the merits of the case.

Bribery and favoritism caused the disappearance and destruction of documents submitted by companies for drug approvals. A Congressional investigative panel embarrassed the FDA by producing the original copy of a generic-drug application that a former FDA branch chief, Charles Chang, had torn in half and thrown in the trash. Chang pleaded guilty in a Baltimore federal court to two counts of interstate travel in aid of racketeering.

The FDA official accepted a paid, round-the-world trip costing over $3,000, and computer equipment worth $8,000, from American Therapeutics Inc., a generic drug maker based in Bohemia, New York. In return, the FDA official sped the company's application through the approval process, while delaying the processing of other applications.

The Congressional investigations revealed major drug companies submitted falsified data, filled generic drug test samples with brand-name products, claiming the products as their own, and winning FDA approval.

THE GREAT GRAPE CATCH—or, Government Intimidation Of Industry and A Country.

As news media attention escalated on the FDA internal corruption, a sudden occurrence shifted public attention in March 1989 to another matter: the great grape catch. The FDA allegedly received a tip that a shipment of grapes from Chile contained cyanide. Like a scene from a school play, a

---

[526] Par Pharmaceutical Inc., and its Quad Pharmaceuticals Inc. subsidiary.

horde of FDA officials converged on a pier in Philadelphia. Pier Superinten-
dent John Hamilton described the scene: "All of a sudden, I saw an army of
guys. They never told us what they were looking for, but it was obvious they
knew where to look."

Out of dozens of ships containing huge shipments of fruit from Chile, the
FDA officials singled out the Almeria Star from an armada of fruit-laden
freighters for inspection. The FDA inspectors went to a row of crates
containing an estimated 280 million grapes, and plucked two grapes that
allegedly had several needle marks on them. These grapes were then taken to
the FDA laboratory and reportedly discovered to contain cyanide, which FDA
officials stated had been injected into the two grapes before they left Chile two
weeks earlier.

FDA officials then issued a warning that consumers not eat any Chilean
fruit, and imposed an embargo against Chilean fruit (March 13, 1989).
Markets in the United States ordered the removal and destruction of Chilean
fruits. U.S. officials tried to pressure other countries to join in the boycott,
but they refused. Farmers in Chile were unable to sell their produce. The
FDA's actions cost Chile over $300 million, inflicting great financial harm
upon Chilean growers and shippers, while increasing the cost of grapes from
an alternate source for U.S. consumers.

Chilean farmers, the Chilean economy, and U.S. consumers lost by this
action. These tactics inflicted catastrophic financial harm upon Chile's
economy. Chilean farmers went out of business due to inability to sell their
crops. In this way the United States halted the entire Chilean fruit harvest to
the United States that was worth almost a billion dollars a year to Chile's
fragile economy, inflicting great economic harm and ruin upon many
Chileans. Chilean leaders went on TV to calm the country, as they tried to
figure out what to do next.

A *Wall Street Journal* article (November 16, 1989) pointed out the
inconsistencies and implausibilities of the FDA's actions that cast "serious
doubt on the FDA's miracle find." The article stated that many people
believed FDA officials fabricated the grape scare, speculating that the FDA's
story was manufactured to show the Pinochet government the power of United
States economic sanctions.

Subsequent laboratory tests conducted by Chilean laboratories revealed
that grapes change color about two days after injection with cyanide. But the
two grapes picked by the FDA officials did not have any color change.
Further, tests revealed that cyanide dissipates rapidly into the air as a gas,
leaving an ugly, unappetizing blemish, and that grapes shriveled and darkened
within two weeks. There were no blemishes on the two grapes picked by the
FDA officials. University of California researchers at Davis, California,
believed the two grapes became contaminated *after* the FDA officials seized
the fruit.

In response to the phony grape claims by U.S. officials, Chile and 2,500
Chilean fruit growers and exporters filed damage claims against the United
States totaling $458 million. The claims argued that the Food and Drug
Administration improperly embargoed all fruit shipments from Chile in 1989.

These administrative claims were the prelude to legal action against the U.S. government.

The Chileans argued that the FDA ignored demonstrated facts about the reaction of cyanide injected in fruit, including its rapid rate of dissolution. The claims stated that "The FDA knew or should have known that it was physically impossible to inject enough cyanide into the two grapes (out of billions) before they left Chile on February 27, 1988, and [for it] still [to] be retained at the levels purportedly detected in the Philadelphia lab on March 12."

Senator Jesse Helms (R-NC) argued that the GAO reports, protecting the FDA actions, were flawed, remarking "I don't believe it happened in Chile. [This is] the most bizarre episode I have ever seen." A Congressional investigation followed, and as could be expected, cleared U.S. officials of any wrongdoing.

ADVANCE WARNINGS

A year earlier, in 1988, George Jones from the U.S. Embassy in Santiago, questioned Chilean attorney Ricado Claro, during lunch, what the Chilean reaction might be to a United States ban on fruit from Chile. White House officials were dissatisfied with certain policies of the Chilean government. Looking back, this question appeared to be a threat for Chile to change its internal affairs to comply with White House demands. A year later the hypothetical happened.

THE TRUTH KEPT FROM THE AMERICAN PEOPLE

Ari Ben-Menashe, former Mossad agent, stated in his *Profits of War*, that he was in Chile at the time, and learned from his CIA contacts that the real reason for the grape setup and embargo was to retaliate against Chile for threatening to halt the chemical and other weapon sales to Iraq by Cardeon Industries of Chile, a company working closely with the CIA.

Chile's General Matthei had planned to put a halt to the sale of chemical and other war supplies to Iraq by Cardeon Industries, a company closely aligned with the CIA. This planned action displeased President George Bush, who reportedly asked his CIA friend, Robert Gates, to retaliate against Chile and force the country to change its plans. Gates was also displeased with Ben-Menashe for having leaked a story to the London *Financial Times*,[527] exposing these chemical weapon sales by Cardoen to Iraq in collaboration with the CIA.

After Chile suffered devastating financial harms from the destruction of its primary agricultural exports, its leaders were forced to capitulate to U.S. demands. Cardeon Industries was allowed to continue shipping chemical weapons to Iraq, as part of the Iraqgate and BNL scandals.

PEDOPHILE ACTIVITIES,
CIA AND HIGH OFFICIALS

In its bag of dirty tricks the CIA has promoted pedophilia for the purpose of blackmailing and controlling people, especially those in high government

---

[527] The exposure of chemical weapon sales to Iraq was published in the *Financial Times* on November 11, 1988.

positions. Several of my CIA and police informants described to me how the CIA made young children available to incriminate people in key positions. Jim Rothstein, a former New York City Vice Squad investigator, revealed the pedophile operations he uncovered, and how the CIA promoted pedophile activity for blackmail purposes as a standard covert practice.

One of the most covered up pedophile operations in which young boys and girls were kidnapped and then used for sex objects, or killed, was the Franklin scandal in Omaha, Nebraska. A concerned Nebraska legislator, John W. DeCamp, published the sordid details in a book entitled, *The Franklin Cover-Up*.[528] The book described the pedophilia ring that took children, mostly boys, on trips to Washington, to the 1992 Republican Convention in Houston, and elsewhere, for use by high government officials.

Several pedophile victims told their stories of sexual misuse of children, including Satanism and killing of little children, describing how Washington officials, including the Justice Department, blocked investigation and prosecution of the perpetrators. The ringleader of the Nebraska pedophile activities was reportedly the prominent black Republican Larry King, who sang the opening song at the Houston Republican convention in 1988.

The book described the killing of children, their exploitation, the involvement of prominent government officials, and the coverup by state and federal prosecutors, including of course Justice Department officials and the establishment media. A one-hour television show was aired on the Franklin activity (November 20, 1992), giving additional support to the documented exposé of the little-exposed problem. Within the CIA covert operations it is common knowledge that numerous U.S. Congressmen and Senators are implicated in pedophile activities. Further details on the pedophile activities were given to me by former FBI agent Ted Gunderson and New York Vice-Squad investigator Jim Rothstein.

SEXUAL ABUSE OF CHILDREN BY PRIESTS

The moral breakdown within the United States is so epidemic that even in the priesthood there it exists, inflicting harm upon children in their care. The crime of priests preying upon children, who looked to the priests for guidance, has been known and covered up for years by the media, the local police, and the church itself. The response of the church hierarchy has been to deny the charges, accusing the victims of lying, and making it possible for other children to be sexually molested. Even after the priests were sent to rehabilitation centers, some of them continued to sexually molest altar boys and other children whose care was entrusted to the church.

The archdiocese of Santa Fe, New Mexico, for instance, knew of pedophilia allegations for years against a former priest, and repeatedly allowed him to molest other children. In one newspaper article[529] attorney Bruce Pasternack reported:

---

[528] *The Franklin Cover-Up*, subtitled Child Abuse, Satanism, and Murder in Nebraska. John W. Decamp. AWT, Inc. Lincoln, Nebraska.
[529] January 10, 1993.

What they demonstrate is proof positive that the Archdiocese of Santa Fe and the Paraclete Center knew their children were going to be raped before they were raped.

Another one of dozens of newspaper articles was headlined, "Catholic Hierarchy Hides From Child Abuse by Priests." Throughout the United States, and especially in the Catholic and Episcopal churches, pedophilia crimes are rampant. With the push to prevent gays from being excluded, pedophile crimes will surely worsen. No thought was given to the financial and emotional trauma that the victimized children would suffer.

The establishment media covered up for this sordid misconduct for years, protecting the churches and the perpetrators. The young victims were charged with making false statements while simultaneously protecting the child molesters. In the late 1980s and 1990s the pattern of sexual abuse of children by priests finally received publicity in the alternate media.

PUBLIC POSTURE VERSUS HARD-KNUCKLE RETALIATION

After years of coverup the Roman Catholic bishops adopted (November 19, 1992) a resolution pledging to address the problem of priests who sexually abuse children. The statement stated in part: "In the course of our assembly this week, we have reflected—once again and more deeply—upon the pain, anguish and sense of alienation felt by victims." "Justice, compassion and charity comprise the foundation of our policy," wrote Cardinal John O'Connor of New York in July 1993,[530] in response to the onslaught of lawsuits about the pedophile activities by their priests.

RE-VICTIMIZING THE VICTIMS

In response to the lawsuits by the victims, the church, through its law firms, went after the victims and the victim's families. After Edward Morris sued the Philadelphia Catholic archdiocese arising out of priest sexual abuse while during eight years while he was a child, the church and the law firm counter-sued Morris's parents, blaming them for, would you believe, failing to discover that the priest was molesting their child.

Morris claimed in his lawsuit that Father Terrance Pinkowski sexually abused him over an eight-year span, telling the young boy that sexual relations were a form of therapy necessary for his spiritual growth in preparation for ordination (Morris had intended to become a priest).

In another example, after Timothy Martinez sued the archdiocese of Santa Fe, the church and the law firm had private investigators questioning neighbors to determine homosexual activities.

Simultaneously with the facade of concern for the child victims, church leaders, through their attorneys, played hard-ball with the victims, using scorched-earth tactics to humiliate and discredit the plaintiffs. These attacks to discredit the victim's charges even occurred after the priests admitted their sex crimes against the children in criminal proceedings.

In case after case, even after the priests have admitted their sex crimes against children in criminal proceedings, or after the priests have been sent to

---

[530] *Wall Street Journal*, November 24, 1993.

church treatment centers for pedophilia (including the Servants of the Peraclete near Albuquerque). One of the victim's attorneys, Jeffrey Anderson of St. Paul, Minnesota, stated of these tactics: "There's a difference between exercising legal rights and prerogatives in lawsuits and intentionally re-victimizing victims by repudiations, rebukes and attacks."

New York state authorities accused Reverend Edward A. Pipala and members of Cardinal John O'Connor's archdiocese in upstate New York of operating a church-affiliated club consisting of several dozen young boys, taking them to sex parties involving sodomy and sexual abuse.

State prosecutors often protected the criminal behavior by the priests, refusing to prosecute.

OTHER CHURCH CRIMES

The scandal surrounding the Vatican Bank showed that the Vatican itself has been heavily involved in corruption, killings, and other criminal acts. After the death of Pope Paul in 1978, Albino Luciani was elected to be the head of the Catholic Church, taking the title of Pope John Paul I. Shortly thereafter he discovered massive fraud and criminal dealings by Catholic bishops and cardinals[531] in charge of the Vatican Bank. He discovered tens of millions of dollars were missing from the bank. He discovered ties to the Mafia and to the secret P2 lodge. Pope John Paul I planned to expose those church officials involved in the corruption. But the exposure of the Vatican crimes was prevented by the mysterious poisoning and death of the Pope thirty-three days after assuming that position (September 28, 1978).

Hiding evidence of the crime, the Pope was hastily embalmed, without any autopsy being performed, and no death certificate issued. Involved in the criminal activities of the Vatican Bank, and threatening to reveal the involvement of many others as the scandal unfolded in Europe, banker Roberto Calvi was found hanged under a bridge in London. Even the CIA had business dealings with the Vatican, funneling large sums of money to the church to aid in covert CIA activities.[532]

DEFECTIVE HEART VALVES

Defective heart valves made by the Pfizer corporation resulted in many deaths.[533] Officials at Pfizer released heart valves that were defective, with fractured or broken wire struts holding the tiny disk in place. When these components fail, blood flow through the heart becomes unregulated and the heart fails. In a majority of the cases where the defective valve fails, the person dies.[534] Over 300 people reportedly died as a result of the defective valves.[535]

An investigation revealed a phantom inspector, who did not exist, had signed off for repair and welding of cracked valve components that were in fact not repaired or welded. During manufacturing, the wire struts welded to

---

[531] Including Bishop Paul Marcinkus, formerly of Chicago; Cardinal Jean Villot and others.

[532] *In God's Name*, David A. Yallop, Bantam Books.

[533] *Wall Street Journal*, November 7, 1991.

[534] Death toll at this writing exceeds 300.

[535] *Wall Street Journal*, November 7. 1991.

the valves often developed cracks, necessitating rewelding. An investigation of records at Pfizer-Shiley Incorporated showed that inspector number 2832 purportedly rewelded and inspected these cracked components. But the inspector had left the company months before the signing of the reports. In addition, the inspector stated that he had never welded any of the parts.

Falsified records were common, according to reports by Shiley workers at the Irvine, California, plant. One Shiley supervisor wrote a memo to his boss stating, "even though no rewelding occurs, the [inspector] signs off the [inspection report] as if it were rewelded. I think we are hiding our worst defect."

RAMPANT CONGRESSIONAL CORRUPTION

In *Above the Law*, [536] author James Boyd described the influence-peddling and buying of votes in Congress. Vested interests pass money under the table—bribes—disguised as honorariums, speech-fees, loans that never come due, and other thinly disguised graft. In its book review, the *Christian Science Monitor*[537] said, "Only the completely cynical can read Mr. Boyd's book without mounting distress."

The review reported the indifference or coverup by the FBI, the Attorney General, and the live-and-let-live philosophy of Congress for their peers. The review also addressed the media coverup, stating "the press doesn't smell too sweet either. It rushed into the kitchen only after the kettle boiled over." Ironically, the *Christian Science Monitor* knew of my allegations from 1965 through 1988, and continued to keep the lid on the scandals. I contacted the *Monitor* in the 1960s, and several times in the late 1980s. They expressed concern, followed by coverup, as described by the *Christian Science Monitor*'s editor-in-chief Earl Foell. He stated the *Monitor* organization has a moral mission to support socially responsible journalism. (*Business Week* September 26, 1988.) In 1990 I wrote again to inquire what they were doing in response to my charges. They never answered. So much for moral missions!

A *Washington Post* article dated September 4, 1969, stated that "Committees in Capital Run Like Swiss Banks." The article continued: "The devious ways that Congress used the District of Columbia [for a] haven for committees that can be used by senators and congressmen to hide embarrassing contributions."

A three-page *U.S. News & World Report* article on November 10, 1969, was captioned: "Scandals in Congress: The Record." The article continued: "Activities of a staff member have put the office of the Speaker of the House high in the headlines. The result is one more entry in the record of scandals that have dogged the U.S. Congress for years." The *New York Times*[538] wrote, "Everybody in D.C.'s Doing the Scandal Shuffle." Two decades later the corruption by government officials is much worse. government corruption has been uncovered in almost every agency in the executive branch, as well

---

[536] Authored by James Boyd and published in 1968.
[537] March 1, 1968. Christian Science Monitor.
[538] October 8, 1989, by R.W. Apple, Jr.

as in Congress and in the federal judiciary.

ABSCAM SCANDAL

Among the many Congressional scandals was Abscam. It broke in February 1980 when the FBI released video pictures of Congressmen[539] taking bribes from an FBI agent posing as an Arab Sheik. Abscam's intent was to expose political corruption, especially of those members of Congress who incurred the displeasure of Justice Department officials. A United States Senator and seven members of the House of Representatives, as well as a number of private attorneys and state and local officials, were implicated as a result of the video taped sting operation.

SHOOTING AMERICAN CITIZENS

In response to Justice Department requests, members of Congress proposed legislation in mid-1989 to authorize federal employees to shoot down private aircraft suspected of drug trafficking, and granting immunity to those federal agents doing the shooting. The legislation provided that if private aircraft do not respond to signals from an intercepting aircraft, they can be legally shot down, even though the pilot of the plane being shot down either did not see, hear, or understand the signals. The Senate voted to authorize the Customs Service and other federal agencies in August 1989 to fire upon small planes that did not respond to interception, making possible the deaths of entire families. This is the type of mindset making possible the Waco massacre and the many other killings on a smaller scale.

SHAM WHISTLE-BLOWER "PROTECTIONS"

This saga of corruption shows the urgent need for legislation protecting and encouraging whistle-blowing against corruption by federal officials and personnel. Past legislation was rendered valueless by placing people in charge of the program who gutted it. In 1978 the Civil Service Reform Act created the Office of Special Counsel (OSC) for the purpose of protecting whistle-blowers from reprisals, and to prosecute those who retaliate. President Reagan gutted the office by appointing Alex Kozinski to head the OSC, and who openly violated the intent and the specifics of the legislation. Nearly half of the office personnel and seventy percent of the attorneys and investigators at the OSC either resigned or were fired. During that time over 7000 federal employees sought assistance from the OSC only two cases were filed, and these were limited to job reinstatement, carefully avoiding any mention of the epidemic government corruption.

"The OSC failed to meet its Congressional mandate," said Senator Levin on February 5, 1987, when he introduced the Whistleblower Protection Act of 1987. "It has not protected employees who have been the victims of unfair personnel practices, and its failure to do so is a reason why federal employees remain afraid to blow the whistle." Congresswoman Patricia Schroeder of Colorado introduced legislation in 1987, known as the Contractor Whistle-blower Protection Act, stated: "We urge [whistleblowers] to come forward;

---

[539] Among those convicted in Abscam included Representatives John M. Murphy (New York); Michael J. Myers (Pennsylvania); Frank Thompson, Jr (New Jersey); Raymond F. Lederer (Pennsylvania); John Jenrette (South Carolina); Richard Kelly (Florida); and Senator Harrison A. Williams, Jr.

we hail them as the salvation of our budget trauma, and we promise them their place in heaven. But we let them be eaten alive."

She should know. I described to her the details of these scandals and the actions taken to silence me through criminal misuse of the federal agencies over which she had oversight responsibilities. She never responded. Representative Barbara Boxer of California promoted the whistleblower legislation and refused to meet her responsibilities when I notified her of the same epidemic corruption that I had brought to Boxer's attention. None of them responded to their responsibility under federal criminal statutes or their oversight responsibilities.

The Cavello Foundation in Cambridge, Massachusetts, who allegedly assists whistle-blowers, wouldn't act when I brought the same information to them. I contacted the government Accountability Project in Washington on June 30, 1988, supplying them with the information, and they wouldn't get involved. GAP staff associate Carina Campobasso expressed concern when I talked to her on the phone, but her subsequent letter stated there was a case-freeze in effect which prevented them from taking on new cases. The massive corruption and harm inflicted upon the United States certainly warranted an exercise of a greater sense of responsibilities than that excuse showed.

A classic example of the need of whistle-blower legislation was the Challenger blowup on January 28, 1986, in which seven astronauts were killed, including school teacher Christa McAuliffe. Following highly sensitive testimony given by engineers from Morton Thiokol, who designed and manufactured the Challenger's solid rocket booster, the engineers were transferred, harassed, and terminated. *Multinational Monitor* stated in its May 1987 issue the consequences of blowing the whistle on the Challenger disaster:

> *Because of the growing reaction to OSC inaction, hostility to its intended mission, and ineffectiveness, Senators Carl Levin, D-Mich., Charles Grassley, R-Iowa, and David Pryor, D-Arkansas, and Representatives Schroeder and Frank Horton, R-N.Y., have spearheaded new reform efforts. These reforms would clarify the role of the Special Counsel as a protector of whistleblowers, not protector of "the merit system."*

The engineers opposed the launching because of their concern about the cold weather's effect on the O-ring seals. They testified that on the eve of the launch, they argued with their own superiors and NASA officials to postpone the launch, without success.

The greatest example of the need for meaningful whistleblower protection is the felony persecution of the whistleblowers in my group, consisting of, among others, Russbacher, Rewald, Riconosciuto, Webb, Abbott, Russell Bowen, John Cole, myself, and others.

For all this corruption to take place, it is necessary for every check and balance, including the watchdog agencies in government, to feloniously cover up, refuse to perform their duty, and obstruct justice. Senate investigators reported in September 1990 that federal inspector generals, who have the responsibilities to uncover and root out wrongdoings in government agencies, usually cover up the misconduct and intimidate those who want to expose it. The report cites "a disturbing pattern of misconduct" by Inspector Generals in a broad array of federal agencies. The report, prepared by Senator Jim Sasser (D-Tenn), chairman of the Subcommittee on General Services, Federalism, and the District of Columbia, stated that the "watchdogs have become political lap dogs."

The report states that instead of meeting its lawful responsibilities, "many Inspector General offices are engaged in damage control for their agencies and political patrols; or are knee deep in the very abuses they are supposed to prevent."

The Inspector-General system was created in 1978 to ferret out waste, fraud, and abuse in government, and to provide a safe harbor for those dedicated federal employees who try to stop government misconduct. As usual, it has been identified as a failure.

REVOLVING DOOR SYNDROME

Part of the reason for influence peddling and corruption arises from the revolving door syndrome. It is seen in many scandals, including HUD, the savings and loan, Defense Department, and in air safety. Ignoring regulatory violations by government employees seeking employment with industry is an accepted fact of life.[540] A *Wall Street Journal* article described government officials appearing before industry groups that are affected by their decisions, seeking clients after their departure from government or for employment positions. These government officials act while in government positions to protect their future benefactors. The revolving door problems were described in a *This World* article on June 2, 1985:

[A] quality control officer nearing the end of a military career was likely to keep his mouth shut if he spotted a problem with a company that might offer him a job after retirement. ... People are frequently looking for the next job, and you're going to do things that make that next job easier to get. ... a Department of Defense attorney ... acknowledged that there was "a lot of concern" about the issue at the

---

[540] NTSB chairman Webster Todd became director of ALPA's department of engineering and air safety; FAA Administrator Butterfield became employed by IASCO, an aviation concern near San Francisco; FAA Administrator Najeebe Halaby became president of Pan American World Airways; FAA chief counsel Bert Goodwin became director of regulatory affairs at ALPA headquarters in Washington; FAA Administrator John Shaffer became a director at Beech Aircraft Corporation; FAA official John Baker became head of the Aircraft Owners and Pilots Association; Donald Madole left the NTSB's Bureau of Aviation Safety to become a partner in a key law firm that profited from airline-crash litigation; NTSB Board member Hogue went with Airline Passengers Association; the bankruptcy judge who ruled favorably for Continental Airlines then left the bench and joined the law firm representing Continental; Robert Remley, a former FAA official who ruled favorably in a 1984 safety audit of Continental (despite contrary inspector reports), went with Continental. Those going to Texas Air Corporation included Richard Hirst as Vice President, who was a former attorney with the CAB; Clark Onstad, Vice President and Chief Lobbyist, who was former Chief Counsel with the FAA; Dewey Roark, General Counsel, who was formerly Special Counsel for regulations in the FAA. The government officials going to Eastern Airlines included John Keyser, Vice President for Regulatory Compliance at Eastern, and former FAA attorney and official (with whom I worked in the FAA in the early 1960s); Phillip Bakes as President and Chief Executive Officer at Eastern Airlines, was former Chief Counsel of CAB, was former counsel to the Congressional Committee which wrote the Airline Deregulation law.

Department. ... [a company] comes around and offers him a job at $50,000 to $75,000 per year. If he stands up and makes a fuss about high cost and poor quality, [the company won't] come to him when he retires.

A *Wall Street Journal* investigative reporting article on January 4, 1989, addressed the revolving door problem:

Competition to Hire Officials Leaving government Is Fiercest for Pair of Lawyers From Trade Office. [Describing the high financial rewards received by government employees going with the industry they formerly regulated and giving as examples two government employees going with industry] it is reliably understood that they each will be paid upwards of $300,000 a year to launch an international trade practice at [a major law firm]."

Another front page *Wall Street Journal* article on January 31, 1989, described the rewards received by employees involved in the savings and loan corruption: "Revolving Door—S&L Mess Isn't All Bad, At Least for Lawyers Who Were Regulators." The article told of an attorney who left government to join a law firm and started at over triple what the government paid.

This reminds me of the Director of the Air Safety Investigative Branch of the Civil Aeronautic Board (now called the National Transportation Safety Board), to whom I reported the criminal activities associated with a series of ongoing airline crashes, and asked him to intervene: attorney Donald Madole. Instead of performing his duty, he covered up, with the result that the crashes and the deaths continued. Madole protected United Airlines, the FAA, the NTSB, and who knows who else. Madole left government service and reportedly became a multi-millionaire, and a partner in the law firm with whom he associated.[541]

Former Reagan aide, Michael Deaver, parlayed his government contacts after leaving government service, and was sentenced to prison for not waiting the required 12 months before using them. But this offense was peanuts compared to the hard crimes committed by those Justice Department attorneys prosecuting Deaver, and the federal judges hearing the case.

Speaking of departing government officials at the Bank Board who helped bring about the savings and loan fiasco, Representative Jim Leach stated: "My impression is that they'll all go out and earn a million dollars. The revolving door at the Bank Board makes the problems at the Pentagon look like peanuts."[542] The Revolving Door problem was addressed by *Newsweek* on February 6, 1989, describing middle and high level officials with the Federal Trade Commission who triple their former government salaries when accepting positions with corporations they formerly regulated.

The *Newsweek* article gave examples of the profitable revolving door syndrome. For instance, John Norris, former Deputy Commissioner, Food and Drug Administration, went from a government salary of $75,500 to an estimated $360,000 yearly salary. Gene Lucero, who supervised enforcement

---

[541] Speiser and Speiser.
[542] January 31, 1989 *Wall Street Journal.*

of Superfund and hazardous-waste laws against private companies, went from $75,000 to an estimated $190,000 a year salary. General Counsel for the Federal Trade Commission, Robert Paul, went from $78,000 to an estimated $240,000. The practice of cashing in their government contacts and knowledge, and working against the public interest, is epidemic.

Former Texas Senator John Tower left the Senate in 1985 after serving as Chairman of the Senate Armed Services Committee, and joined a high-powered consulting firm whose chief clients were major defense contractors. He was paid over $750,000 for his advice to contractors following a very short period of work.

Department of Transportation Secretary James Burnley left government service to join a prominent Washington law firm under suspicious circumstances. He was reported to be actively negotiating to become a member of the law firm of Shaw, Pittman, Potts & Trowbridge at the time he issued an important ruling in favor of Eastern Airlines, one of the firm's major clients in the transportation field.

Before leaving his government position in December 1987, Burnley took the unusual step of personally handling a request by the Air Line Pilots Association to defuse an issue relating to Burnley's new employer. ALPA requested that the Department of Transportation investigate Eastern's "continuing fitness" as a carrier in view of its continuing financial troubles. Such matters are usually dealt with at the Assistant-Secretary level. A week after Burnley intervened personally, he rejected the ALPA petition in a strongly worded order saying it "borders on abuse of the department's processes." He was misusing his government position to carry out the wishes of the airline represented by his future law firm who handled Eastern Airlines and another Texas Air subsidiary, Continental Airlines.

The Air Line Pilots Association accused Burnley of a conflict of interest, accusing him of seeking employment with two law firms having close ties to Eastern Airlines while at the same time denying ALPA's petition for a fitness examination of the airline.

As in each and every one of the other scandals, the country's most expensive attorneys frantically sought to protect their valuable clients.

ALTERING ELECTION RESULTS

In *Votescam*, authors James and Kenneth Collier explained the ease with which election results can be altered in the computerized voting machines. The authors describe how votes can be changed through pre-programmed computerized voting machines to favor a particular candidate. They charge that a cartel of bureaucrats, especially those in the CIA, the establishment media, members of Congress, decide in concert how America's votes are counted and by whom. The book describes how a private corporation, News Election Service (NES), with ties to the establishment media, control the counting of votes. If what they say is true, and it is not far-fetched, elections can be easily corrupted. The corrupt forces in government, and especially those in control of the CIA and Justice Department, can select the winner, regardless of the number of votes actually cast for the various candidates.

Votescam describes how, through the use of the computerized and programmed voting machines, votes can be altered by federal and state officials and government agencies, including the many U.S. intelligence agencies. The authors describe how isolated people, including journalists, are exposing this vote fraud, while the mass media keeps the lid on it, as they have done with almost every scandal described within these pages.

During telephone conversations with the Colliers, they stated that during their many talk show appearances they often recommend that the listeners also read *Defrauding America*. Their reasoning was that this book would make the readers aware of the rampant corruption within the United States and more receptive to accepting the statements made in *Votescam*.

CHAPTER THIRTY

CRIMES OF EPIDEMIC COVERUP

Under federal law it is a crime to cover up for a federal crime, or failure to promptly report information of the crime or crimes to a federal tribunal. The U.S. media and House and Senate members of both political parties kept the lid on every one of the scandals that others, and I, uncovered. Their felony coverup makes possible the continuation and escalation of the criminal activity and the harm inflicted upon the American people.

Even major book publishers engaged in coverup by refusing to print exposé books that address the criminal acts. Most of the large publishers are controlled by a relatively small number of conglomerates that control which books are published and which are banned. The conglomerates have interests throughout our society that are tied in with many of those in control of government and who would suffer financially if the truth came out and their financial contacts affected. These conglomerates do not want to lose these contacts or be adversely effected. An exposure of the vast corruption within these pages would adversely effect many publishers, television and radio networks, plus many individual radio and television stations.

I encountered the publishing house censorship in the mid-1960s, and had to self-publish each of my books to get the information to the public. The pattern of air safety and criminal acts that caused or allowed to occur many of the worst airline disasters would not have happened if the media met their responsibilities to report the valid charges and evidence that I offered. Many papers, such as the *Wall Street Journal*, have excellent investigators and articles, but the editorial sections engage in coverups.

My experience with coverup by NBC commenced in late 1977 when Alan Goldstein and Linda Ellerbee contacted me after reading the U.S. Supreme Court's refusal to vacate the lower court's dismissal of my action against the FAA. Unaware of previous NBC contacts and coverup, they expressed great interest in what I told them, asking for further details, which I sent. That was the end of that.

NBC was one of the media sources that had repeatedly distorted the facts in midair collisions between small planes and airliners, by claiming the small (and much slower) aircraft rammed into the airliner (that was traveling two or three times faster).

The media have people examining federal complaints after they are filed, reporting those that have public interest. They knew of my filings in the U.S. District Courts throughout the United States, which described the corruption described within these pages. Even in those federal actions against members of Congress, and against the U.S. Supreme Court Justices, associated with their coverup and refusal to perform a duty, nothing was printed in the media. The national issues were obviously of extreme importance.

During an appearance on Larry King's television program on June 28, 1989, Leo Demoore, the author of *Senatorial Privilege*, told of the coverup he witnessed as a reporter covering Kennedy's Chappaquiddick accident. He discussed the coverup by the press of the more sensitive and sordid parts of the scandal, claiming that although public attention forced news coverage, most if not all the papers omitted extremely serious misconduct by Kennedy and those who covered up for him, distorting what they did reveal. He said that the press protected Kennedy as much as possible. The press didn't want to hear anything that might blemish Kennedy's image. Demoore made it clear that both the press and the publishing houses wanted the matter kept as quiet as possible.

Demoore had a firm contract with Random House to publish the *Senatorial Privilege*, which had already been accepted in 1985. Suddenly, Random House refused to go to print, claiming they were dissatisfied with the contents, even though they had already expressed complimentary approval of the first half. Demoore felt that unknown people pressured Random House not to publish the book. Random House was also one of the publishers that had tentatively agreed to publish my first printing of *Unfriendly Skies*, and then suddenly refused to do so.

Another of many similar examples happened to journalist Peter Brewton, who had a firm contract with Doubleday to publish *The Mafia, CIA, and George Bush*. Despite assurances that the book would be published by the summer of 1992, before the presidential elections, Doubleday stalled, and then refused to proceed with publication. Brewton then had his book published by SPI Books, a division of Shapolsky Publishers.

CENSORSHIP BY THE PUBLISHING INDUSTRY?

When I finished the first manuscript of *Unfriendly Skies* in the late 1970s, I queried many publishers, several of whom requested to see a copy. Several publishers expressed interest in publishing the manuscript, but each suddenly canceled at the last minute. When Ballantine Publishing Company returned the manuscript, after showing a strong initial interest, they accidentally left an interoffice memorandum in the returned manuscript. One of the editors referred to the manuscript as a "blockbuster." And that first draft submitted in 1976 was mild compared to subsequent manuscripts.

The contents were too sensitive; no one wanted to touch the manuscript. Even when I became a self-publisher, a California book printer refused to print the book, fearing lawsuits. The next printing that came out in 1980 was even more sensitive than the first, and I didn't even bother to look for a publisher; I self-published. The second printing had the benefit of excellent book reviews by top reviewers, including the American Library Association and other influential book reviewers. The second printing also had the benefit of hundreds of talk show appearances, which publishing houses take into consideration in determining the marketability of the book. Still, no publisher would publish the book.

In 1988 I sent over thirty query letters to publishing houses to determine their interest in publishing the highly sensitive third printing of *Unfriendly Skies*. By that time the extent of the air disaster and superimposed government scandal was no secret to the news media. Not a single publisher expressed an interest in even looking at the manuscript. That was odd. In the mid-1960s when I offered the then-primitive manuscript to publishers, at least one out of three wanted to read it. In the late 1980s, when the public's interest was peaked due to the many airline crashes and air safety problems, no publisher was interested in my book. My credentials and exclusive insider knowledge qualified me to be one of the best possible authors for such a publication.

At this same time, a three-page *Time* magazine article in 1989 told of the demand for authors and non-fiction books, and the high bids to get public-interest material. The air safety crisis was a constant topic in the news and on talk shows. My manuscript was the **only** insider book on the subject, unlike any other air safety book.

Strangely, many in the media refused to accept prepaid advertising for my book. I sent prepaid advertisements to various newspapers after the first printing came out in 1978. These were unoffensive advertisements simply listing the title of the book, the price, reviewer's comments, and the address at which it could be ordered. No one could have been offended by that ad.

The newspapers that rejected the book advertisements included the supermarket tabloids that are not exactly the pillars of authenticity, including the *Globe*, *Enquirer*, *Weekly World News*, *Sun*, and others. I couldn't understand how these papers could reject my pre-paid ads when it was their standard practice to print such preposterous articles under such titles as: "Docs Deliver Baby Frozen 600 years;" or "Five Year Old Girl Delivers Baby;" or "Girl Gives Birth To Baboon's Baby! Healthy Newborn Has An Ape's Body—and a Human Brain!" A February 6, 1990, headline in the tabloid *Sun* contained the bizarre "Girl, 6, Gives Birth to a 22-lb. Baby." Even the *Wall Street Journal* refused to accept my advertisements, refusing to give me a reason when I asked. The *Airline Pilot Magazine*, which routinely carries classified ads for aviation related books, refused to accept my advertisements.

A year before I self-published *Defrauding America* I sent out over thirty query letters to every major publisher in the United States, describing the contents and the input from many deep-cover whistleblowers. Almost always a publisher will respond, even if it is with a letter stating they weren't interested. Almost every publisher refused to even do this with my query letters. Very possibly they didn't want to be identified with having refused to assist in getting this sensitive information to the public if the treasonous activities should ever break into the open.

In late 1992 one of the editors for Sheridan Square Press contacted me after being referred by Ari Ben-Menashe of *Profits of War*, asking that I send him some material concerning my manuscript on *Defrauding America*. I sent them an early chapter on the October Surprise, which contained many statements made by CIA operative Russbacher, including the role played by Israel and the Mossad. I never heard from them again, despite four subsequent letters. In April 1993 I requested the chapter back from them that I had sent, and they wouldn't even answer that letter, or send the material back.

SOME IN THE PUBLISHING INDUSTRY
PAID WITH THEIR LIVES FOR THE COVERUP

Among the members of the publishing industry who knew of the air safety corruption that I reported, and whose silence made possible its continuation, were *Playboy* officials. I offered *Playboy* my manuscript in the mid-1970s, depicting the ongoing air safety and government corruption and its relationship to several recent air disasters. They didn't accept the manuscript, or publish any articles on the pattern of corruption I described. Several years later several *Playboy* officials perished in the Chicago DC-10 tragedy resulting from problems that their publicity could have corrected.

After the Chicago DC-10 crash, *Playboy* published a nineteen-page air safety article that complained of the status of air safety, but totally omitted the underlying corruption that brought on the problems. But the article concealed the hard-core safety misconduct that must be addressed before any meaningful corrective actions can be taken. The article was entitled, "Airline Safety, A Special Report," and stated in part:

The closer you look at airline travel, the more it looks like a game of angels and great good luck, rather than skill and know-how and high technology. ... based on the same statistical manipulations, it was safer to walk the tightrope than fly his planes and it was also safer to repair your roof then to take a bath. ... Statistics can devil the hell out of you if you let them, but you pay your money and you take your chances, and in this game, undelivered goods are nonreturnable.

Even the airline pilot's magazine refused to accept advertisement for the book, which could have exposed and corrected the problems that killed many of their own members. The Air Line Pilots Association refused to accept advertisement for my first book. It was ironic that the Association lost a former president, Clarence Sayen, in the United 727 crash into Lake Michigan. This crash was a typical consequence of the rampant irregularities at United Airlines in which their own pilots were victims of the corruption. The Union still wouldn't expose the misconduct, apparently preferring to sacrifice their own members rather than blow the whistle on this sordid scandal. ALPA repeatedly blocked my efforts to improve the safety problem responsible for the death of its former president, many of its pilots, and thousands of people.

BUYING MEDIA COVERUP

Manipulating the news was described in a *Harper's* magazine article (July 1989), explaining in part why I encountered the news gridlock. The article

stated how politicians leak the "news" to favored reporters, who then recipro-
cate by rarely reporting unfavorable articles about those who give them the
"news." The article described the government oligarchy in which power vests
in a few persons, doling out "news." *Harper's* stated:

> By their subjugation of the press, the political powers in America have
> conferred on themselves the greatest of political blessings—Gyges'
> ring of invisibility.

The article detailed how some of the most momentous stories of our times
never get reported, relating the fear of offending government officials who are
the source of a majority of the news stories. The reporters, and their papers,
do not want to lose the benefit of these government news sources.

The release of news by powerful Washington figures is described as a
soup kitchen, where reporters go to get many of their articles. The article told
how self-serving politicians bully and threaten employees of news gathering
agencies not to print a story.

The *Harper's* article described how the CIA's domestic spying under the
transparent guise of "counterintelligence" was kept from the public by the
press for at least ten years, and how the *Associated Press* fired a reporter who
printed the true side of a particular story that was fabricated by Assistant
Secretary of Defense Arthur Sylvester. The story infuriated Sylvester, who
then called the reporter's boss at the AP, who then fired the reporter.
Sylvester was reported to be "the master of the soup kitchen at the time."

Several days after Nixon's reelection, White House aide Charles Colson,
in charge of handing out news releases and intimidating the press, was
infuriated when CBS viewers heard Walter Cronkite detail the high-level
campaign of political sabotage and espionage. Colson called William Paley,
Board Chairman of CBS, and warned him that if they did not stop the second
program, CBS would be stripped of the licenses to operate its five lucrative
television stations. CBS watered down the next show, but not enough to please
Colson. Colson again called Paley, threatening to use the White House's
power to ruin CBS on Wall Street and Madison Avenue. "We'll break your
network," Colson warned. CBS kept these threats and their significance, from
the American public, compounding the harm inflicted upon the American
people.

A January 15, 1990, *Newsweek* article stated that "while the White House
press corps waited to be spoon-fed instructions, scandals in housing programs
and savings and loan regulation went unreported." The article continued:

> No administration really wants reporters snooping through the
> Agriculture Department or other places they can break new ground;
> better to have them hanging around the White House briefing room,
> waiting for handouts. It's this system, rather than any particular
> handler or press secretary, that conditions and corrodes Washington
> coverage. That's why it's up to reporters to redefine the concept of
> news so that it relies more on what they find, and less on what the
> president—or his press secretary—would have them believe.

Occasionally the system goes out of whack, such as in Watergate. For weeks,
most newspapers kept the lid on the relatively minor scandal (compared to

those described in these pages), until the *Washington Post* stirred up public interest to the point where the press could not ignore the drum-beating.

In *The CIA and the Cult Of Intelligence*, the authors describe the pressure and threats upon newspaper and book publishers not to publish matters adversely reflecting upon the CIA or other government agencies. The book tells of the planting of moles in the news media, including radio and television networks, and the pressure not to report government misconduct.

NEWS DISTORTION AND COVERUP

In an in-depth investigative report that is as true today as the day it was published (July 25, 1967), the *Wall Street Journal* described the news distortion and coverup: "*Ethics & the Press*, Conflicts of Interest, Pressures Still Distort Some Papers' Coverage." The in-depth article told how "Advertisers and outside work of newsmen color stories," thereby halting investigations. The article stated in part:

> In Boston and Chicago, newspaper investigations into suspected hanky-panky suddenly are aborted. In one case, a subject of inquiry turns out to be a stockholder of the paper and friend of the publisher. In the other, the investigation threatens to embarrass a politician who could help the paper in a building project.
>
> In Denver, the advertising staff of a big daily wrestles with an arithmetic problem. A big advertiser has been promised news stories and pictures amounting to 25 percent of the ad space it buys; the paper already has run hundreds of column inches of glowing prose but is still not close to the promised allotment of "news" and now is running out of nice things to say.

SHORT-CHANGED READERS

> All this hardly enhances the image of objectivity and fierce independence the U.S. press tries so hard to project. Yet talks with scores of reporters, editors, publishers, public relations men and others reveal that practices endangering—and often subverting—newspaper integrity are more common than the man on the street might dream. Result: The buyer who expects a dime's worth of truth every time he picks up his paper often is short-changed.
>
> All newspapers, including this one, must cope with the blandishments and pressures of special interests who seek distortion or omission of the truth. ... on some papers the trouble starts at the top; it is the publisher himself who lays down news policies designed to aid one group or attack another.
>
> It is plain, however, that a sizable minority [or is it majority] of newspapers still are putty in the hands of their advertisers, that they allow personal as well as business considerations to favor the news to a marked degree, ... that they tolerate staff practices hardly conducive to editorial independence and objectivity. ... blackouts of news involving newspapers are quite common; hardly a working journalist could deny that one of the gravest weaknesses in coverage exhibited by the American press is its coverage of itself. ... another grave fault of a good many papers: Favoritism toward business in general and

advertisers in particular. ... the paper itself, by actual policy or common practice, distorts the news to suit advertisers or literally hands over news space to them. ... Everyone in newspapering pays lip service to the ideal that a paper's news columns should not be for sale, ...a staffer is "on the take" ...

Giving a toast in 1953 before the New York Press Club, the former Chief of Staff of the *New York Times*, John Swinton, stated:[543]

There is no such thing, at this date of the world's history, in America, as an independent press. You know it and I know it. ... The business of the journalist is to destroy truth; To lie outright; To pervert; To vilify; To fawn at the feet of mammon, and to sell his country and his race for his daily bread. You know it and I know it, and what folly is this toasting an independent press? ... Our talents, our possibilities and our lives, are all the property of other men. We are intellectual prostitutes.

The *Wall Street Journal* article described the news distortion of virtually every media in the United States, caused by pressures from vested-interest groups and from financial benefits. The Federal Communications Commission charged NBC-TV with falsely presenting the facts associated with general aviation and airline problems in midair collisions. The FCC charged the NBC staff with twisting and distorting its coverage of the midair collisions, favoring the airlines by distorting the facts. The FAA ordered NBC to take "appropriate steps to achieve fairness," and cease distorting the facts.

I encountered a constant pattern of coverup by the establishment media, starting in the mid-1960s and continuing to this very day. During the sixties when I had hard-core evidence linking criminal misconduct by officials at United Airlines and the FAA with recent airline crashes, none would report the evidence I presented. These media coverups continued into the 1980s and 1990s, and exist at this very moment.

In February 1988, I gave two reporters[544] for the *San Francisco Chronicle* details of the corruption that I had uncovered, providing them with supporting documents. These reporters contacted a friend of mine, falsely stating that they did not write an article on the matters I brought to their attention because I refused to give them supporting material. That was a lie. I had supplied them with a great deal of written material, and withheld nothing. I described to them the corruption I discovered in the aviation area, in Chapter 11 courts, and the persecution judicially inflicted upon me to block my exposure activities. I referred them to specific federal filings at San Francisco and Sacramento that further described the corruption that I had found, and which were now of judicial record. Instead of reporting these charges, they kept the lid on the scandal, making possible the continued corruption against the American people.

"The Complicity of Silence" was the heading on an article in *Lies of Our Times* (June 1993), as it related to the media coverup of the U.S. directed

---

[543] *Contact*, July 20, 1993.
[544] Jeff Palline and Bill Wallace.

assassinations occurring in Central America and particularly the El Mozote massacre in El Salvador (December 1981). The article described how *New York Times* reporter Raymond Bonner sent an article to the home office describing the brutal assassination at El Mozote, primarily of women and children, by the U.S.-trained Atlaeatl Battalion. Bonner was at the assassination site, and personally interviewed the handful of survivors. He then became the target of a media smear campaign to discredit him and to remove him from his reporting activities.

Wall Street Journal editor Robert Bartley savagely attacked Bonner and his reports and especially the one on February 19, 1982. The *Wall Street Journal's* attack upon Bonner caused other newspapers and magazines to instruct their reporters to keep the lid on the massacre, insuring that the massacre of other civilians would continue. The *Wall Street Journal* editorial caused one major newspaper to send copies of that editorial to its correspondents in Central America warning them: "Let's not let this happen to us."

The editors of *Times* then transferred Bonner out of the Central America assignment to quiet him. On March 15, 1993, the U.N.-sponsored Truth Commission on El Salvador released its report on the El Mozote massacre, proving that the massacre had occurred, that it was directed by the CIA, all of which the U.S. media had known and covered up for years.

Earlier in these pages I said the *St. Louis Post Dispatch* sought to cover up for the downing of the U.S. Navy helicopter at Fort Ord that killed three Naval officers from the Pegasus group in the Central Intelligence Agency.

SIMULTANEOUS WRITINGS ON TRAGEDIES, AND COVERUP OF THEIR CAUSES

The press repeatedly prints articles on the sufferings arising from air disasters, while concurrently covering up for the misconduct that made the crashes possible. Some of the best researched articles on the human sufferings associated with air tragedies have been published by the investigative reporters of the *Wall Street Journal*, while simultaneously covering up for the corruption that made the brutalities possible. From 1965 through 1988, I repeatedly made the *Wall Street Journal* aware of the corruption related to a series of specific airline crashes. But instead of publishing the information I gave to them, they covered up, making possible the continuation of the very serious violations I had uncovered.

An article in *Aviation Week & Space Technology* on May 1, 1989 reported:

ATA President Blasts U.S. government's Failure to Reform Aviation Agency. The article stated "The U.S. government has failed inexcusably to respond to reforms recommended by the Aviation Safety Commission a year ago," according to Robert J. Aaronson, the new head of the Air Transport Assn.

The basis for these charges is a fraction of the actual misconduct. No one can blow the whistle on anyone else, without implicating themselves, or vested and protected interests.

PRESSURE ON ADVERTISERS TO REMAIN SILENT

Following a series of Delta Air Line incidents in mid-1987, Delta put financial pressure on the media to stop reporting the many near-crashes of its aircraft. Delta threatened to cancel valued advertising accounts with the newspapers and radio stations making these reports. An *Associated Press* article (August 13, 1987) described Delta's threats to cancel large blocks of advertising. Delta responded by saying there was a "misunderstanding." What else could they say?

Yearly advertising budgets for a major airline approaches one hundred million dollars, insuring that any newspaper, radio station or network will withhold any unfavorable information if possible. Federal Express dropped its ads on ABC prime-time television network after a critical report on ABC's 20/20. The program[545] reported Federal Express mishandled government and military documents and packages, and that drug activities were rampant at the airline.

Federal Express's President Frederick Smith wrote (July 14, 1989) that the company was canceling its prime-time advertising, with the exception of commercials scheduled for the ABC telecast of the World Series and Monday Night Football. Federal Express spent over $40 million a year on advertising, according to the Standard Directory of Advertisers, an industry publication. In another letter, President Smith wrote that this cancellation would cost ABC "in excess of $100 million". It's easy to understand how the news media hesitate to print anything that would dissatisfy a valuable customer.

An *Air Transport World* article (March 1970) described the value of airline advertising: "Airlines are a major source of ad revenue." Airlines such as Delta run full-page ads in the *Wall Street Journal*, which rarely runs articles detrimental to the airlines' interests.

Boston radio station WHDH discovered the consequences of offending Procter & Gamble. The station had broadcast the activities of a local citizen group that were critical of one of the company's products. Procter & Gamble then pulled local ads for all of its products from the station, resulting in the loss of $1 million of advertising revenue. Procter & Gamble reportedly warned that it would pull commercials from any station broadcasting the announcement from the citizen group.[546] The newspaper article stated: "P&G's message reinforced what station managers already believed: don't criticize business, and stay away from controversial topics, or it will cost the station business. Actions such as Procter & Gamble's don't have to happen often before media outlets become self-censoring."

Car makers retaliate against magazines printing articles reporting weaknesses or defects in their products. General Motors, for instance, withdrew advertising for three months after a magazine's editor, David E. Davis, delivered a speech against the auto maker concerning the closure of twenty-one plants, eliminating 74,000 jobs. Toyota Motor Corporation withdrew ads after its models did not make *Road and Track*'s 1991 list of "10 Best List." The loss of this type of advertising can make the difference between profit and loss.

---

[545] *New York Times*, October 18, 1989 report of July 7, 1989 show.
[546] April 1, 1991 San Francisco *Daily Journal*.

THE ADVERTISING DOLLAR MAKES
SMALL PLANES FLY BACKWARDS

The multi-million-dollar advertising revenues may explain the uncanny media reporting of the "ability" of small planes to fly backwards, or catching up and ramming into a jetliner traveling at twice their speed. The news media had attributed this remarkable feat to small planes and their pilots in numerous midair collisions. In the PSA San Diego midair collision, the airliner actually rammed the small plane from the rear. But the news media reported that the small plane crashed into the jet. In the Cerritos midair collision, the DC-9 jet, flying in a northerly direction, rammed into the side of the small plane that was on an easterly heading. The news media reported the small plane crashed into the jetliner. A *Time* article of September 15, 1986, showed the east-bound small plane on a southerly heading toward the oncoming jet, instead of its actual heading of easterly, away from the jet. This misinformation placed the blame for the midair collision on the small plane pilot.

Most of the media would not report anything about the all-night crew partying in the PSA San Diego crash, or the many other wrongdoings.

A *San Francisco Examiner* article by Mark Hertsgaard[547] criticized the press for "framing the news according to what the movers and shakers of official Washington wanted, rather than thinking through the relevant issues for themselves, and [holding] the national political dialogue hostage to the debate within the Washington policy elite." He added, "Journalists got so carried away that instead of being honest brokers of information, many fell into the role of Pentagon cheerleader."

COVERUP IS PROFITABLE

It is unprofitable for the media to report corruption involving those who provide advertising revenue to them, making it profitable for the media to cover up for corruption, regardless of the consequential harm made possible by the coverup. For instance, a disproportionate amount of corruption in the HUD and savings and loan scandals was committed by a group in Denver that included Richmond Homes and MDC Holdings, and its many subsidiaries that were heavy advertisers. This group provided a major share of advertising revenue for the two major newspapers in the Denver area, *Rocky Mountain News* and the *Denver Post*. If either one of the two newspapers reported the corruption, they would lose significant revenue, and subject themselves to government retaliation through any one of numerous government agencies. The indifference of the American public, their ignorance concerning government corruption, their failure to respond in a meaningful manner, doesn't exactly motivate a newspaper to go out on a limb.

MEDIA COVERUP AND DISINFORMATION

The *Washington Post* and reporter Bob Woodward enlarged a White House coverup of the two-bit Watergate burglary into a scandal all out of proportion, and then covered up for the scandals that were a thousand times more serious. The same *Washington Post* kept the lid on the CIA involvement

---

[547] December 30, 1990. Author of *On Bended Knee: The Press and the Reagan Presidency.*

in Watergate, October Surprise, drug trafficking, and the scandals described within these pages. The *Washington Post* and reporter Woodward covered up for CIA-related criminal activities that were far worse than Watergate.

A *Washington Post* article (June 22, 1992) misstated facts relating to the 1980 October Surprise operation. Reporter Bob Woodward and John Mintz sought to squelch the October Surprise story by discrediting CIA whistleblowers and their statements about the October Surprise. Intelligence agency newsletters and magazines described the *Washington Post* as having close ties to the CIA.

Committee Chairman Charles Rangel (D-NY) charged the *Washington Post* with misleading reporting in the Iran-Contra affair. The CIA was after President Nixon, and the *Washington Post* accommodated them. The *Post* also used Mark Hosenball to ridicule the idea that Oliver North and his CIA-associated renegades had done anything wrong, despite the overwhelming evidence that they financially supported the assassination squads and drug trafficking. The *Post* censored a Drew Anderson column describing the actions by Oliver North and his co-conspirators in the Iran-Contra affair, to defuse any public interest and concern into this scandal-riddled CIA operation. Anything unfavorable to the CIA was heavily censored by the *Post*.

WASHINGTON POST DISINFORMATION RIDICULING WHISTLEBLOWERS

The *Washington Post* (June 22, 1992) chastised Presidential candidate Ross Perot for attempting to expose what they implied were non-existing criminal activities by President George Bush, including Bush's role in October Surprise and its progeny, Iran-Contra. I wrote to Katherine Graham, the publisher of the *Washington Post*, pointing out the errors in the articles on October Surprise, advising her that I was a former federal investigator and that my CIA informants had given me considerable information that established the existence of that operation. My letter expressed the opinion that the *Washington Post*, including Bob Woodward, were involved in obstructing justice by the fact that they withheld data, supplied disinformation, and deliberately misstated facts. She did not respond.

The *Village Voice* duplicated the *Washington Post* tactics in an article written by former CIA asset Frank Snepp. The article stated that Russbacher did not know how to start the engines on the SR-71 and therefore could not have been the SR-71 pilot described in the October Surprise plot. Other segments of the media seeking to discredit the October Surprise scandal repeated Snepp's article as if it were proven to be true.

LEGAL PUBLICATION PROTECTING ITS NEWS SOURCE

The San Francisco legal newspaper, *Daily Journal*, was aware of the large-scale Chapter 11 corruption, and addressed it gingerly, carefully avoiding the high-level judicial corruption, and focusing only on the outer peripheral issues. They kept the lid on the judicial involvement in the corruption, protecting their primary sources of news articles. In one article the *Daily Journal* referred to me as a "disgruntled debtor," for my efforts to expose the Chapter 11 corruption that they knew existed, and for filing appeals and oppositions to the corrupt seizure and looting of my assets.

In another article (July 15, 1992) the *Daily Journal* eulogized U.S. District Judge Vaughn Walker, who played a key role in the obstruction of justice in Ninth Circuit courts. The article stated, "Judge Walker a Champion of Law." The *Daily Journal* knew the part played by Walker who aided and abetted the criminal contempt charges in retaliation for exercising my constitutional and statutory rights and responsibilities. In another article the *Daily Journal* eulogized California Court of Appeals Judge Donald King, who played a key role in carrying out the early attacks upon me, as described in earlier pages.

INVESTIGATIVE REPORTERS
SILENCED BY THEIR EDITORS

Marge Sloan, a free-lance investigative reporter who investigated the Denver-based group heavily implicated in the HUD and savings and loan scandals,[548] was told by numerous reporters who had written stories concerning the CIA involvement that their editors killed the articles they had prepared.

Pete Brewton of the *Houston Post*, author of *The Mafia, CIA, and George Bush*, wrote about the block put on many of his stories associating the looting of the savings and loans with the CIA and powerful politicians, including former Texas Senator Lloyd Bentsen (subsequently appointed to President William Clinton's cabinet).

A FEW COURAGEOUS NEWSPAPERS

Several of the alternative newspapers have courageously sought to expose the corruption in government. In some cases they exposed criminality by federal personnel that the mass media then had to address, at least in small part. Among the national newspapers noted for exposing corruption among federal officials that the establishment press covers up is the weekly *Spotlight*.[549] Many of the scandals described in these pages were first identified in the *Spotlight*.

Among those on a local level are included the *Napa Sentinel* (exposing for instance, October Surprise, Iran Contra, and other scandals); the *Arkansas Democrat* (exposing the vast arms and drug trafficking at Mena Airport in Arkansas); the *Houston Post* (who reported the CIA involvement in looting of the savings and loans until pressure caused them to drop the series); and *Playboy* (articles on October Surprise and the CIA). Excellent monthly publications are put out by former intelligence agency personnel, including *Unclassified*[550] and *Covert Action Quarterly*.[551] The problem is that only a relatively small percentage of the American public read these newspapers, magazines, and newsletters.

---

[548] Reference to defrauding the United States should be recognized as defrauding the residents who must pay for these great financial crimes and who suffer the consequences in resulting recessions and depressions.

[549] *Spotlight*, 316 Independence, S.E. Washington, D.C. 20003.

[550] *Unclassified* offices are at 2001 S Street NW, Suite 740, Washington, DC 20009.

[551] *Covert Action Quarterly* offices are at 1500 Massachusetts Ave., NW. # 732, Washington, D.C. 20005.

CENSORSHIP VIA JUSTICE DEPARTMENT THREATS

In early April 1992, the *Now It Can Be Told* show video taped Russbacher for about five hours, during which he described numerous CIA activities in which he participated. These details exposed serious criminal activities within government agencies. Cindy Fry[552] of the *Now It Can Be Told* show stated during a telephone conversation that the producers were warned by Justice Department personnel not to air the Russbacher tapes if they wanted to avoid the consequences. The show never aired, despite the expense involved in taking the crew from New York to the Missouri prison where the taping occurred. Fry added that many people at other network shows had also been threatened by Justice Department personnel not to air any of the Russbacher tapes.

A television station in Missouri had taped Russbacher in April 1992 and made several spot announcements advising the viewers that Russbacher's full taping would appear at ten p.m. over their Jefferson City and Columbia stations. Again, threats from Justice Department officials caused the station to cancel the showing.

The media can be threatened to censor the news in numerous ways:

1. Federal personnel in the Justice Department or other federal agencies can threaten to take retaliatory action against the media through the Federal Communication Commission, IRS, the FBI, or the Justice Department.

2. Refuse to renew their station license.

3. Withhold government business.

4. Withhold news.

5. Pressure advertisers to withdraw business.

6. Management threatening the talk show host.

COVERUP BY STATE OFFICIALS

When necessary, corruption by federal officials can be reinforced by state officials. California authorities aided in the coverup surrounding the killing of attorney Dexter Jacobson by refusing to conduct a meaningful investigation. West Virginia authorities aided in the coverup involving the killing of Danny Casolaro by destroying evidence. Missouri officials aided in the coverup of CIA corruption by removing evidence of CIA proprietaries from the corporate records, and by prosecuting Russbacher and causing his imprisonment. Arkansas officials, including Governor William Clinton, blocked an investigation into the CIA arms and drug trafficking at Mena, Arkansas, that had been demanded by local police and citizens. California authorities aided and abetted the scheme that commenced with the sham lawsuit against me by the covert Justice Department law firm described in earlier pages.

Fearing the consequences, or to benefit from working with those in control of key government agencies, corporate America set no shining example of integrity. Many of these corporations are fronts for the CIA, and find the relationship profitable. An example of this was the part played by the

---

[552] Ganyl Kaufman and Mary Ann Poors, on May 13, 1992.

Pepsico Corporation in the October Surprise scandal, and its drug processing laboratories in foreign countries.

ROSS PEROT COVERUP

Ross Perot appeared to be genuinely interested in helping public spirited causes, including trying to discover if there were any prisoners still alive from the Vietnam War. Perot had been contacted by several people for help in exposing the October Surprise operation, and arrangements were made for Perot to talk to Russbacher via a conference call using my phone. Early on February 7, 1992, Russbacher called me from prison,[553] and I put the call through to Perot in Dallas, as previously requested by Perot. The reason for Perot's interest in Russbacher was to determine if Russbacher sounded legitimate, and to determine if Russbacher was actually involved in the October Surprise operation. After Russbacher got off the phone, Perot and I continued the conversation. In response to Perot's questions I conveyed my confidence in Russbacher's statements, his CIA position, and his role in October Surprise.

Several weeks later, on February 25, 1992, my telephone rang and the caller said, "This is Ross Perot." He then made reference to the earlier phone call, and asked for further information on Russbacher, trying to determine in his mind Russbacher's credibility. I told him what I knew and how I had great confidence in Russbacher's statements.

Perot later appeared on the *Larry King Live* show[554] declaring an interest to run for the President of the United States. Shortly after that talk-show appearance, Perot sent several of his employees to Missouri to personally question Russbacher about the October Surprise operation and to determine if Russbacher actually knew how to fly an SR-71 aircraft. The media picked up on this event and ridiculed Perot for pursuing far-out conspiracy theories, showing the dangers of exposing serious corruption.

Following the visit by Perot's group to Russbacher, the rumor was out that Russbacher didn't even know how to start the engines of the SR-71. I had earlier obtained the formerly secret SR-71 pilot operating manual consisting of over 1,000 pages, and after studying it, questioned Russbacher about such matters as starting the engines. He knew how to start the engines and he knew the other questions that I asked concerning the aircraft. I wrote to Perot stating that he had a duty under federal crime-reporting statutes to expose the corruption that I and CIA whistleblowers had described to him, reminding him that it was his duty to speak out. He never answered.

NADER COVERUP

Ralph Nader's aviation group, consisting of attorneys, kept the lid on the scandal for years, while professing to be active in protecting the public's welfare. I contacted Nader and his group in the mid 1960s, asking for

---

[553] Justice Department officials had charged Russbacher with impersonating a naval officer while he and his wife were billeted at Castle Air Force Base, seeking to continue the imprisonment inflicted upon him as part of the Justice Department scheme to silence this high-ranking officer in the Office of Naval Intelligence and the CIA.

[554]. May 1992.

assistance to expose the corruption related to an ongoing series of airline crashes. Reuben Robertson, an attorney for the group, traveled from Washington to my residence near San Francisco, obtaining information from me. He admitted the gravity of the problem. Despite the recognition of the serious corruption, the Nader group did nothing to publicize and correct the matter. Robertson later accepted a position with the Civil Aeronautic Board, which had been heavily involved in the coverup.

Some years later, after leaving the CAB, Robertson and the Nader group filed a federal lawsuit under the Freedom of Information Act[555] against the FAA in the District of Columbia.[556] The complaint sought information on safety problems discovered during inspections by FAA Washington inspection teams. The FAA refused to release the information, saying it was confidential and against the national interest. This standard phrase to cover up for government corruption was especially bizarre in air safety matters. A federal judge upheld the FAA's position, and refused to require the information to be released. In 1988 I again contacted the Nader group concerning the worsening problems. They wouldn't answer.

A *Forbes* magazine cover story (September 17, 1990) portrayed Nader as overseer to a vast network of organizations financed in part by wealthy lawyers and special interest groups. The story reported Nader controlled twenty-nine organizations with combined revenues exceeding seventy-five million dollars. The *Forbes* article said that Nader had an "umbilical" connection with rich plaintiff's attorneys who receive huge fees in Nader-backed lawsuits against industry. In return, these law firms contribute to his "consumer" organizations.

ATTORNEY DOUBLE-TALK

A conference held in Washington on October 6, 7, 1988, was entitled, "How To prevent, Investigate, and Litigate Aircraft Disasters." One of the speakers on air safety included Donald Madole, a managing partner of one of the nation's largest aviation law firms specializing in airline crashes. Another speaker was Congressman James Oberstar, chairman of the House Investigations and Oversight Subcommittee of Public Works and Transportation—responsible for aviation safety. Another speaker was Richard Witkin, Transportation Editor for the *New York Times*. They all had something in common: coverup of the corruption that made many of the crashes possible.

Donald Madole was an attorney with the Federal Aviation Administration when my predecessor on the United Airlines assignment went to Washington seeking help in correcting the corruption. He was head of the NTSB accident investigating section when I reported additional corruption to him several years and many United Airline disasters later. He covered up for the corruption that made possible many of the subsequent crashes. Oberstar repeatedly refused to receive my evidence of the corruption involving the FAA, which was in his area of responsibility. The *New York Times* had

---

[555] Title 5 Section 552.

[556] *Robertson,III, et al., v. Butterfield, Administrator Federal Aviation Administration, et al.*, C.A. No. 72-2186.

covered up for the corruption that I brought to their attention from 1965 through 1992.

AIRLINE PILOT ASSOCIATION COVERUP (ALPA)

The ALPA knew about the corruption related to a series of airline crashes at United Airlines long before I came on the scene. They were further informed about it after I arrived at United Airlines in 1963. They continued the great American tradition of cover up and refusal to exercise basic responsibilities. As a result, many of their own pilots were killed, blamed for crashes that should have been blamed on corrupt airline and government officials. Their coverup made possible many more crashes and many more deaths from the criminal activities that they knew existed and that they didn't have the basic integrity to expose.

INTERNATIONAL SOCIETY OF
AIR SAFETY INVESTIGATORS

For many years I have been a member of the International Society of Air Safety Investigators (ISASI), whose purported function is air safety, reducing the frequency of airline crashes, and improving accident investigation techniques. This group knew about the corruption other inspectors found. They knew about the judicial actions taken to silence me. Not a single solitary move was taken by this group to either expose what others and I had discovered, or to intervene when I was being sent to prison in retaliation for reporting criminal activities.

At one time the group was composed primarily of present and former members of the FAA, NTSB, and airline pilots with an air safety function, but gradually allowed attorneys as members. At the time that I was being railroaded to prison for having reported the corruption, the San Francisco chapter was taken over by attorneys, the same group that kept the lid on the criminal activities and refused to come to my rescue.

TALK SHOW COVERUPS

At one time talk shows were my best source for exposing the corruption in government. I had appeared as guest on over 1,800 radio and television shows from 1978, when the first *Unfriendly Skies* was published, until about 1990. Suddenly, the talk show hosts that had repeatedly called in the past no longer did so. I sent out hundreds of flyers, as in the past, announcing my availability for the subject of my new book, and the response was silence. Talk show hosts who repeatedly requested my appearance and who had complimented me on my presentation suddenly went quiet, despite the greatly increased interest the topics were generating.

Coverup or news censorship by the radio and television networks was something I discovered in the mid-1960s, and it continues through the 1990s. One example occurred in 1977 when NBC's Alan Goldstein and then Linda Ellerbee contacted me after reading that the U.S. Supreme Court refused me a hearing following my petition for writ of certiorari relating to an action I filed against the FAA. Unaware of previous NBC coverup, they appeared very interested in what I told them and asked me to send further details, which I did. They never responded.

Sudden cancellation of my scheduled appearance was not rare. The producer of one radio station program called me several hours before the show was to start and cancelled my appearance, stating the host was sick. Due to poor coordination, I was later called about two minutes before the start of the show and told to stand by. When I replied, "I thought the show was canceled," the caller checked, and then advised that it had been canceled.

Los Angeles KABC talk-show-host Michael Jackson canceled my appearance hours before I was to appear. As the government corruption became worse in the late 1980s, these cancellations increased in frequency, even though the stations that did not cancel often-times went out of their way to state the seriousness of, and the interest in, the matters we discussed. Radio stations, as with many other business enterprises, receive revenue or licensing from government personnel, and retaliation can easily occur, either directly or indirectly.

"You can't Say Anything Against United Airlines!"

Radio and television stations frequently reminded me not to say anything unfavorable about a major airline, and especially United Airlines. I was to appear on NBC's *Tomorrow* Show, and given a date to appear. During this initial conversation the producer stated that I could not say anything against United Airlines because NBC had a very profitable advertising account with United. I replied that I would concentrate on the misconduct within the two government air safety agencies. But before the appearance I was called and told not to appear.

San Francisco's radio stations, where much of the judicial and Justice Department corruption exists, played their part in the coverup. I sent notices to most of the radio stations in the San Francisco and Sacramento areas, advising them of the contents of *Defrauding America*, and of my availability to speak on the subjects. Despite the extremely serious nature of the charges, my credibility and that of my CIA sources, and the support of the excellent book reviews, not a single one allowed me to appear.

An analogy might be the report of a bomb on a fully loaded 747 scheduled for a departure, and no one would allow the report to be known. These stations knew that if even a small part of the charges were true, that there existed an ongoing scheme inflicting great harm upon the United States and the American people. Their coverup amounted to an obstruction of justice, making them co-conspirators with the very people they were shielding.

When Gary Sick, author of *October Surprise*, appeared as a guest on KGO,[557] a listener called and asked about Gunther Russbacher. Before Sick could respond the host quickly stated that Russbacher had been totally discredited, claiming he did not know how to start the engines on the SR-71. I wrote to the KGO host, explaining that I had quizzed Russbacher on the SR-71, that he did know how to start the engines. I asked the host what information he used to discredit Russbacher and the October Surprise charges. He refused to answer.

---

[557] June 1992.

An interesting incident occurred with Stewart Webb and free-lance investigative reporter Margie Sloan as they appeared on radio station KABC in Los Angeles, on the Michael Jackson show (February 11, 1992). It was being hosted on that date by Dr. David Viscott. The show centered around what the guests learned by examining thousands of documents linking the infamous Silverado Bank Savings and Loan to the CIA, money laundering, and drug trafficking. These dramatic revelations exposed what Justice Department attorneys, White House officials, and much of the media, had sought to keep from the American public.

After the host took a break for a commercial, he disconnected the guests. When the host returned, he shifted the subject to a ball game format, acting as if the guests had never appeared. One listener, finding the guests extremely interesting, called two friends at the beginning of the show to have them listen.

That listener, Ralph Bluthenthal, a former Los Angeles policeman, and Director of the General James Doolittle USO Lounge near the Los Angeles International Airport, subsequently phoned KABC and was told that the two guests had never been on the air. His prior law enforcement background prompted Bluthenthal to call his two friends once again to determine if they had heard the same series of events that he had heard. Upon confirmation, he then called KABC to discover what happened, and was given the run-around by different people. KABC program manager John Dolsa stated "the interview never occurred."

Bluthenthal then asked, "Does that mean, if I request tapes or transcripts of that show, I can't get them?" Dolsa responded, "That show didn't happen." After being cut off, Margie Sloan called KABC and learned that the FBI had contacted the station during the show and warned station personnel to remove the guests.

I had been on KABC's Ray Briem show from midnight to five a.m. the night before and was of course critical of United Airlines. Jackson scheduled a United Airlines pilot and author, John Nance, as guest to follow my appearance a few hours later. Nance's position was that everything was just fine in the aviation field. Other pilots who had been on talk shows with Nance stated to me they found Nance to be constantly covering up for the problems and misconduct as if he was paid to do so.

I had been a guest on KABC numerous times with Ray Briem for five hours at a stretch, and the show was always well received. However, as the scandals of the 1980s escalated, KABC halted my appearances.

KNOWINGLY DUPLICATING MY TITLE

One of the publishing houses to whom I offered my nearly-completed manuscript, *Unfriendly Skies*, in 1988 was Bantam-Doubleday. I inquired whether they would be interested in publishing my manuscript containing highly sensitive material on government corruption, advising them that it will continue carrying the *Unfriendly Skies* title. I also stated that if no publishing house would publish it, I would self-publish. Doubleday responded they were not interested in the subject matter. You can imagine my surprise when I saw the title of *my* book, *Unfriendly Skies*, heavily promoted on the *Today Show* on April 26, 1989. Instead of listing me as the author, it showed the authors to be an airline pilot identified as Captain X and writer Reynolds Dodson.

Doubleday obviously knew my book existed from our prior contacts and its listing in *Books in Print*. They were also aware that I spent years promoting it as a public service to expose government corruption, and that its publication sought to generate public interest in bringing a halt to the ongoing air tragedies. Doubleday published the book using the same title, *Unfriendly Skies*, which I had published for the past decade, and which is listed in trade publications. Doubleday heavily promoted their book as an exposé, expending money far beyond that which was justified by its contents. Doubleday publicized the highly sensitive nature of the book, and because of that alleged fact, the pilot's name was withheld. Captain X appeared on television via computerized composites of his face, to keep his identity secret. It was a good advertising gimmick, but the contents of the book certainly didn't require that secrecy.

It was a snow job to deceive the public. The book didn't contain any specifics, nothing of a sensitive nature, and did not warrant a pseudo author. The book dealt heavily with the dating habits of flight attendants and ramblings by a pilot, suggesting limited experience. Pilots have said to me that they heard Captain X was a United Airlines pilot.

The duplication of a title that was being promoted by an air safety activist for the last decade, periodically updated, was a blatant misrepresentation, deceiving the public. Possibly it was intended to divert attention from my next printing of the same name. And if so, these tactics were contributing factors to continued safety problems and protected the people implicated in the past crash-related misconduct.

Several hours before Captain X appeared on the May 1, 1989, *Larry King Live* show, I talked to Pat Piper, an associate producer on the show, and reminded him *I* was the author of *Unfriendly Skies*, and that Doubleday copied my title. I felt King should address this deception during the show. Piper replied that he had read Doubleday's *Unfriendly Skies*, and complained about its absence of substance, stating he didn't know why Captain X was asked to appear.

King didn't ask Captain X why he copied my title. King did ask why all the secrecy for a book that was rather bland, and portrayed air safety as being in good shape, contrary to the heavy book promotion. Captain X compensated for his lack of substance by his politician's knack for avoiding difficult questions.

I requested an explanation from Doubleday on May 10, 1989, as to why they copied the title of my book. Their law firm replied that they had a right to duplicate any title they wished. While this is true, a major publishing house does not duplicate the title of another book that is being actively promoted. It is my strong belief that *Doubleday* duplicated my title to defuse the scandalous contents in my book.

The *Air Line Pilot* magazine gave Doubleday's version a glowing review.[558] They had refused to address the contents of my book, and had even refused to accept advertising for it when it first came out. The article stated that the book tells it like it is, and that air safety was in good shape. This was contrary to earlier *Air Line Pilot* magazine articles written by their technical staff. The article stated in part:

> There's just a pilot's and copilot's seat. Some 600 functions have been eliminated from the control panels. On the wall to the right, where the engineer was sitting, there's a box with some shelves. Behind that, there's a wardrobe closet. How simple it is! It's not much worse than ... a sports car dashboard! You've got some computer-terminal screens, and they have some weird-looking graphics on them, but other than that it doesn't seem all that complicated, and you have dreams (foolish dreams!) that you might be able to fly this bugger.
>
> In a chapter entitled "The High But Not Necessarily Mighty," the authors discuss "built-in risk factors" like the "noise pollution factor," the "bird factor," and "the airline versus the fork-tail doctor killers." The latter refers to those general aviation aircraft like the Piper Cherokees and Seminoles flying down in "Indian County," many of them, the author claims, owned by rich doctors or movie producers. These aircraft menace his skies, especially in Southern California.

Following this book review, there was a multi-page article relating an interview with Captain X, in which he described how Doubleday approached him to write a book. Captain X had no writing abilities, his airline experience was limited, and he lacked access to and knowledge of the internal problems within government and at United Airlines.

The so-called Captain X described how he and co-author Reynolds Dodson prepared the book's contents. Captain X told of sitting in his backyard and relating "war stories I've told a hundred times before—both to fellow pilots and to friends and relatives."

One of the so-called exposé stories was of the captain correcting a landing by a copilot, an event as routine as getting up in the morning. Captain X said he received some typewritten pages putting in print his back-yard description of the rough-landing story, and the great anxiety it caused him. The article continued: "I've got problems. My company won't want to come within 10 miles of a story about a copilot who almost broke one of its airplanes." First of all a hard landing doesn't normally break an aircraft. Second, a competent captain will correct an approach made by a copilot before it becomes a hard landing. Third, a hard landing occasionally occurs to all pilots, and normally no grounds for disciplinary action.

This embarrassing naivete was evident throughout the book. Nothing in the book constituted an exposé. Captain X continued his description of how *Doubleday* arranged for his participation. His first-person writing suddenly took the position of a third person:

[558] July 1989 *Air Line Pilot*.

He [co-author to Captain X] sent the first chapter, plus an outline, to his agent. His agent in turn sent it to 15 different publishers, and 13 expressed interest in it. Within days, Ren was calling excitedly. Three of the publishers had gone into auction, and the winning bid had been quite considerable. [no legitimate publishers would have gone into auction on such a bland book, when other books far more creditable were on the market.]

I am not always the most patient guy, and a couple of times we almost came to blows over whether a pilot would "shout" or "speak" during the throes of a thunderstorm and whether the emotions that a pilot feels would be fear or hostility. [big deal!]

Now a mini-bureaucracy sprang up, and suddenly I was confronting a new group of personalities. ... When the time came for me to sit down with Doubleday's executives—who still didn't know who I was: as far as they knew I was "Captain X," and to this very day, that is all they know me by—I suddenly found myself sitting in a high-rise conference room staring at a bunch of women who, to my middle-aged eyes, looked like fresh-scrubbed flight attendants.

Captain X made reference to Doubleday's statement that book sales depended on media exposure and advertising, as much as the contents of the book. In this case, far more depended on hype than on contents. Doubleday then arranged for Captain X to be coached in preparation for radio and television appearances.

A Los Angeles newspaper review[559] summarized the contents of what Doubleday called an exposé:

Captain X said the worst is over. Air travel is actually safer than ever as far as Captain X is concerned. The future is bright for aviation.

The book received one of the most unusual book reviews ever written, appearing in the October 1989 *Flight Training* magazine:

This is a bad book. ... I suspect Captain "X" elected anonymity after reading what he dictated, and some residue of both ego and pride required that he divorce himself from it. ... This is a book that simply mocks maturity and professionalism. ... Beware! This is not the way it is. The incidents he reports, and which he allowed to happen (and from which he extricated the airplane) bespeak an impaired captain, unable to recognize acceptable aircraft performance. They are not the compliments to himself that he solicits.

During a radio appearance with host Anthony Hilder in Anchorage on July 19, 1989, Hilder mistakenly introduced me as Captain X, assuming that I was the author of the books that he saw stacked on the floor of local book stores. He had earlier recommended the new book to his listeners.

"Anthony, I'm not Captain X," I explained, and then proceeded to describe the deception by Doubleday. Hilder angrily advised his listeners to return the books they had bought, adding that this explains the reason that he

[559] Los Angeles *Herald Examiner* May 10, 1989.

received complaints from those who read Doubleday's *Unfriendly Skies*, who complained there was nothing to the book.

Callers, including an attorney, stressed the need to sue Doubleday. I didn't have the opportunity to describe that the federal judiciary had me gridlocked, barring me access to federal courts.

The amount of money spent by *Doubleday* to promote the book can be speculated by the reports I received that piles of the book were in bookstores all over the country. Hundreds of thousands of dollars had been spent to flood the bookstores with the duplication of my title.

Author Ralph McGehee states in *Deadly Deceits: My 25 years in the CIA*, "There's a little bit of fear that if you go after the intelligence community, your career is threatened." Several CIA operatives have told me that the CIA had blackmailed Senator Boren, head of the CIA Senate Oversight Committee,[560] with pictures of his alleged homosexual and pedophile activities. In his last senatorial race, Senator Boren faced defeat in a vicious primary battle as his opponent accused him of being a homosexual. Senator Boren was initially opposed to the nomination of Robert Gates as Director of the CIA in 1992. Reportedly the CIA threatened to release pictures of Boren in sexual acts with little boys, after which Boren suddenly changed his position on Gates, saying that Gates was "one of the most candid people we've ever dealt with." This statement was also made after Boren had received several mailings from me describing the role played by Gate in the October Surprise and Iran-Contra operations.

PUBLIC RELATION FIRMS AND THE CIA

The CIA uses public relations firms to perform domestic activities that the CIA is barred by law from doing. Washington-based Hill & Knowlton, for instance, acted as a conduit for propaganda news releases to the media. The firm has numerous CIA and other intelligence agency personnel on its board of directors. Robert Gray, who set up and operated Hill and Knowlton since 1961, had numerous contacts with the CIA and other intelligence groups, and with such CIA personnel as William Casey, Edwin Wilson, Oliver North, and Robert Owen. Gray also formed his own company with CIA contacts and was on the Board of Directors of several covert CIA companies that fronted for Task Force 157, an Office of Naval Intelligence operation.

Covert Action described in its Spring 1993 issue how U.S. intelligence agencies use public relation firms, journalists, and authors to print what they want the American public to hear. The article reported that "In a typical issue of the *Wall Street Journal*, more than half the news stories were based solely on [government-provided] press releases." The article continued: "Reporters were paid by the CIA, sometimes without their media employer's knowledge, to get the material in print or on the air." They reported that news organizations ordered their writers to repeat what was fed to them by the CIA.

A former CIA official whose job was liaison with corporations, Robert T. Crowley, admitted that public relations firms are continuously used by the

---

[560] Chairman of the Senate Intelligence Committee.

CIA "to put out press releases and make media contacts." The CIA's use of U.S. media has been well known in publications related to the intelligence agencies. Much of what is stated as "news" by the media is really press releases from CIA-connected public relation firms. Author Susan Trento wrote:

> Reporters were paid by the CIA, sometimes without their media employers' knowledge, to get the material in print or on the air. But other news organizations ordered their employees to cooperate with the CIA, including the San Diego-based Copley News Service. But Copley was not alone, and the CIA had "tamed" reporters and editors in scores of newspaper and broadcast outlets across the country. To avoid direct relationships with the media, the CIA recruited individuals in public relations firms like H&K to act as middlemen for what the CIA wanted to distribute.[561]

Reporters and the media have become dependent upon government agencies and officials for news handouts, without which they would lose business to those who play the game. This helps explain why scandal after scandal is lightly treated, if at all, by the media.

One of the principal heads of the Hill and Knowlton public relations firm was Robert Keith Gray, who had continuing connections with the intelligence community, and with such CIA figures as William Casey, Oliver North, Edwin Wilson, and others.

PROBLEMS OF WHISTLEBLOWERS

A *Newsweek* (April 1, 1991) article stated: "A Congressional Subcommittee concluded last September that, in 10 recent misconduct cases, the most troubling aspects were the cover-ups, failures to investigate, antipathy to the whistle-blower and a closing of ranks against an accuser." *Newsweek* quoted Associate Dean Paul Friedman of the University of California, San Diego, reporting that "suppression of problems, with hostility toward those who brought accusations," is routine.

In discrediting CIA whistleblowers such as Russbacher, Brenneke, Riconosciuto, Rewald, and others, the mass media knew that they had nothing to prove their CIA status. They do not wear uniforms, do not carry badges or other identifications, and operate in secrecy. The media were aware that it is standard operating procedure for the CIA to deny relationships to any CIA personnel or operation whose cover is blown. The media knew the informants had nothing to gain, and much to lose. Whistleblowers faced sham perjury charges by an utterly corrupt Justice Department gang, and risked joining the list of informers who have been killed or who mysteriously died. Yet, the media refused to accept the charges made by any of the dozens of CIA personnel who had gone public in an attempt to expose corrupt and unlawful activities that were inflicting horrendous harm upon the United States and the American people.

---

[561] Interview with John Stockwell, *Propaganda Review*, No. 6, Winter 1990, p. 14.

TALK SHOW SILENCE

As the first printing of *Defrauding America* came off the press in July 1993, I sent letters to the producers and hosts of over 400 radio stations that had talk shows, including flyers describing the contents of the book and information showing the credibility of the author and the CIA informants. I described my almost 2,000 appearances on radio and television, showing my obvious credibility. Despite the gravity of the information and the obvious harm being inflicted upon the United States, only four replies were received to have me appear.

Every radio and television station in the San Francisco area were sent information about the book and informed of my availability. Despite the fact that the book described in specifics the large amount of corruption in California and federal courts and in the Justice Department, despite the great harm being inflicted upon both the United States and many residents in California, not a single station responded. To have done so would have exposed the corruption in government, and risked disturbing the incestuous relationship between many corporations, the media, and the corruption in government. I had found in the past that the broadcast and news media in the San Francisco area (as in many other areas) caters to or breeds the childish pacifier of the ball games. Homosexuals, lesbians, and ball games, appear to be the primary interest of the San Francisco area media.

The few appearances that I did make on talk shows in other parts of the country were very warmly received by the host and the listeners, with many of the listeners calling the station to have me back again.

PUBLISHER SILENCE

The inordinate silence from the talk show hosts and book reviewers was preceded by the silence I received a year earlier after I sent query letters to about forty book publishers inquiring whether they would be interested in reviewing my manuscript for possible publishing. It is standard industry practice to promptly reply to such a query letter, which in many cases is a not-interested reply. But in this mailing, only four of the forty publishers responded, and they indicated a lack of interest in looking at the manuscript. The thought in my mind is that those who didn't respond simply did not want to be shown in writing as knowing about the highly sensitive book revealing attacks upon the United States in the form of a cabal, and making possible its continuance by refusing to publish such information.

THE PRINTER REFUSED TO PRINT THIS BOOK

After Paul Wilcher's body was found, the printer who was to print this book, Consolidated Printers of Berkeley, California, suddenly fabricated excuses for not proceeding with printing the first issue of *Defrauding America*. This refusal occurred despite the fact that we had a signed contract and they had received half the total cost of the book order. I reminded the printer that copies of the book had been requested by numerous national syndicated writers and networks, and that Consolidated Printers would be suspected of interfering with exposing criminal activities.

MEDIA RESPONSE AFTER THE BOOK'S RELEASE

Over six hundred book reviewers throughout the United States received requests to review *Defrauding America* which I sent to them after the first books came off the press in August 1993. The requests described the charges made in the book, the harm being inflicted upon the United States, the credibility and means of determining the facts by the author and his related band of CIA and other whistleblowers. They were made aware of the many excellent book reviews received by me on my earlier editions of *Unfriendly Skies*. The gravity of the charges, the harm to the United States if the charges were true, were obvious. Yet, out of six hundred requests, only six responded with a request to view a copy of the book.

I sent over 400 letters to book reviewers throughout the United States, offering to send a copy of the book for their review. I described the contents of the book, giving information supporting my credibility, describing the input from my many former and present CIA people. Only five out of over 400 book reviewers responded.

A book reviewer obviously has the discretion whether to review a book or not. But when a book is offered that reportedly reveals subversive and criminal activities against the United States and the American people, and the author and his informants have the credentials that we had, my argument is that the reviewer has a duty to examine the book's contents.

The same absence of response occurred with talk show hosts. I sent out over six hundred flyers advising talk-show producers and hosts of the book, its contents, our expertise, my record of almost 2,000 appearances, along with one especially favorable and in-depth book review. They also had a responsibility. Only about a dozen responded.

Under these conditions of massive irresponsibility, what chance does a concerned citizen, a whistleblower, have of exposing crimes against the United States?

The book and its contents were well received by almost all of the talk shows upon which I appeared. There was a troubling side to the responsibility of talk show hosts to allow the serious charges to be aired. The charges in the book were extremely serious, and if only a fraction of them were true, for instance, an ongoing subversion of the United States was occurring. Obviously, the harm to the United States and the American people continued, made possible by their coverup. The many deep-cover, high-ranking, CIA informants quoted in the book, as well as my background, gave the charges high credibility. Despite all this, only about five percent of the talk show hosts and producers who received the thousands of flyers that I sent to them, announcing my availability, requested a copy of the book for possibly scheduling me as a guest. The other ninety-five percent who were made aware of the serious charges, never responded. At best, this was an irresponsible refusal to perform a duty to the public.

A similar example, perhaps, would be the report of a responsible person that a bomb had been hidden on board a Boeing 747 that was due to depart in a couple of hours. Those who received the information refused to even investigate. The plane later blew up.

PLANTS IN THE ALTERNATIVE MEDIA

Chuck Harder, publisher of Peoples News Bulletin, and talk show host, represented himself as concerned about government corruption, but strangely said very little about it. I sent him a copy of the first printing of *Defrauding America* and asked him to give it a book review. He never answered. A talk show host contacted Harder's office, recommending that his newspaper and radio program give the book publicity. He refused, stating that he gave the book to a psychologist and the psychologist "found holes in it." Upon being told this, I wrote Harder a November 7, 1993 letter asking him what qualifications the person had to determine the truthfulness of the highly supported material stated in the book. Again, he never answered.

CHICAGO TRIBUNE COVERUP

Among the major newspapers that helped to cover up for the CIA corruption exposed by Gunther Russbacher was the *Chicago Tribune*. In a March 17, 1992 article it misstated the facts, covered up for evidence, ridiculed Russbacher for allegedly misrepresenting himself as a Naval officer, and labeled Russbacher a phony. This coverup and misstatement of the facts not only helped keep Russbacher in prison, but covered up for the enormous criminality being perpetrated against the American people, making possible the continued harm suffered by them. I sent the *Chicago Tribune* a copy of the letter that I sent to Attorney General Janet Reno, along with a May 20, 1986 memorandum signed by CIA Director William Casey, identifying Russbacher as a member of the Office of Naval Intelligence. I also sent the *Chicago Tribune* a copy of the first printing of *Defrauding America*, which put them on notice that Russbacher was a Naval officer, and of the charges made by our group of former federal investigators and CIA/DEA/State Department whistleblowers. As expected, the *Chicago Tribune* continued the coverup. This was a major federal crime, made worse by the gravity of the harm inflicted against the United States.

WHO COULD HAVE HALTED
THE ONGOING CRIMINALITY AND RESULTING HARM

The nature and extent of the epidemic corruption within the federal offices of the United States can be very roughly assessed by looking at those who had a duty to act under federal criminal statutes, under their oath of office, under the responsibilities that they assumed and for which they were paid. For instance, in the multi-billion-dollar-a-year looting of Chapter 11 and 13 assets, that converts thousands of people to a state of poverty, it required not only the perpetrators (federal judges, trustees, law firms, attorneys) to corruptly inflict the harm, but the coverup and refusal to act by the media, members of Congress, other attorneys, federal judges, Justices of the U.S. Supreme Court, Justice Department attorneys, and others. Their refusal to act makes them accomplices, and as guilty as the people committing the acts, according to federal criminal statutes. Their continued complicity will make possible the continuation of great harm upon still other victims.

In the CIA drug trafficking that has gone on for decades, which is inflicting great physical harm and death throughout America, and is financially destroying the American way of life, blame goes to the same checks and balances. Drug-related violent crime has reached frightening levels.

The October Surprise conspiracy required the participation and the felony coverup by the same group of checks and balances. The same can be said for Inslaw, the conversion of federal courts and federal agencies into criminal enterprises, the spreading of an ugly mindset throughout state and federal governments, and among the people.

It is virtually impossible under these conditions for any citizen to exercise his or her responsibility under law and under our form of government, to report criminal activities implicating federal personnel.

COPIES OF CHARGES AND SUPPORTING EVIDENCE SENT TO NEWSPAPERS, MAGAZINES AND BOOK REVIEWERS THROUGHOUT THE UNITED STATES

On the premise that anyone who knows of federal crimes is guilty of a felony if they do not promptly report it to a federal tribunal that is not itself involved in the criminal activities, I sent copies of the first edition of *Defrauding America* to many of the primary newspapers and magazines in the United States.[562] Each copy of the book, sent by registered mail, was accompanied by a brief one-page letter outlining the charges, the continuing nature of the criminal activities and the harm resulting from it, and reminded the recipient of their obligations under federal criminal statutes, to make public the charges. The clout that the recipients had, as major publishers, could have forced an exposure of the criminal activities and brought about massive changes in the heads of many government entities. None responded.

[562] Among the recipients of the book were: U.S. News & World Reports; Newsweek; Washington Post; Washington Times; Wall Street Journal; New York Times; New York Post; New York Daily News; Los Angeles Times; San Francisco Examiner; San Francisco Chronicle; Sacramento Union; Sacramento Bee; Dallas News; Dallas Times-Herald; Los Angeles Herald Examiner; Rocky Mountain News; San Jose Mercury; Houston Post; and others.

CHAPTER THIRTY ONE

THE CLINTON GANG

After Bill Clinton took over the White House, the corruption preceding him continued. Suddenly all attention on these crimes halted. One of Clinton's early acts was to carry out what former Attorney General William Barr had started after FBI Director William Sessions threatened to investigate Justice Department corruption. Sessions stated to Senator Boron his intent to investigate Justice Department officials in the BCCI coverup. Two days later the head of the Justice Department, Attorney General William Barr, charged Sessions with ethic violations for allowing his wife to accompany him on government aircraft during speaking engagements, on a space-available basis; and for having billed the federal government for a security fence around the FBI Director's home (which he was authorized to do).

RETALIATING AGAINST THE FBI DIRECTOR

FBI Director William Sessions' investigation of Justice Department officials threatened the power behind the scene. Department U.S. Attorney General William Barr reacted to this danger by charging Sessions with ethic violations for having built a security fence around his home [that was authorized by the government]; for personal phone calls from his office [big deal!]; and for taking his wife along on government aircraft. These were sham charges intended to replace an FBI Director who dared to investigate portions of the inter-related scandals that would bring down powerful people in both political parties.

After the Clinton group assumed office the entrenched power in the Justice Department carried out, through the cooperation of President Bill Clinton, in July 1993, the removal of Sessions, replacing him with one of their own.

Ethic violations, in light of the pattern of hard-core criminality by the three preceding U.S. Attorney Generals (Edwin Meese, Richard Thornburgh, and William Barr), was an exercise in the bizarre. Criminal coverup, obstruction of justice, and other crimes, related to October Surprise, CIA and DEA drug trafficking, Inslaw, BCCI, BNL, were the hallmark of the three prior U.S. Attorney Generals. But this type of conduct became the routine.

The Justice Department's Office of Professional Responsibility knew of these Justice Department crimes, and instead of addressing them, it aided and abetted their coverup.

If FBI Director William Sessions had not been halted, and an honest investigation conducted, the entire inter-related federal corruption in all three branches of government could have been exposed. Sessions had to be replaced. President Bill Clinton and his new lapdog Attorney General Janet Reno, carried out the task. Without granting Sessions a hearing to defend himself, Attorney General Janet Reno and President Bill Clinton fired Sessions for alleged ethic violations. Compare: Bill Clinton covered up for the CIA arms and drug trafficking in Arkansas while he was Governor, obstructing justice in criminal activities inflicting great harm upon the American people. Janet Reno covered up for the criminal activities described within these pages after I brought them to her attention and demanded that she obtain the testimony and evidence of our group of about a dozen CIA whistleblowers.

Clinton continued to use the FBI and Justice Department as a political tool, making these high "law-enforcement" agencies into agencies of corruption. The Office of Attorney General had become a political tool to protect corrupt federal officials for decades. These acts are hard-core criminal violations, and not a matter of presidential discretion or policy decisions.

Pious-sounding Clinton announced that he was replacing Sessions because he lacked credibility, based upon these sham charges. Attorney General Janet Reno repeated Clinton's uttering, just as she did during the debacle at Waco that killed almost a hundred people.

The headline in the September 6, 1993 *Spotlight* reflected the general thinking about why President Bill Clinton replaced FBI Director Sessions: *Sessions Ousted For What He Knew*. The article stated in part:

Alarmed by a British law commission report[563] exposing the "mercenary" links between Israel and the cocaine cartel, pro-Israel officials in the U.S. Justice Department made an all-out effort to suppress it last year. When former FBI Director William Sessions opposed the cover-up–and others like it–he was targeted for elimination by a secret society of dual loyalist Washington bureaucrats. ... Their accounts brought to light the hidden role played in the dispute by the Israel lobby and its invisible network of allies in the national security bureaucracy.

At first Sessions had no idea of the pervasive influence wielded over national affairs by Israel firsters," related Charles Horner, a recently retired Justice Department security official. "He would have been shocked to discover that he owed his own appointment as FBI director to Israel's clout.

---

[563] Blom-Cooper report on the findings of a major British drug probe.

The British investigation was conducted by a British law commission headed by Lord Louis Blom-Cooper, which then conducted a year of hearings. The *London Times* referred to the commission's report as "a scorcher," which found:

* The use of Antigua by the Mossad for drug trafficking and for training and arming the private armies of Columbia's drug barons.

* Lying by CIA officials to the White House, claiming that the Israeli operations in Antigua were to train rebel forces to oust Panama's Manuel Noriega.

* Mossad's training of hundreds of Columbian's into killers for assassination purposes.

* A long standing practice by U.S. authorities to cover for the crimes of the Mossad group, which supported my findings and as described by my CIA and DEA informants.

* Exposed the role played by Israeli Major General Pinchas Shachar in the arms and drug operations. Shachar was the official representative for Israel Military Industries in the United States, with special access to the Pentagon and other guarded U.S. military installations. According to *Spotlight*, Sessions wanted the British report entered into Shachar's file and to suspend his special privileges. Attorney General Barr rejected the recommendation, keeping the American public in the dark about this tentacle of the epidemic drug trafficking that is destroying the sole of the United States.

The *Spotlight* article described how the Bush and Clinton White House sought to ignore the report, just as the many other reports have been hidden from the American public. The U.S. media became accomplices in the coverup.

Justice Department officials referred inquiries to the State Department, claiming it was a foreign affair matter, and the State Department referred inquiries to the Justice Department, claiming it was a criminal matter.

Spotlight wrote that "Sessions [was] considered a loose cannon rather than an asset [and] was targeted for a long ordeal of trumped-up misconduct charges and false slander. Sessions, an outsider, had to go, and be replaced by an insider that could, as Attorney General Janet Reno showed, cover up.

The ethic-violation charges against Sessions came after the Clinton White House, with Attorney General Janet Reno's assistance, brought upon the fiery deaths at Waco; fired the White House travel staff so as to install relatives operating an Arkansas travel operation; shut down part of Los Angeles International Airport for an hour while Clinton obtained a haircut; and other blunders.

President Clinton appointed for FBI Director an insider, who was well familiar with the dirty games of the FBI, the CIA, the Justice Department, and could keep the lid on these scandals: Louis Freeh, a career FBI agent. Clinton now had a U.S. Attorney General and an FBI Director to protect him against his involvement in the serious arms and drug trafficking, the BCCI connection, and God knows what else he had done and what he would eventually commit.

Newly appointed FBI Director Louis Freeh offered advice to the American public in fighting crime: "Play with your friends, be fair and honest, and share your toys."[564]

BETTER CONTROL OF COVERUP

The compartmentalized and vast CIA drug trafficking operations repeatedly risked exposure because of the various agencies responsible for protecting the nation against this debilitating criminal enterprise. Clinton's new FBI director proposed combining the DEA with the FBI. Vice-President Al Gore proposed in September 1993 to merge the DEA into the FBI. This merging would reduce the chance of a renegade DEA agent or administrator from exposing a Justice Department-protected drug operation.

ONLY THE LEADERS CHANGED,
THE GAME WAS THE SAME

Clinton appointed as head of the U.S. Department of Transportation the former Mayor of Denver, Federico Pena, whose primary credentials for the job were that he helped promote the new Denver Airport. But that airport project was riddled with corruption, involving key players from the Denver area HUD and savings and loan scandal, and involved the CIA and its proprietary, Silverado Bank Savings and Loan. Inside CIA sources tell me that Pena was paid a million and a half dollars for his help in getting the Denver voters to approve the Denver Airport project. Pena had been involved with the MDC Holdings and related groups, in which U.S. Attorney Michael Norton was also financially involved.

Former CIA operative Trenton Parker confirmed what other informants stated to me about the bribe money, stating to me on June 7, 1993:

We (Pegasus group of CIA) have a tape recording of Pena, with Millman, ... because Pena's office was bugged, a tape recording where Millman's exact words are, "Ok, here's the million and a half god-damn dollars, now we want the f... airport to go through. Now, get off your butt and let's get this thing going, eh, let's get off our butts and get this thing going." Pena got a million and a half dollars in cash and we have the tape recording, we have the copy of the cancelled check, and we've got from the bank's records of the cancelled check, the actual cancelled check, which was used to pay him off.

Another Clinton appointee Ron Brown, the Secretary of Commerce, was closely allied to these activities. Brown's law firm helped obtain the federal funding for the Denver Airport which was needed to fund the multi-billion-dollar frauds rampant in the Denver area during the 1980s.

In 1993 Brown was identified as having demanded the payment of $700,000 plus a percentage of sales in exchange for his help in lifting the trade embargo against Vietnam. At first, Brown and his attorney denied that Brown has any contact whatsoever with Vietnamese businessman Nguyen Van Hao, who allegedly arranged for the placement of the $700,000 in a secret

---

[564] *Newsweek* September 13, 1993.

bank account. Later, after evidence surfaced that this statement was false, Brown then admitted meeting several times with the Vietnamese business man and Vietnam government contact. After this information surfaced, President Clinton affirmed his support for Brown.

Tim Wirth, another Clinton appointee, was part of the same Denver group, appointed to Under Secretary of State for Global Affairs. He was beholden to Mizel and Brownstein for millions of dollars raised for his various Congressional campaigns since 1974. Wirth was Chairman of the House Banking Committee's Subcommittee on Telecommunications and Finance from 1981 to 1986 while a Congressman from Colorado, during which time he protected the junk bond industry that inflicted such great harm upon the American economy. Wirth's opposition also kept the savings and loan corruption continuing long after the evidence showed the urgency to stop the crooks.

Wirth's opposition to addressing the savings and loan debacle occurred concurrent to his receiving almost $200,000 from several Savings and Loan Associations[565] that cost the taxpayers over $10 billion during the bailout. (All had ties with the CIA.)

Clinton appointed Howard Pastor, former head of a CIA-connected public relations firm of Hill & Knowlton, to Director of Inter-governmental Affairs for the White House. That public relations firm handled the account for the infamously repressive Duvalier regime in Haiti, among others.

For the National Transportation Safety Board, a position that requires good knowledge of aviation safety matters, Clinton appointed a lawyer who lacked any aviation safety or technical experience, Jim Hall. This attorney replaced a board member with aerospace engineer experience and a licensed pilot, Christopher Hart.

Clinton nominated District of Columbia Appeals Court Judge Ruth Ginsberg, who had earlier blocked me from reporting the corruption to a federal court and who dismissed, in clear violation of statutory and case law, my lawsuit seeking relief from the civil, constitutional, and criminal acts judicially inflicted upon me.

"TRAVELGATE" FIASCO

Part of the chaos in the Clinton Administration was the flap with firing the experienced White House travel staff and replacing them with a travel agency in which the Arkansas branch was managed by a twenty-five-year old inexperienced cousin of President Clinton. An interesting side to that flap: the travel agency was World Wide Travel International (WWTI), which CIA operative Russbacher stated was a CIA front. As part of its travel activities WWTI reportedly ships **sealed** containers into the United States on combination freight and passenger aircraft charters. This is one of the tactics my CIA informants stated were used to bring large quantities of drugs into the United States.

---

[565] Silverado, Lincoln, Centrust, and Columbia Savings and Loan associations.

And then we have President Bill Clinton himself. He was ensnared in the CIA arms and drug trafficking by protecting this large operation that existed at Mena Airport in Arkansas, plus his connections with scandal-plagued financier Stephens. What a team!

The true story cannot be told to the American people, without risking impeachment and criminal prosecution of large numbers of federal officials. Assuming, that is, that enough checks and balances exist to carry out these requirements, and that is highly doubtful. Exposing any single one of these scandals to the American public could unleash an unprecedented response adversely affecting some of the biggest crooks that this nation has ever seen.

MYSTERIOUS DEATH OF CLINTON'S AIDE

Involved in the travel department fiasco was attorney Vincent W. Foster Jr., one of Clinton's aides, who was a partner with Hillary Rodham Clinton at the Rose Law Firm in Little Rock. Foster was the Number Two lawyer in Clinton's White House and White House Deputy Counsel. He was involved in several White House fiascos, including the fiasco involving the White House travel staff, their sudden firing, and the improper White House request for an FBI investigation to find fault with the dismissed staff. Foster, with chief White House counsel Bernard W. Nussbaum, played a key role in the selection of Louis J. Freeh to be FBI Director and Judge Ruth Bader Ginsburg for the Supreme Court.

The Rose law firm was reportedly a CIA asset, in which partners included Hillary Clinton, Webster Hubbell, Vincent Foster. Insider reports indicate that Assistant Attorney General Hubbell is the real power in the office of U.S. Attorney General, and that Attorney General Janet Reno is a front carrying out the dictates of the group from the CIA asset, the Rose Law Firm.

On July 20, 1993, Foster's body was found at Fort Marcy, a roadside park along the George Washington Parkway on the west bank of the Potomac River, in Virginia, across from the capital.

If the CIA was involved with World Wide Travel International, and Foster was involved in the fiasco surrounding the White House travel staff, the question arises as to whether some faction of the CIA wanted Foster killed, or to send a message to Clinton.

RHETORIC VERSUS REALITY

Clinton and Reno expressed their concern for the American people and the integrity of the FBI as reasons for firing Sessions. Bill Clinton blocked an investigation and prosecution into the massive arms and drug trafficking in Arkansas involving the CIA and the Drug Enforcement Administration while he was governor. His presidential political campaign was financed by the group that secretly and unlawfully permitted the Bank of Crooks and Criminals to invade the United States and inflict great financial harm upon the American people. His presidency operated along these same lines.

Clinton, in control of the Presidential office of the United States, appointed a new U.S. Attorney General to control the Justice Department: Janet Reno. I put her on notice of the ongoing criminal activities that I discovered, much of it centered in the Justice Department. She received by certified mail a letter outlining the criminal activities described within this book; a copy of the first printing of the book; and a petition to receive testimony and evidence from a group of almost a dozen CIA and DEA whistleblowers, and myself.

I asked for relief from the criminal persecution inflicted upon me and the CIA informants. She refused to respond to the letter. Instead, she repeatedly uttered for public consumption the line Clinton mouthed, that the people must be responsive; that she wanted to hear of any wrongdoings; and other meaningless rhetoric that I have listened to for the last three decades by the nation's most proficient coverup artists.

COVERUP BY ATTORNEY GENERAL JANET RENO

In July 1993 Attorney General Janet Reno received a copy of *Defrauding America* and related information on the criminal activities, along with a letter. The letter, or petition, requested under federal crime-reporting statutes that she receives the testimony and evidence that I and a group of CIA whistleblowers and I wanted to present, relating to the criminal activities against the United States that are described within these pages. Under federal crime-reporting statutes she had a duty to receive this unprecedented group-reporting of the serious crimes against the United States. Her response would indicate whether the highest law-enforcement office in the United States would criminally cover up and obstruct justice relating to the crime-patterns described within these pages.

Her response was as I expected, and the last paragraph in the letter reflected the coverup and obstruction of justice that I had witnessed of this government agency for the past thirty years.

The Criminal Division of the U.S. Department of Justice, writing for Attorney General Janet Reno, wrote:

You allege ... a litany of hard-core criminal activities against the United States by a large and well-orchestrated group of federal personnel in all three branches of the federal government. ... We have carefully reviewed your letters and your book. The allegations you make, while serious, are unsupported by credible evidence and fail to support your claim of persecution. Accordingly, we will take no further action in response to your letters.

Hundreds of people have been sent to their deaths, thousands to prison, on evidence that was a minute fraction of what was described in the book and what the group of CIA and other whistleblowers, and I, were offering to provide to this highest law enforcement official and office in the United States. A corollary to the refusal to receive our evidence would possibly be the refusal to inspect a departing jumbo-jet for a bomb reported by a known and proven reliable informant.

I had been a federal investigator in the past, holding federal authority to make determinations of federal violations. Other members of our unique group, including former CIA and high military officers, were entrusted to carry out highly secret and elaborate operations. If any **one** of the many criminal operations that I reported in the book and in the letters to the Justice Department were true, it would indicate an unprecedented sabotage of the United States by federal officials. It would indicate the existence of ongoing great harm upon America and the American people. Another corollary would be a radar operator reporting on December 7, 1941 a large fleet of unknown aircraft proceeding toward Pearl Harbor, and his report ignored and refused credibility.

U.S. Attorney General Janet Reno, and the U.S. Department of Justice, were obviously engaging in a criminal obstruction of justice and the many federal crimes associated with that duplicity. As I had expected from an examination of Bill Clinton and his appointments, the crimes against the American people would continue.

I responded to this coverup in a September 1, 1993 letter to the Attorney General, reminding her of the serious charges; the credibility of the CIA and other people who have much to lose and nothing whatsoever to gain by making the charges; the harm inflicted upon the United States and its people; and her responsibility under the laws of the United States and of her office. No response.

JUDGE RUTH BADER GINSBURG

President Clinton nominated Judge Ruth Ginsburg to replace retiring U.S. Supreme Court Justice Bryon White. Ginsburg was a judge on the District of Columbia Court of Appeals, and a member of the American Civil Liberties Union. She played a key role several times in preventing me from either reporting the criminal activities described within these pages, or obtaining relief from the felony persecution judicially inflicted upon me, by dismissing several of my appeals without allowing briefs to be submitted.

Every Justice of the U.S. Supreme Court had blocked my attempts to obtain relief from the harms judicially inflicted upon me, and aided and abetted the actions taken to block my reporting of the criminal and subversive acts I had uncovered. Shortly after Ginsburg was appointed to the Supreme Court I put her, again, on notice of the criminality and the part played by federal judges. I sent her a copy of *Defrauding America*; a petition demanding that she receive the testimony and evidence of myself and the small group of deep-cover CIA personnel concerning the well-entrenched corruption against the United States; the corruption and criminal activities by federal judges over whom she had supervisory responsibilities; and the criminal statutes that she would be violating if her actions or inactions blocked our reporting of the crimes. I also requested relief from the judicially inflicted harm I was suffering, including the continued felony persecution in retaliation for having sought to report the crimes and for exercising federal remedies to defend against the judicially inflicted silencing tactics. She refused to respond, making possible the continuation of what is described within these pages.

PETITIONING CALIFORNIA'S NEW SENATORS

I sent petitions to the two new California Senators, Barbara Boxer and Diane Feinstein, demanding that they receive evidence and testimony from my group of CIA whistleblowers and myself, relating to charges that were of such great gravity that no one in a position of responsibility could ignore. Boxer had already been put on notice while she was a Congresswoman from California, and she wouldn't even respond. As Senator, she duplicated her prior inaction when she was a representative. If she had performed her duty she would have exposed her prior coverup, which of course is a felony.

The material that I sent to them strongly indicated the existence of very serious criminal activities against the United States. I asked them for help relating to what was being done to me in retaliation for having sought to report the crimes, including the ongoing federal attempts to put me in prison for making the reports. Feinstein's non-responsive letter dated May 10, 1993, stated:

I wish I could bring you good news with this letter, but I cannot. Instead, I am sorry to tell you that the Federal Bureau of Investigation has advised me that it was unable to take the action you requested. The reasons for the agency's decision are summarized in the enclosed report. I understand your concern, and I am sorry I was not able to affect the decision.

I hadn't asked for an FBI investigation or corrective action, as they had been criminally implicated in these corrupt acts since 1965 when I, as a federal investigator, tried to expose the corruption. I asked, and I expected, Feinstein to show some level of responsibility, and to receive my evidence, and that of my CIA and DEA informants. If even part of my allegations were true, for which I offered evidence, it would show that the United States was being subverted from within by a pattern of coordinated criminal activities. Feinstein was not as dumb as she implied.

Attached to her letter was an April 15, 1993 letter from the FBI addressed to her, in reply to her inquiries:

This is in further response to your inquiry to our San Francisco office on behalf of Mr. Rodney Stich, who makes allegations against the federal government.

Our records indicate that Mr. Stich has been corresponding with the FBI since 1966. During this period, based on information he has furnished in an interview and through correspondence, no evidence of a violation within our jurisdiction has been presented. By letter dated March 5, 1992, he provided the FBI similar information concerning the matters he mentioned in his correspondence to you. The FBI has taken no action in connection with his allegations, and none is anticipated at this time.

This was an almost word-for-word denial sent by FBI Director J. Edgar Hoover to Congressman Waldie in 1967. Never, to this day, has the Justice Department or its FBI Division looked at my evidence or received my testimony.

The information in the papers that I sent to Senator Feinstein was explosive, as shown within these pages. She had a duty to act, and she knew the harm that American people would continue to suffer by her refusal to perform a duty. She had information of crimes against the United States, and solely upon the mealy-mouth response of the FBI, heavily implicated in the criminal activities, she sought to escape her responsibilities as a Senator and under federal crime-reporting statutes. If she was a citizen targeted by the Justice Department, numerous indictments could be handed down against her, including misprision of felonies, obstruction of justice, aiding and abetting, and conspiracy to commit these offenses.

FURTHER COVERUP BY MY CONGRESSMEN

Congressman George Miller knew of my charges for the past twenty years as they related to the aviation criminality and the coverup and obstruction of justice by Justice Department attorneys. Never once would he receive my evidence or provide for an investigation, despite the gravity of the charges. In August 1993 I again put him on notice of the crimes described within these pages, sent him a copy of the book, and demanded that he receives the testimony and evidence of our group. Just as he engaged in a criminal coverup for the past two decades, he continued the practice in 1993.

Congressman Pete Stark who was initially elected on a platform of concern over government misconduct was also notified by me of the aviation-related corruption since 1970, and he also engaged in a coverup. I put him on notice with an August 1993 letter, declaration, and demand that he receives our testimony and evidence. He continued his prior practice of coverup. I knew Stark when he was a banker in Walnut Creek, doing business with Adnan Khashoggi. Stark loaned me money to purchase a home after I left the FAA and moved to California, and his bank loaned money for me to buy various airplanes and various business properties.

My home in Alamo, California, was used by Bill Baker during a fund-raising drive as he was campaigning for State representative. In the mid-1980s I asked him to receive evidence, and provide relief, relating to the judicial attacks upon me by California judges, which have been described in earlier pages. The judicial attacks upon me, misusing the California courts, provided justification for him to investigate. He refused to do so. In 1993, he became a U.S. Congressman from my district, and I put him on notice in August 1993 of the criminal acts described within these pages, demanding that he receives the testimony and evidence of our group. He wouldn't answer.

COVERUP BY OTHER MEMBERS
OF THE CLINTON TEAM

Attorney General Janet Reno blocked an investigation and prosecution of these criminal activities when I submitted the first printing of *Defrauding America* to her, demanding that she receives the testimony of our group of CIA personnel and former federal investigators. Under federal crime statutes she was obligated to receive our testimony. She refused to do so.

On September 7, 1993 I sent to newly appointed FBI Director Louis Freeh a letter, a petition to receive our testimony and evidence, and a copy of the first printing of the book. No response.

On September 14, 1993 I sent a similar letter, petition, and a copy of the book, to newly appointed Supreme Court Justice Bader Ginsburg. Her responsibility to receive our testimony and evidence was not only under general crime-reporting statutes but also her responsibility over federal judges and Justice Department attorneys who were implicated in the criminal activities.

All petitions sent to these federal personnel were sent by certified mail, so that if any of these scandals ever circumvent the massive coverup, the parties implicated in the felony coverup could not deny knowledge of the subversive and activities.

The arrival of the Clinton gang in the White House and at the Justice Department was accompanied by a sudden silence on the many lingering scandals, such as BNL, BCCI, Inslaw, and others. Attorney General Janet Reno and the Justice Department said there was no truth to any of the charges. If the American public and the United States of America were not suffering such great harm from the criminal activities, the obstruction of justice by the Clinton gang could be ignored as "politics as usual."

THE YEAR-OF-THE-WOMAN POLITICIAN

The 1992 elections heralded 1993 as the year of the woman, for changing government for the better. The evidence shows that women running for office are as crooked as the men. Boxer, Feinstein, Reno, Ginsburg, Congresswoman Schroeder from Colorado, were all recipients of my certified mailings. They knew of the serious charges, and did nothing except make possible the continuation of the criminality by their coverup, even though they knew the harms would continue to escalate. So much for the year of the woman!

HYPOCRISY IN THE FACE OF RAMPANT CORRUPTION

Speaking before a NAACP group on November 13, 1993, U.S. Attorney General Janet Reno vowed that the law represented all Americans and that enforcing civil rights laws was a top priority of the Justice Department. She said this as Justice Department people that she controlled and directed were seeking to return me to prison in retaliation for having sought to report the criminal activities described within these pages. At that precise time the U.S. Trustee under her control was liquidating the assets criminally seized from me, and protecting those involved in the criminal enterprise epidemic in Chapter 11 and 13 courts. Reno stated:[566]

The law was a splendid, splendid instrument to do right. If I don't do anything else in the time I have as attorney general, I want to make sure the law and the Department of Justice become an accurate symbol for everyone of what is right. All my life, my mother and father raised me to believe that civil rights enforcement was the most important thing the Department of Justice can do. [Did they really say that!]

Lying to the American public has become as American as "apple pie."

CONTINUED EXPOSURES BY
DEEP-COVER CIA OPERATIVES

After the first printing of *Defrauding America* came out my name become known to other deep-cover people who were concerned about the sordid nature of activities against the United States by people in control of the federal government.

A HIGHER CABAL

For all of these government entities to be implicated, with every known check and balance playing a key role in the coverup and obstruction of justice,

---

[566] November 13, 1993 *Associated Press*.

requires that there be some higher power elite or cabal orchestrating events. Much has been written about these areas, and I leave it for others to speculate. However, there almost certainly is a higher power elite behind the scene that coordinates these criminal operations and prevents an exposure. I've said very little about this, trying to limit what is stated in these pages to that which can be fairly well supported by various forms of evidence.

One speculation has been that there is a determined effort to bring down the lawful government of the United States by inflicting great financial and social damage. Former Nazi intelligence and military officers were brought into U.S. intelligence agencies after World War II. It is possible that through their subsequent high positions within the covert U.S. intelligence agencies that they play a key role in the infliction of great harm upon the American people.

ESCALATING CLINTON EXPOSURES

If Arkansas Governor Clinton did in fact cover up and obstruct justice relating to the enormous CIA drug trafficking in his state it would be fitting that he would be involved in other criminal or unlawful activities. As 1994 started, some of these activities surfaced.

His involvement in a joint investment with a former owner, James McDougal, of a failing Arkansas savings and loan, Madison Guaranty Savings and Loan, exposed suspicious activities (though far-less serious than the felony obstruction of justice in the drug-related crimes). McDougal diverted money from the insolvent savings and loan to Governor Clinton to pay for personal and political debts. Three months before the diversion of funds, Clinton appointed Beverly Schaffer, a lawyer representing Madison, as state regulator overseeing savings and loans. The regulator allowed Madison to stay in business despite taking vigorous actions against other savings and loans in similar financial condition. A few weeks after McDougal diverted money to Governor Clinton, Clinton's savings and loan regulator approved a novel plan for Madison to sell stock, despite its insolvency. In 1989 the federal government took over Madison after it had incurred a loss to U.S. taxpayers of over sixty million dollars.

In 1989 the federal government hired the Little Rock Rose law firm to prosecute McDougal, in which Webster Hubbell, Hilary Clinton, and Vincent Foster, were partners. They falsely represented to the federal government that "the firm does not represent any savings and loan association in state or federal regulatory matters." This was false.

And then there was Clinton's questionable conduct relating to Whitewater Development Corporation, owned by Clinton and McDougal, that started surfacing at the start of 1994. Vincent Foster was involved in all of these matters until his 1993 death. President Clinton was associated with the removal of sensitive documents linked to Foster's death.

CHAPTER THIRTY TWO

CONTINUING DISCOVERIES

In late 1992 and continuing to the date of publication of this revised edition, I discovered still more criminality implicating those already described. I became the focal point for an increasing number of deep-cover whistleblowers reporting the criminal activities that they either witnessed or in which they were ordered to participate. In this chapter I make reference to some of these later discoveries that augment what has already been described. During many hours of statements these former, and even present, deep-cover Intelligence Agency personnel revealed corruption that to most of the American public would be considered delusional. Their statements and writings exposed additional areas of corruption, confirming what I had already learned, and confirm even further the deep-cover role of prior informants. Some of these new informants had either known of Russbacher, for instance, or had served with or under his command.

From this group of nearly a dozen deep-cover people employed by various U.S. Intelligence Agencies I obtained over a thousand hours of statements and hundreds of classified documents, showing the terrible harm inflicted upon the United States and many foreign countries and their citizens. Supplementing what has been stated in earlier pages, I uncovered still more areas of criminal activities, some of which are described here. Much more information has been given to me, but requires further time to coordinate, confirm, and present in a proper form to the reader. In subsequent printings some of this additional information will be presented.

This same group was the target of the coverup and discrediting tactics of the establishment media in the United States, by members of Congress, and by Justice Department prosecutors. The mysterious deaths, murders, and Judicial and Justice Department persecution of whistleblowers continued, fortuitously protecting high U.S. officials, Judges, Justice Department attorneys.

ANOTHER MURDER

While my discovery of additional corruption far beyond what I had earlier uncovered was continuing, one of my close sources mysteriously died, a death that several of my CIA contacts stated was murder. Paul Wilcher, an attorney living in Washington, D.C., was in frequent contact with Gunther Russbacher and myself. He had taped statements made by Russbacher during about six weeks of daily questioning taking place in the Missouri State Prison at St. Charles, Missouri. Fifty-five tapes recorded these conversations, revealing CIA secret operations in which Russbacher was involved, including assassinations overseas and in the United States. Russbacher warned Wilcher that these tapes were never to be revealed to anyone unless he died. I had a set of them in the event something happened to Wilcher's originals.

On June 16, 1993 Wilcher called Russbacher in prison and argued that Russbacher should have his CIA faction release to Paul the copy of the SR-71 video tape that Russbacher stated existed, of the flight from Paris to the United States that was part of the October Surprise operation. Russbacher said to me that his CIA faction delivered the video tape to Wilcher on the evening of either June 17 or June 18, 1993. The possession of that tape, assuming that it exists, would expose parts of the Octopus-like epidemic corruption existing in the federal government, and many people would be threatened.

Other evidence that Wilcher had obtained in May or June 1993, that threatened many members of Congress, were documents sent to him by former BCCI insiders employed in the London office, which listed the members of Congress who had received bribes from the rogue bank.

Wilcher told Garby Leon of Columbia Pictures that he had received these BCCI documents, and also stated to his lady friend, Marion Kindig, that he was investigating the BCCI matter. Former CIA contract agent Michael Riconosciuto said to me that he had given Paul considerable sensitive information about the Justice Department's theft of the Inslaw tapes and other sensitive matters involving the U.S. Intelligence Agencies. Wilcher had played the part of a very concerned citizen, seeking to have Congressman Lee Hamilton of the October Surprise Committee, Congressman Jack Brooks of the BCCI Committee, and other members of Congress, receive his evidence, and encountered a stone wall (i.e., obstruction of justice).

Wilcher had been attending Friday evening news conferences conducted by senior White House correspondent Sarah McClendon, and had taped the meetings. In early June 1993 Wilcher failed to appear at these meetings, and neither Marion Kindig nor McClendon could contact him. Sarah asked Marion to call me to determine if I heard from him, which I hadn't.

GOVERNMENT OCCUPIED AN ADJACENT APARTMENT

Marion Kindig went to his apartment a couple of days earlier, and getting no answer when she rang the door bell, she rang an adjacent apartment seeking to have the person signal the front door to open. She wanted to leave a package on Wilcher's door knob. That adjacent apartment was directly across the hall from Wilcher's apartment. When Marion rang the door bell, it rang into the telephone system, and a recorded message revealed something interesting: "This is a government number that has been disconnected."

I stated to Marion that it is strange to have an official government phone number in an apartment immediately opposite Wilcher's apartment, and then be disconnected when Wilcher disappears. I felt something was suspicious here.

"Do you think Paul is dead?"

A couple of days later, Tuesday evening, June 22, 1993, I called Kindig from Reno after finding a message from her on my home phone recorder. Reaching her at midnight in Washington, she again discussed her concern about Wilcher's disappearance. Marion asked me, "Do you think Paul is dead?" I answered, "Based upon what I know at this time, I would say there is a seventy-five percent chance that he is dead."

I stated to her that since the District of Columbia police would not enter Wilcher's apartment, it was up to her to gain entry, and to do it the following morning. I suggested a way for her to do it. She didn't have to carry out the plan I outlined for her, as the police finally forced their way into Wilcher's apartment, in reaction to McClendon's repeated demands. For an eighty-three year old (or young) woman, McClendon had plenty of drive.

Upon entering Wilcher's apartment the police found Wilcher's body, sitting upright on the toilet, as if he died in that position. Over twenty-five police officers, firemen, and FBI agents were present at Wilcher's apartment that first day, an inordinate amount if it had been a simple death. When Kindig and McClendon arrived, the FBI "assured" them that they had no interest in the case, while they continued to question possible witnesses. The FBI seized all of Wilcher's computer disks, audio tapes, records, letters, which contained evidence relating to October Surprise, BCCI, and related U.S. scandals.

Russbacher advised me, after I mentioned to him that Wilcher was missing, he had his CIA faction enter Wilcher's apartment, which reportedly occurred about two a.m., shortly after I had talked to Marion, at which time they found Wilcher's body. They then left.

Based partly on information given to him by his CIA faction, upon educated guesses, and upon the coroner's autopsy report, Wilcher had left his apartment with persons unknown, and had been eating pizza and drinking Pepsi Cola at the time of his death. He was then placed in the truck of a car in a fetal position, after which rigor mortis set in. He was brought back to his apartment and placed on the stool to look like a normal death. But if a person dies while sitting on the toilet, especially a tall and slim person as Wilcher was, six feet two inches tall, almost invariably the person will fall over and not remain upright.

Sarah McClendon and Marion Kindig went to the morgue to identify the body, which had bruises on the right side of the face, and they said the body was not that of Wilcher. The face was badly swollen, his hair looked different, and his nose appeared to be shaped differently. Several days later, on June 28, Kindig asked the coroner to view the body, thinking that she could identify Wilcher by looking at his teeth. Despite the gruesome condition of the body, which had turned grey, she identified Wilcher by looking at his teeth. The reduction of the facial swelling also made Wilcher's appearance recognizable to her.

The coroner's report, made after the autopsy, could not find, or it didn't report, any known cause of death. But Russbacher's CIA group reported that there was evidence of DMSO containing a neuro-toxin absorbed into the right hand fingers, being the cause of death.

In August 1993 I had written for an autopsy report, but the District of Columbia's coroner's office refused to respond. The refusal of state offices to cooperate when federal involvement exists was a frequent occurrence in various murders or mysterious deaths described within these pages.

Many magazines and newspaper articles should have followed Wilcher's death, as happened after Casolaro's death. Wilcher was well known to Congressional groups as he sought to force them to receive evidence about the October Surprise scandal and its many offshoots. He was known to the Justice Department, and to Attorney General Janet Reno, whom he had sought to meet in early June 1993. He sought to expose the October Surprise, BCCI, and Inslaw scandals. Wilcher's death protected Justice Department officials, members of Congress, and other U.S. officials.

POSSIBLE SCENARIO IN WILCHER'S DEATH

CIA sources reported to me details of Wilcher's death. Wilcher was induced to leave his apartment and go to Vienna, Virginia, where he was questioned as to matters pertaining to BCCI, including the accounts held in the BCCI branch in the Southwest part of London by former Presidents George Bush and Jimmy Carter, and former CIA Director William Webster. Wilcher was allegedly questioned for about two hours, after which he was fed Pizza. This occurred at approximately 3:40 p.m. on June 18, 1993.

Wilcher's death occurred after he was offered a glass of Pepsi-Cola with a mixture of DMSO and curare applied to the glass, which was then absorbed into Wilcher's system through the skin, causing his death. He was beaten in the face to make it look like a mugging, after which the body was placed in the truck of a car, where it remained until the body was returned to Wilcher's apartment. By that time rigor mortis had set in, and Wilcher's body was placed upright on the toilet stool.

Wilcher was a threat to many U.S. officials through his continued investigation and accumulation of evidence, including a video tape of George Bush and Gunther Russbacher in an SR-71 (connected with the October Surprise flight from Paris to the United States); documents of BCCI and BNL; 65 audio tapes of statements made by Gunther Russbacher to Wilcher in mid-1992 in a Missouri prison (copies of which are in my possession, and scattered in many places).

THE PRINTER OF THE FIRST EDITION
SUDDENLY REFUSED TO PRINT THE BOOK

It was June 23, 1993 when the body was found of my friend, Paul Wilcher. That afternoon, and there may be no relationship whatsoever, Consolidated Printers of Berkeley, California, suddenly fabricated excuses for not printing the first edition of *Defrauding America*, despite the fact that we had a signed contract and the printer had received half the total cost. I reminded the printer that copies of the book had been requested by numerous national syndicated writers and networks, and that Consolidated Printers would be suspected of interfering with exposing very serious criminal activities against the United States. Eventually, after a long delay, Consolidated agreed to go ahead with the printing of the book.

SAMPLE OF CONVOLUTED RELATIONSHIP BETWEEN CIA AND THE MILITARY-INDUSTRIAL COMPLEX

Through investigator Stewart Webb I commenced in early 1993 communicating with other CIA and CIA-related informants who continued to provide me information on still other covert and, by now, naturally, unlawful and corrupt activities by people related to espionage activities. One of these sources was John Cole, who worked in management at Granite City Steel company, and which was involved with CIA-related arms and drug trafficking companies. These companies, some of which on the list of the Fortune 500, played major roles in the CIA arms and drug trafficking activities.

It was in the late 1980s that Cole reported to the FBI and U.S. Attorney in Illinois the pattern of criminal activities that he had discovered and documented. To Cole's surprise, his evidence was refused, and no action taken. His persistence in trying to force Justice Department attorneys to take action resulted in the FBI and U.S. Attorney filing criminal charges against him, and stripping him of the assets through forfeiture that were needed to hire legal counsel. Following the standard pattern of those who report corruption of federal officials, Cole ended up in federal prison at Springfield, Missouri, where he met Webb, and then made contact with me.

Cole revealed a convoluted web of intrigue and corruption involving the Central Intelligence Agency, the FBI, Justice Department, military contractors, and even the Japanese crime group, Yakuza.

BRAND-NEW AIRCRAFT AND TANKS SOLD AS SCRAP, UNLAWFULLY SHIPPED OVERSEAS BY THE CIA

One of the schemes involved the sale of brand-new aircraft and tanks by defense industries to CIA proprietaries, which were then shipped to foreign countries, both friendly and unfriendly. Mixed in to the convoluted operations were drug trafficking, arms dealing, money laundering, and looting of America's financial assets.

As Cole sent me hundreds of pages of documents and description of the operation, I discovered that my CIA informant, Gunther Russbacher, was deeply involved through his CIA proprietaries, including National Brokerage Companies in Missouri, and related subsidiaries. Between Cole, Russbacher, and Webb, I discovered still other criminal activities that could provide for a book by themselves. Space limitations require that the operation be described only briefly.

The scheme involving new fighter aircraft involved McDonnell Douglas Aircraft Corporation and General Dynamics. When the CIA needed aircraft (or tanks) for delivery, and sale, to a foreign country, that was barred by U.S. law, the aircraft would be sent as scrap to National Steel and Granite City

Steel. (The same was done with new tanks.) This "scrap" was then shipped,[567] or flown, to foreign countries, including Libya and others who were publicly considered to be enemies of the United States. Large four-engine military aircraft that were labeled scrap were also shipped to these companies and shipped overseas for covert purposes.

Another scheme involved guns seized by police agencies throughout the United States that were shipped to Granite City Steel for the purpose of being melted down. Instead, the guns were secretly shipped to foreign countries for use in CIA operations.

There were many other offshoots of the multi-faceted operations. FBI agents, including FBI agents in the St. Louis office, were reportedly involved in selling stolen automobiles to drug dealers, often trading the cars for drugs. This was allegedly a sting operation to catch drug dealers, but rarely were the drug dealers apprehended. Instead, the drug dealers would be threatened with federal prosecution if they did not cooperate in the drug trafficking controlled by federal personnel, including the CIA.

Money was generated in many ways, including, of course, drug trafficking, arms sales. Financing was sometimes provided by the U.S. Department of Agriculture (as in the sham BNL financing to Iraq that made it possible for Iraq to invade Kuwait), and the Commodity Credit Corporation.

Banks used by the various members of this convoluted group of companies including BCCI and BNL, Nugan Hand, and others. Kissinger Associates played a key role in some of these transactions. Handling some of the transactions funded by the U.S. taxpayers were Kissinger Associates, who arranged for government funding and approval, bank involvement, and other phases of the operation. Money obtained through loans that were guaranteed by the United States under the agriculture programs appeared to go for farm products, but in reality, only a small amount was used in this manner. This practice went on for years, and the BNL and Iraqgate scandals were only one of many such operations paid for by the American taxpayers.

I asked Russbacher if he knew about the operation that Cole was describing to me, realizing that Russbacher was involved, from what Cole had stated. "You are digging up a lot of stuff," Russbacher said. He then enlarged upon what Cole said.

Russbacher described part of the CIA operation called Liberty Loan, which has loan offices throughout the United States. Liberty Loan was a CIA operation, with offices in twenty-two states, that was headquartered in the same building where he had other CIA proprietaries: 7711 Bonhomme, Suite 704, in Clayton, Missouri. Russbacher stated that Liberty Loan no longer exists. "We had to kill it (in 1986). There were too many indictments coming down; the Agency was making phony loans that were receiving attention."

Liberty Loan was tied into a complex scheme involving companies based in Missouri and Illinois, that were tied in with illegal arms sales, drug traffick-

---

[567] Shipping companies included Sioux City in New Orleans; Rock Island Railroad; Stinson Steamship Line, owned by National Steel.

ing, money laundering, stolen cars, and other activities. Surplus military aircraft and weapons were purchased from the government at scrap prices, supposedly to be melted down. Instead, they were shipped or flown overseas for sale to foreign nations, some of whom were friendly to the United States, and some of whom were not.

DOMESTIC AND FOREIGN COUNTRIES IMPLICATED

The CIA used both domestic companies, including its own proprietaries, and foreign companies, in operations inflicting great harm upon U.S. interests, while violating U.S. laws. he companies involved in these covert and criminal operations included, among others, Granite City Steel; National Steel;[568] Bull Moose Tube; Premeian Partners; National Brokerage Companies; Styx Warehouse; Chemitco & Concorde Warehouses, Belgium-owned companies, with locations nationwide, including Austin, Texas, Atlanta, Georgia, Miami, Florida, Denver; and various overseas companies.

There were other corporations that were either legally related or who knowingly participated in the convoluted activities. These included: Southern Air Transportation (S.A.T Miami);[569] Crittenden Air Transportation (C.A.P. Miami); Sarrkes Air Cargo (S.A.C. Miami); Continental Air Transportation (C.A.T. Austin, Texas); Caldwell Air Cargo (C.A.C. Charlotte, North Carolina); Company Air Ways (C.A.W. Atlanta); Bank of Little Egypt (Marion, Illinois);[570] Boatmen's Bank of St. Louis, Missouri;[571] Pan Cargo;[572] Air Ticketing Network;[573] Liberty Loan; Dergo Company of Liechtenstein, owned by Mozar Al Kassar of Damascus, Syria; Permeian Partners Oil Transmission Company; Hiliti Corporation; trucking companies, including TMH and National Steel Carriers, divisions of National Steel; Georgetown Railroad; Wilson Railroad Company; International Mill Service; J.C. Hauling; Gerald Bull of the "Supergun" project; Adnan Khashoggi, well known arms dealer; Liberty Pipe and Tube; among others. Part of the evidence related to these activities is found in federal actions,[574] and in hundreds of pages of factual information that I received by phone and mail.

---

[568] Owned by Nippon Kokon of Japan, and owned in part and influenced by the Japanese crime family known as Yakuza.

[569] CIA proprietary, reportedly hauling drugs from Central and South America into the United States.

[570] Bank president Richard Dodd either committed suicide or was terminated.

[571] Major holder of Bank of Egypt's financial paper, including counterfeit money. President Armstrong ran off to South America.

[572] Reportedly operated by Sarrkes, nephew of King Saud of Saudi Arabia, in shipping hashish and heroin into the United States. The primary drug brought in was reportedly Turkish-Indian-Pakistan type heroin. Sarrkes was a business associate of S. Crittenden of Crittenden Cargo.

[573] With an office in San Francisco, owned by Pakistan personnel, with reportedly a secondary company in Denver called Colorado Satellite TV. These companies reportedly trafficked in heroin and other drugs. The primary type of drugs reportedly brought in was China White.

[574] *United States of America v. Robert Medley*, U.S. District Court, Western District of North Carolina, Nos. C-CR-90-186, 187, 188; *John Cole v. United States of America*, U.S. District Court, Southern District of Illinois, No. 92 CV 638 WLB.

These companies, with their intertwined contacts, and with CIA involvement, and with foreign interests secretly operating within the United States, engaged in many forms of criminality. Aircraft and weapons were stolen from U.S. manufacturers (often with their connivance), and shipped overseas, to friendly and unfriendly governments and factions. Drug shipments to the United States were a part of the web of intrigue.

NAVY SEAL TEAM COMMANDER AS WHISTLEBLOWER

Other concerned deep-cover CIA people came to me with information about serious misconduct, as my efforts became known. One of these was a former commander of Navy SEAL Team Two and formerly Executive Officer of Navy SEAL Team Six: Lieutenant Commander Robert J. Hunt.[575] We started communicating by letter and telephone in June 1993, providing me with documents and information that confirmed some of what other deep-cover operatives had stated to me, and greatly enlarging upon earlier discoveries.

Hunt provided me with ample documentation establishing his CIA/ONI status. Hunt had joined the U.S. Navy when he was seventeen, just as I did, and was later sheep-dipped into the Office of Naval Intelligence and then into the CIA. Hunt served under Commander Richard Marcinko who was commander of Navy SEAL team Six, and who authored *Rogue Warrior*. (Marcinko was one of the founders of the U.S. Navy's top secret SEAL Team Six, a counter-terrorist unit.)

One document, consisting of U.S. government travel orders, dated August 4, 1992, showed his rank and status as commander of SEAL Team Two. The travel orders were for him to proceed from LCRK Naval Air Base to Bahrain and then return, as part of an operation to seize Saddam Hussein. Other CIA and National Security Agency documents were sent to me prior to the publication of this book showing Hunt involved and named in other covert operations, leaving no doubt that he had significant roles in ONI and CIA operations.

In his CIA/ONI role, Hunt worked frequently with Israel's Mossad, and was well known to Israeli personnel. Hunt's CIA/ONI status as commander of Naval SEAT Team Two and his presence during key CIA and White House activities are shown by the documents and letters. Several of them also identify Gunther Russbacher as a member of the activities and being part of the Office of Naval Intelligence, a position and rank ridiculed by key media articles and members of Congress as they sought to cover up for several major criminal enterprises directed at the American people. A few of the documents and letters in my possession follows:

---

[575] Hunt's U.S. Navy serial number was 00254-31-66.

REQUEST AND AUTHORIZATION FOR TDY TRAVEL OF DOD PERSONNEL (Reference: Joint Travel Regulations) Travel Authorized as Indicated in Items 2 through 21.	1. DATE OF REQUEST 4 AUG 92

REQUEST FOR OFFICIAL TRAVEL

2. NAME (Last, First, Middle Initial)	3. POSITION TITLE AND GRADE OR RATING
HUNT, ROBERT J. SSN: 002-54-3166	Cdr, SEAL Team-Two LCDR

4. OFFICIAL STATION	5. ORGANIZATIONAL ELEMENT	6. PHONE NO.
LCRK NAB	COMNAVSPECWARG 305/66 3/32 NORFOLK, VA XVFAA	X7221

7. TYPE OF ORDERS	8. SECURITY CLEARANCE	9. PURPOSE OF TDY
TDY	TOP SECRET	EXERCISE AUGER MACE

10a. APPROX. NO. OF DAYS OF TDY (including travel time)	b. PROCEED O/A (Date)
120	10 AUG 92

11. ITINERARY

FROM: LCRK NAB
TO: BAHRAIN (VIA NAB LITTLE CREEK, VA)
RET: LCRK NAB

12. MODE OF TRANSPORTATION

COMMERCIAL				GOVERNMENT			PRIVATELY OWNED CONVEYANCE (Check one)
RAIL	AIR	BUS	SHIP	AIR	VEHICLE	SHIP	RATE PER MILE
	X			X	X	X	☐ MORE ADVANTAGEOUS TO GOVERNMENT

☐ AS DETERMINED BY APPROPRIATE TRANSPORTATION OFFICER (Overseas Travel only)

☐ MILEAGE REIMBURSEMENT AND PER DIEM LIMITED TO CONSTRUCTIVE COST OF COMMON CARRIER TRANSPORTATION & RELATED PER DIEM AS DETERMINED IN JTR. TRAVEL-TIME LIMITED AS INDICATED IN JTR.

13. ☒ PER DIEM AUTHORIZED IN ACCORDANCE WITH JTR
☐ OTHER RATE OF PER DIEM (Specify)

14. ESTIMATED COST					15. ADVANCE AUTHORIZED
PER DIEM	TRAVEL	OTHER		TOTAL	
$ 7290.00	$ 1570.00	$ 715.00		$ 9,575.00	$ YES

16. REMARKS (Use this space for special requirements, leave, superior or 1st class accommodations, excess baggage, registration fees, etc.)
OFFICER IS AUTHORIZED DELAY ENROUTE. WEAPONS WILL BE TRANSPORTED ACCORDING TO FAA/CAB REGULATIONS. THIS ORDER IS FUNDED BY DEPT OF STATE. REPORT TO USN LIAISON OFFICER, US EMBASSY BAHRAIN. EXPEDITED MOVEMENT DIRECTED IAW MTMC REG 55-355, INDIVIDUAL WILL BE ROUTED VIA MOST EXPEDITONS MODES. SPECIAL CONVEYANCES AUTH. RECIEPTS FOR ALL EXPENSES WILL BE SUBMITTED WITH DD 1351-2 IAW JTR

17. REQUESTING OFFICIAL (Title and signature)	18. APPROVING OFFICIAL (Title and signature)
GREG C. JONES, LT, USN CHIEF ADMIN, CODE 1001/AB	HOWARD J. THOMPSON, VADM, USN COMNAVSPECWARGP TWO

AUTHORIZATION

19. ACCOUNTING CITATION
2122080 24-2400 008040060 DSSN: 5073 APC M778 211A($7290.00)HUN788008X06001
214A($1570.00)HUN788008L06001
219A($ 715.00)HUN788008X06001

20. ORDER AUTHORIZING OFFICIAL (Title and signature) OR AUTHENTICATION	21. DATE ISSUED 08/04/92
MARTIN B. SLYZINSKY CH, ACCTG BR, PBD	22. TRAVEL ORDER NUMBER 8-7009

DD FORM 1 JUN 67 1610

Copy of Hunt's travel document showing his Navy rank and position as commander of Navy SEAL Team Two.

CONSULATE GENERAL OF ISRAEL   קונסוליה כללית של ישראל
CHICAGO   שיקאגו

October 4, 1993

LT. CMDR. Robert Hunt
Seal Team - Four/ONI.
LCRK NAB.
Norfolk, VA. 23505

Commander Hunt

Thank you for taking the time to write me. I have not heard from you in a long
time. I hope all is well with you.

In reference to your request, from N.S.C. regarding our files on May, 1986 operation MAGG PIE I am unable to send them to you, because of the nature of state
security of Israel. Please understand.

Because of our long working relationship and what you have ask for. I will give
you only the names of your agents that were at Tel Avivs Ben-Gurion airport in
may of 1986. our people have made note of Robert McFarlane, Oliver North, Robert
Hunt, George Cave, Howard Teicher, Amiran Nir and two pilots Gunter Russbacher
and John Segal. I hope this will help you in what ever you are doing.please
give me a call if their is any problems (708) 674-8861 wish you the best please
keep in touch you have my number.

Shalom

Yacov Nir
Consulate

October 4, 1993 letter from the Israeli consulate to Commander Hunt,
identifying several of the key participants in the arms-for-hostages activities,
including Robert Hunt and Gunther Russbacher.

EMBASSY OF ISRAEL
WASHINGTON, D.C.

שגרירות ישראל
וישינגטון

November 11, 1993

Lt. Cmdr. Robert Hunt
Seal Team-Four/ONI
LCRK NAB   Re: MAGG PIE
Norfolk, Virginia 23505   Spare Parts

Dear CDR. Hunt:

     This letter is to confirm your previous request from the National Sec-urity Council, as we had stated on May 25, 1986, a delegation headed by Robert C. McFarlane and including Oliver North (NSC), Robert Hunt (ONI), George Cave (CIA) and, Howard Teicher (CIA), left Israel on a plane piloted by Gunther K. Russbacher (ONI) and John R. Segal (CIA).

     On the plane was one pallet of Hawk spare parts. As part of the plan, General Richard Secord remained in Israel with the 707 loaded with the additional twelve pallets of spare parts. Gen. Secord stood ready to deliver them to Iran upon receiving word from the delegation.

     The Iranians however did not release the hostages at the end of the three days of negotiating. The Iranians offered the U.S. delegation the release of two hostages in return for the delivery of the remaining 12 pallets of Hawk spare parts. Col. North was ready to accept the offer, but Robert McFarlane refused and the delegation left Iran. This is all I can provide to you on the subject. Please direct all inquirys to our Office of Foreign Affairs. at 3 Kaplan Street, Kiryat Ben-Gurion, 91919, Jerusalem, Israel.

                   Yours truly,

                   Moshe Ben-Manash
                   Special Envoy to the Ambassador

cc: Office of the Ambassador
     Office of Legal Counsel

MBM/cal

3514 INTERNATIONAL DRIVE, N.W. • WASHINGTON, D.C. 20008 • TEL: (202) 364-5500 • FAX: (202) 364-0607 • TELEX: 23 904158

November 11, 1993 letter from Israel Embassy describing arms-for-hostages activities, and listing Gunther Russbacher and Robert Hunt as ONI.

These confirmations of Robert Hunt and Gunther Russbacher as members of the Office of Naval Intelligence in matters of national interest eliminates any question about their status in ONI and CIA. During the many months that Hunt and I spoke and exchanged letters he made it very clear that he worked extensively with Gunther Russbacher, Oliver North, and several of my other CIA contacts.

Hunt's first assignment was part of the second planned rescue of the American hostages held by Iran in 1980, called Operation Snow Bird. Because the Reagan-Bush group involved in the October Surprise scheme publicized these plans during the 1980 presidential campaign, the rescue operation had to be cancelled.

Hunt initially gave me a limited amount of information, and then as he gained confidence in me, and recognized that I was trying to expose serious corruption by federal officials, he loosened up and gave me additional information. Much of what he said to me was confirmed by other CIA/ONI contacts. Hunt was disturbed by the renegade nature of high officials in the U.S. intelligence agencies, and his cooperation with me was to bring about a halt to these activities.

Hunt was in frequent contact with the Mossad. He gave me a picture of himself and a Mossad agent, which is shown below:

DECLARATION

I, Robert Hunt, declare under penalty of perjury:

1. I am a Lt. Commander in the United States Navy, and have had numerous assignments as a Naval officer, including Commander of Navy Seal Team Two (from 6/85 to 8/87), and Executive Officer of Navy Seal Team Six (from 12/87 to 12/89). My Navy serial number is 002-54-3166. I have been in the U.S. Navy since 1979.

As it relates to Gunther Karl Russbacher:

2. I occasionally worked with or under Gunther Karl Russbacher.

3. During my fourteen years working for the Office of Naval Intelligence (ONI) and National Security Council (NSC), along with regular duty with the U.S. Navy, the Russbacher name was frequently mentioned.

4. I knew him to be an officer in the United States Navy, assigned to the Office of Naval Intelligence, and to the Central Intelligence Agency. It is my belief that when I saw Gunther Russbacher in 1986 that he held the rank of Captain. At that time I was assigned to the National Security Council (NSC).

5. Russbacher acted in part as one of the pilots carrying out duties for the NSC.

6. I saw Russbacher in 1990 while he and I were at Castle Air Force Base.

7. There is no doubt in my mind that Gunther Karl Russbacher was, and probably still is, an officer in the United States Navy, assigned in part to the Office of Naval Intelligence, and the Central Intelligence Agency.

8. For further confirmation of these statements and declarations I can be reached by contacting the following headquarter location (or by contacting Rodney Stich, P.O. Box 5, Alamo, CA 94595, Phone 510-944-1930):

NATIONAL SECURITY COUNCIL
9800 Savage Road

Fort Meade, Maryland 20755

I declare the above statements/declarations to be true and correct, to the best of my knowledge and belief. Executed this ___8___ day of November 1993, in the City of Springfield, Missouri.

Robert J. Hunt
Robert J. Hunt

Subscribed and sworn to before me
18 day of December 1993
Margaret E. Branyan
Notary Public

MARGARET E BRANYAN
NOTARY PUBLIC STATE OF MISSOURI
GREENE COUNTY
MY COMMISSION EXP. AUG. 26,1995

Declaration given by Commander Robert Hunt, at the author's suggestion, stating that he knew Gunther Russbacher as a Naval officer, and occasionally worked with him.

CIA ASSASSINATION SQUADS

During several telephone conversations Hunt enlarged upon what he had written to me, giving me additional information. He described his knowledge of CIA assassination teams, based upon his training of some of the teams, and his involvement with them. Hunt wrote that the training for Operation Ringwind occurred at Camp Perry near Washington, D.C., and his initial handlers were John Michoud of the Office of Naval Intelligence and Blain McCurts of the CIA. Later, Graham Fuller took over. The operation was created by Charles McKee, Matthew Gannon, John McChoud, and Blain McCurts, and put under the control of Robert Gates when he was Deputy Director of the Central Intelligence Agency. Referring to the assassination teams, Hunt said:

> They call it Operation Ringwind, formed in early 1981. It was strictly to take care of all participants in October Surprise until they decide to shut the operation down. And that could be tomorrow morning, or ten years from now. Whoever they think is involved.

Hunt stated that one of Operation Ringwind's operations occurred at Fort Ord, California, on April 30, 1991: the destruction of the Navy helicopter on which Russbacher was to have been. Responding to my question, Hunt said:

> Gunther was at TI [Terminal Island Federal Prison] from my under- standing. My orders were to be at Fort Ord, on such and such a date, I think it was April or May. Our objective was to intercept this aircraft, because I was aware, and I wasn't running this team, I'm not the ringleader, that he was on board with documentation.
>
> I asked an agent back East, "What is this information?" He said "for the president's eyes only." Now, I don't ask questions. And I didn't know Gunther from a hole in the wall. Even if I did, if I had a job to kill my brother, I'd do it. My job was to meet him at Fort Ord, and take him. I mean totally take him; take his information and do away with him.
>
> I hate to say this to you. And I hope Gunther doesn't feel bad in any way. My job was to take the information that he was carrying. It is my guess, from what I've read, that it was a tape of the 71 [SR-71] and a lot of classified documentation. And do away with him. That was the purpose. My job was to infiltrate these people onto the base and give them covert identities and put them into a status where we would not be noticeable on the flight line.
>
> After I came back to the base, all of a sudden I hear an explosion that would just rattle your God damn teeth. I said to these guys, "What is going on here?" And they said they just took care of the situation. My understanding of what had happened, the people in operation Ringwind were actually the people who destroyed that aircraft. From my understanding there were explosives placed on that aircraft before it had left (Alameda Naval Air Station). They knew who they were going to get, they knew the target, and there was only one helicopter involved.

Electronic detonating device and it was probably Simplex. It was probably what we call a rotation cap, which is put into it, and it is set off by signal. And it could have been set up either by signal wave from the tower as they were coming through, or the people on my ground detonated it. I think there was a double backup on that.

Showing the mindset in the intelligence agencies, the blind carrying out of orders, regardless of their unlawful nature, Hunt said:

A lot of people were involved in the October Surprise doings. It is my understanding, I didn't have what you call total profile knowledge, I was told to go to Spot A, Spot B, spot C, and just take care of Mr. so and so, and so-on and so-on. And you know, we never asked questions. If someone said, take care of Rodney, it would be done. If I knew it came from my command or my source, I would certainly not have any problem with that. As I mention those names to you it kind of scares me a little bit. I wonder what would happen if this backfired on me.

In another letter:

It is believed that Parkers' group, 222, had a leak. This is where Operation Ringwind came into place. They were to expose all of the members of Pegasus including Captain G [Russbacher]. As you know, Ringwind was a CIA Hit Team that was put together in the early 1980s.[576] Its primary purpose was to eliminate all people involved in October Surprise. This team trained at Camp Perry, under the guidance of my team and the former head of the FBI Rescue Team. We taught them every deadly sin they know. As for Fort Ord, we were there with them to assist in their operations. It is my belief they put a bomb in that helicopter. BOQ at Fort Ord will reflect my stay there on those dates. As for October Surprise, my involvement was limited.

Hunt stated that the reason for his presence at Fort Ord was to report back to the CIA at Langley what he had seen and heard the night that the helicopter blew up. He stated that he was later contacted for more information by John McChoud (Office of Naval Intelligence) and Blain McCurts (CIA).

The mindset imposed upon people in the intelligence agencies by officials in control of these activities was reflected by a statement made by Hunt in an October 20, 1993 letter:

I remember when I had orders to take him out, I never looked beyond those orders. I just did my job.

FOLLOWING RUSSBACH IN ANOTHER OPERATION

Hunt's handlers told Hunt to follow Russbacher to Castle Air Force Base in 1990, after Russbacher returned from the trip to Moscow. Hunt wrote in various letters, including a July 12, 1993 writing:

I had orders by my handlers to follow Captain Russbacher. Why was uncertain because you never ask. I know he was at Castle Air Base in July of 1990 for a debriefing. He talked about an SR71 flight that left

---

[576] Russbacher stated to me that the head of Operation Ringwind was Robert Gates while he was Assistant Deputy Director of the CIA's Operations Division.

NAS Crows Landing. My guess was that the plane went to Russia. After my debriefing my handlers sent me to Fort Ord in April of 91. You know what happened that night. You know the rest of the story. I think the mission was to do away with Captain Russbacher. I helped the CIA team get into the base to do it. The Team that has been doing all of these hits are CIA. My SEAL Team Six trained these people at Camp Perry. It was called Operation Ringwind. There were eight people involved in it. As far as I know they are still active.

MISSILES FOR PRISONERS

Another operation in which Hunt was involved was Operation Cappuccino, the intent of which was to send TOW missiles from the United States to Iran and cause the release of Ben Weir. In another CIA operation, Hunt was involved with Ya'acov Nimrodi was Operation Espresso. Hunt wrote:

I met a man by the name of Amiram Nir, whom the CIA later killed in Mexico. I was introduced to Ya'acov Nimrodi, along with David Kimche, Al Schmimmer. I was at the King David Hotel in Jerusalem and briefed [Vice President George] Bush fully about the arms sales. Nir [who was later killed by the CIA] taped the whole thing. Bush had known he was being taped. This was in July 1989. I knew because we gave him the recording equipment to do it, and that was another reason they whacked [killed] him.

Hunt described part of the operation, including the meeting which he attended at the King David Hotel at which there were in attendance two assets of the CIA, Charles McKee and Matthew Gannon. McKee and Gannon were subsequently killed on board Pan Am Flight 103 which was blown up over Ireland. Numerous articles have been written about McKee being the primary target of the Pan Am bombing. As part of this operation, Hunt met Amiram Nir, who was later killed by the CIA.

Nir was killed because he tape-recorded a conversation with Vice-President George Bush in Israel describing the sale of arms to Iran, and that Nir intended to release the tape to the media.

ARMS TO THE CONTRAS

Another operation in which Hunt was involved was Operation Tipped Kettle, which consisted of shipping arms to the Contras that had been earlier seized from the PLO by Israel. Hunt stated that Operation Tipped Kettle operated under Morton Abromowitz, Chief of Intelligence in the U.S. Department of State.

BRIBE MONEY FOR FEDERAL JUDGES, TRUSTEES, LAW FIRMS

Earlier pages described the source of bribe money for federal judges, trustees and law firms, involving the Dublin, Ireland corporation, Shamrock Overseas Disbursement Corporation. Hunt described his brief role in that operation, during November 1989, carrying funds from Ireland into a newly opened CIA bank account at the Royal Bank of Canada in Kirkland, Montreal.

SABOTAGED PLAN TO CAPTURE NORIEGA AND MOSSAD AGENT HARARI

Hunt was involved in an operation in Panama to capture Manuel Noriega and Israel's Mossad operative Michael Harari, and bring them to the United States. Harari was heavily involved in drug trafficking with the CIA and DEA, and very probably more to blame than Noriega for drug trafficking into the United States. This secret operation was sabotaged by a rival CIA group, causing Hunt to be shot and four of his men killed. Hunt stated that another faction in the CIA learned of his mission and informed Noriega (or Harari) of the mission. That operation was called Operation Blue Spoon. Hunt wrote:

> *My team and I went to Panama in December 1989, and because of these ..... I lost four of my men and being wounded myself. The Company had told them we were coming. It's a dirty game Rodney and you know it.*

Hunt said:

> *I lost four men that night because [of their mission being revealed to the Mossad and Noriega]. We hit that beach, we were sitting off the coastline actually. We went up from Howard, we were on rafts, and we were told to assault the beach at one o'clock, so we started in early. I said to this guy that we weren't going to hit it at one, we were going to hit it at twelve forty-five [a.m.].*
>
> *So we hit the far end of the beach where the runway comes in on Petella. As we were coming in, all of a sudden a jet takes off. I said "Noriega's gone," and I get on my Comset, my satellite communication phone, and call Joint J-sock, joint operations command center, and I say, "Noriega," we call him Eagle One, I said Eagle One's in flight. They said impossible. There was a ship, it was an LPH, that was monitoring all the flights, and they had E-6 and they confirmed that this aircraft was in the air. We went to the Hangar Three area and there was Noriega's plane. I said, "Harari must have taken off."*

Before rolling aircraft onto the runway to prevent Noriega's plane from taking off, Hunt and his team prepared to "blow up the hangar and cause some confusion." But before they could accomplish this, Hunt explained what happened:

> *All of a sudden it was like a bomb going off. It was incredible. Machine guns started blazing and I thought, "What in the world was going on?" I looked and I had four guys laying on the ground [dead]. I called on the phone for backups, because I had another team at Howard Air Force Base to assist. They were coming in, but they said they were being pinned down by PDF fire, call Spector.*
>
> *I said I can't get Spector in here, call in a Cobra gun-ship or something. So I was calling for both, Spector and a gun-ship. Then I got shot. Before I knew it, Rangers were showing up everywhere. They were popping out of the sky like it was popcorn, and they assisted us. They assisted us in blowing up Noriega's jet. We actually melted the thing right in the hangar. And from there I went off to Bethesda [Naval Hospital], where I stayed for a couple of weeks until I recovered.*

Hunt was absolutely positive that factions within the CIA forewarned Noriega about the operation, resulting in his SEAL Team being trapped, several of his men being killed, and causing failure of the operation. If that advance warning hadn't been given, and the team succeeded in capturing Noriega and Harari, the thousands of deaths that would soon accompany the invasion could have been avoided.

Instead of Noriega having been warned by an unknown CIA faction, I offered the thought that it was the Mossad who was forewarned due to the heavy involvement between the CIA and DEA and the Mossad in drug trafficking into the United States. I suggested to Hunt: "I am wondering if the [CIA informants] were primarily interested in protecting the Mossad's rep, Harari." I added: "I knew there were factions within the CIA that were working with Harari in drug trafficking. The last thing that faction wants is for the Mossad's drug trafficking to be exposed." Hunt replied:

You know, that is a very good theory. I don't doubt that, because I don't think they gave a s... for Noriega. But the Mossad. You know, that's a hell of a theory. I think you are the first one that ever brought that across. They might have really been protecting him. And that is why they had such a PDF force standing there, because Noriega was nowhere in sight. He was gone. From my understanding, he was well into the hills.

ASSASSINATION FOLLOWING SECRET RECORDING OF BUSH IN THE IRAN-CONTRA AFFAIR

Hunt described the flights to Teheran in 1986 seeking to trade arms for the release of American hostages seized in Lebanon. Hunt described a series of flights to Teheran with Colonel Oliver North and others during 1986. Hunt's role was to provide security. During one of these trips to Teheran a hostile group of guards suddenly surrounded the group, and Hunt pulled out his pistol, causing the guards to back off. The first flight to Teheran was the one with the cake and dueling pistols that had received publicity. The second flight carried 80 TOW missiles.

Hunt described sitting in the Hilton Hotel in Geneva with Richard Secord, Oliver North, Amiram Nir, Manuchehr Ghorbanifar, Ya'acov Nimrodi, and an Iranian Intelligence Chief, waited for the 80 TOW missiles to go from Israel to Teheran via Portugal. He described how Secord and Robert McFarlane failed to get landing rights in Portugal, causing the El Al plane carrying the missiles to return to Tel Aviv. Hunt stated that it was decided to send 18 missiles on each flight, for which one American was to be released.

A confidential CIA memorandum signed by CIA Director Bill Bush, dated May 20, 1986, shows Robert Hunt as one of the passengers on the jet flight from Israel's Ben Gurion Airport to Teheran. It also shows Gunther Russbacher as one of the pilots, and identified him as CIA.

Hunt described a meeting occurring in Israel in 1986 at which he had a security role, guarding, among others, then Vice-President George Bush. Bush discovered later that Nir had secretly tape-recorded the meeting, and was planning to expose the activities involving Bush and the CIA. This exposure, and the tape recordings, threatened to expose many high U.S. officials, including Bush, and expose some of the secrets described within these pages. Nir had to be eliminated so as to protect these people and operations.

While at CIA headquarters at Langley, Virginia, Hunt asked Oliver North where Nir was, as Hunt hadn't seen Nir for a period of time. Hunt described this brief conversation:

Colonel North told me that Nir was killed because of his involvement in recording the Jerusalem meeting in 1986. I asked North where was Nir, and he said, "Nir has been taken care of." I said, Why? Because of the Jerusalem meeting.

I was told by the Colonel (Oliver North) himself.

REVEALING CIA METHODS OF INDUCING DEATH

Hunt had previously told me several times that he and his team taught methods of inducing death upon those targeted for sanctions (extermination). I asked Hunt to describe several of the methods used to carry out this operation. He described the use of the chemical, Rohine. He said:

It is used two ways. I have never used that particular one. From my understanding it is self absorbing. It can be put on a letter. It could be put on the rim of a glass, or injected. It has a self-absorbing base. It causes cardiac arrest and leaves no trace.

He described the use of Potassium Chloride, which is injected into the body and reportedly takes the electrolytes out of the brain, causing cardiac arrest.

Hunt described the use of Draino to bring about a person's death. He said:

From what I understand and from how I've seen it used, Draino will cause internal bleeding. It used to be one of the oldest methods, a lot of the pimps would use it on their prostitutes. They would hold them down on the floor and then pour the Draino down the person's throat. This would cause convulsions, and the person's insides start bleeding. It eats up the entire body. That is one method commonly used in the Agency.

ELABORATING ON HIS ROLE IN THE GULF WAR

Hunt described his role in the bombings during the Gulf War in Operation Desert Shield and then Desert Storm and his team's placement of laser homing devices on key buildings in Baghdad. He stated that his Navy SEAL Team and a group of Army Green Berets entered Iraq from Iran, and then proceeding down the Tigris River. His team placed the homing devices on key buildings that were later bombed. He stated that the team left Iraq via that same route.

Hunt wrote: "Let me tell you when that bombing started, it was incredible. I've never been in anything like that in my life."

Hunt described his involvement with the CIA money laundering, describing the dealings with such banks as Israel Discount Bank in Tel Aviv and its branch in Geneva, Switzerland. He described how money from CIA operations in the United States, including the drugs and financial institutions, gets overseas through real estate companies, warehouses, and overseas corporations, using company names. He cited as several of the front companies, Stanford Technology and Brooking Institute. He wrote that these have a "very large CIA involvement; everyone looks at them and thinks they are think tanks, with all of the analysts there."

Hunt described some of the CIA proprietaries that he dealt with, including Doan Helicopters in Florida, outside of Daytona Beach, Florida and Sherman

Aviation out of Fort Lauderdale. He described another CIA proprietary or front in the Reno, Nevada area called CIA Aviation.

HUNT'S ROLE IN TEHERAN FLIGHTS

Hunt described to me his role on the flight to Teheran in 1986, seeking to negotiate with the Iranians to cause the release of Americans held captive after being seized in Beirut. Russbacher had also described his role in that flight, and I compared their statements, which checked out against each other. Hunt stated that the aircraft had been painted in Israel with the colors of the Irish airline, Air Lingus, to cover up for the actual origin of the aircraft. He stated the plane left Israel's Ben Gurion Airport for Teheran on what he thought was about the 25th of May or June of 1986. He identified one of the pilots as Robert John Segal.

Hunt described his role as security and briefing of the pilots. He stated that others on the flight included Oliver North, George Cave, Howard Teicher, Robert McFarlane, among others.

OPERATION AUGER MACE AND SADDAM HUSSEIN

Operation Auger Mace was a Kuwaiti war-game exercise in 1992, which served as a cover for Hunt and his Navy SEAL Team to go into Baghdad for the purpose of capturing Saddam Hussein. Hunt stated:

Our mission there was to go into Baghdad and actually try and bring Saddam back to the United States. The purpose was to help President Bush win reelection. Bush knew at that point in the game that he was in trouble. So we went in Bahrain, and from Bahrain we went to Tel Aviv, working with an Israeli General by the name of Uri Simhoni. He was an attaché at the Israel Embassy in Washington at one time. He was a Major General and with his Intel network we were to go into Baghdad, extract Saddam Hussein, bring him back, similar to what we did with Noriega. This operation was put together with my unit and also a Delta unit, and we were to go in there with the Israeli and extract him from his quarters, right outside of Baghdad, and just take him on out.

CIA DRUG ACTIVITIES AND PAN AM 103

Hunt described his knowledge of CIA drug activities from the Middle East to the United States using Pan American flights. He said:

The money and the drugs were being flown through those Pan Am flights from Europe. Michael Pallack helped coordinate those things. In fact, there is a guy, I only met him once, his name was Major Turnabey, he was the Intelligence Chief for the popular front for the liberation of Palestine. And he had a lot to do with Pallack and his whole gang. They would actually coordinate, do actual drug running, right on through Germany and into the United States.

Hunt described two CIA operatives on Pam Am 103 that he personally knew, who were returning to the United States to report the CIA involvement in drug trafficking. Referring to these two CIA operatives, Hunt said:

These two guys, McKee and the other gentlemen,[577] were involved in Operation Ringwind. They're the ones who helped train all those people in the early eighties. And they were very deep-deep-cover experts in Mideast terrorism. And they were so pissed-off at what was happening they just went in to blow the whistle. When the Agency heard that, I have a gut feeling that the CIA blew the plane up.

I asked, "What type of drug operation did the CIA have, using Pan Am?"" Hunt replied, "Well, they were putting the stuff on Pan Am." Referring to other CIA figures, Hunt said, "And that's where Victor Marchetti and all came in. They were all into this. All these guys, it was just one big giant clique."

BIZARRE SEIZURE OF U.S. NUCLEAR SUBS

Hunt enlarged upon an operation ordered by the White House which caused him and his crew to end up in prison for refusing to disclose the source of the orders. Hunt stated that he and his Navy SEAL Team were ordered by the White House Command Center to test military security by taking over U.S. nuclear submarines that were either in port or at sea. He described the operation and one submarine takeover that sounds like fiction:

There was an organization I was with, called OPO6D. That was the unit designation number, and it came out of an organization called Red Cell, which I may have mentioned in one of my letters. Our unit went to the electric boat company at New London, Connecticut, and took a submarine over, just to prove that we could get into a shipyard like that and do this. I was involved in two submarine takeovers. One was in New London, and that involved a sub in one of the pens being fixed up. The crew was totally on board. We went in and took it over one night to show that we could actually break into a nuclear submarine base like that to show the weakness in base security.

Hunt described the second submarine seizure, and were it not for recognition of intelligence agency capabilities, it would sound like extreme fantasy. The second submarine seizure was in the middle of the Mediterranean. Hunt described that operation:

This was a White House operation, and occurred right in the heart of the Mediterranean. We parachuted out of a C-130. We knew the exact coordinates where the ship was going to be. We jumped probably six miles ahead of this vessel, the U.S.S. Bill Fish, with our rubber boats. We waited for her, and she showed up right on time. I think it was two-thirty in the morning that we took her.

She was running on the surface. We took the crew hostage, took her launch codes, all her data including her navigation data, and tied up the crew. The Navy thought they had a lost sub, they just didn't have any way of communicating. We got out of there and we were rendezvoused, we were picked up. This was in 1987. Later a destroyer or frigate, the John Hancock, intercepted her. The Navy couldn't

---

[577] Believed to include Matthew Gannon and Ronald Lariviere.

believe that something like this could happen.

Hunt continued to explain that operation:

This was a direct order from the White House Command Center, because they wanted to see how vulnerable the U.S. is to an attack or takeover. They play these games in the White House all the time. Now when I was with this unit, the OPO6D unit, I had long hair, a beard, I looked like a real dam terrorist.

You know, it came to a point where we went on this vessel. We blew the locks. They had water-tight doors. We blew up the locks on the conning tower of the island, whatever you want to call it, and the captain was in horror. We jumped down the railing with MP-5 machine guns. Half the crew was asleep at that time of night, the stand-by crew was running it. And there were probably about thirty guys running it. Total horror.

I told the captain right then and there that we want your LK5 codes and your K41 codes. Those are the actual launch codes for the weapon systems. He said "I'm going to refuse to give them to you." I put a gun right into his mouth and said, "I will kill you right here." He opened up the safe. He gave us everything we needed. We were gone in about an hour.

Hunt continued:

The Navy sent vessels looking for the sub. They intercepted her. They boarded it and found the whole crew tied up. Now Naval Intelligence gets involved. The FBI gets into this. The only people who know about this is the White House and a few members of the Joint Chiefs. The White House says just forget it. We know about it. Just hush it up. That is what happened.

Actually, for us, it was a training exercise for the White House to see if something like that could ever possibly happen. And it can, truly can happen. It is like another situation, we took Elliott Abrams hostage one night, right there in Washington, D.C. Now here is the Assistant Secretary of Defense wondering, "How can this happen?" We proved it could happen.

Admittedly, this sounds bizarre, and I would have omitted any reference to it if I had not heard from other deep-cover CIA sources who stated it did happen. I present the information for the reader to accept, withhold a decision, or refuse to believe it.

After several of these ultra-secret operations proved too embarrassing, the White House ordered them halted. Hunt stated that his immediate superior, CIA and ONI operative Richard Marcinko, received the order, but refused to inform him of that fact. As Hunt continued to conduct his ultra-secret operations, other factions in the compartmentalized intelligence community wanted to know the details of his team's operations. The Naval Investigative Service (NIS) sent investigators to seize the records of Hunt's SEAL Team. Hunt's immediate boss, Richard Marcinko, refused the investigators access to the records and orders Hunt and his team to destroy the records.

SENDING TO PRISON THE
COMMANDER OF NAVY SEAL TEAM TWO

A military court proceeding commenced in late 1992, finding Hunt and his team[578] guilty of contempt of court and obstruction of justice for refusing to testify about their operations and for having destroyed records. A Staff Judicial Adjutant (SJA) in Alexandria, Virginia, Hunt and his team were sentenced to six months in prison, with an additional six months for Hunt for contempt of court. Hunt was particularly angry because one of his CIA handlers, Graham Fuller, refused to support Hunt and his team.

Hunt's handlers told him, apparently falsely, that he would be out of prison shortly. This did not occur. This type of assurance was also given to other CIA personnel to keep them quiet, including Gunther Russbacher, Ronald Rewald.

Hunt stated that his pay was cut off, which he discovered upon checking with the Federal Credit Union where his pay was normally deposited. In typical intelligence agency fashion, the records were sanitized and Hunt was told that there was no record of him at the credit union. Ironically, while Hunt was in prison in September 1993, he stated that he received orders to report to the U.S. Navy Base at Norfolk, Virginia, where he was to take command of Navy SEAL Team Four.

MEDIA KNOWLEDGE OF HUNT'S ACTIVITIES

Hunt described the taping by the *60 minutes* show of him and his group, and the show's depiction of the group as phonies, based upon the bizarre nature of the secret activities of the SEAL team. Possibly those implicated in the incredible corruption rely partly on the extreme naivete of the American public, and parts of the mass media, for protection against exposure. The same would apply to the enormity of the criminal activities against the American people described within these pages, that are so gigantic in their implications that no one dares to expose them, partly out of fear that most of those in control of Congress and industry would suffer.

Hunt was also taped by *Current Affairs*, concerning his operation in Panama seeking to kidnap Noriega, and felt, because the scheme was so bizarre, that Hunt and his group were impostors. Using that attitude, it is not difficult to understand how the internal criminal activities against the United States, a virtual *coup de etat*, have gone undetected by the American public.

HOW CIA PERSONNEL CONTACT HEADQUARTERS

Among the many inner workings of the CIA that Hunt described was a system of communicating between Washington and the deep-cover people in the field, called Flashboard. He explained how CIA operatives call into one of several phone numbers at Langley, Virginia, and that a particular code is dialed, after which an operator comes on the line and asks for their code number.

Hunt gave me two numbers, an alphabetical number followed by four numbers. When I asked another CIA operative, Gunther Russbacher, about

---

[578] Except for Petty Officer John Mason, who testified and avoided prison.

these two numbers, he stated that one of them was a security number and one was a sanction number, used for taking out people that the Agency felt to be a danger to its operations.

TAXPAYER-FUNDED ASSASSINATION SQUADS

One of Commander Hunt's ONI duties was teaching assassination squads. He also referred to several private companies funded by the U.S. that were used to train U.S. and foreign personnel to carry out for-hire assassinations (something like the Jewish group known as Murder Incorporated).

One company, known by the acronym, ANV, was based in Jupiter, Florida, and was referred to as the Fish Farm. Shareholders in the company were present and former CIA personnel, reportedly involved in some aspect of CIA related drug trafficking. They included, for instance, Theodore Shackley, who was heavily involved in the CIA Far East drug trafficking and then in the drug trafficking from Central and South America, residing at present in Medellin, Columbia.

ANV was started as a CIA proprietary, and then converted to a private firm for the Agency's standard disavow purposes. ANV conducted much of its training, including assassination squads, on Andras Island in the Bahamas.

The ABC television network sought to run a story on these operations on Andras Island, sending a crew on a helicopter to film the Island from the air. Hunt stated that the ABC helicopter was shot down in 1991 or 1992, killing a woman reporter. The incident was kept from the American public, using national security as an excuse.

ANV functioned as an umbrella organization for various other groups, including the Phantom Battalion (based in Memphis) and the Peregrine Group (based in Texas). Hunt stated there were numerous ties between the groups and the Richard Secord-Theodore Shackley-and Thomas Clines Associates, all of whom were reportedly associated with the opium trade and assassination program in Laos.

One of the companies associated with ANV was known as CSA, founded by Robert C. (Stretch) Stevens, who worked for Shackley for over two decades in various CIA operations. Shackley was heavily involved in CIA drug trafficking from the Far East and in Central and South America.

A para-military group in ANV was known as the Phoenix Battalion, in which Inslaw's president, William Hamilton, was reported an officer. Hamilton reportedly recruited Sam Hall for the Phoenix Battalion.

Some managers of the Daisy Air Rifle Company provided property in Western Arkansas for the groups to use as a training Camp.

Another group under ANV was Peregrine International Associates, founded in 1981 by Guy S. Howard and Ronald R. Tucker founded Peregrine International Associates in 1981. They conducted covert operations with Defense Department approval from 1981 until 1989, when the company folded. Many of Peregrine's personnel were vets of Army Delta Force. The company hired both retired and active duty military personnel on leave to act as "guns"–guys who had no qualm about killing someone.

Peregrine received funds for their operations from U.S. agencies such as Customs, or from foreign governments which may have been drawing on

U.S. military assistance funds [supplied by U.S. taxpayers]. Their assassination targets included drug smugglers acting in competition with CIA and DEA personnel in Peru, Honduras, Belize, and various Caribbean nations. They also armed and trained Contras, and military command units in El Salvador, Honduras and Peru.

Richard J. Meadows served for a time as Peregrine's president. Charles Odorizzo and William Patton, worked for the group. Peregrine's key contacts were retired Army Lt. Gen. Samuel Wilson (former Director of the DIA) and Lt. Col. Wayne E. Long, who as of April 1987 worked as a senior officer in the Foreign Operations Group, which is part of the Army's intelligence support activity office.

OPERATION BLUE GREMLIN

Hunt described other CIA operations to me, including Operation Ho Ho Ho. When I asked Russbacher if he knew about the operation, he enlarged upon it, stating that Operation Ho Ho Ho was the name given to it by those in the field, but that the Agency code name was Operation Blue Gremlin, further identified in communications by the alpha-numeric identification OP BG 1741.5A. They described Blue Gremlin as a planned blowing up of buildings in Teheran in December 1984, but which for various reasons, was never carried out.

ISRAEL'S INFILTRATION OF
THE NATIONAL SECURITY COUNCIL

Hunt had told me earlier that a high official of one of Israel's secret agencies was on the staff of the United States National Security Council, and when I asked who he was, he game me the name: Moshe Ben Lafven, who went under the American name of Steven Croch. If there had been no other scandal described within these pages, the infiltration of one of the most secret government agencies in the United States by a foreign government would be a major scandal.

Hunt had given me considerable information substantiating that my first CIA contact Gunther Russbacher was in fact assigned to the CIA and ONI. Indicating his prior working relationship with the Mossad, the Israeli Embassy in Washington sent two letters to Hunt, which follow:

Hunt and I frequently discussed the absurdity of his imprisonment. As stated earlier, Hunt was sent to prison, along with six members of his team, and with Richard Marcinko, for having destroyed documents relating to the secret activities of Navy SEAL Team Six while on orders from the White House through the National Security Council. Marcinko received a much longer prison sentence because he demanded a trial, while Hunt pleaded guilty to a misdemeanor (and then received a six month prison term plus another six months for contempt of court).

In October 1993 Hunt complained to his ONI handlers about his long prison term, and behind-the-scene activities resulted in an unusual letter from President Bill Clinton to Hunt.

LETTER OF APPRECIATION FROM
PRESIDENT BILL CLINTON TO HUNT

It isn't often that a president of the United States sends a letter of appreciation to an inmate in federal prison, but this happened with Commander Robert Hunt. On November 22, 1993, while Hunt was still in prison and communicating with me, President Bill Clinton sent Hunt a letter "apologizing for the unfortunate circumstances that have you incarcerated." Before ending the letter, Clinton wrote, "I am confident that in time you will realize justice was done." Neither Hunt, nor I, felt it was in the interest of justice for him to be imprisoned for almost a year.

THE WHITE HOUSE

WASHINGTON

November 22, 1993

Lt. Cmdr. Robert Hunt
Office of Naval Intelligence
LCRK, NAB,
Norfolk, Virginia 23505

Dear Cmdr. Hunt:

It gives me great pleasure in writing. I apologize for the unfortunate circumstances that have you incarcerated, but we here at the White House are pursuing a proper channel to effect your release. I truely believe that it's a travesty of justice to our country and its integrity that a career Naval Intelligence Officer, such as yourself, has been mistakingly incarcerated for acting under orders from your superiors. We intend to enact proper controls so as to prevent those mistakes from reoccurring in our administration.

I have had conversation with the Director of the Central Intelligence Agency (CIA) and the Chief of Naval Operations (CNO) regarding the circumstances of your case and they have assured me that a full investigation will be finalized in the near future and they will be in contact with you personally.

You must understand, when handling matters of national security, on a worldwide basis, along with the magnitude of our own government, events do appear to be out of control at times, but let me assure you personally that in most cases there is more to these stories out of the press than meets the eye, and we attempt to make every good faith effort to reach fair resolves. I believe that as a career Naval Intelligence Officer you can relate to the complexity of those processes and the patience one must endure. I am confident that in time you will realize justice was done. My thanks for all your endurance and contributions to the American way of life.

Sincerely yours,

Bill Clinton

BC/sjr

cc: Admiral Frank Kelso II
    Chief, Naval Ops (CNO)

Hunt was released from prison on December 8, 1993, and continued furnishing me with information about the corrupt activities he witnessed inside the U.S. intelligence agencies. His concern about these renegade activities caused him to become somewhat of a renegade, blowing the whistle in an attempt to make the public aware of them and hopefully bring the guilty to justice and cause a halt in the criminal nature of the CIA and other agencies. His statements to me were intended to bring this about.

Hunt enlarged upon the Agency drug trafficking out of the CIA San Francisco office, giving me names of the participants, including federal judges that were reportedly protecting the criminal operations. Hunt added to the names given to me earlier by Russbacher in Operation New Wave. Among the names he gave me were Zenelle International Cosmetics, reportedly based in Danville, California, and its managers, Will and Zen Zenelle. Russbacher confirmed to me the accuracy of this information.

DAILY CONTACTS WITH CIA, FBI, AND OTHER INFORMANTS

I was in almost daily contact with one or more deep-cover high-ranking Agency personnel since late 1990. I became the focal point for CIA whistle-blowers who called and sent me information from all over the United States. These years of contacts gave me an insight into the ugly side of the federal government that is totally unknown by most Americans. This information and supporting documents enlarged upon what I had earlier discovered as a federal investigator for the Federal Aviation Administration, as a private investigator, and what I discovered as I became a victim. It is this combination of events that makes *Defrauding America* one of the most unusual books ever printed as to government corruption.

One of my contacts was a former FBI agent, Darlene Novinger, who had been blackballed out of the FBI after she reported drug involvement by George Bush. During a conversation on December 30, 1993 Darlene stated to me that several high FBI officials with whom she was still in contact recommended that she reads *Defrauding America* to determine the extent of corruption within the CIA and other government agencies. She implied ignorance of the book, even though she had been in frequent contact with me, and furnished me information to include in subsequent editions, a small part of which made it into this edition.

PLANNED ASSASSINATION OF
PRESIDENTIAL CANDIDATE BILL CLINTON?

Because of the sensitivity of a covert operation by a section of the U.S. intelligence agencies, I am identifying the operative who told me about it as "Agent X." I have copies of documents showing this agent's military rank in one of the U.S. intelligence agencies, and am convinced of his status. This agent told me about an operation ordered to be carried out by high Washington personnel in mid-1992, under the code name, Operation Mount Rushmore. He said that it involved the San Francisco law firm of Heller, Ehrman, White, and McCauliffe,[579] and several Mossad agents reportedly working for the firm. Agent X described Operation Mount Rushmore and the apparent major control over it by the Mossad agents and attorneys. The agent said:

[It] could blow the lid right off the White House. The name of it is Operation Mount Rushmore. Operation Mount Rushmore was an attempt to assassinate presidential candidate Bill Clinton when he came into San Francisco. They called it Mount Rushmore because of the heads of the presidents. What I was to do, I was at the Presidio in San Francisco, and I met a Mossad agent who was also involved in this.

And there was a company in Redwood City called EIC. They are on Woodside Road in Redwood City, and the guy who runs it is the owner, Chan Wang. He is a member of an organization called the "Eagles." He is a Chinese guy. It is my understanding that he was financing this entire operation. He was in touch with the law firm of Heller, Ehrman, White, and McCauliffe.

Agent X continued, indicating further Mossad involvement in Operation Mount Rushmore:

There was an attorney I briefly met, whose name was [name withheld at Agent X's request], and he was an attorney at Hiller Erman, and he was handling some part of this operation. From my understanding, these people were organized. I was at the Presidio training some people, and they wanted to do a sanction on candidate Clinton when he came into San Francisco.

Things got screwed up, and the whole operation went sour, and everybody went under ground. The Mossad agent I was in touch with, I never heard from her again. I talked to some people at the State Department and everything was hush-hush and quiet. And it all just dropped off the face of the earth. And then two days later I get orders to go overseas, which are the orders I sent you. After Rushmore went sour, we were told to get the hell out. The State Department wrote the orders and I was gone the next day.

Agent X said, "I was told to go there [San Francisco] last summer and meet a Mossad agent, which I did. I asked, "Why San Francisco," and they said Bill Clinton is coming and we need to talk to you. That is the reason for being

---

[579] Located at 333 Bush Street, San Francisco, California.

in the Bay Area, the Rushmore operation." The agent continued:

Well, here is what happened. I was involved with Operation Ring-wind, which is the team that actually went out and assassinated the people in the very first letter I mentioned to you.[580] I know the names. I try and remember them out of memory, and the notes I make throughout my life. Our operation was with McKee and the other gentlemen who were killed on Flight 103. We actually trained these people at Camp Perry, Virginia. And we also trained them out of Fort Story and at Vint Farm Hill, which is the Intelligence Center. And we briefed them on everything. The object of this unit was to eliminate everyone that was involved in October Surprise.

Everyone who had information pertaining that was not involved militarily, to do away with them. With the military people that were involved, and there were a variety of generals and colonels and so forth, it was handled in a different way. They had training accidents, or they were put so far into retirement that they didn't know what the hell was going on.

And these were the people, there are about seven of them, who are involved in this now. They were actually in the [San Francisco] Bay Area along with myself, and they were going to take care of this operation which involved the Mossad, to take care of Mr. Clinton.

"Why would they want the Mossad in this," I asked.

Agent X answered: "I don't know, and that is one of the things that threw me. Why the Mossad? What do the Israeli have to do with this?" He continued:

When I talked to the Israeli Intel officer he said, "We have our reason." I guess it was because Bush had such a rapport with Israel, they wanted to see him get reelected. And if it involved getting rid of Mr. Clinton, and I hate to say it over a phone, but that is what it came down to.

Agent X continued: "My contacts go back to the early eighties with Duane Claridge and Charles Allen; they were all aware of what was going on."

In subsequent conversations and letters, the agent enlarged upon these statements, stating that the security guard[581] was an employee of the building's managers where the law firm was situated. I checked and learned that the guard's death in front of a BART train at San Francisco's Mission Street station. In a September 20, 1993 letter, Agent X enlarged upon what he had earlier stated and written to me, relating to Operation Rushmore:

I was ordered last summer [1992] to go to San Francisco by Graham Fuller, CIA; Dick Pealer, ONI; and John Kaplin, CIA. These people were my handlers. I was told to go to the Bay Area. I flew from NAS [Naval Air Station] Norfolk to NAS Alameda, where I was to meet

---

[580] Danny Casolaro; Alan Standoff; Barry Kumnick; Dennis Eisman; Alan May; David Mayer; Paul Maresca; Dexter Jacobson; Gary Pinnell; Michael Hand; Ansan Ng; Jonathan Moyle; Arnold Raphel Mohommed Rajai; Cyrus Hashemi; Shahpour Bahktior.

[581] Security guard for 333 Bush Street building.

another Agent. He was the CIA station chief for SF [San Francisco]. His name is Robert Larson. He made arrangements for me at the Presidio. The next day the team arrived, and I wondered why this hit team was in town. I got a call from a woman who said she was Mossad and we needed to meet. So we did; we had lunch. I asked her, her name, and she said it was Anna Colburn. I later found out her real name was Yossi Jameir. We talked about why I was in town, and I asked for what reason. She said they wanted to hit Clinton. When she said that, I got sick. I said to myself, another Kennedy. I then asked her for the technical details.

They would be operating out of Republican Headquarters on Van Ness Avenue, where they could monitor all political moves by Clinton. The lady who would oversee this was Joann Stanhope for the Republican Party. She is also CIA.

Money, who would fund this? A man by the name of Chan Wang. He belongs to an organization called The Eagles. He also owns a real estate company called EIC in Redwood City. The man who would be his in-between was also CIA. His name was Bok Pon. Bok and I hit it off. He told me that Yosi worked for a major law firm called Hiller Ehrman [Hiller, Erman, White, and McCauliffe], and that this firm would handle everything we may need, such as safe-houses, equipment, money, travel, etc. I later found out a major Mossad team was working from the law firm.

Now I have the team assembled. Knowing Clinton was coming to town in the next few weeks, we set up shop. Weapons, escape routs, rendezvous, etc. Clinton was expected to come and stay at the Ritz Carlton. That's when we were going to do it. My men and I took up a position across the street from the Carlton before Clinton's arrival. We photographed the whole area for best possible results. Anyway, three weeks before he was due to arrive, word had it there was a leak. Where, was unknown. So my team and I pulled out in fear of being caught. That night we were told to eliminate all factions involved, including the Mossad agents. This order was given by Bob Larson, [CIA] station chief, San Francisco.[582] The next morning the team and I went to the law firm looking for Yossi. She was not there. She was the first one we were to hit from the firm. We went to her home where we found her.

Three of us: myself, John Aldridge, and Phil Burgess, went in and asked what happened. She didn't know. We told her that we were going to kill her if she didn't talk. Well, she didn't talk. Then you can see what happened next. Next target: Bok Pan. We met him at the office of EIC, hoping to get Wang too. Well, Wang wasn't there, but Bok was. We took him and drove north to talk. We went to the Peppermill in Sarramonte just south of Daly City. He said he knew

---

[582] Larson was later transferred to a position in the Caribbean, and known as "Pogo."

nothing. Then we took Bok over into Mill Valley on the other side of the Golden Gate, where he is now buried in a hill.

Next target: Joann Stanhope. Just as we were about to get her, I get a call on my pager from Flashboard. When I called, they said, "stop operations." When I asked the reason why, they said they found the leak. The leak came from a security guard where Heller Erman had their office. One of the Mossad agents was dating this guard. Our job was to, of course, take care of it. So that night when he got off work at midnight, and he went to catch the Bart train at Market to go home, my friend and I grabbed him and threw him in front of a train. "Job well done," said Washington. Two days later I end up in the Mideast.

Rodney, what I have told you could incriminate me, but I will take the chance and you know why. I have told you a lot of things, and believe me, they are true. ... I know for a fact that the Mossad is still working out of that law firm, for reasons unknown.

The names of the guys in Operation Ringwind are John Aldridge; Phil Burgess; Bob Burdige; Gregg Note; Robert Lister; Fred White; Rodney Harmon; and myself. The names are all CIA.

I forgot to mention that Gene Ferfethen also sponsored this operation. He owned a winery in Napa. He is one of Wang's friends. Together with their money, that how this thing was going to be pulled off. Consider this a self-confession.

When the operation was threatened with exposure, and before the leak was discovered, Agent X stated that the team sent to carry out the operation against Vice-Presidential candidate Bill Clinton proceeded to eliminate those who knew about it.

REFERRING TO THE LEAK

Referring to the leak that caused Operation Mount Rushmore to be shut down, Agent X said:

We found out what happened. One of the security guards at this company was dating one of the Mossad agents, and he came across some information. When we found out this happened, we took care of the situation. We took care of him. We took him and threw him in front of a BART train on Market Street. They thought he committed suicide.

FURTHER QUESTIONING

When the operation was threatened with exposure, and before the leak was discovered, Agent X stated that the team sent to carry out the operation against Vice-Presidential candidate Bill Clinton proceeded to eliminate those who knew about it.

"I believe you said earlier that, in isolating the leak, one person was eliminated." Agent X replied: "We eliminated several people. We did three. One was a guy by the name of Bok Pon. Another one was the Israeli agent Yossi."

"You mean the gal?"

"Yes. And then there was of course the security guard."

"Didn't the Mossad feel irritated by that?"

"We never had any repercussions on it. I had a list of people. I had a guy by the name of Chan Wang I had to take care of. I had Stanhope to take care of. I had Yossi to take care of. I had the security guard to take care of. And if worse came to worse, we were going to take care of the whose law firm itself. Almost like a condor situation."

PLAN TO ASSASSINATE CLINTON A MOSSAD OPERATION?

During a conversation on November 17, 1993 with Agent X, I sought to reconfirm what he had earlier stated about the CIA and Mossad operation to eliminate Vice Presidential candidate Bill Clinton. I asked Agent X: "It appears from what you stated earlier that the Mossad was running Operation Mount Rushmore, and that you received your initial instructions and coordination from them. What are your comments to that?"

Agent X replied: They [Mossad and the Hiller law firm] were the ones actually running the entire operation. From what I understood, and from what I pieced together, they were the ones actually running the whole operation."

Doesn't that sound a little strange?" I asked.

Agent X replied:

Yes, and no. You have to remember, Bush made a lot of friends with Israel. He promised them ten million in aid. The Gulf War, the ten billion in aid, and they didn't want anyone to defeat him [Bush]. They really wanted him to win. The Mossad is a very strong force in San Francisco, from what I can understand. I've never seen such a large contingency in one area. I've seen them in New York. I've seen a few of them in Boston. I know one that actually works for the National Security Council.

"I'm trying to think of the implications of the Mossad directing Operation Mount Rushmore," I said. "There are implications I don't fully comprehend yet."

"We work together a lot of time. It is a very mutual thing in some areas, but not in all areas. When it comes to hard intel [intelligence], no way. But it is like, you give me something and I will give you something." Agent X continued: "If the operation backfired, the Agency would have someone to blame it on. Then they can do a big sting, and catch all these people, and say, look, now you have another Kennedy-type situation. That is my feeling."

WHO ISSUED THE ORDERS

I asked Agent X who issued the orders for this operation. He reply that "The orders came from ONI. I first went out there in July of last year, 1992."

I said that Gunther Russbacher was familiar with the operation and that it was not totally cancelled, "only put on hold." Agent X replied: "Well, it could have been put on hold; my part in it was pulled out. We had a flop in the operation, and we had to sanction several people in it because we had a leak. So when that was done they just pulled the whole unit out of there."

SIGNIFICANCE OF OPERATION RUSHMORE

If Operation Rushmore was indeed a plan to assassinate presidential-candidate Bill Clinton, and involved the CIA and the Mossad, the implications are enormous. It would lend further support to those who argue that JFK's assassination was a CIA operation.

What of Agent X's credibility? CIA documents in my possession establish his intelligence agency connections and officer status. Other CIA contacts confirm Agent X was CIA. He had nothing to gain by giving me the information that he did. Reference to covert CIA operatives who Agent X stated were part of the operation were confirmed as actual CIA operatives by Russbacher and other CIA contacts.

Psychologists recognize the desire by some people to admit past activities or behavior, even though revealing this knowledge may be harmful.

Russbacher confirmed several times to me that Operation Mount Rushmore did exist, and that several people were killed in the operation.

INVOLVEMENT OF FEDERAL JUDICIARY
IN OPERATION MOUNT RUSHMORE

During my many conversations with Agent X the name of U.S. District Judge Marilyn Patel (San Francisco) surfaced. I asked him what role she played in Operation Rushmore. He stated that Patel was in close contact with the parties involved in Operation Mount Rushmore and that he had met her at various social functions in the San Francisco area. [Patel was once on the board of directors of ADL in San Francisco.] Agent X stated:

During the whole Operation Rushmore her name kept coming up constantly. It had something to do with San Francisco and that law firm. Now, the attorneys in that high-power law firm had known her, and were always telling me that if there was a problem, don't worry. They said that if something went sour, she was going to be the overseer and get everyone out of trouble. That is what it all came down to. The name was constantly mentioned. I met her once. In my opinion, she knew everything that was going on with Rushmoor, because of the way that the attorneys from Hiller Erman spoke about her. "Don't worry," they said, "we have friends at 450 Golden Gate (federal building in San Francisco housing the federal courts and the Justice Department)." I said, "Well, who do we know over there?"

"We know Marilyn H. Patel," was their reply. That was how I first met her. "Whenever you do something like what we were going to do [Operation Rushmore], you have to cover every angle. It's like a game of chess. You cover every escape, you cover money, technicalities, what if and what not, every possible avenue. So, if something happened, the case would have got in front of Patel.

I only know her from my trade [CIA covert activities] and what I've done. Whenever you plan an operation like we were going to do, you cover every single angle, I don't care what it is. Who is going to finance it, if something happens who is going to back us up, what contacts in the police department. In fact, the former chief of police there, he is now with a security company called the Phoenix program. Phoenix Security is who he is with now. He was involved in the sense, you know, for contacts, you know it's a big organization.

If Agent X is telling the truth, than we had sections of the CIA, the Mossad, a federal judge, and many others, involved in a scheme to assassinate a presidential candidate. It almost appears as if it was the Mossad who was *directing* the assassination attempt.

Further, we have two of the federal judges that had charged me with criminal contempt of court (for reporting federal crimes) who were identified by my CIA contacts as CIA assets working with agents of a foreign country to assassinate the person who is now our president.

Judge Patel's involvement in a scheme involving the assassination of a presidential candidate who then became president is very much in line with the actions she took to block my reporting of the criminal activities described within these pages. She openly violated numerous criminal statutes as she not only blocked my reporting of these crimes but committed the criminal act of inflicting harm upon me for attempting to make the reports. She caused me to be imprisoned in retaliation for attempting to report federal crimes that I had discovered up to 1990, and her actions were approved by other Ninth Circuit district judges, all of the Ninth Circuit Court of Appeal judges, and the Justices of the U.S. Supreme Court (as previously explained).

INVOLVEMENT AND OBSTRUCTION OF JUSTICE BY OTHER NINTH CIRCUIT FEDERAL JUDGES

Starting in 1974 I discovered federal judges in the Ninth Circuit at San Francisco to be heavily involved in blocking the reporting of the criminal activities I had discovered. It was obvious that the obstruction of justice type of criminal activities perpetrated by federal judges would have other facets. My first CIA contact, Gunther Russbacher, confirmed this fact, as already described. Starting in the later half of 1993, Commander Hunt provided further confirmation of this fact. In December 1993 Hunt was sent to the San Francisco CIA office prior to reporting for his new assignment as an analyst for the National Security Council in Washington. While in San Francisco he discovered massive corruption involving the CIA, federal judges, Justice Department attorneys, law firms, and in the bankruptcy system.

In addition to the federal judges that he had already identified to me, he learned that U.S. District Judges John V. Vukasin, Jr., and Wayne Brazil, were protecting, along with Judges Patel and Walker, the various criminal activities in which the CIA was involved. Hunt was in San Francisco to provide information on a CIA proprietary, COMTEL, that had filed Chapter 7 bankruptcy, leaving behind about fifty million in debt.

Hunt stated that a federal judge appointed as trustee a CIA contract agent, attorney Robert Damir, to prevent the creditors from learning that COMTEL was a CIA operation. After attending a creditors meeting on December 17, 1993, Hunt was aghast at the lawlessness in the proceedings. "Bob, that's what I have been discovering first hand since 1987," I replied. Hunt stated that a CIA law firm in San Francisco was acting to protect the CIA against exposure: Lafayette, McGee, Willis & Greenwages.

Hunt confirmed the existence of CIA drug trafficking directed from the San Francisco CIA headquarters. Hunt stated he saw, during December 1993, over $100,000 in cash on a table in a back room, profits from the drug operation. Hunt stated that many CIA personnel were upset about the CIA's activities, while many others supported them.

FURTHER SUPPORT FOR THOSE WHO BELIEVE
THE CIA WAS INVOLVED IN JFK'S ASSASSINATION

Much has been written about the role of CIA factions in the assassination of President John F. Kennedy. It isn't the purpose of this book to go into that subject. However, the statements of relatively high-ranking former or present ONI and Navy officers relating to the JFK assassination are given within these pages for the reader to ponder.

The role of deep-cover CIA officer, Colonel Trenton Parker, has been described in earlier pages, and his function in the CIA's counter-intelligence unit, Pegasus. Parker had stated to me earlier that a CIA faction was responsible for the murder of JFK, and that Kennedy was advised three weeks before the assassination of a plan to assassinate him in one of three cities that Kennedy would be visiting.

During an August 21, 1993 conversation, in response to my questions, Parker stated that his Pegasus group had tape recordings of plans to assassinate Kennedy. I asked him "what group were these tapes identifying?" Parker replied: "Rockefeller, Allen Dulles, Johnson of Texas, George Bush, and J. Edgar Hoover." I asked, "What was the nature of the conversations on these tapes?"

I don't have the tapes now, because all the tape recordings were turned over to [Congressman] Larry McDonald. But I listened to the tape recordings and there were conversations between Rockefeller, [J. Edgar] Hoover, where Rockefeller asks, "Are we going to have any problems?" And he said, "No, we aren't going to have any problems. I checked with Dulles. If they do their job we'll do our job." There are a whole bunch of tapes, because Hoover didn't realize that his phone has been tapped.

Parker had earlier stated to me that he turned over a full box of files and tapes, documentation, and micro-fiche, for the Pegasus Caribbean operation, to Congressman McDonald, shortly before the Congressman boarded the ill-fated Korean Airlines Flight 007 that was shot down by the Russians.

The November 1993 issue of *Penthouse* magazine had an in-depth article on Parker, in which federal agents sought to frame Parker and charge him with money-laundering. Parker had recognized one of the agents, and converted the Justice Department's scheme into a reverse-sting operation against them, using the techniques taught to him by the CIA. The government agents lost tens of thousands of dollars, not knowing that they had been recognized by Parker and were being taken.

Justice Department prosecutors were unaware of what had occurred, and charged Parker with money laundering. These federal charges were later dropped (in mid-1993) when Parker produced evidence that he was a member of the Office of Naval Intelligence and the CIA.

RUSSBACHER'S HEALTH CONTINUED TO FAIL

In late 1993 Russbacher's health was failing. He badly needed open-heart surgery, and was swallowing Nitroglycerin tablets like candy to get partial relief from angina pain arising from his almost totally blocked arteries. I sought to force various federal and Missouri officials to provide him relief. One of my deep-cover CIA contacts sent me documents showing Russbacher to be an officer in the Office of Naval Intelligence. Russbacher was in prison solely because officials in the U.S. Department of Justice fraudulently charged him with impersonating a Naval officer.

DEMANDING THAT THOSE WITH A RESPONSIBILITY TO ACT, PERFORM THEIR DUTY

Russbacher's health was very bad, and he badly needed coronary bypass surgery. In October and November 1993, I sent letters to Missouri prosecutor Tim Braun, Missouri Governor Mel Carnahan, and U.S. Attorney General Janet Reno. I explained that Russbacher would not be incarcerated if he had not been falsely charged with impersonating a naval officer by Justice Department personnel. I attached to the multi-page letter a copy of a May 20, 1986 government document signed by CIA Director William Casey, identifying Gunther Karl Russbacher as attached to the Office of Naval Intelligence (ONI), showing Russbacher to be a naval officer.

The Immigration and Naturalization Service had a detainer served upon the Missouri prison to seize Russbacher and deport him if he should be released by state authorities. I therefore sent two letters to INS Commissioner Doris Meisner in November 1993, demanding that the INS cancel its detainer on Russbacher and cease their deportation proceedings.

PARTIAL RESPONSE

INS retracted the retainer and cancelled deportation proceedings. Missouri officials at St. Charles (where Russbacher was waiting trial on the check charges),[583] eliminated the nearly half-a-million dollar cash bond, and ordered Russbacher released on his own recognizance, pending a February 7, 1993 hearing. But as Russbacher prepared for his release, St. Louis authorities arrested him on a charge of obtaining a flight on TWA without paying. This charge arose from his covert CIA activities when Russbacher obtained jump-seat authority on a TWA Lockheed 1011 from Philadelphia to St. Louis, enabling him to travel in one of the cockpit jump-seats.

ATTORNEY GENERAL RENO REFUSED TO RESPOND TO MY LETTER AND CHARGES

My letter to Attorney General Janet Reno may have provided relief to Russbacher from the prison sentence and deportation proceedings. I had also sent her the first edition of *Defrauding America*, revealing a pattern of unprecedented criminality in her department, and demanded that she receive testimony and evidence from me and the group of CIA whistleblowers that I represented.

---

[583] The check charges reportedly involved Russbacher writing checks to one of his aliases in the CIA proprietary known as National Brokerage Company. No one lost any money on the matter.

From the desk of Rodney Stich

P.O. Box 5, Alamo, CA 94507; phone: 510-944-1930/820-7250; FAX 510-295-1203
Author of *UNFRIENDLY SKIES–Saga of Corruption* and
DEFRAUDING AMERICA

October 21, 1993

Janet Reno
U.S. Attorney General
Department of Justice
Constitution and Tenth Ave., N.W.
Washington, DC 20530

Certified Mail No. P 299 517 979

Dear Ms. Reno:

Your responsibilities as Attorney General, your responsibilities under federal crime statutes, requires that you provide immediate relief as obviously required by the contents of this letter and the attached documents.

Justice Department prosecutors, in collusion with prior U.S. Attorney Generals and people in control of the Central Intelligence Agency, have fraudulently caused charges to be filed against deep-cover CIA/ONI operative Gunther Russbacher, who is presently in jail at St. Charles, Missouri. I have already described this process, along with the epidemic criminality upon the part of federal officials, in *Defrauding America*, a copy of which was presently sent to you, with a demand that you act upon the criminal activities against the United States. You, of course, chose to keep the lid on these racketeering activities.

I now enclose a copy of a memorandum dated May 20, 1986, from CIA Director Bill Casey, directed to John Poindexter of NSA (National Security Agency), making reference to a secret operation known as MAGG PIE. The body of the document refers to a flight from Tel Aviv's Ben Gurion Airport to Teheran, and named some of the participants, including Robert Hunt (ONI); Bud McFarlane (NSA); George Cave (CIA); and Howard Teicher (CIA). There are several very significant implications arising from this memorandum:

      1. The memorandum identifies the pilots of the aircraft flying to Teheran for the secret arms-for-hostages scheme. One is John Robert Segal (CIA), and the other is "Russbacher Karl Gunther ONI." Russbacher is the ONI deep-cover operative that the U.S. Attorney in Sacramento charged with impersonating a Naval officer when he was billeted at Castle Air Force Base (upon orders of CincPac). Although the U.S. Attorney (who is now a federal judge at Sacramento) dropped these charges, the U.S. Department of Justice of which you head, pressured the State of Missouri to charge Russbacher with impersonating a Naval officer and cause his probation to be rescinded. Russbacher is now in prison, in the beginning of a 21-year sentence (that was itself a fraud as shown by the attached Blunt letter). Justice Department officials knew when they filed the charges of impersonating a Naval Officer, and when they pressured the State of Missouri to revoke Russbacher's probation, that he was in fact a Naval Officer. The intent of the Justice Department officials and the U.S. Attorney General was to discredit Russbacher's exposure of the ongoing serious criminal activities against the United States and the American people. Your Justice Department now has a detainer served upon the State of Missouri prison officials for the purpose of seizing Russbacher and deporting him, if the State of Missouri releases

1

him. But if Russbacher is a Naval Officer, and a member of the CIA and Office of Naval Intelligence as Bill Casey's memorandum shows, he cannot be deported. As the nation's highest law-enforcement officer, you are aware of these crimes against Russbacher. You are aware of the crimes against the United States. Yet, you do nothing, which makes you guilty of far more and far more serious offenses than many who are in federal prison today, some of them for life.

2. Another implication of the memorandum is to show that Vice-President and then President George Bush was lying when he stated repeatedly that he did not know about the Iran-Contra scheme until after the November 1986 downing of the CIA-proprietary aircraft known as the Hasenfus affair. Seven months prior to Bush's alleged first knowledge of the arms-for-hostages scheme, Bill Casey is sending copies of memorandums concerning the conspiracy to none other than "VP Bush." You have a responsibility to expose this relationship and if possible, file criminal charges against Bush for lying and for his involvement in the ugly segments of the Iran-Contra affair, including the massive drug trafficking into the United States.

I expect you to continue the cover up and obstruction of justice, and am notifying you in this manner for inclusion in the next printing of *Defrauding America*. Incidentally, people over whom you have supervisory responsibilities are currently destroying all of my assets (after committing the criminal and civil and constitutional violations involved in their seizure), keeping me a virtual prisoner as I wait a kangaroo-court trial on contempt of court charges (in felony retaliation[1] for having tried to report in 1990 the criminal activities against the United States that I uncovered and in felony retaliation for having exercised federal defenses against the judicial acts taken to silence me.

Also included with this letter, and the May 20, 1986 memorandum from CIA Director Bill Casey, is a letter written by Missouri Secretary of State that admits the charges against Russbacher (via CIA proprietary Southwest Latex Supply) are a sham. Misuse of a state's prosecutors and public offices to silence an officer of ONI is certainly a civil rights violation along with a criminal misuse of state offices. They were probably taking their cue from the Justice Department mindset, but nevertheless, you have a responsibility to immediately intervene.

Among your duties at this time are:

1. Bring about the immediate release of Gunther Russbacher and halt his persecution, stemming from Justice Department initial charges against him.

2. Cancel the detainer placed by INS seeking to deport Russbacher, which would be barred if he was a U.S. citizen and captain in the Office of Naval Intelligence.

3. Publicize the charges I make here and in the book, *Defrauding America*, to focus attention on the serious crimes against the American people.

Title 18 U.S.C. § 241. Conspiracy against rights of citizens
  If two or more persons conspire to injure, oppress, threaten, or intimidate any citizen in the free exercise or enjoyment of any right or privilege secured to him by the Constitution or laws of the United States, or because of his having so exercised the same; ... They shall be fined ... or imprisoned ... or both;

Title 18 U.S.C. § 1512. Tampering with a witness, victim, or an informant —
  (b) Whoever knowingly uses intimidation or physical force, or threatens another person, or attempts to do so, or engages in misleading conduct toward another person, with intent to —
  (1) influence, delay or prevent the testimony of any person in an official proceeding;
  shall be fined ... or imprisoned ... or both. [1988 amended reading]"

Title 18 U.S.C. § 1513. Retaliating against a witness, victim, or an informant. (a) Whoever knowingly engages in any conduct and thereby causes bodily injury to another person or damages the tangible property of another person, or threatens to do so, with intent to retaliate against any person for — (1) the attendance of a witness or party at an official proceeding, or any testimony given or any record, document, or other object produced by a witness in an official proceeding; or (2) any information relating to the commission or possible commission of a Federal offense ..."

2

4. Cause an immediate halt to the final liquidation of my assets that were criminally seized with the help of Justice Department personnel, and as described in further detail in *Defrauding America*.

5. Cause an immediate halt to the felony persecution against me by your goons in the Justice Department as they seek to silence me, aid and abet the underlying criminality, by charging me with contempt of court for having exercised my federal responsibilities and rights.

Without your aiding and abetting, the criminality that I describe and support with massive amount of various forms of evidence could not occur. At this time the complicity of the mass media is protecting you. But the response to *Defrauding America* in the United States, and overseas, may yet circumvent the complicity and duplicity of criminal coverup.

Sincerely,

Rodney Stich

Enclosures:
    May 20, 1986 memorandum from CIA Director Bill Casey.
    May 14, 1989 Blunt letter.
    Book review showing credibility of *Defrauding America*.
    Exhibit of Offutt AFB showing Russbacher as Captain, ONI.

ONE BRIGHT SPOT

The letters I sent, helped by the CIA contact who furnished the documents showing Russbacher to be ONI, brought about Russbacher's release and dropping of deportation proceedings. On December 14, 1993 Russbacher's $450,000 cash bail was eliminated and he was released on his own recognizance, pending a February 7, 1994 hearing on the original charges, which were expected to be dropped. The detainer that Immigration and Naturalization Service (INS) filed with Missouri prison officials was dropped, and an INS agent notified Russbacher that deportation proceedings had been dropped.

Russbacher had emergency bypass surgery several weeks earlier. I felt that after four years of outrageous incarceration he would now be out of prison and able to enjoy life. But Russbacher had other health problems caused by his incarceration. He had suffered several minor heart attacks while incarcerated, which damaged sections of his heart. Although the blockage to coronary blood flow had been circumvented, his pulse rate and blood pressure fluctuated wildly. Doctors who examined Russbacher stated he had a fifty percent chance of surviving for six months. He was discouraged, and so was I. We had fought for so long to get him free, and now he may not live long enough to enjoy it.

Commander Hunt, who had several years earlier been involved in an operation to assassinate Russbacher, worked with me to help Russbacher, including obtaining funds. My phone was used for conference calls between Russbacher and Hunt, and it was obvious to me that they had worked together in deep-cover CIA activities. Their precise knowledge and articulation of deep-cover terms unknown to most people, including most in the intelligence agencies, left no doubt that I was listening to high-ranking deep-cover operatives.

Hunt and Russbacher's intelligence agency status and connections made them privy to some of the most sensitive of past, present, and future operations, and some of this information was passed on to me. Events, some of them very startling, that had yet to occur, are omitted here, but will be included in subsequent editions of *Defrauding America*, if they come to pass.

A LONG WAY TO GO

Obtaining Russbacher's release was only one very small step to expose the awesome criminality against the American public. I appear to be the most active in bringing together many concerned people within the intelligence community, and I wonder whether the three decades of attempting to expose and halt the mushrooming criminality will ever cause the American public to wake up.

THE UGLY SAGA CONTINUES

As this edition of *Defrauding America* goes to press, the criminality continues. I am receiving almost daily reports from the group of concerned deep-cover CIA personnel, some of them in high positions, exposing other forms of corrupt activities by the "Company." Some of these activities are subversive, and inflicting great harm upon the United States. Some of the reports indicates that some very serious events affecting the American people are planned.

The massive corruption by judges, trustees, and attorneys in bankruptcy courts continues. The taxpayer-funded drug trafficking by U.S. intelligence agencies continues. The judicial and Justice Department persecution of potential and actual whistleblowers continues. The harm inflicted upon the American public in general, upon the United States, and upon specific Americans, continues. All of these activities and consequences will continue, and worsen.

Justice Department prosecutors and federal judges continue to charge me with contempt of court in retaliation for trying to expose the enormous corruption in which both groups are implicated. A sentence imposed in 1989 for me to go to prison remains in effect. This judgement, as described in prior pages, arose from a sham contempt of court judgment rendered in retaliation for me filing oppositions and appeals of the corrupt seizure of my assets by federal judges. A contempt of court charge and subsequent Kangaroo Court trial waits for me in the San Francisco federal courts, in retaliation for my attempting to report the criminality I had discovered up to 1990. My multi-million dollar assets are in the final stages of destruction by the group consisting of federal judges, federal trustees, and a group of attorneys and law firms.

Members of Congress and the government checks and balances continue their duplicity of coverup and obstruction of justice. The establishment media continues their coverup, disinformation, and also, obstruction of justice.

In contrast to this huge power-block of corruption, there is a small handful of courageous people seeking to meet their responsibilities as citizens under our form of government. They seek to expose and correct the government criminality described within these pages.

Information on still other subversive and criminal activities committed by federal officials continues to reach me. As these criminal and subversive activities are sufficiently supported, they will be included in subsequent editions of *Defrauding America*. If the public remains indifferent, as it has in the past, the subsequent editions will be even more gloomy than this edition.

CHAPTER THIRTY THREE

IMPLICATIONS AND INDIVIDUAL ACTION REQUIRED

The racketeering activities by corrupt officials and personnel described in these pages make the Godfather movies junior-league. Never in the history of the United States has there been such an epidemic of corruption involving so many federal personnel and offices, inflicting such great harm, upon so many people, and upon the United States itself. Never before have a group of whistleblowers banded together, in this manner, to expose such massive corruption against the American people. Never before has such a group been so openly persecuted, with none of the government and non-government checks and balances exercising their responsibilities to intervene. Never have so many victims been so illiterate as to what was being done to them, and by whom.

CAN ANY OF THIS BE TRUE?

For years insiders have testified before Congress concerning all aspects of the corruption exposed in these pages, and members of Congress have covered up, committing crimes in the process. Many highly documented exposé books have been written about such matters as CIA drug trafficking into the United States, and despite the great financial and physical threat inflicted upon the average American, the most prominent reaction has been coverup and meaningless rhetoric.

The criminal activities against the American people described in these pages are supported by:

1. What I (and other inspectors) discovered as a federal investigator, and the large amount of official government documents I accumulated in that capacity.

2. What I discovered as a victim, as powerful forces in control of federal agencies sought to silence me. These discoveries are supported by large quantities of federal judicial and other records.

3. Statements, often deposition-like, made to me by a almost a dozen deep-cover CIA and DEA personnel during the past few years on an almost daily basis. Some of these people were high-ranking Naval officers, describing to me their role in the various operations, and giving me many documents that assist in proving what they had to divulge.

4. Cross-check between the different informants to confirm what had been told to me.

5. Refusal of the checks and balances to received the testimony and evidence from the group of deep-cover CIA people and myself, when the gravity of the charges, the great harm inflicted upon innocent people if the charges are correct, federal criminal statutes, and duty of office, required positive actions. These obstruction of justice tactics add an element of support to the other forms of evidence.

6. Pattern of persecution, mysterious deaths, and killings, all of which acted to protect those charged in these pages and acted to prevent exposure of the crimes against the American people. These criminal acts also add an element of support to the charges made herein.

7. Dozens of highly documented books, newspaper and magazine articles, on certain segments of the criminal enterprises described within these pages.

HARM INFLICTED UPON PEOPLE
AND GOVERNMENTS OF OTHER NATIONS

The harm inflicted upon innocent people by the epidemic corruption of federal personnel is not theoretical. The American public has suffered, as have innocent people in other countries. The corruption in the federal government filters down to state and local government. It has brought upon the American people death and destruction of personal values and lives through the CIA-engineered drug epidemic. It has inflicted enormous financial harm through such racketeering activities as seen in the savings and loan, HUD, Chapter 11 and 13 courts, and other forms of fraud. Fifty-eight thousand Americans lost their lives in the CIA-engineered Vietnam War, which was "justified" to the American people on the basis that the people of Vietnam wanted another form of government than ours. That was the same line as used in Nicaragua, another CIA operation that conveniently provided for the CIA, and for key CIA people, enormous riches from the then-escalating arms and drug trafficking.

Tens of thousands of people were assassinated in Vietnam, and thousands more in other countries, under orders of the CIA, and funded by the American taxpayers. Without the apathy and indifference of the American public, these crimes could not have been committed, either upon the people of the United States, or the people and victims of other countries.

The CIA trained and funded assassination squads that killed over 40,000 South Vietnamese civilians in the Phoenix program. Many of those killed were innocent women and children, old people, who were no match for the CIA engineered debacle. In Panama, when Colonel Manuel Noriega was learning too much about the CIA drug trafficking, when he demanded a bigger share of the profits, and constituted a threat to U.S. officials by threatened exposure of their activities, President George Bush unleashed the U.S. military. In Central and South America the CIA interfered in the governments of almost every country, financing assassination squads that killed tens of thousands. It has been estimated that about seven million people died throughout the world as a result of CIA-generated confrontations.

THE HARM AND THE HOAX
INFLICTED UPON THE AMERICAN PEOPLE

The unlawful CIA activities in Vietnam resulted in fifty-eight thousand American servicemen being killed and over 100,000 painfully wounded, some maimed or crippled for life. The American public will pay well into the twenty-first century for the corruption involved in the savings and loan and HUD scams, and others. The huge amount of money to finance the Vietnam and other CIA-generated wars must be paid, along with the interest on the money. Through their connections in government, many of the same people who looted the savings and loans bought properties owned by the seized savings and loans at pennies on the dollar. These losses must be paid by the American public who must

Billions of dollars a year are openly looted from unfortunate Americans who exercise the statutory protections of Chapter 11 or 13, and who are then unlawfully and criminally stripped of their assets by the crooked judges, trustees, law firms and the CIA. Thousands of people every year are made penniless and homeless by this and other corrupt activities involved in the inter-related and epidemic corruption.

This harm inflicted upon individual Americans is made possible by the complicity of silence, coverup, refusal to act, by members of Congress, the media, and others. The trickle-down effect from each of these corrupt enterprises results in loss of jobs, homes, reduced standard of living, family break-ups, and all types of adverse consequences few Americans will connect to the criminal activities and coverups by federal personnel.

The CIA-engineered drug trafficking is destroying America, with the help of every check and balance that has known of this criminality for years. Many of these same checks and balances, and especially federal judges and Justice Department prosecutors, are stripping the American public of the constitutional protections on the argument that the drug war requires it. Long prison sentences, destroyed families, informants assassinated, are all part of the game.

ILLITERACY AND LAZINESS OF THE AMERICAN PEOPLE

The public remains apathetic and indifferent to the harm that their conduct makes possible. I watched as they turned a deaf ear to the horror of air tragedy victims; the poverty inflicted upon Chapter 11 and 13 victims; the people assassinated by U.S.-funded assassination squads.

Those who say the public will never respond may be right. By the early 1990s I had been on over 1,800 radio and television appearances, describing the corruption that I discovered during the past thirty years. Callers expressed concern, and then did nothing. The average American male devotes a thousand times more attention to the trivial ball games than the coordinated criminality of their "leaders" in the three branches of the federal government.

The American public is lulled by the babble fed to them into thinking that the laws and Constitution are protectors of human rights. They can't separate fact from fantasy, as the media, members of Congress, and judges articulate their phony concern for justice, while destroying these same rights through corrupt judicial acts.

The entrenchment of corrupt officials in government and in the media had developed a network that will make corrective actions very difficult. Anyone who dares to speak out, as I and members of my group have discovered, are quickly destroyed in full view of the many government and non-government checks and balances whose legal duty includes preventing or stopping such reactions.

PREOCCUPIED WITH PACIFIERS

In our form of government a citizen has a right, and a responsibility, to stay informed as to government conduct, and to speak out and act when people officials commit serious wrongs.

Preoccupied with trivial matters and the refusal to read any of the many documented exposé books, insures that there is very little chance to halt the corrupt groups and activities inflicting such great harm upon the American people and the United States. Unless large segments of the American public become knowledgeable in these matters, and have the backbone to vigorously demand changes, these criminal conditions will continue to inflict great harm, as they have in the past.

SAD STATE OF AMERICAN PRIORITIES

The American public has a sad state of priorities. They have basically ignored every one of the many corrupt activities described within these pages. The greatest interest of a large segment of the American public is the trivia of ball games, the score of their favorite players, or the condition of their pitching arm. They act like children sucking on pacifiers, with the exception that the pacifier is a football or baseball. The important things in their lives are the opiate qualities of sports, with no concern for important issues. Concern is shown for theoretically endangered species of bugs, birds, and cockroaches, or the revelations of author Kitty Kelly, and other relatively meaningless matters. They care not for the victims of the criminality that routinely brings death, financial destruction, human misery, to so many.

A typical and accurate portrayal of the American public's indifference was shown in an October 1991 cartoon in the *San Francisco Examiner*, depicting the inability to get the average American male to face realities. The cartoon portrayed the mania of the average American male, seated before a television set watching a ball game, during the great Oakland, California fire. The cartoon pictured his entire home burned away, with only the fireplace, chimney, the television set, and his chair remaining. As the ball game ends, he calls to his wife, "Alright! the Forty-Niners Won! Now what were you trying to tell me, Dear?" Below the cartoon was the caption: "American Perspective on Priorities." How true!

"If you don't like what is going on in the United States, leave!"

The mentality of many people is reflected by the statements made by talk show host Larry King, "If you don't like what is going on in the United

States, leave!" With that type of mentality, is it any wonder the United States is in such a state of decline? Americans have the right to expect honest government, and the alternative is not for honest Americans to leave the country if corruption of this magnitude exists.

MANY BENEFITTED

Another reason the public has not rebelled against these subversive and criminal activities by government officials is the direct and indirect involvement of people in the financial benefits accruing from being part of the corrupt activities, or in remaining silent. Millions of people benefitted from the looting of the savings and loans; or the CIA and DEA drug trafficking into the United States; or the endemic looting of Chapter 11 assets; or the many other government-funded corrupt activities described in these pages. This is especially true of the law firms and attorneys, who play a major role in the harm inflicted upon the United States.

Exposing the corruption and taking the necessary corrective actions would affect thousands of corporations with ties to those in control of the government. They would suffer economic losses if their benefactors in government were exposed, removed from office, and prosecuted.

The large-scale drug trafficking by the CIA and DEA requires thousands of participants in all walks of life, including the Military, the three branches of the federal government, and state governments. These include people on military bases where the drugs are unloaded; the pilots who knowingly fly the drug-laden aircraft; Justice Department attorneys who not only remain silent, but assist in prosecuting informants and whistleblowers. Hundreds of people in Customs, DEA, members of Congress, know about the criminality, and either say nothing, or engage in deliberate blocking of any exposure. All of these acts are criminal in nature, including misprision of felonies, obstruction of justice, aiding and abetting, and conspiracy.

FIND THE STOLEN MONEY

Almost everyone alive today will go to their grave paying for the hundreds of billions of dollars looted in the savings and loan debacle. Just as the Justice Department and Congress made no attempt to expose the CIA link in this great scandal, neither group made any attempt to locate the stolen money. Only a fraction of the looted money has been located. The two billion plundered from Silverado Bank Savings and Loan, or the three billion looted from the Keating-controlled Lincoln Savings and Loan, are a far cry from the $250 to $500 billion or more that is missing.

To loot a billion dollars the looters must perpetrate a million-dollar swindle a thousand times. To cause a $250-billion-loss the million-dollar fraud must be repeated **two hundred and fifty thousand times**. The amount of money looted from savings and loans is much more than Neil Bush, Charles Keating, and others looted. Where is the money!

My CIA high-level informants state that many billions of dollars (and probably trillions) corruptly obtained by the CIA in the various activities described within these pages are hidden in offshore financial institutions. Some of this money has been reinvested in the United States by foreign corporations that may be fronts for the CIA.

PATRIOTS NEEDED IN OUR FORM OF GOVERNMENT

Never has America needed real patriots more than it needs them now. Our form of government *requires* its citizens to be patriots. The true patriots are those few people who have the courage to fight the epidemic corruption and the overwhelming odds. There certainly are not more than a handful depicted in these pages.

America has an overwhelming percentage of phony patriots. Many of them consider themselves patriots when they display the American flag. The same people won't do a thing about the corruption tearing apart the nation. Possibly the person who is totally ignorant about government corruption has the best excuse for failure to meet his or her responsibility as a citizen. They don't *know* what is going on. Then there is the person who does know, who complains that no one does anything about it, and then promptly duplicates the same cowardice. I've met my share of them, especially in the last ten years. One "friend" was even afraid to talk on the phone about the matters in this book, fearful that harm may come to her. Even close lady friends with whom I thought there was a deep bond, sold out. My children fell into the same group. So much for patriots!

AN ITALIAN-STYLE OUTRAGE IS NEEDED

In 1992 and 1993 the Italian people finally addressed the political corruption in Italy, causing removal from office and imprisonment of hundreds of government officials. This should happen in the United States. But a defect in our government structure makes this unlikely. Italy had a system of magistrates that are not hamstrung by a politically appointed U.S. Attorney General. This highest law-enforcement office in the United States has been criminally misused for decades to cover up for corruption by federal officials, including their own. This misuse of office includes filing false charges to bring about the imprisonment of patriot citizens and whistleblowers.

A change in government structure would be necessary to bring an Italian-style revolt to the United States. No politician wants that to happen, as such a revolt would threaten everyone in Congress and high executive position (as well as in the federal courts, up to and including the Justices of the U.S. Supreme Court). The average American citizen is so far out of the loop, doesn't know what is going on, that correction from outside the system is unlikely.

In Italy, one courageous citizen and one courageous and honest prosecutor started it all, exposing the corruption of epic proportions that reached to almost every corner of Italian society. The owner of a cleaning business, Luca Magni, was tired of the shakedowns, and reported it to a prosecutor who was willing to fight the system. The result: Operation Clean Hands, exposing the scandals of epic proportions involving hundreds of high government officials. Early in the investigations seven politicians and business men killed themselves. A domino effect occurred, ensnaring almost a thousand corrupt politicians.

Many top officials were charged with criminally associating with the Mafia, receiving bribes in exchange for protection, pork-barrel legislation, coverup during investigations. The large number of arrests and investigations caused the Italian cabinet to be reshuffled and eventually replaced. The scandals brought Italy's government to near collapse, with business unsure of the future. The country was beset with gloom, and it took a toll on the nation's psyche.

Italians were calling the charges a revolution against government corruption. Five movies, depicting the corruption, were released in the spring of 1993. Director Daniele Lachetti stated he hoped that his movie would cause the people to wake up and face reality. "We need to rewrite our code of behavior to eliminate the twisted logic that dominates our nation," he told a local magazine writer. This is as true in the United States, or more so.

"Political eruption may bury Italian system," was the headline on a *San Francisco Examiner* article, threatening to sweep away the entire ruling class. "Italian government Is Near Collapse," wrote the *Wall Street Journal* on March 12, 1993. The entire covert operations of the CIA would be subject to dismissal, and the CIA returned to its intended function of being an intelligence-gathering and coordinating agency. Many Justice Department personnel would be fired and sent to prison. Many federal judges would be impeached and prosecuted for crimes, including most of the judges in the Ninth Circuit Court of Appeals, many U.S. District Judges in the Ninth Circuit, and the nine Justices of the U.S. Supreme Court. Large segments of the Congress would be impeached for their duplicity of coverup. Never in the history of the United States would there be such a draconian removal of federal officials and personnel from office.

THE FARCE OF "LIBERTY AND JUSTICE"
FOR ALL IN THE UNITED STATES

"With liberty and justice for all" goes the pledge of allegiance to the United States. Is there really *anyone* who is so unsophisticated to think that there is any truth to those words! Life, liberty, and the pursuit of happiness are the "guarantees" of the Constitution of the United States, and these guarantees have been destroyed by the same groups paid and entrusted to uphold these rights: attorneys in the U.S. Department of Justice and federal judges.

WHAT CAN AND WHAT SHOULD
THE AMERICAN PUBLIC DO?

First, it must quickly educate itself and spend time reading serious articles and books. It won't hurt to start with this one. These activities require taking time away from the American opiates, including the trivial ball games, and get serious about what is going on. While becoming informed, and there isn't much time, consider the following actions that you can take:

1. Send certified letters to each of your U.S. senators and representatives, **demanding** that they immediately take the following parallel actions:

* Instruct the government Accounting Office to conduct emergency and full-blown hearings on the charges made in this book. GAO is the investigative arm for Congress.

* Pass immediate legislation to provide for Independent Prosecutors that have no ties to the Justice Department, including people who are not attorneys, former Justice Department personnel, or judges.

* Demand that the U.S. Attorney General empanel outside investigators to conduct parallel investigations into these charges. Remember that Justice Department officials and attorneys have been heavily implicated in these criminal activities for years and they will engage in various schemes to undermine an investigation. If this is not done, demand removal of the Attorney General.

* Demand that the U.S. Attorney General obtain appointment of Independent Prosecutors to investigate each of these areas, and that witness testimony and hearings be open to the public to prevent a coverup by the investigators. If the Independent Prosecutor legislation has not yet been passed, demand that it be immediately passed.

* Hold news conferences stating that the individual members of Congress will also investigate these charges. It is important that the news media be notified to reduce the probability of coverups.

* Demand that impeachment proceedings, preceded by investigations, be commenced against federal judges and other officials implicated in these wrongful acts.

2. Demand that your senators and congressman introduce the following legislation:

* A statute permitting citizens to sue State and federal judges, in jury trials, for financial damages, if the judges knowingly violate statutory or constitutional protections and cause infliction of financial or other harm upon the person. This statutory right already exists, but judges have rendered it meaningless through self-protective case law holding themselves immune from the consequences of their actions, regardless of how unlawful, criminal or unconstitutional that they may be.

* A statute permitting people whose assets have been corruptly taken from them in Chapter 11 courts to sue the government, and the Judges, Trustees and law firms that played a role in the criminal activities. Have the statute of limitations start to run from the day the legislation is passed, and have an adequate period of time to file administrative claims and initiate court action. Provide for jury trials.

* Make the position of U.S. Attorney General and the U.S. Department of Justice independent from the President of the United States and answerable to a neutral party.

* A statute providing for criminal prosecution and financial liability for prosecutors who falsely charge citizens with criminal offenses.

* Statute providing for an ombudsman, consisting of a panel of citizens with power to take action to force government personnel to act, or to take criminal or other action against corrupt or wrongful actions by federal personnel.

3. Expect the senators and representatives that you contact to stonewall you. Be persistent.

4. If you had a prior claim against an airline or the government as a result of an airline crash associated with fraud, try to find an attorney who will file a claim, or reopen the prior lawsuit, on the basis of government fraud. This

will circumvent the Statute of Limitations. Even if settlement of prior lawsuits occurred, fraud permits reopening the case, or filing actions against parties who were not formerly shown as defendants.

5. If you were a victim of Chapter 11 corruption, file an administrative claim against the United States to activate a Federal Tort Act claim, and consider filing a Bivens action against the United States and the federal personnel responsible. Raise the issue of fraud by federal judges and Justice Department officials so as to circumvent the Statute of Limitations.

6. Make repeated phone calls to your radio and television talk shows bringing up these matters, and encourage them to have the authors of exposé-type books appear as guests. Support the exposure activities of these authors by reading their books. These books can be obtained either through requests to your library or purchase.

7. Recommend copies of this book to your friends, and encourage them to get involved.

8. Don't reelect the same senators and representatives who are now in office. Every Senator in the United States knew of these scandals and engaged in coverup and obstruction of justice. Many representatives did the same.

9. Remove from political office as many attorneys as possible, using them only to write legislation. Their long history of corruption has brought about, or permitted to occur, much of the corruption that is epidemic in the United States.

10. Request that your library stocks multiple copies of this book.

Don't take it anymore; the United States badly needs fewer cowards and more patriots. America needs people like the TV anchorman in the fiction story, *Network*, saying they won't take it any more and do something about it.

WHERE TO EXPECT THE BLOCKS TO EXPOSURE

Highest law-enforcement agency. The highest law-enforcement agency of the United States is the Department of Justice, and the highest official is the U.S. Attorney General. Composed of attorneys, this is probably the most corrupt group in the federal government after the Central Intelligence Agency. Eliminating much of the criminality requires impeachment and criminal prosecution of many Justice Department officials, and our form of government is such that this is highly unlikely.

Congress. Members of Congress have the responsibility to conduct investigations and take corrective actions when an agency of the federal government, enacted by federal legislation is not performing, or performing in a criminal manner. For thirty years I have sought to have Congress received my testimony and evidence relating to very serious federal crimes affecting many people, without success. Even when I demanded under federal crime-reporting statutes that they receive the testimony and evidence of our group, consisting of federal investigators and deep-cover CIA personnel, they refused to even answer. If one member of either house of Congress can be motivated to conduct hearings, receive our testimony and evidence in public proceedings, and publicize our charges, possibly the massive complicity of silence and coverup can be circumvented.

This same Congress has the responsibility to initiate impeachment proceedings against many of the parties implicated in the criminal activities. Again, they have blocked this remedy.

Judicial remedies. Filing federal actions in federal court to report federal crimes by federal officials, and to obtain a court order to order a halt to the corrupt activities, has not only been unsuccessful for me and others (Christic Institute as an example), but highly dangerous. The Christic Institute was ordered to pay over $1 million for having the audacity to exercise federal rights and federal crime-reporting responsibilities. I have been sent to federal prison, with other prison sentences waiting to be carried out, solely because I sought to report the crimes and sought protection against the judicial and Justice Department retaliation. Even the Justices of the U.S. Supreme Court aiding and abetted these criminal activities.

Media. The media is infiltrated and controlled by the very same people in the CIA, the Justice Department, Congress, that are guilty of the crimes. For thirty years I encountered the coverup and obstruction of justice by the establishment media.

Legal fraternity. Various federal statutes permit filing federal actions to report and expose the federal crimes implicating federal officials, and to obtain a judicial order addressing the problem. But attorneys are notorious for closing ranks when scandals of this magnitude implicating the legal and judicial fraternities are involved.

Talk show hosts. Using the talk show hosts to get the message out and motivate the public to take certain actions is one of the best remedies. Only a small percentage of them will be receptive. In the San Francisco area, for instance, where I reside, the legal, judicial, and other corruption is rampant, and its tentacles are everywhere. Despite their knowledge of the charges, the continuing harm that will be inflicted upon innocent people, not a single one called to have me appear. This type of complicity of coverup has made possible the epidemic corruption that now exists.

GOVERNMENT INCAPABLE OF CURING ITSELF

The deterioration, the criminalization, of key government entities, especially the Justice Department, the courts, Congress, and the endemic duplicity of coverup by the media, strongly suggest that the system is incapable and unwilling to correct itself. Unless large groups of Americans quickly educate themselves about the level of corruption, and then take positive and strong corrective actions, the United States will sink farther and farther into the cesspool that now exists. Recovery may then be almost impossible. The scope of the problem is so enormous that even now, with the American public's high level of ignorance about government corruption, and their indifference, it may already be too late. Everything stated within these pages is a harbinger of worse yet to come.

SHOW RESPONSIBLE OUTRAGE

Its long past due when individuals who are not involved in the corruption, and are victimized by it, stand up and act. The American public should be outrages at the enormous and tragic harm inflicted upon them during the past few decades by the merchants of death and destruction who are described within these pages. It is time for responsible Americans to wake up to their responsibilities, to get informed, and take meaningful action. The average American should be outraged by the drug epidemic and its related crime and financial devastation inflicted by and with the protection of those described herein. Outrage should be felt against the great harm inflicted upon people all over the globe by the merchants of death acting through U.S. intelligence agencies. Outrage should be felt against the large percentage of crooked judges, attorneys, law firms, politicians, that inflict these harms upon the American people as a whole, and upon tens of thousands of individuals. Outrage should be felt against the media that covers up for these crimes, without which the harm and criminal enterprises could not exist. How dare they do this to us!

GOAL FOR A FEW RESPONSIBLE AMERICANS

Possibly the reader may find a message in the song, *The Impossible Dream*, in the musical play, *Man of La Mancha*. There is a message and a challenge in the words, that may motivate the very few people who will respond to the challenge of the epidemic corruption in government:

To dream the impossible dream; to fight the unbeatable foe; to bear with unbearable sorrow; to run where the brave dare not go; to reach the unreachable star. This is my quest, to follow that star, no matter how hopeless, no matter how far. To fight for the right, without question or pause. To be willing to march into hell for a heavenly cause. And I know if I'll only be true, to this glorious quest, that my heart will lie peaceful and calm, when I'm laid to my rest. And the world will be better for this; that one man, scorned and covered with scars, still strove with his last ounce of courage, to reach the unreachable stars. To right the unrightable wrong. To try, when your arms are too weary, to reach the unreachable star.

Corny? Maybe. But it is going to take similar courage to combat the epidemic and endemic corruption within government. Surely, only a very few will exercise this courage. In light of the near-total breakdown in America's checks and balances, the media complicity of coverup, and the infiltration of this criminality in every phase of government and non-government activity, the task is not easy.

As long as the author is able, he will expand and update this book to include information received on a continuing basis from an expanding list of former intelligence agencies personnel. The author welcomes input from others, which can be sent to the publisher's address.

EMBASSY OF ISRAEL
WASHINGTON, D.C.

שגרירות ישראל
ושינגטון

October 20, 1993

Michael Maholy
United States Medical Center
1900 Sunshine Expressway
Springfield, Missouri 65807

    Re: Operation "Whale Watch"

Dear Mr. Maholy:

      In reference to your formal request concerning "Operation-Whale Watch"
and through the National Security Council and Central Intelligence Agency, I am
unable to give you full details of this covert mission, although I can forward
to you the names of known agents that we have record of relating thereto.

      These agents include: C.I.A. Intelligence Officers, Michael Maholy,
Dewy Claridge, Steven Tucker, along with two National Security Council (NSC)
officers, Lt. Col. Oliver North and Lt. Robert Hunt. For additional intelligence
if the need arised, a Michael Harair "Mossad" (Retired) was available in a consulting capacity.

      We are unable to provede further detailed information but you must
understand this matter involves high security. We will not jeopardize any of our
intelligence operatives within that country.

      If you have any questions please call our International Affairs Sec-
urity Office at 21 396 Dian-Ben-Row Street, Tel Aviv, Israel.

                    Yours truly

                    Steven Goldburg
                    Security Officer
                    Assistant to the Ambassador

SAG/ft

October 20, 1993 letter from Israel's embassy in Washington, relating to the
CIA drug-trafficking operation known as Operation Whale Watch, and
confirming the CIA status of several of the author's CIA contacts: Michael
Maholy and Robert Hunt.

NATIONAL SECURITY AGENCY
CENTRAL SECURITY SERVICE
FORT GEORGE G. MEADE, MARYLAND 20755-6000

October 25, 1993

Mr. Scott A. Beal
C.I.A. Station Chief
United States Embassy
Costa Rica 9H32

Re: OPERATION "WHALE WATCH"

Dear Mr. Beal:

          In reviewing your letter for verification, dated June 16, 1985, and
due to our highly classified and necessary confidential security measures, we at
Central can only provide names of the agents who were assigned to monitor cable
traffic and special detection devices, including the 7 star-hydro-phone systems
that were placed in position.

          These operatives are: Samuel Thompson, C.I.A., John Plumber, C.I.A.,
Scott Williams, C.I.A., Steven Crow, C.I.A., and Special Agent-in-Charge, Michael
Maholy, C.I.A. In addition, a Lt. Col. Oliver North (USMC, NSC) and a Lt. Robert
Hunt (USN, NSC), were available as back-up for added security if required.

          These Agents were assigned to offshore petroleum drilling rig "Rowan
Houston" during the dates you had stated. The platform was located in Balboa
Harbour, Panama.

          Due to the sensative nature of "Operation Whale Watch" I cannot auth-
orize any further information on this Top-Secret mission, at this time. However,
if you have any further questions, please contact me. I look forward to hearing
from you.

                                        Sincerely,

                                        Steven Bradshaw
                                        Special Assistant-Security Div.
                                        National Security Agency

SB/fp

October 25, 1993 letter from National Security Agency making reference to
the CIA drug trafficking operation known as Operation Whale Watch;
identifying some of the author's CIA contacts; identifying some of the key
participants.